# LIVES

OF THE MOST EMINENT

# PAINTERS, SCULPTORS,

AND

# ARCHITECTS:

TRANSLATED FROM THE ITALIAN OF

## GIORGIO VASARI.

WITH NOTES AND ILLUSTRATIONS, CHIEFLY SELECTED FROM GERMAN AND ITALIAN COMMENTATORS.

BY

MRS. JONATHAN FOSTER.

---

IN FIVE VOLUMES.

VOL. V.

---

LONDON:
HENRY G. BOHN, YORK STREET, COVENT GARDEN.
M.DCCC.LII.

J. HADDON. PRINTER, CASTLE STREET, FINSBURY.

## TABLE OF CONTENTS.

# ERRATUM.

---

*Passage omitted. See Life of Lione Lioni, Vol. V., p.* 439; *after line* 26 *should come the following paragraph.*

A Milanese, named Leonardo, has also accomplished numerous works in Rome, and he has very lately finished two statues of San Pietro and San Paolo in marble, for the Chapel of the Cardinal Giovanni Riccio of Montepulciano; they are considered good figures and are much extolled. The sculptors, Jacopo and Tommaso Casignuola, have executed a statue in several pieces for the tomb of Pope Paul IV. in the Chapel of the Caraffi in the Church of the Minerva; it represents the Pontiff just mentioned, robed in a mantle formed of the [illegible] marble, and the frieze, with the other decorations, is also in vari-c[illegible]ed marbles. Here then we find an addition made to the productions of modern genius, since the sculptors, by means of colours, make their works resemble paintings. This tomb, out of his great goodness and gratitude, has been constructed by that truly excellent and sacred Father and Pontiff Pius V., a man indeed most holy and most worthy to enjoy a long life.

# LIVES

## OF THE MOST EMINENT PAINTERS, SCULPTORS, AND ARCHITECTS.

---

### RIDOLFO GHIRLANDAJO, AND DAVID AND BENEDETTO GHIRLANDAJO,* PAINTERS OF FLORENCE.

[Flourished from the latter part and close of the 15th century, to somewhat past the middle of the 16th century.]

ALTHOUGH it appears to be in a certain sort impossible that he who studiously imitates and carefully pursues the footsteps of some excellent master in our arts, should fail to become very nearly similar, at least in certain points, to the person thus imitated, yet we have very frequently to remark that the sons and brothers of distinguished men do but rarely equal their forerunners; nay, rather, that they do wonderfully degenerate from the same; and this is not, as I believe, because the qualities of their blood have failed to inspire them with the same readiness of mind and an equal amount of genius, but comes rather from a totally different cause—from the too perfect ease and enjoyment secured to them namely, and from that abundance of possessions and indulgences which but too often prevents men from being zealous in their studies and diligent in the labours of their art. Yet I will not affirm this rule to be so entirely without exception, as to preclude the occasional occurrence of the contrary.

David and Benedetto Ghirlandajo were indeed endowed with good genius, and might, without doubt, have pursued the footsteps in art of their brother Domenico; yet they did not do so, but on the death of their said brother they departed to such an extent from the true methods of proceeding, that the one, Benedetto that is to say, wandered long in aimless

* Of David and Benedetto Ghirlandajo, Vasari has already made mention in the Life of Domenico their brother, for which see vol. ii. of the present work, p. 200, *et seq.*

idleness, and the other spent his time in vainly racking his brains about mosaics.

But to speak first of David, who was much beloved by Domenico his brother, and who also loved him exceedingly, both living and dead; David, I say, finished many works which had been commenced by Domenico, some of which he completed in company with Benedetto, more particularly the picture for the High Altar of Santa Maria Novella, the back part that is to say, which is now turned towards the choir: the gradino of the picture was finished in small figures by some of the disciples of Domenico; by Niccolaio* namely, who, beneath the figure of San Stefano, represented with much care and pains a Disputation, in which that saint was engaged; by Francesco Granacci,† and by Jacopo del Tedesco,‡ who, together with Benedetto Ghirlandajo, completed the figure of Sant' Antonino, Archbishop of Florence, with that of Santa Caterina da Siena.§ These artists likewise finished a picture in the body of the Church, Santa Lucia namely, with the head of a Monk, which was placed nearly in the centre of the building, to say nothing of other pictures and paintings of various kinds which are dispersed among the houses of the citizens.

Benedetto subsequently spent many years in France, where he laboured to some purpose and made large gains, insomuch that he ultimately returned to Florence with many privileges and gifts, whereby the king of the first-named country had borne testimony to the estimation in which his abilities had been held there. Finally, having given his attention not only to painting but to military matters, Benedetto died in the fiftieth year of his age.

Now David, although he worked and designed not a little, did, nevertheless, not greatly surpass Benedetto, a circumstance that may have arisen from the fact that he was too

* Bottari considers this Niccolaio to be the person mentioned in the Life of Fra Filippo Lippi, as Niccolò Zoccoli, called Cartoni.

† For the Life of Granacci, see vol. iii. p. 452, *et seq.*

‡ Enumerated among the disciples of Domenico, in the Life of that master, for which see vol. ii. p. 200.

§ These works were removed from the church in the year 1804, and were taken to the Palace of the Medici-Tornaquinci family; they were subsequently sold; when some of the smaller paintings were purchased by Lucien Buonaparte.—*Ed. Flor.*, 1832-8.

wealthy and too much at his ease, and therefore did not keep his thoughts fixed with sufficient firmness on art, who is never to be found in her perfection but by him who zealously seeks her ; being found, moreover, she will not be neglected without at once taking flight.

At the upper end of an avenue in the garden which belongs to the Monks of the Angeli in Florence, there are two figures in fresco by the hand of David Ghirlandajo; they stand at the foot of a Crucifix, and represent San Benedetto and San Romualdo: these works are opposite to the door by which entrance to that garden is obtained.* He did other things of similar kind, but they do not merit that any particular record should be made of them.

But although David would not give much attention to art himself, it was not a little to his credit that he caused his nephew Ridolfo, the son of Domenico, to devote his hours with all study thereto, and to walk in the footsteps of his father, insomuch that this youth, who was the ward of David, and was endowed with a fine genius, received all possible aid from his uncle, who, having engaged him to study the art of painting, supplied him with all the facilities and encouragement necessary to forward his progress in the same, and this all the more readily, as he had begun to repent when too late of not having laboured earnestly himself, and of having consumed his time with mosaic.

For the King of France,† David Ghirlandajo executed a large picture in mosaic on a thick panel of walnut-wood. The subject of this work is the Madonna, with numerous Angels around her, and the mosaic was very highly praised. David passed much of his time at Montaione, which is a fortified place in the Valdelsa, and he dwelt there, principally because in that place he had furnaces, and could

* These works, having suffered by time, were re-painted by a modern artist of very common-place character.—*Masselli.*

† Bottari affirms this to have been the first Mosaic sent into France, but it was to the President de Guisnes, who obtained it when he accompanied Charles VIII. to Naples, and not to the king of France, that the work was sent. This is proved by an inscription, also in mosaic, on the lower part of the picture itself, and which is as follows :—

*Dominus Johannes de Ganai præsidens Parisiensis primus adduxit de Italia Parisium hoc opus mosaicum.*

readily obtain the various woods, glass, &c. which he required for his mosaics; he therefore executed many labours in glass as well as in mosaic, at Montaione, more especially certain Vases, which were given to the Magnificent Lorenzo de' Medici the elder. David likewise produced three heads (those of San Pietro and San Lorenzo namely, with that of Giuliano de' Medici), in a framework of copper, and this is now preserved in the Guardaroba of the Duke.

Ridolfo meanwhile, being frequently engaged in drawing from the Cartoon of Michelagnolo, was reputed to be one of the best artists who studied that work, and was much esteemed by all, but more particularly by Raffaello Sanzio da Urbino, who at that time, he being also a young man of a great name, was sojourning in Florence, as we have said, for the study of his art.

When Ridolfo had designed much and frequently from the above-mentioned Cartoon, and had besides obtained considerable practice in painting, under Fra Bartolommeo di San Marco, he had made so much progress, according to the opinion of the best artists, that Raffaello, being compelled to leave Florence for Rome, whither he had been invited by Pope Julius II., left to Ridolfo the care of finishing the blue drapery, with some other small matters, still wanting to the picture of a Madonna, painted by Raffaello for certain gentlemen of Siena,* and which Ridolfo, having completed the same with very great care, did ultimately send to that city. Nor had Raffaello dwelt any long time in Rome, before he began to make all efforts for prevailing on Ridolfo to repair thither also; but the latter, who had never—as the saying is—"lost sight of the Cupola,"† and could in no wise resolve on living out of Florence, would accept no proposal which might compel him to abandon his abode in his native place.

For the Convent of the Nuns of Ripoli, this artist painted two pictures in oil; the one a Coronation of Our Lady, and

* This circumstance is related, as our readers will remember, in the Life of Raphael. See vol. iii. p. 12.

† The Cupola of the Cathedral that is to say, of which the Florentines are jestingly declared to be enamoured to such a degree that they cannot contentedly draw the breath of life in any place from which it is not visible.

the other a Madonna surrounded by Saints. In the Church of San Gallo he depicted Our Saviour Christ, bearing his Cross and accompained by a large body of soldiers; the Madonna and the other Maries, weeping in bitter grief, are also represented, with San Giovanni and Santa Veronica, who presents the handkerchief to Our Saviour; and all these figures are delineated with infinite force and animation. This work, in which there are many beautiful portraits from the life, and which is executed with much love and care, caused Ridolfo to acquire a great name;* the portrait of his father is among the heads, as are those of certain among his disciples, and of some of his friends—Poggino, Scheggia, and Nunziata for example, the head of the latter being one of extraordinary beauty.†

Now this Nunziata, although he was but a painter of puppets, was nevertheless a man of distinguished ability in certain things, more especially in the preparation of fireworks, and those Girandoli, which, as we have said, were made every year for the festival of St. John. He was besides a most amusing and facetious person, insomuch that every one had pleasure in conversing with him. A citizen came to him one day, and, bemoaning the displeasure caused him by such painters as knew only how to produce improprieties, desired that Nunziata would make him a Madonna, and such a one as should be decent and proper, of respectable years that is to say, and not likely to move any one to light thoughts, whereupon Nunziata depicted him a Madonna with a beard. Another, wishing to have a Crucifix for a room on the ground floor of his house, in which he was accustomed to pass the months of summer, could find nothing to say but, "I want a Crucifix for summer," when Nunziata, perceiving the man to be a simpleton, painted him a figure, wearing no other drapery than a pair of stockings.‡

But we return to Ridolfo, who, having received the com-

* This picture was painted in 1504, and when the artist was but nineteen years old. It was sent in the year 1813 to Paris, where it still remains.

† The picture is now in the Palazzo Antinoni. The Church of San Gallo was demolished, as before related, when the city was menaced by the Prince of Orange.—*Ed. Flor.*, 1832-8.

‡ This Nunziata was the father of that Toto del Nunziata, of whom mention has been already made, and of whom there is more in a subsequent page.

mission for a picture to be painted for the Monastery of Costello, made great efforts to surpass his rivals, and executed that work, the subject of which was the Nativity of Christ, with all the pains and care that he could possibly command; the principal figures are the Madonna, who is in the act of adoring the Divine Child, with San Giuseppo, and two other saints, San Francesco and San Geronimo namely, both kneeling. He added a most beautiful landscape, of a country similar to the Sasso della Vernia, where it was that San Francesco received the stigmata: over the hut wherein is the Infant Saviour, moreover, there are angels singing; the colouring of this work is exceedingly beautiful, and it has great relief.*

About the same time Ridolfo executed a picture which was sent to Pistoja, and commenced two others for the Company or Brotherhood of San Zanobi, who have their seat near the Canonicate of Santa Maria del Fiore; these pictures being intended to stand one on each side of the Annunciation, which had formerly been executed in that place by Mariotto Albertinelli, as we have related in his life. These works Ridolfo brought to conclusion in a manner which was greatly to the satisfaction of the Brotherhood, representing in one of the two, San Zanobi restoring to life a child which had died in the Borgo degli Albizzi, at Florence; this story is depicted with much power and animation, an effect which is heightened by the circumstance that many of the heads are portraits from the life, to say nothing of certain women, whose faces express most truthfully the joy and surprise with which they behold the child revive, and see his spirit return to him.

The second of the pictures painted for the Brotherhood of San Zanobi represents that saint when carried by six bishops from San Lorenzo, where he was first buried, to Santa Maria del Fiore, and when, passing by the Piazza of San Giovanni, an Elm, which had been dried up and dead, being touched by the coffin wherein was the holy corpse, put forth leaves, for such was the will of God, and bore flowers anew. On the place where the tree stood there is now a

* When the Monastery passed from the Cistercian Monks to the Carmelite Nuns of Santa Maddalena de' Pazzi, this picture was stolen from the building.—*Masselli.*

column of marble with a cross upon it, as a memorial of that miracle. This picture was no less beautiful than were those before described as produced by the abovenamed Ridolfo.*

Now these works were all performed by our artist during the lifetime of his uncle David, wherefore that good old man was much rejoiced thereby, and thanked God that he had lived so long as almost to have seen the genius of Domenico living again in Ridolfo. At length, and when, in his seventy-fourth year that is, he was preparing, though then so old, to visit Rome, there to take part in the Holy Jubilee of 1525, he fell sick and died in that same year. He received sepulture from Ridolfo in the Church of Santa Maria Novella, where the other members of the Ghirlandajo family are buried.

Ridolfo had a brother in the Camaldoline Monastery of the Angeli in Florence; and this ecclesiastic, who was called Don Bartolommeo, was a truly upright and worthy man. Ridolfo, who greatly loved him, painted a picture for him in the cloister which looks on the garden; in the Loggia that is to say, wherein are these stories from the life of San Benedetto, which were painted in *Verdaccio* by the hand of Paolo Uccello. The subject of Ridolfo's story, which is on the right of the entrance as you go in by the door of the garden, is the abovenamed Saint seated at table with two Angels beside him; he is waiting until Romano shall send him bread into the grotto, but the devil has cut the cord to pieces with stones. San Benedetto is furthermore depicted as investing a young brother of his order with the monastic habit. But the best of all the figures in that arch of the Loggia is the portrait of a dwarf who was at that time wont to stand at the door of the monastery.

At the same place, and over the Holy Water vase which stands near the entrance of the Church, Ridolfo painted a fresco in colours, Our Lady namely, with the Divine Child in her arms, and little Angels, which are most beautiful, hovering around her; over the door of a small chapel, which is in the cloister opposite to the Capitular buildings also, he painted a fresco in one of the lunettes, San Romualdo that

* These works are still in good preservation, and may be seen in the Public Gallery of Florence (the Uffizj), among the paintings of the Tuscan School.—*Ed. Flor.*, 1832-8.

is to say, with the Church of the Hermitage of Camaldoli in his hand.* No long time after having completed the above, Ridolfo furthermore executed a very fine picture of the Last Supper for the same monks; this work, which is a fresco, is at the upper end of their Refectory: for that painting our artist received his commission from the Abbot Don Andrea Dossi, who had formerly been a monk in the monastery, and who caused his own portrait to be painted in one of the lowermost corners of the picture.

In the little Church of the Misericordia, on the Piazza of San Giovanni, Ridolfo painted three most beautiful Stories from the Life of Our Lady, on a gradino or predella, and these are so delicately executed that they appear to be miniatures. For Matteo Cini the same artist painted a Tabernacle at the corner of his house which is near the Piazza of Santa Maria Novella; the subject of the work is Our Lady with St. Matthew the Apostle and San Domenico; two little sons of Matteo Cini, portraits from the life, are represented as kneeling before the Virgin; this picture although but a small one, is exceedingly pleasing and graceful.

For the Nuns of San Girolamo, of the Order of San Francesco de' Zoccoli, who have their Convent on the height of San Giorgio, this artist depicted two Stories, the one representing San Girolamo in the act of doing penance, while the Nativity of Our Saviour Christ is set forth in the lunette above; and the other, which is opposite to the first, being an Annunciation; in the lunette above the same is Santa Maria Maddalena receiving the sacrament.† In the palace, which is now the property of the Duke,‡ Ghirlandajo painted the Chapel, wherein the Signori hear mass, depicting the Most Holy Trinity in the centre of the vaulted ceiling, with figures of Angels in the form of children, and bearing the mysteries of the Passion, in some of the divisions thereof. There are besides the heads of the twelve Apostles, and in the four angles are the whole-length figures of the Four Evangelists; while on the principal wall of the Chapel is the Angel

* These works were destroyed when the church was restored.—*Bottari.*

† These two paintings are still in their places.—*Masselli.*

‡ Commonly called the Palazzo Vecchio. The chapel here in question is now used for the purposes of the Guardaroba.—*Ibid.*

Gabriel approaching with the Annunciation to the Virgin. Ridolfo added a kind of landscape in the back ground, exhibiting the Piazza of the Nunziata in Florence, and continuing even to the Church of San Marco. The whole work is admirably executed, and has numerous and beautiful decorations; when it was finished our artist painted a picture which was placed in the Deanery of Prato, and represents Our Lady offering her girdle to St. Thomas, who is there seen, together with the other Apostles.*

For Monsignor de' Bonafè, Director of the Hospital of Santa Maria Novella, and Bishop of Cortona, Ridolfo painted a picture to be placed in the Church of Ogniasanti; the subject of this work was Our Lady, with San Giovanni Battista and San Romualdo; and as the Bishop considered himself to have been served well and duly, he caused our artist to execute certain other paintings for him; but of these we need make no further mention. He next copied three pictures which had formerly been painted in the Medici palace by Anton Pollaiuolo, and the subjects of which were taken from the labours of Hercules; these Ridolfo painted for Giovambattista della Palla, by whom they were sent into France.

Having executed these and many other paintings, and finding in his possession all the requisites for mosaic-work, which had belonged to his uncle David, and to Domenico his father, Ridolfo, who had also acquired some knowledge of the processes to be pursued in that work, determined to make an attempt therein. Having completed certain pieces accordingly and finding that he succeeded, he then undertook to decorate in mosaic the arch which is over the door of the Church of the Nunziata, and in this he placed a figure of the Angel who is bringing the Annunciation to the Virgin;†

* Now in the chantry of the Cathedral at Prato. To have been exact, Vasari should have said, St. Thomas with other Saints, and not "other Apostles," since many of the figures do not represent apostles.—*Ed. Flor.*, 1832-8.

† A compatriot of our author remarks that, although this fact, which Vasari may have received from Ridolfo himself, is not to be called in question, yet that it ought to have been mentioned earlier, and the mosaic placed among the works executed during the lifetime of his uncle David, since it was certainly the last-named artist who received the commission for that work from the Monks, and who, if he permitted Ridolfo to execute

but not having the patience required for joining those innumerable little morsels together, he never attempted anything more in that manner.

For the Company of the Woolcombers, Ridolfo painted a picture in their little Church at the upper end of the Campaccio, the Assumption of Our Lady namely, with a choir of angels and the Apostles standing around her tomb; but it happened unfortunately that in the year of the siege, the place wherein this work was executed being filled with young birches for making fascines, the humidity thus occasioned caused the intonaco to fall off, and the picture was totally destroyed. Ridolfo was, however, commissioned to replace it, and then depicted his own portrait therein.

At the Deanery of Giogoli, and in a tabernacle, which looks towards the high road, Ghirlandajo painted a figure of the Madonna with two Angels; and in another tabernacle, which stands opposite to the mill of the Eremite Fathers of Camaldoli, that last being situate on the Ema, and beyond the Certosa, he executed several figures in fresco. But finding that he was now sufficiently employed, and in the receipt of a very good income, Ridolfo would no longer rack his brains for the sake of attaining to what he might have become in the Art of Painting, but rather began to think of living like a gentleman and taking matters easily.

When Pope Leo visited Florence, Ridolfo did nevertheless

the same, presented it to those fathers as his own work. The truth of this assertion is made manifest by the following extract from a book of Records still in the Convent of the Most Holy Annunciation, and wherein we find written as beneath:—

"1509. The Nunziata, on the outside of our church and beneath the Portico, was completed by Davitte di Tommaso, at the cost of the Convent."

And in another book we find, "The Nunziata in mosaic over the principal door of our Convent was finished on the 25th Jan. 1509. It was made by Davit di Tommaso, our painter of mosaic, and some difference respecting the price having arisen between him and the Monks, the Wardens of the Monastery commanded, in the presence of the parties, that a person well acquainted with such matters, should be chosen by each side to be arbiters in that question, and that what they should judge to be just should be accepted in silence and with content.

"These persons therefore having examined the work, and found the figures to be good and well done, adjudged and decreed that the said Monks should pay to the said Davit seventy-eight crowns, that is 546 lire; which sum was given to him."

prepare the Hall and other apartments of the Medici Palace, and executed nearly all the decorations of the same, in company with his disciples and assistants, causing Pontormo to paint the Chapel as we have before related. He also took part in the preparations made for the marriage of the Duke Giuliano and that of the Duke Lorenzo, for whom he executed the scenic ornaments for the dramatic spectacles which were then exhibited. Being much esteemed by those Signori for his abilities, he was subsequently appointed to various offices by their intervention, and was received as an honourable citizen into the council.

Now Ridolfo did not disdain to paint banners, standards, and matters of similar kind, and I remember to have heard him say that he had three times painted the banners for the Potenze,* who were accustomed every year to hold a tournament and give a festival to the city on St. John's day. At a word, he permitted all kinds of things to be done in his workshops, insomuch that they were frequented by numbers of young men, each one of whom could there learn what best suited him.

Antonio del Ceraiolo was one of those who, after having been with Lorenzo di Credi, went to Ridolfo, and having subsequently begun to work for himself, he painted numerous pictures and portraits from the life. In San Jacopo-tra-fossi, there is a picture by the hand of this Antonio, which represents San Francesco and Santa Maddalena, at the foot of a Crucifix ;† and behind the High Altar in the Church of the Servites he painted a picture of the Archangel Michael, which he copied from one executed by Ghirlandajo, in the Ossa di Santa Maria Nuova.

Mariano da Pescia was also a disciple of Ridolfo, and acquitted himself exceedingly well; the picture of Our Lady with the Infant Christ, Sant' Elizabetta, and San Giovanni, which is in that Chapel of the Palace, painted as we have said, for the Signoria, by Ridolfo,‡ is by the hand of Mariano,

* Gentlemen forming a company or association, and popularly called "Le Potenze."

† This work is in the Gallery of the Uffizj at Florence. The figures of the two saints are in tolerable preservation, but that of the crucified Redeemer has suffered much, from the fact that the colour has peeled away in minute scales.

‡ The work of Mariano da Pescia still retains its place.

as are likewise the paintings in chiaro-scuro, which decorate the house of Carlo Ginori, situate in the street which takes its name from that family; the subject of this last-named work has been chosen from the Life of Sampson, and the stories represented therein, are executed in a manner that may be truly called admirable. Nor can it be doubted that Mariano, had he been permitted to enjoy a longer life than was accorded to him, would have become a most excellent painter.

Another disciple of Ridolfo was Toto del Nunziata,* who, in company with his master, painted a picture of Our Lady, with the Infant Christ in her arms, and accompained by two saints, in the Church of San Pietro Scheraggio.

But above all the other disciples of Ridolfo, the one most dear to him was a certain Michele, who had been with Lorenzo di Credi, and was afterwards with Antonio del Ceraiuolo. This youth was one of admirable ability, he worked with the utmost boldness, and was never weary of his labours; continually imitating the manner of Ridolfo, Michele approached him so closely, that whereas he had for a time only a third of the gains, he subsequently received the half of the profit which they made in common. Michele paid to Ridolfo the observance due to a father, nay, he loved and was beloved by his master to such a degree, that he was ever considered as something belonging to Ridolfo, and is still, as he ever has been, known by no other name than that of Michele di Ridolfo.

These two artists then, loving each other as I have said,

* Toto del Nunziata subsequently went to England, as has been related in the Life of Perino del Vaga. Lanzi and other writers speak of him as one of the most distinguished painters who appeared in this country during the sixteenth century, temp. Henry VIII. He was one of the king's serjeant painters (Henry had three), and in a book signed monthly by the king himself we have an entry to the following effect:—"An. reg. xiii., Jan. 23, paid to Antony Toto, by the king's commandment, £20." And again, in a different book:—"To Antony Toto and Bartilmew Penn (Bartolommeo Penne), payntours £12 10s., their quarterly payment between them." Also the following:—"To Antony Toto, his servant, that brought the king a depicted table of Colonia, 7s. 8d." No works of Toto can now be authenticated, so far as is known to the present writer; some of those attributed to Holbein, "whose pencil," remarks Dr. Sarsfield Taylor, "appears, like Aaron's rod, to have swallowed all its contemporaries are believed to be by Toto." See *Origin, Progress, and Present Condition of the Fine Arts in England and Ireland*, vol. i. p. 220.

like father and son, always laboured together, and performed a large number of works in company. For the Church of San Felice—in Piazza, a place belonging to the Monks of Camaldoli, they painted a picture representing Our Saviour Christ and the Virgin in the air;* they are interceding with God the Father for the people praying beneath, and beside whom are kneeling several Saints. In the Church of Santa Felicità, they painted two Chapels in fresco, which are executed with infinite ability; in one of these is seen the Saviour dead, with the Maries around him; and in the other is the Assumption of Our Lady, with certain Saints.† For the Church which belongs to the Nuns of San Jacopo delle Murate,‡ these artists painted a picture, the commission for which they received from Monsignore de' Bonafè, Bishop of Cortona; and in the Convent of the Donne di Ripoli they painted another, representing Our Lady, with certain Saints.

For the Chapel of the Segni, which is beneath the Organ in the Church of the Santo Spirito, they also painted a picture of Our Lady with Sant' Anna and many other Saints; § in a picture for the Company of the Neri they painted the Beheading of St. John the Baptist, and at the *Monachine* in the Borgo San Friano, they executed one of the Annunciation. For the Church of San Rocco at Prato, they painted a picture, the subject of which was Our Lady with San Rocco on one side and San Sebastiano on the other, and for the Brotherhood of San Sebastiano, which is near San Jacopo sopr' Arno, they also executed a painting of Our Lady, with San Sebastiano and San Jacopo. Another work was in like manner undertaken by Ridolfo and Michele, at San Martino alla Palma, and finally they painted one for the Signor Alessandro Vitelli, which last was sent to Città di Castello; this was a figure of Sant' Anna, and it was

* This work is still in the Church of San Felice.

† The paintings executed in these two Chapels have perished.

‡ San Jacopo in Via Ghibellini that is to say. The picture is now in the Academy of the Fine Arts in Florence; it represents the Madonna seated amidst the clouds, with the Infant Christ in her arms; she is accompanied by the SS. Jacopo, Francesco, Lorenzo, and Clara, beneath is the Bishop of Cortona, a kneeling figure, in the habit of a monk.—*Ed. Flor.*, 1832-8.

§ Beneath the organ is the door of the sacristy, but the picture in question is in the fifth Chapel, and on the right of the entrance.—*Ibid.*

placed in the chapel which belongs to the Signor Alessandro, in the Church of San Fiordo.

The paintings of various kinds which proceeded from the workshops of Ridolfo Ghirlandajo were indeed innumerable; and of the many portraits from the life which he sent forth, I will but say that the Signor Cosimo de' Medici, while still but a youth, was portrayed by this artist; that likeness was a very beautiful work, as well as an accurate resemblance: the picture is still preserved in the Guardaroba of His Excellency.* Ridolfo was an exceedingly prompt and rapid painter in many kinds of work, more particularly in the preparations for festivals: when the Emperor Charles V. arrived in Florence, he constructed a triumphal arch at the corner of the Cuculia in ten days; and another arch at the gate of Prato was erected by this artist in a very short space of time, this work being constructed for the marriage of the most Illustrious Lady the Duchess Leonora, and on the occasion of her arrival in Florence, as will be related in the Life of Battista Franco.

In a small cloister at the Madonna di Vertigli,† a place which belongs to the Monks of Camaldoli, and is just without the district of the Monte San Savino, Ridolfo, having with him the above-named Battista Franco and Michele, painted all the events of the Life of Joseph in chiaro-scuro; and in the Church he executed the picture for the High Altar, with a fresco representing the Visitation of Our Lady; this last is perhaps as beautiful a work as any fresco ever executed by Ridolfo. But more than all is the figure of San Romualdo, on the above-mentioned Altar-piece, to be extolled, the venerable aspect of the countenance being indeed most beautiful: our artists painted other pictures in the same place, but it shall suffice us to have mentioned these.

In the palace of the Duke Cosimo, and in the Green Chamber, this artist painted grottesche for the decoration of the ceiling, with landscapes on the walls, which greatly pleased the Duke. Finally, having become old, Ridolfo lived a cheerful and quiet life; he had seen his daughters married and his sons were tolerably prosperous, making their

* The Florentine commentators of our author declare themselves unable to find any trace of this portrait.

† Now called *La Madonna delle Vertiglie.—Ed. Flor.*, 1832-8.

way as merchants in France and at Ferrara. It is true that he found himself to be somewhat heavily afflicted with the gout, insomuch that he was compelled to remain almost always in his house, or if he went out had to be carried in a chair, yet he endured that complaint with much patience, and showed similar equanimity in respect of certain misadventures which befell his sons.

In this his old age Ridolfo still bore much love to all connected with art, and liked to hear of, or, when he could, to see, whatever was most commended in the way of buildings, pictures, and such other works of similar kind as were always in course of execution. One day that the Signor Duke had gone out of Florence, Ridolfo caused himself to be carried in his chair to the palace, where he dined and remained the whole day, examining the whole of that building, which was so greatly altered and transmuted from what it had formerly been, that he scarcely knew it again.* In the evening when he departed, the old man said, "Now shall I die content, since I shall be able to carry to our artists who are in the other world intelligence to the effect that I have seen the dead revived, the deformed made beautiful, the old made young again." Ridolfo lived seventy-five years, and died in the year 1560, when he was buried with his forerunners in Santa Maria Novella.

Michele, the disciple of that master, who, as I have said, is called by no other name than that of Michele di Ridolfo, painted three large arches in fresco over certain of the gates of Florence, and this he did after his master had resigned the practice of art. Over the gate of San Gallo, for example, he painted a figure of Our Lady, with those of San Giovanni and San Cosimo, which are executed in a very able manner; over the gate of Prato, likewise, he painted other figures of similar character; and at that of the Croce he depicted Our Lady with San Giovanni Battista and Sant' Ambrogio.† Pictures and paintings of all kinds were besides produced by this artist in almost unlimited numbers, and all giving proof of ability. I have myself, in consideration of his goodness and sufficiency, employed him several times with others

* Vasari here alludes to the works which, by commission from the Duke, he was himself executing at that time in the palace.

† These works are still in existence.

for the works of the palace,* to my own great satisfaction and that of all besides.

But the thing which most of all pleases me in this Michele is that, to say nothing of his being a truly honest man, of an upright walk and regular life, one who fears God in short; he has always in his workshop a good number of young people to whom he teaches his art with incredible affection.

Carlo Portelli of Loro, in the upper Val d'Arno, was also a disciple of Ridolfo, and by his hand likewise there are numerous pictures in Florence; several of these are in the Church of Santa Maria Maggiore, and there are a vast number dispersed among the other Churches of the city and neighbourhood; in that of Santa Felicità, for example, some are also in the possession of the Nuns of Monticelli. The picture of the Chapel of the Baldesi family in the Cestello† is also by his hand; it is to the right of the entrance, and the subject of the work is the Martyrdom of San Romualdo, Bishop of Fiesole.‡

---

## THE PAINTER, GIOVANNI DA UDINE.

[BORN 1487—DIED 1561-1564.]

In Udine, a city of Friuli, there lived a citizen, Giovanni by name, and of the family of the Nani, who was the first of his kin that had given attention to the calling of an embroiderer, which was afterwards pursued by his descendants with so much distinction, that they were no longer called De' Nani but De' Ricamatori, or the Embroiderers.

To one of that family, a certain Francesco, who lived in the manner of an opulent proprietor, passing his time at the chase and in similar occupations, there was born, in the year

* That now called the Palazzo Vecchio, and which was then the residence of the Duke.

† The Church of Santa Maria Maddalena de' Pazzi, anciently called Cestello. The work of Carlo Portelli, here in question, still retains its place.

‡ Bottari, at the close of the Life of Ridolfo, mentions other works of Michele as existing in the Chapel of the Villa di Caserotta, near Casciano. See the *Roman Edition of our Author*, 1756.

1494,* a son whom he called Giovanni, and who, while yet but a boy, showed so much inclination to the study of design, that the thing was considered extraordinary; for even while hunting or fowling with his father, he would design the figures of the dogs, the hares, the kids, every kind of animal or bird, in short, which fell into his hands, whenever a halt in the chase gave him leisure, and that to such perfection as to amaze all who beheld it.

This disposition being remarked by Francesco his father, the latter took him to Venice, and put him to learn the art of the limner with Giorgione da Castel Franco. Here, while working with Giorgione, the youth heard so much praise bestowed on the productions of Michelagnolo and Raffaello, that he resolved to repair to Rome, come what might, and having procured a letter of good will and favour from Domenico Grimani, who was the particular friend of his father, to Baldassare Cartiglioni, Secretary of the Duke of Mantua, and a special intimate of Raffaello da Urbino, he went to Rome accordingly. Having reached that city he was placed by Cartiglioni in the school of Raffaello, where he acquired a thorough knowledge of the principles of his art, which is a matter of great importance, seeing that when the disciple commences by adopting a bad manner, it rarely happens that he afterwards attains to a good one, or in any case if he do so, it must always be a work of infinite difficulty.

Having passed some time in Rome then, as we have said, and having next acquired a knowledge of the soft, beautiful, and graceful manner of Raffaello, Giovanni, like a youth of good parts as he was, determined to adhere rigidly and by all means to that manner. Wherefore, his genius and power of hand giving good aid to his judicious intention, he made extraordinary progress, and very soon became capable of drawing and painting to such perfection that he rapidly succeeded, at a word, in the successful imitation of whatever

* Giovanni da Udine left a Journal in his native city, written with his own hand, and from which it appears that he was born on the 27th of Oct. 1487. The memoranda of this work bear high testimony to the general accuracy of Vasari, since, with the exception of certain dates, the relation of our author is in strict accordance with the facts as set forth in the Journal of Giovanni.

natural objects were placed before him, whether animals, landscapes, buildings, draperies, vases, implements, foliage, or whatever else the object might be; insomuch that there were none of the young men in that school who could surpass him.*

But above all did Giovanni delight in depicting birds of every kind, and of these he soon completed a book full of so much variety and beauty that Raffaello found a perpetual amusement and interest therein. Now there was at that time with Raphael, a Fleming called Giovanni, who was an excellent master in fruits, foliage, and flowers, all which he executed beautifully, and with the utmost truth to nature, although in a manner that was somewhat hard and laboured; from him, therefore, Giovanni da Udine learned, in a short time, to produce these objects in equal perfection with his teacher; nay, rather, he improved on the manner of the latter by the addition of a certain force and largeness as well as softness, which caused him to succeed in some branches of his art to a degree that was most admirable, as will be presently related. He furthermore learned to execute landscapes, with ruined buildings and the broken relics of antiquity, as also to paint the same landscapes and foliage on cloth, in the manner which has been practised since his time, not by the Flemings only, but by all the Italian painters likewise.

Now Raphael very highly estimated the abilities of Giovanni da Udine, and when occupied with that picture of the Santa Cecilia, now in Bologna,† he caused Giovanni to paint the organ which is in the hand of that saint; this the latter copied from the instrument itself, and with such good effect that his work does really appear to be a relief: he also painted the other musical instruments which are at the feet of Santa Cecilia, and, what is of more importance, he brought his own manner herein to so close a similitude with that of Raphael, that the whole work appears to have been executed by one hand.

* Certain details respecting this master will be found by such of our readers as may desire them, in the work of Count Fabio Maniago, published at Udine, *Storia delle Belle Arti Friulane*, pp. 364, *et seq.*

† See the Life of Raphael, vol. iii. p. 33, *et seq.* See also the Life of Francia, vol. ii. p. 303, *et seq.*

No long time after the completion of the above, excavations were made at San Piero in Vincula, and among the ruins of the Palace of Titus, with the hope of finding statues, when certain subterranean chambers were discovered, and these were decorated all over with minute grottesche, small figures, stories, and ornaments, executed in stucco of very low relief.* These discoveries Raffaello was taken to see, and Giovanni accompanied his master, when they were both seized with astonishment at the freshness, beauty, and excellent manner of these works, seeing that it appeared to them a great marvel to find them in so fair a state of preservation after the lapse of so long a time, but in effect it was not so much to be wondered at, when, we consider that they had never been touched by the air or looked on by the light; which are wont, by means of the changes brought by the seasons, to destroy and consume all things.†

These grottesche then (for they were called *grottesche* because they had first been found in these grottoes or subterranean places), executed with so much care, giving proof of so profound a knowledge in design, and evincing such extraordinary power of fancy, seeing that with those minute ornaments in stucco were mingled portions in colour of the most varied beauty, and exhibiting small figures comprising stories of exquisite grace and sweetness—all these things, I say, did so deeply enter into, and take possession of, the mind and heart of Giovanni, that he devoted himself wholly to the study thereof, and could not satisfy himself with copying the same, neither one time nor twice sufficing him by any means: he succeeded therefore so effectually in imitating these works, and reproduced them with so much grace and facility, that nothing more was now wanting to him than the knowledge of the manner in which the stucco, whereof the grottesche were in part formed, was compounded.

Now, it is true that many before his time had cogitated and puzzled over that matter, but had been able to manage nothing better than a stucco made of gypsum, chalk, Greek

* Certain parts of these works were engraved on copper, and published with explanations in the *Picturæ Antiquæ Romæ*, Rome, 1751.

† And these remains are accordingly now reduced to a deplorable condition, much having been totally destroyed by the humidity of the place. —*Bottari.*

pitch, wax, and pounded bricks, which they then gilded with gold. But they had not succeeded in discovering the true method of making stucco similar to that used for the works discovered in the ancient grottoes and chambers. At the time of which we now speak they were proceeding to construct decorations for the arches and the upper tribune of San Pietro, with lime-stone and puzzolana, as we have related in the life of Bramante, all the carvings of foliage, with the ovoli, and many other members, then being prepared in moulds of clay; wherefore Giovanni began to examine that method of preparation in lime-stone and puzzolana, and to try if he could not succeed in making figures of basso-rilievo therefrom: continuing his experiments accordingly, he finally produced them in all their parts to his wish, with the one exception, that the external surface had not the delicacy and fineness exhibited by the antique, nor had it the whiteness of colour which those works presented.

Giovanni then bethought himself of some remedy for this defect, and decided that it might be requisite to mingle the lime of the white travertine with some substance which should be also white, instead of with puzzolana; he therefore caused flakes of travertine to be pounded, and found that they answered tolerably well, but the work was nevertheless rather of a livid than a pure white. Ultimately, however, having caused the whitest marble which he could find to be ground to an impalpable powder and carefully sifted, he mixed that with lime from white travertine, and found that he had thus indubitably succeeded in producing the stucco of the ancients, with all the properties that were to be desired therein.

Greatly rejoiced with this result, Giovanni then showed Raphael what he had done; and as the latter was then in process of adorning the Papal Loggie, as we have already said, by command of Pope Leo X., he caused Giovanni to decorate all the vaultings of the same with most beautiful ornaments in stucco, surrounding the whole with grottesche similar to those of the antique, all being enriched with the most pleasing and fanciful inventions, and exhibiting the most singular and most varied objects that can possibly be imagined. The whole work was executed in mezzo and basso-rilievo, the decorations being varied by stories, landscapes, foliage, and other fancies, as also presenting borders of much beauty. Giovanni did, indeed, on that occasion exhaust every effort, so to speak, that art can make in works of such a kind, and he not only equalled the antique in this performance,—so far as we can judge from such things as have been hitherto discovered and as we have seen,—but even surpassed them, since these works of Giovanni, for the beauty of their design, for the rich invention displayed in the figures, and for the colouring, whether in stucco or in painting, are indeed to be preferred to those of the ancients; his productions being infinitely superior in these respects to the antiques found in the Colosseum, or painted in the Baths of Dioclesian * and other places known to us.

Nay, where, in the works of any other master, will you find birds more truly natural, so to speak, or which come nearer to the truth, whether as regards the colouring, softness of the plumage, or other praiseworthy qualities, than do those of the friezes and pilasters of the Loggie now in question, where are they to be seen of every kind, and in all instances more truthful and life-like ?† where, indeed, can we see them of equal merit ? We have them exhibited, too, in variety as rich as that of Nature herself, some represented in one manner and some in another, but all of different kinds; many of these exquisite birds, for example, are perched on ears of corn and sheaves of maize, buckwheat, millet, and grain of all sorts ; but not of grain only, they are seen among fruits and berries also, of such kinds as the earth has always produced for the sustenance of birds. As much may be affirmed of the fish and every other manner of water animal and marine monster, which Giovanni represented in the same place ; but since it is impossible to say so much but that it shall still be too little, it were perhaps better to be altogether silent, than to set one's self attempting that which cannot be accomplished.

What, indeed, can I say of the innumerable varieties in fruits and flowers which are here depicted in every possible

* The grottesche and stucco works in the Colosseum and the Baths of Dioclesian have now totally perished.—*Ed. Flor.*, 1832-8.

† The arabesques and stucco work of the Loggie have now suffered greatly : they have been engraved by Santi Bartoli, as well as by Volpato and Ottaviani.—*Ed. Flor.*, 1832-8.

manner and without end? Displaying too, as they do, every tint of colour and change of form which Nature has imparted to them at every season of the year and in all the regions of the world. What again of the infinite assemblage of musical instruments which are also here represented in the most natural fashion? And who does not know,—seeing that the thing is most notorious—who does not know that at the end of the Loggia, where there was a building respecting which the Pope had not yet decided on the mode of completion —that Giovanni had painted a balustrade to imitate and continue the true one of the Loggia, with a hanging carpet over it, and that a groom one day, running in great haste to the Pope, who was then at the Belvedere, where a carpet was required for the use of his Holiness—a groom, I say, running towards this painted carpet from a distance, was about to snatch it from the balustrade, as believing it to be a real one?

At a word, it may truly be asserted, without offence to other artists, that for a work of this kind the paintings here in question are the most beautiful, the most extraordinary, and the most admirable, that have ever been seen by mortal eye. Nay, I will furthermore venture to declare, that this has been the cause why not Rome alone, but every other part of the world also, has been filled with these pictures. For not only was Giovanni more than the restorer, he may even be called the inventor, of stucco work and other grottesche; for by these his productions he has furnished a model from which all who have desired to labour in that branch of art have been able to take their exemplars, to say nothing of the fact, that the young men by whom Giovanni was assisted, and who were in great numbers, one time with another, having learned from him as the true master of that art, did afterwards disseminate their knowledge of the same throughout all the Provinces.

Giovanni was meanwhile proceeding with the lowermost part of the Loggia, wherein he adopted another and different method from that used in the compartments of stucco-work, the pictures on the walls and the vaultings of the first-mentioned Loggie; but these last were no less beautiful, the various divisions representing trellises of cane which supported vines richly covered and laden with grapes mingled with briony and other plants of various kinds, as also with flowers in rich abundance—jasmine, roses, &c., the whole furthermore embellished with different kinds of animals and birds of varied plumage.

Pope Leo then determining to cause the Hall on the ground floor, wherein the Guard of the Lansquenets hold their watch, to be painted, Giovanni, in addition to the friezes which he executed around the same, and which consisted of the Papal Arms, with lions, children, and grottesche, made a species of ornament for the walls, resembling the ancient incrustations used by the Romans for their temples, baths, and similar edifices, as may be seen in the Ritonda, in the Portico of San Piero and in other places, the incrustation made by Giovanni being an imitation of marbles and fine stones of various kinds.

In a Hall near that above-named, and which was used as a waiting-room by the chamberlains, Raffaello da Urbino had painted many beautiful figures of the Apostles, the size of life, standing within certain tabernacles; and over the cornices of that work Giovanni executed numerous animals and birds of the parrot kind, all painted from nature and exhibiting various colours, the originals of those birds being in the possession of His Holiness: he added figures of apes and monkeys also, with civet-cats and other strange creatures. But this work had only a short life, seeing that Pope Paul IV., choosing to make little cabinets and nooks wherein to hide himself, fairly ruined the apartment, and deprived the Palace of a very remarkable work, a thing which would not have been done by that holy man had he been gifted with taste for the arts of design. Giovanni likewise prepared the cartoons for the hangings and arras required for various purposes, and which were afterwards woven of silk and gold in Flanders; the subjects chosen were figures of children sporting amidst festoons of flowers, whereunto are suspended the devices of Pope Leo, with the addition of various animals all copied from nature. He also made the cartoons for certain pieces of arras covered with grottesche, and which are in the first rooms of the Consistory.

While Giovanni was occupied with this work, there was a palace in process of erection for Messer Giovanni Battista dell' Aquila, at the end of the Borgo Nuovo, and near the

Piazza di San Pietro; for the front of this building Giovanni was commissioned to prepare decorations in stucco, and he executed the greater part of the same; a very fine work it was considered to be.* This artist likewise painted the Loggia of the Vigna, which Giulio, Cardinal de' Medici, caused to be constructed under Monte Mario, and made all the ornaments in stucco for that Loggia, wherein there are animals, grottesche, festoons, and arabesques,† which are so beautiful that Giovanni may be supposed to have been desirous of surpassing himself on that occasion;‡ and the Cardinal, who highly estimated his abilities, not only conferred many benefits on the kinsmen of Giovanni, but also gave him a canonicate for himself.§ This benefice was situate at Civitale in Friuli, and was subsequently given by Giovanni to one of his brothers.||

Having at a later period been commissioned to construct a fountain for the same Cardinal at the above-mentioned Vigna,¶ and to make the water flow from the mouth of an elephant's head in marble, Giovanni took for his model in all parts and for every particular the Temple of Neptune, a hall which had been discovered a short time previously, among the ancient ruins of the great palace, and which was decorated all over with stucco work, marine monsters and other products of the sea, copied from nature and executed with the utmost perfection. But in certain respects Giovanni nevertheless did far surpass this ancient hall, seeing that, to a great variety of those animals admirably well done, he added shells and other things of similar kind in vast numbers, and arranged with very great ability.

* These stuccoes have perished.—*Ed. Flor.*, 1832-8.

† The principal difference between the arabesques and the grottesche, as our readers will probably remember, is that the latter added figures to its various fantasies.

‡ Bottari laments, and with reason, that these works, as well as all beside in "in that delicious abode," have suffered grievous injury.

§ Hear! hear!

|| It were to be desired that this second consignee of the Benefice had at least been a churchman, but we have not been able to give our readers the satisfaction of knowing that it was so; on the contrary, the said recipient of clerical dignities is described as simply "Paolo Ricamatori," without any of the additions which denote the ecclesiastic. He is recorded as having "been named Canon in 1522, and died in 1576."

¶ This vigna, or country house, is now called the Villa Madama.

He subsequently constructed another fountain, but in the rustic manner, and having its site in the bed of a stream overhung with shrubs and plants. Here, with infinite skill and judgment, Giovanni caused the water to fall through tufa and other stones in drops and slender streams, which had all the appearance of being entirely natural. In the uppermost part of this grotto or cavern, and amidst the spungeous stones which formed it, he placed a colossal head of a Lion, around which the maidenhair and other climbing plants were so artfully trained as to form a kind of chaplet to the same, nor would it be easy to describe the grace thus imparted to that wild place, which was indeed most beautiful in every part, and inconceivably charming.

Having completed that undertaking, Giovanni received from the Cardinal the dignity of a knighthood of San Pietro, and was then sent to Florence, to the end that, having erected a certain chamber at that corner of the Medici Palace where Cosimo the elder, founder of the edifice, had made a Loggia for the assemblage and accommodation of the citizens, as it was formerly the custom of the most noble families to do, he might then paint and adorn the same with grottesche and stucco-work. Now the Loggia had been constructed after the designs of Michelagnolo Buonarroti, not open, but having the form of a chamber, and being furnished with two grated windows, which were the first of the kind that had been made for palaces, with the external grating of iron curving outwards that is to say. Of this Loggia, Giovanni now decorated all the vaulting with pictures and stucco-work, exhibiting, in a circular compartment thereof, the six balls, which are the arms of the Medici, and giving as supporters three boys in relief, the figures of which are singularly beautiful and graceful in their attitudes. He also represented numbers of admirably depicted animals in the same place, adding many fair devices of the Signori belonging to that illustrious house, with stories in mezzo-rilievo, made of stucco; there were besides compartments, wherein were delineated historical representations in white and black, after the manner of cameos, and so well done that better could not possibly be imagined.

There still remained four arches beneath the roof, which were not decorated with pictures at that time, but were painted many years after by the Aretine, Giorgio Vasari, who was then a youth of eighteen, and working in the service of his first lord, the Duke Alessandro de' Medici. This was in the year 1535; and Giorgio there delineated stories from the Life of Julius Cæsar in allusion to the Cardinal Julius, by whom the work had been commanded, as we have said. On a small vaulting of a coved form, near the above-mentioned Loggia, Giovanni then executed certain ornaments of stucco in very low relief, with several pictures of extraordinary merit, which greatly pleased the painters who were then in Florence, as giving evidence of much boldness and singular facility, while they were full of spirited and fanciful inventions; but being themselves accustomed to a laboured manner of their own and to a servile copying of exact portraits from the life, in everything that they did, the Florentine artists were not disposed to commend them unreservedly and without restriction, they not perfectly entering into the spirit of those productions. Nor did they set themselves to imitate the same, perhaps because they had not the boldness or courage to do so.

Having returned to Rome, Giovanni painted a series of large festoons around the angles and sections of a ceiling in the Loggia of Agostino Chigi, where Raffaello had executed and was then continuing the decorations; Giovanni there represented fruits and flowers appropriate to every season of the year, each season following in regular succession, and the foliage, fruits, and flowers, being all finished to such perfection, that every separate object seen there, appears to be detached from the walls, and is indeed most natural. The variety of kind also in those fruits, grain, &c., is so wonderful, that I will not attempt to enumerate them one by one, and will only say that every sort which has ever been produced by Nature in our part of the world may there be found represented. Among the figures are those of a Mercury in the act of flight, and of a Priapus. Over the former is a gourd enveloped in its tendrils, with pumpkins amidst their flowers, and large bunches of figs, some bursting with their ripeness, and also mingled with flowers: all these fancies being expressed with so much grace, that no one could imagine anything more perfectly done. But what more can I say?—to sum up the whole, I may safely venture to affirm, that in this sort of paintings, Giovanni da Udine has far surpassed all those who have best imitated Nature in works of a similar kind; for, to say nothing of other matters, it was the custom of our artist to depict every object, even to the flowers of the elder, the fennel, and other things, however minute, with an exactitude that is most amazing. In the lunettes, which are surrounded by the above-mentioned garlands, or festoons, are large numbers of animals, with figures of children holding the attributes of the Gods in their hands; but more than all the rest are admired, a lion and a sea-horse; these are foreshortened in a manner which is so beautiful that they are held to be all but miraculous.

The works here in question being completed, Giovanni decorated a bath-room of much beauty, in the Castello Sant' Angelo, and performed many other less important works in the Palace of the Pope; but these, for the sake of brevity, we leave undescribed. The death of Raphael, which grieved Giovanni very much, then ensued, and Pope Leo having also departed, the Arts of Design, with every other kind of talent, were found to have no longer any place in Rome; and Giovanni da Udine employed himself for many months in painting certain matters of little moment, for the Vigna of the above-named Cardinal de' Medici. On the arrival of Pope Adrian in Rome, Giovanni did but prepare the small flags for the Castle, and these he had twice renewed during the pontificate of Leo X., together with the great Standard which floats on the summit of the highest tower.

It is true that Giovanni painted four square banners, when the said Pope Adrian canonized Sant' Antonino, Archbishop of Florence, with St. Hubert, who had been Bishop of I know not what city in Flanders: and of these banners, one, on which is the figure of the above-named Sant' Antonino, was given to the Church of San Marco, in Florence, where the body of that Saint is deposited: another of the banners, bearing the figure of St. Hubert, was placed in the Church of Santa Maria dell' Anima, which is the Church of the Germans in Rome, while the remaining two were sent into Flanders.

But when Clement VII. was created High Pontiff, Giovanni, who had at that time left Rome to avoid the pestilence then raging there, and had gone to Udine, returned instantly to the former city, having been much employed in the service of that Pope, at an earlier period. He was at once appointed to prepare a rich and beautiful ornament, which was to be erected over the steps of San Pietro, for the ceremony of the Coronation of Clement, and it was subsequently commanded that he and Perino del Vaga should paint certain pictures in the vaulted ceiling of the Old Hall; that, namely, which stands opposite to those lower rooms previously decorated by Giovanni, as we have said, and which lead from the Loggia to the rooms of the Torre Borgia. Our artist now therefore, made a beautiful series of divisions in stucco work, with numerous grottesche, and animals of various kinds; while Perino painted the seven planets within the square compartments, formed by those works in stucco.*

The same two artists were also commissioned to paint the walls of that Hall, wherein Giotto, according to that which has been written by Platina, in the Lives of the Pontiffs, did long ago paint figures of certain Popes, who had been put to death for the faith of Christ, and for which cause, that room was once called the Hall of the Martyrs; but scarcely had they completed the ceiling, before that most unhappy sack of Rome took place, and the work could proceed no further; seeing that Giovanni, who had suffered greatly, both in his person and property, had again retired to Udine, with the intention of making a long stay there.

His purpose in that matter was nevertheless interrupted, since Pope Clement VII. having returned to Rome from Bologna, after he had there crowned the Emperor Charles V. caused Giovanni to return thither also; he then made him paint anew the Standards of the Castello Sant' Angelo, and afterwards commanded him to decorate the ceiling of the great Chapel of San Pietro, which is the principal one in that Church, and where the Altar of the Saint is erected.† Meanwhile, Fra Marino, who held the office of the leaden seal, being dead, that office was given to Sebastiano Veneziano, a painter of great name; but a pension of eighty ducats on the same was assigned to Giovanni da Udine,‡ and the

* These stuccoes and paintings have all perished.

† The Chapel having been rebuilt, this work also has been destroyed.

‡ In the Journal of Giovanni he has himself made mention of this precise sum as the pension assigned to him. See Maniago, *Storia delle Belle Arti Friulane.*

troubles of the Pontiff having in a great measure ceased, while the affairs of Rome were also brought into a state of repose, Giovanni was despatched by His Holiness, with many promises of favour, to Florence, there to execute the decorations for the New Sacristy of San Lorenzo, which had been adorned with the admirable sculptures of Michelagnolo, and the tribune of which is covered with deeply sunken squares, diminishing as they approach the central point.

Giovanni put hand to the work accordingly, and completed it to admiration, with the aid of his numerous assistants, adorning the same with rosettes, foliage, and other ornaments in stucco and gold. But in one respect he betrayed a defect of judgment; in the plane or level bordering which forms the ribs of the vaulting namely, and in those which cross the same, and serve to enclose the squares, he painted birds, foliage, masks, and figures of various kinds, which are indeed exceedingly beautiful in themselves, but which, being painted on grounds of different colours, are not to be clearly distinguished from below, by reason of the distance, whereas if he had simply coloured the figures themselves on a plain ground, and without any other addition, they could have been seen, and the whole work would have produced a more cheerful and pleasing effect.*

There now remained to complete only so much of this undertaking as might have been effected in about fifteen days, with some retouching in certain parts—when the news of Pope Clement's death reached Giovanni, who thereupon lost all hope; more particularly in relation to the reward which he was expecting for the work in question. He then perceived, although too late, that the trust of those who put their faith in Courts is too frequently betrayed, and was compelled to acknowledge the constant liability to disappointment of those whose hopes are built on the lives of princes.

Giovanni then returned to Rome, and there indeed he might have lived on the revenues of his offices and other sources of income; he might also have entered the service of the new Pontiff Paul III., or that of the Cardinal Ippolito de' Medici, but he determined to reinstate himself in his native place of Udine, and repaired thither accordingly.

* The whole of these works have long been covered with whitewash.—*Ed. Flor.*, 1832-8.

Here he proposed to live with that brother of his to whom he had given the Canonicate, intending to use his pencils no more: but in that matter also he was compelled to a change of plans, seeing that having taken a wife and become the father of a family, he was in a manner forced, by that instinct which impels a man to desire the future welfare of his children, as well as to feel anxious that they shall be fittingly brought up in his own lifetime, he was compelled, I say, once more to recommence his labours.

He then, at the request of the father of the Cavalier Giovan-Francesco di Spilimbergo, adorned the walls of a room with figures of children, garlands, and other fantasies; after which he decorated the Chapel of Santa Maria di Civitale, with admirable stucco-work and paintings; and for the canons of the Cathedral in that place, he painted two exceedingly beautiful standards. For the Fraternity of Santa Maria di Castello in Udine, Giovanni likewise painted a figure of Our Lady with the Divine Child in her arms, on a rich Gonfalon or Banner; beside the Virgin is a most graceful Angel, who offers to her the above-named Castello, which is on an eminence in the centre of the city.*

In Venice also this artist executed certain works, among which may be particularized a chamber most beautifully adorned with stucco-work and paintings, in the Palace of Monsignore Grimani, the Patriarch of Aquilea. In this room there are besides some admirable stories in small figures from the hand of Francesco Salviati.†

Finally, in the year 1550, our artist, having gone on a pilgrimage to Rome for the most holy Jubilee, travelling on foot, meanly clothed, and in the company of the poorer sort of pilgrims, thus remained in the city several days without being known to any one; but one morning, as he was going to San Paalo, he was recognized by Giorgio Vasari, then proceeding to the same Pardoning, in a coach, with Messer Bindo Altoviti, who was his intimate friend. Giovanni at first denied that he was himself, but being at length com-

* "These works of Giovanni da Udine have long been lost," observes Maniago, *ut supra*, but there is an erudite letter written by the Abbot Mauro Boni, on the above-named Gonfalon, and which was published at Udine in 1797.

† These works still exist.

pelled to admit his identity and confess the truth, he then suffered his case to be known, and allowed that he had great need of Giorgio's assistance with the Pontiff in the matter of his pension, which was withheld from him by a certain Fra Guglielmo, a sculptor of Genoa,* who had succeeded to the leaden seal after the death of Fra Bastiano.

Giorgio mentioned the affair to His Holiness accordingly, when the order for Giovanni to receive his pension was renewed, and subsequently an attempt was made to exchange the same for a canonicate, to be Conferred on a son of Giovanni.† Meanwhile the pension was again withheld by that Fra Guglielmo, and Giovanni repaired from Udine to Florence, just when Pope Pius was elected to the papal chair, hoping that he might there be favoured by His Excellency whose intervention with the Pontiff he expected to obtain by means of Vasari. Having reached Florence therefore, he was made known to the Duke by Vasari, and was permitted to accompany his most Illustrious Excellency to Siena; nay, from that last-mentioned city he went with that Signore to Rome also, whither repaired at the same time the Signora Duchess Leonora. In Rome Giovanni da Udine was so powerfully aided by the Duke, that he was comforted by the obtaining of all that he desired; nay, was furthermore commissioned by the Pope to give the ultimate completion to the last of the Loggie; that namely which is over the one formerly constructed by Pope Leo: he received very handsome appointments while thus employed, and when that work was finished he was commanded by the same Pontiff to retouch all the pictures of the last-mentioned Loggia.

But this was an error, and a very ill-considered thing, seeing that the retouching of those paintings *a secco* caused them to lose all those masterly touches effected by the pencil of Giovanni, when he had been in all the excellence of his best days, and deprived them of that freshness and delicacy

* Guglielmo della Porta, who succeeded Sebastiano Veneziano, as Frate del Piombo, was not a Genoese, but a native of Milan. It is, however, true, that he studied at Genoa under Perino del Vaga.

† This youth, called Raffaello, proved to be a dissipated and worthless man, who was the source of perpetual sorrow to his father. See Maniago, *Storia*, &c., p. 368.

which had rendered the work in the first instance so perfectly beautiful.*

Having completed these labours, and being now in his seventieth† year, Giovanni finished the course of his life also: he died in the year 1564, rendering up his soul to God in that most noble city which had for so many years furnished him with the means of living in honour and with so great a name. Giovanni was always, but more especially towards the close of his life, a man who feared God, and was a good Christian. In his youth he had permitted himself few pleasures, those of hunting and fowling excepted, and while still young it was his custom to repair, on all festival days, with a servant of his, to the chase, sometimes going across the country to a distance of ten miles from Rome: he was, indeed, so successful in shooting with the short gun, or the cross-bow, that he seldom returned home without having first laden his servant with wild-ducks, pigeons, and every other kind of animal to be found in those marshy places. Giovanni was indeed the inventor, as it is said, of the screen formed of a figure of an ox painted on canvas, and behind which the sportsman can fire his piece without being discovered by the object aimed at: his love of fowling and of the chase caused him also to delight in dogs, many of which he reared himself.

This artist, who merits to be extolled among the greatest of his vocation, desired to be buried in the Ritondo, near his master Raffaello da Urbino, that he might not be divided in death from him whom his spirit never willingly abandoned in life; and since both of these masters were excellent Christians, as we have said, so we may believe that they are now met together in eternal blessedness.‡

* Bottari observes very justly in respect to this fact, that if Giovanni succeeded so ill in the re-touching of his own pictures, although an excellent master in his particular walk, we have the less reason to be surprised that the many obscure and incapable persons who have been suffered to retouch the works of able masters should have produced the mischief so frequently lamented.

† The Journal of Giovanni before alluded to shows him to have lived to the age of seventy-seven. See Maniago, *Storia delle Belle Arti Friulane,* as before cited.

‡ In the year 1822, a discourse in eulogy of Giovanni da Udine was pronounced by the Professor Francesco Maria Franceschini, at the Academy of the Fine Arts in Venice. This act of homage took place on the occasion of a distribution of prizes by that Academy.—*Ed. Flor.*, 1832-8.

## THE VENETIAN PAINTER, BATTISTA FRANCO.*

[BORN 1498—DIED 1561.]

THE Venetian, Battista Franco, having given his attention to design in his childhood, repaired to Rome, as one who desired to attain to the perfection of his art, in the twentieth year of his age; and there, having studied for some time with much diligence, and examined the manner of many masters, he resolved to confine himself to copying the designs, paintings, and sculptures of Michelagnolo, and to imitate the works of no other. Wherefore, having set himself to make research, there did not ultimately remain a single design, or sketch, nay not even a copy executed by Michelagnolo, that he did not himself make a copy from; whence it resulted that no long time had elapsed before he was reputed one of the best designers by whom the Chapel of Michelagnolo† was frequented. Nay, what is yet more, Battista would for some time do nothing but draw, and would not paint at all.

But in the year 1536, very great and sumptuous preparations were to be arranged by Antonio da San Gallo, for the arrival of the Emperor Charles V., and all the artists, whether bad or good, were then employed, as we have said, in another place. Then Raffaello da Monte Lupo, who was commissioned to construct the decorations for the bridge of Sant' Angelo, among which were ten statues, to be placed along the bridge,—Raffaello, I say, resolved so to contrive, that Battista likewise should be employed with the rest, having observed him to be an exact designer and a youth of fine parts, for which cause he desired by all means to give him occupation: having spoken respecting the matter to San Gallo, therefore, Raffaello pressed him so much, that Battista received the charge of four large stories in chiaro-scuro, which were to be executed in fresco on the front of the Porta Capena, now called the Gate of San Sebastiano, by which the emperor was to make his entry.

Over this gate therefore, Battista, though he had never then touched colours, painted the arms of Pope Paul III.,

* Zanetti, *Pittura Veneziana*, informs us that the family name of this artist was Semolei.

† The Sistine Chapel in the Vatican that is to say.

with those of the Emperor Charles V., and with a figure representing Romulus, who is placing the papal tiara on the escutcheon of the Holy Father, and an imperial crown over that of the Emperor. The height of the figure of Romulus was five braccia; it was clothed in the antique manner, and had a crown on the head; on the right hand of Romulus stood the figure of Numa Pompilius, and on his left was that of Tullus Hostilius; over all were the words, QUIRINUS PATER. At each side of this gate, moreover, is a tower, and on the walls of those towers Battista furthermore depicted triumphal processions; that of the elder Scipio, decreed to him for Carthage, which he had subjected to the Roman dominion, being on the one side; and the Triumph of Scipio the younger, for the ruin and destruction of the same city, appearing on the other.

Two pictures were painted by the same artist on the exterior face of these towers; in one of them was seen Hannibal under the walls of Rome, but repelled by a tempest, and in the other, that on the left hand namely, was Flaccus entering Rome for the purpose of defending the city against the Carthaginians. All these works, being the first performed by Battista, and, as compared with those of the other masters, were considered very good and much extolled. Nor is there any doubt but that this artist would have surpassed many of his competitors had he begun from the first to paint, and gradually rendered himself familiar with the use of pencils and colours; but his having remained obstinately fixed in a certain opinion entertained by many, who persuade themselves that he who can design may also paint, was to him the source of no little injury. He acquitted himself, nevertheless, much better than did some of those who executed the stories for the Arch of San Marco, of which there were eight, four on each side that is to say, and the best of them were painted partly by Francesco Salviati and partly by a certain Martino,* with other young Germans, who had also come to Rome for the purposes of study.

Nor will I omit to take this opportunity for relating that the above-named Martino, who possessed remarkable ability in the treatment of chiaro-scuro, here produced certain battle-pieces and skirmishes between Christians and Turks, which

* The Hollander, Martin Hemskerck.

exhibited so much boldness, and were enriched with so many beautiful inventions, that it would not have been possible to do better.* It is to be furthermore recorded of this master, that for the purpose of securing the completion of the ornaments within the stated period, he worked with his assistants so zealously that they never quitted their labour; they had consequently a perpetual supply of drink brought to them: this being good Greek wine, the men were constantly inebriated, and this fact of their being perpetually under the influence of wine, together with their practice and zeal for art, caused them to produce wonderful things.

When Salviati, Battista, and the Calavrese† saw the works of these artists, they were therefore compelled to confess that he who desires to become a painter should begin by using the pencils early; and this conviction bringing Battista to a more reasonable manner of viewing the question, he ceased to give so much study to the finishing of his drawings, and resolved that he would sometimes practise himself in colouring also.

Montelupo then went to Florence, where they were in like manner preparing sumptuous ornaments for the occasion of the Emperor's arrival, and Battista Franco accompanied him; but when they reached the city they found the preparations far advanced towards completion: Battista was, nevertheless, set to work, and erected the pedestal for a statue which had been executed by Fra Giovan-Agnolo Montorsoli,‡ to be placed at the corner of the Carnesecchi: this pedestal he covered with figures and trophies. Having thus been made known among the artists as a youth of good parts and fine ability, Battista was much employed at a later period; as he was at the coming of Madama Margherita of Austria,§ wife of the Duke Alessandro, more especially in the preparations made for that event by Giorgio Vasari, in

* He is said to have made drawings of nearly all the Roman churches, and Bottari tells us that in a book possessed by Mariette, there were drawings of San Giovanni Laterano, San Pietro, and San Lorenzo Fuori le Mura, in their ancient state, by the hand of this artist.

† This is perhaps Marco Calabrese, whose life will be found at p. 352 of vol. iii.

‡ The Life of Fra Giovanni Montorsoli follows.

§ Daughter of the Emperor Charles V.

the palace of Ottaviano de' Medici, where the Signora Margherita was to reside.

These festivals being at an end, Battista set himself industriously to draw the statues by Michelagnolo, which are in the New Sacristy of San Lorenzo, whither all the sculptors and painters of Florence were then wont to repair for the purpose of drawing and working in relief: all these figures Battista designed with the most careful study, and he made infinite progress; the error he had committed in not consenting to draw from the life, or to use colours, was nevertheless perceived, and his having never done any other thing besides drawing from statues, and some few objects of similar character, had given him a hardness and dryness of manner, of which it was sufficiently manifest that he could not so entirely divest himself but that everything he did presented a harsh and laboured aspect, as may be seen, among other instances, in a painting on canvas, wherein he has with great care depicted the violence suffered from Tarquinius by the Roman Lucrezia.

While Battista was thus continuing to frequent the Sacristy with other artists, he formed a friendship with the sculptor Bartolommeo Ammannati, who was then studying the works of Michelagnolo in company with many other sculptors, and this intimacy proceeded to such an extent that Ammannati received Battista and Genga of Urbino into his house, where they all lived together for some time, devoting themselves with very great profit to the studies of art.

The Duke Alessandro having met with his death in the year 1536,* and the Signor Duke Cosimo de' Medici being elected in his place, many of the dependants of the departed sovereign remained in the service of the new one, but others did not. Among those who departed was the above-named Giorgio Vasari, who returned to Arezzo with the determination no more to follow Courts, seeing that he had lost his first Lord, the Cardinal Ippolito de' Medici, and afterwards the Duke Alessandro; but he caused Battista to be received into the service of Duke Cosimo, and that artist was set to work in the Guardaroba. There he painted a large picture representing Pope Clement and the Cardinal Ippolito, whose figures he copied from pictures by Fra Bastiano and by

* Assassinated, as our readers will remember, by the treachery of Lorenzino de' Medici.

Titian, with the Duke Alessandro, whom he took from a painting by Pontormo. This work did not attain to the perfection that had been expected; but as in the same Guardaroba, Battista saw that Cartoon of the *Noli me tangere*, which had been made by Michelagnolo, and had been executed in colours by Jacopo Pontormo, he set himself to prepare a similar Cartoon, but with figures somewhat larger, and having done that, he painted a picture from it, in which he acquitted himself much better as to the colouring than he had done in the one above-mentioned; as to the Cartoon, as it was exactly copied from that of Michelagnolo, and done with great patience, it was in fact very beautiful.

The affair of Montemurlo, in which all the exiles and rebels to the Duke were routed and taken prisoners, having then ensued, Battista painted a story of the battle which had been fought, and mingling with the facts certain poetic fancies of his own which displayed good invention, the work was much extolled. It was, nevertheless, easy to perceive that in the deeds of arms, in the taking of the prisoners, and in many other parts, there was very much that was taken bodily from the works and designs of Buonarroti: in the distance was the battle, but in the foreground were the huntsmen of Ganymede, standing with their eyes turned upwards towards the Bird of Jove, who is carrying the youth away to the skies: this part Battista had borrowed from the design of Michelagnolo, and had used it in his picture to signify that the Duke, while still young, had been taken from the midst of his friends by the will of God, and so borne up into heaven: to signify this, I say, or some such matter.

That story, I repeat, was first designed by Battista in a Cartoon; it was afterwards painted by him with extraordinary care in a picture, and is now with his other works in the upper rooms of the Pitti Palace, which his most Illustrious Excellency has caused to be entirely finished. By these and similar labours, Battista Franco was detained in the service of the Duke, until the time when that sovereign took the Signora, Donna Leonora di Toledo, to wife, and he was then employed in the preparations made for those nuptials, for the triumphal arch erected at the Porta di Prato that is to say, where Ridolfo Ghirlandajo caused him to execute certain stories from the Life of the Signor Giovanni, father of the Duke Cosimo. In one of these is seen that Signor making the passage of the rivers Po and Adda; the Cardinal Giulio de' Medici, who was afterwards Pope Clement VII., the Signor Prosper Colonna, and other nobles being present; over this Battista painted the Redemption of San Secondo.

On the opposite side of the arch was another story by the hand of the same artist, and herein was represented the city of Milan with the Camp of the League around it, which, breaking up, leaves the Signor Giovanni in the place. To the right of the arch there was on one side another picture, wherein was a figure representing Opportunity with her hair unloosened; offering those tresses, which she holds in one hand, to the Signor Giovanni: on the other side is Mars, who presents him with the sword. Beneath the arch was also a story by the hand of Battista, the Signor Giovanni that is to say, fighting between the Tesino and Biegrassa upon the bridge of Rozzo, and, like another Horatius, defending the same with incredible valour. On the opposite side was depicted the taking of Caraveggio; and in the midst of the battle was seen the Signor Giovanni passing fearlessly through the fire and swords of the enemies' hosts. Between the columns to the right hand was painted an oval compartment, within which was represented Garlasso, taken by the same leader with a single company of soldiers; and amidst the columns on the left was a Bastion of Milan, also wrested from the enemy by the prowess of the Signor Giovanni. On that front of the arch which was left behind by him who would enter the city gate, was furthermore depicted the same Signor Giovanni de' Medici as seen on horseback beneath the walls of Milan, where he is engaged in single combat with a cavalier, whom he is transpiercing with his lance from one side to the other.

Finally, over the principal cornice, at the point which joins the edge of the upper cornice whereon the pediment is placed, Battista painted another large story, with very great care; this represented the Emperor Charles V., seated on a rock in the centre of the picture, crowned and holding a sceptre in his hand; at his feet lay a figure presenting the river Betis, and holding a vase which poured water from two mouths; near to this was another figure to signify the river Danube, and that river poured its waters into the sea from seven mouths. Of the large number of statues which accompanied the above-described story, and the others executed on the arch in question, I will make no mention, seeing that for the present it must suffice me to name such as were done by Battista Franco; nor is it now any part of my office to describe that which was performed by other artists, and which has moreover been set forth at sufficient length in writing by a different hand. I have besides declared what was needful of the masters by whom the aforesaid statues were executed, it would therefore be superfluous to speak of them further, and the more so as the works are no longer in their places to be examined and judged.

To return, therefore, to Battista: the best of the works executed by that artist in relation to these nuptial solemnities, was one of the ten pictures above-mentioned, and which were in the principal court of the Medici Palace; this was painted in chiaro-scuro, and represented the Duke Cosimo invested with the Ducal ensigns. But with all the care that Battista could take, he was nevertheless surpassed by Bronzino, and by many others who had less knowledge of design than himself, but who were superior to him in power of invention, boldness, and facility in the handling of the chiaro-scuro: for pictures, a remark I have made before, require to be treated with lightness and readiness, every portion of the whole being distributed to its due place with judgment, and giving no evidence of a certain dry weary labour which causes all to appear crude, hard, and displeasing. The too anxious painting over has likewise an injurious effect, since it frequently renders the work obscure and even spoils it, seeing that this perpetual going over the picture deprives it of all that good effect and grace which is the usual result of boldness and facility, qualities which, though they do in a great measure proceed from the gift of nature, may, nevertheless, to a certain extent, be acquired by art.

At a later period, Battista Franco was taken by Ridolfo Ghirlandajo to the Madonna de Ventigli, in Valdichiana, a place which was at that time the succursal to the Monastery of the Angeli in Florence, which belongs to the Order of

Camaldoli, but is now itself the chief seat of a Brotherhood in place of the Monastery of San Benedetto, which, being situate outside of the Pinti Gate, was ruined at the siege of Florence. Here, then, Battista painted in the cloisters the stories which have before been mentioned, while Ridolfo was employed in the execution of the picture and other ornaments for the High Altar; and these being finished, they next, as we have related in the life of Ridolfo, adorned with other paintings that holy place, which is widely renowned and much talked of for the many miracles there performed by the Virgin Mother of the Son of God.

Having subsequently returned to Rome, and just at the moment when the Last Judgment of Michelagnolo had been given to public view, Battista, as being a very zealous student of the manner and works of Buonarroti, most joyfully beheld that production completed, and minutely examined the whole design, to his infinite admiration; nay, he copied and made designs from the entire work. He then determined to remain in Rome, and for the Cardinal Francesco Cornaro, who had rebuilt the palace wherein he was dwelling, and which is situate near San Pietro, but with its portico on the side towards the Campo Santo;*—for this cardinal, I say, Battista painted a Loggia, which looks on the Piazza; he executed a kind of grottesche, over the stucco-work that is to say, covering the space with figures and minute storiettes; a work which the artist completed with great care and pains, nor did it fail to be considered a very beautiful performance.

About the same time, which was in the year 1538, Francesco Salviati had painted a story in fresco for the Brotherhood of the Misericordia,† but had still to give the last touches to his work.‡ He had also undertaken to execute others, which it was the purpose of many private persons to have painted in the same place; but the rivalry which was

* This Palace was demolished on the re-building of San Pietro.—*Bottari.*

† Now called San Giovanni Decollato.—*Ed. Flor.*, 1832-8.

‡ Which represented the Visitation of the Madonna. It has been spoiled by re-touching.—*Bottari.* This work was engraved by Bartolommeo Passerolli, and by one of the engravers Matham, James (or Jacob) that is to say.

just then existing between Francesco and Jacopo del Conte* caused these works to remain incomplete. This state of things becoming known to Battista, he thought to have here found an opportunity of proving himself to be greater than Francesco, nay, the greatest master in Rome. Thereupon he set his friends to work, and using every means he could find, did so contrive that Monsignore della Casa, having been shown one of his designs, commissioned him to execute a picture: he set hand to the work accordingly and painted a fresco, the subject of which was San Giovanni Battista taken by Herod and cast into prison.

But in despite of all the pains that were taken with his picture by Franco, it was considered to be far from approaching the merit of those by Salviati, seeing that it gave evidence of an excessively laboured treatment, and was in a hard, melancholy manner, being moreover without order in the composition, and wholly destitute of the grace and charm of colouring by whch those of Francesco were distinguished. And from this failure we may safely conclude that those are falling into a great error who, when in pursuit of art, consider themselves to have done all when they have given close attention to depicting exactly, and with all its muscles well developed, some torso, leg, arm, or whatever other part may be in question, and believe that the being well acquainted with so much renders them masters of the whole. Yes; such people are, without doubt, deceived, for a part is not the whole; and he only exhibits perfection in his work who, having well delineated the parts, knows how to bring the whole into harmony and true proportion, and who besides is careful that the composition and grouping of his figures, with the expression given to each and all, shall be such as will render clearly the effect desired without formality and without confusion.

Another point to be carefully secured is that the heads shall be powerful, animated, graceful, and exhibiting beauty withal, as well as truth of expression; nor must the manner be crude and hard: the nude parts must be sufficiently darkened in the shadows that they may have the due degree of relief, the figures must retire and fall into the distance

* Of this artist, who was a disciple of Andrea del Sarto, there is more hereafter.

exactly in the proportions required, to say nothing of the truth to be observed in perspective, of landscapes and many other parts, which all demand the utmost care for the production of a good picture. He who takes from the works of others, moreover, should be careful to do so in such sort that the portions borrowed shall not be too easily recognised. Battista therefore discovered, when it was too late, that he had been expending his time unduly over the minutiæ of muscles, &c., and in drawing with an over-strained diligence, while he did not give sufficient regard to the demands of the art in its other departments.

Having completed the picture above-mentioned, for which he obtained but little commendation, Battista transferred himself to Urbino, where, by the intervention of Bartolommeo Genga, he entered the service of the Duke. By that sovereign he was then commissioned to paint a large vaulting in the Church and Chapel attached to the Palace of Urbino, and setting hand instantly to the work, without further consideration, and without making any division by compartments, he began to prepare the designs, as the idea of the work presented itself, but taking the invention from the Judgment of Buonarroti: he thus made a Glory in Heaven, in imitation of that work, with Saints resting on clouds, which were scattered over the whole surface of the vaulting, and with all the choir of angels assembled around a figure of Our Lady, who, being in the act of ascending into heaven, is there awaited by Jesus Christ, who is about to place a crown on her head. Standing around in divers groups are the Patriarchs, the Prophets, the Sybils, the Apostles, the Martyrs, the Confessors, and the Virgins; all which figures, in their various attitudes, appear to be rejoicing and congratulating each other on the arrival of that glorious Virgin Mother.

Now this was a subject which certainly presented a most happy occasion for Battista to have proved himself an able artist, as he might have done, had he chosen a better path, taken pains to obtain practice in the handling of fresco colours, and governed himself with better order and more judgment in his labours than he displayed. But in this work he proceeded much as he had done in all those previously executed,* reproducing for ever the same figures, the same draperies, and the same accessories. The colouring was, besides, entirely destitute of beauty, and every part was executed with a laboured difficulty which deprived it of all grace; wherefore, the work being finished, was found to give but little satisfaction to the Duke Guidobaldo, nor did it in any wise content Bartolommeo Genga, or the other artists who had expected great things from this man, and the rather as he had shown them a most beautiful design in the beginning, for which cause they had been looking for a painting of equal excellence.

It may indeed be affirmed with truth that for preparing a beautiful design Battista had no equal, and might be therein considered an accomplished man. Remarking that this was the case, Duke Guidobaldo thought the designs of Battista might probably be used with good effect by those who were then so admirably working in vases and other pottery at Castel Durante, and where prints from the designs of Raffaello da Urbino,† and other able artists, had been copied with the most perfect success; he therefore caused Battista to prepare a large number of designs, and these being used for that kind of clay or china work, which is of better appearance than anything of the sort elsewhere made in all Italy, turned out to be of admirable excellence. Great numbers of vases were accordingly prepared, and of such sorts as might be suitable for the credenza or beaufet of a royal house, nor could the pictures executed thereon have been more effective or of better workmanship had they been painted in oil by the best masters.

Of these vases therefore, which, as respects the quality of the clay, do greatly resemble those anciently made in Arezzo, at the time of Porsenna, king of Tuscany that is to say; the

* The pictures executed by Battista Franco in Urbino were destroyed when the Cupola was taken down.—*Ed. Flor.*, 1832-8.

† Many of our readers will remember to have seen a collection of these vases in the Pharmacy and Laboratory at Loretto, the designs of which they will remember to have been told were by Raphael Sanzio, but the best authorities are disposed to think that the designs made expressly for these works were by Raffaello dal Colle and other artists of good ability, but not by the world's Raphael Sanzio. See the *Dissertations* of Lanzi on this subject, with the works of Thiersch, Millengen, Panofka, &c. See also the learned work of Passeri published in the last century.

above-named Duke Guidobaldo sent a quantity sufficient for the double furnishing of a credenza, to the Emperor Charles V., with one to the Cardinal Farnese, brother to the Signora Vittoria, his duchess.* Now, it is fit we should know that, as regards this kind of paintings on vases, the ancient Romans did not possess any examples, so far as we can judge; for the vases of their times, used to hold the ashes of the dead, or for other purposes, which are now found, are covered with figures which are hatched and grounded on one sole colour, whether black, red, or white, but never exhibit the lustre of a vitrified surface, nor do they possess the beauty and attraction of the varied pictures which have been, and still are seen in our times.† Nor must it be affirmed, that the Romans may perchance have possessed such, but that the paintings have been destroyed by time in the long period during which they have remained buried, since we know well that ours are capable of resisting the utmost force of the weather, and of every other evil influence, insomuch that they might be kept beneath the ground for 4000 years, so to speak, without sustaining injury to their paintings. Vases and pictures of this kind are produced, as is well known, throughout all Italy; but the best earths and the most beautiful vessels are, nevertheless, those found and made, as I have said, at Castel Durante,‡ a place in the State of Urbino, and at Faenza.§ The best among them are of a pure white, and have but few pictures, what there are being in the centre or round the vase; they

* Numbers of these vases are still to be found in various places, and they are greatly prized for the beauty of their paintings, which are for the most part from the works of the great masters.—*Ed. Flor.*, 1832-8.

† The vases here alluded to had their origin in the ancient Etruria and in the Greek colonies. Those belonging to the latter have figures of superior design, and their surfaces are covered with a shining varnish. The richest collection of the particular kind of vases here alluded to is in Naples, but they abound, as our readers will remember, in other cities also (Rome, Munich, Berlin, London, &c.) They have largely occupied the pens of writers, among whom are Inghirami, Gerhard, La Borde, and those cited in a previous note. See also Mrs. Hamilton Gray's elegant work on the Tombs and Antiquities of Etruria.

‡ Since erected into a city, and now called Urbania.—*Masselli.*

§ Whence the French "Faience."

are, moreover, always of very graceful character, and exhibit the most careful execution.*

But let us now return to Battista Franco. In the solemnities for the nuptials of the Signor Duke of Urbino, with the above-named Signora Vittoria Farnese, and which took place at the city of Urbino, our artist was employed by Genga, who had charge of all the preparations, and who, having erected arches of triumph, caused Battista to paint all the stories with which they were decorated, a work accomplished by that artist with the aid of his disciples. But the Duke, being apprehensive that Battista would not be ready in time, sent for Giorgio Vasari, who was at that moment in Rimini, painting a large chapel in fresco, with the altar piece of the same in oil, for the White Monks of Monte Oliveto; the preparations for those nuptials being a very great undertaking; the Duke, I say, desired Giorgio to go to Urbino for the purpose of assisting Genga and Battista in the works required. Vasari was, however, indisposed at the time; he wrote to the Duke therefore, excusing himself, and begging his Excellency to have no fear, since Battista had so much skill and knowledge that he would without doubt have the whole work finished within the appointed time, as did indeed prove to be the case.

But when Vasari had completed his undertaking in Rimini, he repaired to Urbino, there to visit the Duke, and to make his excuses in person to that Sovereign. His Excellency then caused him to examine the above-mentioned chapel, to the end that he might estimate the value of the work, when Giorgio praised it highly, and extolled the merit of the artist, who was largely satisfied with the great liberality of the Duke. Battista was not in Urbino at the moment, he having gone to Rome, where he was engaged in making designs, not only from the statues, but from all the other antiquities of that city, with intention to prepare a large book of the same, which he subsequently effected, and the work was highly commended.†

Now, while Battista was thus occupied, it came to pass

* Vases of this kind are called among the Italians *Majolica*.

† Richardson, *Account of Statues*, &c., 1722, affirms that Battista Franco designed the antiquities of Rome for the purpose of having them engraved or etched on copper.—*Ed. Flor.*, 1832-8.

that Messer Giovan Andrea dall' Anguillara,* a man who had distinguished himself greatly by a certain sort of poesies, had formed a society composed of men possessing fine genius in various walks, and was causing exceedingly rich scenic ornaments and other decorations to be prepared in the large Hall of Sant' Apostolo, where he proposed to arrange the performance of dramas by different authors before the gentlemen, nobles, and other distinguished personages of the city. There were to be places for spectators of different degrees, but for the Cardinals and other great Prelates certain rooms were prepared where, by means of gratings and jealousies, or blinds, those churchmen could see all that was done without being seen.

In the Society, or Company, were painters, architects, sculptors, and men who had to recite the dramas, as well as to perform other offices; wherefore to Battista Franco and Ammannato, who had also been elected members of the Company, there was given in charge the arrangement of the scenic decorations, with stories and ornaments of pictures which Battista executed so well, with the aid of some statues by Ammannato, that he was very highly extolled. But it was found that the great cost of that place exceeded the means of the Society, wherefore Messer Giovanni Andrea and the other members were compelled to remove the scenes and other decorations from Sant' Apostolo, and take them to the Strada Giulia, where Battista re-arranged everything in the new Church of San Biagio; when that being done, several dramas were performed, to the inexpressible satisfaction of the people and courtiers of Rome. From this commencement it was that the Dramatic Companies, called the "Zanni,"† who go about reciting comedies, took their rise.

After these things, in the year 1550 that is to say, Battista Franco, with Girolamo Sicciolante, of Sermoneta,‡ received a commission from the Cardinal di Cesis, to paint the Arms of Pope Julius III., who had been newly created High Pontiff, on the façade of his Palace; they added to

* Anguillara translated Ovid's Metamorphoses into the *Ottava-rima*.—*Ibid.*

† The contraction of Giovanni in the Bergamasco dialect. The Zanni in comedy is always a stupid, blundering Bergamese servant.—*Masselli.*

‡ There is further mention of Sicciolante at the close of the work, where Vasari speaks of certain artists then living.

the escutcheon three figures, besides several Children, which were much commended. Having completed that work, Battista next painted stories of Our Lady and of Jesus Christ, in a Chapel which had been constructed in the Church of the Minerva, by a Canon of San Pietro; and these, which were in a division of the vaulting, were the best paintings which Battista had then produced.* On one of the two walls of the same Chapel he furthermore painted the Nativity of Our Saviour Christ, with the Shepherds, and a Choir of Angels singing above the hut or cabin wherein is the Divine Child; on the other, he depicted the Resurrection of Christ, with numerous Soldiers standing in various attitudes around the sepulchre. Over each of the above stories there are lunettes, in which Battista painted colossal figures of Prophets; and, finally, on the wall behind the Altar, our artist represented Christ Crucified, with Our Lady, San Giovanni, San Domenico, and other Saints, in all which he acquitted himself well, and after the manner of an excellent master.

But his gains being small, and the expenses of living in Rome very great, Battista, after having executed some pictures on cloth, which had not much success, determined on returning to Venice, his native place, thinking, perhaps, that by a change of abode he should also change his fortune. In Venice, his fine manner in drawing caused him to be esteemed an able artist, and he very soon received the commission for a picture in oil, to be placed in the Chapel of Monsignore Barbaro, Patriarch elect of Aquilea, which chapel was in the Church of San Francesco della Vigna. The subject of this work was the Baptism of Our Saviour Christ in the river Jordan, by St. John the Baptist; the figure of the Almighty Father is seen in the air, and beneath are two Children who hold the vestments of Jesus; in the angles is the Annunciation, and at the foot of the figure is the painted semblance of a cloth, beneath which are numerous small figures, all nude; angels, demons, and souls in purgatory namely, with a motto of which the words are as follow :—*In nomine Jesus omne genuflectatur.*

This work, which was reputed to be a good one,† caused

* These paintings are in the third chapel on the right.—*Bottari.*

† Certain of the authorities, among whom is the accomplished churchman last quoted, declare that this work is, on the contrary, entirely devoid of merit.

Battista to acquire great credit and reputation ; it was, indeed, the cause of his receiving another commission, seeing that the Barefooted Friars, who have their house at that place, and to whom is committed the care of the Church called Sant' Jobbe in Canareio, caused Battista to paint a figure of Our Lady, in the Chapel belonging to the Foscari family, in that Church of Sant' Jobbe. The Virgin is seated with the Divine Child in her arms, and on one side of her is San Marco ; there is a female Saint on the other side, and in the air above are Angels scattering flowers. For the tomb of the German merchant Cristofano Fuccheri, which is in the Church of San Bartolommeo, Battista painted a picture, wherein he represented the God Mercury, with figures of Abundance and Fame.* He also painted a picture for Messer Antonio della Vecchia, a Venetian gentleman, representing Our Saviour Christ crowned with Thorns, and surrounded by Pharisees, who are deriding him: the figures are of the size of life, and are very beautiful.

Meanwhile, the steps which lead from the first floor upwards in the Palace of St. Marco, having been constructed of masonry, after the designs of Jacopo Sansovino, as will be related in the proper place, and having been adorned with various ornaments in stucco, which formed compartments for paintings, by the sculptor Alessandro,† a disciple of Sansovino, Battista was employed to paint certain minute *grotteschine*, over every part thus divided. In the larger spaces he painted a considerable number of figures in fresco, which have received a fair share of commendation from artists, and having completed these, he then decorated the ceiling of the Vestibule to that staircase. No long time afterwards, there were given, as we have said above, commissions for three pictures each, to the most renowned painters then in Venice, which were to be executed for the Library of San Marco, with the condition that he who should the most clearly distinguish himself in the opinion of those Magnificent Signori, should receive a collar or chain of gold, in addition to the

* The paintings executed in Sant' Jobbe and San Bartolommeo have now disappeared.—*Ed. Flor.*, 1832-8.

† This is Alessandro Vittoria of Trent, an admirable sculptor, of whom there is further mention at the close of the Life of Jacopo Sansovino.—*Ibid.*

stipulated price; when Battista painted three stories between the windows of that Library, to which he added two figures of Philosophers; and in these works he acquitted himself exceedingly well, although he did not obtain the prize of honour, as we have before related.*

These works being all completed, Battista received from the Patriarch Grimani a commission to paint a Chapel in San Francesco della Vigna, the first on the right hand namely as you enter into that Church; and Battista set hand to the work accordingly; he began by preparing very rich compartments of stucco, by means of which he divided the whole of the vaulting, which he then filled with stories and figures in fresco; over all these he laboured with extraordinary diligence, but whether it were that some precaution needful to his health had been neglected, or that Battista worked too much at frescoes, perhaps upon very fresh walls—for the villas of certain among the nobles, as I have heard say, before he had completed the above-mentioned chapel, our artist died, and the paintings, remaining unfinished, were afterwards brought to conclusion by Federigo Zuccaro, of Sant' Agnolo-in-Vado, a young painter of great excellence; he is indeed considered to be one of the best in Rome.†

On the walls of this chapel then, Federigo painted a story in fresco, the subject chosen being Santa Maria Maddalena converted by the preaching of Christ, as he did also another representing the Resurrection of her brother Lazarus;‡ both are very graceful pictures: he then, having finished the walls, depicted the Adoration of the Magi on the Altar-piece, a work which was highly commended. Battista Franco died in the year 1561, and many of his designs, which are truly worthy of praise, having been engraved, he has derived from them a very great name and reputation.§

* In the Life of San Michele; see vol. iv. p. 450.

† Vasari names him again in the Life of Taddeo Zucchero, but the ambition of Federigo was not satisfied with the praises bestowed on him, and in certain annotations which he has affixed to a copy of these Lives which was in his own possession, he has attacked our author in the bitterest manner.—*Masselli.*

‡ Zanetti, *Pittura Veneziana*, declares that he can find no trace of the manner of Zuccaro in the picture of Lazarus.

§ Bartsch, *Le Peintre-Graveur*, enumerates nearly a hundred engravings from the works of Battista Franco.

In the same city of Venice, and almost at the same time, there lived and does yet live, a painter called Jacopo Tintoretto,* who is a great lover of all the arts, and more particularly delights in playing on various musical instruments; he is besides a very agreeable person, which is proved in all his modes of proceeding; but as to the matter of painting, he may be said to possess the most singular, capricious, and determined hand, with the boldest, most extravagant, and obstinate brain, that has ever yet belonged to the domain of that art. Of this there is sufficient proof in his works, and in the fantastic composition of his stories, which are altogether different from and contrary to the usages of other painters; nay, he has been more than ever extravagant in some of his more recent inventions, and in those strange caprices of his fancy, which he has executed almost as it were by hap-hazard and without design; insomuch that one might suppose, he well nigh desired to show that the art is but a jest. He will sometimes present as finished, sketches which are such mere outlines, that the spectator sees before him pencil marks made by chance, the results of a bold carelessness rather than the fruits of design and of a well-considered judgment.

This artist has painted every kind of picture, whether in fresco or oil, with portraits taken from the life also, and he executes works of all prices, in such sort that in this manner of his he has undertaken, and does undertake, the greater part of the pictures painted in Venice. It is to be observed, too, that in his youth Tintoretto† had proved himself to possess great ability by the execution of many excellent pictures, insomuch that if he had properly used the advantages which he derived from nature, and had judiciously cultivated them by study, as those have done who have pursued the beautiful manner of his predecessors, and not depended on mere facility of hand as he has permitted himself to do, he would have been one of the best masters that Venice has ever possessed. Nor, proceeding as we have

* The name of Tintoretto was Jacopo Robusti. He was the son of Battista Robusti, and was born in 1512. Ridolfi, *Vite de' Pittori Veneti.*

† Tintoretto, "the little dyer;" so was this artist called (after the Italian fashion of that period, and one not entirely unknown, as many of our readers can avouch, to the present day), from the trade of his father Battista Robusti, who was a dyer. *Italice,* "Tintore."

said, does even this prevent him from being a bold and clever artist, of a most sprightly mind, a vivid fancy, and pleasing cheerful manner.*

When therefore the Venetian Senate had commanded that Jacopo Tintoretto, and Paolo Veronese, then a youth of whom high expectations were entertained, should each paint a picture for the Hall of the Council, while Orazio, the son of Titian, was also commissioned to execute another, Tintoretto depicted a story of Frederick Barbarossa crowned by the Pope; he represented the ceremony as taking place within a magnificent building, while around the Pontiff is a large number of cardinals and nobles of Venice, all portraits from the life; beneath these figures are seen the musical band of the Pope. In all this he acquitted himself in such a manner, that his work may bear comparison with those of the other masters, not excepting that of the above named Orazio, the son of Titian.

The subject of the picture painted by the last-mentioned artist was a Battle fought at Rome, and near the Castello Sant' Angelo, on the banks of the Tiber, by the Germans of the Emperor Frederick Barbarossa on the one part, and the Romans on the other; and in this, among other things, is to be observed the foreshortened figure of a horse, which is leaping over a soldier in full armour. It is a group that may be truly called most beautiful; but some affirm that Orazio was assisted in the work by Titian his father. Near the picture of Orazio is that by Paolo Veronese, of whom we have made mention in the Life of Michele San Michele, and who in his work represented the same Federigo Barbarossa appearing at Court to kiss the hand of the Pope Ottaviano, as in contempt of Pope Alexander† III. In addition to this picture, which is a very beautiful one, the same Paolo painted four large figures over

* He was a disciple of Titian, but was dismissed by that master because he would in no wise give obedience to his commands; a highly probable reason, the character of the disciple considered; yet there are not wanting those who affirm that the great artist was jealous of his pupil. Tintoretto wrote the following words on a wall of his workshops (the refined "studio" had not then been invented), "The design of Michael Angelo and the colouring of Titian."

† Our readers will not fail to recall the feuds with which these "men of peace" disturbed the repose of the world at this period.

a window; they represent Time; Concord or Union, holding a bundle of rods; with Patience and Faith; and in all these figures he acquitted himself so well that too much could not be said of their merit.

No long time after the completion of these works, another picture being required for the same Hall, Tintoretto took such steps, by the intervention of friends and other means, that the commission to execute the work was given to him, when he completed it in a manner that was most admirable; and this picture merits to be enumerated among the best he ever executed: so powerful in this artist was the will with which he then set himself to equal, if not to surpass, such of his competitors as had also laboured in that place. And the subject of the work which he thus depicted, (to the end that the same may be recognized, even by those who are not of the art,) was Pope Alexander excommunicating Barbarossa and laying his dominions under the interdict, with the same Barbarossa, who nevertheless emboldens his people to refuse all further obedience to the papal mandate.*

Among other singular things in this picture may be remarked as beautifully executed, the part where Pope and Cardinals are seen casting candles and flaming torches from a high place, as is ever done when any one is excommunicated, while a vast crowd of nude figures are seen below struggling and fighting to obtain those torches: all which is rendered in the most admirable manner.† There are besides various relics of antiquity, as pedestals and other objects, with portraits of different gentlemen dispersed over the pictures; these last are extremely well done, and the work is altogether such as to have won grace and favour for Tintoretto from all who have seen it.

It followed in consequence that this artist received a commission for two paintings in oil, to be placed beneath the work of Pordenone in the principal chapel of the Church of San Rocco; these were to be of extent equal to the entire

* And recalling what that "interdict" was, we perceive that obedience was not refused without good and sufficient cause.

† These paintings were destroyed in the conflagrations of 1573 and 1577, but there is still a picture by Tintoretto in the ancient Hall of the Great Council; this represents the Ambassadors before Frederick Barbarossa. There is also the famous picture of the Paradise by that master, with some others in the ceiling.—*Note to the Venetian Edition of Vasari.*

width of the chapel, about twelve braccia each that is to say. In one of these our artist painted a perspective view, as of a large Hospital filled with beds, wherein the sick, who are receiving medical attendance from San Rocco, are lying in various attitudes: among these are certain nude figures which are very well done, with a dead body foreshortened, which is most admirable. In another is a story, also from the life of San Rocco, in which there are many very beautiful and graceful figures; the work is so good a one, in short, that it is accounted to be one of the best ever executed by that painter. In the centre of the above-named Church, moreover, there is a picture of almost equal size with those before mentioned, and likewise by the hand of Tintoretto. This represents Our Saviour Christ healing the Sick at the Pool of Bethesda, and is a work which is also considered to be an extremely good one.*

For the Church of Santa Maria dell' Orto, where the Brescian painters, Cristofano and his brother,† painted the ceiling as I have before related, Tintoretto executed the decorations of two walls, which will be found in the principal chapel, they are in oil, on cloth, and extend from the cornice above the seats, even to the ceiling, a height of twenty braccia that is to say. The picture on the right represents Moses returning from the Mount, where he has received the Laws from the hand of God, when he finds the people adoring the golden calf: and that on the left exhibits the Universal Judgment at the last day; the latter, an extravagant invention, which is truly fearful and terrible, in its diversity of figures which are of each sex and every age; the souls of the condemned, as well as of the blessed, are beheld in various parts in the distance. The boat of Charon is likewise depicted in this work, but in a manner altogether different from that of those usually seen, and of a beautiful as well as unusual form. Indeed had this fanciful invention been executed after a correct and well-regulated design, and if the painter had given due attention to each part and to

* These works retain their place, as do other pictures still remaining in the same church, and by the same artist, but which are not mentioned by Vasari.—*Ed. Flor.*, 1832-8.

† Cristofano and Stefano Rosa have been mentioned in the Life of Garofalo, see vol. iv. p. 536, *et seq.*

all the details, as he has to the general whole, this picture, expressing the amazement, terror, and confusion of that day, would have been a most wonderful production. He who does but glance at it for a moment is even now astonished at the power displayed; but if it be examined minutely, the work has all the appearance of having been painted as a jest.

For the same church, on the doors which close the organ that is to say, Tintoretto painted Our Lady ascending the steps of the Temple; this work, which is in oil, is the most carefully executed, most delicately finished, and most cheerful looking picture to be found in all the church. Our artist likewise painted the doors of the organ in Santa Maria Sebenigo; the subject of that work was the Conversion of St. Paul, but it was not executed with much care.* In the Carità is a Deposition from the Cross by the same hand;† and in the Sacristy of San Sebastiano, Tintoretto painted Moses in the Wilderness, with other stories on the presses of that place;‡ this he did in competition with Paolo of Verona, who executed numerous pictures on the ceiling and walls of the church. The works thus commenced were continued at a subsequent period, by the Venetian painter Natalino,§ and by others.

In the church of San Jobbe, Tintoretto painted the three Maries, with San Francesco, San Sebastiano, and San Giovanni, as he did a Landscape at the altar of the Pietà;‖ and on the doors of the organ in the church of the Servites¶ he

* There are other pictures by Tintoretto still in the Church of Santa Maria Zebenico, but not that here mentioned by Vasari.—*Note to Ed. Ven.*

† Even Zanetti, *Pittura Venesiana*, does not mention this work, which shows that it had disappeared so early as his day (1771.)

‡ There is no picture by Tintoretto in the Church of San Sebastiano, with the exception of the Israelites attacked by the Serpents.—*Ed. Ven.*

§ This painter, who, according to Ridolfi, was a disciple of Titian, excelled in portrait painting. Lanzi informs us that he died young. See *History of Painting* (English Edition), vol. ii. p. 170.

‖ "No such picture has ever existed in the Church of San Jobbe," says a Note to the *Venetian Edition* of our author. Vasari has perhaps been thinking of one by Giovanni Bellini on the same subject, and which was removed from San Jobbe to the Academy of the Fine Arts in Venice.

¶ This church is now suppressed. On the doors of the organ there were two Saints, and an Annunciation, but not Cain slaying his brother.—*Note to Ed. Venet.*

depicted figures of Sant' Agostino and San Filippo, with Cain slaying his brother Abel beneath. At the altar of the Sacrament in the Church of San Felice, in the ceiling of the Tribune that is to say, Tintoretto painted the four Evangelists, and in the Lunette over the altar he depicted an Annunciation. On another Lunette in the same place, he represented our Saviour Christ in Prayer on the Mount of Olives; and on the wall is the Last Supper of our Lord with his Disciples,* by the same hand. In San Francesco della Vigna this artist painted a Deposition from the Cross; Our Lady is in a swoon, the other Maries stand around her, and there are also figures of certain Prophets.†

In the Scuola of San Marco near SS. Giovanni e Paolo are four large pictures by Tintoretto; the first exhibits San Marco appearing in the air and delivering a man who was his votary from grievous torments, which an executioner is seen to be preparing for him; but the irons which the tormentors are endeavouring to apply break short in their hands, and cannot be turned against that devout man. This picture exhibits a great number of figures, many well executed foreshortenings, much armour, with buildings, portraits from the life, and other objects of similar kind, which render the work one of infinite interest.‡ The second picture also displays the figure of San Marco as floating in the air, and delivering one of his votaries from peril; the danger in this case has arisen from a storm at sea; but the painting is not executed with the care perceptible in that previously named.

In the third picture is a torrent of rain, with the dead body of one who has in like manner been devoted to San Marco, and whose soul is seen to be ascending into heaven; here also we have a composition, the figures of which are not without a fair share of merit. In the fourth painting, in which San Marco expels an unclean spirit, there is the perspective view of an extensive Loggia, at the end whereof is a fire by which the Loggia is illuminated, and the reflec-

* In San Felice there is but one picture by Tintoretto, that of the Demetrius, which has been lately restored by Comiani.—*Ed. Venet.*

† The fate of this work is not known.—*Note, in loc cit.*

‡ Now in the Academy of the Fine Arts in Venice, and may be considered the masterpiece of Tintoretto. It has been engraved in outline for the before-cited work of Zanotto, and there is a lithographed plate of the same in the collection of forty great pictures of the Venetian School.

tions of that light fall on various parts of the edifice.* In addition to these stories, there is a figure of San Marco on one of the altars, by the hand of the same artist, and which is also a tolerably good painting.

These works, then—with many others which I leave undescribed, because it shall suffice me to have made mention of the best—have been executed by Tintoretto with such extraordinary promptitude that, while people had been supposing him to have only just begun, he had in fact finished his performance. It is to be furthermore remarked, that this artist always contrives by the most singular proceedings in the world to be constantly employed, seeing that when the good offices of his friends and other methods have failed to procure him any work of which there is question, he will nevertheless manage to obtain it, either by accepting it at a very low price, by doing it as a gift, or even seizing on it by force. An instance of this kind happened no long time since, when Tintoretto, having painted a large painting on cloth and in oil, representing the Crucifixion of Christ, for the Scuola of San Rocco,† the men of that Brotherhood then determined to have some magnificent and honourable work executed on the ceiling of the apartment, proposing moreover to give the commission for the same to such of the painters then in Venice as might be expected to do it in the best manner and after the most beautiful design.

They consequently sent for Giuseppo Salviati and Federigo Zucchero, who were then in Venice, with Paolo Veronese and Jacopo Tintoretto, commanding that each of them should prepare a design, and promising that the work should be adjudged to him who should acquit himself the best. But while the other artists were giving themselves with all diligence to the preparation of their designs, Tintoretto made an exact measurement of the space for which the picture was required, and taking a large canvas, he painted it without saying a word to any one and with his usual celerity, puting it instantly

* Two of these Stories are now in the ancient Hall of the Library of San Marco, one on each side of the door of entrance namely.—*Ed. Venet. note.*

† One of the finest, if not the very finest of Tintoretto's works. The school of San Rocco may indeed be truly called a gallery of the works of Tintoretto.—*Ed. Venet.*

up in the place destined to receive it. One morning, therefore, when the Brotherhood had assembled to see the designs and to determine the matter, they found that Tintoretto had entirely completed the work, nay, that he had fixed it in its place; whereupon, becoming very angry with him, and observing that they had required designs and had not commissioned him to do the work, Tintoretto replied that this was his method of preparing designs, that he did not know how to make them in any other manner; and that all designs and models for a work should be executed in that fashion, to the end that the persons interested might see what it was intended to offer them, and might not be deceived: he added, that if they did not think proper to pay for the work and remunerate him for his pains, he would make them a present of the same. At the last, therefore, though not without much opposition, he contrived so to manage matters, that the picture still retains its place.

The subject of this painting is the Almighty Father descending with bands of Angels from Heaven to embrace San Rocco;* and in the lowermost part of the picture are numerous figures, to represent or signify the other principal Schools† or Companies of Venice; the Carità for example, that of San Giovanni Evangelista, the Misericordia, San Marco, and San Teodoro; all which was executed after the usual manner of Tintoretto. But since it would lead us too far, were we to describe all the works performed by the artist here in question, this shall be the close, and we will content ourselves with having said thus much of Tintoretto, who is certainly a very clever man and highly commendable painter.

* This is in the ceiling of that room in San Rocco, called the "Albergo," and in which is the Crucifixion mentioned above.—*Ed. Venet.*

† We have more than once remarked in previous notes that these Schools are not of necessity places of education, as indeed most of our readers well know; they are more usually charitable institutions for the tendance of the sick, the burial of the dead, the release of captives from the infidel, and other purposes of similar kind. It may be added, that the revenues of more than one among them have been appropriated by the Austrians to military purposes, and many of their spacious buildings have been turned into barracks.

About the same time there was a painter in Venice called Bazzacco,* who was a creature of the Casa Grimani and by especial favour, this artist, after he had been many years in Rome, received commission to paint the ceiling of the large Hall of the Cai† of Ten; but conscious that he could not complete the work himself, and would have need of aid, Bazzacco took for his companions Paolo da Verona, and Battista Zelotti,‡ dividing among them and himself nine pictures in oil, which were to be executed for that place, four compartments of an oval form in the angles that is to say, four oblong squares, and a larger oval in the centre. This last, together with three of the squares, Bazzacco gave to Paolo Veronese, who represented Jove launching his thunderbolts at the Vices, with other figures therein; and two of the smaller ovals, with one square, Bazzacco kept for himself; the two remaining ovals he gave to Battista. In one of these compartments is Neptune, the God of the Sea, the others have each two figures, symbolical of the grandeur and repose then enjoyed by Venice.

Now all these artists acquitted themselves very well in that work, but the best of them was Paolo Veronese; for which cause he received a commission from the Signori to paint the ceiling of a chamber which is beside the above-mentioned Hall.§ Here he depicted a figure of San Marco floating in the air, in the lowermost part is Venice surrounded by Faith, Hope, and Charity; the painting is in oil, and Paolo had for his assistant therein the above-named Battista Zelotti. But though a beautiful picture, this work is not equal to that executed by Paolo in the Hall first-

* This artist was a native of Castel Franco, and consequently, a compatriot of Giorgione. Bottari corrects Vasari, who, in his first or second edition called him Brazacco, but Lanzi, quoting the Padre Federici, declares our author, Bottari, Ridolfi, Zanetti, and Guarienti to be all equally wrong, affirming his true name to have been Ponchio. In despair for the loss of his wife, this artist became a monk on her death, and never touched pencil more.

† Cai, Venetian for Capi, or *Chiefs.*

‡ Called in early editions of our author, *Farinato;* but by the authority of Ridolfi and other competent writers, Bottari corrected this error in his edition of our author, Rome, 1759, and later commentators have given their assent to that emendation.

§ This is the ceiling of the Hall called *Della Bussula.—Ed. Venet.*

mentioned. In the Umiltà* he then executed a painting entirely alone; on a large oval compartment of the ceiling namely, where he painted an Assumption of Our Lady, with other figures, a very lightsome, pleasing, and well considered performance.†

In like manner, belonging to our own time, is another good painter of that same city, Andrea Schiavone namely.‡ I call him good, because he has certainly produced many a good work, sometimes unhappily when in much want and distress.§ Schiavone has always imitated the manner of good masters to the best of his power, but the greater part of his pictures have been painted for the houses of private gentlemen, and I propose to speak only of those which are public.‖ In the Church of San Sebastiano at Venice, and in the chapel

* A church which has been demolished.

† Vasari has spoken of Paul Veronese in the Life of San Michele, as our readers will remember, and mentions him frequently on different occasions, sometimes as a young man of much promise, again as surpassing all his competitors in some particular work, but always in terms of commendation. Bottari argues from this and other circumstances that Vasari frequently made additions to what he had previously written, as circumstances came to his knowledge, without giving himself the trouble to re-arrange or re-write the life thus interpolated.

‡ Andrea Schiavone, whose surname was Medola, was a disciple of Titian. "He died," remarks Baldinucci, "after a life of much suffering as well as much labour." His works, by which the merchants enriched themselves, barely supplied himself with the means of existence. He was born of poor parents at Sebenico in Dalmatia, in the year 1522, and dying at the age of sixty, was buried by the charity of his brother artists. There are three pictures by this master in the Bridgewater Gallery, and one in the Sutherland Collection. There are also two at Burleigh, which may be considered fair examples of his manner. Moschini, *Guida di Venezia*, tells us that in the Registers of the Academy he is called *Andrea di Niccolo da Curzola*; and in a print engraved by himself, and representing Heliodorus, we have the following inscription by his own hand, *Andreas Sclavonus Meldola fecit*.

§ This passage has been sometimes differently construed, and Vasari is made to say (by his Italian commentators) that Schiavone "sometimes painted a good picture *by mistake*." It is true that the text may *bear* such a reading, but we think that our readers, considering the history of the hapless artist, and the favourable opinion expressed of him by our author, will admit the reading adopted by the present writer to be the true one.

‖ Zanetti, *Pittura Veneziana*, remarks that the colouring of Schiavone was so much admired by Tintoretto that he kept a painting by that artist in his studio, and recommended others to do so, but he also advised them to draw better than their model, whose poverty had unhappily prevented him from studying design.

of the Men of the Cà Pellegrini,* Schiavone has painted a figure of San Jacopo with those of two Pilgrims;† and in the Church of the Carmine he has executed a picture of the Assumption, with a large number of Angels and Saints.‡ This is on the ceiling of the Choir; and in the same Church, at the Chapel of the Presentation that is to say, he has depicted Our Saviour Christ, as an Infant presented by the Virgin Mother in the Temple.§

The last mentioned painting comprises many portraits from the life, but the best figure in it is that of a Woman clothed in a yellow vestment, who is suckling a child. This is executed with a sort of facility and in a certain manner not unfrequently used in Venice, the group being merely dashed in or slightly sketched, without being finished at all. In the year 1550 this artist was commissioned by Giorgio Vasari to paint a large picture in oil, the subject being the Battle which had been fought a short time previously between Charles V. and Barbarossa.‖ That work, which is among the best ever executed by Andrea Schiavone, and is indeed a truly beautiful painting, is now in Florence in possession of the heirs of the Illustrious Ottaviano de' Medici, to whom it was sent as a gift by Vasari.¶

* Cà Pellegrini. The House of the Pellegrini Family.

† Pellegrini, pilgrims. The picture represents Our Saviour Christ proceeding with the two disciples to Emmaus.

‡ Piacenza, in his notes to Baldinucci, asserts that the figures of the Madonna, with those of SS. Peter, Paul, Elias, and the Four Evangelists, were removed from the Church of the Carmine to the Church of Santa Teresa ; but Moschini, whose authority is much respected, makes no mention of that circumstance.

§ According to Lanzi, this picture was not painted by Schiavone, but by Tintoretto, who so closely imitated the manner of the first-named artist therein, that even Vasari himself was deceived. See *History*, &c., English Edition, vol. ii. p. 173.

‖ The subsequent fate of this work is not known.

¶ Many works by this master will be remembered by our readers as enriching the galleries of Venice. There are three according to Guarienti—according to Rosa, four—of his pictures at Dresden ; with others, according to Förster, at Vienna.

## GIOVAN-FRANCESCO RUSTICI, SCULPTOR AND ARCHITECT OF FLORENCE.

[Born about the middle of the 15th century.—Died at the age of eighty, towards the middle of the 16th century.]

It is a remarkable fact, that almost all young men who studied their art in the Garden of the Medici, and were favoured by the Magnificent Lorenzo the Elder, became distinguished in their several vocations, a circumstance that cannot be attributed to any other cause than the extraordinary, or rather the infinite, judgment of that most noble person, the true Mecænas and protector of all men of genius, and who, to the power of discriminating elevation of character and mind, added that of duly promoting and rewarding them.

It thus happened, that as the Florentine citizen, Giovan-Francesco Rustici, acquitted himself very creditably in his youth, not only in design but in modelling in clay also, so by the Magnificent Lorenzo, who readily perceived his quickness of intellect and good parts, he was placed for the purposes of study with Andrea del Verrocchio, with whom, in like manner, had studied Leonardo da Vinci; the youth of the latter gave evidence, as will be remembered, of the rarest ability, and he was early endowed with extraordinary genius.

Now, the fine manner and admirable dispositions of Leonardo pleased Rustici greatly, and as it appeared to him that the expression of his heads and the movements of his figures were more graceful, as well as more animated, than those of any other whose works he had ever seen; so, when he had learned the art of casting in bronze, had obtained some acquaintance with the laws of perspective, and could work in marble, he attached himself to Leonardo da Vinci. This occurrence did not, however, take place until after Andrea Verrocchio had gone to Venice for the execution of the works which, as we have before related, were executed by his hand in that city.

Becoming thus fixed with Leonardo, and serving him with the most affectionate submission, Rustici was greatly beloved by that master, who found him to be upright, sincere, and liberal of mind, as well as diligent and patient in the labours of his art; insomuch that Leonardo would eventually do nothing, small or great, but that which seemed good in the eyes of Giovan-Francesco. Descending from a noble family, the youth had sufficient means wherewith he might have lived at his ease; he attached himself to the studies of art, therefore, more from the desire of honour, and out of love for the same, than from any wish for gain. Nor, to speak the truth of the matter, does it often happen that those artists who have not glory, and honour, but the making of profit, for their ultimate or even principal aim, become truly excellent, even though they may have been endowed with good powers and a fine genius.

The condition of him who must be constantly at his labours, to the end that he may live, as is the case of vast numbers who are bowed down by poverty and the cares of a family—who must work, I say, not only when fully disposed to do so, and when the spirits and power are equally ready to serve them, but at all times, for actual need, and that from morning till night; this is a state of things proper, not to men who place honour and glory before them as their end and aim, but to drudges, as the saying is, and mechanics hired by the day.

Works of merit are indeed not to be accomplished but with long and mature consideration, and, taking this view of the matter, Giovan-Francesco, in his more advanced age, was wont to say, that a man should first think, and then make his sketch; he should afterwards prepare his designs, and having done that, should leave them without casting an eye upon them for weeks and months; then, having selected the best, he may put them in execution. This is a method which cannot be adopted by every one, nor is it one common to those who work only for gain. Rustici would also remark that an artist ought not lightly to permit the examination of his works before they are finished, by all who may come about him; nor should he be ready frequently, or without consideration, to change and alter at the suggestion of others.

Giovan-Francesco acquired much valuable knowledge from Leonardo, and, among other things, the method of delineating horses, in which he delighted so greatly that he copied these animals in clay, in wax, in full relief, and in half relief; at a word, in every manner that one can possibly imagine. We have some drawings of horses by his hand in our book, which are admirably well designed, and bear ample testimony to the skill and ability of Giovan-Francesco: he was exceedingly ready in the management of colours also, and produced pictures which are very good, although his principal vocation was sculpture.

The residence of Rustici was in the Via de Martelli,* and he lived on terms of much amity with all the members of that family, which has ever been rich in men of ability and excellence, but he was more particularly intimate with Piero de' Martelli; for whom he made certain small figures in full relief, a Madonna among the rest, seated amidst the clouds, with the Divine Child in her arms, and surrounded by Cherubim. At a later period Giovan-Francesco painted a figure similar to the above-mentioned, in oil and of a large size, adding a sort of garland formed of Cherubim, which encircles the head of the Virgin in the manner of a diadem.

The Medici family having returned to Florence, Rustici made himself known to the Cardinal Giovanni,† by whom, as one who had been the protégé of his father Lorenzo, Giovan-Francesco was received with much kindness. But the fashions of a court were not to his liking; they were indeed entirely distasteful to his calm and upright nature, which had no tinge of ambition or self-seeking; he preferred to live a life apart, and after the manner of a philosopher, enjoying the repose and quiet of solitude: but he did not refuse occasional recreation, and frequented the society of such among his fellow citizens as were known to him; he often met the friends of his art likewise, nor did he neglect to labour when he felt the disposition to do so and found an opportunity for exertion.

On the arrival of Pope Leo X. at Florence, in the year 1515, for example, being requested to execute certain statues by his intimate friend Andrea del Sarto, he did not refuse to comply, but completed the same, when they were pronounced to be most beautiful. They found favour more particularly

* Our readers will remember that the members of the distinguished family to whom this street owes its name were the early and zealous patrons of Donato, who repaid their protection by the most affectionate gratitude. See the Life of that master, vol. i. of the present work.

† Afterwards Pope Leo X.

in the eyes of the Cardinal Giulio de' Medici,* and caused that Prelate to give Giovan-Francesco a commission for a statue of Mercury in bronze, about one braccio high: this figure, which was entirely nude, was intended to be placed on the summit of the Fountain in the principal court of the Medici Palace; it stands on a ball, and is in the act of taking flight.† In the hands of the statue Giovan-Francesco placed an instrument, which was made to turn round by the water which the figure poured down upon it, and the matter was managed on this wise: the leg and torso of the Mercury were perforated for the admission of a tube, and this being carried up to the mouth, the water rising through the same, fell on the above-mentioned instrument, which was balanced very nicely, and had exceedingly thin plates of metal in the form of a butterfly's wings attached to it, the water falling on it then, as I have said, caused the same to turn about; and this, for a small work, obtained considerable praise.

No long time after having completed the Mercury, Giovan-Francesco made the model of a figure to be cast in bronze for the same Cardinal: this was to have been a David, similar to that which Donato had executed for the Illustrious Cosimo the Elder, as we have said; the work of Rustici being destined for the first court of the Medici Palace, whence that of Donato had been removed. The model gave much satisfaction, but a certain dilatoriness in the mode of proceeding of Giovan-Francesco, caused this work to fail of being cast in bronze, and the Orpheus in marble of Baccio Bandinelli was erected in its stead; the David made in clay by Rustici, which was an admirable thing, came eventually to an evil end therefore, and that was a great pity.

Giovan-Francesco executed an Annunciation in mezzo-rilievo, with a perspective view of extraordinary beauty, in a very large medallion; in this work he was assisted by the painter Raffaello Belli, and by Niccolò Soggi; when it was

* This member of the Medici family was also subsequently elected supreme pontiff, as our readers will remember, and took the name of Clement VII.

† Bottari has confounded this figure with that of Giovanni Bologna, an error into which we must by no means fall, although we cannot ascertain the fate of the work in question.—*Ed. Flor.*, 1832-8.

cast in bronze, it proved to be a performance of such extraordinary beauty that nothing better could possibly be seen, and it was sent to the King of Spain. In a medallion of similar size, but in marble, Rustici next produced a figure of Our Lady, in alto-rilievo, the Virgin has the Divine Child in her arms, and San Giovanni, also a little child, is beside her ; this was placed in the first Hall of the Magistrates of the Guild of Por Santa Maria.

These works having brought Giovan-Francesco into high credit, the Consuls of the Guild of Merchants, who had at that time caused certain hideous figures of marble, made in 1240, which had stood over the three gates of the Church of San Giovanni to be taken down, as we have before related ; these Consuls, I say, having commissioned Andrea Contucci of Sansovino, to execute those which were to replace the old ones, over that door of San Giovanni which looks towards the Misericordia, now gave Rustici the statues which were to be erected over the door which is at the side opposite to the Canonicate of the church, and commanded that he should prepare three figures in bronze, each four braccia high; these figures to be of similar subjects to the old ones, a San Giovanni preaching namely, and represented as standing between a Pharisee and a Levite.

Now this work was one entirely after the heart of Giovan-Francesco, first, because it was of so much importance, and was to be erected in a place of such great renown, and next, on account of the competition with Andrea Contucci : he set hand to it therefore immediately, and made a small model, but this he greatly surpassed by the excellence of the work itself, to which he gave all the consideration which so important an undertaking demanded, and at which he laboured steadily with infinite diligence. The work being finished, was considered to be in all its parts the most perfectly composed and best arranged performance of the kind that had ever then been seen, the figures exhibiting an absolute perfection of form, and the aspect of the faces having singular grace as well as infinite majesty and force : the nude arms and lower limbs are likewise most admirably executed, and are conjoined to the trunks in a manner so entirely irreproachable, that better could not be ; and, to say nothing of the beauty given to the hands and feet, how graceful are the attitudes, and what heroic gravity have those heads !*

While Giovan-Francesco was modelling this work in clay, he would permit no one to be about him but Leonardo da Vinci; and he, whether in the preparation of the moulds, the securing of these with their irons, or whatsoever other part of the process was in hand, never left his side; some are therefore of opinion—but they know nothing beyond what I here say—that Leonardo worked at this group with his own hand, or that he at the least assisted Rustici with his counsel and good judgment. These statues, which are the best and most perfectly executed of any that have ever been produced in bronze by a modern master, were completed at three castings, and were chiselled at that house of the Via de' Martelli, in which, as we have said, Giovan-Francesco had his abode; as were also the ornaments which surround the figure of San Giovanni, with the two columns, the cornices, and the devices of the Guild of the Merchants, which all form part of the work. †

Near the figure of San Giovanni, which is one of singular power and animation, is that of a bald and somewhat corpulent man, also very finely done; the right hand of this figure is placed on his side, one of the shoulders is partially nude, with the left hand he holds a scroll before his eyes, and standing with the left leg crossed over the right, he is waiting in a most thoughtful attitude for the moment when he may utter the reply which he has manifestly prepared for the Baptist.‡ The vestments of this figure exhibit textures of two kinds; one of a slight and thin fabric, which floats about the nude parts of the form; the other much thicker and firmer, of which the mantle worn over the lower vestments is composed; the folds of these draperies are singularly

* The praises bestowed by Vasari are in no degree exaggerated. Cicognara, writing two centuries and a half after him, has spoken of these works in the following terms :—"Three of the most admirable figures produced by Sculpture in the commencement of the age here in question, are to be seen on that gate of the Florentine Baptistery which looks towards the House of Works, and these may truly be accounted among the most perfect productions exhibited by the Art of that period." See *Storia della Scultura*, &c.

† All still retain their places.

‡ In the *Storia* of Cicognara, above cited, this figure is engraved in outline. See Plate LXXII.

flowing and easy, they are also very judiciously arranged; of equal merit is the second figure, that of the Pharisee namely, the hand is placed on the beard, which it presses back in a certain manner, and the face wears an expression of infinite gravity, while it likewise gives evidence of much astonishment at the words of the preacher.*

While Rustici was occupied with this work, he became weary of having to make daily application for money to the Syndics of the Guild above-named, or to their deputies, and the rather as the same persons were not always in attendance, and are besides, for the most part, men who have but little regard for distinguished ability, and do not care greatly for the merits of the work before them. Giovan-Francesco became weary of this I say, and to finish the undertaking, he sold an estate belonging to his patrimonial inheritance, and which he possessed at San Marco Vecchio, a place situate at a short distance from Florence. Yet notwithstanding all these labours, expenses, and cares, he was but very poorly rewarded by those Syndics and by his fellow citizens. One of the Ridolfi, who was a chief of that Guild, more particularly showed himself adverse to the interests of Rustici, moved by some private pique, or perhaps offended because the latter did not pay him honour enough; perhaps also, because Giovanni would not let him see the figures in progress whenever he desired to do so. Be this as it may, Ridolfi was always found to be the opponent of Rustici in every question arising between him and the Syndics.

That which ought to have redounded to the honour of Giovan-Francesco was consequently turned to his injury, seeing that, whereas he had merited a double degree of reverence, as a distinguished artist no less than a noble and citizen of eminent station, his having become a sculptor deprived him, with the ignorant and foolish, of that honour and respect which were due to his birth. When his work had to be estimated, therefore, and when Giovan-Francesco on his part had chosen Michelagnolo Buonarroti for that office, the Court of Syndics, by the persuasion of Ridolfi, selected Baccio d'Agnolo to perform the same duty on their part. Of this, Rustici complained bitterly, remarking to the Syndics, in full council assembled, that the per-

* This figure will also be found in Cicognara, *loc cit.*

mitting a wood-worker and artisan to estimate the work of a sculptor and statuary, was too extraordinary a proceeding; nay, he did all but inform those personages that he considered them little better than a herd of stupid oxen; whereupon Ridolfi replied, that the choice had been well made, and that Rustici was himself a proud and insolent person.

But what was more unjust than all, has yet to be related: the work, which deserved full two thousand crowns, was estimated at five hundred only, and even that sum was never entirely paid to Giovan-Francesco: four hundred were all that he could ever obtain, nor did he receive that until it was extorted by the intervention of Giulio, Cardinal de' Medici. At the spectacle of so much baseness, Rustici withdrew almost in despair, and resolving never more to accept any commission from the Civic Magistrates, or indeed from any Company which might render him liable to have more than one person to deal with.

He now lived a very solitary life, and made his dwelling in the rooms of the Sapienza, which is near the Monastery of the Servite monks, where he employed himself with certain small works by way of amusing his leisure, and that he might not be wholly idle. But he also wasted both time and money in attempting to freeze mercury, and this he did, in company with Raffaello Baglioni, a genius of similar character.

In a picture, three braccia long and two high, Giovan-Francesco painted the Conversion of St. Paul. This work, which is in oil, exhibits a large number of horses ridden by soldiers who accompany the Saint; and among them are seen varied and beautiful attitudes with many fine foreshortenings: it is now, with other productions of Giovan-Francesco, in the possession of the heirs of the above-named Pietro Martelli, to whom it was presented by the artist. There is a small picture by the same hand, and representing a Hunt, which is the property of Lorenzo Borghini, by whom it is held in the utmost estimation, as a most fanciful and beautiful performance, which it certainly is; Lorenzo being one who greatly delights in the productions of our arts.

For the Nuns of Santa Lucia, in the Via di San Gallo, Giovan-Francesco executed a figure in clay of Our Saviour

Christ, appearing to Mary Magdalene in the Garden; this work, which is a mezzo-rilievo, was afterwards vitrified by Giovanni della Robbia, and was placed within a frame of macigno on an altar in the Church of the above-mentioned Nuns. For Giacomo Salviati the elder, who was an intimate friend of Il Rustici, that master executed a large medallion in marble, to be placed in the chapel of his palace, which is situate above the bridge at the Badia. He also produced numerous medallions filled with figures of terra cotta in full relief, to say nothing of many other beautiful decorations, which were, for the most part, nay rather, almost all, destroyed by the soldiery in the year of the siege, when the palace was set on fire by those who were adverse to the party of the Medici.

Giovan-Francesco had a great love for that place, and would sometimes stroll out of Florence in his long gown* until he would get even to the Palace; having cleared the city, he would throw the gown over his shoulder, and, thus accoutred would pass slowly forward lost in thought, until he reached his favourite spot. One day among others, he was going along that road, when, feeling himself too warm, he concealed that long robe of his in a sloe-bush, and never thought of it again until he had been at the Palace two days. He then sent one of his servants to seek the gown, and seeing the man return after having found it, he exclaimed: "Ah! the world has got to be too good! it must be coming to its end, and can't last much longer!"

Giovan-Francesco was a man of exceeding kindness, and very charitable to the poor, insomuch that he would suffer none to depart unconsoled. His money was kept in a sort of basket, whether he had little or much, and from this he would give, according to his ability, to all who asked of him. Wherefore it chanced one day that a poor man, who very often went to beg assistance from Il Rustici, and saw him constantly going to that basket for the alms which he bestowed, said, whispering to himself and without expecting to be heard,—"Ah! my God! if I had but what that basket contains, I should soon be out of my difficulties." Giovan-

* *In lucco.* The mode of dress thus described is said to have been peculiar to the Florentine citizens of a certain rank, and consisted in a long loose robe or gown, usually of a dark colour.

Francesco heard this, and having looked at him fixedly for a moment, he said—"Come hither, and I will content thee." He then emptied the basket into the skirt of the poor man's garment, and said, "Go, and may God grant his blessing." He then sent to Niccolò Buoni, who was his most intimate friend, for more money; indeed the whole of his affairs were arranged by this Niccolò, who received and kept account of his rents, and of the income which he received from the *Monte*,* as well as of the produce of his farms. This Niccolò sold at the right season, and it was his custom to give Rustici what money he wanted every week; these sums Giovan-Francesco would throw into the drawer of his desk, which he never locked, all who might want any for the necessities of the house taking therefrom without restraint, as they happened to require it.

But, returning to the works of Il Rustici, I have to relate that he executed a singularly beautiful Crucifix in wood, the size of life, which he proposed to send into France; but the work remained in the keeping of Niccolò Buoni, with other bassi-rilievi and designs, being left with him when Giovan-Francesco determined to quit Florence, which he fancied was no longer a favourable abode, and thinking, perhaps, that in changing his residence he should change his fortune also. The Crucifix is still in the possession of Buoni, therefore, together with the other productions just alluded to. For the Duke Giuliano, by whom he was always much favoured, Il Rustici executed a portrait of himself, in mezzo-relievo; this was a profile which Giovan-Francesco cast in bronze, and it was considered to be an admirable work; the present possessor of the same is Messer Alessandro, the son of Messer Ottaviano de' Medici.

To the painter Ruberto di Filippo Lippi, who was his disciple, Giovan-Francesco gave many works by his hand, bassi-rilievi, namely, with models and designs; among others a Leda, a Europa, a Neptune, and a most beautiful Vulcan, with a small work in basso-rilievo, exhibiting the nude figure of a man on horseback, which is singularly beautiful. This is now in the study of Don Silvano Razzi, at the Angeli.

* For an explanation of what is meant by this word *Monte*, to give which would require a greater space than could be afforded to the compass of a note, the reader is referred to Ranke, *History of the Popes*, vol. i.

The same artist also produced an exceedingly beautiful female figure, two braccia high, intended to represent a Grace; but what became of it is not known, nor can the hands into which it has fallen be ascertained.

Horses in clay by this artist, and similar to those before-mentioned, some bearing riders, and some fallen, with the cavaliers lying beneath them, abound in the dwellings of the citizens, these works having been presented to the persons possessing them, by Giovan-Francesco, who was not as men are for the most part discourteous and avaricious, but most liberal and obliging, to those who were of the number of his friends—Dionigi da Diacceto, for example, a very excellent and much respected gentleman, who like Niccolò Buoni took charge of Rustici's affairs, and was very much the friend of the latter, received many bassi-rilievi as gifts from his hands.

There was never a more amusing or more fanciful person than Giovan-Francesco, nor could there well be a man who had more delight in animals. He had a hedgehog among others, which he had rendered so tame that it would lie under the table like a dog, but sometimes rolled itself against people's legs, after a fashion that made the owners glad to draw them back into their own keeping: he had an eagle also, with a raven, which had been taught to speak so plainly, that he was frequently taken by those who heard and did not see him, for a human being. Giovan-Francesco also gave his attention to necromancy;* nay, according to what I am told, he caused his disciples and servants to suffer excessive terrors thereby, and was thus enabled to keep them in such

* An Italian commentator on the works of Vasari would have us be certain that the latter here means to speak only of sleight of hand, and that commentator may be right; but he who has read the Life of Pierino da Vinci (see vol. iv. p. 220), to say nothing of many other passages to a similar effect, that might be cited from our author's works, will at once perceive that Vasari's belief in necromancy, chiromancy, *et id genus omne*, is a thing which may not be denied. That he had most high and reverend authority for his belief is however as undeniable; hear, for example, what the Spaniard, Mendoza, among others,—and writing of Vasari's time—has to say on that subject:—"He (the Pope) will decide no question, he will take no journey, hold no sitting of the Consistory, do nothing, in short, without first consulting the stars; nay, the matter has come to such a pass, that very few Cardinals would transact an affair of any kind, were it but to buy a load of wood, except after consultation duly held with some Astrologer or Wizard."

perfect obedience, that he was thereby permitted to live without cares as regarded his domestics. He had a room constructed almost in the manner of a fishpond, and in this he kept numerous snakes and serpents of various kinds, which could not get out; and here he found the greatest amusement, more particularly in the summer, from standing to look at these creatures; observing their fierce gambols, and the strange contortions they made, with indescribable pleasure and interest.

In his rooms at the Sapienza, Giovan-Francesco Rustici was accustomed to assemble a company of gentlemen, who called themselves the Brotherhood or Society of the Paiuolo,* their numbers were limited to twelve, and these were Rustici himself, Andrea del Sarto,† the painter Spillo, Domenico Puligo, the goldsmith Robetta,‡ Aristotile da Sangallo, Francesco di Pellegrino, Niccolò Buoni, Domenico Baccelli, who played and sang most admirably, and the sculptor Solosmeo;§ Lorenzo' called Guazzetto,‖ the painter, was also of the number, as was Roberto di Filippo Lippi, who was their steward. Each of these members was permitted to bring four of his friends to their suppers and amusements of different kinds, but not more.

Now the order observed in these suppers was this (and I describe it the more willingly, because the custom of forming such companies is now almost wholly abandoned and laid down): every member was enjoined to contribute one dish to the repast, and in this dish it was always expected that he should display some new or ingenious invention; having brought his contribution, each member presented the same to the lord of the feast, who was always one of the members,

* A cauldron or pot for boiling meat, &c.

† The Italian annotators affirm it to have been before this company that Andrea del Sarto read the translation or imitation of the Batrachomyomachia, attributed to his pen, and this would appear probable from the fact that at the close of each canto the author addresses his thanks to the "Signore and Companions of the Pajuolo," for the patient hearing accorded to his verses.

‡ Best known for his engravings. Mr. Young Ottley mentions his works with approbation, and Bartsch has enumerated certain of his plates. See also Zani, *Enciclopedia Metodica delle Belle Arti*.

§ Solosmeo has been more than once mentioned in these Lives, but more particularly in that of Baccio Bandinelli. See vol. iii. p. 263, *et seq.*

‖ A disciple of Rustici, of whom there is further mention hereafter.

and who, on receiving it, made it over at once to some one among them, whomsoever he pleased, receiving from him at the same time his own dish in return, which in like manner the lord then presented to another of the members, selecting at his good pleasure as before. When all were at table, each offered to the other of his dish, as was reasonable, thus every one had a portion of all, if it so pleased him; but he who, in his choice or invention, had stumbled upon that previously chosen by another, was chastised for his fault.

One evening, among others, that Giovan-Francesco was giving a supper to these his companions of the Paiuolo, he commanded that they should substitute for the table an immense Cauldron, made from a large vat, within which all the guests found ample space, while the dishes were arranged in such a manner that they also appeared, as did the guests, to be floating in the water of the cauldron; the viands thus presented in the centre of the cauldron were illuminated from above, from the handle of the pot that is to say, which had the form of a bow, and whence there proceeded so bright a light that all the company could clearly examine each other's faces thereby. When all were thus most commodiously seated within the cauldron, there was seen to rise from the centre of the same, a tree with numerous branches, whereon were placed the first course of the meats composing the supper; and when that course was despatched the tree descended below, where were situated musicians sounding various instruments. Immediately afterwards the tree rose anew, presenting the second course; and again in like manner the third, continuing thus through the whole supper, servants being meanwhile in constant attendance and serving to all the finest and most generous wines.

This invention of the Cauldron, which was admirably managed, and decorated with pictures and paintings on canvas, was much commended by the members of the society: the particular contribution of Rustici on that occasion was a boiler or stew-pan formed of pastry, and wherein Ulysses was seen to be plunging his father, for the purpose of making him young again; the two figures of Ulysses and Laertes being represented by two boiled capons, which were most dexterously made into the forms of men by adding the limbs and various parts required, each member being composed ot things suitable and good to eat, and all affixed with due care to the bodies of the capons.

Andrea del Sarto presented on the same occasion a temple of eight sides, resembling the Baptistery of San Giovanni in form, but raised upon columns. The pavement of this temple was an enormous dish of jelly, divided into compartments of various colours to represent mosaic; the columns, which appeared to be of porphyry, were very large and thick sausages, the capitals of the columns were made of Parmesan cheese, the cornices were of sugar-work, while the tribune was formed out of sections of Marchpane. In the centre of the temple was a singing desk, made of cold veal, the book was formed of Lasagna,* the letters and musical notes being made of pepper-corns; the singers standing before the desk were roasted thrushes and other small birds placed upright, with their beaks wide open as in the act of chanting, they wore a sort of shirt resembling the tunic of the choristers, and this was made of a kind of net-work, contrived in the thinnest parts of a caul of hog's lard; behind them stood two very fat pigeons as contra-bassi, with six ortolans, which represented the soprani, or trebles.

The dish presented by Spillo was the figure of a Tinker made from a great goose, or other bird of similar sort; and this man, so contrived out of a goose, carried with him all the tools required for the mending of a cauldron in case of need. Domenico Puligo brought a roasted pig, but so treated as to resemble a scullery maid watching a brood of chickens, and having her distaff and spindle beside her; she being there for the purpose of washing the aforesaid cauldron. Robetta produced an anvil made out of a calf's head, with all the requirements of the same; this was to serve for the better maintenance in order of the cauldron, and was extremely well managed, as indeed were all the contributions (at a word, and that I may not have to enumerate each viand one by one), which were presented at that supper, as well as at the many

* The Lasagna is a kind of thin paste, resembling that used for macaroni, which, being cut into slices and dried, is boiled in water, or, by my richer friend, in his good strong gravy or broth, and being thus boiled, *may* be eaten, to the much delectation of him, my said friend, with fresh butter and grated cheese: it *may* be thus eaten, I say, but rarely is so, save in the sunny land of Italy.

other festivals given by the Company or Brotherhood of the Paiuolo, or Cauldron.

Another Company, which was that of the Trowel, and of which Giovan Francesco was also a member, had its origin in the manner following. One evening, in the year 1512, a joyous band had assembled at supper in that garden which the humpbacked fifer, Feo d'Agnolo, who was a right merry fellow, then had in the Campaccio; there were met, with this Feo, Ser Bastiano the pig-feeder, Ser Raffaello of the Shambles, the Barber Ser Cecchino, Girolamo del Giocondo, and Il Baia; these good souls being all busily employed in the eating of their *Ricotta.** While thus appropriately occupied, it chanced that Il Baia espied a heap of mortar which had been left in the garden at no great distance from their table, and in which the mason had left his trowel sticking when he quitted his work on the previous day. Taking up a morsel of the mortar on the point of that trowel therefore, Il Baia popped the same into the mouth of Feo, who sat gaping wide, in the expectation of a great lump of Ricotta, which another of his comrades was about to place therein. This being perceived by the company, they all began to cry, A Trowel! A Trowel! with the utmost force of their voices.

Out of this circumstance it was that the Company of the Trowel took its origin; and it was determined to make the society consist of twenty-four members; twelve of that number being selected from those who, as was the phrase at that time, "went for the Great,"† and twelve from such of

* Another dainty, little known beyond the country of its birth; yet not a few of my readers will remember to have turned in their despair, from the wickedly-nauseous butter of certain Italian towns (whose names, as we are doing a little evil-speaking, the present writer refrains from particularizing) to the white and not uninviting *looking* Ricotta, a preparation of milk, somewhat resembling curd, or a something between that and cream cheese. This contrivance, my readers may have essayed perchance, but few will have felt themselves greatly consoled thereby for the loss of their good English butter. It is nevertheless much eaten by Italians of the lower orders, sometimes with a preparation of wine, sugar, and spices, by way of sauce; a re-inforcement respecting the merits whereof, the experience of this deponent doth not enable her to speak.

† The phrase, "to go for the Great," was originally applied in Florence to those families whose names had been inscribed on the ancient rolls of the principal Guilds, and who were consequently considered of greater importance than those of others among the citizens. It afterwards came to be used as expressing every distinction of what kind soever.—*Masselli.*

the citizens as "went for the Little;" it was furthermore decreed, that the ensign of the Company should be a trowel, to which they afterwards added one of those little black vessels, with large heads and a certain species of tail, which are also called in the Tuscan language *Cazzuole* or *Trowels*. For their patron saint, these brethren of the Cazzuola chose Sant' Andrea, whose festival they celebrated with great magnificence and a splendid supper, given according to the rules laid down by their society.

The first members of the company were, for those of the Great, Jacopo Bottegai, Francesco Rucellai, and Domenico his brother; Gio Battista Ginori, Girolamo del Giocondo, Giovanni Miniati, Niccolò del Barbigia, and Mezzabotte his brother; Cosimo da Panzano, and Matteo his brother; Marco Jacopi, and Pieraccino Bartoli. While for those of the Little the members were, Bastiano Sagginotti, Ser Raffaello del Beccaio, Ser Cecchino de' Profumi; the painters Giuliano Bugiardini, and Francesco Granacci, Giovan-Francesco Rustici, the hunchback Feo, with the musical performer Talina his companion; the fifer Pierino, a certain Giovanni who was one of the city trumpeters, and the artilleryman Baia. The associates of the company were, Bernardino di Giordano, Il Talano, Il Caiano, Maestro Jacopo del Bientina, and the brazier Messer Gio Battista di Cristofano, both heralds of the Signoria: to these were added Buon Pocci and Domenico Barlacchi.*

The Company had not been many years in existence before the festivals given by it, and the amusement occasioned thereby, had so greatly increased its reputation that the following personages were made members of the Brotherhood of the Trowel: the Signor Giuliano de' Medici, Ottangolo Benvenuti, Giovanni Canigiani, Giovanni Serrestori, Giovanni Gaddi, Giovanni Bandini, Luigi Martelli, Paolo da Romena, and the hunchback Filippo Pandolfini. With these were at the same time admitted in quality of associates, the painter Andrea del Sarto, Bartolommeo, a musician and trumpeter; Ser Bernardo Pisanello; the cloth-shearer Piero, Il Gemma, who was a shopkeeper; and lastly, the physician, Maestro Manente da San Giovanni.

* "A man of so facetious a humour," remarks Bottari, "that his brilliant sayings were collected, and submitted to the press."

The feasts held by these companions at different times were innumerable, but I propose to make mention of some few among them only, and that chiefly for the benefit of those who are not acquainted with the usages of those societies which are now, as I said before, almost wholly extinct. The first supper given by the men of the Trowel, and which was arranged by Giuliano Bugiardini, was held at the place called L'Aia, or the threshing floor of Santa Maria Nuova, where the bronze doors of San Giovanni were cast, as we have before related. Now, the lord of the feast had commanded that all the guests should be permitted to appear in whatsoever habiliments might best please them, but if any two should chance to present themselves in the same garb they were to be punished for that misdeed; the Company, therefore, appeared in the most fanciful and most eccentric, but also most beautiful, vestments that can be imagined.

The hour of supper having arrived, the guests were placed at table in order according to the character of their clothing; those who wore the dress of princes were placed first, the rich and noble followed, and those who had attired themselves as poor men were sent to the lower end; but with regard to the jests and sports that were enacted after the supper, let every one picture to himself what these were, for they may be more easily imagined than described.

At another feast, which was arranged by the above-named Bugiardini and Giovan-Francesco Rustici in concert, the men of the Company appeared, as had been commanded by the lord of the feast, some in the dresses of master masons, and some in the garb of hod-men and other labourers; those who "went for the Greater," bearing the trowel by way of a knife for the table, and having a hammer in their girdle; and those who "went for the Lesser," with a pail or a hod and the windlass or lever in their hands, the trowel being carried in the girdle.

When the whole Company had reached the first chamber, they were shown, by the Signore or lord of the feast, the ground-plan of a building, which they were to erect for the Society, and the masters seating themselves at table around this plan accordingly: the labourers then immediately began to bring them the materials for laying the foundations, hods or pails that is to say, full of boiled Lasagne and Ricotta prepared with sugar, for lime to make mortar; the sand was represented by a mixture of cheese, pepper, and spices of different kinds; for gravel they brought coarse sugar-plums and pieces of Berlingozzo cake; the bricks, great or small, and the tiles, were represented by loaves of bread and cakes, which were served in, or rather thrown out from, baskets and hods brought on hand-barrows.

After this there was borne in the pedestal or socle of a column, but the construction of that basement was not approved by the stone-cutters, who, declaring it to be not well executed, adjudged it to be taken to pieces, whereupon they threw themselves on the same, and found it to be entirely composed of pasties, livers, cutlets, and other eatables of similar kind; all which being placed before the masters by the labourers, were eaten accordingly. Next was presented a column wound around with the tripe of calves, and this ornament being removed, the boiled veal and capons of which the column was composed were consumed; when the master builders proceeded to eat the base, which was of Parmesan cheese; and the capital, which was marvellously compounded of pieces carved from roasted capons and slices of veal, the mouldings being most fancifully made of tongues.

But why do I linger over all these particulars? Let it suffice to say, that after the column there was presented on a car, a piece of an architrave very completely formed, with frieze and cornice so admirably arranged, and for the construction of which so many kinds of eatables were employed, that to enumerate the whole of them would make much too long a story; it shall be sufficient to say, therefore, that when it was time to break up the party, after many peals of thunder, there fell a most cleverly contrived shower of rain, which instantly drove all these builders, masters, and workmen from their labours, and every man departed to his home.

Another time, and when Matteo da Panzano was master of the feast, the supper was ordered after the manner following:—Ceres, seeking Proserpine her daughter, who had been carried off by Pluto, entered the apartment wherein all the men of the Trowel were assembled, and presenting herself before the Signore, she begged that he, with his guests, would be pleased to accompany her to the infernal regions. To this request, after much discussion *pro* and *con*, the Society consented, and agreed to follow her guidance; they then proceeded to a somewhat darkened chamber, where, in place of a door, they found the open mouth of a serpent, the head of which filled all one side of the room; and having assembled around this door, while Cerberus kept barking, Ceres inquired if her lost child were there, and having received the reply that she was, the mother added that she desired to receive her daughter back.

But to this there came answer from Pluto to the effect that he would not give her up; this reply being accompanied by an invitation for Ceres and all her company to the nuptials, which were then about to be solemnized; and that bidding having been accepted, they all passed through the above-described mouth, which was full of teeth, and, moving on hinges, permitted only two of the guests to pass at a time, after which it closed again. By degrees, however, the whole assembly got in, when they found themselves in a vast chamber of a circular form, which had but one small glimmer of light in the centre, and this burnt so faintly that the guests could not distinguish each other without difficulty; here they were forced into their seats, which surrounded a table covered with black, by a most hideous-looking devil, who drove each to his place with a huge toasting-fork, when Pluto commanded that, in honour of his wedding, the pains of hell should cease during all the time that those guests remained there, a command which was obeyed accordingly.

Now, around that chamber there had been painted all the gulphs and caverns of the regions of the damned, with their several pains and torments; in an instant therefore, and with the swiftness of a flash of lightning, fire being set to a match prepared for the purpose, there sprang up flames in each of those cavernous dungeons, when the mode and manner in which the dwellers in those dismal abodes were tormented became at once fully apparent.

The viands to be consumed at that infernal supper, moreover, were all presented under the forms of the most abominable, disgusting, and repulsive looking animals; but beneath the hideous covering of pastry, or other materials, there were, in fact, concealed the most exquisite meats, in the richest and most costly variety. The skin, I say, and the external parts, caused these eatables to appear as if nothing less than serpents, adders, lizards, newts, great venomous spiders, toads, frogs, scorpions, bats, and animals of similar kind, were to be forced upon the guests, but within these articles were found to be the most choice and inviting preparations; these were placed before each guest with a fire-shovel, under the direction of the huge devil before-mentioned, while a comrade of his brought wines of the finest quality in vessels of hideous form, and these he poured into ladles looking like such as are used for melting glass, and which served the guests as beakers.

After these first dishes, which were but as a species of "antepast," or foretaste, there were fruits placed on the table as if for dessert, pretending that the supper (which had scarcely commenced) was already finished—with sweetmeats of various kinds; but these fruits and confections which were cast about and rudely scattered all over the table, were apparently relics of the dead, although in fact the seeming bones were most delicate compositions of sugar, &c. This being done, command was given by Pluto (who announced that he was then going to his repose), to the effect that the ordinary pains should recommence and the condemned be tormented anew; whereupon the lights by which the places of torture had been previously shown were instantaneously extinguished, aye, in less than the twinkling of an eye, and at the same moment there arose sounds of infinite horror, groans of the suffering, fearful cries, and exclamations full of terror. Then, in the midst of that darkness, and holding a faint light which did but just permit him to be seen, appeared the form of that Baia, the artillery-man of whom I have before spoken, and who was one of the guests, but had now been condemned to hell by Pluto, because in preparing fire-works and "girandole" he had always confined his inventions to a representation of the seven mortal sins and things appertaining to the realms of the infernal king.

While all were occupied with that spectacle and in listening to those outcries, lamentations, and moanings, the whole of the grizly sight was swept away; and lights then appearing, there was seen in its stead the most royal and magnificent preparation for a supper, which was instantly laid with all respect before the guests by well-appointed and watchfully obedient servants. At the end of the feast, a ship laden with choice confections appeared, and this the masters thereof, as men who were selling their merchanize, distributed among the company; when all were thus disposed of the guests were conducted into the upper rooms, where a much renowned comedy called Philogenia, for which very splendid and beautiful scenic decorations had been prepared, was performed; after which all departed, in the dawn of the morning, and having been infinitely delighted, to their respective homes.

Two years had elapsed from the time of the feast above described, when, after many festivals and dramatic performances, it again came to the turn of the same person to be "Signore," when, by way of reproving some of the members who had gone to unreasonable expenses for those suppers, and, as the phrase goes, had "eaten themselves up alive" in the same; he caused his feast to be arranged as follows:—At the Aia, or threshing floor of Santa Maria, where the Company was accustomed to hold its assemblies, he caused figures such as are commonly depicted on the walls and at the entrances of almshouses and hospitals, to be painted on the building, outside of the door: that of the Director, or Spedalingo, among others, who was represented as in the act of charitably and kindly receiving certain pilgrims and poor men. This picture was displayed on the evening of the feast, and when the members began to arrive; having knocked, and being received by the Spedalingo, the guests were then ushered into a great room, such as are used in almshouses, with its beds ranged on each side, and all the rest of the furniture being of the sort usually found in places of that kind.

In the centre of the chamber, and gathered about a great fire, were Bientina, Battista dell' Ottonaio, Barlacchi, Baia, and others selected from the most facetious of the companions, all clothed in the garb of idle, worthless beggars, and poor wretched rogues. These men assumed the appearance of not supposing themselves to be visible to the general company of the guests, who soon began to assemble, and of whom, in their turn, they took no notice whatever, but carried on a discourse relating entirely to the men of the society by whom they were surrounded. These they assailed without mercy, by no means sparing themselves, although their remarks consisted of the most biting sarcasms, being levelled more especially against those who had thrown away their property, and squandered more of their substance than it was advisable to spend, in festivals, suppers, &c. When all the members of the Company were assembled, and this discourse had come to an end, there appeared to them their patron, Sant' Antonio, who, delivering them from the Poor-house, conducted them into a chamber, magnificently prepared, where they all supped joyously together.

That being done, Sant' Antonio pleasantly advised them, to the end that they might keep safely out of the Poor-house, and not make waste of their property by superfluous expense—he recommended them, I say, to content themselves for the future with one great feast in the year, that done, their patron Saint disappeared from amongst them. Nor did the Company fail to obey the injunction thus given; for many years they had only one supper annually; but this was a very magnificent one, with a dramatic representation by way of close; and at various times there were performed by them, as we have related in the life of Aristotile da San Gallo, the Calandra of Messer Bernardo, Cardinal di Bibbiena, the Suppositi and the Cassaria of Ariosto, the Clizia, and the Mandragola of Macchiavello. with many others.

On a certain time, when Francesco and Domenico Rucellai were Signori of the feast, they performed the Harpies of Fineo; the Signore who succeeded them causing a Disputation on the Trinity by certain Philosophers to be represented, and therein they exhibited Sant' Andrea, who commanded that all Heaven should be opened to the gaze of the beholders, with all the choirs of Angels. A most truly beautiful and extraordinary spectacle it was. By Giovanni Gaddi, who received aid from Jacopo Sansovino, Andrea del Sarto, and Giovann Francesco Rustici, the punishment of Tantalus, in the infernal regions, was represented; and while he feasted the Company, they all appeared in the habiliments proper to the various Gods of Olympus, exhibiting besides all the remainder of the Fable with many fanciful inventions of gardens, the Elysian fields, effectively arranged fire-works, and other matters, to describe the whole of which would make too long a story.

The invention exhibited by Luigi Martelli also, when he, being Signore, gave his supper to the Company in the house of Giuliano Scali,* at the Porta a Pinti, was also a very fine one, seeing that he there represented Mars, who, to denote his cruelty, was shown entirely covered with gore, in a room filled with the bleeding members of the human form; while in another chamber were seen Mars and Venus, whom Vulcan has covered with a net, and having done so, assembles all the Gods to make them witnesses of the affront offered to him by Mars and his wicked wife.

But, after this digression, which, for many causes, does not appear to me to be altogether out of place, although it may seem to many to be too long, it is time that I should return to the life of Giovan-Francesco Rustici.

In the year 1528, the Medici being driven from Florence, our artist no longer found his residence in that city to his liking, and having left the charge of all his affairs to Niccolò Buoni, he departed, with his disciple Lorenzo Naldini, called Guazzetto, to France, where, being made known to the king by Giovambattista della Palla, who was then in that country, and by the particular friend of Rustici, Francesco di Pellegrino, who had repaired thither but a short time previously, he was received most willingly by the sovereign, who instantly gave him a pension of five hundred crowns per annum, and for whom Rustici executed certain works, of which, however, we cannot obtain exact notices. He also received commission to cast a Horse in bronze, to be double the size of life, and on which the statue of King Francis was to be seated; to this work he set hand accordingly, producing various models which pleased tne monarch greatly: nay, continuing his labours, Giovan-Francesco then prepared the great model for the figure, of which he had made the mould, and was even ready for casting, the preparations for which had been made in a large palace, given to Giovan-Francesco for his accommodation by King Francis. But, whatever the cause may have been, the

* This house now belongs to the Conte della Gherardesca, and is very near the palace occupied by that noble at the Pinti gate.—*Ed. Flor.*, 1832-8.

work was not finished when the King died; and on the accession of King Henry to the throne our artist was one of the many persons who were deprived of their pensions, the expenses of the Court being considerably decreased.

It is said that Giovan-Francesco, being then old, and not in very good circumstances, lived for some time on the rent which he received for the large palace and its adjacent buildings, for which he was indebted to the generosity or King Francis; but Fortune, not content with all that this man had before endured, was preparing for him a very great blow in addition to the rest, seeing that King Henry presented the palace above-mentioned to the Signor Pietro Strozzi, and Giovan-Francesco would have found himself in a most grievous strait, had it not been for the compassion of that noble, who, grieving much for the distress of Rustici (the latter having made himself known to Pietro), came in happy hour to the rescue, and that in his utmost need; Strozzi installing him in an abbey, or some place of that kind, which belonged to his brother.* There the needy old age of Giovan-Francesco was not only guarded from want, but he was very comfortably served and cared for, as befitted his condition and merits, even to the end of his life.

Il Rustici died at the age of eighty, and his possessions came for the most part into the possession of the above-named Signore, Piero Strozzi; but I will not omit to mention, that while Antonio Mini,† a disciple of Buonarroti, was living in France, and receiving much aid as well as kindness from Giovan-Francesco, there came into the hands of the latter many designs and models by Michelagnolo, one portion of which was, at a later period, in the possession of the sculptor, Benvenuto Cellini, who was then in France, and who afterwards brought those effects to Florence.

Giovan-Francesco Rustici, as I have before said, was not

* The Cardinal Lorenzo Strozzi, brother of Piero the Marshal, and of Leone the Governor of Capua and Admiral of France, both, or rather, all three, being sons of the renowned Filippo Strozzi, who killed himself, or was slain in the Lower Fortress during the reign of Cosmo I., and is regarded by many writers as the Florentine Cato.—*Ed. Flor.*, 1832-8.

† This disciple of Michael Angelo received from his master the famous Cartoon of the Leda, which he sold to the King of France, as we have said before.—*Ed. Flor.*, 1832-8.

only without an equal for the casting of works in metal, but he was moreover a man of excellent life: of incomparable goodness to all men, he was more especially a most charitable friend of the poor; wherefore it is but just and by no means surprising, that he, in his need, should be assisted with the utmost liberality, when in want of money and all other things, by the above-named Signor Piero; for it is not to be questioned, being true above all other truth, that even in this life, the good that we do to our neighbour for the love of God, is often restored to us by twice a thousand fold.

Rustici designed most admirably, as may be seen, not only from the specimens in our own book, but also from those in the collection of the very reverend Don Vincenzio Borghini.

The above-named Lorenzo Naldini, called Guazzetta, who was the disciple of Rustici, has executed many works of sculpture in France,* and these are declared to be admirable; but I have not been able to ascertain the particulars of the same, any more than of those performed by his master, who cannot, as we must needs believe, always have remained idle during the many years of his abode in France, nor could he even have been constantly occupied with the house of which we have made mention.

Now Lorenzo Naldini possessed some houses in that suburb which lies before the gate of San Gallo, in Florence; but these, together with other dwellings of the people, were ruined and demolished during the siege.† This grieved him so much, that when, on revisiting his country in the year 1540, he passed through that gate, Lorenzo covered his head with the cape of his cloak, when he came within a quarter of a mile of the place, and shut his eyes that he might not see the ruin and devastation of his home. The guards at the gate, seeing him thus muffled, inquired the cause, and being told wherefore he had so concealed his face, they laughed at him for his pains. After remaining in Florence some few months, Lorenzo, taking with him his mother, then returned to France, where he still lives, and is continuing his labours.

* Where he formed a particular intimacy with Rosso, as has been related in the Life of that painter. See vol. iii. p. 321.

† That of the year 1530.

## THE SCULPTOR, FRA GIOVANN' AGNOLO MONTORSOLI.

[BORN 1428—DIED 1563-4.]

To a certain Michele, the son of Agnolo, of Poggibonzi, and at a village called Montorsoli, which is situate about three miles from Florence on the road to Bologna, where Michele had a good and tolerably large farm, there was born a male child, to whom he gave the name of his own father and the boy's grandfather, Agnolo that is to say. The child growing up and evincing a decided inclination for design, he was placed by his father, who acted in pursuance of advice given him by various friends, to learn stone carving with certain masters who were then occupied among the quarries of Fiesole, very nearly opposite to Montorsoli; continuing his labours under these men, therefore, in company with Francesco del Tadda,* who was then a youth, and with others, many months had not elapsed before the young Agnolo knew perfectly well how to handle his tools, and executed not a few works proper to that vocation.

Having subsequently, and by means of Del Tadda, become known to Maestro Andrea, a sculptor of Fiesole,† the latter was so greatly pleased with the character of the child, that he began to give him instructions; and his affection for the boy increasing, he kept him in his workshop for three years. About that time Michele, the father of Agnolo, being dead, he set off with other young stone-cutters to Rome, whither many of that calling then repaired; and there, having set himself to work in the building of San Pietro, he carved several of those rosettes which are in the great cornice that passes entirely around the Church, which he did to his great advantage, receiving good pay for the same. Departing afterwards from Rome, I know not why, he engaged himself in Perugia with a master stone-cutter, by whom, at the end of a year, he was entrusted with the care of all the undertakings passing through his hands: but knowing that his continued abode

* The name of this artist was Francesco Ferrucci. He was of the same family with the artist of his name who is mentioned in a note to the Life of Tribolo, as being the first to execute statues in porphyry. See vol. iv. p. 182.

† Who was also of the Ferrucci family.

in Perugia was not advisable, since he was not learning anything there, Agnolo removed to Volterra, having found a favourable opportunity for doing so, and there worked at the tomb of Messer Raffaello Maffei, called Il Volterrano;* and for this monument, which was in course of being executed in marble, Agnolo carved ornaments, which clearly showed that he would some day render himself remarkable, and produce works meriting remembrance.

That sepulchral monument being completed, Agnolo, hearing that Michelagnolo Buonarroti was then employing the best carvers and stone-cutters that he could find, for the buildings of the Sacristy and Library of San Lorenzo, —Agnolo, I say, departed from Volterra and repaired to Florence, where he at once began to work. But he had no sooner done so, than Michelagnolo perceived that the youth, from whose hand he had seen various ornaments, was one of a bold spirit and excellent genius, who performed more work in one day than was produced by many older and more experienced masters in two, wherefore Buonarroti caused to be paid to him, though still but a mere boy, the same salary that was given to those of advanced age.

These buildings having been suspended in the year 1527, by the outbreak of the plague and other causes, Agnolo, not knowing what else to do with himself, set off for Poggibonzi, where his father and grandfather had received their birth, and there he remained for some time with his uncle, Messer Giovanni Norchiati, a pious and learned man,† in whose house he employed his time solely in drawing and studying. But finding that the world seemed all to be turning upside-down, he formed the resolution of becoming a monk, and devoting his time to the calm pursuits of the cloister and the salvation of his own soul; whereupon he betook himself to the Hermitage of Camaldoli. This life he tried for a time; but finding that he could not support the discomforts thereof, nor endure the perpetual fasts, and that abstinence from all the enjoyments of life which was there

* A man renowned for his learning and the excellence of his life.—*Bottari.*

† Chaplain, and afterwards canon of San Lorenzo as will be seen hereafter.—*Ibid.*

the rule, he would not remain. Yet during the time that he did abide in that place, he made himself particularly acceptable to those fathers, because he was of an excellent disposition. The amusement of Agnolo while at the Hermitage, consisted in carving the heads of men and different animals, with other fanciful inventions, on the upper ends of the stick or staff which each of those good fathers was accustomed to carry, when he proceeded from Camaldoli to the Hermitage, or went into the woods for amusement, at which time the rule of maintaining silence is dispensed with.

Having left the Hermitage with the permission and good favour of the Principal, but feeling still strongly disposed to become a monk, Agnolo then repaired to La Vernia, where he also remained for some time, frequenting the choir and holding converse with the fathers. But neither did that mode of life suit him on a further acquaintance; wherefore, having received certain intimations in respect to the manner of proceeding observed by various religious communities in Florence and Arezzo, he visited some of these on leaving La Vernia; and finding that he could not continue his care for the welfare of his soul with the desired attention to the studies of design, in any other convent so conveniently as in that of the Ingesuati of Florence, he presented himself to those fathers, and entered their monastery, which is situate at the Pinti Gate; he was very willingly received by those monks, the more so as they, labouring much in the painting of glass windows, had great hope that in him they should find a very useful and valuable assistant.

Now it has not been the custom with the Padri Ingesuati to read Mass, but according to their manner and the rule of their order, they keep a priest, who performs that office every morning; their Chaplain at that time being a Servite Monk named Fra Martino, who was a man of fair judgment and respectable life. This chaplain, perceiving the genius and aptitude of the youth, considered that he would not find exercise for the same among the Frati Ingesuati, who do nothing but say paternosters, make glass windows, distil herbs for sweet waters, dig their gardens, and perform other works of similar kind, but do not study or cultivate letters, wherefore he did and said so much that Agnolo went forth from the Ingesuati, and finally took the monastic habit among the

Servite Monks, in the Monastery of the Nunziata at Florence. This he did on the 7th day of October, in the year 1530, receiving the name of Giovann' Agnolo.

In the year 1531, having acquired the requisite knowledge of such ceremonies and offices as are practised there, while he also studied the works of Andrea del Sarto which are in that place, Giovann' Agnolo made what they call his profession; and the following year, to the entire satisfaction of those fathers, and after having received the full consent of his kindred, he sang his first mass with much pomp and ceremony.

On the expulsion of the Medici, the wax figures of Leo, Clement, and other members of that most noble family which had been placed in the Cloisters of the Servites in pursuance of a vow, had been much injured by some young people, more out of their folly than from the bravery and good motives which they would fain have had attributed to them, when the Monks resolved that those works should be restored; and Giovann' Agnolo, with the aid of some others among them, who had given their attention to the making of images, undertook to repair such as were old and injured by time, while he moulded anew the Popes Leo and Clement, whose figures, as he made them, are still to be seen in that place.* Shortly afterwards he executed figures of the King of Bossina,† and of the old Signor da Piombino; in these works Fra Giovann' Agnolo gave evidence of having made considerable progress in his art.

In the meanwhile Michelagnolo was in Rome with Pope Clement, by whom he had been summoned, because his Holiness desired that the works of San Lorenzo should be continued; the Pontiff also required Buonarroti to find him a young man who could restore some ancient statues which were in the Belvedere and had been broken; whereupon Michelagnolo, remembering Fra Giovanni, proposed him to the Pope, and his Holiness requested his presence by a brief to the General of his order, who granted it, because he could not do otherwise, but with a very ill will. The young monk

* They are no longer there, having been removed during the last century. —*Ed. Flor.*, 1832-8.

† This is probably the last King of Bosnia, Matthias Huniades, whose power was annihilated at the Battle of Mohacz, in the year 1527.

having arrived in Rome accordingly, was at once set to work in certain rooms of the Belvedere which were assigned to him by the Pope as his abode and place of labour; here he restored the left arm of the Apollo and the right arm of the Laocoon, both of which are in that place he made arrangements for the restoration of the Hercules also.

Now Pope Clement was then accustomed to frequent the Belvedere very much, repairing thither almost every morning for his diversion, or to perform his devotions; the monk therefore, profiting by these occasions, made a portrait of his Holiness in marble, which was so good a one, that the work obtained for him much praise. He became very acceptable to the Pontiff also, and the rather because the latter observed that Fra Giovanni was most studious of his art, and found too that he occupied a part of every night in making designs, to the end that he might have something new to show his Holiness every morning, nor did Pope Clement fail to take infinite pleasure in those productions.

About that time a Canonicate of San Lorenzo in Florence, which is a Church that was built and endowed by the Medici, had fallen vacant, when Fra Giovann' Agnolo, who had laid aside his monkish vestments, obtained it for Messer Giovanni Norchiati his uncle, who was a chaplain in that Church as we have said.

Pope Clement having then determined that Buonarroti should return to Florence, there to finish the works of the Sacristy and Library of San Lorenzo, gave him orders, seeing that many of the statues were still wanting there, as will be related in the Life of Michelagnolo, to the effect that he should secure the services of the most able men that could be found, but more particularly of the Frate, Giovann' Agnolo: Buonarroti, being commanded to proceed as Antonio San Gallo had done, when engaged on the completion of the works at the Madonna di Loretta.

Michelagnolo and the Frate repaired to Florence accordingly, and in the execution of the statues of the Duke Lorenzo and of Giuliano, Buonarroti availed himself constantly of Giovann' Agnolo's assistance in the polishing of the same, and in the performance of certain delicacies of execution connected with the hollowing out and placing in such relief as to be entirely detached from the marble beneath, of certain parts in those works; on which occasion Giovann' Agnolo found means to acquire the knowledge of many things from that truly divine master Buonarroti, by whose side he would stand during long hours, attentively watching his labours and observing the most minute circumstance connected with them.

Among the other statues still wanting to the completion of that work, were those of SS. Cosimo and Damiano, which were to stand one on each side of Our Lady; Michelagnolo, therefore, took measures for the execution of the same, and gave one of them, the San Damiano, to Raffaello da Montelupo; * the other, San Cosimo, he commissioned Il Frate Giovann' Agnolo to prepare. The latter set himself to his labours with very great care accordingly, and made a large model of the figure, which was retouched in many parts by Buonarroti, or rather Michelagnolo himself made the head and arms in clay, these being still in Arezzo in the hands of Giorgio Vasari, who preserves them among his most valued possessions, as proof of his regard to the memory of so great a man.† It is true that there are not wanting those who have censured Michelagnolo for that circumstance, saying that he had given evidence of but little judgment in confiding the commission for that statue to Giovann' Agnolo, and had made a bad choice; yet the result proved not only that Michelagnolo Buonarroti had chosen most judiciously, but that the Frate was a very able man.

Having completed and erected in their places the statues of the Duke Lorenzo and of Giuliano, which he did with the assistance of Giovanni Agnolo, Michelagnolo was recalled by the Pope, who desired that he should make arrangements for the execution in marble of the façade of San Lorenzo; he returned to Rome therefore, but had not been there long before Pope Clement died, when all those undertakings were left unfinished. The statue of the Frate Giovann' Agnolo was meanwhile given to public view at Florence with the rest; and, unfinished as it was, that work obtained very high commendation.‡ Of a truth, indeed, whether it is to be

* See the Life of Raffaello da Montelupo, vol. iii. p. 140.

† Now unhappily lost, with the many other precious works of art collected by Vasari.—*Ed. Flor.*, 1832-8.

‡ Cicognara speaks in terms of high praise of the head of that figur but does not express satisfaction with other parts. He has given an outline

attributed to the diligence and care of the artist, or to the assistance of Michelagnolo, this figure proved to be the best ever executed by the Frate among all that he produced in his whole life, and is without doubt entirely worthy of the place assigned to it.*

Buonarroti, being freed from his engagements at San Lorenzo by the death of the Pontiff, now turned his thoughts towards the fulfilment of that which he had contracted for the sepulchral monument of Julius II.; but knowing that he should have need of assistance in his work, he sent for the Frate, who did not however proceed to Rome until he had first entirely completed the figure of the Duke Alessandro in the Nunziata. This he executed in a very beautiful manner, and one altogether different from that adopted by those artists who had previously treated the same subject; he has represented the Duke in his armour that is to say, and kneeling on a casque of the Burgundian fashion, as if in the act of recommending himself to the protection of the Madonna, beside whom he is placed. Having finished this work the monk then went to Rome, where his assistance was the utmost value to Michelagnolo, in the preparation of that sepulchral monument for Pope Julius alluded to above.

The Cardinal Ippolito de' Medici was meanwhile given to understand that Cardinal Tournon was desirous of taking with him a sculptor required at that time for the service of the King of France, and therefore proposed to him the Frate Giovann' Agnolo, who being earnestly advised by Michelagnolo with many arguments to accept the appointment, did accordingly consent to accompany the Cardinal de Tournon to Paris. Arrived in that city, he was introduced to the King, and very favourably received by that monarch, who very soon afterwards assigned him a pension in addition to his stipend, with orders that he should at once commence the execution of four large statues. But of these the Frate had not yet finished the models, when the King, being at a distance, and occupied on the borders of his kingdom, in wars with the English, he found the treasurers disposed to refuse him his pension; in effect, he could neither obtain his

engraving of the work in the *Storia della Scultura*, plate LXV. See also tomo ii. p. 309.

* The work is still in its place.

appointments nor anything else that he required, and with which the monarch had commanded that he should be supplied.

Offended by this treatment, and perceiving that men of ability were as much despised and maltreated by the ministers of that magnanimous king, as they were valued and honoured by the sovereign himself, Giovann' Agnolo departed, and this notwithstanding that all the arrears of his stipend were paid to him by the treasurers (who were made aware of his displeasure), even to the uttermost farthing. Before he left Paris, however, Giovann' Agnolo declared his purpose of doing so, bv his letters to the King as well as to the Cardinal.

From the capital of France he proceeded to Lyons, and thence by Provence to Genoa, but did not remain there long, leaving that city in company with several of his friends, with whom he visited Venice, Padua, Verona, and Mantua, where, to his great pleasure, he saw and sometimes designed, many fine buildings, sculptures, and paintings. But that which pleased him more than all in Mantua, was the examination which he had opportunities for making of the paintings executed in that place by Giulio Romano, some of which he copied with much care. Having afterwards been informed, (while at Ferrara and Bologna,) that his brethren of the Servites were holding a general Chapter of their Order in Budrione, he repaired thither to meet the many of his acquaintance, who were certain to be found there, more particularly the Florentine Maestro Zaccheria, who was his most intimate friend; and at the entreaty of this Maestro Zaccheria, Giovanni Agnolo there produced in a day and a night, two figures in *terra*, of the size of life, representing Faith and Charity, which were coloured to imitate white marble, and served as ornaments to a Fountain contrived by him, with the aid of a great copper vessel, for the occasion. This fountain continued to throw water during the whole of the day on which the Chanter was held, to the reat honour and glory of the Frate.

With the same Maestro Zaccheria, Giovann' Agnolo then returned to Florence, and to his Convent of the Servites, where he executed two figures, also in *terra*, and larger than life, which were placed in two niches of the Chapter House; these represented Moses and St. Paul, and were very highly extolled.* He was afterwards sent to Arezzo, by Maestro Dionisio, who was then General of the Servites, and was eventually made Cardinal by Pope Paul III.; that Dionisio considering himself under great obligations to Angelo the General of his Order at Arezzo,† by whom he had been brought up and instructed in good letters; and having commissioned Giovann' Agnolo to erect a magnificent sepulchral monument of macigno stone in the Church of San Piero, in that city,‡ for the said Aretine General, adorning the same with many carvings and statues. On the Sarcophagus is the figure of the General Angelo, a portrait from the life, with two nude figures of children, in full relief, represented as weeping while they extinguish the torches of human life; there are besides other ornaments, which render that work extremely beautiful; but it was not entirely completed when Giovann' Agnolo was recalled to Florence, and compelled to depart, his presence being required in the last-named city, by the preparations which the Duke Alessandro was then making for the expected arrival of the Emperor Charles V., who was at that time returning victorious from Tunis.

Having reached Florence, the Frate at once proceeded to construct a colossal figure of eight braccia high, which he placed on a broad pedestal at the Bridge of the Trinità; this, which represented the River Arno, was in a recumbent position, and appeared to be rejoicing with the Rivers—Rhine, Danube, Biagrada, and Ibero,§ (which had been made by other artists) at the coming of his Majesty; this figure of the Arno was a very good and beautiful one. The same Frate made a statue, twelve braccia high, for the angle of the Carnesecchi, a Jason, Leader of the Argonauts, namely; but this, being as it was of immoderate size, and the time for its preparation being short, was not of equal perfection with the first-mentioned, nor indeed was another, representing Royal Gladness, which the Frate added at the corner of

* These figures are still in the Chapter House, which is now called the Chapel of the Painters, &c. They stand one on each side of Bronzino's picture representing the Most Holy Trinity.—*Masselli.*

† The general of the Servites here meant is the Cardinal Dionisio Laurerio, of Benevento.—*Bottari.*

‡ This monument still retains its place.—*Ed Flor.*, 1832-8.

§ The Ebro, or as some say the Tiber, for authorities differ on that point, which we leave to the research of our readers.

the Cuculia. The rapidity with which he had completed these works was nevertheless taken into the account, and Giovann' Agnolo obtained much credit for his labours from artists, as well as from the people generally.

Giovann' Agnolo afterwards returned to finish his work at Arezzo, and having there heard that Girolamo Genga* was about to execute a monument in marble at Urbino, the Frate went to seek him; but no conclusion having been arrived at, he turned his face towards Rome, where however he did not long delay, but went on to Naples, with the hope of being commissioned to construct the sepulchral monument of Jacopo Sannazzaro, a Neapolitan gentleman, and poet of truly singular merit and admirable qualities. Now Sannazzaro had built a magnificent and very commodious habitation, at a place which enjoys a most beautiful, nay rather, an exquisite view on the Margoglino† that is to say, which is situate at the end of the Chiaja, in the city of Naples, and directly faces the shore; this dwelling, which had the form proper to a monastery,‡ with a very beautiful little church,§ was enjoyed by Sannazzaro during his life;|| at his death he bequeathed it to the Servite Monks, commanding the Signor Cesario Mormerio, and the Conte di Lif,¶ executors of his will, to construct his sepulchral monument in the church which had been erected by himself as we have said, and desiring that therein, where the above named fathers were always to officiate, his own remains should be deposited.

The question of making this tomb being then discussed,

* Whose Life will be found in vol. iv. of the present work, p. 398

† Now called the Mergellina.

‡ The Palace was built by Frederick of Arragon, and that prince, on his accession to the throne, presented it to Sannazzaro, who had been his secretary.

§ The Church was dedicated to Santa Maria del Parto, by Sannazzaro himself, who, as our readers will remember, was the author of the Latin poem, *De Partu Virginis*. At a later period it was taken from the Servite Monks, and given to a secular body.

|| This is not strictly correct, the palace having been razed to the ground by Philibert de Chalons, Prince of Orange, in the struggle between the Imperialists, commanded by himself, and the French, led by Marshal Lautrec. Sannazzaro did indeed erect the building "in the form of a monastery," on the ruins of the palace, and he also did ultimately dispose of the same, as Vasari proceeds to relate.

¶ The Count D'Aliffe that is to say.—*Ed. Flor.*, 1832-8.

the Servite Monks proposed to the executors that the commission for the same should be given to Giovann' Agnolo, and he, going, as we have said, in that expectation to Naples, the work was finally accorded to him :* his models were indeed found to be much better than those which had been prepared by many other sculptors, and he consequently received a good share of the 1000 crowns advanced for them. Giovann' Agnolo then sent Francesco del Tadda, of Fiesole,† an able carver, to superintend the excavation of the marbles, having given him directions to get forward with all such rough hewings, dressings, and carvings, as should be demanded for the work, to the end that it might proceed with the greater rapidity.

While the Monk was thus making his arrangements for the construction of the above-mentioned sepulchre, the Turkish army entered Apuglia, and the people of Naples, being thrown into no small terror by that event and by the near vicinity of the foe, orders being given for the fortification of the city ; four men of eminent distinction, and whose judgment was much relied on, being charged with the care of the works. These persons, requiring the assistance of an able architect, bethought themselves of the Frate, but some slight rumour of what was intended having reached his ears, and he not thinking that it beseemed a man of religion as he was, to meddle with matters of war, left Naples, but first gave the executors of Sannazzaro's testament to understand that he would prepare his tomb either at Carrara, or Florence, and would take care that it should be finished and erected in its place within the appointed time.

He thus departed, as I have said, from Naples, and repaired to Florence, where he at once received commands from the

* Piacenza (in his additions to Baldinucci) affirms that the commission for this tomb was first given to Girolamo Santacroce, of whom Vasari has made mention in vol. iii. p. 253, *et seq.*, and that he had commenced the work, but being interrupted by death, Montorsoli was then appointed to replace him, in consequence of the protection accorded to his pretensions by the Servite Monks. But Domenici, who is the authority best informed, as regards Neapolitan affairs, maintains that the monks favouring their co-religionist, and the executors their fellow citizen, the dispute which ensued, was adjusted by the two candidates dividing the work between them. Domenici has indeed assured us that he saw the contract for this arrangement in the archives of the building.

† See note *, p. 86, of the present Life.

Signora, Donna Maria, Mother of the Duke Cosimo, to the effect that he should finish the figure of San Cosimo, which he had formerly commenced under the direction of Buonarroti, for the tomb of the Magnificent Lorenzo the Elder;* Whereupon, having set hand to the same, he completed it entirely; and that being done, the Duke, who had then constructed the more important part of the conduits for the great fountain of his Villa at Castello, also required his services: and the matter was on this wise. The decorations of the summit of that Fountain were to consist of a figure of Hercules, in the act of strangling Antæus, out of whose mouth, in place of breath, there issues water, which ascends into the air to a considerable height; and for this it was that the Frate was commanded to make a model of tolerably large size; that model pleased his Excellency greatly, when Giovann' Agnolo received commission to execute the work, and was ordered to repair to Carrara for the purpose of excavating the marbles.

For Carrara the Frate departed accordingly and with great good will, seeing that he had thus an opportunity for getting forward with the above-mentioned monument of Sannazzaro, more especially with a story in figures of mezzo-rilievo, which he desired to prepare with his own hand. While Giovann' Agnolo was thus at Carrara it chanced that the Cardinal Doria wrote from Genoa to the Cardinal Cibo, who was also at Carrara; and his letter was to the effect that as Bandinelli had never completed the Statue of Prince Doria, and as he, Cardinal Doria, had no one ready to finish it, so he begged that Cibo would endeavour to procure some able artist by whom that work might be accomplished, he being very anxious to have it done. On the receipt of this letter, Cibo, who had long before obtained some knowledge of the Frate, used many efforts to prevail on him to go to Genoa; but he declared that he neither could nor would do anything for the service of his most reverend Lordship,

* From these words we (the Florentine Editors of the Passigli Edition of Vasari) are first made aware of the fact that the group of the Madonna, with the two Saints, Cosimo and Damiano, was intended for the tomb of Lorenzo the Magnificent, whom Vasari, as our readers will have remarked, always calls "the Elder," to distinguish him from Lorenzo, Duke of Urbino, whose sepulchral monument had been erected by Michael Angelo in the same place.

until he had first fulfilled the promise which he had given to the Duke Cosimo, and had completed the engagement which he had made with that Signore.

While these matters were in discussion, the Frate had got rapidly forward with the Tomb of Sannazzaro, and having also sketched for Duke Cosimo the Hercules in marble, he then proceeded with it to Florence, where, with much promptitude and diligence, he conducted it to such a degree of forwardness that little more was required for the entire completion of the figure, which would indeed have been presently finished had Giovann' Agnolo continued to work at it. But a rumour had got abroad, to the effect that the marble statue was not by very much so beautiful as the model had given cause to expect that it would be, and that the Frate would find infinite difficulty in fixing the legs of the Hercules to the trunk, seeing that they were not adapted to the torso which he had prepared for them. This went so far, that Messer Pier-Francesco Riccio, the Majordomo,* from whom Giovan' Agnolo was accustomed to receive his stipend, permitting himself to be influenced more readily than a grave man should do, became very backward in his payments to the Frate, listening too credulously to Bandinelli, who left nothing undone that could injure the Monk, by way of avenging himself for the wrong which, as it appeared to him, he had received from Giovann' Agnolo in the promise which the latter had given to finish the Statue of Prince Doria, so soon as he should have fulfilled his engagement with the Duke.†

There was also an opinion prevailing that the favour enjoyed by Tribolo, who was executing the decorations for the Castello, was in no way serviceable to the Frate; however this may have been, Giovann' Agnolo, a proud and choleric man, perceiving himself to be maltreated by Riccio, set off at once for Genoa, where he was instantly commissioned by the Cardinal and the Prince to execute the Statue of the latter, which was to be placed on the Palazzo Doria. He

* Of whom there has before been mention, more particularly in the Life of Tribolo, and who is alluded to in subsequent pages, but rarely to his honour.

† A fact alluded to in the Life of Baccio Bandinelli, for which see vol. iv.

set hand to the work accordingly, but without altogether neglecting the Tomb of Sannazzaro, for which Tadda was executing the remainder of the carvings and decorations at Carrara; and while these were in course of preparation, the Frate finished the Statue of Doria, to the great satisfaction of the Prince and all the people of Genoa.

Now the above-mentioned statue was intended, as we have said, to be placed on the Piazza Doria, but the Genoese made so much ado in the matter, that notwithstanding the protestations of Giovann' Agnolo, the figure was in fact erected on the Piazza della Signoria. It was in vain that the Frate declared the statue to have been executed with a view to its being placed on a pedestal and in an isolated position in the midst of an open space, adding, that it could not therefore have its due effect if placed, as was now proposed, at the angle of a wall; all that he could say availed nothing. Yet to tell the truth, it is certain that there cannot be a more injurious act than that of placing a work intended for some particular place in a different position, seeing that the artist, as he proceeds with his labour, has a view to the place where the sculpture or painting is to be fixed, and accommodates himself thereto in respect to the lights and other circumstances.

After this, and when the Genoese had seen the stories and other figures which Giovann' Agnolo had executed for the Tomb of Sannazzaro, which pleased them greatly, they determined that the Frate should have the commission for a figure of San Giovanni Evangelista, which was to be placed in their Cathedral Church; and when this was completed, they were so abundantly satisfied therewith, as to declare themselves amazed by its beauty.*

Leaving Genoa, Fra Giovanni at length proceeded to Naples, there to erect the Tomb of Sannazzaro in its place, and the manner of that monument is on this wise: at the outer angles of the base are two pedestals, on each of which are carved the arms of Sannazzaro, and between them is a stone tablet of a braccio and a half in width, on which is

* It was placed in one of the four principal tribunes of the cathedral. —*Masselli.*

inscribed the epitaph* which was written by Jacopo Sannazzaro himself, the tablet is supported by two little boys. On each of the two pedestals, moreover, is a Statue of marble, four braccia high; these figures are seated, and represent, the one Minerva, the other Apollo.† Between these figures, and in the midst of two consols, which stand at the sides, is a basso-rilievo two braccia and a half in the square; and here are sculptured Fawns, Satyrs, Nymphs, and other figures singing, and sounding various instruments, after the manner described in Sannazzaro's very learned Poem of the "Arcadia," and in the pastoral verses of that most eminent man.

Above this rilievo is an Urn, of a round form and very beautiful character, being richly adorned moreover, nay covered, so to speak, with sculptures; in this Urn are the remains of the Poet; and over it, placed on a pedestal in the centre, is the bust of Sannazzaro, a portrait from the life, with these words beneath it, ACTIUS SINCERIS; the portrait is accompanied by two boys, bearing wings in the manner of Loves; and having books around them. In two niches, which are beside the Tomb and in the walls of the Chapel, are two figures in marble, standing on pedestals, and representing, the one St. James the Apostle, the other San Nazzaro.‡ The Frate having erected this

* The epitaph to be read on this tomb is by Bembo, and is as follows:—

*Da sacro cineri flores. Hic ille Maroni*
*Syncerus Musa proximus ut tumulo,*
*Vixit an.* LXXII. *obiit* MDXXX.

Beneath these lines are inscribed the following:—

*Fr. Io. Ang. Flor. Or. S. fa.* *Masselli.*

† "Exceedingly beautiful statues," remarks an Italian commentator, "beneath which are now inscribed the names *David* and *Judith*. It is said that this change of names was effected by the monks, to save the works from the rapacity of a Spanish governor, who, pretending that, being heathen gods, they were not well-adapted to that sacred place, was on the point of making himself master of them."

‡ "These two statues," remarks the Italian quoted above, "which allude to the baptismal and family names of the poet, Jacopo Sannazzaro (Azzio Sincero being his academical name), are works of the most common-place character, and cannot be attributed with truth either to Santacroce or Montorsoli, whose abilities have been rendered manifest by so many other works, that there is no excuse for doing them the injury of attributing these to their hand. Engenio, whose injudicious partiality for his native country has induced him to attempt the degradation

work, in the manner here described, the above-named Signori executors declared themselves to be most perfectly satisfied, as did the whole city of Naples.

Giovann' Agnolo then remembered that he had promised Prince Doria to return to Genoa, there to erect the sepulchral monument of that Sovereign himself. This was to be constructed in the Church of San Matteo, and the Frate was furthermore to decorate the entire church. He departed from Naples, therefore; and having arrived in Genoa, at once prepared the models for such works as the above-named Signori had commanded, and which pleasing the latter greatly, Giovann' Agnolo set hand to the same, Prince Doria allowing him a good stipend, and the monk being assisted by a fair number of masters. Thus dwelling in Genoa, Giovann' Agnolo made many friends among the Genoese nobles and men of distinction, but more especially with certain physicians, and these persons were of great use to him, seeing that they dissected large numbers of human bodies; and, mutually aiding each other, they studied architecture and the laws of perspective in common; by which means Giovann' Agnolo rendered himself most excellent in his art.

Labouring in this manner, the days of the monk passed on, the Prince going frequently to the place where he was at work, finding much pleasure in his conversation, and ultimately conceiving a great friendship for him. Now about this time one of the nephews of Giovann' Agnolo, whom he had left in the custody of Maestro Zaccheria, was sent to him at Genoa, and this one, called Angelo,* was a youth who then gave promise of fair ability and very good dispositions. At the same time there was sent to the Frate by the same Maestro Zaccheria, another young man called Martino, the son of Bartolommeo, a tailor. Both these youths whom the monk instructed as carefully as he might or

of Montorsoli, by comparing these statues with those executed in other places by Santacroce, has found no one to support his opinion. Dominici indeed, *Vite dei Pittori Scultori e Architetti Napolitani*, denies that they are by either of the two artists above-named, nor does Vasari attribute them to Montorsoli, but merely mentions them as being among the other sculptures in the chapel which he is describing."

* Or Agnolo; the two being identical, and merely different forms of the same name.

could have done had they been his own sons, he now set to work on the undertaking which he had in hand; and having at length completed the several parts, he constructed the chapel, erected the tomb, and arranged all the ornaments which he had prepared for the Church. The nave of that building forms a single cross at the upper part of the same, and at the lower end there are three crosses; the High Altar is in the centre, being wholly isolated in its upper part.

The Chapel of which there has been mention above, is supported at the angles by four large pillars, which also serve to sustain the cornice passing around it, and above which rise four round arches, turned immediately over the pillars. Of these arches, three are occupied by windows of no great size, and over them passes a cornice of a round form, which forms four angles between arch and arch at the lower edge, but takes the form of a basin or depressed cupola in the upper part.

For the four sides of the Altar, Fra Giovann' Agnolo had prepared rich ornaments in marble, and above them he placed an exceedingly beautiful and splendidly decorated vase, also in marble, for the most holy Sacrament, two Angels of the natural size, and in marble like the rest, standing on each side thereof. Around the edge is a decoration formed of various stones inlaid on the marble ground, and exhibiting a beautiful and varied arrangement of marbles in different colours, and other precious stones, as for example, serpentines, porphyries, and jaspers. At the upper and principal wall of the Chapel, moreover, Giovann' Agnolo prepared a base or socle, richly encrusted with similar vari-coloured marbles and stones, which extends from the floor to a height equal to that of the summit of the altar, and this forms the basement to four columns of marble which enclose three spaces; the central and largest of which contains a tomb, holding the relics of I know not what Saint; while in those on each side are two statues in marble representing two of the Evangelists.

Above the range of columns here described is a cornice, and over the cornice four more columns, but of smaller size: these support another cornice, divided into three square compartments, corresponding with the open spaces between the first range of columns: in the central compartment is the Resurrection of Our Saviour Christ in full relief; the figures, which are in marble, being larger than life. On the sides are ranges of columns in like manner, and in the middle, above the before-mentioned tomb, is a figure of Our Lady in mezzo-rilievo, with the Dead Christ: on each side of the Madonna are figures representing King David and St. John the Baptist, St. Andrew and the Prophet Jeremiah occupying the spaces at the opposite end. In the lunettes of the arches and above the greater cornice where are the windows, is a rich decoration in stucco-work, with figures of Children who appear to be employed in adorning those windows. In the angles beneath the cupola are four Sybils also in stucco, works in which material likewise decorate the whole of the vault, being formed into grottesche of various kinds.

Beneath this chapel is a subterraneous chamber, into which there is a descent by means of marble stairs; and having entered it, you perceive a marble tomb at the upper end with figures of Angels in the form of children above it; and here were to be deposited, after his death, the remains of the above-named Signore, Andrea Doria, as I believe has been done. On an altar placed opposite to the Tomb is a beautiful Vase in bronze, cast and polished most admirably by whomsoever may have done it,* and within this vase is laid a piece of the wood of the most holy cross whereon our Saviour Christ was crucified, that morsel of the cross having been given to the Prince Doria by the Duke of Savoy. The walls of this sepulchral chamber are wholly encrusted with marble, and the vault is decorated with stucco-work and gold, exhibiting stories from the life and great deeds of Doria himself;† the pavement also is composed of vari-coloured marbles and precious stones, the divisions of the same corresponding with those of the vault.

In the transept of the church above are two sepulchral monuments in marble, with tablets in mezzo-rilievo: in one of these lies entombed the Signore, Count Filippino Doria,

* The present writer has not been able to obtain even a conjecture from any writer of authority with respect to the author of this work.

† The stucco-work on the vaulting of the chapel does not represent the actions of Doria, but of other Genoese rulers.—*Piacenza.*

and in the other is buried the Signor Giannettino, also of the Doria family. Against the pillars at the commencement of the middle aisle are two beautiful pulpits in marble, and throughout the side aisles are distributed chapels of admirable architecture, the whole of them being richly adorned with columns and other ornaments, by all which this fabric is rendered a truly rich and magnificent edifice. Having completed the church, Prince Doria then caused the Frate Giovann' Agnolo to set hand to his palace, making large additions to the building, and also laying out very beautiful gardens, which were in like manner committed to the superintendence of the Frate.

Finally, Giovann' Agnolo constructed a fish-pond before the front of the palace, and for this he prepared an ornament in marble; the subject chosen, and which was executed in full relief, being a Marine Monster, by which water in vast quantities is poured into that fish-pond. He likewise executed a colossal figure of Neptune* in stucco, which was placed on a pedestal in the garden of the prince: two Portraits of the same Doria, and two of the Emperor Charles V., which were taken into Spain, are also to be enumerated among the works of Giovann' Agnolo.

While this artist abode in Genoa, Messer Cipriano Pallavicino, the Signor Abate Negro, Messer Giovanni da Montepulciano, and the Signor Prior of San Matteo, were all of the number of his friends, as, at a word, were all the first nobles and gentlemen of that city, wherein the Frate acquired both fame and riches: of Messer Cipriano Pallavicino in particular it may be remarked that, as he possesses much judgment in matters concerning our arts, so does he willingly associate himself with the most eminent artists, whom he favours upon all occasions.

Having finished the above-mentioned works, Fra Giovann' Agnolo departed from Genoa and repaired to Rome, there to visit Buonarroti, whom he had not seen for many years, and also to try if he could by any means renew his connexion with the Duke of Florence, in such sort that he might return thither to complete the Hercules which he had left unfinished. But having arrived in Rome, where he bought himself the dignity of a Knighthood of San Pietro, he there heard, by

* The figure is not of Neptune, but of Jupiter.—*Piacenza.*

letters which he received from Florence, that Baccio Bandinelli, pretending to want marble, and affecting to consider the Hercules as a piece of marble spoiled, had broken it to pieces by permission received from the Majordomo Riccio, and had used it to make cornices for the tomb of the Signor Giovanni, which was then in process of construction: hearing of this act of Bandinelli, I say, Giovann' Agnolo was so much displeased that he would not then even hear of revisiting Florence, since it appeared to him that the presumption, arrogance, and insolence of that man had been and was too easily supported.

While the Frate was thus passing his time in Rome, the Messinese were deliberating on the construction of a Fountain which they desired to have erected on the Piazza of the Cathedral, and resolving to have this work richly decorated with statues, they had despatched messengers to Rome with command to select a sculptor of eminence for that service. These men had engaged Raffaello da Montelupo, but he falling sick just at the time when he was on the eve of departing with them for Messina, they determined to take Giovann' Agnolo instead, who had indeed given himself infinite pains and made much interest to obtain the commission for that work.

The Frate first placed his nephew Angelo, who turned out to have much less ability than the uncle had expected, with a joiner in Rome; he then departed for Messina with his disciple Martino, and they arrived in that city in the month of September, 1547. They were at once accommodated with rooms, and without loss of time they began to prepare the conduits for bringing the water, which was to come from a distance, as also to arrange matters for the excavation of marbles in Carrara, and for the transport of those marbles from that place to Messina. With the aid of numerous stone-cutters, therefore, they brought that fountain, in due time, to completion, and the manner of the work is on this wise.

The fountain has eight sides or faces, four larger or principal namely, and four smaller; two of the four greater, projecting forwards, present an angle to the centre, and the other two receding, are connected with a level or plane surface which joins the four remaining and smaller sides, making in all the eight above-mentioned. The four angular faces which project forward, forming a kind of ressault, leave space to four plane surfaces which all recede; and in the midst is a Basin of considerable size, which receives water in great abundance from four river-gods of marble: these figures are so placed that they surround the body of the basin and are seen on all the eight faces of the fountain.

The whole fabric of the fountain is raised on four steps, which have twelve sides or faces, eight larger, which present an angular form, and four smaller on which are placed vases. Beneath the four river-gods are balusters five palms high, and on each corner (of which there are in the whole twenty) there is placed the ornament of a Terminal figure. The circumference of the first basin is a hundred and two palms, and the diameter of the same is thirty-two palms; in each of the above-mentioned twenty angles there is a story in marble carved in basso-rilievo, the subjects of poetical invention, but appropriate to the place, and all touching waters and fountains—Pegasus that is to say, the blow of whose foot produces the Fount of Castaly, Europa borne through the sea, Icarus attempting to fly across and falling into the same, Arethusa turned into a Fountain, Jason traversing the Sea with the Golden Fleece, Narcissus changed into a Fountain, Diana surprised in the Bath and turning Actæon into a Stag, with other subjects of similar character.

In the eight angles which divide the ressaults from the steps of the fountain, two flights of which ascend towards the vases and the river-gods, while four are directed on the angular planes, are eight Marine Monsters in various forms: they are raised on socles in a recumbent position, with the fore-paws stretched in front of them, and reposing on masks, whence there pours water into smaller vases, or basins of a circular form. The river-gods, which are ranged on the edge, and which are placed on socles of such a height as to give them the appearance of being seated in the water, are the Nile, with seven children, the Tiber, surrounded by a vast number of palm-trees and trophies, the Ebro, with various symbols of the victories obtained by Charles V., and the Cremano, near Messina, from whose bed has been taken the water to supply this fountain. They are accompanied by figures of Nymphs and by stories, all giving proof of much thought and careful consideration. At the height of ten palms from the ground there are sixteen very ample jets of water, eight of them are thrown by the masks above-mentioned, four by the river-gods, and four by fishes seven palms high, which stand erect in the basin, and with their mouths turned outwards, cast water from the same towards the side of the larger planes.

In the centre of the octangular basin, and on a socle formed to receive them, are Syrens, one at each angle namely, they have wings instead of arms, and these meeting in the centre support four Tritons, eight palms high,* the tails of the latter are intertwined, and in their hands they hold an immense Tazza, into which † water is poured from four gigantic masks superbly sculptured. From the centre of that Tazza there rise two very hideous masks, purporting to represent Scylla and Charybdis; on these rest the feet of three Nymphs, nude figures, each six palms high, who bear the last Vase of the Fountain on high with their arms. In the Vase just mentioned are four Dolphins, their heads downwards, and their tails borne aloft to form a basement, whereon is a ball, from the midst of which proceed four heads, and these cast the waters of the fountain into the air, as do also the Dolphins before mentioned, on which are mounted four nude figures of children. Lastly, and on the uttermost summit of the Fountain, is an armed figure representing the Constellation Orion, bearing on a shield the arms of the city of Messina, of which it is related, or more properly fabled, that Orion was the founder.

This then is the Fountain of Messina, but it is manifestly not so easy to describe it in words as it would be to show it by a drawing: ‡ the Messinese, meanwhile, were so entirely satisfied with the work that they commissioned Fra Giovann'

* Here there would seem to be a slight inaccuracy, since, to judge from a plate of this Fountain given in the *Architecture Moderne de la Sicile*, by Hittorff and Zanth, Paris, 1822, the Tritons are supported, not on the wings, but on the interlaced tails of the Syrens; and this may even be gathered from Vasari's own words, since he says, "the tails of the Tritons are *also* intertwined." It is to be remarked, however, that the present writer has not seen the Fountain in question, and cites the work of Hittorff and Zanth from memory only, not having it at hand.

† The masks pour the water into the lower basin rather.

‡ See the *Architecture Moderne*, as above cited, where, if the present writer remembers correctly, the various details and accessories are to be found, as well as the ground-plan of the work.

Agnolo to construct a similar fountain on the Strand near the side of their Custom-house: this also proved to be a very magnificent and beautiful production. It has eight sides like the first, but is nevertheless entirely different from the above described erection. The steps, for example, are divided into four ranges, the three which ascend the larger facets having rectangular fronts, and those on the smaller sides of the fabric presenting a semicircular form: above these flights of steps stands the fountain with its eight sides. The balustrade of the larger and lowermost basin, also exhibiting an octangular figure, has a richly sculptured pedestal at each of its angles, and in the centre of four out of the eight faces or planes is another pedestal of similar character. On the sides to which you mount by the circular steps there is a marble vase or basin of an oval shape into which there falls water in vast abundance from two masks, which are fixed on the basement of the carved balustrade. In the centre of the principal vase of this fountain is a pedestal, of proportions justly adapted thereto, and on this pedestal are exhibited the Arms of Charles V., with a Sea-horse at each angle of the basement, from between the feet of which spring jets of water; in the frieze of the same, beneath the upper cornice that is to say, are eight large masks, which pour streams of water downwards. On the summit is a figure of Neptune, five braccia high; the sea-god holds his trident in his hand, and beside him is a Dolphin.

On the two sides* of the great basin are two other pedestals, on which are Scylla and Charybdis, in the forms of two monsters, with heads of Dogs, and surrounded by Furies, the whole extremely well done,† and this work also, when brought to completion, gave entire satisfaction to the Messinese, who, having found a man to their mind, had no sooner beheld their fountains completed,‡ than they determined to commence the façade of their Cathedral, which they also carried forward to a considerable height.§ They

* The two longer sides namely, for the fountain is not a regular octangle, it has two longer and six shorter planes.

† They still retain their places, and are in good preservation.

‡ The second Fountain will also be found described in the work of Hittorff and Zanth before cited.

§ This, according to more than one authority of good credit, is an error; the façade of the Messinese Cathedral having been commenced in 1320.

subsequently commissioned Giovann' Agnolo to construct twelve chapels within the Church; for these he was required to select the Corinthian order, and they are placed six on each side, all being decorated with statues of the apostles five braccia high, and executed in marble. Of these chapels four only were finished by the Frate, the two statues of San Pietro and San Paolo being entirely by his own hand, and both very good figures: he was also commanded to place a figure of our Saviour Christ, in marble with rich decorations around it, at the upper end of the principal chapel, with a story in basso-rilievo to be placed beneath the statues of the twelve apostles; but for that time he did not proceed further with the work.

On the Piazza of the same Cathedral, Giovann' Agnolo superintended the erection of a church to San Lorenzo; the architecture of this fabric proved to be exceedingly beautiful, and he was very highly commended for the same. The Tower of the Pharos, which is on the shore of the sea, was also constructed under his direction, and while these works were in course of progress, he likewise superintended the building of a chapel in the Church of San Domenico, for the Captain-General Cicale, executing for that fabric a figure of the Madonna, in marble, as large as life. For the cloister of the same church, and in a chapel belonging to the Signore Agnolo Borsa, Giovanni Agnolo also executed a basso-rilievo in marble; this story, which was finished with great care, was in like manner considered to be a very fine work.

The Frate furthermore conducted water by the wall of Sant' Agnolo, to a fountain, for which he prepared a colossal figure in marble with his own hand; the statue though large, is that of a Child, and it pours water into a basin which is very richly decorated as well as judiciously arranged for its purpose; this likewise was reputed to be a highly creditable production. At the Wall of the Virgin he likewise constructed a fountain, the water from which falls

We are doubtless, therefore, here to understand that Montorsoli was commissioned to re-commence the suspended work of a restoration, previously contemplated and resolved on, and undertaken at that moment because the Messinese had, as our author says, "found a man according to their taste."

into a basin; this he adorned with a figure of the Madonna, by his own hand. For the fountain which is erected near the Palace of the Signore, Don Filippo Laroca, Giovann' Agnolo sculptured the figure of a Boy from a certain stone much used in Messina: the Child is surrounded by marine animals, and pours water into a vase. He also executed a statue, four braccia high, of the Virgin Martyr, Santa Caterina; this work, which was an exceedingly beautiful one, was sent to Taurinima,* a place which is situate some four and twenty miles from Messina.

While Giovann' Agnolo thus dwelt at Messina, he had for his friends and associates the above named Signore, Don Fillipo Laroca, and Don Francesco, who was of the same family with Messer Bardo Corsi, Giovanfrancesco Scali, and Messer Lorenzo Borghini; all three Florentine gentlemen then in Messina. Serafino da Fermo was also one of his intimates, as was the Grand Master of Rhodes, who frequently invited them to go to Malta, and would willingly have made him a knight; but the Frate replied that he had no mind to confine himself to that island; he had indeed become dissatisfied with himself, for not wearing the habit of his Order, and frequently entertained thoughts of returning to the Cloister. Indeed, I know of my own knowledge, that if he had not been in a certain manner forced to defer his purpose, he would have retaken the habit, as I have said, and returned to live in the manner of a pious monk. When, therefore, it was decreed, in the year 1557, and during the pontificate of Pope Paul IV., that all the apostates, or, more properly, all those who had left their monasteries, and laid down the habit, should be compelled to return under the heaviest penalties, Fra Giovann' Agnolo abandoned the work which he had in hand, and, leaving his disciple Martino, in Messina, he departed from that city in the month of May, and repaired to Naples, proposing thence to return to the Monastery of the Servites.

But before completing that arrangement, and to the end that he might devote himself entirely to God, Giovann' Agnolo bethought himself of the best mode in which he might suitably dispose of his large gains. He first gave certain of his nieces, who were very poor, in marriage, as he

* Taormina.

did some other young girls belonging to his native place, or to the neighbourhood of Montorsoli, and furthermore commanded that a sum of 1000 crowns should be given to that nephew, Angelo, of whom we have before made mention as having been left in Rome, for the purpose of buying him a Knighthood of the Lily :* he also disbursed a considerable amount of money for two Hospitals in Naples, giving to each a large sum in alms ; and to his own Monastery of the Servites he left 4000 crowns to buy a farm, endowing those Monks with that likewise which had belonged to his own forefathers at Montorsoli, but on condition that twenty-five crowns yearly should be paid to each of two of his nephews, who were like himself monks of that Order, with certain other charges, of which we shall make further mention hereafter.

All these matters being settled, Giovann' Agnolo presented himself openly in Rome, and resumed the habit of his Order, to the infinite delight of his brethren, and more especially of Maestro Zaccheria. He then repaired to Florence, where he was also received with indescribable rejoicing and gladness, by his kinsfolk and friends. But although the Frate had now determined to devote the remainder of his days to God and to spend his life in the service of Our Lord, remaining quietly at peace in the enjoyment of a Knight's revenue,† which he had reserved to himself; yet this was not so easily effected as he had supposed it might be. For being pressingly invited to repair to Bologna by Messer Giulio Bovio, the uncle of Vascone Bovio, to the end that he might direct the construction of the High Altar in the church of the Servites, with a richly decorated tomb, he could not refuse to comply with that entreaty, and the less as the work to be performed was for a church of his own Order.

The above-named altar was to be of marble, and to stand entirely isolated, the tomb was in like manner to be encrusted with marble, and furthermore to be enriched with elaborate ornaments of vari-coloured stones. Giovann' Agnolo re-

* For certain details relating to these knighthoods, their origin, the mode of their distribution, the incomes derived from them, &c., the reader is referred to vol. iv. of the present work, p. 169, *et seq.* See also Ranke, *History of the Popes*, English Edition, vol. i. p. 309, *et seq.*

† See Ranke, *loc. cit.*

paired to Bologna accordingly, and having set hand to the work, he completed the same within the space of twenty-eight months; constructing the above-named altar, which occupies the entire space between pillar and pillar, and enclosing the whole choir of the monks, which is all of marble, both on the inner and outer side. In the centre he placed a nude figure of Our Saviour Christ, two braccia and a half high, with other statues at the sides.*

The architecture of this work is of a truly beautiful character, every part being well arranged, and all so carefully conjoined, that no better workmanship could be executed. The pavement also, beneath which is the sepulchre of Bovio, is formed in well fancied compartments, and there are chandeliers in marble of much beauty, with small figures and minute stories in relief, which are also of considerable merit; the whole fabric is rich in carvings, but the figures—to say nothing of their being small, which arises from the difficulty experienced in the transport of large masses of marble to Bologna—are not equal to the architecture, nor do they deserve very high commendation.†

While Fra Giovann' Agnolo was occupied at Bologna with this undertaking, he gave much consideration to the question as to where, among the dwellings belonging to his Order, he might most commodiously pass the remainder of his days; a matter on which he had come to no definite resolution, when his most intimate friend Maestro Zaccheria, who was then Prior of the Nunziata at Florence, desiring much to attract him to that place and to fix him there, spoke of his friend to the Duke Cosimo, recalling to the memory of his Excellency the great merits of the monk, and entreating him to command his services. To this the Duke replied with much favour, and added, that he would find occupation for Giovann' Agnolo, so soon as he should have returned from Bologna: when Maestro Zaccheria wrote him an account of all that had passed, sending him also, shortly after-

* These are the figures of St. Peter and St. Paul standing upright, with those of Adam and Moses, seated at the sides of the altar. The local writers speak highly of their beauty and excellence. See Giordani.

† Many authors affirm these statues to be exceedingly beautiful. Certain compatriots of our author, defending him from the charge sometimes brought against him by cavillers, of partiality to the Florentines, point out the opinion here given as one among many proofs of his strict impartiality.

wards, a letter from the Cardinal Giovanni de' Medici,* in which that Signore encouraged him to return and distinguish himself in his own country, by some important work.

Having received these letters, and remembering that Messer Francesco Riccio,† after having lived for many years in a state of idiocy, had at length died, while Bandinelli also had departed this life; the Frate, to whom these two persons had not been very kindly disposed, wrote replies to the effect that he would not fail to return for the service of his most Illustrious Excellency, so soon as he possibly could, but adding that he desired to be useful in matters that were not of a worldly character, and would be glad to employ himself in some sacred work, seeing that his whole heart was turned to the service of God and of his saints.

In the year 1561, therefore, Fra Giovann' Agnolo at length returned to Florence, when, as the Duke and Cardinal were at Pisa, he repaired with Maestro Zaccheria to that city, there to present his duty to their most illustrious lordships. He was received by each of those Signori with the most affable kindness; and the Duke, having added that, on his own return to Florence the Frate should be at once employed on some work of importance, Giovann' Agnolo went back to the last-named city.

Shortly afterwards, and by the intervention of Maestro Zaccheria, Giovann' Agnolo obtained permission from his brethren of the Nunziata to erect in the chapter-house of that convent, where he had many years before produced the figures of Moses and of San Paolo in stucco,‡ as we have related above, a very beautiful sepulchre, occupying the centre of the place, and destined for the tomb of himself and such other professors,§ persons belonging to the arts of design, painters, sculptors, and architects, as might be unprovided with a burial-place of their own; proposing to make an arrangement, as he subsequently did, for the settlement of his property on the monks, under the condition that on certain festival days, as well as on ordinary occasions, they should there perform mass for the good of the souls of

* Giovanni, the son of Cosmo I.—*Bottari.*
† See *ante*, p. 98, note *.
‡ See *ante*, p. 94, note *.
§ See vol. iv. of the present work, p. 382.

those to be interred in that Chapter-house. He stipulated, moreover, that on the festival of the Most Holy Trinity in each year, high mass should be read and a solemn festival held, while, on the day following, the office for the dead should be performed; all being intended for the good of the souls of the persons above-mentioned.

This plan was imparted by Fra Giovann' Agnolo to Maestro Zaccheria and to Giorgio Vasari, who was their intimate friend; when they held much discourse together concerning the affairs of that Company or Brotherhood of Artists which had been instituted in the time of Giotto,* and had established their rooms in Santa Maria Nuova at Florence, as appears by a memorial still to be seen at the high altar of the Hospital,† which has remained from those days even to our own: eventually, they resolved to take that opportunity for reviving and restoring the Company, which, having been removed from their place at the high altar above-mentioned, had been transported (as will be related in the Life‡ of Jacopo Casentino) to that part of the vaults beneath the Hospital of Santa Maria Nuova, which are close to the corner of the Via della Pengola; but finally, driven thence also, the place having been taken from them by Don Isidoro Monteguti, director of the hospital,—the Brotherhood had almost entirely dispersed, and no longer held its assemblies.§

But the Frate, Maestro Zaccheria, and Giorgio Vasari, having then discoursed, as I have said, at much length, on the state of that Company, Giovann' Agnolo proceeded to speak of the matter with Il Bronzino, Francesco Sangallo, Ammannato, Vincenzio de' Rossi, Michele di Ridolfo, and many other painters and sculptors of the first rank, and having explained his intentions, all the most noble and excellent artists belonging to the vocations of design were

* The Company was in fact founded in the year 1349, about twelve years after the death of Giotto that is to say.—*Ed. Flor.*, 1832-8.

† It is no longer there.—*Ibid.*

‡ Or rather, "as has been related." See the Life of Jacopo di Casentino, vol. i.

§ From the records of receipt and outlay of the Brotherhood, it would seem that the payments for these solemnities were still made, but the zeal of the members having cooled, they were probably not much frequented.—*Masselli.*

found, when the morning of the Most Holy Trinity had arrived, to have assembled themselves in the above-named Chapter-house. Here, a most solemn festival had been arranged. The tomb before-mentioned being then completed, and the altar so nearly finished that it wanted nothing with the exception of certain figures in marble, which were to be placed thereon.

A solemn mass was then said, after which a fine oration was made by one of the Servite fathers in praise of Fra Giovann' Agnolo, and of the magnificent liberality which he had displayed in the gift thus bestowed on the above-named Company, conferring on them, that is to say, that chapter-house, that tomb, and that chapel, wherein, and to the end that they might at once take possession thereof, it was then determined to deposit the body of Pontormo, which had previously reposed in the first small cloister of the Nunziata, but was now to be laid at rest within the tomb in question. High mass and the oration being finished, the Company all went into the church, where the remains of the above-named Pontormo had been placed on a bier; this was raised on the shoulders of the younger members, and each man taking a light in his hand, they first passed in procession around the Piazza, and then bore the corpse to the chapter-house, where, in place of the cloth of gold with which it had been previously adorned, they found it all hung with black, whereon were paintings of the dead and other objects of similar character: after this manner was the above-named Pontormo deposited in the new sepulchre.*

The Company being then dismissed, it was arranged that the first meeting should be held on the following Sunday, by way of making a commencement; when the laws of the Society were to be examined, a selection was to be made from the best among the members who were then to serve as administrators, and an Academy to be instituted, where the inexperienced might learn, while those already competent

* On the stone which closes the sepulchre are sculptured the instruments used in the arts of design, and around it is the motto, *Floreat semper vel invita morte.* The Tuscan laws do not now permit burial in churches, and the last artist interred there was the celebrated architect, Gaspero Paoletti, who was buried in that place in the year 1813, during the French domination.—*Ed. Flor.*, 1832-8.

might be impelled to further efforts and acquirements by an honourable and commendable emulation.

Now Giorgio had meanwhile made mention of these matters to the Duke, begging him to favour and promote the study of those noble Arts (as he had done that of Letters, by the re-opening of the University of Pisa, by the institution of a College for students, and by the establishment of the Florentine Academy), when Vasari found His Excellency perfectly well disposed to favour the undertaking, insomuch that nothing better could be desired.

But some time afterwards the Servite Monks, having thought further of the business, resolved, and gave the Company to understand as much, that they would not permit their Chapter-house to be used for any other purpose than those of holding festivals, hearing mass, and burying the dead; in regard to the assemblies and sittings, therefore, the monks declared that they would have no proceeding of the kind in their convent.

Of all this Giorgio Vasari then spoke to the Duke, requesting him to bestow a place of assembly on the Company, whereunto His Excellency replied that he had been thinking of providing one for them, where they might not only establish their Brotherhood, but might also have space enough, to give evidence of their ability in the works which they might execute therein. A short time afterwards, therefore, the Duke wrote to Messer Lelio Torelli,* to the Prior, and to the Monks of the Angeli, giving them to understand that they were to accommodate the aforesaid Company in the Temple which had been commenced in their monastery by Filippo Scolari, called Lo Spano.† The monks obeyed, and the Company was furnished with certain rooms, wherein they assembled many times with the good favour of those fathers, who received them even in their chapter-house also on several occasions and with infinite courtesy.

It chanced, nevertheless, at no very distant period, that some of the monks showed themselves to be by no means satisfied at this assemblage of the Company within their

* "Messer Lelio Torelli, of Fano, Auditor to the Duke Cosimo, excellent in letters, profound in the laws, remarkable for sagacity."—*Bottari.*

† Of this temple, commenced by Filippo Brunelleschi, there has already been mention in vol. i. of the present work.

borders, seeing that the monastery was thereby in a certain sort embarrassed and rendered dependent; as to the Temple which the artists talked of filling with their works, the monks, so far as they were concerned, thought it just as well that it should remain as it was. His Excellency therefore caused it to be signified to the men of the Academy, which had already made a commencement, and had solemnized the festival of San Luca in that Temple; that since the monks of the Angeli, from what he could learn, did not receive them very willingly in their house, he would himself take care to provide them with a place of their own. The Signor Duke added further, like a truly magnanimous prince as he is, that he would not only ever continue to favour the said Academy, but would himself be the head thereof, its chief, its guide, and its protector; appointing to that end a representative of his person, who should be constantly present at the meetings of the body; and should be chosen year by year as lieutenant of His Excellency. Acting on this suggestion, there was then elected as the first of these representatives, the Reverend Don Vincenzio Borghini, Director of the Hospital of the Innocents; for all which favours and proofs of affection granted by the Signor Duke to his new Academy he received the thanks of the same through a deputation of ten belonging to the oldest and most eminent of their number.

But of this matter I will not speak further on the present occasion, seeing that the reform of the Company and the rules of the Academy are treated of at great length in the report prepared by the men chosen and selected for that purpose from the whole body, with the assistance of the above-named representative or deputy of the Duke, and confirmed by subsequent reference to His Excellency. I will but add the names of the members to whom the reform and the preparation of rules was committed; and these were, Fra Giovanni' Agnolo, Francesco da Sangallo, Agnolo Bronzino, Giorgio Vasari, Michele di Ridolfo, and Pier Francesco di Jacopo di Sandro.*

I must, however, not omit to mention, that as the old seal and arms, or rather device of the Company, the winged Ox

* This is the same Pier-Francesco who is mentioned among the disciples of Andrea del Sarto.—*Ed. Flor.*, 1832-8.

lying down namely, which is the animal that always accompanies St. Luke the Evangelist, was displeasing to many among them, so they determined to choose another, and every member was called on to give his opinion on the subject, either by word of mouth or in a drawing. The most singular fancies, and the most beautiful as well as whimsical and extravagant of inventions, were accordingly presented. It is, however, not yet decided as to which of all among these proposals will be finally accepted.*

Martino meanwhile, the disciple of Giovann' Agnolo, having arrived in Florence from Messina, departed this life in the first-named city, but a few days after his arrival there; he was then buried in the new sepulchre which his master had constructed, and where no long time after, in the year 1564 that is to say, that Father, Fra Giovann' Agnolo himself, was likewise interred with the most honourable obsequies. Among the solemnities was a very fine oration in praise of that excellent sculptor, and this was publicly pronounced in the Church of the Nunziata, by the most reverend and very learned Maestro Michelagnolo.

Our arts may indeed be truly said to be deeply indebted in many ways to Fra Giovann' Agnolo, who bore infinite love to the same as well as to the artists by whom they are exercised; for, to say nothing of all besides, how largely serviceable has already been, and still more will be, that Academy to which he, in the manner above-described, may be almost said to have given origin, and which is now under the protection of the Signor Duke Cosimo, by whose command the society is at this time holding its assemblies in the new sacristy of San Lorenzo, wherein there are so many works in sculpture, by Michelagnolo Buonarroti.

Here then there have been, and still are, very many admirable productions displayed by our artists, moved as they are by emulation among themselves, and by the wish to prove themselves not unworthy academicians. In the obsequies of the above-named Buonarroti himself, for example,

* The device of the above-named Company and Academy of the Fine Arts, was eventually, and still is, formed of three chaplets intertwined, to indicate the three arts of design, with the following motto :—

*Levan di terra al ciel nostro intelletto.*

They raise our minds from earth to heaven.

which were, I do not say magnificent only, but little less than regal in their splendour, they very greatly distinguished themselves, and still more on occasion of the Nuptials of the most Illustrious Signor, the Don Francesco Medici, Prince of Florence, and of the most exalted Queen, Joanna of Austria, wherein they did indeed perform admirable works, as has been fully and with good order related by others, and as will be repeated in a more suitable place and more at length, by ourselves.

And now, since not only from the life of the above-mentioned Father Fra Giovann' Agnolo, but also from those of others, of whom we have before held discourse, it has been shown, and is continually seen, that a truly good monk is useful to the world; not only in letters, in the education of youth, and in the councils of the Church, but also in the arts and other noble vocations, wherein they have by no means cause to be ashamed of comparison with others;—since it is thus, I say, we may perhaps be suffered to declare that those who too broadly affirm the contrary, and declare that monks select their mode of life because they are incapable, from poverty of spirit, of taking care of themselves, have done so unadvisedly, and that such opinion is maintained rather from anger or from some private pique, than with any good reason and from a love of truth. But may God forgive them for that error. Fra Giovann' Agnolo lived sixty five years, and died on the last day of August, 1563.

---

## THE FLORENTINE PAINTER, FRANCESCO SALVIATI.

[Born 1510—Died 1563.]

The father of Francesco Salviati,* whose life we are now about to write, and who was born in the year 1510, was a good man, called Michelagnolo de' Rossi, a weaver of velvets. He had not only this son, but many other children besides, both male and female; and having therefore great need of assistance, had determined within himself that Fran-

* So called from the favour and protection accorded to him by the Cardinal of that name. See vol. iv. p. 378. See also Bryan, *Dictionary of Painters and Engravers*, article "Salviati."

cesco should by all means learn his own trade of weaving velvet.

But the youth, whose mind was turned to other matters, had a mortal dislike to the labours of that calling, although the trade had in old times been exercised by persons—I will not say noble,—yet, who were at least, in good and easy circumstances, nay, rich men, as is well known. Francesco did, nevertheless, fulfil the desire of his father in that matter, but with much ill will, and being oftentimes in the society of the sons of Domenico Naldini, a very honourable citizen (who had his house in the Via de' Servi, and was the neighbour of Michelagnolo), Francesco was remarked to be much inclined to adopt the courteous and elegant manners of those with whom he thus associated; he likewise displayed a decided love for the arts of design.

In these dispositions the boy was much encouraged by a cousin of his named Diacceto, who was a goldsmith, and a youth of some ability in drawing, for the latter not only taught Francesco what little he knew, but also furnished him with numerous designs by various artists of eminence, and over these Francesco laboured secretly day and night with indescribable zeal, but entirely without the knowledge of his father. The fact became known nevertheless to Domenico Naldini, who after having well examined the child, said so much to Michelagnolo his father, that the weaver finally agreed to place his boy in the shop of his uncle, there to learn the art of the goldsmith, when the facilities afforded him for drawing were turned to such extraordinary account by Francesco, that at the end of a few months, he was found to have made an amount of progress at which every one who beheld it was amazed.

Now there was at that time a society of young goldsmiths and painters in Florence, who were accustomed occasionally to meet together and proceed on festival days or at other times to copy or design from the best works, wherever these were to be found dispersed about the city; but among all these young men, there was none who exerted himself with more zeal and love on these occasions than Francesco. The youths composing this society were Nanni di Prospero delle Corniuole,*

* Nanni di Prospero delle Corniole was a relation of the renowned Giovanni delle Corniole, of whom favourable mention has been made in

the goldsmith Francesco di Girolamo, of Prato, Nannoccio of San Giorgio,* and many others, who proved at a later period to be very excellent masters in their vocations.

At this period, Francesco and Giorgio Vasari, being at that time both children, formed an intimacy in the following manner. In the year 1523, Silvio Passerini, the Cardinal of Cortona, chancing to pass through Arezzo, Antonio Vasari, who was his kinsman, conducted his eldest son Giorgio to pay his duty to that prelate. The Cardinal, therefore, finding that this child, who was then but nine years old, had been so carefully instructed in the first rudiments of learning, by Messer Antonio da Saccone and by the excellent Aretine poet, Messer Giovanni Pollastra,† that he could repeat a large part of the Æneid of Virgil by heart, while he had also been brought forward in drawing by the French painter Guglielmo da Marcilla ;‡ seeing this, I say, the Cardinal made an arrangement with Antonio Vasari, to the end that the latter should himself conduct the child to Florence.

Here Giorgio was placed in the house of Messer Niccolò Vespucci, a knight of Rhodes, whose dwelling was beside the Ponte Vecchio and near the Church of the Sepulchre; he was then sent to study under Michelagnolo Buonarroti. This circumstance attracted the notice of Francesco, who was at that time living in the lane beside the residence of Messer Bivigliano (where his father employed many workmen in a large house, with its front looking on the Vacchereccia, which he had rented there); and, as every creature loves its like, he contrived in such sort, that by means of Messer Marco da Lodi, who was a gentleman belonging to the above-named Cardinal of Cortona, he established an acquaintanceship with the said Giorgio, Messer Marco having showed to Giorgio a portrait, which pleased the boy very greatly, and which had been executed by Francesco, who had shortly before devoted himself to painting under the discipline of Giuliano Bugiardini.§

the Life of Valerio Vicentino, for which see vol. iii. p. 467, *et seq.* This appears from a document discovered by Manni, and cited by Bottari.

* Of whom there is further mention hereafter.

† Already more than once alluded to, as in the Life of Rosso, and of Lappoli, for which see vol. iii. p. 304, and vol. iv. p. 146.

‡ Whose Life will be found in vol. iii. p. 65.

§ For the Life of this artist see vol. iv. p. 296, *et seq.*

Vasari, meanwhile, had not been suffered to neglect the pursuit of learning and the sciences, but, by order of the Cardinal, he passed two hours of each day with Ippolito and Alessandro de' Medici, under the instructions of their preceptor Il Pierio, who was a most able man.* With respect to the friendship contracted, as I have said, between Vasari and Francesco, this was such that it never ceased to exist between them, although their emulation of each other, with a certain haughtiness of manner, of which the said Francesco sometimes gave evidence in speech, caused many people to think otherwise.

When Vasari had been some few months with Michelagnolo, that excellent man was summoned by Pope Clement to Rome, there to receive the Pontiff's orders for the commencement of the Library of San Lorenzo, when Giorgio was placed by him, before his departure, with Andrea del Sarto, pursuing the studies of design under that artist. Vasari then assisted Francesco in secret, by lending to him the drawings of his (Vasari's) master, the former having no greater delight than that of studying the same, as in fact he did, night and day. At a later period also, and when Vasari was sent by the Magnificent Ippolito to learn drawing with Baccio Bandinelli, who was well content to have that youth with him, and instructed him gladly; the boy gave himself no rest until he had succeeded in getting Francesco likewise admitted, which he ultimately did, to the great profit of them both, seeing that they made more progress, thus drawing together, in one month, than they would have done in two years had each been working alone. A similar remark may be made in regard to another youth who was with Baccio Bandinelli at the same time, that Nannoccio dalla Costa San Giorgio namely, of whom mention has been made immediately above.†

* "Pierio Valeriano or Giovanni Pietro Bolzani of Belluno. His master Sabellius gave him the name of *Pierio*, in allusion to the Muses, under their appellation of the *Pierides*, he having been a lover of those ladies from his infancy." For this learned note we are indebted to a compatriot of our author, whose name escapes the memory of the present writer.

† This is that Nannoccio of whom it has already been related, in the Life of Andrea del Sarto namely, that he went into France with the Cardinal de Tournon.

In the year 1527, when the Medici were expelled from the city of Florence and there was much fighting in defence of the Palace of the Signoria, a large bench or form being cast down from on high, with intent that it should fall on those who were attacking the door, it chanced, as Fortune would have it, that the missile fell upon the arm of the David, in marble, by Buonarroti, which is on the platform, and the arm was thereby broken into three pieces. These fragments having been thus suffered to remain lying on the earth for three days without having been lifted up by any man, Francesco repaired to the Ponte Vecchio to seek Vasari, and having imparted his purpose to him, the two boys, children as they were, advanced into the Piazza, without thinking of the dangers to which they thus exposed themselves, and from the midst of the soldiers on guard they gathered up the three pieces of that arm, and carried them into the house of Michelagnolo the father of Francesco, in the lane beside the dwelling of Messer Bivigliano. From this place it was that the Duke Cosimo, in course of time, regained those fragments which he then had fastened to the statue by means of copper nails.

The House of Medici being thus in exile, and with them the above-named Cardinal of Cortona, Antonio Vasari took his son back to Arezzo, and this to the no small regret of Francesco and himself, who loved each other like brothers. They were, however, not separated long; seeing that the plague, which broke out in the following August, caused the death of the father of Giorgio with that of all the rest of his house, when Vasari was so earnestly pressed to return to Florence, by the letters of Francesco, who had himself been on the point of dying in the pestilence, that the said Giorgio finally agreed to do so. There, for the space of two years, impelled by their necessities and by the desire of improvement, they laboured with indescribable zeal and industry, insomuch that they both made very remarkable progress; taking refuge meanwhile, as did also the above-named Nannoccio da San Giorgio, in the workshops of the painter Raffaello del Brescia,* where Francesco executed numerous small

* "The name of this artist would have been lost," remark the Florentine Editors of the Passigli Edition of our author, "had it not thus dropped from the pen of Vasari." Lanzi, vol. ii. p. 226, has made men-

pictures, he being most of all in need of exertion, as having to provide himself with the means of life.

In the year 1529, as it did not appear to Francesco that he was doing any great good in the workshops of Brescia, he went, as did Nannoccio, to Andrea del Sarto, with whom they remained during all the time of the siege, but in the midst of such grievous privations, that they afterwards both repented the not having accompanied Giorgio, who spent that year at Pisa, and amused himself during four months by studying the art of the goldsmith, under the above-named Manno. Vasari subsequently repaired to Bologna; and this he did at the time when Charles V. was there crowned Emperor by Pope Clement VII. About the same period, Francesco, who had remained in Florence, painted on a small panel a votive picture for a soldier who had made his vow thereof at a moment when, being in his bed, he had been attacked by other soldiers who designed to kill him. The work was a thing of no moment, but Francesco had studied it most carefully, and finished it to perfection: this picture fell into the hands of Giorgio Vasari not many years ago, when the latter presented it to the reverend Don Vincenzio Borghini, director to the Hospital of the Innocents, by whom it is very highly valued.

For the Black Friars of the Badia, Francesco painted three small pictures in a Tabernacle of the Sacrament, which had been made by the wood-carver Tasso, in the manner of a Triumphal Arch. The subject of one of these little stories was the Sacrifice of Abraham; that of the Second was the Fall of the Manna; and of the Third, the Hebrews eating the Paschal Lamb on the eve of their departure from Egypt; these works were executed in such a manner that they gave a foretaste of what Francesco was afterwards to become.* He subsequently painted a picture of Dalilah cutting off the hair of Sampson, for Francesco Sertini, by whom the work was sent into France; in the background of this painting is seen the same Sampson, when, casting his arms around the

tion of a Fra Raffaello da Brescia, an Olivetine monk, who painted in the Choir of San Michele in Bosco, at Bologna. Artists of this name are however very numerous; there are no fewer than thirty enumerated by Zani. See the *Enciclopedia Metodica*.

* This work is unhappily lost.—*Ed. Flor.*, 1832-8.

Columns of the Temple, he brings that building down upon the Philistines; and the picture was one of such merit that it served to make Francesco known as the most deserving among all the young painters who were then in Florence.

No long time afterwards, the master in clock-making, Benvenuto della Volpaia, being in Rome, was requested by Cardinal Salviati the elder to find him a young painter, whom he might retain in his house, and who would paint for him such pictures as it might please him to command, when Benvenuto proposed to that Prelate the Florentine Francesco, who was his friend, and whom he knew to be the most capable of all the young painters of his acquaintance; and this Benvenuto did all the more willingly, as the Cardinal had promised him to give every facility for study, and all kinds of assistance, to the young artist who might be selected. The qualities of Francesco as they were described by Benvenuto della Volpaia, being approved by the Cardinal, the latter commissioned Benvenuto to send for him, and gave him money for that purpose; Francesco was summoned accordingly, and his manner of proceeding in his works, as well as his character and habits, proving agreeable to the Cardinal, that Prelate commanded that he should have apartments prepared for him in the Borgo Vecchio, with a stipend of four crowns per month, and a place at the table of the gentlemen belonging to the Cardinal's household.

The first works undertaken for Cardinal Salviati by Francesco (to whom it appeared that he had met with a piece of singular good fortune) were, first a picture of Our Lady, which was considered very beautiful; and next the Portrait of a French Nobleman, who is represented in chase of a hind which, being hard pressed, is taking refuge in the Temple of Diana; of this last work, I have myself the drawing by his hand, which I keep as a memorial of Francesco in my book of designs. These paintings being completed, Cardinal Salviati caused our artist to make the Portrait of one of his nieces in a singularly beautiful picture of Our Lady; this Signora, the Cardinal had given in marriage to the Signor Cagnino Gonzaga, whose portrait was in like manner depicted by Francesco.

Finding himself thus in Rome, Francesco had now no more earnest desire than that of seeing his friend Giorgio Vasari in the same city; and in this respect Fortune proved herself favourable to his wishes, but still more so to those of the aforesaid Giorgio himself. And the matter happened on this wise: the Cardinal Ippolito, having parted in great anger from Pope Clement VII. for causes which were set forth at the time, did nevertheless return to Rome before any long period had elapsed, accompanied by Baccio Valori. He then passed through Arezzo, where he found Giorgio, who had at that time been left without his father, and was passing his time in the best manner that he could; the Cardinal, therefore, desiring that the youth should make progress in art, and wishing moreover to have him near his own person, gave orders to Tommaso de' Nerli, who was commissary in Arezzo, to the effect that he should send Vasari to Rome so soon as he should have finished a Chapel in fresco, which he was at that time painting for the Monks of San Bernardo of the Order of Monte Oliveto in Arezzo, a commission which was instantly attended to by Nerli.

Arrived in Rome, therefore, the first thing which Giorgio did was to seek Francesco, who joyfully described to him the great favour in which he stood with the Cardinal his Lord, and declaring that he was now in a place where he could study to his heart's content; he added, moreover, "Not only do I enjoy the present, but I hope still better things for the future, for besides that I now have thyself in Rome, thee with whom, as with a near friend, I may take counsel and confer on matters relating to our art; there is also the prospect of my admission into the service of the Cardinal Ippolito de' Medici, from whose liberality and from the favour of the Pope I may expect still greater things than I now possess; nay this last will certainly happen, if a young man who is now expected from abroad * should fail to arrive."

* "From abroad." It is without doubt well known to most of our readers that an Italian of the old times considered every man a foreigner, if born or dwelling, I do not say in the next state, but in the neighbouring towns of his own state; nay, it is well if he did not, or perhaps do not even now consider him as a "natural enemy" also. It has not unfrequently happened to the present writer, when remarking on some one of those trifling impositions or vexations of whatever kind, whereunto the traveller is "heir," to be asked what better could be expected, for "is he not a Bergamasco, a Cortonese, an Urbinate, a Perugino!" a native of some town or village in short, at least half a league removed from the one entitled to

Now Giorgio knew that the youth thus expected was himself, and that the place to which Francesco was looking forward had been reserved for him; but he would not say any thing of that fact for the moment, seeing that a certain doubt had entered his mind as to whether the Cardinal might not have another person in view besides himself; he was therefore unwilling to advance an assertion which might afterwards be found incorrect. Vasari had brought a letter from the above-mentioned Commissary Nerli to the Cardinal, but this, in the five days during which he had then been in Rome, he had not yet presented; at length, however, he went with Francesco to the palace, where, in what is now the Hall of the Kings, they found Messer Marco da Lodi, who had formerly been in the service of the Cardinal of Cortona, as we have said, but had since entered that of the Medici. Presenting himself to Messer Marco, therefore, Vasari told him that he had brought a letter from the Commissary at Arezzo, which was to be delivered to the Cardinal, and which he begged Messer Marco to present. While the latter was promising to do this immediately, it so chanced that the Cardinal himself came in, and Giorgio, hastening towards him, delivered the letter at the same time that he kissed his hands. He was very favourably received by the Prelate, who instantly commanded the Steward of the Household, Jacopone di Bibbiena, to find rooms for him, and to give him a place at the table of the Pages. It seemed a little strange to Francesco that Giorgio had not confided the matter to him, but he was nevertheless persuaded that he had acted from right motives, and done what he thought the best; when the said Jacopone, therefore, had given Giorgio rooms behind the Santo Spirito, which was very near to the dwelling of Francesco, the two young men worked hard together throughout the winter, studying the productions of art in company, to the great profit of both, insomuch that they left nothing, whether in the Palace * or elsewhere, that they did not fully copy, or at least partially design. It is true that when the Pope was in the Palace they could not do this so commodiously as they might have desired, but no

rejoice in the birth of him who made the remark. The tendencies of so deplorable a state of things as this will be obvious to all.

* The Vatican.

sooner did His Holiness ride forth, which was his very frequent custom, to the Magliana,* than they gained admission, by means of their friends, to the rooms so often mentioned, and there they would remain from morning till night without anything better to eat than a morsel of bread, and being very nearly frozen with the cold.

The Cardinal Salviati having subsequently commanded Francesco to paint in fresco that chapel of his palace wherein he heard mass every morning, and the subject chosen being stories from the Life of San Giovanni Battista, Francesco set himself to study the nude figure from the life; this he did in a bathing house that was near his dwelling, still accompanied by Giorgio, and at that time they also made several dissections in the Campo Santo.

The spring having at length appeared, and the Cardinal Ippolito being despatched by the Pope into Hungary, that Prelate gave orders before his departure, to the effect, that Vasari should be sent to Florence, there to execute certain pictures, and copies of pictures, which were then to be forwarded to Rome. But in July of that year, what with the fatigues he had borne in the winter, and the heats of the summer, Vasari fell sick, and was carried in a litter to Arezzo, much to the grief of Francesco, who became ill also and was on the point of death. He did, nevertheless, recover at length, and then received a commission, by the intervention of the master in wood-carving, Antonio Labacco, to paint a fresco for Maestro Filippo da Siena, in a niche over a door behind the Church of Santa Maria della Pace. The subject of this work is our Saviour Christ, speaking with San Filippo, and in two angles are the Virgin with the Angel of the Annunciation. The execution of the whole work pleased Maestro Filippo very greatly, insomuch that it caused him to offer a second commission to Francesco, a large picture namely, to be painted in the same place. This was likewise a story of the Madonna, her Assumption that is to say, and it occupied one of the eight sides of the Church above mentioned, which compartment had not previously received any decoration.†

* Then a villa of the Popes; the building, which was situate at about four miles from Rome, on the banks of the Tiber, was afterwards turned into a Convent for the Nuns of Santa Cecilia.—*Bottari.*

† These works have perished.—*Ibid.*

Now Francesco, reflecting that he had to execute this work, not only in a place of great publicity, but one in which there were paintings by men of the highest eminence, Raffaello da Urbino, Il Rosso, Baldassare da Siena, and others, gave his utmost attention to the same; and, painting it in oil on the wall, he spared no pains or study to bring it to perfection, for which cause he succeeded in producing a picture which has been highly extolled, and is, indeed, a very beautiful one.* Among other figures therein, one (with the hands joined) is the Portrait of the above-named Maestro Filippo, and is justly held to be most excellent. And now, as Francesco was in the service of Cardinal Salviati, as we have said, and was known to be his creature, he began to be called Cecchino† Salviati; and being soon known by no other name, he retained that appellation to the day of his death.

Pope Clement VII. being now dead, and having been succeeded by Pope Paul III., Messer Bindo Altoviti caused the Arms of the new Pontiff to be painted on the front of his house near the Bridge of Sant' Agnolo; the commission for that work was given to Francesco, who executed the same, together with certain nude figures of vast size, in so good a manner, that he gave infinite satisfaction. He took the Portrait of the aforesaid Messer Bindo likewise, about the same period, and this also was a very good figure, as well as a fine likeness: it was subsequently sent to Altoviti's Villa,‡ at San Mizzano, in the Valdarno, where it still remains.

At a subsequent period, Francesco painted an exceedingly beautiful picture in oil for the Church of San Francesco a Ripa; this work, the subject of which is an Annunciation of Our Lady, he finished with extraordinary care. On the occasion of the Emperor's arrival at Rome also, in the year 1535; he painted certain stories in chiaro-scuro for Antonio San Gallo; these were placed in the Arch erected

* The work here described having suffered very greatly, was ultimately replaced by one in stucco.—*Bottari.*

† Cecchino is the diminutive of "Cecco," the Italian "Frank."

‡ This portrait is lost, but a German commentator remarks that it might be discovered by seeking among the protraits attributed to Francesco, and comparing that most likely to be the work in question with one of Altoviti, by Raphael, now in the Pinecotheca at Munich, and which was long considered to be the likeness of Raphael himself.

at San Marco, and, as we have said before, were the best of all the pictures prepared for these festivals.

Now the Signor Pier Luigi Farnese had at that time been made Lord of Nepi, and, desiring to adorn that city with new buildings and pictures, he took Francesco into his service, giving him apartments in the Belvedere, and causing him to paint certain stories from the Life of Alexander the Great in water-colours on cloth; these were afterwards sent into Flanders, there to be woven into cloth of arras and tapestries. For the same Signor of Nepi Francesco also decorated a large and handsome Bath-room, with numerous stories and figures painted in fresco.

When the above-named Signor Pier Luigi was subsequently made Duke of Castro, Francesco was furthermore employed to superintend the rich and magnificent preparations made for his first entry into the city, when he constructed a Triumphal Arch, among other works, covering the same with stories, figures, and statues, all arranged with infinite judgment, and executed by artists of ability, more especially by Alessandro, called Scherano, a sculptor of Settignano. Another Arch in the form of a Façade was erected at the Petrone, with a third on the Piazza; and these were constructed, so far as regarded the wood-work, by Battista Botticelli. For these festivities, moreover, Francesco prepared the scenic decorations, with five perspective views for the performance of a dramatic spectacle which was exhibited on that occasion.

About this time, Giulio Camillo,* who was then in Rome, had made a book of his Compositions, for the purpose of sending them into France to King Francis, and he now caused this book to be adorned with pictures by Francesco, who executed his task with all the zeal and diligence which it was possible to bestow on a work of such a character.

Now the Cardinal Salviati desired to possess a work by the hand of Fra Damiano, of Bergamo, who was a lay-brother of the Monastery of San Domenico at Bologna, a picture made of tinted woods, or "in Tarsia" that is to say. He therefore sent Fra Damiano a design in red chalk, which he had caused Francesco to make of the subject that he

* Giulio Delminio of Portogruaro in Friuli, a man of great learning. He died at Milan in the year 1544, aged sixty-five.—*Masselli.*

desired to have represented: this was King David Anointed by the Prophet Samuel; it is a truly beautiful composition, and the best ever designed by Cecchino Salviati.

It was about this period that Giovanni da Cepperello, and the Hunchback Battista da Sangallo, had caused the Florentine painter, Jacopo del Conte, who was then a youth, to paint a story of San Giovanni Battista for the Company of the Misericordia, in the Church of San Giovanni Decollato, which is situate beneath the Capitol in Rome, the work being executed in the second church that is to say, and where the said Company was accustomed to hold its sittings; the particular event there represented by Jacopo del Conte was the Appearance of the Angel to Zaccheriah; and the same persons now commissioned Francesco to paint another story from the life of the same Saint beneath that above-mentioned—the Visitation of our Lady to Sant' Elizabetta namely. This work, which was completed in the year 1538, was executed in fresco, and is in so fine a manner that it merits to be numbered among the best and most thoughtfully-considered paintings ever produced by Francesco: whether we examine the composition of the picture, the careful attention to rule in the arrangement, the diminution, and due receding of the figures, the fine perspective and admirable architecture of the buildings, the beauty of the nude figures, the lovely expression of the heads, the grace of the draperies, or, at a word, the whole painting in each of its parts, we find it to be of such merit that we cannot be surprised if all Rome remained in astonishment at the perfection thereof.*

Around a window in the same place Francesco painted certain fanciful decorations in imitation of marble, with little stories of minute figures which have infinite grace. And as it was not the habit of Francesco to waste his time, while thus employed with the work in question, he executed many other designs, and likewise coloured a picture of Phaeton, with the Horses of the Sun, which had been designed by Michelagnolo.

All these productions were shown by Salviati to Giorgio, who had gone to Rome for two months on the death of the

* This beautiful picture was much injured by re-touching, but we have fortunately very faithful engravings of it.—*Ed. Flor.*, 1832-8. It has been engraved by B. Basseroli G. Ghisi and J. Mathani.

Duke Alessandro, and whom he told at the same time, that when he had finished certain pictures which he had then in hand, he would return to his country, once more to behold his kindred, his friends, and his acquaintance; the rather as his father and mother, to whom he was of the utmost value, and whom he assisted greatly, were still alive. Francesco had, besides, afforded help to his parents in the settlement of his two sisters, one of whom had been given in marriage, and the other had been established as a nun in the Convent of the Monte Domini, where she still is.

The works to be first completed by Francesco as abovementioned were San Giovanni as a Youth, which he was painting for the Cardinal Salviati his Lord, and a Crucifixion of Our Saviour on cloth, which was to be sent into Spain, with a picture of the Madonna, undertaken by Francesco for Raffaello Acciaiuli.

Arriving accordingly in Florence, where he was received with great joy by all his kinsfolk and friends, it chanced that he reached the city exactly at the moment when all were engaged in preparing for the marriage of Duke Cosimo with the Signora Donna Leonora di Toledo; wherefore he was invited to execute one of the stories exhibited in the court, a commission which he accepted very willingly. The subject treated by Francesco was that in which the Emperor is seen to place the Ducal Coronet on the head of Duke Cosimo; but our artist, being seized with a desire to visit Venice, and leaving Florence for that purpose before the undertaking was completed, made over that work to Carlo Portelli da Loro,* by whom it was finished in accordance with the design of Francesco, which design is now in our book, with many others by the same hand.

Departing from Florence, Francesco repaired to Bologna, where he found Giorgio Vasari, who had arrived in that city two days previously, having then returned from Camaldoli, where he had painted the two pictures which are in the screen of the Church of Camaldoli, and commenced that of the High Altar. Giorgio was also taking order for the execution of three large pictures in the Refectory of the Fathers of San Michele in Bosco, where he kept Francesco

* Carlo Portelli of Lora, a village in the Valdarno, was a disciple of Ridolfo Ghirlandaio, in whose Life he is named.

with him for two days, during which time attempts were made by certain of his friends to procure for him the commission for a picture which the men of the Hospital of Death had then to give. But notwithstanding these efforts, and although Salviati prepared an exceedingly beautiful design for the picture above-named, yet those men, as having but little judgment in such matters, did not know how to profit by the opportunity which *Messer Domeneddio** had sent them of securing to the city of Bologna a work by the hand of so able an artist.

Finding this, Francesco left the place in some anger; but before his departure he deposited some very beautiful designs in the hands of Girolamo Fagiuoli, to the end that the latter might engrave them on copper and cause them to be printed.† Having arrived in Venice, he was very courteously received by the Patriarch Grimani and by Messer Vettor his brother, both of whom conferred on him many favours. After the lapse of a few days he received from the Patriarch a commission to paint a figure of Psyche in oil, within an octangular frame, four braccia in extent; in this picture incense and vows are offered to Psyche as to a goddess, in acknowledgment of her beauty, and the octangle was placed in a small apartment in the house of that Signore, the ceiling of the apartment having been adorned in its centre with festoons, by the hand of Cammillo Mantovana,‡ a painter, who, for the execution of landscapes, flowers, foliage, fruits, and objects of a similar description, was at that time considered most excellent.

The above-mentioned octangle was placed in a room of the Patriarch's house, and was surrounded by four pictures, each two braccia and a half square, and all exhibiting stories from the Life of the above-named Psyche, which had been exe-

* I leave the untranslateable naïveté of this *Messer Domeneddio* in its original purity; no form of words in our own language could express the name of the Supreme Creator with equal simplicity, and at the same time avoid an unpardonable air of burlesque, which last would indeed be a wide departure from the meaning of our author, as well as a grave offence. Monseigneur St. Jacques and Madame La Sainte Vierge will occur to our readers as instances of the same kind of expression, all better left to their own forms of untransmutable simplicity.

† Mentioned in the Life of Soggi, for which see vol. iv.

‡ Named with praises in the Life of Genga, for which see vol. iv.

cuted, as we have related in the Life of Genga, by Francesco da Furlì; but that octangle is not only beyond all comparison the most beautiful of those pictures, but is, indeed, the most exquisite painting in all Venice.* Francesco subsequently executed certain small figures in fresco, some nude and others draped, in a room wherein Giovanni Ricamatore, of Udine,† had produced numerous works in stucco, and these frescoes are also very graceful.

In a picture executed by Francesco, for the Nuns of the Corpus Domini, at Venice,‡ he delineated the figure of Our Saviour Christ, lying dead, with the Maries around him, and an Angel in the air above, who is holding the Mysteries of the Passion. He also painted the Portrait of the Poet, Messer Pietro Aretino, who sent that likeness, as being a very beautiful production, to Francis King of France, accompanying the same with certain verses in praise of him who had produced the portrait.§ For the Nuns of Santa Cristina, at Bologna, who are of the Order of Camaldoli, Salviati painted a very beautiful picture, comprising many figures; this he did at the request of Don Giovanfrancesco da Bagno, Confessor of those Nuns, in the Church of whose Convent this truly exquisite work has been placed.||

His abode in Venice having subsequently become distasteful to Francesco, as to one who remembered what it was to dwell in Rome, and the place appearing to him not well suited to the men of design, he departed, with intention to return to Rome; in his way he made a round by Verona and Mantua, visiting the numerous antiquities to be found in the one, and in the other the works of Giulio Romano; he then proceeded to Rome by the route of the Romagna, and reached that city in the year 1541. Here, having rested

* This beautiful work is still in the Grimani Palace, but the dissent against our author's judgment as to this being the *most* beautiful one to be found at that time in Venice, which has been recorded by Lanzi, has been concurred in by almost every subsequent authority of value.

† Giovanni da Udine, for whose Life see *ante*, p.16.

‡ This church has been suppressed.

§ This portrait, according to Förster, is not now to be found among the collection of pictures in the Louvre.

|| Still in the church. It represents Our Lady enthroned with the Divine Child, and certain Saints beside her, together with the *Beata* Lucia da Stifonte, foundress of the Convent.

himself for some time, he recommenced his labours, and the first works which he executed were portraits; those of Messer Giovanni Gaddi namely, and of Messer Annibale Caro,* both of whom were his very intimate friends: having finished these, he painted an exceedingly beautiful picture for the Chapel of the Clerks of the Chamber in the Papal Palace.

In the Church of the Germans also,† Francesco commenced a Chapel in fresco for a merchant of that nation, painting the Apostles receiving the Holy Spirit in the vaulting above, and in a picture which reaches to about half the height of the wall, he represented Our Saviour Christ arising from the dead and surrounded by the sleeping soldiers. These figures are lying about near the tomb in various attitudes, and are foreshortened in a very bold and beautiful manner. On one side of this picture is the figure of San Stefano, and on the other that of San Giorgio; they stand in two niches, and are by the same Francesco. Beneath is San Giovanni Elemosinario bestowing alms on a naked beggar; on one side of the Saint is the figure of Charity, and on the other is the Carmelite Monk, Sant' Alberto, placed between figures intended to represent Logic and Prudence. Finally, Francesco painted the figure of the Dead Christ with the Maries, as the Altar-piece of that Chapel.‡

Now Salviati had formed a friendship with the Florentine goldsmith, Piero di Marcone; and having become his gossip, sent to his other gossip, the wife of this Piero, the present of a very beautiful design, on the occasion of her giving birth to the child for whom he stood godfather. The subject was intended for painting in one of those circular trays on which food is presented to a woman in child-bed, and represented, in a square compartment subdivided into upper and lower ranges, the whole history of the human life; the figures were of great beauty, and each was accompanied by a garland or festoon appropriate to the respective ages and

* Who mentions this portrait in a letter to be found in the third volume of the *Lettere Pittoriche*, lett. XCVI.

† Santa Maria dell' Anima.

‡ These paintings have suffered much in their colouring, that of the altar more particularly.—*Bottari.*

seasons. Among these peculiarly arranged divisions were two long ovals, wherein were the figures of the Sun and Moon, and between them was a figure representing or typifying Isaias,* a city of Egypt: this figure, standing before the temple of the goddess Pallas, implored the gift of Wisdom, as if the artist proposed to signify that the blessing to be first of all entreated for the children who should be born was that of wisdom and goodness. The design for this work was always preserved with great care by Piero as a beautiful and valuable jewel, which indeed it was.

No long time after the completion of that painting, the above-named Piero and other friends, having written to Francesco to the intent that he would do well to return to his native land, since it was almost certain that he would there be received into the service of the Duke Cosimo, who had no masters about him but such as were slow and irresolute, he finally determined (but principally confiding in the favour of Messer Alamanno Salviati, brother of the Cardinal, and uncle to the Duke,) to reinstate himself in Florence. Having returned accordingly, before he attempted any other thing, Francesco depicted for the above-named Messer Alamanno, an exceedingly beautiful figure of Our Lady, which he executed in a room then held by Francesco del Prato,† in the House of Works of Santa Maria del Fiore, and where that Francesco, from having been a goldsmith and master in Tarsia, had just then set himself to the casting of small figures in bronze and to painting, in both which he succeeded to his no small honour as well as profit.

In this place then, I say, where Francesco dal Prato was installed by virtue of his office as superintendent of the wood-works performed in the cathedral, laboured Francesco Salviati also: and among other pictures he painted a Portrait of his friend Piero di Marcone, with that of Avveduto del Cegia, the fur-dresser, who was likewise his friend. This Avveduto has, indeed, very many of the works of Salviati in

* Sais or Sai, an ancient city of Egypt. Bottari observes that he thinks the goddess must be Isis, rather than Pallas, the place of the former being appropriately fixed between the Sun and Moon. See *Roman Edition of Vasari*, 1759.

† An artist of this name is mentioned by Averoldo and Chizzola, *Guida di Brescia*, as the author of a *Sposalisio*, in the Church of San Francesco at Brescia.—*Ed. Flor.*, 1832-8.

his possession, more especially a portrait of Francesco himself, painted in oil with his own hand, and which is exceedingly natural.

The before-mentioned picture of Our Lady being completed, was placed in the shop of the wood-carver Tasso, who was then Architect of the Palace. It was there seen by a large number of persons, who all extolled it highly, but that which most of all contributed to obtain for it the name of an extraordinary work was, that Tasso himself, who was in the habit of censuring almost every thing that was done, praised this production without measure; nay, what was still more to the purpose, he told Messer Pier-Francesco Riccio, the Majordomo, that it would be certainly advantageous for the Duke, if his Excellency were induced to give some work of importance to Salviati; whereupon this Messer Pier-Francesco, with Cristofano Rinieri, who had the ear of the Duke, performed their parts so zealously, that when Messer Alamanno spoke to his Excellency, informing him that Francesco desired permission to paint the smaller Hall of Audience, that namely which stands before the Ducal Palace,* requiring no other payment for his labours than the credit of having performed them, Duke Cosimo was content that this privilege should be conceded to him.

Francesco then commenced his work by the preparation of small designs wherein he represented the Triumph of Furius Camillus with many other stories from the life of the same, that done, he began to divide the chamber to be adorned into suitable compartments, but arranging them with no small difficulty, seeing that some of the spaces left by the windows and doors were high and others low, insomuch that it was no easy matter to contrive in such sort that the stories should be secured from suffering by that irregularity. In the wall wherein is the door of entrance, there were two large spaces divided by the door; and opposite to this, where there are three windows which look on to the Piazza, there are four compartments, but no one of them is more than about three braccia in extent. At that end of the Hall, moreover, which is to the right of him who enters by the door, are two win-

* Commonly called in these days the Palazzo Vecchio (Old Palace) The Hall here in question now makes part of the Guardaroba, and the pictures painted by Salviati are still in good preservation.—*Masselli.*

dows looking into another part of the Piazza, and here there were three spaces of similar extent, about three braccia each that is to say; while at the other end, which is opposite to this now in question, there stands the marble door which gives entrance into the Chapel, with a window and a grating of bronze, so that there remained only one space wherein there could be represented any work of moment.

In this last-mentioned space, on the wall of the Chapel therefore, where there is a decoration of Corinthian columns supporting an architrave and forming a recess, from the ceiling of which there hang two rich festoons, with two pendants of different fruits very naturally represented, on which is seated a naked Child supporting the Ducal Arms—those of the Houses of Medina and Toledo namely;—in this space, I say, Francesco painted two stories, the one on the right showing Camillus commanding that Schoolmaster* to be given up to his scholars for punishment; and that on the left exhibiting the same Leader, who makes his way through the ranks of the Gauls, while the army is engaged in combat, and the camp with its stockades and tents is in flames around him. Beside this, and beneath the same range of columns, our artist depicted a group the size of life, representing Opportunity seizing Fortune by the forelock, with certain of the devices of his Excellency, and many other ornaments, all executed with admirable grace and facility.

On the principal façade, that namely wherein are the two large spaces, divided by the chief door of entrance, Francesco executed two large and very beautiful stories; in the first are seen the Gauls, who, weighing the tribute gold of the Romans, throw a sword into the scale, to the end that the weight may be the greater, when Camillus, indignant at this wrong, flies to arms, and by the force of his valour delivers his country from the yoke. This is indeed a singularly beautiful story, rich in figures, adorned with landscapes, and furthermore embellished by the addition of antiquities; as for example, Vases of great beauty, painted to imitate gold and silver. In the story beside that just described, is

* We need not waste the time of our readers with the well-known history of "that Schoolmaster," whose appropriate punishment for the traitorous betrayal of his scholars into the hands of the enemy is here alluded to.

Camillus in his triumphal Chariot drawn by four Horses, with Fame above, placing a chaplet on his head; before the chariot walk priests richly clothed, some of these bear the Statue of the Goddess Juno, others carry vases in their hands, with certain trophies and spoils of infinite beauty. Around the chariot are prisoners in vast numbers, and finely varied attitudes, while behind all, come the soldiers of the army bearing their weapons: among these men is one presenting the portrait of Francesco himself, so admirably painted that it seems to be alive. In the distance to which the triumphal procession extends itself, is seen a very beautiful representation of Rome. Over the door between these two Stories is a picture in chiaro-scuro, the figure of Peace namely, with prisoners engaged in the destruction by fire of a pile of arms; the whole executed by Francesco with so much thought and care, that a more beautiful work could scarcely be seen.*

On the wall towards the east, and in the two larger spaces, our artist depicted two niches; in one of which he painted the figure of Mars fully armed, and with a nude figure, intended to represent a Gaul, lying beneath him: on the head of this last is a crest formed of the bird of Gaul, a cock namely, in its natural shape. In the second niche is Diana, wearing a short tunic of furs, she is in the act of drawing an arrow from her quiver, and at her feet is a hound. In the two angles which connect the wall in question with the neighbouring walls, are two figures, both representing Time; one of these is adjusting the weights of a balance, the other is tempering a liquid by pouring it from one vase into another.

In the last portion now to be described, that namely which is opposite to the chapel and looks towards the North, is on one side, the Sun figured in that manner which is customary

* In the first of these two stories is a Soldier, fallen to the earth, and transfixed with a lance, but the admirably drawn and beautifully coloured torso of this figure had been destroyed by the swelling and scaling away of the intonaco, which had fallen to the ground; it was, however, gathered up carefully, and every morsel was so nicely conjoined, and so successfully replaced by Baldassare Franceschini, called the Volterrano, by whom every, the most minute of all those innumerable morsels into which the intonaca had separated, was gathered and restored to its due position, with such extraordinary care and patience, that there is scarcely a trace of the misfortune now to be seen.—*Bottari.*

among the Egyptians, and on the other the Moon in a similar manner; between them is Good Fortune or Prosperity, signified by a nude figure of a youth placed on the summit of a wheel, beside which are represented, on one side, Envy, Hatred, and Malevolence; on the other, Honour, Pleasure, and all the other delights of life, as described by Lucian.

Above the windows is a frieze consisting of nude figures the size of life; they are of great beauty, and exhibit various forms as well as attitudes: there are likewise certain stories, all from the life of Camillus. Opposite to the figure of Peace burning the arms of War, as before described, is that of the River Arno; it holds the Cornucopia with one hand, and, lifting the edge of a curtain with the other, it displays the city of Florence, with all the Pontiffs and other great men of the House of Medici. Francesco furthermore added a kind of socle which passes entirely around the Hall beneath the pictures and niches, the decoration thereof consisting of terminal figures in the form of women sustaining festoons of fruit and flowers. In the centre of the basement are oval compartments filled with figures engaged in adorning the Sphynx and the River Arno.

Now in this work Francesco was desirous of leaving to his native land a memorial worthy of himself and of so great a Prince; he therefore devoted the utmost care and attention which he could possibly command to the execution of the same, and although he had to encounter many vexations in the course of its progress, he did finally bring it to a fortunate completion. Francesco was of a melancholy temperament, and when he was painting he did for the most part feel very unwilling to have any one near him. On this occasion, however, almost doing violence to his nature, he compelled himself to be more liberal, and affecting an unwonted sociability at the commencement of the work, he suffered Tasso, and others of his friends who had done him any service, to come about him with much familiarity, permitting them to stand and look on while he worked, Francesco meanwhile showing them all the courtesies that he could think of But when he had gained a footing in the Court, and thought himself in favour, he returned, as they say, to his usual habits, indulging his choleric and sarcastic nature, and no longer showing the least respect to any one. Nay, what is worse than all, as with the most bitter words (a thing which furnished his adversaries with an excuse for their enmity), he was accustomed to censure and decry the works of others; so he did not scruple to exalt himself by perpetual boastings, and to praise his own productions to the skies.

These unpopular modes of proceeding giving umbrage to many persons, but more especially to certain artists, attracted so much odium to Francesco, that Tasso and some others, who, from being his friends had become his enemies, began to give him no small cause for disquietude. It is true that they still continued to praise his excellence in art, which was not to be denied, and admitted the promptitude and facility with which he executed his works, doing them well no less than quickly; but they were still by no means at a loss for subjects of blame, and although they could not undo the good they had done him, and, having suffered him to gain a footing and make his way, could not remove or injure him, they yet soon began to give him trouble and offer him molestation in various ways.

Nay, there were even many artists as well as others who were not ashamed to band themselves together and form a party against him, disseminating a report among the nobles and great people, to the effect that the work on which he was employed in the Hall would not prove to be a successful one, seeing that he proceeded by mere readiness of hand and did not bestow the due amount of care and study on what he was doing. But herein they accused him most wrongfully, since, although he did not linger over his compositions as it was their fashion to do, yet it could not truly be affirmed that he did not study them, nor could any man rightfully declare that he had not rich powers of inventing as well as executing his pictures, which last he did with infinite grace. These his adversaries, however, not being able to eclipse the abilities of Francesco by the excellence of their works, did their best to overwhelm him by censure and reproaches such as we have described.

The truth and real power do nevertheless always prevail in the end. Francesco first of all did but make a jest of these rumours, but at a later period, and when they began to pass beyond what was reasonable, he complained, on more than one occasion, to the Duke: still his Excellency paid but little attention to the matter, as it seemed to Francesco; and his adversaries perceiving, as they thought, that his favour had decayed, took courage thereupon, and sent forth a rumour to the effect that the stories which he had painted in the Hall were to be thrown to the earth, as by no means giving satisfaction to the rulers.

All these injuries, directed against him by his enemies with incredible envy and calumny, at length began to produce their effect, and at the last Francesco was so much annoyed by them that, had it not been for the kindness of Messer Lelio Torelli, Messer Pasquino Bertini, and others of his friends, he would certainly have left the court clear for those evil speakers, which was exactly the thing that they desired. But those his well-wishers above-named encouraged him to complete the works of the Hall, with others which he had in hand, and prevented him from departing; their efforts being aided by those of others among his friends who were at a distance from Florence at the time, but to whom he had written the history of these persecutions. Among the latter was Giorgio Vasari, who in reply to a letter wherein Salviati complained of this matter, exhorted him to take patience, reminding him that goodness is refined to excellence by persecution, as gold is made perfect in the fire, consoling him by the assurance that a time would come when his genius and high superiority must needs be acknowledged, and adding, that he must henceforth complain of no other than himself, who had not sufficiently studied the humours of those around him, and had failed to appreciate correctly the character of the people, but more particularly that of the artists of his own country.

Thus it happened that, notwithstanding all the vexations and annoyances by which the poor Francesco was assailed, he did nevertheless complete that Hall, the engagement that is to say which he had made to decorate the walls; for as to the ceiling or wood-work, there was no need that he should do anything, since it was already most richly carved and adorned with gilding, and exhibited work, than which none of that kind could possibly be finer. To make all suitable, moreover, the Duke commanded two new windows of glass to be made, with ornaments of his own arms and devices, accompanied by those of the Emperor Charles V.

These were executed by Battista del Borro, an Aretine painter of high distinction in that branch of art, and by whom they were completed to perfection.

After having brought this undertaking to an end, Francesco painted for his Excellency the ceiling of that Hall in which the family dines during the winter season, adorning the same with numerous devices and figures of small size in tempera: our artist also painted an exceedingly beautiful study, which opens on the green chamber; he took portraits of the Duke's children moreover, and one year he prepared the scenic decorations, perspective views, &c., for a dramatic spectacle which was exhibited in the great Hall, all which he did in a manner so entirely different from and superior to those which had been previously seen in Florence, that they were considered to surpass everything of the kind before attempted. Nor is this to be wondered at, seeing that Francesco always gave proof of great judgment, with the most rich and varied power of invention, in all his works; nay, what is of still higher importance, he had a more profound knowledge of design and a more beautiful manner than any artist who was then in Florence; he handled the colours also with infinite ability, and finished his works most admirably well.

The Head, or rather Portrait, of the Signor Giovanni de' Medici, father of the Duke Cosimo, which is now in the Guardaroba of his Excellency, is also by the hand of Francesco, and may be justly described as a truly meritorious work. For his intimate friend, Cristofano Rinieri, Francesco made a picture of Our Lady, which is also very beautiful; this painting is suspended in the Hall of Audience, now used by the Council of Ten. For Ridolfo Landi our artist painted a figure of Charity, which is so admirable that nothing could well be more so;* and for Simon Corsi he painted a Madonna, which was in like manner very highly extolled.

* Borghini, in his *Riposo*, makes mention of a figure of Charity as then (1584) adorning the Hall of the Council of Ten, whence a doubt has arisen whether Vasari may not have incorrectly stated the *locale* of Francesco's Charity, which he should have given, as many writers believe, to the Hall of the Council instead of the Madonna, which was more probably painted for Ridolfo Landi. There is a figure of Charity by Francesco now in the Gallery of the Uffizj at Florence.—*Ed. Flor.*. 1832-8.

For the Knight of Rhodes, Messer Donato Acciaiuoli, with whom Francesco always lived on terms of unusual intimacy, he painted certain small pictures, which are held in much esteem; and on a larger panel, the same artist depicted a figure of our Saviour Christ showing to St. Thomas, who does not believe that he has risen from the dead, the marks of those wounds which had been received by our Lord from the Jews. This picture was taken into France by Tommaso Guadagni, and was placed in the Chapel of the Florentines in a certain Church of Lyons.*

At the desire of the above-mentioned Cristofano Rinieri and of Giovanni Rozzi, the Flemish master of tapestry-work, Francesco painted all the Story of Tarquinius and the Roman Lucretia, in a vast number of Cartoons, which, being afterwards executed in cloth of arras woven in gold and silks of various kinds, proved eventually to be an admirable work.

When this came to the ears of the Duke, who was at that time employing the above-named Maestro Giovanni to make him cloth of arras of similar kinds in Florence for the Hall of the Dugento, and had caused Bronzino and Pontormo to prepare Cartoons for the same from the story of the Hebrew Joseph, as we have before related;—when the Duke heard this I say, he commanded that Francesco also should prepare a Cartoon, the subject given to him being the interpretation of the seven fat and the seven lean kine: our artist gave all his attention to the work accordingly, and carefully took into consideration all the peculiarities required for a production of that sort, and which are necessary to the successful imitation of the Cartoon by the tapestry-worker; for these cloths of arras demand considerable fancy in the invention, with figures carefully detached and standing forth one from another, to the end that they may display good relief; they must likewise be cheerful as to colouring and the vestments, also, should be rich and varied.

This piece of the tapestry in question, and the others, having been found to succeed well, his Excellency then resolved to establish the art of making such hangings in Florence, and accordingly commanded that it should be

* Waagen, *Künstler und Kunstwerker in Frankreich*, speaks of this work, which is now in the Louvre, as one of very little importance.

taught to several boys, who, having now arrived at mature age, are at this time producing most excellent works in tapestry for the Duke. An exceedingly beautiful picture of the Madonna, painted in oil, was also executed by Francesco, and is now in the chamber of Messer Alessandro, son of Messer Ottaviano de' Medici.

For the above-mentioned Messer Pasquino Bertini, Francesco made another picture of Our Lady on cloth with the Divine Infant, and San Giovanni, also a child; they are smiling, and amusing themselves with a parrot which they have in their hands; a very fanciful and graceful work. For the same person he likewise made a most beautiful and graceful design of a Crucifix, about one braccio high; with a Magdalen at the feet thereof: this is in a manner so new and pleasing that it is considered quite a wonder; the design was given by Messer Salvestro Bertini to his intimate friend Girolamo Razzi, who is now Don Silvano,* when two pictures were painted from it by Carlo da Loro, who subsequently executed many more from the same design. These works are now dispersed about Florence.

Now Giovanni and Piero d'Agostino Dini had caused a very rich chapel in macigno to be constructed in the Church of Santa Croce, at the right hand as you enter the church, with a sepulchral monument for Agostino and others of their house, and gave the altar-piece for the same to Francesco: he depicted thereon Our Saviour Christ taken down from the Cross by Joseph of Arimathea and Nicodemus; at the foot is Our Lady, who has fainted, and is surrounded by San Giovanni, the Magdalen, and the other Maries. This work was completed by Francesco with so much art and care, that not only is the nude figure of Our Lord Christ a most beautiful one, but the other figures also are so well disposed, and have a force of relief and a beauty of colouring so remarkable, that they cannot well be sufficiently extolled.† It is true that the work was at first much cen-

* This is the Camaldoline Monk, Don Silvano Razzi, well known for the many works published by him, and often mentioned as having assisted Vasari in the preparation of these Lives.

† This work still retains its place. Our readers may consult the before-cited *Riposo* of Borghini, Florentine Edition of 1730 where it has been highly eulogized; see p. 85 and p. 410.

sured by the enemies of Francesco, but it has nevertheless acquired for him a very great name in all parts, and those who have since treated the same subject in rivalry of our artist have found it impossible to surpass him.

Before leaving Florence Francesco likewise painted the Portrait of the above-mentioned Messer Lelio Torelli, with some few other matters of but little importance, of which I do not know the particulars. But one among these productions is to be specified as exceedingly beautiful, a Conversion of St. Paul namely, which the artist had designed in Rome long before: this he caused to be engraved on copper in Florence by Enea Vico of Parma, and the Duke was content to retain him in the city until that work should be accomplished, with payment of all his accustomed appointments and allowances.

At that time, which was in the year 1548, Giorgio Vasari was in Rimini, employed on the execution of those works in oil and fresco, whereof there is mention in another place, when Francesco sent him a long letter, giving a circumstantial account of all his affairs, and most especially describing the manner wherein things had passed at Florence: he spoke more particularly of a design which he had prepared for the principal Chapel of San Lorenzo, which chapel was then to be painted by order of the Signor Duke. But Francesco added that in relation to the chapel he felt certain that some one had done him infinite mischief with his Excellency, declaring, among other things, that he was sure the Majordomo, Messer Pier Francesco, had never laid his design for the same before the Duke. The consequence of this had been, he furthermore affirmed, that the work had been given to Pontormo, and he finished with the remark that for these causes he was returning to Rome, much dissatisfied with the men and artists of his native country.

Having returned to Rome, and re-instated himself in that city accordingly, Francesco there bought himself a house near the Palace of Cardinal Farnese, amusing himself meanwhile with the execution of works which were of no great importance. He then received a commission from the above-mentioned Cardinal, by the intervention of Messer Annibale Caro and Don Giulio Clovio,* to paint the chapel of the

* The Life of this admirable miniaturist, who has been so frequently mentioned, will be found in the present volume.

Palace of San Giorgio: here he first prepared singularly beautiful compartments in stucco-work, and in the very graceful ceiling of the chapel he depicted stories from the Life of San Lorenzo in fresco, the figures of the work being very numerous as well as beautiful. Francesco also executed an Altar-piece painted in oil and on stone for the same chapel, and in this he depicted the Nativity of Our Saviour Christ, introducing in that work, which was a singularly fine one, the Portrait of the before-mentioned Cardinal, taken from the life.

At a subsequent period, Francesco was commissioned to execute another work in the Chapel belonging to the Brotherhood of the Misericordia, to which we have previously alluded.* Here Jacopo del Conte had painted the Preaching and the Baptism of St. John, and had acquitted himself exceedingly well therein, although he had not surpassed Francesco. The Venetian Battista Franco and Piero Ligorio † had also produced works in that place, and Francesco Salviati now commenced a painting which is close beside his former production, the story of the Visitation namely. But although a well-conducted work, this picture, the subject of which is the Birth of St. John, is by no means equal to the earlier performance. For Messer Bartolommeo Bussotti our artist painted two figures in fresco at the upper end of the same chapel, the Apostle St. Andrew and San Bartolommeo, two very fine figures;‡ these he executed one on each side of the altar on which Jacopo del Conte depicted a Deposition from the Cross, which is an admirable work, nay, the best that Jacopo had then produced.

In the year 1550, and when Julius III. had been elected High Pontiff, Francesco undertook certain stories in fresco for the Arch erected on the upper end of the staircase at San Pietro, on the occasion of the Pope's coronation, and these were very beautiful. In the same year the Company of the Sacrament caused a Sepulchre to be represented in the Church of the Minerva, with several ranges of steps and

* In the Church of San Giovanni Decollato namely.

† An excellent architect and painter in fresco of considerable merit.—*Lanzi.*

‡ These figures have been re-touched, as has the Birth of St. John.—*Bottari.*

rows of columns; for this Francesco painted certain stories in *terretta*, which were considered superlatively beautiful. For a chapel at San Lorenzo in Damaso, Salviati painted two Angels in fresco; they are supporting a canopy, and of one of these angels we have the design by Francesco in our book of drawings. In the Refectory of San Salvator del Lauro at Monte Giordano, our artist painted the Marriage of Cana in Galilee, at which Our Saviour turned water into wine, on the principal wall. There are numerous figures in this work, and on the side walls are certain Saints, with St. Eugenius the Pope, who was of that order, and other founders and distinguished brethren of the same. Over the door of the Refectory, moreover, and on the inner side, he painted a picture in oil, the subject of which is St. George killing the Dragon, a work conducted with much facility, delicacy of finish, and beauty of colouring.

A large picture was sent by our artist about the same time to Messer Alamanno Salviati, who was then in Florence; the subject of this work is Adam and Eve at the Tree of Life eating the forbidden fruit, and the picture is a very beautiful one.* For the Signor Ranuccio, of the House of Farnese, and Cardinal of Sant' Agnolo, Francesco painted two sides of a small apartment which precedes the great Hall of the Farnese Palace, a work in which he displayed much fancy. On one of these sides the artist depicted Signor Ranuccio the elder, who receives the Baton of Captain-general of the Holy Church from the hands of Pope Eugenius IV., with figures of the Virtues; and on the other is Pope Paul III., who was also of the House of Farnese, and by whom the Baton of the Church is conferred on the Signor Pier Luigi, while the Emperor Charles V. is seen in the distance, accompanied by Alessandro Cardinal Farnese, and by other nobles, whose portraits are taken from the life. In this work Francesco, in addition to the above-described and many other stories, painted a figure of Fame with other figures, which are very beautiful, but it is to be remarked that the whole was not completed by himself, but was ultimately finished

* The fate of this work is not known, but Bottari suggests that it may have been taken to France, he having found a work on that subject mentioned in Lepicié, *Catalogue raisonne des Tableaux du Roi*, Paris, 1752.

by Taddeo Zucchero of Sant' Agnolo, as will be related in the proper place.*

The Chapel which Fra Bastiano had commenced in the Church of the Popolo for Agostino Chigi, but which, as we have related in his Life, he had not finished, was completed by Francesco; and for the Cardinal Riccio da Montepulciano, this artist painted an exceedingly beautiful Hall, in his Palace situate in the Strada Giulia, representing various stories from the life of David therein; the work, which is in fresco, consists of numerous pictures, one of which presents Bathsheba as seen in the Bath, with many other female figures, while David stands looking at them. This story is a good and graceful composition, nor do I know a work more rich in respect of its invention. In another picture is the death of Uriah; in a third is the Ark, with men sounding musical instruments as they walk before it; and finally, after many others, there follows a Battle-piece, showing David in combat with his enemies, and extremely well composed; at a word, the whole work is full of grace, exhibiting the richest fancy with many singular and ingenious inventions, the groups are arranged with much judgment, and the colouring is most agreeable. Francesco was indeed so well aware of the bold and copious powers of invention with which he had been endowed, that, perceiving his hand to be always obedient to his genius, he would gladly have occupied all his time with some great and extraordinary work.

If Francesco was sometimes peculiar in his conduct towards his friends, that circumstance arose principally from the fact that, being versatile and unstable in certain matters, that which pleased him to-day became insufferable to him on the morrow; it is also to be remarked that he completed few works of importance in respect to which he had not to endure a contention before the price demanded for the same could be settled, and for this cause he was disliked and avoided by not a few.

At a subsequent period it chanced that Andrea Tassini was required to send a painter to the King of France, and in the year 1554 he applied to Giorgio Vasari, but neither

* The work was not finished by Salviati, because that master died before its completion, when two of the Stories, those opposite to the large window, were given to Taddeo Zucchero by the Cardinal Santangelo Farnese.

promises of great pay nor high promotion could prevail with that artist, who replied that he would on no account depart from the service of his Lord the Duke Cosimo. Tassini, therefore, at length agreed with Francesco, on the understanding that if the latter were not amply satisfied in France, he was to be remunerated in Rome by Tassini. But before Francesco would depart for France, having the conviction that he should return from that country no more, he sold all that he possessed, his house, his furniture, and everything besides, with the exception of the offices to which he had been nominated, these he retained.

The affair did nevertheless not turn out as he had expected: when he arrived in Paris he was received most courteously by Messer Francesco Primaticcio, Abbot of San Martino, who was then painter and architect to the King, but, as it is said, he was at once perceived to be a very singular person, and among other things it was observed that he never cast his eyes on the works of any other master, Rosso, or whomever it might be, that he did not openly and decidedly censure them. Every one then began to expect that some very great thing would be produced by himself; and the Cardinal of Lorraine, who had caused him to be sent for, set him to execute certain pictures in his Palace of Dampierre; for this work Francesco then prepared numerous drawings, and finally setting hand to the painting, he executed various pictures in fresco over the cornices of several apartments, and also decorated a study with stories which are said to be of high merit: but be the cause what it may, he did not receive any great commendation for these labours. Francesco was indeed never much liked in France, he being of a disposition altogether opposed to that of the men of the country, seeing that by as much as the joyous and jovial companions who live freely with all, and appear willingly at festivals and banquets, are acceptable to them, by so much, are, I will not say, disliked or avoided, but at least, less welcome to them, all such as, like Francesco, are of a melancholy temperament, reserved manners, infirm health and peevish temper. And if for some of these things he deserved indulgence, as, for example, that his constitution did not permit him to frequent feasts and festivals, yet he might have been more courteous in his demeanour, and more friendly in conversation; but besides that he failed on these points, he did more, for whereas it was his duty, according to the custom of that country and court, to show himself abroad, and pay his respects to such as treated him amicably, Salviati, on the contrary, expected to be courted by all the world and thought himself fully entitled to be so distinguished. At length, perceiving that the King was engaged in war, as was also the Cardinal, and that the stipend and promises made to him were not paid or fulfilled, he resolved to depart; and after having been in France twenty months, he returned to Italy.

Salviati then repaired to Milan, where he was courteously received by the Aretine Messer Lione, in a house which the latter has built for himself, and which he has decorated finely with casts in stucco from works of high character, enriching it, moreover, with statues, ancient and modern, as will be related in its due place. There Francesco remained fifteen days, and having rested himself sufficiently, he then set off to Florence, where, having found Giorgio Vasari, he told the latter how well he had done in refusing to visit France, and furthermore related to him such things as were well calculated to make any one change his mind, however great had previously been his desire to go thither.

Leaving Florence, Francesco then repaired to Rome, where he entered an action against those who had guaranteed him his appointments in France, and compelled them to make good all that should have been paid to him by the Cardinal of Lorraine. Having received these sums, he purchased offices with the same, in addition to those which he had previously possessed, and now determined to think only of taking care of himself, knowing, as he did, that he was exceedingly unhealthy, and had entirely destroyed his constitution. He would nevertheless have employed his leisure gladly on some great work, but that not presenting itself, he amused himself for a time in the execution of small pictures and portraits.

Pope Paul IV. being dead, Pope Pius IV. was then elected; and that Pontiff, taking considerable pleasure in architecture, commanded the Cardinals Alessandro Farnese and Emulio to cause the Great Hall, called the Hall of Kings, to be completed by Daniello da Volterra, who had already commenced the same. Now the Cardinal Farnese above-named, made all possible effort to procure the half of this work for Francesco, and this caused a long contention between Daniello and Salviati, but Michelagnolo Buonarroti having taken part with the former, the question was not brought to an issue for some time. In the meanwhile Giorgio Vasari arrived in Rome with the Cardinal Giovanni de' Medici, son of the Duke Cosimo, and to him Francesco related his numerous misadventures, more particularly describing the trouble in which he then found himself; when Giorgio, who greatly prized the abilities of this man, pointed out to him that he had up to that time very badly conducted the affair, and advised him to refer the matter to his (Vasari's) guidance, Giorgio promising to contrive in such sort that Salviati should certainly have the half of the Hall of Kings, and this he did the more readily as Daniello could not have completed so great a work alone, he being a slow, irresolute person, nor yet altogether equal, perhaps, to Francesco, in versatility and force of genius.

Matters standing thus, and nothing further being done for the moment, Giorgio was himself invited not many days subsequently, by the Pope, to execute a portion of the works for that Hall, but he replied that he had already undertaken to paint one, three times as large, in the Palace of his Lord the Duke Cosimo, and remarked besides, that he had been so badly treated by Pope Julius III., as no longer to know what it might be reasonable to hope or advisable to do with respect to certain men; adding that he had painted a picture of Christ on the Sea of Tiberias, calling Peter and Andrew from their nets, for the same Pontiff, the price of which had never been paid, and praying that His Holiness would cause the painting (which had been taken by Pope Paul IV. from the Chapel of the Belvedere, where it had been placed by Julius, and was now to be sent to Milan) to be either paid for or restored to him, Giorgio.

To this Pope Pius made answer, that whether these things were true or not, he knew nothing of the picture in question, and desired to see it; whereupon it was brought, and being examined by His Holiness in a very bad light, the latter decided that the painting should be returned. That affair being settled, the discourse respecting the Hall was then resumed, when Giorgio plainly told the Pope that

Francesco was the first and best painter in Rome, and that as none could serve His Holiness better than Salviati, it would be well to secure him. As to the favour shown to Daniello by Buonarroti and the Cardinal, this Vasari declared they did out of their friendship for the latter, and from no other cause. But to return for a moment to Vasari's picture above-named: Vasari had but just left the Pope when it was sent after him to the house of Francesco, who afterwards caused it to be forwarded to Arezzo, where, as we have said elsewhere, it has been placed, after having received a rich and costly frame, in the Decanal Church of that city.

The affair of the Hall of Kings remaining in the condition described above; when the Duke Cosimo left Siena to repair to Rome, Vasari, who had accompanied His Excellency so far, very earnestly recommended Salviati to his care, and begged the Duke to do him what favour he could with the Pope, writing to Francesco at the same time, as to the mode in which he ought to proceed when the Duke should arrive in Rome. And now Francesco did in nowise depart from the line of conduct prescribed to him by Vasari; he went to pay his respects to the Duke, who received him with a most friendly aspect, and shortly after mentioned him with so much kindness to His Holiness, that he was at once commissioned to decorate the half of the Hall above-mentioned. Setting hand to his work, accordingly, the first thing Francesco did was to destroy a story which had been commenced by Daniello, an action which caused no small displeasure between them: then the Pontiff, as we have said, employed the architect Piero Ligorio for his buildings, and the latter had in the first instance greatly favoured Francesco; but Salviati, paying no regard to Piero any more than to others, when once he had commenced his work, caused the architect, from having been his friend to become in a certain sort his enemy, a fact of which manifest evidence was soon perceived. Piero now began to intimate to the Pope that there were many young and able painters in Rome to whom, as he desired to have that Hall off his hands, he would do well to give the separate paintings, one to each artist, and by this means the work would come to an end.

These proceedings of Piero, to whom it was evident that the Pope listened favourably, caused infinite displeasure to

Francesco, insomuch that he angrily retired from the work and its contentions, believing that he had not been held in sufficient esteem. He mounted his horse, therefore, and without saying a word to any one, left Rome, and went to Florence, where he lodged himself in a tavern, not showing the least consideration for any one of his friends, proceeding as if he had not belonged to the place, and had no acquaintance, or any one for whom he cared within the city. At a later period, it is true that he did present himself to the Duke, by whom he was so well received that some good result might reasonably have been expected, had Francesco been of a different disposition, or if he had given ear to the counsel of Vasari, who advised him to sell the offices which he held in Rome, and to settle in Florence, there to enjoy himself among his friends, and thus escape the danger he was in of losing all the fruits of his toils, as well as his life itself. But Francesco, incited by the desire of vengeance, and listening to his anger and obstinacy alone, resolved to return to Rome, come what might, before the lapse of many days; but he did so far comply with the entreaties of his friends as to leave that tavern, and retire to the house of Messer Marco Finale, Prior of Sant' Apostolo.

Here he painted for Messer Jacopo Salviati—principally for his amusement—a picture of the Madonna, with the Dead Christ, in colours, on cloth of silver. Our Lady is accompanied by the other Maries, and the work was considered a singularly beautiful one. He also repainted a Medallion of the Ducal Arms, which Messer Alamanno had formerly caused to be placed over a gate of his Palace; and for the above-named Messer Jacopo he prepared a beautiful book, filled with costumes of fanciful characters, comprising head-dresses and decorations of various kinds, both for men and horses, to be used in the different maskings then held, receiving innumerable courtesies from the kindness of that Noble, who did, nevertheless, complain much of his strange proceedings, seeing that he could never prevail on Francesco to take up his abode in his house on this occasion, as he had done at other times.

Finally, Francesco being resolved on returning to Rome, Giorgio, as his friend, reminded him that, being rich, advanced in years, and of very weak health, he ought now to think of living in quiet, and should carefully shun the strifes and contentions of active life; all which he might have done most conveniently, he having acquired both honour and profit enough, if he had not been too avaricious and eager for gain. Vasari furthermore advised him to sell the greater part of his offices, and to arrange his affairs in such sort, that in all cases, and whatever might happen, he might be in a condition to remember his friends, and those who had served him faithfully. Francesco promised to proceed discreetly, both in act and word, confessing that Giorgio told him the truth, but as it usually happens with men of dilatory habits, he did nothing in the matter.

Arrived in Rome, Francesco found that the Cardinal Emulio had commissioned other artists to execute the Stories of the Hall, having given two of them to Taddeo Zucchero, of Sant' Agnolo, one to Livio da Forli,* another to Orazio da Bologna, one to Girolamo Sermoneta, and others to other masters. Hereupon Francesco sent an account of what had been done to Vasari, inquiring of him if he thought it advisable that what he, Salviati, had commenced before his departure from Rome to Florence should now be completed. Vasari made answer to the effect, that since so many small designs and large cartoons had been made, it would be well to finish, at least, one of the pictures, notwithstanding that the greater part of the work had been accorded to so many others, all of whom were inferior to himself; and adding, that Francesco would do wisely in approaching, so far as he could, to the pictures executed by Buonarroti, on the front and ceiling of the Sistine Chapel, and to those of the Pauline. Vasari furthermore assured him, that when once his work had appeared, those executed by the others would be thrown to the ground, and the whole undertaking made over to himself, to his no small honour and glory: he entreated him, moreover, not to think of profit in this case, nor to regard the vexations which he might receive from those who had the superintendence of the works, seeing that the honour to be acquired was worth more than all besides. The letters written on this occasion by Vasari, with the replies, both copies and originals, are still preserved among those which we retain as memorials of so great a man and so intimate a

* A disciple of Perino del Vaga. See Baglioni, *Vite de' Pittori*, &c.

friend as was Francesco; those by our own hand having been found among the effects left behind him by Salviati.

But all these efforts did not prevent Francesco from becoming angered by the passing events, nor could he form any fixed resolution as to what it would best suit him to do: thus troubled in mind, afflicted in body, and much debilitated by the frequent use of medicines, he finally fell sick of a mortal disease, and in a short time was found to be at the last extremity, while he had yet not given himself time to make any very exact dispositions in respect to his worldly affairs. To one of his disciples, called Annibale, the son of Nanni di Baccio Bigio, he left sixty crowns per annum, secured on the Monte delle Farine, with fourteen pictures, all his designs, and other effects relating to art. The remainder of his property he left to the nun Gabriella, his sister, but, as I have heard, she did not receive even "the cord of the sack," as the proverb goes. It is certain, nevertheless, that one picture by her brother must have fallen into her hands; it was painted on cloth of silver, and surrounded by an embroidered border, having been executed by Francesco for the King of Portugal or of Poland, I know not which, and having been given to her to keep in memory of him. All his other possessions, as, for example, the offices which he had purchased with the fruits of all his heavy labours, were wholly lost.

Francesco died on St. Martin's day, the 11th of November, 1563, and was buried in San Geronimo, a church near to which was his dwelling. His death was a great loss to art; for although he was fifty-four years old, and in very bad health, he yet passed his time in continual labour and study; nay, at the very end of his life he had begun to work in mosaic. He was indeed very fanciful, and had a love for attempting various novelties; had he happened to meet with a prince willing to lend himself to his humour, and who would have given him occupations according to his own heart, Salviati would, without doubt, have accomplished extraordinary things, seeing that he was, as we have said, most richly gifted with inventive power, and abundantly skilled in every branch of his art. Francesco imparted infinite grace to all his heads, of whatever character they might be, and understood the nude form as well as any painter of his time. He had a most graceful manner in the arrangement of his draperies, and in his works the nude form is always seen through the vestment whenever the occasion demands that it should be so. He clothed his figures also in a new and varied manner, displaying much fancy in the choice of head-dresses, buskins, and ornaments of different kinds. He handled the colours, whether in oil, tempera, or fresco, in such a manner that he may be truly affirmed to have been one of the most able, spirited, bold, and yet careful artists of our day. Of this we, who have held close intercourse with him for so many years, are fully competent to bear testimony; and, although from the desire which all conscientious artists feel to surpass each other, there was always between us an amicable emulation, yet the affection of a true friendship was never wanting to us, even when each was labouring in rivalry of the other, through the most renowned cities of Italy, a fact of which proof may be seen in the numerous letters from the hand of Francesco, which I still retain in my possession.

Salviati was of an amiable disposition in his youth, but subsequently became suspicious and intolerant; possessing sufficient acuteness and penetration on certain points, he was yet credulous on others: if the conversation turned on matters of art, he would often express himself, whether in jest or earnest, in terms calculated to give offence, and sometimes profoundly wounded those with whom he was speaking. He delighted in the society of men of learning and other distinguished persons, but the meaner kind of artists were ever most unwelcome to Francesco, even though some of these persons were of good repute as to certain branches of art. He avoided such men as he perceived to be habitual slanderers of private character, but if brought into contact with them would fall upon and tear them without mercy; but most of all did he abhor the cozenings and trickery sometimes practised by artists, and of which, having been in France and heard somewhat of that matter, he was but too well qualified to speak. There were times when, to escape the attacks of his constitutional melancholy, he sought the society of his friends, and did his utmost to be cheerful. After all, indeed, the suspicious, irresolute, and unsocial dispositions of which he so frequently gave proof, were injurious only to himself. His most intimate friend in Rome was the Florentine goldsmith, Manno, a person of high distinction in his calling, and no less remarkable for integrity and goodness of heart. Manno had a large family, and if Francesco had disposed of his property as might have been wished, and not spent the best fruits of his labours on offices to leave them to the Pope,* he would have given a great part of them to the children of that good artist and excellent man. The before-mentioned Avveduto dell' Avveduto, the furrier, was also among the intimates of Salviati, and was the most affectionate as well as most faithful friend that ever he possessed, nay, had he been in Rome when Francesco died, the affairs of the latter might perchance have been arranged in a manner altogether different.

The Spaniard Roviale was a disciple of Francesco Salviati, in company with whom he executed numerous works; and in the church of Santo Sprito in Rome, this Roviale painted a picture, entirely without assistance, the subject of that work being the Conversion of St. Paul. Salviati was much attached to Francesco the son of Girolamo del Prato, in whose company he practised drawing while yet a child, as we have related above. This Francesco was endowed with a brilliant genius; he drew better than any goldsmith of his time, and was in nowise inferior to his father Girolamo, whose works on plates of silver were admitted to surpass those of every other person. Nay, Girolamo, as it is said, succeeded easily in whatever he undertook; and among other things, is reported to have had a manner of beating out such plates with a mallet, and after placing them on a plank beneath a covering of wax, pitch, and tallow, he procured a material partly hard and partly soft, which he would then beat with irons, towards the inside or the outside as was required, and thus produced whatever forms he wished; heads, busts, arms, legs, trunks, or whatever other portion of the figure might be demanded by those who were in the habit of causing votive images of saints or other figures to be made, for the purpose of affixing them to the holy images of any place wherein they might have received some favour, or found that their supplications were heard with more than common effect. But Francesco di Girolamo

* These offices, as Vasari calls them, were in fact a species of annuity, which returned to the apostolic camera, or treasury, on the death of those who had purchased them. See Ranke, as before cited.

did not give his principal attention to the preparation of votive images or offerings, as did his father; he occupied himself in works of Tarsia likewise, and inlaid steel with gold or silver, after the fashion of Damascus, representing foliage, figures, or whatever else he pleased; and making, among other works, an entire suit of armour, to be used by a foot-soldier, for the Duke Alessandro de' Medici. Among many other medals of great beauty by the hand of this artist, were those bearing the head of the above-named Alessandro, which were placed in the foundations of the Fortresses at the Gate of Faenza, with some others, on which the head of Pope Clement VII. appeared on the one side, and a nude figure of our Saviour Christ on the other, accompanied by the instruments used in the flagellation of our Lord. Francesco del Prato found great delight in works of sculpture also, and likewise cast certain small figures in bronze, which were singularly graceful; these came ultimately into the possession of the Duke Alessandro. The same artist polished and brought to high perfection four figures, all of the same size, which had been commenced by Baccio Bandinelli; a Leda namely, a Venus, a Hercules, and an Apollo, all which were given to the above-named Duke.

The art of the goldsmith having at length become distasteful to Francesco di Girolamo, he, not having the means requisite for pursuing that of the sculptor, which demands considerable resources, then devoted himself to painting, being already a good designer as we have said. Francesco held intercourse with but few people, nor did he wish to let it be known that he was proposing to practise painting; he therefore kept the works he attempted to himself; at this time it was that Francesco Salviati came to Florence, and worked in the rooms which Francesco di Girolamo del Prato occupied in the House of Works to the Cathedral, where Salviati painted his picture for Messer Alamanno; and Francesco del Prato, having thus an opportunity of seeing his methods of proceeding, betook himself to paint with more zeal than ever, and executed a very beautiful picture, the subject whereof was the Conversion of St. Paul: this is now in the possession of Guglielmo del Tovaglia. He subsequently delineated, in a picture of similar size, the Fall of Serpents by which the people of Israel were afflicted; and in another he represented Jesus Christ delivering the Holy Fathers from the Limbo or Gates of Hell. These two last-mentioned works, which are exceedingly beautiful, are now in the possession of Filippo Spini, a gentleman who greatly delights in our arts. Francesco del Prato executed many other small works; he drew, also, much and well, as may be seen by certain sketches from his hand, which are preserved in our book of Designs. He died in the year 1562, and his death grieved the whole Academy deeply; for, besides that he was a person of great ability in art, there perhaps never lived a more excellent man than was Francesco del Prato.

Giuseppe Porta of Castel Nuovo, in the Garfagnana, was in like manner a disciple of Francesco Salviati, and he also, from respect to his master, was called Salviati. This Giuseppe was conducted to Rome in the year 1535, and while yet a boy, by an uncle of his, who was then Secretary to Monsignor Onofrio Bartolini, Archbishop of Pisa; he was there placed with Salviati, with whom in a short time he learned not only to draw well but to paint admirably. Having afterwards accompanied his master to Venice, he formed so many intimate acquaintances among the gentry of that place, that, having been left there by Francesco, he determined to adopt the city of Venice for his home, and having taken a wife there, has continued to make it his abode; nay, he not only remains there still, but has so rarely departed from it as to have performed few works in any other place than Venice.

Giuseppe Salviati has decorated the House of the Loredani family, which is situate on the Campo di San Stefano, with stories in fresco, which are of great beauty, and executed in an admirable manner. He has also painted the House of the Bernardi family at San Polo, with another behind San Rocco, which is an excellent work. The same artist has painted three very large façades in chiaro-scuro; these, which he has covered with stories, are situate, the first at San Moisè, the second at San Casciano, and the third at Santa Maria Zebenigo.* The entire Palace of Priali, a large and rich building at Treville, near Treviso, has also been decorated both within and without by Giuseppe Salviati; but of this palace we shall speak at length in the life of Jacopo

* These works have been destroyed by the salt winds prevalent here.—*Venetian Edition of Vasari.*

Sansovino. At Piere del Sacco likewise, Giuseppe has produced a very beautiful façade, and at Bagnuolo, a place belonging to the Monks of the Santo Spirito at Venice, he has painted a picture in oil; while for the same fathers he has executed the ceiling and wainscot of the Refectory in their Monastery of Santo Spirito, representing a very fine Cenacolo, or Last Supper, at the upper end of the same, and covering the remainder of the walls with pictures in various compartments.

In the Palace of San Marco, Giuseppe has painted the Sybils, the Prophets, the Cardinal Virtues, and Our Saviour Christ with the Maries. All these works, which are in the Hall of the Doge, have been very highly extolled; and in the beforementioned Library of San Marco there are two* pictures by the hand of this artist, which he painted in concurrence with other Venetian painters of whom mention has before been made. Having been invited to Rome by the Cardinal Emulio on the death of Francesco Salviati, Giuseppe completed one of the largest stories in the Hall of the Kings,† and commenced another. At a later period, and when Pope Pius IV. was dead, Giuseppe returned to Venice, where the Signoria has given him a ceiling in the Palace to decorate, and this he is to cover with pictures in oil; the vaulting in question being that at the summit of the new staircase.

The same artist has produced six very beautiful paintings in oil, one of which is at the Altar of the Madonna, in the Church of San Francesco della Vigna;‡ the second is at the High Altar in the Church of the Servites; the third, in the Friars Minors; the fourth, in the Madonna dell' Orta; the fifth, at San Zaccheria; and the sixth, at San Moisè. Guiseppe has also painted two pictures at Murato; both of which are executed with great care and in a fine manner. But of this artist, since he still lives and is becoming a very excellent master, I will not for the present add more, except to remark that he has also devoted himself to the study of Geometry, in addition to that of painting, and the Volute of

* There are three pictures by Salviati in the Library of San Marco.—*Venetian Edition of Vasari.*

† It is that which represents Frederick Barbarossa receiving the benediction of Pope Alexander III. on the Piazza of San Marco at Venice.

‡ There are two paintings by Giuseppe Salviati in the Church of San Francesco della Vigna.—*Ed. Venet.*

the Ionic Capital, which has just appeared in copper-plate, is by his hand.* In this we are shown how this member should be turned after the antique measure, and there is very shortly to be published a work by this same Giuseppe, which he has composed on the subject of Geometry.†

A Roman, named Domenico, was also a disciple of Francesco Salviati, and was of much assistance to his master in the Hall which the latter painted at Florence, as well as for other works. In the year 1550, this Domenico engaged himself to the Signor Giuliano Cesarino, and has not hitherto worked on his own account.

---

## DANIELLO RICCIARELLI, PAINTER AND SCULPTOR OF VOLTERRA.

[BORN 1491, *circa*.—DIED 1566.]

DANIELLO RICCIARELLI acquired some knowledge of design in his youth from Giovanni Antonio Razzi, at the time when the latter was executing certain labours in Volterra; but on the departure of Razzi he made much sounder and more rapid progress under Baldassare Peruzzi, although, to say the truth, he did not at that time derive any very great benefit from his studies with either of these masters, seeing that by so much as he was impelled to exertion by a firm will and eager desire for knowledge, by as much was he impeded by the want of natural genius and readiness of hand. In his first works at Volterra we perceive much, nay, infinite industry, but not the promise of a grand or beautiful manner; neither grace, loveliness, nor power of invention are to be perceived in these paintings, as they are in those of so many other artists even at the earliest hour. Born to be painters, these last have given evidence of boldness, facility, and the commencement of a good manner, even in their very first attempts. The early works of Daniello, on the contrary, offer proof of having been produced by

* The rules for the Ionic column were first published by Marcolini, in fol. Venice, 1552. They were then translated into Latin by Poleni, and were inserted in his *Esercitazione Vetruviane*.—*Bottari*.

† This work the author is said to have burnt, not having time to complete it, and not choosing to leave it in an imperfect state.—*Ibid*.

a slow and melancholy hand; they are manifestly executed with much patience and at great cost of time; but the traces of heavy labour are also clearly apparent.

But to come to particulars: leaving out of the account such pictures as do not merit attention, I find that in his youth Daniello painted the façade of a house in Volterra, belonging to Messer* Mario Maffei; this he executed in chiaro-scuro, acquiring a fair name and much credit by the work. Having finished this, and seeing that there was no one in Volterra with whom he could enter into competition, while there were also no works in that city,† whether ancient or modern, from which he could learn much, he resolved on making every effort to reach Rome, where he had heard that there were not many artists much engaged at that time in painting, with the sole exception of Perino del Vaga. But prior to his departure, Daniello desired earnestly to prepare some painting which he might take with him, and ultimately produced a picture of Christ scourged at the Column. This work, which was in oil, comprised many figures, and having given all his wonted diligence to its completion, for which he used many models and portraits from the life, he took it with him to Rome.

Arrived in the city, Daniello had not been there any very long time before the picture just mentioned was made known, by means of certain of his friends, to the Cardinal Triulzi, who was so highly satisfied therewith, that he not only purchased the same, but conceived a great liking for Daniello, whom he despatched shortly afterwards to one of his dwellings, a large building called the Salone, which he had erected outside Rome, and which he was then causing to be decorated with stucco-works, fountains, and pictures by Giovanni Maria da Milano, and other artists, who were employed there precisely at that moment, all busied in adorning the same with stuccoes and *grottesche*. Having reached this place therefore, Daniello, incited by the spirit of emulation, and also desiring to serve effectually that Noble, from whom he might reasonably hope much honour as well as profit, began at once to paint various stories in the different apartments

* Monsignore rather. Mario Maffei was a high dignitary of the church.

† The works of Signorelli, Ghirlandajo, and some few others, which were then in Volterra, might have induced an exception to this somewhat hasty remark; to say nothing of architectural monuments.

and galleries, all which Daniello executed in company with the other artists before alluded to; more particularly may be mentioned certain *grottesche*, which our artist filled with innumerable figures of women, all of very minute dimensions.

But that in which he was most especially successful was a story of Phaeton, in fresco, the figures of which were as large as life; there is indeed a River-god of colossal dimensions, which is an excellent figure. Now the Cardinal very frequently visited all these works while they were in course of execution, and as he took with him, now one person and now another, that circumstance caused Daniello to be made known to, and to form a friendship with, not a few among these visitors. At a somewhat later period it chanced that Perino del Vaga, who was then painting the Chapel of Messer Agnolo de' Massimi at the Trinità, required the aid of a young man for that work; and Daniello, who desired to learn all that he could, and was besides attracted by the promises of Perino, engaged himself to that artist, assisting him to execute many things in the above-named Chapel, all which Daniello performed with infinite diligence. Meanwhile, and before the sack of Rome, Perino having painted the Ceiling of the Chapel of the Crucifix in San Marcello, as we have said, depicting therein the Creation of Adam and Eve in figures as large as life, with figures of two Evangelists, San Giovanni and San Marco namely, which were much larger; the men of the Company who had commissioned him to execute that work, determined, when Rome had been restored to a state of quiet, that these figures, which were not finished, should then receive the requisite additions, the San Giovanni still requiring completion from the middle upwards. But Perino had at that time other work on hand, and having prepared the Cartoons, he caused Daniello to proceed with them; when the latter first finished the San Giovanni, and subsequently added the two figures of the other Evangelists, San Luca and San Matteo, with two Boys holding Chandeliers between them. There are besides two Angels from his hand, within the arch of that side of the wall in which are the windows; they are represented as in the act of flight, and hovering, suspended on their wings, they display the instruments used in the Crucifixion of our Lord: the arch itself was very richly adorned by Daniello with *grottesche*, and many small nude figures of great beauty: he acquitted himself, in short, in the most creditable manner throughout the whole work, although it is true that he took much time to finish it.*

The same Perino subsequently gave to Daniello the Frieze of a Hall in the Palace of Messer Agnolo Massimi; and here too, the latter depicted various stories, these were from the Life of Fabius Maximus, he executed the stucco-work compartments likewise, with the other ornaments, so well, that the Signora Elena Orsina, beholding that work, and hearing the ability of Daniello much extolled, gave him the commission for painting a Chapel belonging to her, in the Church of the Trinità at Rome, which is situate on that hill whereon the monks of San Francesco di Paola have their abode. Wherefore, Daniello, putting forth his utmost diligence, in the hope of producing an excellent work, and one which should make him known as an able artist, did not shrink from bestowing on it the labour of many years. Now, from the name of that Lady, the Chapel had received the title of the "Cross of Christ Our Lord;" and the subject of the Stories depicted therein was taken from the Life of Sant' Elena; thus, in the first picture, Daniello exhibits Our Saviour Christ deposed from the Cross, by Joseph and Nicodemus, with the other Disciples; the Swooning of the Virgin Mary is also represented, she is supported in the arms of the Magdalen; and the other Maries are around her. In this work our artist showed much judgment, and did indeed prove himself to be a man of ability; for, to say nothing of the composition, which is excellent, the figure of Christ is an admirable one, very finely foreshortened, the feet projecting forward, while the remainder of the person falls back. The figures of those who are removing the Saviour are, in like manner, very ably foreshortened, a work of no small difficulty; they stand on ladders and hold the body, which they have taken down, involved amidst its draperies, their own forms being partly draped also, but partly nude, and in some of these nude parts, which are very gracefully done, these figures give evidence of much ability in the artist.

Around this picture Daniello then executed a rich frame of stucco work, exhibiting numerous carvings, with two figures, which support the Fronton with their heads, while

* These works still remain in the Chapel of the Crucifix above-named.

with one hand they hold the Capital, and with the other they appear to be placing the shaft which supports it, and which, half-resting on the base, is already attached to the capital; the whole work is performed with incredible care and pains. In the arch above the picture, Daniello painted two Sybils in fresco, and these are the best figures of the whole; they stand, one on each side of the window, which rises above the centre of the picture, and gives light to the chapel. The ceiling of the chapel is divided into four compartments by fanciful, beautiful, and richly varied designs in stucco and *grottesche*, to which are added very new and original masks and festoons: within these compartments are four stories of the Cross and of St. Helena, the Mother of Constantine. The first of these represents the fabrication of the three Crosses, which took place before the Passion of our Lord; in the second is St. Helena commanding certain Hebrews to show her these Crosses; in the third she is giving orders to the effect that those who, having knowledge of the same, have refused to impart it to her, shall be cast into a well; and in the fourth are seen the Hebrews pointing out to her the place wherein all the three Crosses were buried. These four Stories are beautiful to an extraordinary degree, and are executed with remarkable care.

On the side-walls of the chapel are four other stories—two on either side that is to say—each being divided into two parts by the cornice which forms the impost of the arch, on which reposes the vaulting of the said chapel. In one of these stories is St. Helena, who is causing the Holy Cross, with the other two Crosses, to be drawn from a well; in the second is the Cross of the Saviour distinguished by its cure of a sick person. The pictures which are beneath exhibit, one, the above-named St. Helena, who recognizes the Cross of Christ by its resuscitation of a dead man; and the other, which is opposite to it, the Emperor Heraclius, walking barefoot and divested of his imperial robes, as he bears the Cross of the Redeemer through the gate of Rome.* Here are seen large numbers of women and children, with men also kneeling in adoration of the Cross: many Barons

* The legend has it "gate of Jerusalem," and not of Rome; it adds that the Emperor was arrested by miracle as he was about to leave the gate, and was forced, also by miracle, to direct his steps towards Mount Calvary.

of the Emperor are also present with an Esquire, who holds the horse of the Monarch. Of the dead man raised to life by the Cross of our Lord, as above-mentioned, it is to be remarked that Daniello bestowed infinite pains on the muscular development of this form, having studied the anatomy, and exhibited every minutia of the various parts with marvellous exactitude. He did as much for the figures of those who are placing this dead man upon the Cross, and for the bystanders, who remain astounded at the miracle they behold. He furthermore imagined a most fanciful bier, or *cataletto*, with a skeleton of the human form embracing the same, all which gives proof of rich invention, and is executed with infinite care and diligence.

Beneath these pictures, and serving as a species of socle or basement for each, are two female figures in chiaro-scuro, made to imitate marble, and singularly beautiful: they appear to support the stories. In the space beneath the first arch, and on the front of the chapel, are two figures standing upright; they are of the size of life, and represent, one San Francesco di Paola, the Founder of the Order by which Divine Service is performed in that church; and the other St. Jerome in his robes as a Cardinal. These are two beautiful figures; but the same may, indeed, be averred with truth of all in the work, which Daniello completed with incalculable pains and study, after having spent therein the space of seven years.

But paintings executed in this manner have always a something of laboured hardness, and the work in question is altogether wanting in that graceful facility which alone is capable of entirely satisfying the spectator. Wherefore, Daniello himself, admitting the pains which he had bestowed on the work, and fearing the censures to follow, which in fact he did not escape,—Daniello, I say, finished all by adding beneath the feet of the two Saints, partly from caprice, but partly also as a kind of defence, two smaller stories in stucco-work of basso-rilievo, wherein he designed to show that his imitation of his friends Michelagnolo Buonarroti and Fra Bastiano del Piombo, whose precepts and methods of action he did indeed closely follow, ought to suffice for his defence (even though his proceedings were laborious and slow), against the attacks of those envious and malignant persons whose evil nature often betrays itself when they least expect it. To this end our artist represented in one of these stories a crowd of Satyrs engaged in weighing legs, arms, and other members of the human form in a balance, making note of such as are of just weight, and referring all they find wrong, incorrect, or defective, to Michelagnolo and Fra Bastiano, who are holding judgment thereon.* In the other Story is Michelagnolo looking at himself in a glass, the signification of which is sufficiently clear.†

In the two angles of the outer arch, Daniello executed two nude figures in chiaro-scuro, which are equal in excellence to those presented by the other portions of the work. This last having been given to public view after the lapse of the long time we have specified, was upon the whole much commended, and admitted to be a fine as well as a difficult performance; Daniello being at the same time acknowledged to merit the name of an excellent artist. Having completed this Chapel, the Cardinal Alessando Farnese caused the master to make a Frieze of much beauty in one of the rooms of his palace. In this chamber and three others of great size, which follow consecutively, rich ceilings had been prepared under the direction of Maestro Antonio da Sangallo; and here Daniello was now commanded to paint a story with figures on each wall, in addition to the frieze. The subjects chosen were a Triumph of Bacchus, a Hunting party, and other exercises of similar character; all which pleased the Cardinal greatly, and that prelate caused the artist to add the Unicorn in the lap of a Virgin, which is the impress of his most illustrious family, to the various divisions of the work. These labours caused the noble in question, who has ever been the friend of all able and dis-distinguished men, to show much favour to Daniello, and he would doubtless have done even more for him had he not been so dilatory in his mode of working; yet this was not the fault of Daniello, seeing that such was his nature and genius; nor could he ever content himself with doing much and badly,

* This description is not strictly accurate. In one of these bassi-rilievi Satyrs are weighing, not detached limbs, but the actual figures represented in the pictures above, while other Satyrs are chasing the enemies of the painter from the place. The second basso-rilievo is no longer in its place.—*Bottari.*

† It signified namely that Michael Angelo beheld his very self re-produced in the pictures above, an import more likely to be "sufficiently clear" in Daniello's day than in our own.—*Ibid.*

preferring, on the contrary, and with good reason, always to do little and well. In addition to the favour of the Cardinal, Daniello enjoyed that of the Signor Annibale Caro, who laboured so earnestly on his behalf with the Signori Farnesi his lords, that they were ever ready to afford him protection and to give him their aid.

For Madama Margherita of Austria, the daughter of the Emperor Charles V., Daniello executed certain decorations in the Palazzo de' Medici at Navona; these were in that Study or Library of which we have made mention in the Life of Indaco, and consisted of eight stories from the acts of Charles V., which Daniello painted in eight compartments of that room, completing them with so much diligence and success that, for a work of that character, one could scarcely find a more advantageous example. In the year 1547, and when Perino del Vaga had died, leaving unfinished the Hall of the Kings—which, as we have said, is in the Papal Palace near the Sistine and Pauline chapels—Daniello, by the intervention of certain nobles and friends of his, Michelagnolo more especially, was appointed by Paul III. to fill Perino's place, with a stipend similar to that which had been received by the latter, and was commanded first to commence those ornaments of the walls which were to be executed in stucco, with certain figures in full relief, that were to be placed on the summit of some gables belonging to the same apartments.

Now the walls of this great Hall are broken by six large doors, three on each side, and it has but one end remaining free from interruption. Daniello, therefore, contrived a sort of Tabernacle over each of these doors; this he constructed in stucco-work of great beauty; and within them all he proposed to paint figures of those Kings by whom the faith of Christ has been defended, one in each tabernacle. He then designed to depict stories on the walls, all relating to such monarchs as had benefited the Apostolic Church by victories or tributes. There were thus to be six pictures, and six tabernacles or niches. All these niches being finished, Daniello then, with the aid of others, completed the rich decorations in stucco-work, which are seen in other parts of that hall, while he was also preparing and studying the Cartoons for such paintings as he designed to delineate therein. This being done, he commenced the execution of one of the stories, but did not paint more than about two braccia, with two of the kings in the tabernacles over the doors. For, although much pressed to hasten his movements by Cardinal Farnese as well as the Pope, he conducted the work very slowly, not considering that Death but too frequently steps in to spoil designs which are too long deferred; insomuch, that when Pope Paul departed this life in 1549, there was no part of the work completed but that indicated above.

At this time it became necessary to clear the Hall for the Conclave which was to assemble there, the whole space being filled with the scaffoldings and wood-work erected for the execution of the paintings and stuccoes; all these impediments had now to be removed, and the pictures were consequently given to view. The decorations being thus seen by every one, the stucco-work was very greatly extolled, as indeed it merited to be; but not so the two pictures of the Kings, which were far from approaching the excellence of the paintings executed at the Trinità, insomuch that Daniello, with all those fine appointments and rich stipends, was adjudged to have rather retrograded than made improvement in his manner.

In the year 1550 Julius III. was created High Pontiff, when Daniello put himself forward by means of his friends, in the hope of retaining the same salaries, and of being permitted to continue the works of the Hall; but the Pope did not show the wished-for disposition towards him, and put off the question continually; nay, when he afterwards turned his attention to matters of art, his Holiness sent to summon Giorgio Vasari, who had already been in his service —when that Pontiff was Archbishop of Sipontino namely— Daniello was nevertheless employed some time after, and the matter happened on this wise. His Holiness resolved to construct a fountain at the head of the Corridor of the Belvedere; and the design presented by Michelagnolo, which was a figure of Moses striking the Rock whence he causes the waters to flow, did not please him, seeing that its execution was likely to occupy much time, since it was to be sculptured in marble. It was therefore decided, in pursuit of the counsel of Giorgio, that a divine figure of Cleopatra made by the Greeks, should be used for the purposes of that fountain, when the charge of the work, by the intervention of Buonarroti, was given to Daniello of Volterra, with orders that a grotto in stucco-work should be first erected, and the figure of Cleopatra then placed within it.*

Daniello set hand to the preparations accordingly, but, although earnestly requested to hasten, his proceedings were so exceedingly dilatory that he did but complete the decorations in stucco and painting, leaving many other things, which the Pope wished to have done, in a state of suspension for so long a time, that all interest in the undertaking departed from the mind of His Holiness, and the work was not finished at all, everything being suffered to remain as we now see it.

In the Church of Sant' Agostino, Daniello painted a fresco of the size of life in one of the Chapels; a figure of St. Helena namely, who is causing the holy Cross to be restored to the light of day. He likewise added figures of St. Cecilia and St. Lucia in two niches of the side walls; but these figures were painted in part only by himself, having been principally executed after his designs by the young men who were with him; the work does therefore not display so high a degree of perfection as do some other of Daniello's performances.

About the same time, a Chapel in the Church of the Trinità, which stands opposite to that of the Signora Elena Orsina, was entrusted to Daniello by the Signora Lucrezia della Rovere. Having first prepared certain compartments by means of stucco-work, Daniello then caused the Vaulting to be decorated with Stories from the Life of the Virgin, by Marco da Siena and Pelegrino da Bologna, while on one of the walls he commissioned the Spaniard Bizzera to depict a Nativity of the Madonna, and permitted his own disciple, Giovan Paolo Rosselli, of Volterra, to represent the Infant Christ presented to Simeon, on the other. This last-named artist likewise painted Gabriello, the Angel of the Annunciation, and the Birth of Christ, in the uppermost range of Arches. On the angles of the outer side, moreover, our artist placed two large figures, with two Prophets, beneath the Pilasters. The façade of the Altar Daniello painted with his own hand; here he depicted Our Lady ascending the steps of the Temple; and on the principal wall he also painted the Virgin, borne to heaven by numerous Angels, under the

* This figure is now in the Sculpture Gallery of the Vatican.

forms of most beautiful Children, the Apostles meanwhile standing beneath and watching her Ascension. But the space at his command not affording room for all the figures he desired to have, and he wishing also to display a new invention in that work, caused the Altar of the Chapel to represent the Tomb, and arranging the Apostles around it, he used the floor of the Chapel, at that point namely where the Altar commences, for the place whereon they rested their feet; and this method of proceeding has pleased some people, but the greater and more judicious portion of the judges it has not pleased. One wall of this Chapel still remained to be finished, and that, after he had made the Cartoons, he caused to be painted by Michele Alberti, his disciple, who was a native of Florence.

Now the Florentine Monsignore, Messer* Giovanni della Casa, a most learned man, as his very graceful and erudite works, both in Latin and in the vulgar tongue, sufficiently demonstrate, began to write a Treatise on the subject of Painting,† and desiring to enlighten himself as to certain minutiæ by reference to men of the profession, he caused Daniello to prepare the model of a David in *terra*, to which all possible care was given, and which was finished with the most delicate nicety; he afterwards commissioned him to paint, or rather copy, that figure of David in a picture, wherein were represented the two sides, back and front namely, in a singularly fanciful manner, but the work was a very beautiful one. This picture is now in the possession of Messer Annibale Rucellai.‡ For the same Messer Giovanni, Daniello painted a Dead Christ, with the Maries; and in a picture on cloth to be sent into France, he represented Eneas, who being on the point of removing his vestments for the purpose of retiring to rest, is accosted by Mercury, who is supposed to be addressing to him the words found in the verses of Virgil. For the same prelate he painted another picture, also in oil, a San Giovanni in the Desert namely, as large as life; and that figure, which is one of infinite beauty, was highly prized by the Signor Cardinal to the end of his days, as was also a San Jerome, likewise by Daniello, and beautiful to a marvel.

* *Sic.*

† The fate of this work is unknown.

‡ It is not now in the Rucellai Palace, nor can the present locality of this work be ascertained.—*Ed. Flor.*, 1832-8.

Pope Julius III. being dead, and Paul IV. being elected Supreme Pontiff, the Cardinal di Carpi sought to procure the permission of His Holiness for the completion by Daniello, of the Hall of Kings; but that Pontiff not taking any pleasure in pictures, made answer to the effect that it was much better to fortify Rome, than to spend money in painting it. He consequently caused the great gate of the Castle to be commenced, after the designs of Salustio, the son of Baldassare Peruzzi of Siena, his architect; but he likewise commanded that five statues, of four bracia and a half high, should be placed in the niches of that work, which was in travertine, and formed a sumptuous and magnificent triumphal arch, when one of these statues, representing the Angel Michael, was given to Daniello; the commissions for the remaining three having been accorded to other artists.*

Meanwhile Monsignore Giovanni Riccio, Cardinal of Monte Pulciano, having resolved to construct a Chapel, in San Pietro-a-Montorio, exactly opposite to that which Pope Julius had caused to be erected there after the designs of Georgio Vasari, proposed to confide the altar-piece, the stories in fresco, and the statues in marble, to Daniello; wherefore that artist, who had now determined to abandon painting and devote himself entirely to sculpture, departed for Carrara, there to superintend the excavation of the marbles for the work in question, as well as for the Statue of San Michele. On this occasion he visited Florence, and there saw the works which Vasari was in process of executing in the Palace of Duke Cosimo, with other performances to be seen in that city, where he was received with infinite courtesy and attention by many friends, more especially by the above-named Vasari, to whom Buonarroti had recommended Daniello in his letters. Thus abiding in Florence, and seeing how greatly the Signor Duke delighted in the arts of design, Daniello conceived the purpose of attaching himself to the service of his Most Illustrious Excellency, and the Signor Duke having replied to those by whom he was recommended, to the effect that he might be introduced by Vasari, it was so done. Then Daniello, offering himself at that audience to the service of his Excellency, the latter replied most amicably, that he accepted him very willingly, and that so

* No one of these statues was ever placed in the position here indicated. —*Bottari*.

soon as he, Daniello, should have fulfilled his engagements in Rome, he might present himself anew, and should be instantly received.

For the remainder of that summer Daniello remained in Florence, where he had been lodged by Giorgio in the house of Simon Botti, the intimate friend of Vasari. It was at this time that Dllo anie cast in plaster, nearly all those marble figures, from the hand of Michelagnolo, which are in the new Sacristy of San Lorenzo; he also made a beautiful figure of Leda, for the Fleming, Michael Fugger: our artist then repaired to Carrara, whence he despatched the marbles required for his future purposes to Rome; and, that done, he returned to Florence. Now Daniello, when he had first come to Florence, had brought with him from Rome a young disciple of his, called Orazio Pianeti, an amiable and very clever youth, but this Orazio—whatever may have been the reason thereof—had no sooner arrived in Florence than he died, a circumstance which caused his master, who loved him greatly, very heavy sorrow. Having now returned to Florence, therefore, and being able to do nothing more for this poor boy, he executed a bust of him in marble, having taken an admirable portrait of his face, from a cast formed after death,* and this being finished, he placed it with an epitaph in the Church of Santa Michele Bertelli, on the Piazza degli' Antinori. In this action Daniello proved himself to be a man of rare goodness, and much more the friend of his friend, than it is usual to find people now-a-days, seeing that there are but few who value anything in friendship beyond their own convenience and profit therein.

After these things, and considering that it was now a long time since he had visited his native place of Volterra, Daniello repaired thither, and this he did before returning to Rome. In Volterra, he was most amicably received by his kindred and friends; and being requested to leave some memorial of himself to his native city, he executed the story of the Innocents in small figures, and this picture he placed in the Church of San Piero.† Subsequently, and believing that he should never more return to Volterra, he sold what little of his paternal estate he possessed there, to his nephew Lionardo Ricciarelli, who having been with him

* This bust is unhappily lost.

† This work is now in the Gallery of the Uffizj, in Florence.

to Rome, and having there learned to work admirably well in stucco, afterwards laboured with many others in the service of Giorgio Vasari, whom this Lionardo aided in the works then executing for the Palace of the Duke.

The return of Daniello to Rome, took place at the time when Pope Paul IV., offended by the nude figures in the Last Judgment of Michelagnolo, was on the point of having that work utterly destroyed; but being assured by certain of the Cardinals, and other men of judgment, that it would be a pity to deface them, he consented to their employing Daniello, who contrived to make a sort of slight covering for the figures,* finishing that work under Pope Pius IV., when he likewise altered the figures of Santa Caterina and San Biagio, the defects of which, as to the particular now in question, were more especially conspicuous.

Meanwhile, the Statues for the Cardinal of Montepulciano were commenced, as was also that of San Michele, for the Great Gate; but Daniello did not proceed with the rapidity which he could and ought to have evinced, he being one whose mind was ever vacillating between project and project. At this time, Henry the King of France having been killed in a tournament, and Caterina de' Medici having become Regent of that kingdom, the Signor Ruberto Strozzi came into Italy and to Rome, where he set himself to fulfil the desire of Caterina, for some befitting monument which she proposed to have erected in memory of her husband, and to that end she had commanded Ruberto to confer with Buonarroti. Arrived in Rome, therefore, Ruberto conversed long of that matter with Michelagnolo, who, being then old, could not take such an undertaking on himself, but counselled Strozzi to give the commission to Daniello, whom he promised to aid by his advice and assistance in all things connected with the work.

This last offer being greatly prized by Strozzi, the subject was deliberated maturely, and it was finally resolved that Daniello should cast a Bronze Horse, all in one piece, though the height was to be of twenty palms, and the length about forty: on this horse was then to be placed the figure of Henry, fully armed, and also of bronze. That determined, Daniello made a small model in clay, according to the suggestions and with the advice of Michelagnolo, when the group gave

* A service for which he obtained among the jesters of the time, the name of *Il Braghettone*, or the breeches-maker.

great satisfaction to the Signor Ruberto, who wrote an account of the whole matter, which he sent to France. Finally, an agreement was entered into between Ruberto and Daniello, as to price, time of completion, and all other minutiæ, when the master instantly set hand to the work with all his accustomed care and study. Commencing with the Horse, he made the form in clay, exactly as it was to be, refusing all other engagements, to devote himself to this alone; having formed the model, he prepared to cast it, and for a work of that importance he took care to obtain the advice of many founders, for the purpose of assuring the success of the operation.

It was at this time that Pius IV. having been called to the pontifical throne on the death of Paul, made it known to Daniello that he desired him to finish the Hall of the Kings, to which end the artist was enjoined to lay aside every other undertaking. Thereunto Daniello replying that he was then much occupied, being pledged to the Queen of France, but that he would prepare the Cartoons and cause the work to be carried forward by his disciples, and would besides take care to do his own part therein, that reply displeased the Pontiff, who began to think of committing the whole work to Salviati. Rendered jealous by the intimation of that purpose, Daniello took such measures, by means of the Cardinal del Carpi and of Michelagnolo, that the half of the Hall was at length given to him to paint, but the other half was accorded to Salviati, although Daniello made all possible efforts to obtain the whole, to the end that he might have gone about his work without competition and in tranquillity, after his usual leisurely manner of proceeding. Finally however, the question of this work was handled in such a manner, that Daniello did nothing whatever, in addition to what he had accomplished long before, and that Salviati never finished the little which he had commenced, nay, even that little was destroyed for him by the malignity of others.

After four years of preparation, Daniello was at length ready, so far as he was himself concerned, to complete the casting of the Horse, but he was compelled to make a delay of several months by the fact that his stipend was not paid by Strozzi, and the metal, with other materials, were not provided in sufficient abundance. All these things were, however, finally procured, and Daniello embedded the form, which was of an immense bulk, between two founding furnaces erected in a very convenient locality which he had obtained at Monte Cavallo. For a certain time the molten mass ran well into the mould, but the weight of metal suddenly bursting the body of the horse, the material gushed forth in all directions. This misfortune caused Daniello much grief in the first instance, but eventually finding means to remedy the disaster, he recovered his self-possession; at the end of two months, therefore, he prepared to cast his work for the second time; and on this occasion, his ability prevailing against the malice of Fortune, he completed the cast of the Horse (which is a full sixth larger than the Horse of Antoninus on the Capitol) in one unblemished mass. Perfectly equal and of similar thickness throughout, this vast work did not weigh more than 20,000 pounds, which is sufficiently remarkable, its size considered.

But the toils and discomforts which Daniello, who was of a somewhat feeble and melancholy temperament, had endured for this work, were shortly afterwards succeeded by a fearful catarrh; this harassed him cruelly, and whereas it might have been expected that he should now be content and happy, seeing that he had overcome incalculable difficulties, and had produced so extraordinary a work, he was, on the contrary, so much depressed that it appeared certain he could never rejoice any more, however perfectly his affairs might prosper; nay, at the end of two days this affection deprived him of life, an event which took place on the 4th of April, 1566. He had nevertheless had time to prepare for his death, and having confessed very devoutly, he requested to have all the other Sacraments of the Church, proper to his circumstances, administered to him; this being done, he made his will, desiring that his body should be buried in the new Church, which had been commenced at the Baths by Pius IV. for the Carthusian Monks, commanding likewise that the Statue which he had begun for the Great Gate, should be placed over his grave, and giving the care of these things to the Florentine, Michele degli' Alberti, and to Feliciano di San Vito of the Campagna of Rome, to whom he left the sum of two hundred scudi for that purpose.

Both of these persons then set themselves with the most affectionate assiduity to the fulfilment of his wishes, bestowing on him the most honourable sepulture in the place, and after the manner which he had requested.* To the same persons, Daniello left all his property connected with art, his moulds, models, designs, and every other his effects of that kind. They were, consequently, in a condition to offer the Ambassador of France the completion of the Monument aforesaid within a determined limit of time, the Horse namely, with the figure of the King to be placed upon it. And of a truth, since both these artists have long laboured under the care and discipline of Daniello, a very creditable work may reasonably be expected at their hands.†

Biagio da Carigliano of Pistoja was also a disciple of Daniello, as was likewise Giovampaolo Rossetti of Volterra, who is a person of much genius and great diligence in his vocation; and having retired to Volterra some years since, he has there executed, and continues to execute, works highly deserving of praise. Marco da Siena‡ also made considerable progress while working with Daniello; he has now gone to Naples, having chosen that city for his home, and being constantly occupied there. Another disciple of Daniello is Giulio Mazzoni of Piacenza, who commenced his studies with Vasari, when the latter was painting a picture in Florence for Messer Biagio Mei, which was subsequently despatched to Lucca, where it was placed in the Church of San Piero Cigoli; Mazzoni was also with Giorgio, when the latter was painting the picture of the High Altar at Monte Oliveto in Naples, with a great work in the Refectory of the same place, the Sacristy of San Giovanni Carbonaro and the doors of the Organ in the Episcopal Church, to say nothing of other works.

This Giulio, having afterwards learned to work in stucco from Daniello, and in this respect becoming the equal of his master, has decorated the whole of the inside of the Palace belonging to Cardinal Capodiferro, with his own hand, producing admirable works there, not in stucco only but in painting also, stories namely, both in oil and fresco; and these

* The statue was not on the tomb in the time of Bottari, who declares himself unable to ascertain its fate.

† The Horse, which was not much approved, was in fact sent to Paris, but received the statue of Louis XIII., and not of Henry II.—*German Edition of Vasari.*

‡ See Della Valle, *Lettere Sanesi*, vol. iii.

have procured him high commendations which are fully merited.* The same artist has executed the bust of Francesco del Nero in marble, a portrait taken from the life, and so good a one that it does not seem possible to produce a better, from all which we may fairly hope for him the most distinguished success; nay, there can be no doubt but that he will ultimately attain to the highest point of perfection in our arts.

Daniello was a well-conducted and upright man, but so profoundly intent on his studies that he gave but little thought to the remaining circumstances of his life. He was of a melancholy disposition, and in his habits much inclined to solitude. He died at about the age of fifty-seven. I have endeavoured to procure his portrait from those before-mentioned disciples of his, who have taken it in plaster, and when I was in Rome last year they promised that I should have it; but notwithstanding the many letters and messages that I have since sent, they have neglected to forward it to me, thereby showing but little consideration for the memory of their dead master. I have nevertheless been unwilling to be entirely baffled by this ingratitude of theirs, and have therefore added that portrait of Daniello (who was a very good friend of mine) which is given above, although it does not resemble him very closely. It shall nevertheless remain as the proof that I have done my best, and as that also of the little care and regard displayed on this occasion by Michele degli Alberti and Feliciano da San Vito.

---

## TADDEO ZUCCHERO, PAINTER OF SANT' AGNOLO IN VADO.

[BORN 1529—DIED 1566.]

At the time when Francesco Maria was Duke of Urbino there was born to the painter, Ottaviano Zucchero, who dwelt in the territory of Sant' Agnolo, a portion of that state, a male child, to whom he gave the name of Taddeo; and this child having learned to read and write with tole-

* The palace here in question is on the Campo di Fiore in Rome, and is now called the Spada Palace.

rable accuracy in the tenth year of his age, the father then took him into his own charge, and began to teach him the principles of design. But Ottaviano soon perceived that his son was endowed with a genius of no common order, and might very probably become a much better artist than he believed himself to be; he placed him therefore with a certain Pompeo of Fano, his intimate friend, but a very ordinary painter, whose works as well as manners pleased the young Taddeo so little, that he left him, and returned to Sant' Agnolo, where he assisted his father (as he did also in other places) to the utmost of his power.

Increasing in judgment, however, as he advanced in years, Taddeo perceived that he could acquire but little under the discipline of his father, whom he also found that he could but slightly assist (although being charged with a family of seven boys and a girl, he much needed help) with the trifling amount of knowledge which he then possessed; he therefore determined to set off for Rome. This he did all alone at the age of fourteen, but being in the first instance known to no one, and not knowing any one himself, he suffered no little discomfort; nay, he seems to have been treated far from well by such few acquaintances as he did make. In this strait he applied to Francesco, called Sant' Agnolo, who was then working for a daily payment at *grottesche* for Perino del Vaga, and whom Taddeo approached with all humility, entreating him, since he was a kinsman, to be be pleased to give him aid.

What he desired was, however, not done. On the contrary, Francesco, as kinsmen sometimes will do, not only refused to aid him by word or deed, but even reprehended and repulsed him harshly. Notwithstanding all this, the poor youth did not lose courage, nor did he waver in his purpose, but supported himself, or rather, starved on * during many months in Rome, by hiring himself to grind colours, now in one workshop, and now in another, for miserable wages, and

* The scenes from the Life of Taddeo, in the drawings of his brother Federigo, very touchingly set forth the grievous circumstances of his life at this period. In one of these we find him drawing from the ancient statues of Rome by moonlight; in another, overcome by home-sickness, by weariness of heart, and by the burning heat of the sun, he has sunk in sleep on the edge of a river, and awaking in a state of delirium, he fills his empty wallet with the pebbles of the shore, which he believes to be paintings of Raphael, and which he carries joyfully away upon his back.

sometimes practising a little drawing, as he best could. It is true that he did at last succeed in fixing himself as a disciple with a certain Calabrian called Giovan Piero, but he did not derive much profit from doing so, since this man, with his wife, a most ill-tempered woman, kept him to the grinding of colours day and night. They furthermore caused him to suffer from actual want of food, and to the end that he might not have sufficient for his hunger, or take bread when he desired it, they hung their loaf in a basket suspended from the ceiling and furnished with bells, which jingled whenever the basket was touched, thus serving as a kind of spy to betray such hands as might invade the same. All this would nevertheless have given but little trouble to Taddeo, if he could have been allowed the time to copy certain works of Raffaello da Urbino, which were in the possession of that miserable master of his.

The above-mentioned, and many other strange proceedings, caused Taddeo to leave Giovan Piero, and he then resolved to work for himself, taking refuge among the different workshops of Rome, wherein he had now begun to be known, and expending one part of the week in working to live, while he employed the remainder in drawing, more especially from the works of Raphael, in the house of Agostino Chigi, and in other Palaces of Rome. And as at this time it often happened to him that when the night came he had no place wherein to lay his head, so did he take shelter many a night in the Loggie of the above-named Chigi, or in other places of the same kind. These sufferings did not fail permanently to affect his health, nay, had he not been supported by the force of his youth, they would most probably have killed him altogether; as it was they caused him to fall dangerously ill, and as Francesco Sant' Agnolo, his kinsman, did not help him then any more than he had done before, the poor Taddeo, that he might not finish his life amidst the wretchedness by which he was then surrounded, was compelled to return to Sant' Agnolo and to the house of his father.

But not to waste more time over matters which are not of primary importance, and having sufficiently shown the pains and sufferings with which Taddeo acquired his art, I will but say, that being at length recovered, he returned once more to Rome and resumed his studies, but this time he took somewhat better care of himself than he had previously done, and having acquired much knowledge under a certain Jacopone,* he began to obtain some credit. His relative Francesco, who had behaved so cruelly towards him, then perceiving that he was becoming an able man, made friends with him by way of making use of his services, and the good Taddeo, who was of an excellent disposition, forgot all his wrongs, when these two agreed for a certain time, to work together. Taddeo therefore preparing the designs, and both together painting numerous friezes in fresco for chambers and Loggie, they did not fail to help each other considerably.

Meanwhile the painter Daniello da Parino,† who had formerly worked many years with Antonio da Correggio, and had also had much intercourse with the Parmigiano, Francesco Mazuoli, had undertaken to paint in fresco a Church situate at Vitto beyond Sora, on the borders of the Abruzzi; with the Chapel of the Virgin in the same place. He therefore, being in want of an assistant, engaged Taddeo for that purpose, and took the latter with him to Vitto. And herein Daniello da Parino, although not the best painter in the world, was yet of great use to our artist, seeing that, having attained to mature age, and having also observed the methods of Correggio and Parmigiano, and the softness with which they finished their works, he had acquired so much facility of hand that showing those methods to Taddeo and instructing him by his words also, he did him service as we have said; nay, more perchance than he might have done by working before him. In this Church, then, Taddeo Zucchero painted the four Evangelists, two Sybils, two Prophets, and four Stories, of no great size, the subjects of which were taken from the Life of our Saviour Christ and the Virgin Mother.

Having subsequently returned to Rome, it chanced that a certain Roman gentleman, Messer Jacopo Mattei, was conversing with Taddeo's kinsman Francesco Sant' Agnolo in relation to a part of his house, which he desired to have painted in chiaro-scuro, when Francesco proposed Taddeo for that office, and on the gentleman remarking that he seemed too young, Francesco replied that a trial might be made of him in two stories, which, if they were not well done might be de-

* A disciple of Raphael, and zealous copyist of that master's works, but who left few of his own.

† Daniello di Par.—*Bottari.*

stroyed, but if satisfactory might remain as a commencement. Having set hand to the work therefore, these two stories proved successful to such a degree that Messer Jacopo was not only satisfied but astonished; nay, when the work was completed, which was in the year 1548, Taddeo Zucchero was highly extolled by all Rome, and with very good reason, seeing that since Polidoro, Maturino, Vincenzio da San Gimignano and Baldassare da Siena, there had been no artist who had equalled what Taddeo, still but a youth of eighteen, had there produced. The stories of these works, which were from the Life of Furius Camillus, will be best comprehended hy the following inscriptions.

The first is as follows :—

TUSCULANI PACE CONSTANTI VIM ROMANAM ARCENT.

The second :—

M. F. C. SIGNIFERUM SECUM IN HOSTEM RAPIT.

The third :—

M. F. C. AUCTORE INSENSA URBS RESTITUITUR.

The fourth :—

M. F. C. PACTIONIBUS TURBATIS PRÆLIUM GALLIS NUNCIAT.

The fifth :—

M. F. C. PRODITOREM VINCTUM FALERIO REDUCENDUM TRADIT.

The sixth :—

MATRONALIS AURI COLLATIONE VOTUM APOLLINI SOLVITUR.

The seventh :—

M. F. C. JUNONI REGINÆ TEMPLUM IN AVENTINO DEDICAT.

The eighth :—

SIGNUM JUNONIS REGINÆ A VEIIS ROMAM TRANSFERTUR.

The ninth :—

M. F. C. . . . ANLIUS DICT. DECEM . . . SOCIOS CAPIT.*

From this time until the year 1550, when Pope Julius III. ascended the Papal throne, Taddeo Zucchero was employed in works of no great importance, but from which the gains that he made were nevertheless considerable. In that year, which was the year of the Jubilee, Ottaviano, the father of Taddeo, with his mother and a little son of theirs, came to Rome, partly to take their portion of the most Holy Jubilee, and partly to visit Taddeo. Having passed some weeks with the latter they returned home, leaving with him the boy above-mentioned, who was called Federigo, to the end

* These works have totally perished.

that his brother might cause him to study letters, but Taddeo considering his abilities better suited for painting, as has been shown to be the truth, by the admirable progress which this Federigo has made,*—Taddeo, I say, after he had made the child acquire the first principles of learning, then set him to study design, furnishing him meanwhile with better assistance and more ample support than he had himself enjoyed.

Taddeo was meanwhile to paint four Stories behind the High Altar in the Church of Sant' Ambrosio of the Milanesi; they are in fresco of no great size, represent events from the Life of that Saint, and are accompanied by a frieze of Termini, these last consisting of Boys and Girls.† Immediately after the completion of this work, which was an exceedingly good one, he commenced the decoration of a façade beside Santa Lucia della Tinta, which is near the Orso; this he covered with stories from the Life of Alexander the Great, beginning with his birth, and exhibiting, in five stories, the most remarkable events of his career; this work was very highly commended, although it had to endure comparison with one from the hand of Polidoro, which was close beside it.‡

At that time Guidobaldo Duke of Urbino, having heard the fame of this youth, who was his vassal, and desiring to bring the Chapel of the Cathedral of Urbino, of which the ceiling had been painted by Battista Franco, as we have said, to a conclusion, invited his said vassal to Urbino; then the latter, leaving Federigo with persons in Rome who were charged to be watchful over his progress, and doing as much for another of his brothers, whom he placed with some friends who were goldsmiths, repaired to Urbino, and was there received with much favour by the Duke, who instantly laid before him the works which he wished him to design for other places as well as for the Chapel abovenamed. But Guidobaldo, as Captain-general of the Venetian

* Vasari never speaks of this artist but with his unvarying impartiality, although Federigo had conceived an envious hatred of Vasari, which sufficiently appears in the bitter sarcasms appended by him, in the form of marginal notes to the second edition of our author's book.

† This work also has been destroyed in the various reparations of the church.

‡ These works also have perished by the injuries of time and the weather.

Signoria, had at this time to visit Verona and the other fortified places of that dominion, wherefore he took our artist with him, and Taddeo then copied for his Excellency that picture from the hand of Raffaello which, as we have related in another place, is in the Palace of the Counts of Canossa. He afterwards commenced a very large picture on cloth for his Excellency; the subject of that work is the Conversion of St. Paul, but this he never finished, and it remains still incomplete in the house of Ottaviano his father.

Having then returned to Urbino, Taddeo recommenced the designs for the Chapel. They were scenes from the Life of Our Lady, as may be seen from certain of them, drawn in chiaro-scuro with a pen, which are in the possession of Federigo. But whether it were that the Duke thought our artist too young, or whatever else may have been the cause, certain it is that Taddeo remained with his Excellency two years without doing anything but some few pictures in a writing chamber or study, at Pesaro, with a great Escutcheon of Arms in fresco, which he painted on the front of the Palace, and the Portrait of the Duke, the size of life, in a large picture, all of which works were very fine ones. At length, however, and when his Excellency was on the point of his departure for Rome, there to receive the Baton of Commander for Holy Church from the hands of Pope Julius III., he left directions with Taddeo, to the effect that the latter should proceed with the above-named Chapel, commanding furthermore, that he should be provided with all that he might require for that purpose. But the ministers of the Duke, proceeding as such men usually do, delaying all things and impeding him at every point, that is to say, caused him at length to leave Urbino, after he had lost two years of his time. He then repaired to Rome, where, having found the Duke, he dexterously excused himself without casting censure on any other person, promising his Excellency that he would not fail to complete the undertaking in due time.

In the year 1551, Stefano Veltroni of Monte Sansavino, having been commanded by the Pope, and directed by Giorgio Vasari, to adorn with grottesche the apartments of the Vigna which had belonged to the Cardinal Poggio, and were situate on the hill without the Porta del Popolo,—Stefano Veltroni, I say, summoned Taddeo, whom he caused to paint the central picture of his work. This represented a figure intended to signify Opportunity, who, having taken Fortune by the forelock, is on the point of cutting off the hair with his shears; this is the device of the above-named Pontiff; and in the delineation of the same, Taddeo Zucchero acquitted himself exceedingly well. Subsequently, and when Vasari had prepared the design (which he had done before any of the other artists), for that Court and Fountain in the new Palace, afterwards carried into execution by Vignola and Ammannato, the masonry being undertaken by Baronino, and many pictures being painted therein by Prospero Fontana,* as will be related hereafter; on that occasion I say, Taddeo Zucchero was also frequently employed, and this was the cause of future benefit to our artist, seeing that the Pope, being highly satisfied with his methods of proceeding, gave him further occupation. This was in the Belvedere, and consisted in small figures, which serve as the friezes of the apartments, together with an open Loggia; which stands behind that turned towards Rome, and where Taddeo painted all the Labours of Hercules, in figures as large as life. This work which was in chiaro-scuro, was destroyed under the Pontificate of Paul IV., for the purpose of building a Chapel with certain chambers on the site of the Loggia.

At the Vigna of Pope Julius, and in the principal apartments of the Palace, Taddeo painted Stories in the centre of the ceilings; one, representing Mount Parnassus, may be more particularly mentioned. In the Court of this Vigna likewise, our artist executed two Stories in chiara-scuro; they represent the Rape of the Sabines, and stand one on each side of the marble door which enters the Loggia, at that point where the descent to the Fountain of the Acqua Vergine commences. All these works were highly and deservedly extolled.†

Now Federigo Zucchero had repaired to Urbino while Taddeo was at Verona with the Duke Guidobaldo, and between that place and Pesaro he had continued to abide from that time; but Taddeo caused him to return to Rome after the completion of the pictures above-named, and there he availed himself of the services of the youth on a large

* See Malvasia, *Felsina Pittrice*. See also Baldinucci, *Vite*, &c.

† They have now (1759), with other admirable works of this noble edifice, been very grievously injured by barbarous maltreatment.—*Bottari*.

frieze and other decorations in the Great Hall, which were then in process of execution. Federigo laboured also in the Palace of the Giambeccari family, whose house is above the Piazza di Sant' Apostolo. Taddeo likewise caused him to paint other friezes, which he was then preparing, at the Obelisk of San Mauro, for Messer Antonio Portatore. These works were very rich in figures and other ornaments, and were considered exceedingly beautiful.

During the Pontificate of Pope Julius, Maestro Mattinolo, the Master of the Post, had bought a piece of ground in the Campo Marzio, where he had built a very commodious house, the front of which he now caused Taddeo to paint in chiaro-scuro. Here our artist depicted three Stories relating to Mercury, the Messenger of the Gods, which were very beautiful; the remainder of the decorations he made others execute from designs by his own hand. Meanwhile, Messer Jacopo Mattei had caused a Chapel to be built in the Church of the Consolation, which is beneath the Capitol, and gave it, knowing the abilities of Taddeo, to that artist to paint: and this he undertook to do very gladly, although the price was but moderate, because he wished to prove to certain persons who had declared him unable to execute anything but façades and other works in chiaro-scuro, that he could handle the colours also.

Having set hand to this work therefore, Taddeo would never go to it except at such times as he felt himself fully disposed, and in the humour to do something good, employing the remainder of his time on works which did not interest him so much on the score of his honour; in this leisurely manner he completed the same, after having been occupied on it during four years. In the ceiling he depicted four Stories in fresco, from the Passion of Our Saviour Christ. They are not of great size, but are so admirable from the rich originality of the invention, the correctness of the design, and the beauty of the colouring, that the artist was seen to have herein surpassed all his previous efforts. The subject of this portion of the work is the Last Supper, the Washing of the Feet, the Prayer in the Garden, and the Betrayal by Judas. On one of the side-walls, in figures the size of life, we have Christ Scourged at the Column; and on the other is Our Saviour brought out to the people by Pilate, with the words *Ecce Homo*. Over this last, and within an arch, is Pilate washing his hands; and on the opposite side, also within an arch, is Christ led before Annas. On the wall behind the Altar, is the Crucifixion of our Lord with the Maries at the foot of the Cross and our Lady in a swoon. Beside the Virgin Mother stand certain of the Prophets, and in the arch above the ornaments in stucco are two Sybils; these four figures last-mentioned appear to be holding discourse concerning the Passion of Christ. There are besides four half-length figures in the ceiling, intended to represent the four Evangelists; and these also, which are accompanied by decorations in stucco, are very beautiful. When the work was given to view, which happened in 1556, Taddeo was but twenty-six years old, and the performance being then, as it still is, considered a singularly fine one, he was at once declared by the artists to be an excellent painter.

That undertaking being finished, Taddeo Zucchero was commissioned by Messer Mario Frangipane, to paint a chapel which he had in the church of San Marcello; and on this occasion, as on many others, Taddeo employed many of those young artists from distant parts, who are constantly to be found in Rome, and who go about working for daily wages, not only to gain their bread, but to learn their art also. Our artist likewise painted certain apartments in fresco in the Palace of the Pope, those which are occupied by the Cardinal Caraffa namely, and which are situated in the great tower over the guard-room of the Lansquenets. This work he executed under the Pontificate of Paul IV.; as he did also some small pictures in oil: among these were two, the Nativity of Christ, and the Flight into Egypt, which were ultimately sent to Portugal by the Ambassador of that country.

It then happened that the Cardinal of Mantua desired to have the interior of his palace, which is situated near the Portuguese arch, adorned with paintings, which he desired to have executed with great rapidity; he therefore entrusted that work to Taddeo Zucchero, to whom he agreed to pay an appropriate remuneration; when our artist, setting hand to the same with a large number of assistants, conducted it in a short time to completion, and herein he did not fail to evince great judgment in the use which he made of so many heads, all united to expedite so great a work; he displayed so much knowledge, moreover, in the arrangement of the different manners, that the whole undertaking appears to have been executed by one hand. At a word, our artist satisfied the Cardinal perfectly, and at the same time disappointed the expectations of those who had believed him unequal to the charge of so great a work.

In like manner Taddeo painted stories of figures in fresco to decorate certain niches of the chambers in the palace of Messer Alessandro Maffei, which is near the Botteghe Scure, causing his brother Federigo to execute certain other stories, to the end that the latter might become accustomed to working for himself. Wherefore, encouraged by this, Federigo painted a Mount Parnassus entirely alone, a work which he accomplished in the house of a Roman gentleman called Stefano Margani, whose dwelling is at the foot of the steps which lead to the Ara Cœli. When Taddeo perceived that Federigo could thus proceed by himself, and prepare his own designs, almost entirely without aid from any one, he procured him a commission for the painting of a Chapel from the men of the Company of Santa Maria dell' Orto-a-Ripa in Rome, but making it almost appear that he intended to execute the work himself, since it was certain that to Federigo alone the commission never would have been given, he being still but a youth, and to satisfy those men Taddeo did paint a Nativity of Christ in that chapel; but the rest was entirely executed by Federigo alone; the latter acquitting himself in such a manner as to give evidence of the ability which is now made manifest in his works.*

About the same time, the Duke of Guise, who was then at Rome, desiring to find a good painter and able man, who might paint a palace which he had in France, Taddeo was proposed to him for that purpose, whereupon, having seen certain of his works, and his manner having pleased His Excellency, the Duke agreed to give him a stipend of 600 crowns per annum, and it was settled that Taddeo, when he had finished his works then in hand, should proceed to France and enter his service. And so, indeed, our artist would have done,

* "The frank impartiality of Vasari," remarks a compatriot of our Author, "comes in remarkable contrast with the envious acrimony of Federigo, who has but proved his own abjectness of mind, and fixed a deep stain on his reputation, while basely seeking to villify the upright biographer."

the money for his outfit and expenses having been deposited in a bank for that purpose, if the wars which immediately succeeded had not broken out in France, and if that Duke himself had not died very soon afterwards. Taddeo then returned to the work of Frangipane in San Marcello, but was not able to continue it without interruption for any long time, because the Emperor Charles V. having also died, and orders having been given for the solemnization of magnificent funeral rites in Rome (that Monarch being Emperor of the Romans), Taddeo was called on to paint stories from the Life of Charles, with numerous trophies and other ornaments, all which, executed with great beauty and decorum, our artist completed in the space of twenty-five days. For this labour, therefore, and for that of Federigo and the other assistants whom he had employed, Taddeo received the sum of 600 golden crowns.

No long time after these things, Taddeo painted two large chambers at Bracciano for the Signor Paolo Giordano Orsini; they were richly decorated in gold and stucco-work, and the subjects of the pictures executed by our artist were the Loves of Cupid and Psyche in one room, and in the other Stories from the Life of Alexander the Great. These last had been commenced by other artists; but of those which remained to be done, he caused Federigo his brother to take charge; and the latter acquitted himself therein to his great credit. For the Signor Stefano del Bufalo, Taddeo then painted certain frescoes in a garden near the fountain of Trevi, the Mount Parnassus namely, with the Muses around the Fountain of Castaly; this work also was considered a very fine one.

Now, the Superintendents of Works to the Cathedral of Orvieto, had caused certain Chapels to be constructed in the Nave of their Church, as we have related in the Life of Simone Mosca, with ornaments of marble and stucco-work: they had besides commissioned Girolamo Mosciano of Brescia to paint some pictures therein, being induced thereto by the intervention of friends; but having now heard of the reputation of Taddeo Zucchero, they invited him to Orvieto, whither he repaired accordingly, taking with him Federigo. Having commenced his labours in that city, therefore, our artist executed two colossal figures; one representing Life in Action, the other Life in Contemplation; both executed with the bold facility of hand peculiar to this artist, and always seen in such works as he had studied but little. While Taddeo was engaged with these, Federigo painted three stories from the Life of St. Paul in the recess of the same chapel. These paintings were but just completed, when the brothers both fell sick, and left Orvieto, but with the promise to return in the month of September. Taddeo then repaired to Rome, and Federigo to Sant' Agnolo, where he arrived with a slight fever; but having been cured of this at the end of two months, he also then proceeded to Rome.

Passion week was then approaching, and the two brothers painted the whole Passion of Christ in Stories of chiaroscuro within the space of four days; the occasion of the work was a magnificent solemnity prepared for Holy Thursday and Good Friday, and the site thereof was the Oratory of Sant' Agata, which is behind the Banchi, and belongs to the Company of Sant' Agata dei Fiorentini; the paintings occupied the whole of the ceiling and recess, and there were figures of prophets and other decorations which astonished all who beheld them.*

The Cardinal Alessandro Farnese having then brought his Palace of Caprarola to a happy termination, under the care of the architect Vignola, of whom we shall speak further shortly, gave the commission for painting the whole to Taddeo Zucchero, and the conditions of their agreement were as follows:—Taddeo was not to resign the engagements which he had in Rome, but was himself to make all the designs, cartoons, divisions, and arrangements for whatever works were to be executed in that place, whether in painting or stucco. Furthermore, Taddeo was to select the men who were to be employed, but all these men were to be paid by the Cardinal. Taddeo was to repair to Caprarola to work there himself during two or three months of the year, and was to proceed thither at other times whenever his presence should be required, and to see how the whole affair was proceeding; he was also to retouch such of the paintings as were not to his mind: for all this the Cardinal engaged to pay him a stipend of two hundred crowns yearly.

And now, having an appointment so considerable, with the

* Bottari informs us that even in his day, these works had been so completely ruined by re-touching that they could scarcely have been more injured had they been whitewashed.

favour of so great a Noble, Taddeo resolved to give himself some quiet of mind, and determined no longer to accept, as he had hitherto done, all the most abject works that could be proposed to him in any part of Rome; being moved thereto principally by his desire to escape the reproaches addressed to him by many of the art, who declared that a certain avaricious rapacity had caused him to undertake whatever offered, that he might make large gains by the labour of others; whereas it would have been more creditable to him had he left these things to be done by those who were seeking support and opportunity for study from such works, as he had himself done in his first youth. But against these reproaches Taddeo defended himself by declaring that what he did was on account of Federigo, and of that other brother, the care of whom he had also on his shoulders, and for whom he wished to secure the means of learning his profession.

Having however, now resolved to restrict his operations, he set himself to serve the Farnese, and to finish the Chapel of San Marcello, but he procured from Messer Tizio da Spoleti, the Master of the Household to that Cardinal, a commission for his brother Federigo, the façade of a house namely, which Messer Tizio had built on the Piazza of the Dogana, near Sant' Eustachio, a circumstance which greatly rejoiced Federigo, who had long desired nothing more earnestly than to have some work which should be altogether his own. On this front then, Federigo painted the Story of Sant' Eustachio, causing himself to be baptized, together with his wife and children, and in the centre of the story, which is an excellent work, he represented the same Saint, when, being at the Chase, he beholds the figure of Our Saviour Christ on the Cross between the horns of a Stag.* But when Federigo executed this picture he was but twenty-eight† years old, wherefore Taddeo, who reflected that these paintings were in a very public place, and that the credit of Federigo was at stake, not only went often to see how he was proceeding, but would frequently retouch and amend certain parts with his own hands.

This was endured patiently for some time by Federigo, but one day he fell into a transport of rage, and seizing a

* These works are now nearly effaced.

† Or rather eighteen, as indeed Vasari must have written, this being doubtless a mistake of the copyist or an error of the press.

hammer, he dashed something—I know not what—that had been painted by Taddeo, to pieces, and in his anger remained several days before he would return to the house. These things becoming known to their friends, the latter took such measures that the brothers were eventually reconciled, with the understanding that Taddeo might correct or retouch the designs or cartoons of Federigo at his pleasure, but was not to lay a hand on the works which the latter was executing in oil, in fresco, or in any other manner.

Having finished the painting of the above-mentioned house, Federigo was universally extolled, and the work acquired for him the reputation of being an excellent painter. Taddeo was then commissioned to restore those Apostles which had been long before executed in terretta by Raffaello, in the Sala dei Palafrenieri, but which had been destroyed by order of Paul IV.; having completed one of these figures, Taddeo then caused all the others to be executed by Federigo, who acquitted himself exceedingly well in that work also. They afterwards painted in company a Frieze in one of the Halls of the Palace at the Ara Cœli; this was a fresco in colours. Now it was about this time that the treaty was in progress for giving the Signora Donna Virginia, daughter of the Duke Guidobaldo of Urbino, as a wife to the Signor Federigo Borromeo, when Taddeo was sent for to take the Portrait of the lady, which he did to admiration. Before his departure from Urbino he also prepared all the designs for a Credenza, which Duke Guidobaldo subsequently caused to be made at Castel Durante, and sent to Philip King of Spain.

Returning to Rome, Taddeo presented the portrait of Donna Virginia to the Pope, who was greatly pleased therewith; but such was the discourtesy of the Pontiff, or of his ministers, that the poor artist was not paid even the expenses which he had incurred. In the year 1560, the Pope expected the Signor Duke Cosimo, with the Signora Duchess Leonora his Consort to pay him a visit; and intending to lodge their Excellencies in the rooms which had been erected by Innocent VIII. (and which look on the first Court, as well as on that of San Pietro, having Loggie in front of them, which look on the Court of the Benediction), the care of such pictures and other ornaments as were required for that occasion was given to Taddeo, who was also commissioned to gild the new ceilings by which the old ones, ruined by time, had been replaced. In this certainly great and important work, Federigo, to whom his brother confided almost the entire charge of the same, acquitted himself exceedingly well, but he incurred a great danger in the execution thereof, for, while he was painting grottesche in the above-mentioned Loggia, he fell from a scaffold, and was for some time in danger of losing his life.

No long time after this, the Cardinal Emulio, to whom the Pope had entrusted the care of the matter, commissioned numerous young artists, to the end that the work might be rapidly accomplished, to paint the small Palazzo which is in the wood of the Belvedere, and which was commenced under the Pontificate of Paul IV., being adorned with many ancient Statues and a beautiful Fountain ; the architecture and design by Pirro Ligorio. The young men who worked (to their great honour) in that place, were Federigo Barocci of Urbino, a youth of the highest hopes, with Lionardo Cungi and Durante del Nero, both of Borgo San Sepulcro, who executed the paintings in the rooms of the first floor. The Florentine painter Santi Titi, painted the first room above the spiral staircase, acquitting himself admirably well, and the principal apartment, which is near that just mentioned, was painted by the above-named Federigo Zucchero the brother of Taddeo ; one beyond it being entrusted to the Sclavonian, Giovanni dal Carso, an excellent master of *grottesche*.

But although each of the above-named artists acquitted himself exceedingly well, they were nevertheless all surpassed by Federigo Zucchero in certain Stories which he painted from the Life of Christ : the Transfiguration for example, the Marriage of Cana in Galilee, and the Centurion kneeling before Christ. There were still two Stories remaining, and these were executed, the one by Orazio Sammacchini, a Bolognese painter, and the other by Lorenzo Costa of Mantua. The small Loggia, above the Fish-pond in the same place, was painted by Federigo Zucchero, and he afterwards executed a Frieze in the principal Hall of the Belvedere, that namely which is attained by the spiral staircase, and which exhibits stories of Moses and Pharaoh, which are really beautiful. Of this work Federigo, no long time since, gave the design, drawn and painted by his own hand, to Don Vincenzio Borghini, by whom it is very highly prized as the work of an excellent painter. In the same place this artist also painted the Angel destroying the First-born of Egypt, availing himself of the aid of many assistants, that the work might be the more rapidly finished.

But when the labours above-described were estimated, the toils of Federigo and of the other young men, were not considered, as they ought to have been, seeing that there are many among our artists, whether in Rome, Florence, or elsewhere, who, blinded by envy, will not acknowledge the merits of others, yet are not by any means aware of the defects existing in their own works; but such persons often cause the rising genius of many a youth to be repressed, while they make others cool in their studies and become negligent in their modes of operation.

At a later period Federigo painted two figures larger than life in the Office of the Ruota; these represented Justice and Equity, being used in the manner of supporters to the Arms of Pope Pius IV.: he was very highly commended for this work, and during the time when Federigo was occupied therewith, Taddeo Zucchero was engaged in the completion of his engagement at Caprarola, and was proceeding with the Chapel of San Marcello. His Holiness meanwhile having determined that the Hall of the Kings should by all means be finished, after the many contentions which had arisen respecting it between Daniello and Salviati, as we have related, gave at last a command to the Bishop of Forlì, to the effect that what he desired should be accomplished: the above-mentioned Prelate thereupon wrote to Vasari, (and this was on the 3rd of September, 1561), giving him to know that the Pope, resolving to finish the Hall of Kings, had commanded him, the Bishop, to find men for the same, who should rid his hands once for all of that work. He added that, moved by their ancient friendship and by other causes, he now begged Giorgio to repair without delay to Rome, if he could obtain the good pleasure and permission of the Duke his Lord, seeing that he might thereby give satisfaction to His Holiness, while he secured honour as well as profit to himself. The Bishop requested, moreover, that a reply to this letter might be returned as speedily as possible.

The answer of Vasari was to the effect that he was doing

exceedingly well in the service of the Duke, by whom his labours were remunerated in a manner altogether different to that which he had experienced in Rome and from the Pontiffs. Vasari added, that things being so, he had determined to continue in the service of his Excellency, for whom he was about to commence a much larger Hall than was that of the Kings: he furthermore remarked that, as to the matter in question, the Bishop need suffer no want of men in Rome who were fully capable of serving him. Having received that reply from Vasari, and having conferred respecting the whole matter with His Holiness, it was finally determined that the Cardinal Emulio should undertake the distribution of the work; when it was divided, as has been declared, among numerous young artists, some of whom were already in Rome, while others had to be summoned from other places.

The two principal Stories of the Hall were given to Giuseppe Porta, of Castelnuovo in the Garfagnana, who was a disciple of Salviati; while to Girolamo Sicciolante, of Sermoneta, was also given one large picture with another of smaller size. The Bolognese Orazio Sammacchini likewise received a small story, as did Livio da Forlì,* and the Bolognese Giovan Battista Fiorini,† all which coming to the ears of Taddeo, and he knowing that he had been excluded because the Cardinal Emulio had been told that he thought more of gain than of glory, or of the complete execution of his works, now used all his interest with Cardinal Farnese, to the end that he also might obtain a share of the work. But Farnese, not wishing to take any part in the matter, replied that the labours then in progress at Caprarola might suffice Taddeo for that time, and declared moreover that he did not think his, the Cardinal's, works ought to be neglected on account of the emulation and strife awakened among the artists by that Hall of the Kings. He added, that when works of art were carefully executed, it was those productions that gave name to the place they occupied, not the place that gave a name to them.

Notwithstanding all this, Taddeo pressed the matter so much with the Cardinal Emulio, that he did finally obtain a small picture over one of the doors; but not all his impor-

* This Livio da Forli is our Livio Agresti.

† See Malvasia, *Felsina Pittrice*

tunity, nor any other of the means employed by him, availed to procure him one of the larger stories. And in this respect it has been said that Emulio acted with foresight, since it was at that time his hope that all the other artists were to be surpassed by Giuseppe Salviati, and he was disposed to give him the whole work, nay, even to destroy all that had been done by others, if there should appear to him to be good cause for so doing. But when each of the artists had brought his work towards completion, the Pope desired to see them, and all being given to view he perceived, that Taddeo had acquitted himself better than the rest, when all the Cardinals and the best artists being of the same opinion, His Holiness commanded the Signor Agabrio to cause one of the large pictures to be given by Emulio to that master, for which cause he was entrusted with that end of the Hall in which is the door of the Pauline Chapel. Our artist commenced his work accordingly, but did not finish what he had begun, because, the death of the Pope supervening, that Hall had to be cleared for the Conclave, as we have said, although many of the stories were still unfinished. With respect to that commenced by Taddeo, the design of it, executed by his own hand, and sent to us by himself, is now in our book of drawings.

About the same time, and among other small works, Taddeo painted a very beautiful figure of our Saviour Christ, in a picture which was to be sent to Caprarola, for the Cardinal Farnese, but which is now in the possession of Federigo, who declares that he means to retain it while he lives.* This picture receives its light from weeping Angels, holding torches.† But since we are to speak of the works executed by Taddeo at Caprarola when discoursing of Vignola, by whom the fabric was erected, we will not now say more on that subject.

Federigo had meanwhile been invited to Venice, where he agreed with the Patriarch Grimani to finish the chapel of San Francesco della Vigna, which had remained imperfect, as we have said, at the death of the Venetian Battista Franco. But before commencing his work at the chapel, he

* In the year 1760 this picture was in the possession of the Marquis Vitelleschi.—*Bottari*.

† The work was afterwards copied on a wall of the Chapel at Caprarola, where it serves as the altar-piece.—*Ibid.*

decorated the Staircase of the Patriarchs with small figures placed with infinite grace behind certain ornaments in stucco: this done, he painted two Stories in fresco, that of Lazarus and the Conversion of the Magdalen namely, in the above-mentioned chapel, the designs for which, by the hand of Federigo, we now have in our book.* The Altar-piece for the chapel, which he painted in oil, is an Adoration of the Magi. At a somewhat later period, Federigo executed certain pictures in a Loggia at the Villa of Messer Giovan Battista Pellegrini, which is situate between Monselice and Chioggia, and where Andrea Schiavone has also left many works, as have the Flemings, Lambert and Walther. Those now executed there by Federigo were very highly extolled.

His brother having thus departed, Taddeo continued the frescoes in the Chapel of San Marcello, at which he worked all the summer, and where he finally painted the Altar-piece in oil. The subject chosen was the Conversion of St. Paul; and the Saint, a figure in a very fine manner, is seen fallen from his horse and bewildered at the splendour and voice of Christ, who appears surrounded by a Glory of Angels, and is in the act of uttering the words,—"Saul, Saul, why persecutest thou me?" Those around him are standing, in equal amazement, all looking terrified and confounded by the miracle passing before them. In the ceiling our artist depicted three Stories in fresco from the Life of the same Saint, within certain compartments, formed of stucco-work. One represents St. Paul when, being led prisoner to Rome, he disembarks on the Island of Melita, and the serpent seizes his hand as he is in the act of kindling a fire. In this picture numerous figures of mariners, almost entirely nude, stand around the ship. The second exhibits the miracle of the youth, who, having fallen from the window, and being brought to St. Paul dead, is, through the power of God, restored by him to life. The third presents the beheading and death of the Saint.

The walls beneath are in like manner adorned with two Stories in fresco, one shows St. Paul curing a lame man, the other is a Disputation, wherein the Saint causes a Magician to be struck with blindness, both truly beautiful pictures;

* The first of these Stories only is now in existence, the other has been whitewashed.—*Ed. Venet.*

but these being left unfinished by the death of Taddeo have been completed by Federigo, who has lately given them to view, and that to his no small credit. About the same time Taddeo painted certain pictures in oil, which were sent into France by the Ambassador of the French King.

The death of Francesco Salviati having caused the smaller Hall of the Farnese palace to remain unfinished, wanting two Stories that is to say at the entrance, which is opposite to the great window, the Cardinal Sant' Agnolo Farnese gave the commission for the work to Taddeo, who conducted it very successfully to its conclusion, although he did not surpass Francesco, nor indeed did he equal that master in the paintings of the apartment in question, as certain envious and malignant persons have gone about Rome affirming that he has done, with the hope of diminishing the glory of Salviati by their calumnies. Taddeo indeed, made efforts to excuse himself for not having done better in that work, by declaring that it had been painted principally by his disciples, and that the only part executed by his own hand was the design, with some few other portions; but these excuses were not accepted, for in so manifest a rivalry no man will entrust the credit of his art and reputation to weaker and less capable hands than his own, since that would be to incur a certain defeat.

It was now that the Cardinal Sant' Agnolo, a man of a truly profound judgment in all things, and of the most admirable goodness,—it was now I say, that he perceived the extent of the loss incurred by the death of Salviati; for although the latter was proud, obstinate, and ill-tempered, he was truly excellent in all things appertaining to his art. Finding, nevertheless that the best artists were now almost wholly wanting in Rome, the Prelate determined at length, and as there were no others, to give the commission for painting that Hall to Taddeo, who accepted it gladly, proposing therein to give evidence, by every effort he could make, of the ability and knowledge which he possessed.

Now the Florentine Lorenzo Pucci, Cardinal Santi Quattro, had caused a chapel to be constructed in the Church of the Trinità, and here Perino del Vaga had painted the ceiling, with figures of Prophets and two Boys, who supported the Arms of that Cardinal, on the outside of the Chapel. But the work being still incomplete, three sides of the Chapel remaining to be painted, the Fathers sold the same to the Archbishop of Corfu at the death of the Cardinal, and without having any regard to what was just and reasonable in the matter; when the commission for the pictures still wanting was given by that Archbishop to Taddeo Zucchero. It may be true that, from respect to the Church and from other causes, it would have been well done to find means for completing the chapel, but the Fathers ought not to have consented that in the part already finished the Arms of the Cardinal should be removed for the purpose of substituting those of the Archbishop, seeing that these last might easily have been placed in some other position, without offering so manifest an injury to the respected memory of that excellent Cardinal Santi Quattro.

Finding that he had so many works on hand, Taddeo now daily urged the return of Federigo from Venice, where the latter, after having finished the Chapel of the Patriarch, was on the point of making an agreement to paint the principal façade in the Hall of the Grand Council, wherein Antonio Veneziano had formerly laboured. But the rivalry and contentions, established on this occasion by the painters of Venice, prevented Federigo from receiving that commission; while at the same time those painters did not secure it for themselves, notwithstanding the favours which they had taken pains to seek, in the hope of obtaining it.

Meanwhile Taddeo, had a great wish to visit Florence, and see the numerous works which he understood to be there in progress for Duke Cosimo, more especially the commencement of the Great Hall, at which his friend Giorgio Vasari* was then labouring. Wherefore he gave out that he was going to Caprarola, to look after the work he was engaged in there; but on the Festival of San Giovanni he arrived at Florence in company with the young sculptor and architect, Tiberio Calsagni, who was a native of that city. Here, to say nothing of Florence itself, which pleased him greatly, Taddeo Zucchero was infinitely delighted with the works of the many excellent sculptors and painters to be found there, ancient as well as modern; he was so much interested moreover by the numerous undertakings at that time in progress,

* "Against this passage," says Bottari, "Federigo has written '*false friend and malignant detractor*;' a description which applies admirably to himself."

that he would gladly have remained there several months. He then saw the arrangements and preparations of Vasari for the decoration of the above-mentioned Hall; forty-four large pictures namely, of four, six, seven, and ten braccia each, and in which Giorgio was executing figures, the greater part whereof were six and eight braccia high, all of them executed in less than a year; although he had no other aid than that of the Fleming Giovanni Strada and Jacopi Zucchi, who were his disciples, with the exception of some which he obtained from Battista Naldini, and these works being thus seen by Taddeo gave him great pleasure, and inspired him with new courage. He then returned to Rome and set hand to the Chapel of the Trinità, with the determination to surpass himself in the Stories of Our Lady, which were to be painted there, as we shall presently relate.

Now Federigo, although much entreated to leave Venice and return to Rome, could not refuse himself the pleasure of passing the Carnival then approaching, in the first-mentioned city, and in company with the architect Andrea Palladio. The latter had just completed an uncovered Theatre in woo , after the manner of the Colosseum, for the Signori of the Company of the Calza, and wherein there was to be performed a tragic drama; Palladio therefore caused Federigo to prepare twelve large pictures, each of seven feet and a half square, for the scenic decoration of the same; these pictures exhibited numerous events from the Life of Hyrcanus, King of Jerusalem, as the subject of the drama demanded, and in this work Federigo acquired great credit for the rapidity with which he had executed his work, as well as for the excellence of the same. At a later period, and when Palladio had gone into Friuli, there to found the Palace of Civitale, of which he had already prepared the model, Federigo also journeyed thither, for the purpose of visiting that district; in which he copied or designed many of the works which had pleased him.

Finally, and after having seen many things in Verona, as well as in other cities of Lombardy, Federigo came to Florence, arriving exactly at the time when the richest and most beautiful works were in progress, as a preparation for the arrival of the Queen Joanna of Austria. It was then the pleasure of the Signor Duke that he should paint a singularly fanciful picture of a Hunt on a large piece of canvas, which covered the scene at the head of the Hall; this was in colours, but Federigo also executed certain pictures in chiaro-scuro, all which gave infinite satisfaction. Having then proceeded from Florence to Sant' Agnolo, for the purpose of revisiting his friends and relations, Federigo at length departed for Rome, where he arrived on the 16th of January. But he was not of any great use to Taddeo at that time, seeing that the death of Pope Pius IV. with that of the Cardinal Farnese, had interrupted the works in the Hall of Kings, as well as those of the Farnese Palace; wherefore Taddeo, who had finished another apartment at Caprarola, and almost completed the Chapel of San Marcello, was proceeding, but quite at his leisure, with the Assumption of Our Lady, and the Apostles who are standing around her bier.

In the meantime Taddeo had secured the commission for a Chapel in the Church of the Reformed Priests of Jesus, which was at the Obelisk of San Mauro, to be painted in fresco by Federigo, and to this work the latter instantly addressed himself. The elder brother, meanwhile, feigning to be angry at Federigo's long delay, appeared to be but little moved by his return, although he did in truth rejoice in it greatly, as was afterwards made clearly manifest. It was a vexatious annoyance to Taddeo, for example, to have the cares of a house on his shoulders, and this trouble Federigo had been accustomed to take wholly on himself; the return of the latter, therefore, relieving him as it did from inconveniences of that kind, left him free to give his attention with a quiet mind to his labours. The friends of Taddeo were at that time earnestly advising him to marry, but he, accustomed to a life of freedom, and fearing, what sometimes happens, that together with the wife, he might bring a thousand cares and anxieties into his house, could never resolve on taking that counsel; nay, he now seemed to give himself up wholly to his works at the Trinità, and had not a thought but for the Cartoon which he was preparing for the principal façade, and the subject of which was the Ascent of Our Lady into Heaven.

Federigo was then painting a picture of San Piero in Prison, for the Signor Duke of Urbino* with another, repre-

* This is now in the Pitti Palace

senting Our Lady in Heaven, surrounded by Angels, which was to be sent to Milan, and a third, wherein was a figure intended to signify Opportunity, painted for Perugia. The Cardinal of Farrara had at that time many painters and masters in stucco-work, employed at an exceedingly beautiful Villa, which he has at Tigoli, and he ultimately despatched Federigo thither also, giving him a commission to paint two rooms, one of which is dedicated to Generosity, the other to Fame. Here our artist acquitted himself extremely well, and depicted a great variety of most fanciful and beautiful inventions. That done, he returned to Rome, and resumed his work of the Chapel, which he has now brought to completion, having adorned it with a Choir of Angels hovering in splendour around a figure of the Almighty Father, by whom the Holy Spirit is sent down on the Virgin, who receives the Annunciation from the Angel Gabriel. On each side of the Madonna are three Prophets, larger than life, which are very fine figures.

Taddeo meanwhile continued to labour at the Assumption of Our Lady, which he was painting in fresco at the Trinità, and it might almost have seemed as if he had been impelled by nature to make his utmost efforts for that work, as for the last which he was to accomplish. And of a truth it proved to be the last; he fell ill of a malady which at first seemed to be but of slight importance, merely the result of the great heats experienced that year; yet eventually, it became very serious, and he died in the month of September, 1566. Taddeo had, however, first received the Sacraments of the Church, as a good Christian should; he had moreover taken leave of the greater part of his friends; but these things done, he departed, leaving behind him his brother, Federigo, who was at that time also suffering from illness. Thus in a short time have our arts, but more particularly that of painting, suffered severe losses, seeing that Michelagnolo, Salviati, Daniello, and Taddeo have all been taken from the world.

The works of Taddeo Zucchero give evidence of great boldness, he had a soft and harmonious manner, totally free from the crudeness but too often seen. His compositions were rich, the heads and hands beautiful, and the nude form betrayingn one of the hardness into which some artists fall, while seeking to display their knowledge of anatomy, and comprehension of art. To these persons there not unfrequently happens something similar to that which befell the stranger, who, by his laborious efforts to speak like the Athenians, was discovered, by a mere woman of the people, to be no Athenian.* Taddeo Zucchero coloured also with much grace, and had a light and easy manner of handling; he was richly aided by Nature, but he would sometimes rely too implicitly on that circumstance. He was so anxious to possess something of his own, that for a long time he would accept whatever offered, for the sake of gain; but among the works thus multiplied, there were many—nay, rather an infinite number, well meriting the highest praise: this painter had always numerous disciples and other artists, working at his undertakings, as indeed was indispensable, for without such aid he could not have fulfilled his engagements. He was of a sanguine temperament, hasty, given to anger, and of a somewhat free life; but his aberrations were of no immoderate character, nor did he permit them to offend the public eye: affectionate towards his friends, he was ever ready to aid them, and spared no pains to do so, whenever the opportunity presented itself.

The work of Taddeo Zucchero, at the Trinità, had not been given to view at the time of his death, and the Great Hall of the Farnese Palace also remained unfinished, as did likewise the works of Caprarola; but all these undertakings were left in the hands of Federigo his brother, whom the masters or owners of those places have permitted to complete them, as he may he expected eventually to do; and of a truth Federigo will be no less the heir of the talents than of the property of Taddeo. The latter received sepulture from his brother, in the Ritonda† of Rome, near the Tabernacle, wherein is buried his fellow countryman, Raffaello da Urbino; and certainly they are placed well, one beside the other, seeing that as Raphael died at the age of thirty-seven, and on the same day on which he was born, so also did Taddeo depart this life in his thirty-seventh year, having been born on the first of September, in the year 1529, and dying on the second of the same month, in the year 1566. It is the purpose of Federigo to

* Our readers will not have forgotten the Lesbian Theophrastus, by referring to whom Vasari proposes to reprove the too servile imitators of Michael Angelo; but it is nevertheless certain that he must himself be reckoned among them.

† The Pantheon, that is to say.

repair the other Tabernacle, if he be permitted to do so, and there to erect some memorial to his most affectionate brother, to whom he acknowledges himself to be under infinite obligations.

And now, since I have before made mention of Jacopo Barozzi, of Vignola, and have said that the most Illustrious Cardinal Farnese has had his magnificent, nay, regal Villa of Caprarola built after the designs of that architect, I will not omit to add that this Bolognese painter and architect, who is now in his fifty-eighth year, was placed to study the art of painting in Bologna, during his childhood, and in his youth; but he did not greatly profit, partly because he had not received a right direction at first setting off; but also in part because he was more decidedly disposed to architecture than to painting, as may be seen from the few works which he has executed in painting, as compared with his architectural designs; his inclination to the study of perspective and architecture, was indeed very strong, insomuch that he not only acquired the first principles almost without assistance, but mastered the most subtle difficulties also, in a very short time; many beautiful designs are thus to be found, executed by Jacopo, before he had become known, and principally for Messer Francesco Guicciardini, who was then Governor of Bologna, or for others of his friends: these designs were afterwards executed in tarsia, by the Dominican Fra Damiano da Bergamo.

Having subsequently proceeded to Rome, intending to study painting, in the hope that he might thence obtain the means of assisting his poor family, Vignola first worked at the Belvedere, with the Ferrarese Jacopo Melighini, architect to Paul III., for whom he made designs. But there was then in Rome a Society of Nobles and Gentlemen, who met for the purpose of reading Vitruvius, and by these—among whom was Marcello Cervini (afterwards Pope), Monsignor Maffei, Alessandro Manzuoli, and others,—Vignola was subsequently employed to take measurements of all the Roman antiquities, and to execute other works under their direction, from all which he gained profit as well as practice in art. The Bolognese painter, Francesco Primaticcio, had meanwhile arrived in Rome, and by him also Barozzi was much employed in modelling a great part of the Roman Antiquities, the moulds of which were sent into France, where statues in bronze, resembling those of the antique, were afterwards cast from the same. These preparations completed, Primaticcio returned to France, taking Vignola with him, and employing him in architectural works, as well as in the casting of the bronze statues above-mentioned, all of which Barozzi did with much diligence and good judgment.

Two years later our artist returned to Bologna (as he had promised the Count Filippo Pepoli that he would do), there to work at the fabric of San Petronio. But here he consumed several years in disputes with his competitors, without having done anything, with the exception of the Canal which was constructed after his designs, and by means of which the vessels, which previously could not come within three miles of Bologna, were enabled to enter the city. Nor has a more useful or more praiseworthy undertaking than is this Canal ever been executed, although Vignola, who was the inventor of that work, was but poorly renumerated for his pains.

In the year 1550 Julius III. was elected Pope, when Barozzi, by the intervention of Vasari, was appointed architect to His Holiness, from whom he received charge of the Acqua-Vergine, and of all the works at the Vigna of the Pope, His Holiness receiving Vignola into his service all the more readily, as he had known him when he, Julius, was Legate at Bologna. In these works for the Pontiff, Barozzi underwent great fatigues, but was as before very poorly remunerated. At length his abilities were made known to the Cardinal Farnese, by whom he was ever afterwards greatly favoured, and who would have everything in his Palace of Caprarola, arranged after his designs and invention. Nor was the judgment of the Prelate in selecting so good an architect, less remarkable than his greatness of mind in constructing so noble and magnificent an edifice, which is not indeed in a position to be much enjoyed by the public, being in a remote and solitary district, but is nevertheless admirably placed for one who desires to escape for a time from the toils and vexations of cities.*

This edifice has the form of a pentagon; it is divided

* The paintings in the Farnese Palace at Caprarola were published in Rome by G. Prenner, in the year 1748. The work consists of thirty-six copper-plate engravings, the subjects being events from the lives of the most illustrious members of the Farnese family.

into four parts, exclusive of the principal front wherein is the great door; behind which is a Loggia eighty palms long by forty broad, and at one end of the same is a spiral staircase the steps of which are ten palms in width, while the space in the centre, which gives light to the whole, is of twenty palms. This spiral stair ascends from the ground to the third or uppermost floor, it is supported on double columns, and adorned with rich and varied cornices: at the lower end we have the Doric Order which is followed successively by the Ionic, Corinthian, and Composite, all richly decorated with balustrades, niches, and other fanciful ornaments which render it very graceful and beautiful.

Opposite to this Staircase and on the other side of the entrance, is a range of rooms commencing with a circular vestibule of size equal to that of the Staircase, and leading to a Hall on the ground floor, eighty palms long and forty broad. This is called the Hall of Jupiter, and is adorned with stucco-work and painted with Stories of Jupiter, his birth that is to say, and his infancy, when nursed by the Goat Amalthea; the coronation of the latter is added, with two other stories, one on each side of these, showing Amalthea received among the number of the Celestial Signs in one, and in the other a story of the same Goat, both of which allude, as do the others, to the name of that Palace, Caprarola. The walls of this apartment are furthermore decorated with perspective views of buildings drawn by Vignola and painted by his son-in-law; they are very beautiful, and cause the Hall to appear much larger than it is. This room is succeeded by one of forty palms only, which is likewise adorned with stucco-work and paintings, all referring to the Spring. From this room and turning the angle towards the apex of the Pentagon, where a Tower has been commenced, we proceed to three large rooms each forty palms long and thirty wide. In the first of these are stucco-work and paintings to intimate the Summer; in the second is depicted the Autumn; and the third, which is sheltered from the north, is adorned in like manner with paintings and stucco-work symbolical of the Winter.

We have hitherto spoken of that half of this pentagonal edifice which is on the right, and immediately over the basement of the building wherein are the kitchens, cellars, larders, offices for the servants, and so forth; we have now to remark that on the opposite or left hand are the same number of rooms of a similar size. Within the five angles of the Pentagon, Vignola has constructed a circular court into which there come the external doors of all the apartments in the building, and these doors all open into a circular Loggia or Gallery eighteen palms broad. This Loggia passes around the Court, the diameter whereof is ninety-five palms five inches. The pilasters of the Loggia, between which are niches, and which support the arches and vaulting, occupy fifteen palms for each couple with its central niche; and the space between the arches is also of fifteen palms. From this Loggia the ascent is by four spiral staircases, reaching from the foundation of the building to its summit, to the great convenience of the Palace. There are also reservoirs for collecting the rain water, and in the centre is a very large and handsome cistern, to say nothing of the windows, and other conveniences which make this building appear, as it is, a most beautiful and commodious edifice. The villa, which is approached by steps of an oval shape, holds the position, and has the form of a Fortress; it is surrounded by a ditch and draw-bridges of original invention and new form, these lead into gardens enriched with many beautiful fountains, mingled with shrubberies and parterres of most pleasing effect, and adorned, at a word, with all that could be demanded by a truly regal Palace.

We now ascend the great winding staircase from the court to the apartments above it, and here we find rooms of equal number with those below; there is also a chapel which stands opposite to the principal staircase. In the Hall, which is over that of Jupiter and of the same size, are rich ornaments in stucco by the hand of Taddeo and his disciples, with paintings by the same, all relating to the illustrious men of the House of Farnese. The ceiling is divided into six compartments, which enclose paintings, four of a square and two of a round form, these are in immediate contact with the cornice which surrounds the Hall, and in the centre of them are three oval pictures with a parallelogram divided into two small squares, in one of which is depicted the figure of Fame, in the other that of Bellona. In the first of the three ovals, meanwhile, there is the figure of Peace; that in the centre exhibits the ancient Arms of the House of Farnese, with the Casque, which is surmounted by a

Unicorn; in the third oval is a figure representing Religion.

Of the six stories abovementioned, the first represents Guido Farnese surrounded by numerous figures, all well executed; beneath it is the following inscription:—

*Guido Farnesius urbis veteris principatum civibus ipsis deferentibus adeptus, laboranti intestinis discordiis civitati, seditiosa factione ejecta, pacem et tranqillitatem restituit anno* 1323.

In a long square is the figure of Pietro Niccolò Farnese, the liberator of Bologna, the inscription beneath which is as follows:—

*Petrus Nicolaus sedis Romanæ potentissimis hostibus memorabili prælio superatis, imminenti obsidionis periculo Bononiam liberat, anno salutis* 1361.

The square next to this shows Piero Farnese, when made Captain General of the Florentines, the inscription being as follows:—

*Petrus Farnesius reip. Florentinæ imperator magnis Pisanorum copiis capto duce obsidionis occisis urbem Florentiam triumphans ingreditur, anno* 1362.

In the circular picture opposite to that before-described is another Pietro Farnese, who defeats the enemies of the Roman Church at Orbatello; this also has its appropriate inscription. In one of the two other squares, which are of equal size, is the Signor Ranieri Farnese elected Captain-general of the Florentines in the place of the Signor Pietro his brother, with this inscription:—

*Rainerius Farnesius a Florentinis difficili reip. tempore in Petri fratris mortui locum copiarum omnium dux deligitur, anno* 1362.

And in the remaining square is Ranuccio Farnesi appointed General of the Church by Pope Eugenius IV., with the inscription which follows:—

*Ranutius Farnesius Pauli III. papæ avus Eugenio 4 P. M. rosæ aureæ munere insignitus pontificii exercitus imperator constituitur, anno Christi* 1435.

In addition to these Stories, the whole ceiling is filled with most beautiful figures, to say nothing of the stucco-work, gilding, and other ornaments. The walls beneath have eight pictures, two on each. In the first, which is at the right of the entrance, is Pope Julius III. confirming the Duke Ottavio, and the Prince, his son, in the possession of Parma and Placentia, which he does in the presence of the Cardinal Farnese; in that of Sant' Agnolo, his brother; the Chamberlain, Santa Fiore; the elder Salviati, Chieti, Carpi, Polo, and Morone, all of whom are portrayed from nature, are likewise present. Beneath them is the following inscription:—*

*Julius III. P. M. Alexandro Farnesio auctore Octavio Farnesio eius fratri Parmam amissam restituit, anno salutis* 1550.

In the second Picture is Cardinal Farnese, making his Entry into the City of Worms, as Legate to the Emperor Charles V., who is coming forth, together with the Prince, his son, to meet the Prelate. His Majesty is attended by a large number of his Barons, and with them is the King of the Romans. On the wall to the left of the entrance, the first story exhibits the war undertaken in Germany against the Lutherans, in the year 1546, when the Duke Ottavio Farnes was Legate; this also has its inscription. The second, on this side, has the Cardinal Farnese, with the Emperor and his Sons; they are all four under a Canopy, which is borne by figures, each one a portrait from the life, and among them is that of Taddeo, the artist of the work. There are besides many Barons and other Nobles in this picture. On one of the two façades at the end of the Hall are two Pictures, between which is an oval compartment containing the portrait of King Philip, with the following inscription:—

*Philippo Hispaniarum regi maximo ob eximia in domum Farnesiam merita.*

Of the two Stories above-mentioned, one presents the Duke Ottavio espousing Madama Margherita, and has Pope Paul III. in the centre: in this picture there are the portraits of Cardinal Farnese the younger; Cardinal di Carpi; the Duke Pier Luigi; Messer Durante; Eurialo da Cingoli; Giovanni Riccio, of Montepulciano; the Bishop of Como; the Signora Livia Colonna; Claudia Mancina; Settimia; and Donna Maria de Mendoza. The second picture exhibits the Duke Orazio taking to Wife the Daughter of King Henry of France, with the inscription which follows:—

*Henricus II. Valesius Galliæ rex Horatio Farnesio Castri duci Dianam filiam in matrimonium collocat, anno salutis* 1552.

In this Story, beside the portrait of Diana the Bride, who wears the regal mantle, and of her husband, Ottavio, there are those of the Queen, Catherine de' Medici; of Margaret, the King's Sister; of the King of Navarre; the Constable; the Dukes of Guise and Nemours; the Prince of Condè,

* This story is not given in the work of Prenner above cited.

Admiral of France; and the younger Cardinal of Lorraine; with those of another Guise who had not then been made a Cardinal; of the Signor Piero Strozzi; of Madame de Montpensier; and of Mademoiselle de Rohan.

The end of the Hall opposite to this, has in like manner two Stories, with an oval compartment between them; and in this Oval is the portrait of Henry King of France, with the following inscription:—

*Henrico Francorum regi max. familiæ Farnesiæ conservatori.*

In one of the Stories, that to the right, namely, Pope Paul III. invests the Duke Orazio, who is kneeling before him, with a sacerdotal Robe, and makes him Prefect of Rome; the Duke Pier Luigi, and other Nobles, stand around. The inscription is as follows:—

*Paulus III. P. M. Horatium Farnesium nepotem summæ spei adolescentem præfectum urbis creat. anno sal.* 1549.

Here also are numerous Portraits, the Cardinal of Paris,* for example, with Visco, Morone, Badia, Trento,† Sfondrato, and Ardinghelli. Beside this Story is that which represents the same Pope Paul conferring the Baton of General on Pier Luigi and his Sons, who were not yet Cardinals. We have here the following portraits: the Pope; Pier Luigi Farnese; the Chamberlain; the Duke Ottavio; Orazio, Cardinal of Capua; Simonetta; Jacobaccio; San Jacopo; Ferrara; the Signor Ranuccio Farnese, who was then a youth; Giovio; Molza, and Marcello Cervini, who was afterwards Pope; the Marquis of Marignano; the Signor Giovan Battista Castaldo; Alessandro Vitelli, and the Signor Giovan Battista Savelli, are likewise portrayed from the life in this work.

We now come to the smaller Hall, that namely which is above the Hall of Spring, and the ceiling of which is richly adorned with stucco-work and gilding; in the centre is the Coronation of Paul III., with four compartments forming a Cross, and bearing the following inscription:—

*Paulus III. Farnesius pontifex maximus Deo et hominibus approbantibus sacra tiara solemni ritu coronatur, anno salutis* 1534, *iij. Non. Novemb.*

Four Stories complete the decoration; in the first, the Pope confers his benediction on the Galleys which departed in the

* The Cardinal Jean Bellay, Archbishop of Paris, that is to say.—*Bottari.*

† The Cardinal Cristofano Madruzio, Bishop and Prince of Trent.—*Ibid.*

year 1535, from Civitavecchia to attack Tunis. In the second, the same Pope excommunicates the King of England; this happened in 1537, and the picture is accompanied by an appropriate epitaph. In the third are the Galleys which the Emperor and the Venetians, with the sanction and assistance of the Pope, despatched against the Turks in the year 1538. The fourth exhibits the people of Perugia, entreating pardon from the Church, after having rebelled against it, in the year 1540. The walls of this room exhibit four large Stories, one on each wall; between them are the windows and doors. The first of these pictures represents the great Emperor Charles V., who, returning victorious from Tunis, kisses the feet of Pope Paul—of the Farnese family; this happened at Rome in the year 1535. In the second is the same Pope at Busetto, where he makes peace between Charles V. and Francis I. King of France, an event which took place in 1538. The portraits in this work are*—the elder Bourbon; the Kings Francis and Henry; the elder Lorenzo; Cardinal Tournon; the younger Bourbon; and two sons of King Francis. In the third, Pope Paul makes the Cardinal di Monte, Legate to the Council of Trent, and in this also there are numerous portraits. The last picture, which is between the two windows, has the same Pontiff, who, in preparation for the Council, elects a certain number of Cardinals, among whom are four, who afterwards successively occupied the Papal throne, Julius III. namely, Marcellus, Paul IV., and Pius IV. To say all at a word, this room is adorned with every embellishment best calculated to enrich such an apartment.

The first chamber beside the Hall above-described, and which is a dressing room, is also richly decorated with stucco-work and gilding; in the centre is a Sacrifice with three nude figures, and one of Alexander the Great, who casts vestments of furs upon the fire. There are many other Stories in the same place, some of them exhibiting the discovery of textures for clothing from vegetable substances, but to describe them fully would lead us too far. From this room we enter a bed-room, for which Taddeo, when about to paint it, received the following directions from the Commen-

* Bottari informs us that the re-touching which these works had undergone had greatly injured them at the time when he wrote, 1759–61, *circa*.

ator Annibale Caro, who furnished them by commision
om the Cardinal.

"The subjects," observes Annibale, "which the Cardinal
as commanded me to give for the paintings of his Palace
f Caprarola, cannot be rendered sufficiently intelligible in
ords, wherefore I propose to describe them as briefly as I
an on paper; and first, for the room with a level ceiling
he only one of which I have yet received the charge), it
ppears to me that, since it is the bed-chamber of his most
lustrious Lordship, there should here be executed subjects
ppropriate to the place, and also out of the common way,
hether as regards the invention or workmanship. And
rst, to express my idea generally, I would have Night
ere, seeing that this subject, being both appropriate and
ncommon, would be different from those in the other rooms;
would also afford you an opportunity for executing many
eautiful and extraordinary specimens of your art, and the
ather, as strong lights and deep shadows are wont to give
uch relief and effect to the figures. The time of this
Tight I would have approaching the Dawn, since the
isibility of the objects represented would thus be probable;
ut before descending to the particulars of these objects,
re must first consider the situation and divisions of the
hamber.

"Let us suppose it then to be divided (as it is) into a
eiling and walls; the first has a concave oval in the centre,
rith four large corbels in the angles; between the corbels
re four lunettes, and if we now give its name to each of the
arts, according to the division which we shall make of the
vhole chamber, we can then more readily distinguish every
art. Let us then divide these parts into five; the first
hall be 'the head,' and this we will suppose to be towards
he Garden; the second, or opposite to this, we will call 'the
oot,' the third, 'the right,' and the fourth, 'the left;' the
ifth part, which we will suppose to be amidst all these, shall
e called 'the centre.' We shall thus be able to distinguish
very part by its name. We will also determine the place
n the floor which should be occupied by the bed, and this,
s I think, should be along the wall at 'the foot,' with its
head towards 'the left.' Having thus named all the parts,
we will first give directions for the work generally, and then
for each point in particular. The oval concave of the ceiling

shall represent Heaven (as the Cardinal has judiciously decided); the remainder of the vaulting shall appear as if not separated from the rest of the chamber, but shall be adorned with fine architectural ornaments, which you will devise. The four lunettes I would have also appear to be concave; and since the oval represents Heaven, these shall represent Air, Earth, and Sea, as though these were seen *beyond* the chamber by those *within* it. But since the ceiling is not a lofty one, and the lunettes are too small to contain any but minute figures, I would have each divided longitudinally into three parts, suffering the outermost part to continue in the line of the corbels, and deepening the centre beneath that line, in such sort that this should appear to be a high window, through which figures and stories of correctly proportioned size should appear as if seen, as I have said above, on the outside of the room by those within it. The two extremities of the lunettes (which we will henceforth call their Horns), shall remain level, and on each of them shall be a figure seated or recumbent, and seeming to be either inside or outside of the room, as you shall find advisable.

"And now, to speak again of the chamber as a whole, I would say that I think it ought to be somewhat obscure in itself and receive no light but from the concave oval and the lunettes: the light that is to say being partly from the celestial bodies, and partly from the fires of the earth, which shall be made as I will describe hereafter. I would also have you to observe, that from the half of the room downwards I wish the obscurity to increase in proportion as you approach 'the foot,' where the Night shall be: as also of the upper half, in proportion as you approach 'the head,' or where the Aurora shall be, so is all gradually to become clearer and clearer.

"Having thus disposed of the whole, let us now consider the parts, giving to each its due place. In the oval of the ceiling there shall be made the Aurora at 'the head'—as I have said; and I find that this may be done in many ways; but I select that which appears to me the most graceful for painting. Let there be figured then, a maiden of such beauty as the poets labour to express by their words, composing her of roses, of gold, of purple, of dew, and of such like charms of colour and complexion. As to her vestments, we have to consider, if out of many we would select the most suitable, that, as this maiden has three seasons and three distinct colours, so also has she three different names; Alba (white), Vermiglia (red), and Rancia (orange). This justly weighed, I would make her a vest to the girdle that should be of a clear white and very slight texture, nay, as it were transparent: from the girdle to the knee, she should have a tunic of scarlet, with knobs and escaloped edges to imitate the reflections which are seen in the clouds, when the dawn is of an empurpled colour. From the knee to the foot, her vestment should be of a golden tint, to represent the day-break, when it has become orange. But I warn you that these vestments must be open from above the knee downwards, that they may show the nude limbs; and the vest as well as tunic, must be moved by the wind, forming folds and waving about. The arms must be naked and rosy; fair coloured wings must rise from the shoulders; on the head must be a crown of roses, and in the hands a lamp or lighted torch, or perhaps it were better to let a Cupid bearing a torch go before her, while another coming after her shall awaken Tithon with his torch. She must be seated on a golden seat in a chariot, also gilded, and drawn by a winged Pegasus or by two horses, for she is depicted in both ways. The colours of the horses must be, one a shining white, the other a radiant red, to denote the names given to them by Homer of Lampos and Phæton. She shall be represented as rising from a tranquil Sea, which shall appear to be rippled, luminous, and glancing. In the right horn of the lunette, on the wall behind her, shall be Tithon her husband, and in the left horn of the same shall be Cephalus her lover. The first a gray-beard reclining on a golden bed, or better still, lying in a cradle, as one who from extreme age has returned to childhood, and let his attitude be that of one who would gladly retain Aurora, and who looks after her as if her departure grieved him. But let Cephalus be a most beautiful youth, wearing a short doublet, and with half-boots on his feet; he shall have a javelin with a gilded point in his hand, and with his dog beside him shall be about to enter a grove, as not caring for Aurora, because of the love which he bears to his Procris.

Between Cephalus and Tithon, in the window of the lunette behind Aurora, there shall be seen to appear some few rays of the Sun exhibiting a splendour more radiant than that of Aurora, but these shall be partly hidden by a large Woman, who shall appear before them: this woman is to signify Vigilance, and must be presented in such sort that she shall appear to be illumined from behind by the rising Sun; and as it is her purpose to anticipate him, she shall seem to be hurrying through the window and into the chamber. Her form shall be that of a tall, active, and powerful woman; her eyes shall be well opened, and her brows arched; she shall be clothed to her feet in a transparent vest, bound round her at the waist; with one hand she is to rest on a spear, and with the other she may gather up the folds of her vest: let her stand firmly on the right foot, and holding the left suspended, let her thus appear to move with a prompt yet firm step. She shall raise her head as if to look at Aurora, and shall appear to be indignant that the latter has risen before her. On her head she shall bear a helmet surmounted by a Cock, which shall be crowing and clapping his wings. All this shall appear to be behind Aurora. But before her, in the sky of the concave oval that is to say, you shall make little figures of Maidens one behind another, and some of them being more in shadow, while others are less so, according as they shall be nearer to or farther from Aurora: these are to signify the Hours which precede her and the Sun. These Hours shall have the vestments and garlands of Virgins; they shall be winged, and have their hands filled with flowers, as if they were scattering the same.

"On the opposite side shall be Night, and as Aurora rises, so must Night descend; as the one shows her face must the other turn her back; let the first rise from a tranquil sea, while the other must sink into a cloudy and troubled deep. The horses of Aurora must advance; those of Night must be departing. At a word, the whole presentment of the latter must differ from that of Aurora. Her complexion dark, her mantle and horses black, as also shall her wings be, and these last must be open, as if she were flying. Her hands shall be borne aloft, and in the one she shall hold an infant sleeping, which shall be white to signify Sleep; while in the other she shall have a black child, also asleep, to signify Death, because Night is said to be the mother of both. She shall appear to be sinking with the head foremost into shadows that must be constantly deepening; and the heavens around her shall be thickly strewn with stars. Her chariot shall be of bronze, with the wheels divided into four spaces, to intimate the four watches of the night. And as, in the wall behind her, Aurora has Tiphon and Cephalus, so shall Night have Oceanus and Atlas. The first shall be on the right, and shall be represented by a large and powerful man, with hair and beard dishevelled and streaming; while from both there shall proceed the heads of dolphins, which shall also compose his head-dress, with the addition of sea-weed, shells, corals, and other marine products; he shall repose on a chariot drawn by whales. Tritons shall precede him with their trumpets. Sea-nymphs shall surround his car; and monsters of the deep shall follow him. Or, if not all these things, then as many of them as may be permitted by your space, which appears to me but little for such a purpose.

"The Atlàs, which shall be on the left of Night, you shall represent as a Mountain, with the breast, arms, and all the upper part of the body, that of a strong, muscular, bearded man, in the act of supporting the Heavens, which is his usual attitude. Lower down, and opposite to the Vigilance which we have placed beneath Aurora, should be Sleep; but as, for certain reasons, it appears to me that Sleep should be reserved for the bed, we will here place Repose, and the rather as I find that Repose has been adored, and has had a temple dedicated to her, but I do not find the form in which she is presented, unless indeed it be that of Security. Yet I think it is not so, seeing that Security is of the mind, and Repose of the body. Let us then make our Repose in the figure of a maiden, mild of aspect, and not recumbent, but seated, as one weary and dozing, with her head supported by the left arm. Let her have a spear leaning against her shoulder, but with its lower end on the earth, and let her right arm hang freely along the staff; one leg must be crossed over the other, but let her attitude be that of one who is reposing for the restoration of her strength, not from idleness. She shall have a crown of poppies, and a sceptre, which shall be at some distance from her, but yet only so as that she may resume it readily; and as Vigilance bears a crowing Cock on her head, so shall our Repose have a brooding Hen, to show that she is in her duty even while at rest.

"Within the central oval and to the right hand, there shall be a figure of the Moon, represented as a maiden of eighteen, tall, and of a virginal aspect, not unlike that of the Apollo. Her hair shall be long, thick, and slightly waving; or she shall have the Phrygian cap on her head, with two wings on it, which shall be placed towards the front, and fall over the ears. There shall also be two small horns on the front, like those of the crescent moon; or, according to Apuleius, she should have a small polished mirror on her brow, with serpents at certain distances, and a few ears of corn on the upper edge. Her coronal shall be of dittany, according to the Greeks; or, according to Martianus, of varied flowers; nay, as some will have it, of helichrymum. There are some who would have her clothed in a vesture that should reach even to her feet, others will have it shortened to the knee, and there are who will have a cincture at the waist, and the vestment crossed beneath the girdle, after the manner of the Nymphs. Her mantle shall be clasped on the shoulder, and she shall have buskins neatly decorated. Pausanias, alluding, as I think, to Diana, clothes her with the skin of the deer; but Apuleius, taking her perchance for Isis, gives her a slight veil of many colours, white, yellow, and red, with a second vesture, wholly black, yet clear and shining; he sprinkles it, moreover, with stars, placing the moon in the centre of them, and adorning the edge with fruits and flowers, pendent in the manner of a knotted fringe. You may take either of these habits at your pleasure. Let her arms be naked, or with large sleeves; place a lighted torch in her right hand, and in her left a drawn bow, which last Claudian declares to be of horn, while Ovid maintains it to be of gold: make it which you please, but fail not to fix the quiver on her shoulders. Pausanias also places two serpents in her left hand, but in Apuleius she holds a golden vase, the handles whereof are serpents, which appear to be swollen with venom: the foot of the vase is adorned with palm leaves. But here also, I think, Apuleius must be alluding to Isis, wherefore I would have you give her the bow, as I have said. Let her be mounted on a chariot drawn by horses, of which one shall be black, the other white; or, if you desire variety, by a mule, according to Festus Pompey; or by oxen, according to Claudian and Apuleius; but if you have these last, let their horns be very small, and let them have a white spot on the right side. The attitude of the Moon must be that of one looking from the heaven of the oval towards the horn of the lunette on the garden side, where her lover Endymion must be placed; nay, she shall bend forwards from her chariot as if to embrace him; and not being able to effect this, because of the enclosure, she shall be regarding him tenderly, and enlightening him with her beams.

"For Endymion you must make a beautiful youth, in the garb of a shepherd, and he must be lying asleep at the foot of Mount Latmos. In the second horn of the lunette shall be the god Pan, who is in love with Luna, and whose form is familiar to you. His pipe must be round his neck, and let him extend his hands, wherein there shall be a skein of white wool, toward the Luna; for with this it is feigned that he obtained her love, and by this present he hopes to induce her to descend and dwell with him. The remaining space of the window shall be filled with a Story of the Sacrifices offered at night by the Lemures, who believed that evil spirits were thus driven from their houses. And the rite was performed on this wise; with raised hands and bare feet, they walked round and round, scattering black beans, which they first turned about in their mouths and then cast behind them, striking meanwhile on basins and other instruments of copper, whereby they made a loud noise.

"On the left side of the oval shall be Mercury, in his usual form, with the winged cap and wings at his feet, the caduceus in his right hand, and a purse in his left. He shall be entirely nude, with the exception of the short mantle on his shoulders; his form that of a beautiful youth, but of a simple comeliness, and wholly without art; his countenance cheerful, the eyes very spirited; a slender person, beardless chin, and rosy complexion. Some give him wings at the ears, and make feathers of gold proceed from his hair. Be the attitude at your pleasure, provided you show that he is descending from heaven to bring sleep; and turning towards the bed, let him seem to touch the canopy thereof with his rod.

"Opposite to Mercury place the Lares his sons, the protectors of private dwellings: two youths, namely, clothed with the skins of dogs, but with short vestments thrown over the left shoulder, yet returning under the right arm, to show that they are unencumbered and ready to guard the houses confided to them. Let them be seated beside each other, with spears in their hands, and a dog between them. Above them, let there be a small head of Vulcan wearing a cap, and having the pincers of a smith beside it. In the other horn shall be a Battus turned into stone, for having betrayed the theft of cows committed by Mercury. This must be the figure of an old Shepherd pointing with a finger of the right hand towards the place where the cows were hidden, and leaning with his left arm on a slight wand or rod; from the middle downwards let him be of the black or touch-stone, into which he was converted: let the remainder of the space be occupied by those sacrifices offered to Mercury by the ancients, to the end that they might obtain uninterrupted sleep. To figure these, you must have an Altar, with the Statue of the God thereon; at his feet must be a fire, into which those around are throwing wood for burning; they hold cups of wine in their hands, and of this wine they pour out a part, but the other part they drink.

"In the centre of the Oval (that all the Heaven may be filled), let the Twilight appear, as the medium between the Aurora and the Night; and to signify this, I find that you must make a youth entirely naked (he is sometimes winged and sometimes not); he must have two lighted torches in his hand, one of which he extends towards the Aurora, and the other towards the Night. Some make this youth with the two torches to be riding on a Horse, either of the Sun or of Aurora; but that would not suit our purpose; wherefore we will have him as I say, and turning towards the Night: but beneath his feet shall be a large star, which may be considered that of Venus, seeing that Venus and Phosphor, Hesperus and Twilight, appear to be one and the same; take care, however, that from this figure to the Aurora all the minor stars shall have disappeared.

"We have hitherto spoken of such things as must appear to be outside of the Chamber, we now come to that which is to appear as within it; and first, of the portion above the bed, where we will have Sleep depicted; but to do this, we must first describe the dwelling thereof. This, Ovid places in Lemnos or among the Cimbri; Homer, in the Ægean Sea; Statius, in the country of the Ethiopians; and Ariosto, in Arabia. But wherever the place may be, it shall suffice you to represent a Mountain, of which we are to suppose that a perpetual darkness reigns there and the sun never shines. At the foot of this is to be a deep cavity, through which must pass water, as it were dead and without movement, to show that it does not murmur; or you can make it of a dark colour, because we mean it to signify an arm of the River Lethe. Within this cavity let there be a bed, which, as it is feigned to be of ebony, shall be black, and covered with black draperies. In this bed there shall be laid Sleep or Somnus, a youth of the most perfect beauty; and let this figure be most placid as well as most beautiful. Some will have him nude, others give him two vestments, a black above and a white below. Under his arm he has a horn, from which a dark liquid appears to be poured over the bed, and this denotes Oblivion, although there are who would make it full of fruits. In one hand let him have a wand, in the other three heads of poppies. Let him sleep like one who is sick, with the head and hands falling listlessly, wholly abandoned to a deep slumber. Around his bed let there be Morpheus, Icelus, and Phantasy, with a large number of dreams, for all these are his sons; and these dreams may be minute figures, some of fair aspect, and others hideous, as being things that are in part pleasing and in part afflictive. Let them have wings and turn their feet backward to mark their instability, and to show how inconstant they are. Let these phantoms hover around the bed, making a species of representation or drama, by transforming themselves into things possible and impossible. Morpheus is called by Ovid the artist and inventor of figures, and therefore I would make him in the act of forming masks with all kinds of strange faces, some of which he sets on feet. Icelus is said to transmute himself into various shapes; and him I would represent in such sort that while in the whole he should seem a man, yet should he also exhibit the parts of a wild beast, a bird, and a serpent, as Ovid describes him. Phantasy is also declared to transform himself into all sorts of insensate objects; he too may therefore be depicted as described by Ovid, partly of stone namely, partly of water, and partly of wood. There shall, furthermore, appear to be two doors in this concavity; one of ivory, whence proceed the false dreams; and one of horn, from which issue true ones: the true shall be more distinct, more lucid, and of more correct forms; the false shall be confused, dark, and imperfect or indistinct of outline.

"On the corbel, between the wall at 'the foot' and that at 'the right,' shall be painted Brizzo,* the Goddess of auguries and interpreter of dreams. I do not find her dress depicted, but she may have the form of a Sybil, seated at the foot of the Elm described by Virgil, as concealing innumerable images amidst its leaves, suffering the same to fall from its branches and hover around the Goddess; and these shall be of more or less distinctness, as above said, some darker, some lighter, some broken, and others almost wholly imperceptible, thereby to represent the visions, dreams, oracles, phantoms, and other nonentities, seen while sleeping. These five modes of such appearances are indicated by Macrobius, and Brizzo is to appear absorbed in the care of interpreting them: she must be surrounded by men who offer her baskets filled with every kind of gifts, fish only excepted. On the corbel between the wall of 'the head' and that of 'the right,' may be conveniently placed Harpocrates the God of Silence, seeing that he, being the first object perceived by those who enter the room, will thus warn them to make no noise. The figure of Harpocrates is a youth or boy of a somewhat dusky colour, as being a God of the Egyptians; he must press one finger on his lip to command silence, and may have a branch of the peach-tree in his hand, adding, if you please, a garland of its leaves; they feign that he was born with weak legs, and that having been killed, his mother Isis restored him to life. Some, therefore, paint him extended on the earth; others, lying in the lap of his mother, with his limbs bound up: but I would have him standing up and supported in some fashion, or seated perhaps, as is that one which belongs to the Cardinal Sant' Angelo, and which has wings, with a Cornucopia. He must have figures around him, presenting him, as was the custom, with first fruits of lentils and other vegetables, but more particularly of peaches. Some make this God as a figure without a face, wearing a small cap on the head, and clothed in the skin of a wolf, all covered with eyes and ears. Take whichever of these two you like best.

"On the last corbel, between the wall of 'the head' and

* Brizo (from *βριστιν, slumber*) was the mid-day sleep or the slumber of infants. She made known the future in dreams, and was morre especially worshipped by the women of the Island of Delos, but it was essential that no fish should be offered on her altars.

that of 'the left,' will be appropriately represented Angerona, the Goddess of Secresy, seeing that she will be thus conveniently placed for admonishing all who leave the Chamber to keep whatever they may have heard and seen there secret, as it behoves them to do who serve the great. Her figure is that of a woman placed on an Altar, with the mouth tied and sealed. I know not what vestments are given her, but I would wrap her in one long robe, covering her from head to foot, and fastened on the shoulders. Let there be priests around her, since these were accustomed to offer sacrifice to her in the Curia, to the end that she might prevent all men from betraying, to the injury of the Republic, whatever had passed there.

"There now remains only to add, that I would have the whole work surrounded by a frieze of *grottesche* or Stories of minute figures; the subjects being in harmony with those above described. In the Stories I would have such things exhibited as are done by men, and even by animals, at the hour pre-supposed; thus, as appropriate to the Dawn, I would have artists, mechanics, and workmen of every kind, who, having risen thus early, are about to re-commence their labours. Smiths to their anvils, the learned to their studies, the hunter to the chase, and the muleteer to the road. But, above all, I would here have that little old woman, whom Petrarch describes, as with skirts tucked up and barefoot, she has risen to begin her spinning, and is first lighting her fire. Or, if you like to make *grottesche* of animals, let them be singing-birds, geese going forth to the pasture, cocks announcing the morn, and such like messengers of the day. In the frieze of the wall at 'the foot,' you might make, as in harmony with the darkness, people who go bird-catching by candle-light, spies, adulterers, and rogues who clamber into windows: then for *grottesche* you may take porcupines, hedgehogs, owls, and badgers, with a peacock expanding its tail, which signifies a star-lighted night: also, bats, screech-owls, horned owls, and such like. For the frieze of the right hand wall, as things in harmony with the Moon, you might have fishers of the night, and those who steer by the compass, with necromancers, witches, and such like; for *grottesche*, a distant light-house, nets still wet, and with fish within them, crabs, which seek their food by moonlight, and, if the space permit, an elephant kneeling in adoration of the moon.

"Lastly, on the frieze of the left hand wall you may have mathematicians with their instruments, thieves, coiners, treasure-seekers, shepherds in their still closed folds, lying around their fires, with objects of similar character. For animals, I would have wolves, foxes, apes, lap-dogs, and whatever other creatures of that malicious and traitorous nature there may be found.

"Now in this part I have spoken my thoughts thus at hazard, merely to intimate the kind of inventions that may here be employed; but as none of them need to be more minutely described, I leave you to imagine them at your own pleasure, knowing that painters are by their nature well-endowed and graceful in all such phantasies. Having thus completed the whole work, therefore, I do not think of anything more to say to you, unless it be that you should consult with Monsignore the Cardinal respecting all, arranging everything after his taste, and adding or diminishing as may be required. Seek, also, on your own part, to do yourself honour. Fare you well."

But although these fine inventions of Caro were fanciful and ingenious, Taddeo could but execute such of them as the place would contain. It is, however, true that these were the principal part, and they were completed by him with much grace and in a good manner. Beside the chamber here described, and in the last of the three which is dedicated to Solitude, our artist, with the aid of his assistants, depicted our Saviour Christ, preaching to the Apostles in the deserts and woods: to the right we have San Giovanni, an exceedingly well executed figure. In a Story opposite to this are those hermits who have retired to the wilderness to avoid the conversation of men, some even taking out their own eyes, that they may no more see the world, while others are labouring to disturb them, and some are throwing stones at the hermits. Here also we have the Emperor Charles V., a Portrait from the Life, with the following inscription:—

*Post innumeros labores ociosam quietamque vitam traduxit.*

Opposite to Charles is the Portrait of the last Grand Turk,

who delighted much in solitude, with the inscription which follows :—

*Animum a negocio ad ocium revocavit.*

Near this last is Aristotle, beneath whom are these words :—

*Anima fit sedendo et quiescendo prudentior.*

Opposite to the above and beneath another figure, by the hand of Taddeo, are written the following :—

*Quæ ad modum negocii, sic et ocii ratio habenda.*

Beneath another we find :—

*Ocium cum dignitate. Negocium sine periculo.*

Opposite to which is a figure with the words :—

*Virtutis et liberæ vitæ magistra optimo solitudo.*

Another picture bears the legend :—

*Plus agunt qui nihil agere videntur.*

And the last exhibits the words :—

*Qui agit plurima, plurimum peccat.*

At a word, this chamber is richly adorned with beautiful figures, as well as with stucco-work and gilding.

But to return to Vignola. The many works which he has written and published, or is now writing,* together with the admirable edifices he has constructed, bear ample testimony to his excellence in architecture, but of this we shall speak further in the Life of Michelagnolo. Returning now to Taddeo, we have to relate that he performed many other works in addition to those we have mentioned, but of these it is not needful now to speak. We may nevertheless mention the chapel which he painted in the Church of the Goldsmiths, which is situate on the Strada Giulia, with a façade in chiaro-scuro, which he painted at San Jeronimo, as he did the Chapel of the High Altar in Santa Sabina. Federigo, his brother, was meanwhile employed on a picture of San Lorenzo extended on his gridiron,† which is in the richly decorated chapel of that Saint in the Church of San Lorenzo-in-Damaso. Paradise is seen to open in this painting, which is expected to prove a very fine one. And, that I may not omit anything which can be useful or

* His Treatise on the Five Orders is called by Milizia "L'Abbicci dell' Architettura."

† Not on his gridiron, but in discourse with San Damaso.—*Bottari.*

pleasing to those who shall read this my work, to what I have already said I will add this also: While Taddeo was working, as we have related, at the Vigna of Pope Julius, and at the façade of Mattiolo the Postmaster, he painted two pictures, of no great size, for Monsignore Innocenzio, the most Illustrious Cardinal di Monte; one of these, which is a very beautiful painting, is now in the Guardaroba of the Cardinal, with many other truly admirable works, ancient and modern; the other has been given away: but as regards the works here in question I will not omit to mention a picture which is as fanciful a production as any whereof we have spoken.*

In this painting, which is about two braccia and a half high, nothing is seen by him who regards it from the ordinary point of view, with the exception of certain letters on a scarlet ground, having the Moon in the centre of them; but if you approach the picture and look at it in a mirror, which is placed over the same in the manner of a canopy, you may clearly perceive the Portrait of Henry II., King of France, somewhat larger than life, and as natural as may be; if you lean your brow on the upper part of the frame and look thus at the work, you again see the King, but in the opposite direction to that given by the glass. Nor can this portrait be distinguished unless as thus regarded from above, seeing that it is painted on twenty-eight most slender ridges, which are raised between the lines of the above-mentioned letters. These words, too, have a second meaning besides that which appears at first view. If you look at either extreme of the lines or in the centre you shall find letters of larger size than the others, which altogether make the following inscription:—

*Henricus Valesius Dei gratia Gallorum rex invictissimus.*

Messer Alessandro Taddei, a Roman and secretary to the Cardinal, and my friend Don Silvano Razzi, who have given me information respecting this picture and many other things, assure me that they do not know from what hand it proceeds, but they say that it was given by Henry II. to Cardinal Caraffa, when the latter was in France, and was

* Vasari, who now proceeds to describe these "rarities" of Cardinal Monte's Museum, returns no more to Vignola, but our readers will find that accomplished architect mentioned with due honour by the difficult and, exacting Milizia, *ut supra*

afterwards presented by Caraffa to Cardinal di Monte, by whom it is prized as a remarkable thing, which it is. The words painted in the picture, and which are seen by those who look at it in the ordinary manner, are the following:—

*HEus tu quid viDes nil ut reoR*
*Nisi lunam crEscentem et E*
*Regione pos Itam quæ aX*
*Intervallo. GRadatim utI*
*Crescit nos Admonet ut iN*
*Una spe fide eT charitate tV*
*Simul et ego Illuminat I*
*Verbo Dei crescAmus doneC*
*Ab eiusdem Gratia fiaT*
*Lux in nobis Amplissima quI*
*ESt æternus iLLe dator luciS*
*In quo et a quO mortales omneS*
*Veram lucem Recipere sI*
*Speram^s in vanUM non sperabiM^s*

In the same Guardaroba is a beautiful portrait of Sophonisba Anguisciola, by her own hand, and which had been presented by herself to Pope Julius II. There is also in this collection an exceedingly ancient book, which merits great esteem; it contains the Bucolics, Georgics, and Æneid of Virgil, in characters so old, that many learned men in Rome and elsewhere have judged it to have been written in the time of Cæsar Augustus, or but shortly after, wherefore it is no marvel that the Cardinal should hold it in veneration.*

And this shall be the end of the Life of the painter Taddeo Zucchero.

---

## THE FLORENTINE, MICHELAGNOLO BUONARROTI, PAINTER, SCULPTOR, AND ARCHITECT.

[BORN 1474—DIED 1563.]

WHILE the best and most industrious artists were labouring, by the light of Giotto and his followers, to give the world

* This is the renowned Codice Mediceo, now in the *Biblioteca Laurenziana*. The opinion most common among the learned is that it was written in the fourth century. Towards the middle of the fifth century it was in the possession of the Consul, Tertius Rufus Apronianus Asturius, who has corrected in red ink certain errors in orthography committed by the copyist.

ensamples of such power as the benignity of their stars and the varied character of their fantasies enabled them to command, and while desirous of imitating the perfection of Nature by the excellence of Art, they were struggling to attain that high comprehension which many call intelligence, and were universally toiling, but for the most part in vain, the Ruler of Heaven was pleased to turn the eyes of his clemency towards earth, and perceiving the fruitlessness of so many labours, the ardent studies pursued without any result, and the presumptuous self-sufficiency of men, which is farther from truth than is darkness from light, he resolved, by way of delivering us from such great errors, to send to the world a spirit endowed with universality of power in each art, and in every profession, one capable of showing by himself alone what is the perfection of art in the sketch, the outline, the shadows, or the lights, one who could give relief to Paintings, and with an upright judgment could operate as perfectly in Sculpture; nay, who was so highly accomplished in Architecture also, that he was able to render our habitations secure and commodious, healthy and cheerful, well proportioned, and enriched with the varied ornaments of art.

The Almighty Creator was also pleased to accompany the above with the comprehension of the true Philosophy and the adornment of graceful Poesy, to the end that the world might select and admire in him an extraordinary example of blamelessness in life and every action, as well as of perfection in all his works: insomuch that he might be considered by us to be of a nature rather divine than human. And as the Supreme Ruler perceived that in the execution of all these sublime arts, Painting, Sculpture, and Architecture, the Tuscan genius has ever been raised high above all others, the men of that country displaying more zeal in study, and more constancy in labour, than any other people of Italy, so did he resolve to confer the privilege of his birth on Florence, as worthy above all other cities to be his country, and as justly meriting that the perfections of every art should be exhibited to the world by means of one who should be her citizen.

In the Casentino, therefore, and in the year 1474, a son was born, under a fated and happy star, to the Signor Lodovico di Lionardo Buonarroti Simoni, who as it is said, was descended from the most noble and most ancient family of the Counts of Canossa;* the mother being also a noble as well as excellent lady. Lodovico was that year Podestà, or Mayor of Chiusi-e-Caprese, near the Sasso della Vernia, where St. Francis received the Stigmata, and which is in the diocese of Arezzo. The child was born on a Sunday, the 6th of March namely, at eight of the night, and the name he received was Michelagnolo, because, without further consideration, and inspired by some influence from above, the father thought he perceived something celestial and divine in him beyond what is usual with mortals, as was indeed afterwards inferred from the constellations of his nativity, Mercury and Venus exhibiting a friendly aspect, and being in the second house of Jupiter, which proved that his works of art, whether as conceived in the spirit or performed by hand, would be admirable and stupendous.

His office, or Podesteria, having come to an end, Lodovico returned to Florence, or rather to the Villa of Settignano, about three miles from that city, where he had a farm which he had inherited from his ancestors. The place is rich in stone, more especially in quarries of the *macigno*, which are constantly worked by stone-cutters and sculptors, for the most part natives of the place, and here Michelagnolo was given to the wife of a stone-cutter to be nursed. Wherefore, jesting with Vasari one day, Michelagnolo once said, "Giorgio, if I have anything good in me, that comes from my birth in the pure air of your country of Arezzo, and perhaps also from the fact that with the milk of my nurse, I sucked in the chisels and hammers wherewith I make my figures."

Lodovico had many children, and as he possessed but slender revenues, he placed his sons as they grew up with wool and silk weavers. When Michelagnolo had attained the proper age he was sent to the school of learning kept by Messer Francesco of Urbino; but the genius of the boy disposing him to drawing, he employed his leisure secretly in that occupation, although reproached for it, and sometimes beaten by his father and other elders, they, perhaps, not perceiving his ability, and considering the pursuit he had adopted an inferior one and unworthy of their ancient family.

* See the magnificent work of Count Pompeo Litta, *Le Famiglie celebri Italiane*.

At this time Michelagnolo formed a friendship with Francésco Granacci, who, although also but a boy, had placed himself with Domenico Ghirlandajo to learn the art of painting; and being fond of Michelagnolo, Granacci supplied him daily with the designs of Ghirlandajo, who was then reputed one of the best masters, not in Florence only but through all Italy. The desire of Michelagnolo for art thus increased from day to day, and Ludovico, finding it impossible to divert him from his drawings, determined to try if he could not derive benefit from this inclination, and being advised by certain friends, he decided on placing him with Domenico Ghirlandajo.

Michelagnolo was now fourteen years old. His life has been written * since this book of mine was first published, by one who affirms that, for want of sufficient intercourse with him, many things have been related by me which are not true, and others omitted which should have been told, more especially respecting this point of time; Domenico Ghirlandajo, for example, being accused of base envy by the said writer, and declared to have given Michelagnolo no assistance in his studies. But that this is indeed false may be shown by certain entries which Lodovico the father of Michelagnolo, wrote with his own hand in one of Domenico's books, which book is now in the possession of his heirs: the words in question are these:—"1488, I acknowledge and record, this 1st day of April, that I, Lodovico di Lionardo di Buonarroti have engaged Michelagnolo my son to Domenico and David di Tommaso di Currado, for the three years next to come, under the following conditions: That the said Michelagnolo shall remain with the above-named during all the said time, to the end that they may teach him to paint and to exercise their vocation, and that the above-named shall have full command over him, paying him in the course of these three years twenty-four florins, as wages, in the first six namely, in the second eight, and in the third ten, being in all ninety-six lira." Beneath this entry is the following, also written by Lodovico: "The above-named Michelagnolo has received two florins in gold this sixteenth day of April. I, his father, Lodovico di Lionardo, having received twelve lira and twelve soldi on his account."

These entries I have copied from the book itself, to show

* By Ascanio Condivi, that is to say.

that what I then wrote, as well as what I now propose to write, is the truth, nor do I know any one that has had more intercourse with Michelagnolo than myself, or who has been more truly his friend or a more faithful servant to him than I have been; neither do I believe that any man can show a greater number of letters by his hand than he has written to me, or any written with more affection. This digression I have made for the sake of truth, and it shall suffice for all the rest of the Life. We will now return to the history.

The ability as well as the person of Michelagnolo increased to such an extent, that Domenico was amazed thereat, since it appeared to him that Michelagnolo not only surpassed his other disciples, of whom he had a large number, but even equalled himself, who was the master. One day for example, as one of Domenico's disciples had copied with the pen certain draped female figures by Ghirlandajo, Michelagnolo took that sheet, and with a broader pen he passed over one of those women with new lines drawn in the manner which they ought to have been in order to produce a perfect form. A wonderful thing it was then to see the difference of the two, and to observe the ability and judgment of one who, though so young, had yet so much boldness as to correct the work of his master. This sheet I now keep as a relic, having obtained it from Granacci, to put it in my book of designs with other drawings by Michelagnolo. And in the year 1550, being in Rome, I showed it to Michelagnolo, who knew it at once and was rejoiced to see it again, but remarked out of his modesty, that he knew more when he was a boy than at that time when he had become old.

Now it chanced that when Domenico was painting the great Chapel of Santa Maria Novella, he one day went out, and Michelagnolo then set himself to draw the scaffolding, with some tressels, the various utensils of the art, and some of those young men who were then working there. Domenico having returned and seen the drawing of Michelagnolo, exclaimed, "This boy knows more than I do," standing in amaze at the originality and novelty of manner which the judgment imparted to him by Heaven had enabled a mere child to exhibit; for the work was, in truth, rather such as might have fully satisfied the artist, had it been performed by the hand of an experienced master. But if it was possible to Michelagnolo to effect so much, that happened, because all the gifts of nature were in him enhanced, and strengthened by study and exercise, wherefore he daily produced works of increased excellence, as began clearly to be made manifest in the copy which he made of a plate engraved by the German Martino,* and which procured him a very great name. This engraving was one which had just then been brought to Florence, and represented St. Anthony tormented by devils. It is a copper-plate, and Michelagnolo copied it with a pen, in such a manner as had never before been seen. He painted it in colours also; and, the better to imitate the strange forms of some among those devils, he bought fish which had scales somewhat resembling those on the demons; in this painted copy also he displayed so much ability that his credit and reputation were greatly increased thereby. He likewise copied plates from the hands of many old masters, in such sort that the copies could not be distinguished from the originals, for Michelagnolo had tinged and given the former an appearance of age with smoke and other things, so that he had made them look old, and when they were compared with the original, no difference could be perceived. All this he did, that he might give his own copies in the place of the old works which he desired to possess from the hand of their authors, admiring in them the excellence of art and seeking to surpass them, when engaged in the execution of his own works; by which he acquired a very great name.

Lorenzo the Magnificent retained at that time the Sculptor Bertoldo at his garden on the Piazza, not so much as Curator and Guardian of the many fine antiquities collected there at great cost, as because Lorenzo desired to form a good School of Painters and Sculptors; wherefore he wished that the students should have for their chief and guide the abovenamed Bertoldo, who had been a disciple of Donato. It is true that he was old and could not work, but he was an able and highly reputed artist, not only for the ability and diligence which he had shown in polishing the bronze pulpits of Donato his master, but also for the numerous casts in bronze of battle-pieces and other smaller works, which he had executed for himself, and in the treatment of which there was then no one in Florence who could surpass him.

* Martin Schön, or Schongauer, is the "Martino Tedesco" of our Author.

Having a true love for art, Lorenzo grieved that in his time there should be found no great and noble sculptors who could take rank with the many painters of high fame and merit then existing, and he resolved, as I have said, to form a School. To this end he requested Domenico Ghirlandajo to send to the garden any youth whom he might find disposed to the study of sculpture, when Lorenzo promised to provide for his progress, hoping thus to create, so to speak, such artists as should do honour to his city.

By Domenico, therefore, were presented to him among others, Michelagnolo and Francesco Granacci, as excellent for this purpose. They went to the garden accordingly, and found there Torrigiano, a youth of the Torrigiani family, who was executing in terra certain figures in full relief which Bertoldo had given him. Seeing this, and aroused to emulation, Michelagnolo began to attempt the same; when Lorenzo, perceiving his fine abilities, conceived great hope of his future success, and he, much encouraged, took a piece of marble, after having been there but a few days, and set himself to copy the head of an old Fawn from the antique. The nose of the original was much injured, the mouth was represented laughing, and this Michelagnolo, who had never before touched the chisel or marble, did in fact copy in such a manner, that the Magnifico was utterly amazed. Lorenzo, furthermore, perceived that the youth had departed to a certain extent from the original, having opened the mouth according to his own fancy, so that the tongue and all the teeth were in view; he then remarked in a jesting manner to the boy, "Thou shouldst have remembered that old folks never retain all their teeth, some of them are always wanting." Michelagnolo, who loved that Signore, as much as he respected him, believed in his simplicity that Lorenzo had spoken in earnest, and no sooner saw his back turned than he broke out a tooth, filing the gum in such sort as to make it seem that the tooth had dropped out,* he then waited impatiently the return of the Signor. When the latter saw what was done he was much amazed, and often laughed at the circumstance with his friends, to whom he related it as a marvel, resolving meanwhile to assist Michelagnolo and put him forward.

* Now in the Florentine Gallery, in the Hall of Inscriptions namely.—*Masselli.*

He sent for Lodovico, therefore, requesting the latter to entrust the youth to his care, and saying that he would treat him as a son of his own, to which Lodovico consented gladly; when Lorenzo gave orders that a room in his own house should be prepared for Michelagnolo, and caused him to eat at his own table with his sons and other persons of worth and quality. This was in the second year of Michelagnolo's engagement with Domenico, and when the youth was fifteen or sixteen years old; he remained in the house of Lorenzo the Magnificent four years, to the death of Lorenzo namely, which took place in 1492. During all this time Michelagnolo received from the Magnifico an allowance of five ducats per month, and was furthermore presented for his gratification with a violet-coloured mantle; his father, likewise, had an office in the Customs conferred on him. But indeed all the young men who studied in the garden received stipends of greater or less amount from the liberality of that magnificent and most noble citizen, being constantly encouraged and rewarded by him while he lived.

At this time and by the advice of Politiano, Michelagnolo executed a Battle of Hercules with the Centaurs in a piece of marble given to him by Lorenzo, and which proved to be so beautiful, that whosoever regards this work can scarcely believe it to have been that of a youth, but would rather suppose it the production of an experienced master. It is now in the house of his family,* and is preserved by Michelagnolo's nephew Lionardo, as a memorial of him, and as an admirable production, which it certainly is. Not many years since, this same Lionardo had a basso-rilievo of Our Lady, also by Michelagnolo, and which he kept as a memorial of his uncle; this is of marble and somewhat more than a braccia high; our artist was still but a youth when it was done, and designing to copy the manner of Donatello therein, he has succeeded to such an extent that it might be taken for a work by that master, but exhibits more grace and higher powers of design than he possessed. That basso-rilievo was afterwards given by Lionardo to Duke Cosimo,† by whom it

* The Casa Buonarroti is in the Via Ghibellina, and still belongs to the descendants of the great artist.—*Ed. Flor.*, 1832-8.

† Who subsequently gave it to the younger Michael Angelo, and the latter, constructing a Gallery, which still remains, in his house, adorned the same with paintings, depicting the actions of his great ancestor, at a cost of 20,000 crowns.—*Bottari.*

is highly valued, and the rather as there is no other basso-rilievo by his hand.

But to return to the garden of Lorenzo the Magnificent. Of this place, adorned with valuable antiques and excellent pictures, collected there for study and pleasure, Michelagnolo had the keys, and proved himself more careful as well as more prompt in all his actions than any of the other young men who frequented the place, giving proof of boldness and animation in all that he did. He laboured at the pictures of Massaccio in the Carmine also for many months, copying them with so much judgment that the artists were amazed thereat; but envy now increased with his fame; respecting this we find it related that Torrigiano, having formed an intimacy with Michelagnolo, and becoming envious of his distinction in art, one day, when jeering our artist, struck him so violent a blow in the face that his nose was broken and crushed in a manner from which it could never be recovered, so that he was marked for life; whereupon Torrigiano was banished Florence as we have before related.

On the death of Lorenzo, Michelagnolo returned to his father's house in great sorrow for his loss; here he bought a large piece of marble from which he made a Hercules, four braccia high, which was much admired, and after having remained for some years in the Strozzi Palace, was sent to France, in the year of the siege, by Giovan Battista della Palla. It is said that Piero de' Medici, the heir of Lorenzo, who had been long intimate with Michelagnolo, often sent for him when about to purchase cameos or other antiques; and that, one winter, when much snow fell in Florence, he caused Michelagnolo to make in his court a Statue of Snow, which was exceedingly beautiful.* His father, seeing him thus honoured for his abilities, and beginning to perceive that he was esteemed by the great, now began to clothe him in a more stately manner than he had before done.

For the Church of Santa Spirito, in Florence, Michelagnolo made a Crucifix in wood, which is placed over the lunette of

* Condivi adds that Piero kept him in the Casa Medici, as his father had done, but whereas Lorenzo had given him such men as Politian for his associates, Piero coupled his name with that of a Spanish lacquey, boasting of these two as his most useful domestics. "The calling him to make a statue of snow," remarks Bottari, "was a childish and unworthy action."

the High Altar.* This he did to please the Prior, who had given him a room wherein he dissected many dead bodies, and, zealously studying anatomy, began to give evidence of that perfection to which he afterwards brought his design. Some weeks before the Medici were driven from Florence, Michelagnolo had gone to Bologna, and thence to Venice, having remarked the insolence and bad government of Piero, and fearing that some evil would happen to himself, as a servant of the Medici: but finding no means of existence in Venice, he returned to Bologna, where he had the misfortune to neglect the countersign, which it was needful to take at the gate, if one desired to go out again; Messer Giovanni Bentivogli having then commanded that all strangers, who had not this protection, should be fined fifty Bolognese lira.† This fine Michelagnolo had no means of paying, but he having, by chance, been seen by Messer Giovan Francesco Aldovrandi, one of the sixteen members of the government, the latter, making him tell his story, delivered him from that peril, and kept him in his own house for more than a year.‡ One day, Aldovrandi took him to see the Tomb of San Domenico, which is said to have been executed by the old sculptors, Giovanni Pisano§ and Maestro Niccolò dell' Arca: here, as it was found that two figures, of a braccio high, a San Petronio, and an Angel holding a candlestick namely, were wanting, Aldovrandi asked Michelagnolo if he had courage to undertake them, when he replied that he had; and having selected a piece of marble, he completed them in such sort that they are the best figures of the work, and he received thirty ducats for the two. He remained, as we have said, a year with Aldovrandi, and to have obliged him would have remained longer, the latter being pleased with his ability in design, and also with his Tuscan pronunciation in reading, listening with pleasure while Michelagnolo read the works of Dante, Petrarch, Boccaccio, and other Tuscan authors. But our artist, knowing that he was losing time at

* No effort has enabled us to ascertain the fate of this Crucifix.—*Ed. Flor.*

† See Marini, *Sigilli*, tomo i.

‡ Michael Angelo was then about twenty years old.

§ Niccolò Pisano, and not Giovanni. See Förster, *Beiträge zur neueren Kunstgeschichte*, p. 14. See also Davia, *Storico Artistico intorno all' arca di San Domenico*, Bologna, 1838, where documents will be found which prove that the tomb, commenced in 1267, was ultimately completed by Fra Guglielmo of Pisa.

Bologna, returned to Florence,* where he executed a San Giovanni in marble for Lorenzo di Pier Francesco de' Medici; after which he commenced a Sleeping Cupid, also in marble and the size of life. This being finished was shown as a fine work, by means of Baldassare del Milanese to Pier-Francesco, who having declared it beautiful, Baldassare then said to Michelagnolo, "I am certain that, if you bury this Statue for a time, and then send it to Rome so treated, that it may look old, you may get much more for it than could be obtained here;" and this Michelagnolo is said to have done, as indeed he very easily could, that or more, but others declare that it was Milanese who, having taken this Cupid to Rome, there buried it, and afterwards sold it as an antique to the Cardinal San Giorgio for two hundred crowns. Others again affirm that the one sold to San Giorgio was made by Michelagnolo for Milanese who wrote to beg that Pier-Francesco† would give Michelagnolo thirty crowns, declaring that sum to be all he had obtained for it, thus deceiving both him and Michelagnolo.

Cardinal San Giorgio had, meanwhile, discovered that the Cupid had been made in Florence, and having ascertained the whole truth, he compelled Milanese to return the money and take back the Statue, which, having fallen into the hands of the Duke Valentino, was presented by him to the Marchioness of Mantua, who took it to that city, where it is still to be seen.‡ San Giorgio, meanwhile, incurred no small ridicule and even censure in the matter, he not having been able to appreciate the merit of the work; for this consisted in its absolute perfection, wherein, if a modern work be equal to the ancient, wherefore not value it as highly? for is it not a mere vanity to think more of the name than the fact? But men who regard the appearance more than the reality, are to be found in all times. The reputation of Michelagnolo increased greatly from this circumstance, and he was invited to Rome, where he was engaged by the Cardinal San Giorgio, with whom he remained nearly a

* Condivi adds that there were other motives; the threat of a Bolognese sculptor to avenge himself on Michael Angelo for the loss of those statues, and the fact that the latter could now remain securely in Florence, where quiet had been restored.

† Lorenzo di Pier-Francesco.

‡ It is no longer to be found there.

year, but that Prelate, not understanding matters of art, did nothing for him.

At that time a Barber of the Cardinal, who had been a painter, and worked tolerably in fresco, but had no power of design, formed an acquaintance with Michelagnolo, who made him a Cartoon of St. Francis receiving the Stigmata, and this was painted by the Barber very carefully; it is now in the first Chapel of the Church of San Pietro, in Montorio.* The ability of Michelagnolo was, however, clearly perceived by Messer Jacopo Galli, a Roman gentleman of much judgment, who commissioned him to make a Cupid, the size of life, with a Bacchus of ten palms high; the latter holds a Tazza in the right hand, and in the left he has the skin of a Tiger, with a bunch of grapes which a little Satyr is trying to nibble away from him. In this figure the artist has evidently brought to mingle beauties of a varied kind, labouring to exhibit the bold bearing of the youth united to the fulness and roundness of the female form;† and herein did he prove himself to be capable of surpassing the statues of all other modern masters.

During his abode in Rome, Michelagnolo made so much progress in art, that the elevation of thought he displayed, with the facility with which he executed works in the most difficult manner, was considered extraordinary, by persons practised in the examination of the same, as well as by those unaccustomed to such marvels, all other works appearing as nothing in the comparison with those of Michelagnolo. These things caused the Cardinal Saint Denis, a Frenchman, called Rovano,‡ to form the desire of leaving in that renowned city some memorial of himself by the hand of so famous an artist. He therefore commissioned Michelagnolo to execute a Pietà of marble in full relief; and this when finished, was placed in San Pietro, in the Chapel of Santa Maria della Febbre namely, at the Temple of Mars.§ To this work I think no sculptor, however distinguished an artist, could add a single grace, or improve it by whatever

* See Titi, *Pitture di Roma.*

† See Bianchi, *Ragguaglia della Galleria Medicea,* Firenze, 1759. See also Cicognara, *Storia della Scultura Moderna.*

‡ Bottari tells us that it was not Cardinal Rohan, but the Cardinal Grolaye de Villiers, by whom this work was ordered.

§ Where the temple of Mars had been that is to say. The Pietà is now in the chapel which stands opposite to the baptismal font.

pains he might take, whether in elegance and delicacy, or force, and the careful perforation of the marble, nor could any surpass the art which Michelagnolo has here exhibited.

Among other fine things may be remembered—to say nothing of the admirable draperies—that the body of the Dead Christ exhibits the very perfection of research in every muscle, vein, and nerve, nor could any corpse more completely resemble the dead than does this There is besides a most exquisite expression in the countenance, and the limbs are affixed to the trunk in a manner that is truly perfect; the veins and pulses, moreover, are indicated with so much exactitude, that one cannot but marvel how the hand of the artist should in a short time have produced such a work, or how a stone which just before was without form or shape, should all at once display such perfection as Nature can but rarely produce in the flesh.* The love and care which Michelagnolo had given to this group were such that he there left his name—a thing he never did again for any work—on the cincture which girdles the robe of Our Lady; for it happened one day that Michelagnolo, entering the place where it was erected, found a large assemblage of strangers from Lombardy there, who were praising it highly; one of these asking who had done it, was told "Our Hunchback of Milan;" hearing which, Michelagnolo remained silent, although surprised that his work should be attributed to another. But one night he repaired to Saint Peter's with a light and his chisels, to engrave his name as we have said on the figure, which seems to breathe a spirit as perfect as her form and countenance, speaking as one might think in the following words:—

> Beauty and goodness, piety and grief,
> Dead in the living marble. Weep not thus;
> Be comforted, time shall awake the dead.
> Cease then to weep with these unmeasured tears,
> Our Lord, and thine, thy father, son, and spouse,
> His daughter, thou his mother and sole bride.†

From this work then Michelgnolo acquired great fame; certain dullards do indeed affirm that he has made Our Lady

* This admirable figure has been cast by the Cavaliere Camuccini, and presented by him to various Academies of Art.

† The obscurity of these lines has not escaped the lash of our author's compatriots.

too young, but that is because they fail to perceive the fact that unspotted maidens long preserve the youthfulness of their aspect, while persons afflicted as Christ was do the contrary; the youth of the Madonna, therefore, does but add to the credit of the master.

Michelagnolo now received letters from friends in Florence advising him to return, since he might thus obtain that piece of marble which Pier Soderini, then Gonfaloniere the city, had talked of giving to Leonardo da Vinci, but was now preparing to present to Andrea dal Monte Sansavino, an excellent sculptor who was making many efforts to obtain it. It was difficult to get a statue out of it without the addition of several pieces, and no one, Michaelagnolo excepted, had the courage to attempt it; but he, who had long wished for the block, no sooner arrived in Florence than he made every effort to secure the same. This piece of marble was nine braccia high, and unluckily, a certain Maestro Simone da Fiesole* had commenced a colossal figure thereon; but the work had been so grievously injured that the Superintendents had suffered it to remain in the House of Works at Santa Maria del Fiore for many years, without thinking of having it finished, and there it seemed likely to continue.

Michelagnolo measured the mass anew to ascertain what sort of figure he could draw from it, and accommodating himself to the attitude demanded by the injuries which Maestro Simone had inflicted on it, he begged it from the Superintendents and Soderini, by whom it was given to him as a useless thing, they thinking that whatever he might make of it must needs be preferable to the state in which it then lay, and wherein it was totally useless to the fabric. Michelagnolo then made a model in wax, representing a young David, with the sling in his hand, as the ensigns of the Palace, and to intimate that, as he had defended his people and governed justly, so they who were then ruling that city should defend it with courage and govern it uprightly. He commenced his labours in the House of Works, at Santa Maria del Fiore, where he formed an enclosure of planks and masonry, which surrounded the marble; there he worked perpetually, permitting no one to see him until the figure

* Gaye, *Carteggio inedito*, vol. ii. p. 434, calls the master who sketched this Colossus, *Agostino Gucci*.

was brought to perfection. The marble having been much injured by Simone, did not entirely suffice to the wishes of Michelagnolo, who therefore permitted some of the traces of Simone's chisel to remain; these may be still perceived,* and certainly it was all but a miracle that Michelagnolo performed, when he thus resuscitated one who was dead.

When the Statue was completed, there arose much discussion as to how it should be transported to the Piazza de' Signori, but Giuliano da Sangallo, and Antonio his brother, made a strong frame-work of wood, and, suspending the figure to this by means of ropes, to the end that it might be easily moved, they thus got it gradually forwards with beams and windlasses, and finally placed it on the site destined to receive the same. The knot of the rope which held the Statue was made in such sort that it ran easily, but became tighter as the weight increased, a beautiful and ingenious arrangement, which I now have in my book of designs: a secure and admirable contrivance it is for suspending great weights.†

When the Statue was set up, it chanced that Soderini, whom it greatly pleased, came to look at it while Michelagnolo was retouching it at certain points, and told the artist that he thought the nose too short. Michelagnolo perceived that Soderini was in such a position beneath the figure, that he could not see it conveniently, yet to satisfy him, he mounted the scaffold with his chisel and a little powder gathered from the floor in his hand, when striking lightly with the chisel, but without altering the nose, he suffered a little of the powder to fall, and then said to the Gonfaloniere who stood below, "Look at it now." "I like it better now," replied Piero; "you have given it life." Michelagnolo then descended, not without compassion for those who desire to appear good judges of matters whereof they know nothing. The work fully completed, Michelagnolo gave it to view, and truly may we affirm that this Statue surpasses all others whether ancient or modern, Greek or Latin; neither the Marforio at Rome, the Tiber and the Nile in the Belvedere, nor the Giants of Monte Cavallo, can

* More particularly on the back.

† Parenti, in his MS. work, the *Storia Fiorentina*, attributes this mechanism to Cronaca. See also Gaye, who shows that four days were employed in removing the statue to its place.

be compared with it, to such perfection of beauty and excellence did our artist bring his work. The outline of the lower limbs is most beautiful. The connexion of each limb with the trunk is faultless, and the spirit of the whole form is divine: never since has there been produced so fine an attitude, so perfect a grace, such beauty of head, feet, and hands; every part is replete with excellence; nor is so much harmony and admirable art to be found in any other work. He that has seen this, therefore, need not care to see any production besides, whether of our own times or those preceding it. For this Statue, Michelagnolo received from Soderini the sum of four hundred crowns; it was placed on its pedestal in the year 1504, and the glory resulting to the artist therefrom became such as to induce the Gonfaloniere to order a David in bronze, which, when Michelagnolo had completed, was sent to France.*

About the same time our artist commenced, but did not finish, two Medallions in marble, one for Taddeo Taddei, which is now in his house;† the other for Bartolommeo Pitti, which was presented to Luigi Guicciardini‡ by Fra Miniato Pitti of Monte Oliveto his great friend, and whose acquaintance with Painting as well as with Cosmography and other sciences, is very extensive. These works also obtained high approbation, as did likewise a marble Statue of St. Matthew, which Michelagnolo then sketched for the Superintendents of Works to Santa Maria del Fiore, and which, merely sketched as it is, gives clear evidence of the perfection to which the finished performance would have attained, and serves well to teach the Sculptor how figures are to be drawn from the marble in such sort that they shall not prove abortions, and also in a manner which leaves to the judgment all fitting opportunity for such alterations and ameliorations as may subsequently be demanded.§

* The history of this work will be found in Gaye, *Carteggio inedito d'Artisti*, vol. ii., where there is a letter from the Signoria of Florence respecting it, with another from Pandolfini, to the effect that the aforesaid Signoria had refrained from sending the same, because the Duke de Nemours, for whom it was destined, *had lost the French king's favour.*

† It was subsequently purchased by Sir George Beaumont, and is now in the Academy of Arts.

‡ This is now in the Florentine Gallery of the Uffizj.

§ Let our readers consult the notes appended by Vigenero (who was intimately acquainted with Michael Angelo) to his Translation, *Les Images*

About this time Michelagnolo cast a Madonna in ~~bronze~~ for certain Flemish merchants called Moscheroni, persons of much account in their own land, and who paid him a hundred crowns for his work, which they sent into Flanders. The Florentine citizen, Agnolo Doni, likewise desired to have some production from the hand of Michelagnolo, who was his friend, and he being, as we have before said, a great lover of fine works in art, whether ancient or modern; wherefore Michelagnolo began a circular painting of Our Lady for him; she is kneeling, and presents the Divine Child, which she holds in her arms, to Joseph, who receives him to his bosom. Here the artist has finely expressed the perfection of delight with which the mother regards the beauty of her Son, and which is clearly manifest in the turn of her head and fixedness of her gaze: equally obvious is her wish that this contentment shall be shared by that pious old man who receives the babe with infinite tenderness and reverence. Nor did this suffice to Michelagnolo, since the better to display his art, he has assembled numerous undraped figures in the back-ground of his picture, some upright, some half recumbent, and others seated.* The whole work is, besides, executed with so much care and finish, that of all his pictures, which indeed are but few, this is considered the best.†

When the picture was completed, Michelagnolo sent it, still uncovered, to Agnolo Doni's house, with a note demanding for it a payment of sixty ducats. But Agnolo, who was a frugal person, declared that a large sum to give for a picture, although he knew it was worth more, and told the messenger

&c. *de deux Sophistes Grecs*, Paris, 1614. Here, among other interesting and valuable observations, he will find the following: "Of this matter" (sketching) "I may add that I have seen Michael Angelo, although then sixty years old, and not in robust health, strike more chips from the hardest marble in a quarter of an hour, than would be carried off by three young stone-cutters in three or four times as long; a thing incredible to him who has not seen it. He would approach the marble with such impetuosity, not to say fury, that I often thought the whole work must be dashed to pieces; at one blow he would strike off morsels of three and four inches, yet with such exactitude was each stroke given, that a mere atom more would sometimes have spoiled the whole work.

* "None of which," remarks an Italian annotator, "have any business here; and, speaking with all due deference to the great master, the introduction of them is a most reprehensible licence."

† This picture, which is called hard and displeasing by the compatriots of the master, is now in the Tribune of the Uffizj.

that forty ducats which he gave him was enough. Hearing this, Michelagnolo sent back his man to say that Agnolo must now send a hundred ducats or give the picture back; whereupon Doni, who was pleased with the work, at once offered the sixty first demanded. But Michelagnolo, offended by the want of confidence exhibited by Doni, now declared that if he desired to have the picture, he must pay a hundred and forty ducats for the same, thus compelling him to give more than double the sum first required.

When the renowned painter, Leonardo da Vinci, was painting in the Great Hall of the Council, as we have related in his Life, Piero Soderini, who was then Gonfaloniere, moved by the extraordinary ability which he perceived in Michelagnolo, caused him to be entrusted with one portion of that Hall,* when our artist finished a façade (whereon he represented the War of Pisa), in competition with Leonardo. For this work Michelagnolo secured a room in the Hospital of the Dyers at Sant' Onofrio; and here he commenced a very large Cartoon, but would never permit any one to see it in progress. The work exhibited a vast number of nude figures bathing in the River Arno, as men do in hot days, and at this moment the enemy is heard to be attacking the Camp. The soldiers who were bathing, spring forth in haste to seize their arms, which many are portrayed by the divine hand of Michelagnolo as hurriedly doing. Some are affixing their cuirasses or other portions of their armour, while others are already mounted and commencing the battle on horseback.

Among the figures in this work was that of an old man who, to shelter himself from the heat, has wreathed a garland of ivy round his head, and, seated on the earth, is labouring to draw on his stockings, but is impeded by the humidity of his limbs. Hearing the sound of the drums and the cries of the soldiers, he is struggling violently to get one of the stockings on, the action of the muscles and distortion of the mouth evince the zeal of his efforts, and prove him to be toiling all over, even to the points of his feet. There were drummers, and other figures also, hastening to the Camp with their clothes in their arms, all dis-

* In a letter from Soderini to the Cardinal of Volterra, Michael Angelo is called "a young man who stands above all of his calling in Italy; nay, in the world." See Gaye, *ut supra.*

playing the most singular attitudes; some were standing, others kneeling or stooping forward, or half-suspended between all these positions; some were falling down, others springing high in the air and exhibiting the most difficult foreshortenings. There were innumerable groups besides, all sketched in different manners, some of the figures being merely outlined in charcoal, others shaded off, some with the features clearly defined, and lights thrown in, Michelagnolo desiring to show the extent of his knowledge in that vocation; and of a truth the artists were struck with amazement, perceiving, as they did, that the master had in that Cartoon laid open to them the very highest resources of art: nay, there are some who still declare that they have never seen anything equal to that work, either from his own hand or that of any other, and they do not believe that the genius of any other man will ever more attain to such perfection. Nor does this appear to be exaggerated, since all who have designed from and copied that Cartoon (as it was the habit for both natives and strangers to do), have finally become excellent in Art.

As proof of this, may be cited Aristotele da Sangallo, the friend of Michelagnolo, Ridolfo Ghirlandajo; Raffaello Sanzio da Urbino; Francesco Granaccio; Baccio Bandinelli; and the Spaniard, Alonzo Berughetta.* These were followed by Andrea del Sarto; Franciabigio; Jacopo Sansovino; Il Rosso; Maturino; Lorenzetto; and Tribolo, who was at that time but a child; with Jacopo da Pontormo, and Perino del Vaga, all of whom were excellent masters.

The Cartoon having thus become a study for artists, was removed to the great Hall of the Medici Palace, but this caused it to be left with too little caution in the hands of the artists; insomuch that, at the time of Giuliano's sickness, and when no one was thinking of such things, it was torn to pieces, as we have before related,† and scattered over different places, among others in Mantua, where certain fragments are still to be seen in the house of M. Uberto Strozzi, a Mantuan gentleman, by whom they are preserved with

* For notices of this artist, who rose to great eminence in Spain, see the work of his compatriot Palomino, *Vidas de los Pintores y Estatuarios eminentes Espanoles.*

† See the history of this criminal action in the Life of Baccio Bandinelli, vol. iii. of the present work.

great reverence, as indeed they well deserve to be; for in looking at them one cannot but consider them rather of divine than merely human origin.*

The fame of Michelagnolo had now, by his Pietà, by the Colossal Statue in Florence, and by his Cartoon, become so much bruited abroad, that in 1503, when our artist was about twenty-nine years old, he was invited to Rome with great favour by Julius II., who had succeeded Alexander VI. on the papal throne. Here His Holiness, who had caused one hundred crowns to be paid to Michelagnolo by his agents for travelling expenses, commissioned him to prepare his Sepulchral Monument, but he had been several months in Rome before he was directed to make any commencement. Finally, it was determined that a design which he had made for that Tomb, should be adopted, and this work also bore ample testimony to the genius of the Master, seeing that, in beauty, magnificence, superb ornament, and wealth of statues, it surpassed every other sepulchre, not excepting the Imperial tombs, or those of antiquity. Encouraged by this success, Pope Julius ultimately determined to rebuild the Church of San Pietro, for the purpose of worthily installing the monument above-mentioned within it, as has been related elsewhere.

Michelagnolo then set hand to his work with great spirit, repairing for that purpose, with two of his disciples, to Carrara, to superintend the excavation of the marbles, having first received one thousand crowns in Florence from Alamanno Salviati, on account of those works.

In those mountains, then, he spent eight months without receiving any additional stipend or supplies of any kind, amusing himself meanwhile by planning all manner of immense figures to be hewn in those rocks, in memorial of himself, as did certain of the ancients, invited thereto by the vast masses before him. Having finally selected all that he required, he loaded them on ships, which he despatched to Rome, where they filled the entire half of the Piazza, which is towards Santa Caterina, and the whole space between the church and the corridor leading to the Castello, where Mi-

* There are nineteen figures from these Cartoons, which were engraved and published by Schiavonnetti in 1808. Certain groups from them are also engraved by the old engravers, Marcantonio, Agostino Veneziano, &c. See the *Life of Michael Angelo*, by Duppa. See also Waagen, *Kunstwerke und Künstler in England*.

chelagnolo had his studio, and where he prepared the Statues and all other things needful for the Tomb. And to the end that His Holiness might come conveniently to see the artist at work, there was a drawbridge constructed between the corridor and the studio, a circumstance which gave rise to so close an intimacy, that the favourable notice thus bestowed on Michelagnolo having awakened great envy among the artists of his own calling, occasioned him much vexation and even persecution. Of this work, Michelagnolo finished four Statues and commenced eight others, either during the life or after the death of Pope Julius; and as the arrangements made for this work give proof of extraordinary powers of invention, we will here describe the principal features thereof.

For the greater magnificence of the effect, it was decided that the tomb should be wholly isolated, a passage remaining entirely around it, the fabric being eighteen braccia in extent on two sides, and twelve on the other two, the dimensions thus presenting a square and a half: a range of niches passed entirely around it, and these were interchanged by terminal figures, clothed from the middle upwards, and bearing the first cornice on their heads, while to every one was bound a captive in a strange distorted attitude, the feet of these prisoners resting on the projection of a socle or basement. These captives were intended to signify the Provinces subjugated by Pope Julius, and brought by him into the obedience of the apostolic Church. There were other statues, also bound, and these represented the Fine Arts and liberal Sciences, which were thus intimated to be subjected to death no less than was that Pontiff, by whom they had been so honourably protected. On the angles of the first cornice were four large figures, representing Active Life and Contemplative Life, with St. Paul and Moses.*

Above the cornice the fabric gradually diminished, exhibiting a frieze of stories in bronze, with figures of angels in the form of boys, and other ornaments around them; and over all, at the summit of the work, were two figures, one of which, having a smiling aspect, represented Heaven,

* Our readers will not need to be reminded that Vasari here speaks of what was to be, rather than what was. He is unhappily not describing a work finished, but only the design of one proposed, and even executed in part, but never completed.

and bore a bier on the shoulder: the other represented Cybele, who appeared to be weeping at her misfortune of being compelled to remain in a world deprived of all genius by the death of so great a man, while Heaven was smiling because his soul had passed to the celestial regions. The fabric was so arranged that a free passage remained between the niches, the spectator passing in or out by the ends of the quadrangular edifice, which was of an oval form, and resembled a temple in that part destined to receive the dead body of Julius. Finally, there were to be added forty statues in marble, to say nothing of the numerous stories, angels, and other ornaments, or of the richly carved cornices and architectural decorations.

To forward the progress of the work, moreover, Michelagnolo had arranged that a portion of the marbles should be sent to Florence, where it was his custom to pass a part of the summer, by way of avoiding the malaria of Rome, and where he did in fact complete the several pieces required for one entire side of the monument. In Rome also he finished two of the captives, which were indeed divine, with some other statues, so good that better have never been seen. But as these figures were not used for the Tomb, Michelagnolo afterwards gave the two captives above-mentioned to the Signor Roberto Strozzi, in whose house he lay sick, and by whom they were sent to King Francis. They are now at Cevan,* in France. Our artist likewise commenced eight Statues in Rome with five in Florence, and finished a figure of Victory, with a prisoner lying beneath her feet. This is now in the possession of Duke Cosimo, to whom the group was presented by Leonardo, the nephew of Michelagnolo, and who has placed it in the Great Hall of his Palace painted by Vasari.†

The Moses, in marble, five braccia high, was also completed by Michelagnolo, and never will any modern work approach the beauty of this statue; nay, one might with equal justice affirm, that of the ancient statues none is equal to this. Seated in an attitude of imposing dignity, the

* St. Econen rather. The figures are now in the Louvre. See Duppa, *Life of Michael Angelo*, London, 1816.

† It is still in the Palazzo Vecchio, and in the "Great Hall" of the text. Engravings of this group will be found in Cicognara, vol. iii. plate LVII.

Lawgiver rests one arm on the Tables, and with the other restrains the flowing beard, that, descending softly, is so treated as to exhibit the hair (which presents so great a difficulty in sculpture) soft, downy, and separated, hair from hair, in such sort, as might appear to be impossible, unless the chisel had become a pencil. The countenance is of the most sublime beauty, and may be described as that of a truly sacred and most mighty prince; but to say nothing of this, while you look at it, you would almost believe the figure to be on the point of demanding a veil wherewith to conceal that face, the beaming splendour of which is so dazzling to mortal gaze. So well, at a word, has the artist rendered the divinity which the Almighty had imparted to the most holy countenance of that great Lawgiver. The draperies also are most effectively raised from the marble ground, and are finished with beautiful foldings of the edges: the muscles of the arms, with the anatomical development and nerves of the hands, are exhibited to the utmost perfection; and the same may be said of the lower limbs, which, with the knees and feet, are clothed in admirably appropriate vestments. At a word, the sculptor has completed his work in such sort that Moses may be truly affirmed more than ever now to merit his name of the friend of God.* Nay, the Jews are to be seen every Saturday, or on their Sabbath, hurrying like a flight of swallows, men and women, to visit and worship this figure, not as a work of the human hand, but as something divine.†

Having at length made all his preparations, and approached the conclusion of the same, Michelagnolo erected one portion of the Tomb, the shorter sides namely, at San Pietro in Vincola. It is said that while he was employed on that

* For the much that has been written in reprehension or defence of Vasari's exaggerated admiration for his master, Michael Angelo, and respecting that great artist himself, our readers are referred to the severe Milizia, *Dell' Arte di Vedere*, on the one hand; and to Moreni, *Memorie sul risorgimento delle Arti in Toscana*, on the other. The Abate Cancellieri, *Lettere sopra la Statua di Mosè*, and Frèart, in his *Idée de la Perfection de la Peinture*, may also be consulted on the different sides of the same question; and among the defenders of Michael Angelo our own Reynolds may be read with advantage. See more particularly his Lectures delivered before the Academy.

† Neither Cancellieri nor Bottari will admit the truth of this assertion, both remarking that it cannot be correct, since Jews do not enter the Roman churches.

operation, a certain part of the marbles arrived from Carrara, where they had been suffered to remain, and as it was necessary to pay those who had delivered them, our artist repaired to the Pope, as was his custom. But finding His Holiness engaged with important intelligence just received from Bologna, he returned home, and paid with his own money, expecting to receive the order for it from the Pontiff immediately. He went to the palace a few days after therefore, but was again desired to wait and take patience, by a groom of the chambers, who affirmed that he was forbidden to admit him. A Bishop who stood near observed to the attendant that he was perhaps unacquainted with the person of the man whom he refused to admit; but the groom replied that he knew him only too well. "I, however," he added, am here to do as my superiors command, and to obey the orders of the Pope." Displeased with this reply, the master departed, bidding the attendant tell His Holiness when next he should inquire for Michelagnolo, that he had gone elsewhere. He then returned to his dwelling, and ordering two of his servants to sell all his moveables to the Jews, and then follow him to Florence, he took post-horses that same night, and left Rome.

Arrived at Poggibonsi, a town on the road to the first-named city, in the Florentine territory, and consequently in a place of safety, the master made a halt; five couriers followed him one after another with letters from the Pope, and orders to convey him back, but no entreaty and no threat of the disgrace that would await him in case of refusal, would induce him to return. He was, however, finally prevailed on to write in reply, when he declared that His Holiness must excuse his returning to his presence, which he was resolved not to do, seeing that he, Julius, had driven him forth like a worthless person, which was a mode of treatment that his faithful service had not merited; he added that the Holy Father might seek elsewhere for some one who should serve him better.

Having reached Florence, Michelagnolo set himself to complete the Cartoon for the Great Hall, at which he worked during the three months of his stay in the city, Piero Soderini, the Gonfaloniere, being anxious to see it finished. The Signoria meanwhile received three Briefs, with the request that Michelagnolo might be sent back to

Rome,* but the latter, doubting what this eagerness of the Pope might portend, entertained, as it is said, some intention of going to Constantinople, there to serve the Grand Seigneur, who sought to engage him, by means of certain Franciscan Monks, for the purpose of constructing a bridge to connect Constantinople with Pera. But the Gonfaloniere labouring to induce Michelagnolo to repair to the Pope instead, and the master still refusing, Soderini at length prevailed on him to do so by investing him with the character of Ambassador from the Florentine Republic,† and recommending him also to the care of his brother, the Cardinal Soderini, whom he charged to introduce Michelagnolo to His Holiness; he then sent the artist to Bologna, in which city Pope Julius had already arrived from Rome.

But there are some who ascribe Michelagnolo's departure from Rome, and his disputes with the Pope, to the following cause.‡ The artist would never suffer any one to see his works while in progress, but he suspected that his people sometimes permitted strangers to inspect them in his absence, and one day when the Pope, having bribed Michelagnolo's assistants, was entering the Chapel of his uncle Pope Sixtus, which he was causing our artist to paint, as will be related hereafter, the latter, who had that day hidden himself, because suspicious of his young men as we have said, rushed upon him with a plank of the scaffolding,§ and nôt perceiving whom it was that he was turning out, drove His Holiness forth in a fury. Let it suffice, however, that for one cause or another, Michelagnolo fell into discord with the Pope, and then, beginning to fear for his safety, departed from Rome as we have said.

Arrived at Bologna, his feet were scarcely out of the stirrups before he was conducted by the servants of the

* One of these will be found in the third volume of the *Lettere Pittoriche*, published by Bottari, and from a letter of Soderini's cited by Gaye, *Carteggio*, &c., this would appear to have been the only one written.

† The letters of Soderini, as cited by Gaye, do not mention the sending of Michael Angelo to Rome as ambassador, but recommended him as the dear fellow citizen of the writer, very warmly, to the good offices of the Cardinal.

‡ In his first edition, Vasari assigns the following as the only cause. That given above appears first in the second editions of our author's work.

§ He threw down a plank from the scaffolding rather, by way of startling the intruder.—*Bottari*.

Pontiff to the presence of His Holiness, who was at the Palace of the Sixteen. He was accompanied by a Bishop, sent by Cardinal Soderini, who was himself too ill to fulfil that office. Having reached the presence, Michelagnolo knelt down before His Holiness, who looked askance at him with an angry countenance, and said, "Instead of coming to us, it appears that thou hast been waiting till we should come to thee," in allusion to the fact that Bologna is nearer to Florence than is Rome. But with a clear voice and hands courteously extended, Michelagnolo excused himself, having first entreated pardon, admitting that he had acted in anger, but adding that he could not endure to be thus ordered away; if he had been in error, His Holiness would doubtless be pleased to forgive him.

Now the Bishop who had presented Michelagnolo, thinking to aid his excuses, ventured to remark that such men as he were always ignorant, knowing and being worth nothing whatever, once out of their vocation; but this threw the Pope into such a rage that he fell upon the Bishop with a stick which he had in his hand, exclaiming, "'Tis thou that art the ignoramus, with the impertinencies thou art pouring forth, and which are such as we should ourselves not think of uttering; he then caused the Bishop to be driven out by the usher in waiting, with blows of his fist.* This offender having departed, the Pope, his rage thus cooled upon the prelate, bestowed his benediction on Michelagnolo, who was detained in Bologna by numerous gifts and promises, His Holiness ultimately giving him the commission for a Statue in bronze, being a Portrait of that Pontiff himself five braccia high. In this work, our artist displayed high powers of art, the attitude is majestic and graceful, the draperies are rich and magnificent, while the countenance exhibits animation, force, resolution, and an imposing dignity.

This Statue was placed in a niche over the Gate of San Petronio, and it is said that while Michelagnolo was engaged therewith, he received a visit from the distinguished gold-

* The accomplished churchman above-cited expresses a doubt, as well he may, respecting this story of sticks and fistycuffs, seeing that the luckless gentleman thus gratified was nothing less than a bishop. He prefers, therefore, the version of Condivi, who makes the Pope salute the Bishop as an "ignorant" namely, and bids him, "Get out of my sight and be hanged to thee."

smith and painter Francia, who had heard much of his fame and works, but had never seen any one of them. Measures were accordingly taken for obtaining permission, and Francia had leave to see the statue above-mentioned. He was much struck by the knowledge of art displayed, but on being asked what he thought, he replied that it was a fine casting and a beautiful material. Hearing which, Michelagnolo supposed that he was praising the bronze, rather than the artist and remarked to Francia: "I am as much obliged for it to Pope Julius who gave it me, as you are to the shopkeepers, who supply you with your colours for painting;" he furthermore added angrily, in the presence of all the gentlemen standing near, that Francia was a dunce. It was on this occasion that Michelagnolo remarked to a son of Francia, who was a very beautiful youth: "The living figures made by thy father are handsomer than those that he paints."

Among the gentlemen present at this visit, was one who asked Michelagnolo which was the larger, the statue of that Pope or a pair of oxen. "That depends on what the animals may be," replied the artist; "for if they are Bolognese oxen it is certain that our Florentines are not such great brutes as those are." The statue was finished in the clay model, before Pope Julius left Bologna for Rome, and His Holiness went to see it, but, the right hand being raised in an attitude of much dignity, and the Pontiff not knowing what was to be placed in the left, inquired whether he were anathematizing the people or giving them his benediction; Michelagnolo replied, that he was admonishing the Bolognese to behave themselves discreetly, and asked His Holiness to decide whether it were not well to put a book in the left hand. "Put a sword into it," replied Pope Julius, "for of letters I know but little." The Pontiff left a thousand crowns in the Bank of M. Antonmaria da Lignano, for the purpose of completing the figure; and after Michelagnolo had laboured at it for sixteenth months, it was placed over the door of San Petronio, as we have before-mentioned when describing the size of the statue. The work was eventually destroyed by the Bentivogli, and the bronze was sold to the Duke Alfonso of Ferrara, who made a piece of artillery called the Julia; of the fragments: the head only was preserved, and this is now in the Duke's Guardaroba.*

* The ultimate fate of this head cannot now be ascertained with certainty.

The Pope having returned to Rome and Michelagnolo being still engaged with the Statue, Bramante, who was the friend and kinsman of Raffaello, and but little disposed to befriend Michelagnolo, availed himself of his absence to influence the mind of Julius, whom he saw to be much inclined to works of Sculpture, and hoping so to contrive that, on the return of Michelagnolo, His Holiness should no longer think of completing the Sepulchre, Bramante suggested that for a man to prepare his tomb during life was an evil augury and a kind of invitation to death. At a word, the Pontiff was persuaded to employ Michelagnolo on his return in the painting of that Chapel, which had been constructed in the Palace and at the Vatican, in memory of his uncle Pope Sixtus. Bramante and the other rivals of Michelagnolo, thinking they should thus detach him from his Sculpture, in which they saw that he was perfect, and throw him into despair, they being convinced that by compelling him to paint in fresco they should also bring him to exhibit works of less perfection, (he having but little experience in that branch of art), and thus prove himself inferior to Raphael. Or even supposing him to succeed in the work, it was almost certain that he would be so much enraged against the Pope as to secure the success of their purpose, which was to rid themselves of his presence.

When Michelagnolo returned to Rome, therefore, he found Julius no longer disposed to have the Tomb finished, but desiring that Michelagnolo should paint the ceiling of the Chapel. This was a great and difficult labour, and our artist, aware of his own inexperience, did all he could to excuse himself from undertaking the work, proposing at the same time that it should be confided to Raphael. But the more he refused the more Pope Julius insisted; impetuous in all his desires, and stimulated by the competitors of Michelagnolo, more especially by Bramante, he was on the point of making a quarrel with our artist, when the latter, finding His Holiness determined, resolved to accept the task. The Pope then ordered Bramante to prepare the scaffolding, which the latter suspended by ropes, perforating the ceiling for that purpose. Seeing this, Michelagnolo inquired of the architect how the holes thus made were to be filled in when the painting should be completed; to which Bramante replied that they would think of that when the time came, and that it could not be done otherwise. But Michelagnolo, perceiving that the architect was either incapable or unfriendly towards himself, went at once to the Pope, whom he assured that such a scaffolding was not the proper one, adding that Bramante did not know how to construct it; and Julius, in the presence of Bramante, replied, that Michelagnolo might construct it himself after his own fashion. The latter then erected his scaffolding on props in such a manner that the walls were not injured, and this method has since been pursued by Bramante and others, who were hereby taught the best way in which preparations for the execution of pictures on ceilings, and other works of the kind could be made, the ropes used by Bramante and which Michelagnolo's construction had rendered needless, the latter gave to the poor carpenter, by whom the scaffolding was rebuilt, and who sold them for a sum which enabled him to make up the dowry of his daughter.

Michelagnolo now began to prepare the Cartoons for the ceiling, His Holiness giving orders to the effect that all the paintings executed on the walls by older masters in the time of Pope Sixtus, should be destroyed,* it was furthermore decided that Michelagnolo should receive fifteen thousand ducats for the work, an estimation of its value which was made by Giuliano da San Gallo. But the extent of the work now compelled Michelagnolo to seek assistance; he therefore sent for men to Florence, resolving to prove himself the conquerer of all who had preceded him, and to show modern artists how drawing and painting ought to be done. The circumstances of the case became a stimulus to his exertions, and impelled him forward, not for his own fame only, but for the welfare of Art also. He had finished the cartoons, but deferred commencing the frescoes until certain of the Florentine painters who were his friends should arrive in Rome, partly to decrease his labour by assisting in the execution of the work, but also in part to show him the processes of fresco-painting, wherein some of them were well-experienced. Among these artists were Granacci, Giuliano Bugiardini, Jacopo di Sandro, and the elder Indaco, with Agnolo da Donnino, and Aristotile da Sangallo.

* This command was not obeyed, since many of those paintings still exist.—*Ed. Flor.*, 1832-8.

These masters having reached the city, the work was begun, and Michelagnolo caused them to paint a portion by way of specimen, but what they had done was far from approaching his expectations or fulfilling his purpose, and one morning he determined to destroy the whole of it. He then shut himself up in the chapel, and not only would he never again permit the building to be opened to them, but he likewise refused to see any one of them at his house. Finally therefore, and when the jest appeared to them to be carried too far, they returned, ashamed and mortified, to Florence. Michelagnolo then made arrangements for performing the whole work himself, sparing no care nor labour, in the hope of bringing the same to a satisfactory termination, nor would he ever permit himself to be seen, lest he should give occasion for a request to show the work; wherefore there daily arose, in the minds of all around him, a more and more earnest desire to behold it. Now Pope Julius, always greatly enjoyed watching the progress of the works he had undertaken, and more than ever desired to inspect anything that was purposely concealed from him: thus it happened that he one day went to see the chapel, as we have related, when the refusal of Michelagnolo to admit him, occasioned that dispute which caused the master to leave Rome, as before described.

Michelagnolo afterwards told me the cause of this refusal, which was as follows: When he had completed about one-third of the painting, the prevalence of the north wind during the winter months had caused a sort of mould to appear on the pictures; and this happened from the fact that in Rome, the plaster, made of travertine and puzzolana, does not dry rapidly, and while in a soft state is somewhat dark and very fluent, not to say watery; when the wall is covered with this mixture, therefore, it throws out an efflorescence arising from the humid saltness which bursts forth; but this is in time evaporated and corrected by the air. Michelagnolo was, indeed, in despair at the sight of these spots, and refused to continue the work, declaring to the Pope that he could not succeed therein, but His Holiness sent Giuliano da Sangallo to look at it, and he, telling our artist whence these spots arose, encouraged him to proceed, by teaching him how they might be removed.

When the half was completed, Pope Julius, who had subsequently gone more than once to see the work (mounting ladders for that purpose with Michelagnolo's aid), and whose temper was hasty and impatient, would insist on having the pictures opened to public view, without waiting until the last touches had been given thereto, and the chapel was no sooner thrown open than all Rome hastened thither, the Pope being the first; he had, indeed, not patience to wait until the dust caused by removing the scaffold had subsided. Then it was that Raffaello da Urbino, who was very prompt in imitation, having seen this work, instantly changed his manner, and to give proof of his ability, immediately executed the Prophets and Sybils in the Church of the Pace.* Bramante also then laboured to convince Pope Julius that he would do well to confide the second half of the Chapel to Raffaello. Hearing of this, Michelagnolo complained to the Pope of Bramante, enumerating at the same time, without sparing him, many faults in the life, as well as errors in the works, of that architect; of the latter, indeed, he did himself become the corrector at a subsequent period.† But Julius, who justly valued the ability of Michelagnolo, commanded that he should continue the work, judging from what he saw of the first half, that our artist would be able to improve the second materially; and the master accordingly finished the whole, completing it to perfection in twenty months, without having even the help of a man to grind the colours.‡ It is true that he sometimes complained of the manner in which the Pope hastened forward the work, seeing that he was thereby prevented from giving it the finish which he would have desired to bestow; His Holiness constantly inquiring when it would be completed. On one occasion, therefore, Michelagnolo replied, "It will be finished when I shall have done all that I believe required to satisfy Art." "And we command," rejoined the Pontiff, "that you satisfy our wish to

* On the contrary, in the Prophets and Sybils, Raphael proposed rather to show the difference between his style and that of Michael Angelo. In the Isaiah of Sant' Agostino he did indeed imitate that master, but on this subject enough has already been said in the Life of Raphael.

† The works of Bramante were sometimes deficient in strength, a grave error, without doubt, and in this respect Michael Angelo may have amended them, but he did not "correct" or improve the design of Bramante.

‡ The truth of this assertion has been much questioned. See the *Diario* of Paris di Grassio, as given in the *Kunstblatt* for 1844, No. 105. See also Gaye, *Carteggio inedito d'Artisti*, vol. ii. p. 487.

have it done quickly;" adding finally, that if it were not at once completed, he would have him, Michelagnolo, thrown headlong from the scaffolding.

Hearing this, our artist, who feared the fury of the Pope, and with good cause, desisted instantly, without taking time to add what was wanting, and took down the remainder of the scaffolding, to the great satisfaction of the whole city, on All Saints' day, when Pope Julius went into that Chapel to sing mass: but Michelagnolo had much desired to retouch some portions of the work *a secco*, as had been done by the older masters who had painted the stories on the walls; he would also gladly have added a little ultramarine to some of the draperies, and gilded other parts, to the end that the whole might have a richer and more striking effect. The Pope, too, hearing that these things were still wanting, and finding that all who beheld the Chapel praised it highly, would now fain have had the additions made, but as Michelagnolo thought reconstructing the scaffold too long an affair, the pictures remained as they were, although the Pope, who often saw Michelagnolo, would sometimes say, "Let the Chapel be enriched with bright colours and gold; it looks poor." When Michelagnolo would reply familiarly, "Holy Father, the men of those days did not adorn themselves with gold; those who are painted here less than any, for they were none too rich; besides which, they were holy men, and must have despised riches and ornaments."

For this work Michelagnolo received from the Pope, in various payments, the sum of three thousand crowns, and of these he may have spent twenty-five in colours. He worked with great inconvenience to himself, having to labour with the face turned upwards, and injuring his eyes so much in the progress of the work, that he could neither read letters nor examine drawings for several months afterwards, except in the same attitude of looking upwards. I can myself bear full testimony to the effects of such work, having painted the ceilings of five large apartments in the Palace of Duke Cosimo; and if I had not made a seat with a support for the head, and occasionally laid down to my work, I should never have been able to finish them; as it was, I weakened my sight, and injured my head so much that I still feel the bad effects of that toil, and I wonder Michelagnolo endured it so well; but his zeal for his art increased daily, while the knowledge and improvement which he constantly perceived himself to make, encouraged him to such a degree that he grudged no labour, and was insensible to all fatigue.

The division of the work in the Chapel is after this manner: There are five corbels on each side thereof, and one on the wall at each end.* On these are figures of the Prophets and Sybils; and in the centre of the ceiling is the History of the World from the Creation to the Deluge, with the Inebriation of Noah. On the lunettes are the Genealogy of Christ. In these compartments Michelagnolo has used no perspective foreshortenings, nor has he determined any fixed point of sight; but has rather accommodated the division to the figures, than the figures to the division; he has been satisfied with imparting the perfection of design to all his forms whether nude or draped, and this he has done effectually, insomuch that a finer work never has been, and never can be executed; nor will it be without difficulty that its excellence shall be imitated. Of a truth, this Chapel, as thus painted by his hand, has been and is the very light of our art, and has done so much for the progress thereof, that it has sufficed to illumine the world, which had lain in darkness for so many hundreds of years. Nay, no man who is a painter now cares to seek new inventions, attitudes, draperies, originality, and force of expression, or variety in the modes of representation, seeing that all the perfection which can be given to each of these requisites in a work of this character by the highest powers of art are presented to him here, and have been imparted to this work by Michelagnolo. Every beholder who can judge of such things, now stands amazed at the excellence of the figures, the perfection of the foreshortenings, the astonishing roundness of the outlines, and the grace and flexibility, with the beautiful truth of proportion, which are seen in the exquisite nude forms here exhibited; and the better to display the resources of his art, Michelagnolo has given them of every age, with varieties of expression and form as well as of countenance and feature; some are more slender, others fuller; the beautiful attitudes also differ in all, some are seated, others are in motion, while others again are supporting festoons of oak-leaves and acorns, adopted as the impress and device of Pope Julius,

* Vasari here calls the ressaults between the lunettes, "corbels," (*peducci*.)

and denoting that at that time, and under his government, there flourished the age of gold; seeing that Italy was not then in the condition of trouble and misery, which she has since endured. Between them the figures bear medallions in relief, to imitate bronze and gold, the subjects being stories taken from the Book of Kings.

In addition to all this, and furthermore to display the perfection of his art as well as the greatness of God, Michelagnolo likewise depicted a story exhibiting the division of the Light from the Darkness. The majesty of the Supreme Creator is displayed in the awful dignity of his attitude; Self-sustained, He stands with extended arms, and a countenance at once expressive of power and love. The second picture, evincing admirable judgment and ability, portrays the Almighty when He creates the Sun and Moon. His figure is here supported by numerous Angels in the form of Children, and there is infinite power of art displayed in the foreshortening of the arms and legs. Next follows the Benediction of the earth, and the Creation of the animal races. Here the Creator is represented as a foreshortened figure on the ceiling, and this form appears to turn with you into whatever part of the Chapel you may proceed. The same figure recurs in the story of the division of the Water from the Earth. Both are exceedingly beautiful, nay, they are such, and of invention so perfect, that no hand but that of the most divine Michelagnolo could have been worthy to produce them.

Then next comes the Creation of Adam. God the Father being here borne by a group of Angels, represented by little boys of very tender age entirely nude; yet these appear to sustain the weight, not of one figure only, but of the whole world; so imposing is the majesty of that most venerable form, and such is the effect produced by the peculiar manner of the movement imparted thereto; one arm is thrown around certain of the children,,as if he were supporting himself thereby, and the other is extended towards Adam, a figure of extraordinary beauty, whether as regards the outline or details, and of such character that one might believe it to have been just newly created by the great Father of all, rather than the mere production of the mind and pencil even of such a man as Michelagnolo. The Story beneath this is the Creation of our mother Eve; and herein are the two nude forms of our first parents, the one held captive in a sleep so profound that it resembles death, the other just awakened to the most animated life by the Benediction of God; and the pencil of this most admirable artist here has shown clearly, not only the difference between Sleep and wakeful vitality, but also the appearance of stability and firmness, which is presented, humanly speaking, by the Divine Majesty.

There next follows the Story of Adam, yielding to the persuasions of a figure, half woman and half serpent, and taking his death as well as our own in the forbidden fruit; he is furthermore exhibited in this picture as driven, with Eve, out of Paradise. And here, in the figure of the Angel, is displayed with grandeur and dignity, the execution of the mandate pronounced by an incensed Deity; while in Adam we have regret for his fault, together with the fear of death; and in the woman that shame, abasement, and desire to obtain pardon, which are expressed by the compression of the arms, the clasping of the hands, the sinking of the head towards the bosom, and the turn of her imploring countenance towards the avenging Angel: all showing, likewise, that her fear of God's justice predominates over her hope in the Divine Mercy.

Not less beautiful is the Story of the Sacrifice of Cain and Abel, wherein there are figures in great variety of attitudes; one brings wood, another is bent down and seeking to kindle the fire into flame by his breath, some are cutting up the victim; and these figures are painted with all the care and forethought which distinguish the others. Equally conspicuous are the art and judgment of the master in the Story of the Deluge; wherein there are numerous dead corpses mingled with other figures, all betraying the terrors inspired by the fearful events of those days, and seeking in various manners to escape with their lives. Among these heads are many, the expression of which proves them to be in despair of redeeming their days from destruction; fear, horror, and disregard of all around them are legibly impressed on their features. In others again, compassion is seen to prevail over their fears, and they are aiding each other to attain the summit of a rock, by means of which they hope to escape the coming floods. There is one figure in particular, which is labouring to save another, already half dead, and the action of which is so perfect, that Nature herself could show nothing more life-like.

Nor would it be easy adequately to describe the Story of Noah, lying inebriated before his sons, one of whom derides the helplessness of the Patriarch, while the other two throw their mantles over him; this is a work of incomparable excellence; it could be surpassed by none but the master himself, and as if encouraged by what he there perceived himself to have accomplished, he subsequently prepared for yet greater efforts, proving his superiority in art, more than ever indisputably, by the figures of the five Sybils and seven Prophets, each of which is more than five braccia high; the variety of attitude, the beauty of the draperies, and every other detail, in short, exhibits astonishing invention and judgment; nay, to those who comprehend the full significance of these figures, they appear little less than miraculous. The Prophet Jeremiah is seated with the lower limbs crossed, and holding the beard with one hand, the elbow of that arm being supported by the knee, while the other hand is laid on his lap: the head is bent down in a manner which indicates the grief, the cares, the conflicting thoughts, and the bitter regrets which assail the Prophet, as he reflects on the condition of his people. There is evidence of similar power in the two boys behind him; and in the first Sybil, that nearest the door namely, in whom the artist has proposed to exhibit advanced age, and not content with enveloping the form in draperies, has been anxious to show that the blood has become frozen by Time, and has furthermore placed the book which she is reading very close to her eyes; by way of intimating that her power of sight is weakened by the same cause.

After the first Sybil follows the Prophet Ezekiel, a very old man, whose attitude is singularly noble and beautiful; he too is much wrapped in draperies, and holding a scroll of his prophecies in the one hand, he raises the other, and turns his head at the same time, as in the act of preparing to utter high and holy truths; behind him are two Boys, who hold his books. The Sybil following Ezekiel is in an attitude exactly opposite to that of the Erethryan Sybil first described; she is holding her book at great distance, that is to say, and is about to turn a leaf; her limbs are crossed over each other, she is deeply pondering on what she is preparing to write, and a boy standing behind her is blowing at a brand of wood, with which he is about to light her lamp. The countenance of this figure has an expression of extraordinary beauty, the draperies and head dress are finely arranged, and the arms, which are of equal perfection with the rest of the person, are nude. Next to this Sybil is the Prophet Joel, who is profoundly absorbed in attention to a scroll which he holds in his hand, and is reading, with an expression of countenance which proves him to be perfectly satisfied with what he finds therein, and has all the effect that could be produced by the face of a living man, whose thoughts are firmly riveted on some question of moment.

Over the door of the Chapel is the aged Prophet Zacharias, who, seeking through the written page for something which he cannot find, remains with one foot lifted, and the other dropped down, while the anxiety and eagerness with which he seeks what he requires, and cannot discover, have caused him to forget the inconvenience of the painful attitude which he has taken. The figure has the aspect of a beautiful old age, the form is somewhat full, and the drapery, of few and simple folds, is admirably arranged. The Sybil opposite to Zacharias, and turning towards the Altar, is putting forward certain writings, and with the boys her attendants deserves equal praise with those before described. But he who examines the Prophet Isaiah shall see features truly borrowed from nature herself, the real mother of art; one of the limbs is crossed over the other, he has laid one hand within a book, at the place where he has been reading, is resting the elbow of the other arm on the volume, and leaning his cheek on his hand, he replies to the call on his attention, made by one of the boys standing behind him, by a mere turn of the head, without disturbing himself further. From this figure, at a word, the observer, who studies it well in every part, may acquire all the rules demanded to constitute the guiding precepts of a good painter. The Sybil next to the Prophet Isaiah is of great age, but also of extraordinary beauty; her attitude, as she zealously studies the book before her, is singularly graceful, as are those of the boys who are ministering around her.

But not imagination herself could add anything to the beauty of a figure representing the Prophet Daniel, and which is that of a youth, who, writing in a great book, is copying certain passages from other writings, with indescribable eagerness of attention; the weight of the book is supported by a boy, who stands before the Prophet, and the beauty of that child is such that no pencil, by whatever hand it may be borne, will ever equal it. As much may be said for the Lybian Sybil, who, having completed the writing of a large book taken from other volumes, is on the point of rising with a movement of feminine grace, and at the same time shows the intention of lifting and putting aside the book, a thing so difficult that it would certainly have proved impossible to any other than the master of this work.

And what shall I say of the four pictures which adorn the angles of the Corbels on this ceiling? In the first is David, exerting all his boyish force in the conquest of the gigantic Philistine, and depriving him of his head, to the utter amazement of numerous Soldiers, who are seen around the Camp. Equally beautiful are the attitudes in the picture of Judith, which occupies the opposite angle, and wherein there is the lifeless body of Holofernes, so recently decapitated that it seems yet to palpitate with life. Judith meanwhile is placing the head of the General in a basket, which is borne by an old servant, on her head. The handmaid is tall of stature, and is stooping to facilitate the due arrangement of her burden by the hands of her mistress. She is endeavouring at the same time to uphold, and also to conceal, what she bears, being impelled to the last-mentioned act, by the sound arising in the tent from the body of Holofernes, which although dead, has drawn up an arm and a leg, thereby causing the sound in question. The face of the servant betrays her fear of some one entering from the Camp, as well as the terror caused her by the dead body, a picture which is certainly most remarkable.

But more beautiful and more divine than even this, or indeed than any of those yet described, is the Story of the Serpents of Moses, which Michelagnolo has placed above the left side of the Altar, and wherein there are represented the dropping of the Serpents on the people, their stings and the bites they inflict, as is also that Serpent of Brass, which Moses himself erected on a staff. In this picture the different modes in which death seizes the sufferers is rendered vividly apparent, many of those not yet dead are obviously hopeless of recovery; others die convulsed with the fear and horror which that acrid venom has caused them. Many are throwing up their arms in agony; some appear to be paralysed: unable to move, they await their coming doom ; and in other parts are beautiful heads, giving utterance to cries of desperation, and cast backwards in the horrors of hopeless anguish.

Those who, looking towards the Serpent erected by Moses, perceive their pains to be alleviated, are also admirably depicted. They turn their eyes on their deliverer with infinite emotion, and one of these groups may more particularly be specified, that of a Woman namely, supported by one who sustains her in such a manner that the effectual assistance rendered by him who gives aid is no less manifest than is the pressing need of her who endures that fear and pain. The story of Ahasuerus, reclining in his bed and causing the Chronicles to be read, has equal merit. The figures are very fine, and among them are three men, seated at a table eating, who represent the deliberation of those who sought to free the Jewish people, and to compass the death of Haman. The figure of the latter is likewise seen foreshortened in a very extraordinary manner ; the stake which supports his person, and the arm which he stretches before him appearing not to be painted, but really round, and in relief, as does also the leg, which he projects outward, and the portions of the body which are bent inward. This is indeed a figure which, among all beautiful and difficult ones, is certainly the most beautiful and most difficult.*

But it would lead me too far were I to describe all the admirable compositions to be admired in these stories. The Genealogy of the Patriarchs, for example, commencing with the sons of Noah, for the purpose of showing the descent of Our Saviour Christ, and in which we have an indescribable variety of figures, vestments, expressions, and phantasies of various kinds, original as well as beautiful. All bear the impress of genius, many of the figures exhibit the most remarkable foreshortenings, and every one of the details is most admirable. Who could behold without astonishment the powerful figure of Josiah, which is the last in the chapel,

* "There doubtless must have been infinite difficulty in the execution of this figure," remarks an Italian commentator, "since it is painted in the angle of the chapel, and is partly on one wall and partly on the other."

and where, by the force of art, the vaulting, which in fact does here spring forward, is compelled, by the bending attitude of that figure, to assume the appearance of being driven backwards and standing upright? such is the knowledge of design here displayed. Oh, truly fortunate age, and thrice happy artists! Well may I call you so, since in your day you have been permitted to dispel the darkness of your eyes by the light of so illustrious a luminary, and behold all that was difficult rendered clear to you by so wonderful and admirable a master! The renown of *his* labours renders *you* also known, and increases your honour, the rather, as his hand has removed that bandage which you had before the eyes of your minds, previously full of darkness, and has delivered the truth from that falsehood which was over-shadowing your intellect. Be thankful to Heaven therefore, and strive to imitate Michelagnolo in all things.

When this work was completed, all the world hastened from every part to behold it, and having done so, they remained astonished and speechless. The Pope rewarded Michelagnolo with rich gifts, and was encouraged by the success of this undertaking to project still greater works; wherefore, the artist would sometimes remark, in respect to the extraordinary favours conferred on him, that he saw well the Pope did esteem his abilities, and if he should now and then inflict some rudeness by a peculiar way of proving his amicable* feeling towards him, yet he always cured the wound by gifts and distinguished favours. On one occasion, for example, when Michelagnolo requested leave from his Holiness to pass the festival of San Giovanni in Florence, and begged also to have some money for that purpose, Pope Julius said, "Well! but when will this chapel be finished?" "When I can, Holy Father," replied our artist, and the Pope, who had a staff in his hand, struck Michelagnolo therewith, exclaiming, "When I can—when I can! I'll make thee finish it, and quickly, as thou shalt see." But the master had scarcely returned to his house to prepare for his journey to Florence, before the Pontiff sent Cursio,† his

* Bottari dissents from this reading and would have the *amorevolezza* of our author changed for *amarezza*, or *amarevolezza*, but the present writer considers the reasons of the annotators who reject that supposed emendation, to have greater weight than those adduced by the accomplished churchman, and has consequently adhered to the text, as left by Vasari.

† Or rather Accursio, as Condivi properly calls him.—*Masselli*.

chamberlain, with five hundred crowns to pacify him, having some fear lest Michelagnolo should play him a prank, as he did before. The chamberlain excused Pope Julius moreover, declaring that these things must all be considered favours and marks of kindness; and as Michelagnolo knew the disposition of the Pontiff, and was, after all, much attached to His Holiness, he laughed at what had happened, the more readily as things of this kind always turned to his profit, and he saw well that the Pope did his utmost to retain him as his friend.

The Chapel being finished, Pope Julius, before he felt the approaches of death, commanded the Cardinals Santi Quattro* and Aginense, his nephews, to see that his Tomb (when he died) should be constructed after a simpler design than that at first adopted. And now Michelagnolo set himself anew to the work of that sepulchre with all the better will, as he hoped at length to bring it to a conclusion, unimpeded by those fatiguing obstacles which had hitherto assailed him; but he was tormented, on the contrary, with unceasing vexations and turmoils in that matter, which cost him more labour and trouble than any other work of his whole life; nay, for some time it caused him to be charged with ingratitude towards that Pontiff by whom he had been so highly valued and favoured. Having returned to the chapel, Michelagnolo worked at it continually, and arranged a part of the designs for the fronts of the fabric, but envious Fortune would not permit this monument to have a conclusion in harmony with the magnificence of its commencement. Pope Julius died, and on the creation of Pope Leo that work was laid aside, for this Pontiff, no less enterprising and splendid in his undertakings than Julius, was anxious to leave in his native city of Florence, of which he was the first Pope, some great memorial of himself, and of that divine artist who was his fellow citizen. At a word, he desired to complete some one of those admirable constructions which only a great prince, such as he was, can attempt; and as he therefore commissioned Michelagnolo to execute the façade of the Church of San Lorenzo in Florence, which had been built by the House of Medici, the Tomb of Pope Julius was of

* The Cardinal Santi Quattro was Lodovico Milero Valentino, and not Pucci, who was created Cardinal by Leo X., the successor of Julius.—*Ed. Flor.*, 1832-8.

necessity left unfinished, Leo not contenting himself with the counsels or even the designs of Michelagnolo, but requiring him to act as superintendent of the works. Yet the master did not yield without such resistance as was possible to him, alleging his engagements with the Cardinals Santi Quattro and Aginense, to whom he was already pledged in respect of the Tomb; but His Holiness replied that he was not to think of them, he (the Holy Father) having provided for that matter, and in effect he did procure the release of Michelagnolo by those prelates, promising them that he should continue his preparations for the Sepulchre, by working at the figures destined for it in Florence, as he had previously done. All this was, nevertheless, much to the dissatisfaction of the Cardinals, as well as Michelagnolo, who left Rome with tears in his eyes.

Much talk, nay innumerable discussions, arose on the subject of the works to be executed in Florence also, seeing that an undertaking like that of the Façade of San Lorenzo ought certainly to have been divided among many persons; in regard to the architecture more especially, several artists repaired to Rome, applying to the Pope for the direction thereof. Baccio d'Agnolo, Antonio da San Gallo,* Andrea and Jacopo Sansovino, with the graceful Raffaello da Urbino, having all made designs for that building: the latter did indeed afterwards visit Florence for a similar purpose.

But Michelagnolo determined to prepare the model himself, and not to accept any guide, or permit any superior in the matter of the architecture:† this refusal of all aid was nevertheless the occasion of such delays that neither by himself nor by others was the work put into operation, and the masters above-named returned, hopeless of a satisfactory conclusion, to their accustomed avocations. Michelagnolo then repaired to Carrara, but first he was empowered to receive a thousand crowns from Jacopo Salviati, and presented himself for that purpose accordingly. Now it chanced that Jacopo was at that moment shut up in his room, engaged on matters of importance with certain of the citizens, but Michelagnolo would not wait for an audience,

* Giuliano da San Gallo, and not Antonio.—*Bottari.*

† A model, long believed to be that here mentioned, will be found in the Florentine Academy of the Fine Arts, but many doubts have lately arisen as to its authenticity

ad departed, without saying a word, for Carrara. Hearing f the master's arrival in Florence, but not seeing him, alviati sent the thousand crowns after him to Carrara, he messenger requiring that a receipt should be given to im. But Michelagnolo replied, that the money was for xpenses on the Pope's account and not his own, adding hat the messenger might carry it back if he chose to do so, ut that he, Michelagnolo, was not in the habit of giving eceipts and acquittances for others; whereupon the man ecame alarmed, and returned to Jacopo Salviati without ny receipt.

While Michelagnolo was at Carrara, where he was causing marbles to be excavated for the tomb of Pope Julius, which he proposed ultimately to complete, as well as for the façade of San Lorenzo, he received from Pope Leo a letter to the effect that there were marbles, of equal beauty and excellence with those of Carrara, to be found in the Florentine dominions, at Serravezza namely, on the summit of the highest mountain in the Pietra Santa, called Monte Altissimo.* Now Michelagnolo was already aware of that circumstance; but it seems he would not attend to it, perhaps because he was the friend of the Marchese Alberigo, Lord of Carrara, or it might have been because he thought the great distance to be passed over would cause loss of time, as indeed it did. He was nevertheless compelled to go to Serravezza, although protesting that the difficulty and expense would be greatly increased thereby, as proved to be the case in the beginning. But the Pope would not hear a word of objection. A road had then to be constructed for many miles through the mountains, and for this rocks were to be hewn away, while it was needful to drive piles, in marshy places, many of which intervened. Michelagnolo thus lost several years in fulfilling the Pope's desire; but finally he procured five columns of fine proportion from these quarries, one of them being now on the Piazza of San Lorenzo, in Florence,† the others lie on the shore. Another result of the matter was to make the Marchese Alberigo a

* After having been long abandoned, the quarries on Monte Altissimo have lately (1838) been re-opened, and are now worked with great activity.—*Ed. Flor.*, 1832-8.

† An opinion was said to prevail in old times, to the effect that some of the marbles in question were actually buried in the Piazza San Lorenzo itself.—*Masselli.*

bitter enemy of Michelagnolo, although the latter was so little to blame.

Other marbles, besides the columns above-named, were subsequently procured at Serravezza, where they have been now lying more than thirty years; but Duke Cosimo has given orders for the completion of the road, of which there are still two miles to make, over ground very difficult to manage, when the transport of marbles is in question; but there is also another quarry, which was discovered at that time by Michelagnolo, and which yields excellent marble, proper for the completion of many a noble undertaking. He has likewise found a mountain of excessively hard and very beautiful vari-coloured marble in the same place of Serravezza, and situate beneath Stazema, a villa constructed amidst those hills, where Duke Cosimo has formed a paved road more than four miles long, for the purpose of bringing the marbles to the sea-shore.

But to return to Michelagnolo, who had now again repaired to Florence. Losing much time, first in one thing and then in another, he made a model, among other things, for those projecting and grated windows with which are furnished the rooms at the angle of the Palace, in one of which Giovanni da Udine executed the paintings and stucco-work which are so much and so deservedly extolled. He also caused blinds, in perforated copper, to be made by the goldsmith Piloto, but after his own designs, and very admirable they certainly are.* Michelagnolo consumed many years, as we have said, in the excavation of marbles; it is true that he prepared models in wax and other requisites for the great undertakings with which he was engaged at the same time, but the execution of these was delayed until the monies, appropriated by the Pontiff for that purpose, had been expended in the wars of Lombardy; and at the death of Leo the works thus remained incomplete, nothing having been accomplished but the foundations of the Façade, and the transport of a great column from Carrara to the Piazza di San Lorenzo.

The death of Pope Leo X. completely astounded the arts and artists, both in Rome and Florence; and while Adrian VI. ruled, Michelagnolo employed himself in the last-named city with the Sepulchre of Julius. But when Adrian

* These copper blinds are not now to be found.—*Masselli.*

was dead, and Clement VII. elected in his place, the latter proved himself equally desirous of establishing memorials to his fame in the arts of sculpture, painting, and architecture, as had been Leo and his other predecessors. It was at this time, 1525, that Giorgio Vasari, then a boy, was taken to Florence by the Cardinal of Cortona, and there placed to study art with Michelagnolo; but the latter having been summoned to Rome by Pope Clement, who had commenced the Library of San Lorenzo; with the New Sacristy, wherein he proposed to erect the marble tombs of his forefathers, it was determined that Giorgio should go to Andrea del Sarto, before Michelagnolo's departure; the master himself repairing to the workshop of Andrea, for the purpose of recommending the boy to his care.

Michelagnolo then proceeded to Rome without delay, being much harassed by the repeated remonstrances of Francesco Maria, Duke of Urbino, who complained of the artist greatly: saying that he had received sixteen thousand crowns for the Tomb, yet was loitering for his own pleasure in Florence without completing the same: he added threats, to the effect that if Michelagnolo did not finish his work, he, the Duke, would bring him to an evil end.* Arrived in Rome, Pope Clement, who would gladly have had the master's time at his own command, advised him to require the regulation of his accounts from the agents of the Duke, when it seemed probable that they would be found his debtors, rather than he theirs. Thus then did that matter remain; but the Pope and Michelagnolo taking counsel together of other affairs, it was agreed between them that the Sacristy and New Library of San Lorenzo in Florence should be entirely completed.

The master thereupon, leaving Rome, returned to Florence, and there erected the Cupola which we now see, and which he caused to be constructed in various orders. He then made the Goldsmith Piloto prepare a very beautiful ball of seventy-two facettes. While he was erecting his cupola, certain of his friends remarked to him that he must be care-

* For details respecting these matters the reader may consult Bottari, *Lettere Pittoriche*, tomo iii. See also Moreni, in his introduction to the work of Frèart before cited, with the annotations of Ciampi to a book published in 1834 from the MS. of a letter by Michael Angelo now in the Biblioteca Magliabecchiana, and entitled *Lettera di Michelangelo per giustificarsi contra le' calunnie de' nemisi suoi sul proposito del Sepolcro di Papa Giulio II.*, &c. &c..

ful to have his lantern very different from that of Filippo Brunelleschi: to which Michelagnolo replied, "I can make a different one easily; but as to making a better, that I cannot do." He decorated the inside of the Sacristy with four Tombs,* to enclose the remains of the fathers of the two Popes, Lorenzo the elder and Giuliano his brother, with those of Giuliano the brother of Leo, and of Lorenzo his nephew.† Desiring to imitate the old Sacristy by Filippo Brunelleschi, but with new ornaments, he composed a decoration of a richer and more varied character than had ever before been adopted, either by ancient or modern masters: the beautiful cornices, the capitals, the bases, the doors, the niches, and the tombs themselves, were all very different from those in common use, and from what was considered measure, rule, and order, by Vitruvius and the ancients, to whose rules he would not restrict himself. But this boldness on his part has encouraged other artists to an injudicious imitation, and new fancies are continually seen, many of which belong to *grottesche* rather than to the wholesome rules of ornamentation.

Artists are nevertheless under great obligations to Michelagnolo, seeing that he has thus broken the barriers and chains whereby they were perpetually compelled to walk in a beaten path, while he still more effectually completed this liberation and made known his own views, in the Library of San Lorenzo, erected at the same place. The admirable distribution of the windows, the construction of the ceiling, and the fine entrance of the Vestibule, can never be sufficiently extolled. Boldness and grace are equally conspicuous in the work as a whole, and in every part; in the cornices, corbels, the niches for statues, the commodious staircase, and its fanciful divisions—in all the building, at a word, which is so unlike the common fashion of treatment, that every one stands amazed at the sight thereof.

About this time Michelagnolo sent his disciple, Pietro Urbano of Pistoja, to Rome, there to execute a figure of Christ on the Cross, which is indeed a most admirable work:

* Michael Angelo constructed two monuments only. Our author most probably describes the work from a design which was never fully completed. —*Bottari.*

† The Tombs executed by Michael Angelo are those of Giuliano, Duke of Nemours, brother of Leo X., and of Lorenzo, Duke of Urbino.

it was afterwards erected beside the principal Chapel in the Minerva* by M. Antonio Metelli.

Then followed the Sack of Rome and the exile of the Medici from Florence: and in this change, those who governed the City resolving to rebuild the fortifications, made Michelagnolo Commissary-general of the whole work.†

In that capacity he prepared numerous designs, adding much to the defences of the city, and more especially surrounding the hill of San Miniato with bastions: these he did not form in the usual manner, of turf, wood, and bundles of faggots, but first constructed a basement of oak, chestnut, and other strong materials, using rough bricks very carefully levelled: he had previously been despatched by the Signoria of Florence to Ferrara, there to inspect the fortifications of artillery and munitions of Duke Alfonso I., when he received many proofs of favour from that Noble, who begged the master to execute some work for him at his leisure; which Michelagnolo promised to do.

Having returned to Florence, he proceeded with the fortifications of the city, and although impeded by numerous engagements, he yet contrived to paint the picture of a Leda for the Duke of Ferrara. This work, which was in tempera, proved to be a divine performance, as will be related in due time. He also continued secretly to labour at the Statues for the Tombs in San Lorenzo. Michelagnolo remained about six months at San Miniato, hastening forward the defences of the Heights, seeing that the city would have been lost, had the enemy made himself master of that point; he consequently devoted the most zealous attention to the works. The before-mentioned Sacristy was also making progress, and Michelagnolo occupied a portion of his time in the execution of seven Statues for that place, some of which he completed wholly, others only in part. In these, as well as in the architecture of the Tombs, all are compelled to admit that he has surpassed every artist in all the three vocations. Among the Statues, either rough-hewn, or finished in marble by Michelagnolo for that Sacristy, is one of Our Lady. This is a seated figure with the limbs crossed, the Infant Christ being placed astride on the uppermost, and

* The figure still retains a place in the Church, but is now behind the High Altar.

† See Varchi, *Storia*, lib. viii.

turning with an expression of ineffable sweetness towards the mother, as if entreating for the breast; while the Virgin, holding him with one hand and supporting herself with the other, is bending forward to give it him. The figures are not finished in every part, yet, in the imperfection of what is merely sketched, there clearly appears the perfection which is to be the final result.

But still more did he surprise all beholders by the Tombs of the Dukes Giuliano and Lorenzo de' Medici, in which he appears to have proceeded on the conviction that Earth alone would not suffice to give an appropriate burial-place to their greatness, he would therefore have other powers of the world to take part, and caused the Statues to be placed over the Sarcophagus in such rich sort as to overshadow the same, giving to the one Day and Night namely, and to the other the Dawn and the Twilight. All these Statues are beautiful, whether in form or attitude, while the muscular development is treated with so much judgment, that if the Art of Sculpture were lost, it might, by their means, be restored to all its pristine lustre. The Statues of those Princes, in their armour, also make part of the ornaments; Duke Lorenzo, thoughtful and reflective, with a form of so much beauty that eyes of mortal could see nothing better; and Duke Giuliano, haughty of aspect, but with the head, the throat, the setting of the eyes, the profile of the nose, the chiseling of the mouth, and the hair, so truly divine, as are also the hands, arms, knees and feet, with all besides indeed, accomplished by our artist in this place, that the spectator can never be satisfied with gazing, and finds it difficult to detach his eyes from these groups; and, of a truth, he who shall examine the beauty of the buskins and cuirass, must believe it to be celestial rather than of this world.*

But what shall I say of the Aurora?—a nude female form, well calculated to awake deep melancholy in the soul, and to make the Art of Sculpture cast down her chisel. Her attitude shows her to have hastily risen from her bed, while she is still heavy with sleep; but in thus awakening, she had found the eyes of that great prince closed in death; wherefore she turns in bitter sorrow, bewailing, as an evidence of the great suffering she endures, her own unchangeable beauty.

* The reader who cannot give our respectable Giorgio credit for the extravagance and bathos of this phrase, is reluctantly referred to the original.

Or what shall I say of the Night?—a statue not rare but unique. Who, in any period of the world's history, has ever seen statues, ancient or modern, exhibiting equal art? Not only is there here the repose of one who sleeps, but the grief and regret of one who has lost a great and valued possession. This is the Night that obscures all those who for a certain time expected, I will not say to surpass, but to equal Michelagnolo. In this figure is all that somnolency which one remarks in the sleeping form, as moulded by Nature herself; wherefore many verses, both in Latin and the vulgar tongue, were made in praise of our artist's work by most learned persons, as, for example, those which follow, and of which the author is not known.*

> The Night that here thou seest, in graceful guise
> Thus sleeping, by an Angel's hand was carved
> In this pure stone; but sleeping, still she lives.
> Awake her if thou doubtest, and she'll speak.

To these words Michelagnolo, speaking in the name of Night, replied as below:—

> Happy am I to sleep, and still more blest
> To be of stone, while grief and shame endure;
> To see, nor feel, is now my utmost hope,
> Wherefore speak softly, and awake me not.

Certain it is, that if the enmity, which constantly exists between Fortune and Genius, had suffered this work to attain completion, Art might have proved to Nature that she is capable of far surpassing her on every point.

While Michelagnolo was thus labouring with the utmost zeal and love at such works, came the siege of Florence, which too effectually impeded the completion thereof; this took place in 1529, when he could do little or nothing more, the citizens having charged him with the care of the fortifications, as we have said. He had lent the Republic a thousand crowns; and, as he made one of the Council of War, called the Nine, he turned all his mind and thoughts to the perfecting and strengthening of the defences. But at length, and when the enemy's troops had closed round the city, while all hope of aid was gradually disappearing, and the difficulties of maintaining the place increased, Michelagnolo, who felt himself to be in a position not suited to him, resolved, for the

* The author was Gio Battista Strozzi. See *Notizie degli Uomini illustri dell' Accademia Fiorentina.*

safety of his person, to leave Florence and repair to Venice, without making himself known to any one by the way.* He departed secretly, therefore, by the road of Monte Miniato, no one being informed of his purpose, and having with him only his disciple Antonio Mini, and the goldsmith Piloto, his faithful friend. They all bore a sum of money, each having fastened his portion into his doublet; and having reached Ferrara, the master halted to refresh himself.

Here the suspicions usual in time of war, and the league of the Emperor and Pope against Florence, caused the Duke Alfonso of Ferrara to keep strict watch, and he required to be secretly informed every day by the hosts of all the strangers whom they lodged; a list of all foreigners, with the countries to which they belonged, being carried to him daily. It thus happened, that although Michelagnolo desired to remain unknown, yet the Duke, made aware of his arrival by this means, greatly rejoiced thereat, because he had become his friend. That prince was a man of a high mind, and delighted in works of genius all his life long. He instantly despatched some of the principal persons of his Court to invite Michelagnolo, in the name of his Excellency, to the Palace, where the Duke then was; these Signori being ordered to conduct him thither with his horses and all his baggage, and to give him commodious apartments in the Palace. Michelagnolo, thus finding that he was no longer master of his movements, put a good face on the matter, and accompanied the Ferrarese nobles to the presence of their lord, but without removing his baggage from the hostelry. The Duke received him graciously, but complained of his reserve and secrecy; subsequently making him rich gifts, he did his utmost to prevail on him to settle in Ferrara; but to this Michelagnolo could not agree, when the Duke requested that he would at least not depart while the war continued, and again offered to serve him to the utmost of his power.

Unwilling to be outdone in courtesy, our artist thanked the Duke with the utmost gratitude, and turning to his two

* Varchi tells us that Michael Angelo had discovered treasonable intentions on the part of Malatesta Baglione, Captain-general of the Florentines (who was in treaty with the Pope for the betrayal of the city), and had made this circumstance known to the Gonfaloniere Carduccio; but not finding the attention he expected, then resolved to secure his own safety by flight. For numerous details respecting this event, see also Gaye, *Carteggio*, vols. ii. and iii.

travelling companions, he remarked that he had brought 12,000 crowns with him to Ferrara, and that if these could be of any service to the Duke, they were to consider his Excellency as much master of them as himself. The Duke then led the master through the Palace to amuse him as he had previously done at an earlier visit, showing him all the fine works in his possession, among others his own Portrait by the hand of Titian, which Michelagnolo greatly extolled: but the latter could not be prevailed on to accept rooms in the Palace, and insisted on returning to his inn. The host then received various supplies, secretly sent from the Duke for the better accommodation of our artist, and was forbidden to accept any remuneration when his guest should depart.

From Ferrara Michelagnolo repaired to Venice, where many of the most distinguished inhabitants desired to make his acquaintance; but he, who had never any very high opinion of their judgment in matters concerning his vocation, left the Giudecca, where he had taken up his abode, and where, as it is said, he prepared a design, at the entreaty of the Doge Gritti, for the Bridge of the Rialto, which was declared to be one of original invention and extraordinary beauty.* He was meanwhile earnestly entreated to return to his native city, and not to abandon his works there; a safe conduct was likewise sent him, and, moved by love of his native place, he did eventually return, but not without danger to his life. At this time Michelagnolo finished the Leda, which he was painting, as I have said, at the request of the Duke Alfonso, and which was afterwards taken into France by his disciple Antonio Mini.† He also repaired the Campanile of San Miniato, a tower which effectually harassed the enemy during the siege with its two pieces of artillery. The Imperialists then assailed it with heavy cannon, and, having all but effected a breach, would soon have destroyed it utterly, had not Michelagnolo found means to oppose sacks of wool and thick mattresses to the artillery; but he did eventually defend it with success, and it is standing to this day.

* Many distinguished artists are said to have given designs for this Bridge, but they were all found to be too costly, and it was constructed in 1591 after the designs of Antonio da Ponte.

† Certain details respecting this painting, which has been mentioned in previous pages of the present work, will be found in Waagen, *Künstler und Kunstwerke in England*.

We find it furthermore related that Michelagnolo at that time obtained the block of marble nine braccia high, which Pope Clement, in the contention between Baccio Bandinelli and himself, had promised to the former. This being now the property of the Commonwealth, he demanded it from the Gonfaloniere, who granted his request, although Baccio had already made his model and diminished the stone considerably by the commencement of his rough-hewn sketch. Michelagnolo now prepared a model on his part, which was considered a very fine one; but on the return of the Medici, the marble was restored to Bandinelli. The war having been brought to an end, Baccio Valori, commissioner of the Pope, received orders to arrest and imprison some of the more zealous among the citizens, the Court itself causing Michelagnolo to be sought in his dwelling, but he, doubtful of their intentions, concealed himself in the house of a trusted friend, where he remained several days.*

But when the first bitterness of resentment had subsided, Pope Clement, remembering the ability of Michelagnolo, commanded that he should be sought anew, but with orders that no reproaches should be addressed to him, nay, rather that he should have all his early appointments restored, and should proceed with the works of San Lorenzo, M. Giovambattista Figiovanni, an ancient servant of the house of Medici, and prior of San Lorenzo, being named superintendent of the work. Thus re-assured, Michelagnolo, to make a friend of Baccio Valori, commenced a figure in marble of three braccia high; an Apollo namely, drawing an arrow from his quiver, but did not quite finish it; it is now in the apartments of the Prince of Florence, and although, as I have said, not entirely finished,† is a work of extraordinary merit.

About this time there came to Michelagnolo a gentleman of the Duke Alfonso of Ferrara, who, having heard that the master had completed a beautiful work for him, and being unwilling to lose such a jewel, had sent the gentleman in question to secure it, who had no sooner arrived in Florence than he sought out our artist, to whom he presented the

* The Senator, Filippo Buonarroti, assured Bottari that his great ancestor had lain concealed in the bell-tower of the Church of San Niccolò, beyond the Arno, for a considerable time.

† Now in the western Corridor of the Uffizj.

letters of his lord. Having received him courteously, the master then showed him the Leda; her arm thrown around the swan, and with Castor and Pollux proceeding from the egg; a large picture in tempera. The Duke's messenger, expecting, from what he had heard of Michelagnolo, to see some great thing, but who was incapable of comprehending the excellence and power of art displayed in that figure, remarked to the master, "Oh, this is but a very trifling affair." Whereupon our artist, knowing that none have better judgment in a matter than those who had long experience therein, inquired of him what his vocation might be. To which the gentleman, secretly smiling and believing himself not to be known for such to Michelagnolo, replied, "I am a merchant;" at the same time making a sort of jest of the question, and speaking with contemptuous lightness of the industry of the Florentines. "Aye, indeed," replied Michelagnolo, who had thoroughly understood the sense of his words; "then you will make a bad bargain for your master this time; be pleased to take yourself out of my sight."

In those days Antonio Mini, the disciple of Michelagnolo, had two sisters to marry, when the master presented the Leda to him, some few days after the conversation just related, with the greater part of the designs and cartoons which he had made, a most noble gift indeed. When Antonio afterwards took it into his head to go to France, therefore, he carried with him two chests of models, with a vast number of cartoons finished for making pictures, some of which had been painted, while others still remained to be executed. The Leda he there sold, by the intermission of certain merchants, to Francis the King of France; and it is now at Fontainebleau; but the cartoons and designs were lost, seeing that Antonio died before he had been long in France, when those treasures were stolen, and our country was thus deprived, to her incalculable injury, of those admirable works of art. The Cartoon of the Leda* has, however, returned to Florence, and is in the possession of Bernardo Vecchietti. There are four pieces of the Cartoons of the

* The original Cartoon of the Leda remained for a long time in the possession of the Vecchietti, but was purchased by an Englishman about the middle of the last century, and brought to England. See Borghini, *Riposo.*

Chapel also, which have been brought back by the sculptor Benvenuto Cellini, and are now held by the heirs of Girolamo degli Albizzi.*

Michelagnolo now thought it fitting and proper that he should repair to Rome, there to take the commands of Pope Clement, who, though much displeased, was yet the friend of distinguished men; His Holiness accordingly forgave all, and ordered him to return to Florence with a commission to give the ultimate completion to the Library and the Sacristy of San Lorenzo. By way of facilitating the progress of the work moreover, the large number of Statues required for it were distributed among other masters. Tribolo received two; one was given to Raffaello da Monte Lupo; and another to the Servite monk, Fra Giovan Agnolo, all sculptors;† but Michelagnolo assisted each of them, making rough models in clay for them all. While these masters, therefore, were zealously occupied with their works, Michelagnolo proceeded with the Library, the ceiling of which was finished after his models by the Florentines Caroto and Tasso, both excellent carvers and masters in wood-work; the shelves for the books being executed at the same time by Battista del Cinque and Ciapino his friend, also good masters in their vocation; while, to give the work its final perfection, the famous Giovanni of Udine was invited to Florence; when he, assisted by his disciples and certain Florentine masters, adorned the Tribune with stucco-work;‡ all these artists labouring zealously to bring the edifice to completion.

Michelagnolo, on his part, was anxious to have his statues also in readiness, but the Pope then summoned him to Rome, for the purpose of adorning the walls of the Chapel of Sixtus with pictures, as he had already done the ceiling for Pope Julius II. On the first of these walls, or that behind the Altar, Pope Clement commanded him to paint the Last Judgment, proposing that in this picture he should display

* Of Michael Angelo's drawings, seventy-nine are now in the Gallery of the University at Oxford, others are in the British Museum; there were also a certain number in the possession of the King of the Netherlands at the Hague, and others will be found at Vienna.

† The whole of the statues were not completed, and there still remain twelve empty niches; the nine finished and erected are seven by Michael Angelo, and two by Tribolo and Raffaello da Montelupo.

‡ All the stucco-work has disappeared, but the wood-carving still remains.

all that the art of design is capable of effecting; while on the opposite wall, and over the principal door, the Pontiff directed that the Fall of Lucifer, and that of the Angels who sinned with him, should be depicted, with their Expulsion from Heaven and Precipitation to the centre of Hell. Of these subjects, it was found that Michelagnolo had long before made sketches and designs, one of them being afterwards put into execution, in the Church of the Trinità in Rome, by a Sicilian painter, who had been many months with Michelagnolo, and had served him in the grinding of his colours. The picture, which is in fresco, is in the Transept of the church, at the Chapel of San Gregorio namely; and although badly executed, there is nevertheless a certain force and variety in the attitudes and groups of those nude figures raining down from heaven; and of the others, which having fallen to the centre, are then turned into frightful and horrible forms of Demons, which certainly give evidence of extraordinary power of fancy and invention.

While Michelagnolo was thus busied with his painting of the Last Judgment, no day passed that he did not have contentions with the agents of the Duke of Urbino, who accused him of having received sixteen thousand crowns for the Tomb of Pope Julius II. He was much grieved at this charge, and though now become old, wished to finish the tomb, since so unlooked-for an opportunity had been presented to him of returning to Rome, whence indeed he desired never to depart, not being willing to remain in Florence, because he greatly feared the Duke Alessandro de' Medici, whom he knew to be no friend of his; nay, when the latter had intimated to him, through the Signor Alessandro Vitelli, that he must repair to Florence, there to select a better site for the forts and citadel, Michelagnolo replied that he would not go thither, unless compelled to do so by Pope Clement.

An agreement being finally arrived at, in respect to the Tomb of Julius, the matter was arranged on this wise:* the edifice was no longer to be an isolated fabric, but merely a single façade, executed as Michelagnolo should think best, he being held nevertheless to supply to it six Statues by his

* For minute details, which cannot here find place, see Duppa's *Life of Michael Angelo*; or Condivi, *Vita di Michelagnolo*, Rome, 1553. See also Ciampi, *Lettera di Michael Angelo*, as before cited.

own hand. By this contract* the Duke of Urbino allowed Michelagnolo to work during four months of the year for Pope Clement, whether in Florence or wherever else it might please the Pontiff to employ him; Michelagnolo now believed himself to have obtained quiet, but he was not allowed to continue his work of the Tomb in peace, because Pope Clement, eager to behold the ultimate effort and force of his art in the Chapel, kept him perpetually occupied with those paintings. Yet, while giving the Pontiff reason to suppose him fully employed with them, he did secretly work on the Statues for the Sepulchre.†

In the year 1533, Pope Clement died,‡ when the works proceeding at the Library and Sacristy in Florence, which, notwithstanding all the efforts made, were not yet finished, were at once laid aside. Michelagnolo then believed himself to be free and at liberty to give all his attention to the Tomb of Pope Julius, but Paul III. being created High Pontiff, no long time elapsed before our artist was summoned by His Holiness, who received him with great favour, declaring that he wished the master to enter his service and remain near his person; Michelagnolo excused himself, saying, he was engaged by contract to the Duke of Urbino until the Tomb should be completed; but Paul, much displeased, replied, "For thirty years have I had this wish, and now that I am Pope will you disappoint me? That contract shall be torn up, for I will have you work for me, come what may." Hearing this, Michelagnolo was tempted to leave Rome and find means for the completion of the Tomb elsewhere.§ Yet, prudent as he was, and fearing the power of the Pontiff, he resolved to try if he could not content him with words, and so keep him quiet (seeing that he was already so old), until some new change might ensue.

Pope Paul meanwhile, determined to have some important work executed by Michelagnolo, went one day to his house with ten Cardinals, and then demanded to see all the Statues

* The Duke's letter to Michael Angelo, dated March 6, 1542, will be found in Gaye, *loc. cit.* vol. ii.

† For details respecting Michael Angelo's occupations of this period, and the invitation which he received from Federigo Gonzaga, Duke of Mantua, see Gaye, *ut supra*, vol. ii.

‡ Pope Clement died on the 25th Sept., 1534.—*Bottari.*

§ For highly interesting details of this period, which cannot here find place, see Condivi, *Vita di Michelagnolo*, as before cited.

for the Tomb of Julius; they appeared to him to be most admirable, more particularly the Moses, which, as the Cardinal of Mantua remarked, was sufficient of itself to do honour to the late Pontiff. The Cartoons and designs for the walls of the Chapel were next examined, these also amazed the Pope with their beauty, and he again pressed Michelagnolo to enter his service, promising to persuade the Duke of Urbino to content himself with three Statues by the hand of Michelagnolo, who might cause the remaining three to be executed after his own models by other good artists. And His Holiness did accordingly so arrange with the Duke's agents, that a new contract was signed by that prince; but Michelagnolo proposed, of his own free will, to pay for the three Statues wanting, as well as for the masonry of the sepulchre, depositing one thousand five hundred and eighty ducats in the Bank of the Strozzi for that purpose. This he might have avoided, had it pleased him to do so; but having done that, he thought he had made sufficient sacrifices for so laborious and vexatious an undertaking as this Tomb had proved to be, and he then caused it to be erected, at San Pietro in Vincola, in the following manner.

The lower basement, with its carved decorations, has four pedestals, which project forwards to the extent required for giving room to a figure representing a Captive, which was originally to have been placed on each, but for which a terminal figure was now substituted; the lower part had thus a poor appearance, and a reversed corbel was therefore added at the feet of each. Between the termini are three niches, of which the two outermost have a circular form, and were to have received figures of Victory; instead of which, the one had now Leah, the daughter of Laban, as the representative of Active Life; in one hand she holds a mirror, to denote the circumspection which we should give to our actions; and in the other a garland, to intimate the virtues which adorn our lives while in this world, and render them glorious after death. The opposite niche received Rebecca, the sister of Leah, as denoting Life in Contemplation;* her hands are joined, her knees are bent, and her face is turned upwards as in ecstacy of spirit. These

* The reader will find numerous details of great interest respecting this portion of the work in Condivi, *loc. cit.*

Statues were executed by Michelagnolo himself in less than a year.

In the centre is the third niche, but this is of a square form, having been originally intended to serve as the entrance to the oval temple, wherein the quadrangular sarcophagus was to have been erected. In this niche there is now placed the beautiful and majestic Statue of Moses, of which we have said enough. Over the heads of the terminal figures, which serve as capitals, there are the Architrave, Frieze, and Cornice, which project over the termini and are richly carved in foliage, ovoli, denticulations, and other ornaments. Above the cornice is a second compartment without carving of any kind, but with termini of a different form, and other figures, standing immediately over those below, they stand in the place of pilasters with varied cornices. In the centre of this compartment, which is similar to and accompanies that below in all its parts, is an opening corresponding with the niche wherein is the Moses; and here, supported by the ressaults of the cornice, is a marble sarcophagus on which is the recumbent Statue of Pope Julius II. executed by the sculptor Maso dal Bosco.* Immediately over this and within a niche is the figure of Our Lady holding the Divine Child in her arms, and executed, after the model of Michelagnolo, by the sculptor Scherano da Settignano. These are tolerably good statues; and in two other niches, also of a square form, are two larger statues, a Prophet and a Sybil namely, both seated; they are placed immediately over the figures representing Active Life and Life in Contemplation. These were made by Raffaello da Montelupo, as we have said in the Life of Baccio his father, but did not give satisfaction to Michelagnolo.

This part of the Tomb was surmounted by a richly decorated cornice, which formed the summit of the whole, and projected considerably over the whole front of the work. At the ends of the same, and above the Termini, stand Candelabra of marble; and in the centre, or over the Prophet and Sybil, are the Arms of Julius II. Within each of the niches, however, it has been necessary to make a window for the convenience of the monks who serve the church; the choir being behind this monument, these windows permit the voices to be heard in the church, and allow the divine

* This is believed to be Maso Boscoli, the disciple of Andrea Sansovino.

offices to be seen. Upon the whole, then, the work has turned out to be a very good one, although wanting much of the magnificence promised by the first design.*

Michelagnolo had now resolved, since he could not do otherwise, to enter the service of Pope Paul III., who commanded him to continue the paintings ordered by Pope Clement, without departing in any manner from the earlier plans and inventions, which had been laid before His Holiness; for the latter held the genius of Michelagnolo in great respect; nay, the love and admiration which he felt for him were such that he desired nothing more earnestly than to do him pleasure. Of this there was a proof in the fact that Pope Paul desired to have his own Arms placed beneath the Statue of the Prophet Jonas, where those of Julius II. had previously been. But when the master, not wishing to do wrong to Julius and Clement, declined to execute them there, saying that it would not be well to do so, His Holiness yielded at once, that he might not give Michelagnolo pain, acknowledging at the same time the excellence of that man who followed the right and just alone, without flattery or undue respect of persons; a thing to which the great are but little accustomed.

Michelagnolo now caused an addition to be made to the wall of the Chapel, a sort of escarpment, carefully built of well-burnt and nicely chosen bricks, and projecting half a braccio at the summit, in such sort that no dust or other soil could lodge on the work. But I do not propose to enter into details as regards the compositions or inventions of this story, because there have been so many prints, great and small, made from it that I need not waste my time in describing the same.† Let it suffice to say that the purpose of this extraordinary master was no other than the representation by the pencil of the human form, in the absolute perfection of its proportions, and the greatest possible variety of attitude, with the passions, emotions, and affections of the soul, expressed with equal force and truth: it was sufficient to him to treat that branch of art wherein he was superior to all, and to lay open to others the grandeur of manner that might be attained in the nude form, by the display of what he could himself effect in the difficulties of design, thus

* Ciacconio, tom. iii. p. 247, has given an engraving of this Tomb.

† The largest print of this work is that published in fifteen plates, to be united into one, by C. M. Metz, in 1803.

facilitating the practice of art in its principal object, which is the human form. Keeping this end in view, he gave but slight attention to the attractions of colouring, or to the caprices and new phantasies of certain delicate minutiæ, which some painters, and not perhaps without good show of reason, have been especially careful to cultivate. Many, indeed, who have not possessed Michelagnolo's distinction in design, have sought by the variety of their tints and shades of colouring, by many fanciful and varied inventions, or, in short, by some other method of proceeding, to make their way to a place beside the first masters; but Michelagnolo, taking firm ground on the most recondite principles of art, has made manifest to all who know enough to profit by his teaching, the means by which they may attain perfection.

But to return to the story. Michelagnolo had brought three-fourths of the work to completion, when Pope Paul went to see it; and Messer Biagio da Cesena, the master of ceremonies, a very punctilious man, being in the Chapel with the Pontiff, was asked what he thought of the performance. To this he replied, that it was a very improper thing to paint so many nude forms, all showing their nakedness in that shameless fashion, in so highly honoured a place; adding that such pictures were better suited to a bath-room, or a road-side wine-shop, than to the chapel of a Pope. Displeased by these remarks, Michelagnolo resolved to be avenged; and Messer Biagio had no sooner departed than our artist drew his portrait from memory, without requiring a further sitting, and placed him in Hell under the figure of Minos, with a great serpent wound round his limbs,* and standing in the midst of a troop of devils: nor did the entreaties of Messer Biagio to the Pope and Michelagnolo, that this portrait might be removed, suffice to prevail on the master to consent; it was left as first depicted, a memorial of that event, and may still be seen.†

* Round the waist that is to say, and not round the limbs, Michael Angelo having followed the reading of Dante, his devoted admiration of whom is well known.

† The Pope is said to have replied to Messer Biagio's plaints by the comforting assurance that, "If the painter had put thee into Purgatory, I would have done all I could for thee, but since he hath sent thee to Hell, it is useless for thee to come to me, since thence, as thou knowest, *nulla est redemptio.*"

It chanced about this time that Michelagnolo fell from a no inconsiderable height of the scaffolding around this work and hurt his leg, yet in the pain and anger this caused him he would suffer no surgeon to approach his bed; wherefore the Florentine physician, Maestro Baccio Rontini, the friend of Michelagnolo, and a great admirer of his genius, who was a very eccentric person, taking compassion on his state, went one day to knock at the door of the house. Obtaining no reply, either from his neighbours or himself, he strove to make his way in by a secret entrance, and from room to room at length arrived at that wherein the master lay. He found him in a desperate state, but from that moment he would not leave his bed-side, and never lost sight of the patient until he had effectually cured the injured leg.

His malady overcome, and having returned to his work, the master laboured thereat continually for some months, when he brought it to an end, giving so much force to the figures of the same, that they verified the description of Dante,—"Dead are the dead, the living seem to live." The sufferings of the condemned and the joys of the blessed are exhibited with equal truth; wherefore, this painting being given to view, Michelagnolo was found to have surpassed not only all the early masters who had painted in that Chapel, but himself also, having resolved, as respected the ceiling which had rendered him so celebrated, to be his own conqueror; here, therefore, he had by very far exceeded that work, having imagined to himself all the terrors of the last day with the most vivid force of reality. For the greater pain of those who have not passed their lives well, he has represented all the Passion of our Saviour Christ, as presenting itself to their view; the cross, the column, the lance, the sponge, the nails, and the crown of thorns, being all borne in the air by nude figures; whose difficult and varied movements are executed with infinite facility. The seated figure of our Lord, with a countenance terrible in anger, is turned towards the condemned, on whom he thunders anathema, not without great horror on the part of Our Lady, who, wrapt in her mantle, is the witness of that destruction.

There are, besides, a vast number of figures, Prophets, and Apostles, surrounding the Saviour; those of Adam and St. Peter are more especially conspicuous, and they are believed to have been made so; the one as the first parent of those thus brought to judgment, the other as being the founder of the Christian religion. At the feet of Christ is a most beautiful figure of San Bartolommeo, holding forth the skin of which he was deprived; with a nude figure of San Lorenzo, and those of other saints male and female, to say nothing of the many other forms of men and women, some near and some at greater distance, who embrace each other and express their joy; they, by the grace of God and as the reward of their good works, having secured eternal blessedness. Beneath the feet of our Saviour are the seven Angels with the seven trumpets, described by St. John the Evangelist; and as they summon all to judgment, the terrible expression of their faces causes the hair to stand on end. Among the angels, there are two holding the Book of Life; while near them on one side, and not without admirable forethought, are the seven mortal sins in the form of demons: they are struggling to drag down to hell the souls which are flying, with beautiful attitudes and admirable foreshortenings, towards heaven.

Nor has our artist hesitated to show the world how, in the resurrection of the dead, these forms retake their flesh and bones from the earth itself, and how, assisted by others, already risen to life, they are soaring into the heavens, the blessed spirits above also lending them aid; every part exhibits the peculiarities that may be supposed best suited to such a work: the master having made sketches and endured fatigues of all kinds, as indeed may be clearly perceived throughout the whole. This is, perhaps, more particularly manifest in the barque of Charon, who stands in an attitude of furious anger, striking with his oars at the souls which are dragged into the boat by the devils; as Michelagnolo's most beloved author, Dante, has described him, when he says,—

> Charon, the demon, with the eyes of brass,
> Calls the sad troops, and having gathered all,
> Smites with raised oar the wretch that dares delay.

Nor would it be easy adequately to describe the variety displayed in the heads of those devils, which are truly monsters of hell. In the sinners also, the crimes they have committed, with their fear of eternal punishment for the same, are equally manifest; and, to say nothing of the beauty of this work, the harmony with which it is executed is so extraordinary that the pictures appear as if all painted in the same day, while the delicacy of their finish surpasses that of any miniature. But of a truth the number of the figures, with the grandeur and dignity of the composition, are such, while the expression of every passion proper to humanity is so fully and so wonderfully expressed, that no words could do the work justice. The proud, the envious, the avaricious, or the luxurious, are easily distinguished by one who examines with judgment, the master having given his attention to every point, and maintained the truth of Nature in each expression, attitude, and circumstance, of whatever kind; a thing which, however great and admirable, was not impossible to Michelagnolo, who was ever prudent and observing. He had seen many men and lived much in the world, thereby acquiring the knowledge which philosophers seek to obtain from books and reflection.

The man of judgment and one well versed in Art will here perceive the latter in all its force, and will discover thoughts and emotions in these figures such as were never depicted by any other than Michelagnolo himself. Here we may learn how the attitude may be varied even in the most extraordinary gestures of young men and old, male and female; and who can fail to perceive herein the greatness of his art, as well as the grace which had been imparted to him by Nature, when they move the hearts of the ignorant almost as they do those of men well versed in the matter? Foreshortenings are here seen which give the appearance of the most perfect relief, with a softness and delicacy of every part, showing what paintings may be when executed by good and true masters: but in some of these figures there are outlines turned by Michelagnolo in a manner that could have been effected by no other than himself. At a word, we have here the true Last Judgment, the real Condemnation, the effectual Resurrection. For our arts this work is, in short, the example of a great picture sent by God to men, thereby to show them how Fate proceeds, when spirits of the highest order are permitted to descend to this our earth, bearing within them the grace and divinity of knowledge as innate, or a part of themselves. Those who had before believed themselves acquainted with Art, are led bound and captive by the work before us, and, gazing on the evidence of power in these contours, they tremble and fear as if some great Spirit had possessed himself of the art of design; examining these labours, their senses are bewildered at the mere thought of what other paintings executed, or to be executed, must needs appear, when brought into comparison with this paragon.

Truly fortunate may that man be esteemed, and happy are his recollections, who has been privileged to behold this wonder of our age. Thrice blessed and fortunate art thou, O Paul III., since God has permitted that under thy protection was sheltered that renown which the pens of writers shall give to his memory and thine own! How highly are thy merits enhanced by his art!* A great happiness, moreover, has most assuredly been his birth for the artists of our time, since by the hand of Michelagnolo has been removed the veil of all those difficulties which had previously concealed the features of Painting, Sculpture, and Architecture: seeing that in his works he has given the solution of every difficulty in each one of those arts.

At this work Michelagnolo laboured eight years. He gave it to public view on Christmas day, and (as I think) in the year 1541. This he did to the amazement and delight, not of Rome only but of the whole world. For myself, I, who was at Venice that year, and went to Rome to see it, was utterly astounded thereby.†

Now Pope Paul had caused a Chapel, called the Pauline, to be built by Antonio da Sangallo, as we have before related, in imitation of that erected by Nicholas V., and he now resolved that Michelagnolo should there paint two large stories; in one of them our artist accordingly depicted the Conversion of St. Paul: Our Saviour Christ is seen in the air above, with a multitude of angels, nude figures, exhibiting the most graceful movements. On the earth beneath them lies Paul, fallen from his horse, stunned and bewildered; some of the soldiers standing around are about to raise him up, while others, terrified by the voice and the majesty of Christ, are betaking themselves to flight: their movements and attitudes are of singular beauty; the horse

* Let our readers take patience, remembering that Michael Angelo was the revered and beloved master of our excellent Giorgio.

† Michael Angelo caused a copy in oil to be made by Marcello Venusti, for the Cardinal Alessandro Farnese, and from the Palace of that House this picture ultimately came into the possession of the King of Naples. Of the numerous engravings from the Last Judgment we have not space here to make mention.

likewise, endeavouring to fly from the place, appears to hurry after him the servant who is seeking to restrain the velocity of his course; the whole story indeed offers evidence of extraordinary power and design. In the second picture is the Crucifixion of St. Peter, a most beautiful figure bound naked to the Cross. The executioners have made a hole in the earth wherein they are about to fix the cross, that the martyr may remain crucified with his feet in the air; a picture full of fine thought and consideration.*

The attention of Michelagnolo was constantly directed towards the highest perfection of art, as we have said elsewhere; we are therefore not here to look for landscapes, trees, buildings, or any other variety of attraction, for these he never regarded; perhaps because he would not abase his great genius to such matters. These were his last pictures, they were painted in his seventy-fifth year, and as he told me himself, at great cost of fatigue, seeing that painting, and more especially fresco, is not the work of those who have passed a certain age. Michelagnolo now arranged that Perino del Vaga, a most excellent painter, should decorate the ceiling with stucco-work and painting after his designs, and to this Pope Paul III. consented; but the work being delayed, nothing more was done, as indeed has been the case with many undertakings, which the irresolution of artists or the indifference of princes has caused to be left unfinished.

Pope Paul had begun to fortify the Borgo, and had called Antonio Sangallo, with many of the Roman nobles, to counsel in that matter, but knowing that Michelagnolo had directed the fortifications of San Miniato at Florence, he determined, after many disputes, to ask his opinion also. Thinking differently to Sangallo and most of the others, Michelagnolo nevertheless uttered his thoughts plainly, when Sangallo told him that sculpture and painting were his arts, and not fortification: to this Michelagnolo replied, that of sculpture and painting he knew but little; of fortification, on the contrary, the much he had thought of it, with what he had accomplished, had taught him more than had ever been known by Sangallo and all his house put together. He then proceeded, in the presence of all, to point out the errrors that had been committed. One word calling forth another, the Pope was compelled to

* These paintings, which had been much injured by dust and smoke, have of late years been carefully cleaned.—*Förster.*

impose silence on every one; but no long time afterwards, Michelagnolo brought the whole fortification of the Borgo, designed in such sort as to throw light over all that remained to be done; and this, opening the eyes of each person concerned, caused the great gate of Santo Spirito, designed by Sangallo, and then near its conclusion, to be discontinued and to remain unfinished.

The active spirit of Michelagnolo could not endure to continue unoccupied; and not being able to paint any longer, he set himself to work on a piece of marble, whence he proposed to extract a Pietà, consisting of four figures larger than life; doing this for his amusement and pastime as he said, and because the use of the hammer kept him in health. Our Saviour Christ, as taken from the Cross, is supported by the Virgin Mother, who is powerfully aided by Nicodemus, a figure standing beneath, with the feet firmly fixed on the earth. One of the Maries also, perceiving that the powers of Our Lady are about to fail, comes also to her aid, as, overcome by her grief, she can no longer support the form of her Son. A dead body equal to this of Christ could not possibly be found; sinking with the limbs in perfect abandonment, the attitude is different from that of any other, not of Michelagnolo's own execution only, but of any that has ever been made. The work is such as has rarely been extracted from a single stone, it is a truly beautiful as well as laborious one, but, as will be related hereafter, it suffered many mishaps,* and ultimately remained unfinished; although Michelagnolo had intended this group to serve as his own monument, and to be placed at the altar near which he hoped to be laid to his final rest.

In the year 1546, it chanced that Antonio da San Gallo died; a Director for the fabric of San Pietro was required, and there were various opinions as to who should be entrusted with the office; at length, and, as I believe, inspired by God, His Holiness resolved to send for Michelagnolo. Being asked if he would undertake the work, the master replied that he would not, architecture not being his vocation; but when entreaties were found useless, the Pope commanded him to accept the trust, and to his infinite regret

* It remained for many years in the sculpture room of the Chapel of St. Lorenzo, but in the year 1722, it was placed behind the High Altar in the Cathedral of Florence.

he was compelled to obey. One day among others that he had gone to the building accordingly, to see the model in wood prepared by Sangallo, and to examine the fabric, the whole party of the Sangallicans came to meet him, and in the best terms they could find, expressed their satisfaction at his appointment, remarking that the model before them was a field on which he need never want pasture. "You speak well," replied Michelagnolo, intending to imply (as he declared to one who was his friend) that the pasture was good for sheep and oxen and other animals who know nothing of art.* Nay, he would often publicly declare that Sangallo had left the building without lights, and had heaped too many ranges of columns, one above the other on the outside; adding, that with its innumerable projections, pinnacles, and divisions of members, it was more like a work of the Teutons than of the good antique manner, or of the cheerful and beautiful modern style; he furthermore affirmed that fifty years of time, with more than 300,000 crowns in the cost, might very well be spared, while the work might be completed with increased majesty, grandeur, and lightness, to say nothing of better design, more perfect beauty, and superior convenience.

He made a model also, to prove the truth of his words, and this was of the form wherein we now see the work to have been conducted; it cost twenty-five crowns, and was finished in a fortnight; that of Sangallo having exceeded four thousand, as we have said, and occupied several years in the making. From this and other circumstances, it was indeed easy to see that the Church had become an object of traffic and a means of gain, rather than a building to be completed; being considered, by those who undertook the work, as a kind of bargain to be turned to the best account. Such a state of things could not fail to displease so upright a man as Michelagnolo; and, as the Pope had made him Superintendent against his will, he determined to be rid of them all. He therefore one day told them openly that he knew well they had done and were doing all they could, by means of their friends, to prevent him from entering on this

* See Platner and Bunsen, *Beschreibung der Stadt Rom.*, vol. ii. p. 151, where the opinion of Michael Angelo as to this model will be found in a letter from himself to a certain Messer Bartolommeo; or the original of that letter may be consulted in the *Lettere Pittoriche*, tom. vi. p. 26.

office, but that if he were to undertake the charge, he would not suffer one of them to remain about the building. These words thus publicly spoken, were taken very ill, as may readily be supposed, and awakened so much hatred against Michelagnolo, that this, increasing daily as the whole arrangement of the work was seen to be changed both within and without, permitted Michelagnolo to have no peace, his adversaries constantly inventing new methods of tormenting him, as will hereafter be seen.

At length the Pontiff issued a *Motu-proprio*, by which he appointed him Superintendent of the fabric, with full authority to do or undo, decrease, extend, or change as it should seem good to him, and furthermore commanding that the whole government of those who were employed should be in his hands. Thereupon Michelagnolo, seeing the confidence which the Pope placed in him, desired to prove himself worthy thereof, and had a clause inserted in the *Motu-proprio*, to the effect that he performed his office for the love of God, and would accept no reward, although the Ferry of the river at Parma,* which had formerly been given to him by the Pope, had been lost to him by the death of the Duke Pier-Luigi, and he had received only a Chancery of Rimini, which brought him in but a small revenue, in its stead. But that circumstance he did not regard; and although Pope Paul more than once sent him money as a stipend, he would never accept any, a fact to which Messer Alessandro Ruffini, then Chancellor of the Pope, and Messer Pier Giovanni Aliotti, Bishop of Forli, have borne witness.

The model of the Church made by Michelagnolo was finally approved by the Pope, and this, although it decreased the circumference of the building, yet did in fact give it greater space, to the satisfaction of all who have judgment, although some, who profess to be judges, but in reality are not, are far from being pleased therewith. It was now found that the four principal piers constructed by Bramante, and left unaltered by Antonio da Sangallo, which had to support the weight of the Tribune, were too weak. Michelagnolo therefore, partly filled them up; and near them he made two spiral staircases, with steps of ascent so easy and so slightly inclined, that the asses used for carrying the

* This must be of Piacenza, and not Parma.—*Ed. Flor.*, 1832-8.

materials to the summit could mount and descend them, while men could go up on horseback to the platform of the arches. He formed the first cornice over the arches of travertine in a circular form, a beautiful work, of the most graceful effect, and quite different from the others; nor could there be anything better of that kind. He then commenced the two great recesses of the Transept; but whereas, by the order of Bramante, Baldassare, and Raffaello, there were to be eight niches or tabernacles on the side towards the Campo Santo, as we have said, an arrangement followed by Sangallo, Michelagnolo reduced them to three, with three chapels, raising over them a vaulting of travertine, and a range of windows, giving full light, varied in their form, and of very magnificent effect. But as these are finished, and are besides to be published by engravings, as are all the designs of Michelagnolo and of Sangallo likewise, I will not give myself the trouble of describing them, which is indeed unnecessary. Let it suffice to say, that where our artist made changes he caused all to be constructed with the utmost exactitude, adding a degree of strength which should leave no pretext for any other to disturb his plans. And this was the foresight of a prudent man, for it does not alway suffice to do well, unless further precaution be taken; seeing that the presumption and boldness of such as might be supposed—if you regard their words rather than their works—to know something, may cause many inconvenient changes.

Now the Roman people desired, under the favour of Pope Paul, to give some more decorous, beautiful, and convenient form to their Capitol, proposing to adorn it with columns, and flights of steps, having balustrades and broad stairs; to say nothing of the ancient statues wherewith it was to be further decorated. For this the advice of Michelagnolo was requested, and he made them a rich and beautiful design; this comprised a fine front in travertine, on the side of the Senate-house, towards the east namely, with a double flight of steps, ascending to a platform, whence you enter the middle of the Great Hall, the rich and varied balustrades of those steps serving at once as a support and a bulwark. And, for the further decoration of the same, he added antique figures of recumbent River-gods, nine braccia high, the Tiber and the Nile namely; these he has raised on pedestals, and between them there is to be the statue, in a large niche, of Jupiter.* On the south side, where is the Palace of the Conservators, and by way of bringing the building to a square form, there followed a rich and varied façade, with a Loggia of columns, and niches beneath, and here many antique statues are to be placed; doors, windows, and numerous ornaments are likewise in preparation, many of which are finished. A similar façade is to be erected opposite to this, on the north side beneath the Ara Cœli; and on the west, there is to be a flight of steps of very easy ascent, the whole surrounded by a balustrade; and here will be the principal entrance, which is further to be adorned by a range of pedestals, whereon the magnificence of those statues, in which the Capitol is now so rich, will be displayed.

In the centre of the Piazza, and on a pedestal of an oval form, is erected the Horse of bronze so much talked of, whereon there sits the figure of Marcus Aurelius, which Pope Paul III. caused to be removed from the Piazza of the Lateran, where it had been placed by Sixtus IV. By all these alterations and additions the edifice has now been rendered so beautiful that it merits to be accounted among the finest of Michelagnolo's works, although it is at present only in course of completion, not by himself, but by M. Tommaso de Cavalieri, a Roman gentleman, who has been and is one of the most faithful friends of Michelagnolo, as will be related hereafter.

While Antonio da Sangallo lived, Pope Paul had permitted him to continue the building of the Farnese Palace; but the upper cornice on the outside was still wanting, and His Holiness now desired that this should be added by Michelagnolo, after his own design, and under his direction. That master, therefore, not wishing to disoblige the Pope, who esteemed and favoured him so much, made a model in wood, seven braccia long, and of the exact size which the cornice was to be. This he caused to be fixed on one of the angles of the Palace that the effect might be seen, when, as the Pontiff and all Rome with him were much pleased therewith, it was put into execution, and so much of it as we now see was completed, proving to be the most beautiful and varied cornice ever erected, either by the ancients or moderns. On the death of Sangallo, Pope Paul desired, as we have said,

* These figures are now in the Vatican.

that Michelagnolo should undertake the charge of the whole Palace, where he constructed the great window with its beautiful columns of vari-coloured marble, which is over the principal entrance, adding a large escutcheon, also in marble, and bearing the arms of Paul III. the founder of that edifice.

He continued the great Court also, constructing two ranges of columns over those first erected, with the most beautiful windows, and a great variety of rich ornaments, ending with the great cornice; all of these works being so beautiful, that this Court, by the labour of Michelagnolo, has now become the finest in all Europe. Our artist likewise enlarged the great Hall, and made arrangements for the vestibule, which he vaulted after a new manner, in the form of a half oval. It chanced that in this year an antique group of Hercules, in marble, standing on a mountain, and holding a bull by the horns, was discovered at the warm baths of Antoninus; a second figure is assisting Hercules, the group is seven braccia square: around the hill are nymphs, herdsmen, and different animals. The whole work is certainly one of great beauty, the figures being in full relief: it was adjudged to have been intended for a fountain, and Michelagnolo advised that it should be placed in the second Court, where, being restored, it might be used for the same purpose. This advice pleased every one, and by command of the Signori Farnesi, the group is now receiving the most careful restoration to that effect.*

It was at this time that Michelagnalo proposed the erection of a bridge, to cross the Tiber at the point where it would form a road from the Farnese Palace in the Trastevere, to another palace belonging to the same family; when a view might be obtained from the principal entrance on the Campo di Fiori across the Court, and comprising the Fountain, the Strada Julia, this bridge, and the beautiful gardens, even to the opposite gate which opens on the road of the Trastevere; a magnificent idea, and one fully worthy of that Pontiff, as well as of the genius and judgment of Michelagnolo.

In the year 1547, Bastiano Viniziano, the Monk of the leaden seal, departed this life; and as the Pope was then pro-

* Our readers will not need to be reminded that this group, known as the *Toro Farnese*, is now in Naples. They will also perceive that the figure here called Hercules is that of Dirce.

posing to have the antique Statues of the Vatican restored, Michelagnolo favoured the Milanese sculptor, Guglielmo della Porta, a youth of great promise, who had been recommended to him by Fra Bastiano, and with whom Michelagnolo was himself much pleased; he presented him to Pope Paul, therefore, from whom Guglielmo received a commission to restore two of the Statues in question,* and Michelagnolo afterwards caused the office of the leaden seal to be conferred on Della Porta, who continued the restoration of the statues also, as we now see them in the palace; but, forgetful of all these benefits, Fra Guglielmo subsequently became one of the master's most eager opponents.

The death of Pope Paul took place in the year 1549, when Julius III. was elected High Pontiff; and Cardinal Farnese then commissioned Fra Guglielmo to construct a vast Sepulchre for his kinsman Paul III. That artist proposed to erect it under the first arch of the new Church beneath the Tribune.† But this interfered with the plans of the architect, and was in effect not the proper place for the Tomb; wherefore, Michelagnolo judiciously advised that it should not be constructed there; this caused Fra Guglielmo, who thought our artist acted from envious motives, to conceive a bitter hatred against him, but time has proved Michelagnolo right, and the fault was all with Guglielmo, who, having the opportunity for producing a fine work, failed to make use of it, as I shall mention further elsewhere, and can here plainly show. For it chanced that in the year 1550, I had gone to Rome by order of Pope Julius III., there to enter the service of that Pontiff, and the more gladly as I could thus be near Michelagnolo, when I took part in the council held respecting that matter of the Tomb, which Michelagnolo wished to have placed within one of those niches, where now stands the Column of the Possessed, and which was indeed its proper position. I had also laboured to secure from Pope Julius the selection of

* Among the statues thus restored was the Hercules of Glicon, so well known as the "Farnese Hercules," the legs of which he executed so well, that when the antique legs were discovered (in 1560) Michael Angelo would not suffer them to replace those of Guglielmo, and they were deposited in a room of the Vatican.

† For details which cannot here find place, the reader who shall desire such, may consult Bricolani, *Descrizione della sacrosanta Basilica Vaticana*, p. 60.

he opposite niche as the place of his own sepulchre, which ras to correspond in manner with that of Paul III., but the pposition of Fra Guglielmo caused his own work to remain nfinished,* while the construction of that of Pope Julius ras likewise prevented; results which had all been predicted y Michelagnolo.

In the same year Pope Julius resolved to erect a marble hapel in San Pietro-a-Montorio, with two sepulchral monuaents, the one for his uncle Antonio Cardinal di Monte, and he other for Messer Fabiano his grandfather, who had laid he foundation of greatness for that illustrious house. For hese works Vasari made the designs and models, when Pope Julius, who admired the genius of Michelagnolo and loved Vasari, commanded that the former should fix the price to be paid for those labours, and Vasari entreated the Pontiff to prevail on Michelagnolo to take the work under his protection. Now Vasari had proposed that Simon Mosca should be employed to prepare carvings for this Chapel, and that Raffaello di Montelupo should execute statues; but Michelagnolo advised that no carvings of foliage should be added, nor any decorations of that kind used among the architectural portions of the monuments, remarking that where there are marble statues there should be no other ornament. Vasari meanwhile was afraid the work would look poor; but when he afterwards saw it completed, he confessed that Michelagnolo had displayed judgment, nay, great judgment.

The master was also unwilling that Raffaello da Monte Lupo should have the commission for the statues, remembering that he had not acquitted himself well in those which he had executed under his own guidance for the Tomb of Pope Julius II. He therefore preferred to see them confided to Bartolommeo Ammannati, whom Vasari was likewise seeking to put forward for that occasion, although Michelagnolo had a touch of personal dislike against him, as well as against Nanni di Baccio Bigio. But this displeasure, if we consider all things, had arisen from slight causes, these artists having offended from love of art rather than from a desire to wrong him. Being youths that is to say, they had taken several drawings by Michelagnolo from his disciple Antonio

* It was subsequently completed, and in the niche destined by our author for the tomb of Pope Julius III., that of Pope Urban VIII. has been erected.

Mini, but these were afterwards restored by the intervention of the Council of Eight, and the master himself had employed the intercession of his friend Messer Giovanni Norchiati, canon of San Lorenzo,* to save the boys from any further punishment. Michelagnolo was once talking to Vasari about this matter when the latter told him laughingly, that he did not consider the young men so very blameable, and would himself have taken, not some drawings only, but all that he could have laid hands on, acting from the love of art and in the hope of improvement only, seeing that those who would make progress must proceed with force of will, and should be rewarded for their zeal rather than punished as are those who steal money or property of that kind. The matter was thus turned into a jest, and the work being commenced that year, Ammannato went with Vasari to Carrara, to prepare the marbles.

Vasari was at this time in the company of Michelagnolo daily, and one morning in the Jubilee year, the Pope in his kindness gave them both a holiday, to the effect that they might accompany a cavalcade which was riding forth to visit the Seven Churches, and might thus receive the absolution together. In doing this they had much useful and pleasing discourse, while going from one church to another, respecting the arts and other vocations, and Vasari wrote the whole dialogue, which he intends to publish at some future day, with other matters concerning art.† In the same year, Pope Julius confirmed the *Motu-proprio* of Paul III. in respect to the fabric of San Pietro, and although the Sangallican faction found great fault with what Michelagnolo had ordered for the building, the Pontiff would at that time hear nothing of all they could say; Vasari having assured him that Michelagnolo had given life to the edifice (as was the truth), and persuading His Holiness to do nothing in respect to his design for San Pietro, without the full concurrence of the master, a promise to which Pope Julius, having once given it, constantly adhered. Nor would he suffer anything to be done without Michelagnolo's advice either at the Vigna Julia or the Belvedere. The flight of steps now used was at that time constructed at the last-mentioned palace, in

* Author of a Commentary on Vitruvius and a Vocabulary of the Arts (never completed), as also of the *Trattato dei Dittonghi Toscani*.

† This design was never accomplished.

place of the semi-circular staircase previously existing there, and which, having ascended eight steps, turned inwards and ascended eight more, as designed by Bramante. This was erected in the great recess in the centre of the Belvedere, but Michelagnolo now designed the beautiful quadrangular staircase with a balustrade of peperino marble, as we still see it.

It was in this same year that Vasari completed the printing of his book, comprising the Biography of the Painters, Sculptors, and Architects; but he had written the life of no surviving artist (although many were very old), Michelagnolo alone excepted. He now presented his work to that master, who received it very gladly, many facts derived from his own lips having been recorded therein, for he, being of so advanced an age, and having so much judgment as well as experience, was well able to afford much information. No long time afterwards, having read the book, Michelagnolo sent Vasari the following sonnet, which he had written, and which, in memory of his affection, I think it well to add in this place :—

> If with the chisel and the colours, thou
> Hast made Art equal Nature, now thy hand
> Hath e'en surpassed her, giving us her beauties
> Rendered more beautiful. For with sage thought
> Now hast thou set thyself to worthier toils,
> And what was wanting still, hast now supplied,
> In giving life to others; thus depriving
> Her boast of its last claim to rise above thee.
> Is there an age whose labours may not hope
> To reach the highest point? yet by thy word
> All gain the limit to their toils prescribed.
> The else extinguished memories thus revived
> To new and radiant life, by thee, shall now
> Endure, with thine own fame, throughout all time.

Vasari, having soon afterwards returned to Florence, remitted the charge of laying the foundations at San Pietro-a-Montorio to Michelagnolo; but to Messer Bindo Altoviti, then Consul of the Florentines and a great friend of Vasari, the latter remarked that it would have been much better if the Tomb of Pope Julius had been erected in the Church of San Giovanni de' Fiorentini, Giorgio added, that he had already spoken on the subject to Michelagnolo, who wished to promote the change, seeing that this would be a good opportunity for completing that Church. The proposal pleased Messer Bindo, who, being admitted to much familiarity by the Pope, pressed it zealously on His Holiness, urging that it would be much better to construct the Chapel and Tomb in the Church of San Giovanni than at Montorio, because the Florentines, impelled by the motive for action thus presented, would at length be induced to supply the monies needful for the completion of the Church; seeing, that if His Holiness would make the principal Chapel, there were merchants who would make six more, and so on by degrees, until all should be finished. The Pope changed his mind accordingly, although the model had been made and the price of the work agreed on; and going to Montorio, he sent for Michelagnolo. Thereupon Vasari, who was daily writing to the latter and obtaining intelligence of all that was going on there, in reply, received the following, dated August 1, 1550, wherein he notifies the Pontiff's change of purpose, and these are the words themselves as they came from his own hand :—

"My dear Messer Giorgio,—With respect to the foundations at San Pietro Montorio, I write you nothing, seeing that the Pope will not hear of them, and I know you are well advised thereof by your man that is here. But I desire to tell you what follows, and that is, that yesterday morning the Pope having repaired to the said Montorio, sent for me : I met him on the bridge as he was returning, and had a long conversation with him in regard to the Tombs confided to you. At length he told me that he had determined not to construct them on the Mount, but in the Church of the Florentines, desiring to have my opinion and designs for the same ; whereupon I encouraged him in that purpose, considering that the Church would thus be finished. Respecting your last three letters, I have no pen that can reply to such high matters; but if I should rejoice to be what you make me, it would be principally that you might have a servant who should be worth something. Yet why should I marvel that you, being the restorer to life of dead men should add life to those who are still living? But to shorten my words, such as I am, I am wholly yours,

"Michelagnolo. *Rome.*"

While these affairs were in course of arrangement and the Florentines in Rome were labouring to raise money, certain difficulties arose; there was nothing concluded and the matter began to cool. But Vasari and Ammannato had now caused all the marbles to be excavated at Carrara, whereupon they were sent to Rome, and Ammannato with them, Vasari writing by him to Buonarroto, desiring the latter to get an order from the Pope as to where the work was to be executed, and having received it, to let the foundations be laid. As soon as Michelagnolo had read this letter, he spoke to our Lord the Pope, and wrote to Vasari as follows :—

"My dear Messer Giorgio,—As soon as Bartolommeo had arrived, I went to speak to the Pope, and seeing that he wished the Tombs to be at Montorio, I began to look out for a builder from San Pietro. But when Tantecose* heard of it, he desired to choose one after his own mind; whereupon I withdrew, not wishing to struggle with one who commands the winds, and who is so light-minded a man that I think it better not to involve myself in any question with him. At all events, the Church of the Florentines is no longer to be thought of. Return as soon as you can; and, meanwhile, fare you well. Nothing further remains to say, 15th Oct. 1556."

Michelagnolo called the Bishop of Forlì† *Tantecose,* because he liked to meddle with every kind of matter; being principal chamberlain to the Pope, he had under his care all the medals, jewels, cameos, small figures in bronze, and other things of similar kind, but he would fain have had everything depend on himself. Michelagnolo avoided him carefully, finding the Bishop's meddling always unfriendly to himself, and fearing lest the ambition of the prelate should involve him in some trouble. Be this as it may, the Florentines in Rome lost an excellent occasion for completing their Church. God knows when they may have such another, and the failure gave me indescribable vexation. I would not omit the mention of the matter, desiring to show how constantly Michelagnolo sought to benefit those of his country as well as to assist his friends and brother artists.

Scarcely had Vasari returned to Rome, and the year 1551 had not well commenced, before the Sangallican faction had formed a plot against Michelagnolo, making interest to

* Mr. Busy-body, Much-a-do, or whatever may best express a meddling disposition; Tante-cose meaning simply "many things."

† Or perhaps Messer Pier Giovanni Aliotti.—*Bottari.*

prevail on the Pope to assemble all concerned in the building of San Pietro, declaring, with false calumnies, that they could show His Holiness how Michelagnolo was spoiling the edifice. He had constructed the recess of the King, where the three chapels are that is to say, and had placed three windows in the upper part; but these people, not knowing what he was proposing to do in the vaulting, with their feeble judgment had given the old Cardinal Salviati, and Marcello Cervino, who was afterwards Pope,* to understand that San Pietro would be left with insufficient light. All being assembled accordingly, the Pope told Michelagnolo that the deputies declared that part of the church to be unduly deprived of light, when the master replied that he would like to hear those deputies speak. "We are the deputies," replied Cardinal Marcello; and Michelagnolo rejoined, "Monsignore, in the vaulting above, and which is to be of travertine, there are to go three other windows."—"You have never told us so," returned the Cardinal; to which Michelagnolo responded, "I neither am nor will be obliged to tell either your lordship or any other person what I intend or ought to do for this work; your office is to procure money, and to take care that thieves do not get the same; the designs for the building you are to leave to my care." Then turning to the Pope, he said, "Holy Father, if the labours I endure do not benefit my soul, I am losing my time vainly for this work;" to which the Pope, who loved him, replied, laying his hands on the shoulders of the master, "You will be a gainer both for your soul and in the body; do not doubt it."

Having rid himself of those who desired to unseat Michelagnolo, the love of the Pope for that master increased daily, and he commanded that Vasari, as well as himself, should repair to the Vigna Julia, on the very day following that of the assembly above described. Here the Pontiff had much conversation with them, discussing all the admirable improvements since effected there, nor did he meditate or decide on any work of design without the opinion and judgment of Michelagnolo. And among other occasions, that artist once going thither, as he frequently did, with Vasari, they found the Pope, with twelve cardinals, by the Fountain of the Aqua Vergine, when His Holiness would

* Marcello survived his election to the papal chair a few weeks only.

compel Michelagnolo to be seated near him, however humbly he excused himself, the Pontiff always doing every possible honour to his genius.

Pope Julius likewise made him prepare the model for a palace, which His Holiness wished to build near San Rocco, proposing to make the Mausoleum of Augustus serve as a part of the masonry; nor would it be possible to find the design of a façade more varied, original, rich or beautiful than is this, seeing that Michelagnolo, as may be remarked in all his works, would never restrict himself to any laws, whether ancient or modern, as regarded architecture, he being one who had ever the power to invent things no less beautiful than varied and original. This model is now in the possession of the Duke Cosimo de' Medici, to whom, when he went to Rome, it was given by Pope Pius IV., and who has deposited it among his most valued possessions. This Pontiff regarded Michelagnolo so highly that he constantly defended him against all the Cardinals and others who sought to do him injury. He also required every other artist, however able or distinguished, to wait on Michelagnolo at his own house: nay, his consideration for our artist was so great that, fearing to demand too much, he refrained from asking many a work, which the master, notwithstanding his age, might very well have performed.

In the time of Pope Paul III. Michelagnolo had received a commission from that Pontiff to repair the foundations of the Bridge of Santa Maria, which had been weakened by time and the perpetual flow of the waters. The piers had been carefully repaired, or rather refounded, by means of coffer-dams, and a great portion of the work had been concluded, at a great expense for timber and travertine. Under the pontificate of Julius III. there was question in the Council of bringing this bridge to an end: certain among those present proposing that the architect, Nanni di Baccio Bigio, should finish it by contract, they alleging that it would thus be done in a short time and at small cost. The Clerks of the Chamber pretended, moreover, that this would be a relief to Michelagnolo, who was now old, and cared so little for the matter that the work, at the rate it then proceeded, could never be brought to an end. The Pope was no lover of disputes, and not thinking of the consequences that might ensue, he gave the desired authorization, bidding them manage the matter as an affair of their own. The fabric, with all the materials collected, was then committed, without Michelagnolo knowing anything of what was going forward, to Nanni, who had full power to treat it as he pleased, when he not only neglected the precautions needful to the security of the foundations, but even removed and sold a great part of the blocks of travertine with which the bridge had been anciently strengthened and paved (a thing which greatly added to the stability and duration of the structure), supplying the place of those blocks with gravel, and materials of similar kind, so that there was no want of solidity in appearance. Nanni also made bulwarks and other external defences, causing the Bridge to be seemingly well restored, while in fact it had been much weakened and deteriorated. Five years afterwards, however, and when the flood of 1557 came down, the whole fabric fell to ruin, in such a manner as to prove the error of judgment which the Clerks of the Chamber had committed, and the injury which Rome had suffered from their disregard of Michelagnolo's advice. He had indeed frequently predicted the ruin of the bridge to his friends, and I remember that when we were one day crossing it on horseback, he said, "Giorgio, this bridge shakes beneath us, let us be gone, that it may not fall while we are on it."

But to return to a subject before touched on: when the work of Montorio was, to my great satisfaction, completed, I returned to Florence to the service of Duke Cosimo; this was in the year 1554. The departure of Vasari grieved Michelagnolo, as indeed it did Georgio, and as no day passed wherein the adversaries of the master did not labour to vex him, now in one way and now in another, so did these two not fail to write to each other daily. In the April of the same year Vasari gave Michelagnolo notice, that a son had been born to his nephew Leonardo, the child, whom Georgio had accompanied to his baptism, having been attended by a most honourable train of noble ladies, and receiving the name of Buonarroto. To this letter Michelagnolo replied by the following:—

"My dear Friend Giorgio,—I have felt much pleasure in reading your last, seeing that you still remember the poor old man, and also because you were present at the triumph of which you write, and have seen the birth of another Buonarroto. For this intelligence I thank you as much as I can or may, although I am displeased by so much pomp, seeing that no man should laugh when the whole world is in tears. I think, too, that Leonardo should not rejoice so much over the birth of one who is but beginning to live; such joy should be reserved for the death of one who has lived well. Do not be surprised if I have not replied immediately; and for the many praises you send me, if I could only deserve one of them, I should then think that in giving myself to you, soul and body, I might perhaps have given you something that might, in some small measure, repay the much wherein I am your debtor: but I must acknowledge you my creditor for more than I can ever pay, and being old I have now no hope of acquitting myself. In the next life we may nevertheless regulate our account, wherefore I pray you to take patience, and am wholly yours. Things here stand much as before."*

So early as the time of Paul III. Duke Cosimo had sent Tribolo to Rome to try if he could persuade Michelagnolo to return to Florence, there to finish the Sacristy of San Lorenzo; but the master had excused himself, saying that he was become old, might no longer endure the fatigue of labour, and could not leave Rome. Tribolo then inquired as to the steps for the Library of San Lorenzo, for which Michelagnolo had caused many of the stones to be prepared, but for which no model, nor any certain indication of the form in which they were to be constructed, could be found. It is true that there were some few sketches of a pavement and other things in *terra*, yet the correct and final design of the work could not be ascertained. But not all the entreaties of Tribolo, although he brought in the name of the Duke, could move Michelagnolo to say more than that he did not remember.

The Duke then commanded Vasari to write to the master, since it was hoped that for love of him Michelagnolo would perhaps say something which might enable them to bring

* The German translator of our author gives a different reading of this passage, which we add, together with the original; let our reader take his choice:—*E le cose di quà stan pur così.* Of this the German translator makes, "Und so geht's in der *Welt* ! !" (which is the way of the world); a reading which the original, as our readers perceive, may bear, but the notes of exclamation are the German's, and not the Italian's, a circumstance which, in this case, makes a material difference.

the work to conclusion. Vasari wrote to him accordingly as the Duke desired, adding, that of all which had to be done Vasari was to be the director, and would do everything with the utmost fidelity, taking care of every minutia, as of a work of his own. To this Michelagnolo replied by sending the plans for the work in a letter written by his own hand on the 28th of September, 1555.

"MESSER GIORGIO, MY DEAR FRIEND,—About the Staircase whereof there has been so much said, believe that if I could remember how I had arranged it I should not require so many entreaties. There is a certain stair that comes into my thoughts like a dream ; but I do not think it is exactly the one which I had planned at that time, seeing that it appears to be but a clumsy affair ; I will describe it for you here nevertheless. I took a number of oval boxes, each about one palm deep, but not of equal length and breadth. The first and largest I placed on the pavement at such distance from the wall of the door as seemed to be required by the greater or lesser degree of steepness you may wish to give to the stair. Over this was placed another, smaller in all directions, and leaving sufficient room on that beneath for the foot to rest on in ascending, thus diminishing each step as it gradually retires towards the door ; the uppermost step being exactly of the width required for the door itself. This part of the oval steps must have two wings, one right, the other left. The steps of the wings to rise by similar degrees, but not to be oval in form. The ascent by the middle flight, from the centre to the upper part, shall be for the Signore ; the turn of the wings must be towards the wall.* But from the centre downwards to the pavement, they shall be kept at the distance of about three palms, in such sort that the basement of the vestibule shall not be infringed upon in any part. What I am writing is a thing to be laughed at, but I know well that you will find something suitable to your purpose."*

* Gaye, *Carteggio*, makes it doubtful whether Vasari finished these steps or not; and a Florentine commentator says, "Although Michael Angelo had left the steps, the balustrade, and many other parts of this work in a state of preparation, it is manifest that Vasari did not succeed in comprehending the master's wish. He constructed a magnificent flight of steps without doubt, but not that intended by Michael Angelo. See Ruggieri, *Studio d'Architettura civile*; also Rossi, *Libreria Medicea-Laurenziana*.

In those days Michelagnolo wrote to Vasari, to the effect that, Julius III. being dead, and Marcellus being elected in his place, the faction adverse to himself was beginning to torment him anew. The Duke hearing this, and being displeased by those proceedings, made Giorgio write to Michelagnolo, bidding him leave Rome and come to Florence, where his Excellency would ask nothing more from him than occasional advice respecting his buildings and other works of art, but was ready to grant him whatever he might desire without wishing him to lay a hand upon anything.* Messer Leonardo Marinozzi, private secretary to the Duke, was also the bearer of a letter to that effect from his Excellency, as well as of one from Vasari. But Marcellus having died, and Pope Paul IV. being elected High Pontiff, Michelagnolo, who had gone to kiss the feet of the new Pope, had received the most amicable offers from His Holiness; and desiring to see the completion of San Pietro, while he also thought himself bound in a certain sort to that employment, the master wrote to the Duke, excusing himself for that he could not then enter his service; and to Vasari he sent the following words:—

"Messer Giorgio, my dear Friend,—I call God to witness how much against my will it was that I was put into the Fabric of San Pietro ten years since by Paul III.; had they subsequently continued to work at that edifice, as they then did, I should have now brought it to such a state that I might be permitted to think of returning home; but for want of money the work has been retarded, and that at a time when the most laborious and difficult part of it has come to be executed: insomuch, that to abandon it now would be no other than a great shame and sin, whereby I should lose the reward of all those toils which for the love of God I have endured for the last ten years. I make you this discourse in reply to your letter, and because I have a letter from the Duke which makes me not a little to marvel that his Lordship should write with so much kindness;† I thank God and his Excellency so much as I may and can.

* The reader will find the letters of Duke Cosimo to Michael Angelo in Gaye, *Carteggio inedito*, vol. iii.; they give evidence of much kindness in the prince, and of his great respect for the master.

† See Gaye, as above cited.

But I depart from my subject, I have indeed last my memory and understanding; writing is besides a great trouble to me, seeing that it is not my vocation. The conclusion is this: to make you comprehend what would follow if I were to abandon the above-named building and depart hence. Firstly, I should rejoice many a worthless scoundrel; and lastly, I should cause the ruin, or perhaps indeed the final suspension, of the edifice."

Michelagnolo furthermore wrote to Vasari, telling him, for his excuse with the Duke, that having a house and many other comforts in Rome, worth some thousands of crowns, and suffering besides from many infirmities of age, he was unfit for the fatigues of travelling, as Messer Eraldo his physician, to whom, after God, he owed it that he was yet in life, could testify. He added, that for all these causes he was unable to leave Rome, and had, indeed, courage for nothing more than to die and be at rest. In other letters from his hand, which Vasari has kept, he begs the latter to excuse him to the Duke; and did himself also write to his Excellency, as I have said. Nay, had he been in a condition to travel, he would have repaired instantly to Florence; and the kindness shown to him by Duke Cosimo had moved him so deeply that I do not believe he would in that case have found resolution to depart again.

Meanwhile he pressed forward the works of San Pietro in various parts of the building, desiring to bring it to such a state that the arrangement thereof could no more be changed. About this time he was told that Pope Paul IV. bethought himself of having certain parts of the Paintings in the Chapel altered, His Holiness considering that the figures in the Last Judgment where shamefully nude. When Michelagnolo, therefore, received a message from the Pope to that effect, he replied: "Tell His Holiness that this is a mere trifle, and can be easily done; let him mend the world, paintings are easily mended."

The office of the Chancery at Rimini was now taken from our artist, but he would not speak of the matter to His Holiness, who knew nothing about it, his Cupbearer having withdrawn it from Michelagnolo, with the intention of paying him a hundred crowns per month instead, by way of stipend, for his services at San Pietro; but when the first month of that stipend was sent to the master's house, he refused to receive the money. In the same year there happened to Michelagnolo the death of Urbino, his servant, or rather his companion, for such he had become.* This man had entered his master's service at Florence, in the year of the Siege, and after Antonio Mini, his disciple, had gone to France; he was a most zealous servant, and in the twenty-six years of his abode with his master the latter had made him rich, and had loved him so much, that although so old, he had nursed him in his sickness, and slept at night in his clothes beside him, the better to watch for his comforts. When Urbino died, therefore, Vasari wrote to Michelagnolo to console him, and the master replied in these words:—

"My dear Messer Giorgio,—I can but ill write at this time, yet to reply to your letter I will try to say something. You know that Urbino is dead, and herein have I received a great mercy from God, but to my heavy grief and infinite loss. The mercy is this, that whereas in his life he has kept me living, so in his death he has taught me to die, not only without regret, but with the desire to depart. I have had him twenty-six years, have ever found him singularly faithful, and now that I had made him rich, and hoped to have in him the staff and support of my old age, he has disappeared from my sight; nor have I now left any other hope than that of rejoining him in Paradise. But of this God has given me a foretaste, in the most blessed death that he has died; his own departure did not grieve him, as did the leaving me in this treacherous world, with so many troubles. Truly is the best part of my being gone with him, nor is anything now left me except an infinite sorrow. And herewith I bid you farewell."

Under Paul IV., Michelagnolo was much employed in many parts of the fortifications of Rome; and for Salustio Peruzzi, to whom that Pontiff had entrusted the construction of the Great Gate of the Castello Sant' Angelo, now half ruined, as we have related elsewhere, he undertook to distribute the statues required for that work, as well as to see and correct the models of the sculptors. At this time the French army approached Rome, and Michelagnolo, believing

* In all things not appertaining to art, Michael Angelo permitted himself to be managed entirely by this trusted friend and servant.

that he might himself come to an evil end, together with the City, resolved to depart with Antonio Franzese, of Castel Durante, whom Urbino had left him at his death to serve him. He fled secretly from Rome accordingly, retiring into the mountains of Spoleto, where he visited several abodes of the Hermits. At that time Vasari wrote to him, sending him a little work which the Florentine citizen, Carlo Lenzoni, had left at his death to Messer Cosimo Bartoli, who was to have it printed, and dedicated to Michelagnolo.* It was just then finished, and Vasari, who despatched it to Michelagnolo, received the following in reply:—

"MESSER GIORGIO, MY DEAR FRIEND,—I have received Messer Cosimo's little book, and in this shall be an acknowledgment, which I beg you to present to him with my service.

"I have in these last days undertaken a visit in the Mountains of Spoleto, to the Hermits abiding there, at great cost of labour and money, but also to my great pleasure, insomuch that I have returned to Rome with but half my heart, for of a truth one finds no peace or quiet like that of those woods. More I have not to tell you. I rejoice that you are well and happy, and recommend myself to your friendly remembrance. This 18th day of Sept., 1556."

Michelagnolo worked for his amusement almost every day at the group of four figures, of which we have before made mention; but he broke up the block at last, either because it was found to have numerous veins, was excessively hard, and often caused the chisel to strike fire, or because the judgment of this artist was so severe, that he could never content himself with anything that he did, a truth of which there is proof in the fact that few of his works, undertaken in manhood, were ever completed; those entirely finished having been the productions of his youth. Such for example were the Bacchus, the Pietà of the Madonna della Febbre, the Colossal Statue at Florence, and the Christ of the Minerva, which are finished to such perfection, that a single

* This work, the title of which is *Difesa della Lingua Toscana e di Dante*, was most appropriately dedicated to Michael Angelo (but by Giambullari rather than Lenzoni, who did not complete the work), that master's profound study of, and affectionate veneration for the great poet being well known.

grain could not be taken from them without injury;* while the Statues of the Dukes Giuliano and Lorenzo,† with those of Night, Aaron, Moses, and the two figures belonging to the latter, altogether not amounting to eleven statues, have still remained incomplete. The same may be said of many others; nay, Michelagnolo would often remark, that if he were compelled really to satisfy himself in the works to be produced, he should give little or nothing to public view. And the reason of this is obvious, he had proceeded to such an extent of knowledge in art, that the very slightest error could not exist in any figure, without his immediate discovery thereof; but having found such after the work had been given to view, he would never attempt to correct it, and would commence some other production, believing that the like failure would not happen again; this then was, as he often declared, the cause wherefore the number of pictures and statues finished by his hand was so small.

When he had broken the Pietà, as related above, he gave it to Francesco Bandini, and this happened about the time when the Florentine sculptor, Tiberio Calcagni, had been made known to Michelagnolo, by the intervention of that Bandini, and of Messer Donato Giannotti, for he being one day in the house of the master, where the broken Pietà still remained, inquired, after a long discussion, wherefore he had destroyed so admirable a performance? to this our artist replied, that he had been moved thereto by the importunities of Urbino his servant, who was daily entreating him to finish that work: there had besides been a piece broken off the arm of the Madonna; and these things, with a vein which had appeared in the marble and had caused him infinite trouble, had deprived him of patience, insomuch that he not only broke the group, but would have dashed it to pieces, if his servant Antonio had not advised him to refrain, and to give it to some one even as it was. Hearing this, Tiberio

* "Among the works of Michael Angelo's youth," observes a German annotator, "is the beautiful group of the Virgin and Child in the Church of Notre Dame at Bruges, originally destined for Genoa. It was seized by a Dutch privateer, and taken to Amsterdam, where it was purchased by a merchant of Bruges, and presented to the church above-named. It was taken to Paris, with other spoils, by the French, but was subsequently restored, and is now in the church."

† These two statues are finished, as are the allegorical figures which accompany them.—*Ed. Flor.*, 1832-8.

spoke to Bandini, who desired to have something from his hand; and by means of the latter, Antonio received the offer of two hundred crowns in gold, on condition that he should prevail on Michelagnolo, to permit that Tiberio, aided by the models of the master, should complete the group for Bandini, by which means the labour already expended on it would cease to be lost.

Michelagnolo presented them with the broken marbles accordingly, and they instantly carried them away, when the parts were put together by Tiberio, certain portions, I know not what, being added: but the death of Bandino, of Michelagnolo, and of Tiberio himself, caused the work to remain unfinished after all. It is now in the possession of Pierantonio Bandini, son of Francesco, and may be seen at his Villa of Montecavallo.* But to return to Michelagnolo, it now became needful to find some other block of marble, that he might daily have opportunity for amusing himself with his chisel; he took a much smaller piece therefore, wherein he commenced another Pietà, but in a different manner.†

Now the architect, Piero Ligorio, had entered the service of Pope Paul IV., and, busying himself with the fabric of San Pietro, he disturbed Michelagnolo anew, going about declaring that the latter had fallen into second childhood. This offended our artist exceedingly, he would fain have then returned to Florence, and was much pressed to do so by Giorgio; but feeling that he had become old, for he had then attained his eighty-first year, he excused himself to Vasari, to whom, writing in his ordinary manner, he sent several spirited sonnets, setting forth that the end of his days was nearly come, that he must now be careful to direct his thoughts to suitable objects, that his letters must prove him to be at his eleventh hour, and that no thought arose in his mind which did not bear the impress of approaching death. He added in one of his letters, "God has willed that the burden of my life must be endured for some time longer. I know you will tell me that, being old, I am unwise to attempt the making of sonnets, but since they say I am in my dotage, I do but perform my proper office. I see well the love you bear me, and do you, on your part, know to a certainty that I would gladly rest my weak frame by the

* The fate of this work cannot now be ascertained.—*Ed. Flor.*, 1838.

† This is the group mentioned in a previous note. See *ante*, p. 292.

ones of my father, as you exhort me to; but if I departed ence I should cause great injury to the fabric of St. Peter, which would be a shame as well as heavy sin; yet when all s so far completed that nothing can be changed, I hope still o do as you desire, if indeed it be not sinful to disappoint a et of rogues who are expecting me daily to leave the world."

With this letter there came the following sonnet:—

"Now in frail bark, and on the storm-tossed wave,
Doth this my life approach the common port,
Whither all haste to render up account
Of every act,—the erring and the just.
Wherefore I now do see, that by the love
Which rendered Art mine idol and my lord,
I did much err. Vain are the loves of man,
And error lurks within his every thought.
Light hours of this my life, where are ye now,
When towards a twofold death my foot draws near?
The one well-known, the other threatening loud.
Not the erst worshipped Art can now give peace
To him whose soul turns to that love divine,
Whose arms shall lift him from the Cross to Heaven."

From this we see that Michelagnolo was drawing towards God and casting from him the cares of art, persecuted as he was by those malignant rivals, and by certain among the Commissioners for San Pietro, who would fain, as he said himself, be making themselves more than rightfully busy in the matter.* Vasari replied to Michelagnolo's letter, by order of Duke Cosimo, in few words, but still encouraging him to return to his own country; to his verses Giorgio replied by a sonnet of similar character. And Michelagnolo would now without doubt have left Rome very gladly, but he had become so weak, that although he had determined on doing so, as will be related hereafter, yet the spirit was more willing than the frame, and his debility kept him in Rome. Now it happened in June, 1557, that in the construction of the vaulting over the apsis (which was in travertine, and after Michelagnolo's own designs), there was found to be an error, he not being able to visit San Pietro so frequently as before, and the principal builder having constructed the entire vaulting on one centre, instead of using several, as he ought to have done. Thereupon Michelagnolo, as being the friend and confidant of Vasari, sent him the designs for the

* "They desiring," remarks Bottari, "not to benefit the fabric, but to restore the old corruptions of the expenditure for their own profit."

vaulting as made by himself, and with the words beneath written at the foot of two of them.

"The chief builder took the measure of the arch, which you will find marked in red, for that of the whole vaulting, but when he came to the centre of the half-circle, which is at the summit of the same, he perceived his error as here seen in the design marked in black. But with this error it is that the work has been proceeding, insomuch that a large number of the stones will have to be displaced; for in the whole vaulting there is no masonry of bricks, all is in travertine, and the diameter of the arch, exclusive of the cornice which borders it, is twenty-two palms. This mistake has been committed because my advanced age prevents me from visiting the building so frequently as I could wish, although I had prepared an exact model of the work, as I do of every thing; and whereas, I thought that part of the fabric was finished, it will now not be completed during the whole winter. If a man could ever die of shame and grief, I should not be living now. I beg you to account to the Duke for my not being at this moment in Florence."

On another of the designs, wherein Michelagnolo had drawn the plan of the building, he wrote as follows:—

"MESSER GIORGIO,—To the end that the difficulty of the vaulting may be the more clearly comprehended, it becomes needful to describe the construction from the ground upwards. It was necessary to divide it into three sections, corresponding with the windows beneath, which are separated by piers; and these sections you see proceeding in the form of pyramids towards the inner centre of the highest point of the vaulting, being in perfect harmony with the basement and sides thereof. But it was needful that the work should be regulated by a large number of centres for supporting the arches, which should have been constantly changed on all sides, and from point to point, for all which no fixed rule could be given; the circles and squares approaching the centre of their deepest part having to be diminished, and to cross each other in so many directions, and to proceed to so many points, that it is without doubt exceedingly difficult to find the true proportions for bringing all to perfection. Yet, having the model—which I make for all things, they ought not to have committed so great an ror as to attempt constructing all those three sections with ne centre for the arches; a mistake which has compelled the emoval of many stones, which we have still the shame and xpense of taking down. The entire vaulting, with its various ections and ornaments, are, like the lowermost part of the hapel, wholly of travertine, a thing not customary in ome."

The Duke Cosimo, perceiving all these hindrances, no onger pressed Michelagnolo to return to Florence, declaring hat the satisfaction of the master, and the continuation of San Pietro, were matters of greater interest to him than any ther consideration, and begging that Michelagnolo would ive himself no further anxiety. Whereupon, the latter vrote to Vasari, telling him that he thanked the Duke with ll his heart for that great kindness, and adding, "God give ne grace to serve him with this my poor person, for my nemory and understanding are gone to await him elsewhere." The date of this letter was August, of the year 1557. Thus Michelagnolo perceived that the Duke esteemed his life and honour more than his presence, which was nevertheless so highly acceptable to him: all these things, with many others which it is not necessary to repeat, we learned from letters written by his own hand.

Our artist was now much pressed to make his final arrangements known, and as he saw that little was done at the building (although he had partly advanced the internal frieze of the windows, and the double columns outside, which form the circle above the round Cornice* whereon the Cupola is to be placed, as will be related hereafter), he was encouraged by his best friends, as the Cardinal di Carpi, Messer Donato Giannotti, Francesco Bandini, Tommaso de' Cavalieri, and Lottino;† nay, he was even constrained by them, to make at least a model of the Cupola; since, as he might perceive, the erection of the same was suffering delay. Several months elapsed nevertheless, before he could resolve on anything; at length he made a beginning, and by degrees produced a small model in clay, to the end that after this,

* "This is the beautiful drum of travertine, some of the stones of which having shown cracks in certain parts, no man knows how or when produced, gave rise to the report that the cupola was about to fall."—*Bottari.*

† Author of the *Avertimenti Civili.*

and by the aid of the plans and sections which he had likewise prepared, there might eventually be made a much larger one in wood. Such a model was accordingly constructed in somewhat less than a year, and under Michelagnolo's guidance, by Maestro Giovanni Franzese, who worked at the same with much zeal and care. The dimensions and minute proportions of this smaller structure, measured by the ancient Roman palm, corresponded in every particular with those of the great Cupola, all the parts being executed with extreme nicety; the members of the columns, the bases, capitals, doors, windows, cornices, ressaults, and every other minutia, being represented in such sort that no better work of the kind could be effected. It may indeed be affirmed that, not in all Christendom, nor indeed through the whole world, is there a grander or more richly decorated structure than will be that now in question.

And since we have taken the time to notify objects of so much less importance, I think it will be our duty as well as profitable to our readers, to describe the design according to which Michelagnolo proposed to construct this Church and Cupola; wherefore, with such brevity as we may, we will give a simple narration thereof, to the intent that if, which may God not permit, this undertaking should continue to be impeded in the lifetime of the master, as it has hitherto been, and should have a similar fate after his death, so shall my writings, such as they may be, avail to assist the faithful executors of his designs, and restrain the malignity of those presuming persons who may desire to alter them,† they may also enlighten and give pleasure as well as aid to those who love and delight in these vocations.

To commence then, I say that, according to the model made under the directions of Michelagnolo, the internal diameter will be a hundred and eighty-six palms from wall to wall, reckoning above the great circular cornice in travertine, which passes around the inside and rests on the four double piers, or pilasters; these rise from the floor with their carved capitals of the Corinthian Order, being with their architrave, frieze, and cornice, also in travertine. This cornice turning around the great recesses, reposes on the

† "It has indeed been changed, nevertheless," remarks Bottari. "The Cross which Michael Angelo made Greek is now Latin; and if it be thus with the essential form, judge ye of the details!"

ur large arches, those of the three niches, and that of the ıtrance namely, which form the Cross of the Church. rom that point upwards commences the Cupola itself, which ›rings from a basement of travertine, with a platform six alms broad, forming a wall or passage around the building. 'hat basement presents a circle in the manner of a well, the ıickness thereof being thirty-three palms eleven inches, ıe height to the upper cornice eleven palms ten inches; the pper cornice is about eight palms, and it projects about ix palms and a half. Through this basement there are ıade four entrances by which the ascent to the Cupola is ommenced, and these are placed above the arches of the Cribunes, the thickness of the basement being divided into hree parts. The innermost division measures fifteen palms, he outermost eleven palms, and that in the middle seven ›alms eleven inches, which make the thirty-three palms ›leven inches before mentioned.

The middle portion of the basement is unencumbered and serves as a passage, its height is equal to twice its breadth, t has a coved ceiling, and in the line of the four entrances it has eight doors, each joined by four steps, one leads to the level of the cornice of the first basement, which is six and a half palms broad, another conducts to the inner cornice, eight and three quarters palms broad, which encircles the Cupola. These doors give commodious access to the inside as well as outside of the edifice. The distance from one to another forms the segment of a circle of two hundred and one palms, and these being four, the entire circle is one of eight hundred and four palms. This basement, whereon repose the columns and pilasters, and which forms the interior frieze of the windows, is fourteen palms one inch high, and on the outside there is a slight cornice above and below, which does not project more than ten inches, and is entirely of travertine. In the thickness of the third part, above that of the interior, and which we have described as being fifteen palms broad, there is a staircase four and a quarter palms broad in each quarter of the circle; it has two branches, the one turning one way and the other in the opposite direction; these staircases lead to the level of the columns, above which, and immediately over the centre of the basement, there rise eighteen * large piers entirely of travertine, each adorned

* Since the drum is octagonal, there cannot be more than sixteen piers. —*Ed. Flor.*, 1832-8.

with two columns on the outside and two pilasters within, as will be mentioned hereafter, and between these the whole space is left for the windows which are to give light to the Cupola.

On the side looking towards the centre of the Cupola these great piers present a surface of thirty-six palms, but on the other side of nineteen and a half palms only,* each has two columns on the exterior side, the dado at the foot of these measuring eight palms and three quarters, and eight and a half palms in height; the base is five palms eight inches broad, and . . . . palms eleven inches high; the shaft of the columns has forty-three and a half palms in height; the diameter is five palms six inches at the base, and above four palms nine inches: the Corinthian capital is six and a half palms high, or with the mouldings nine palms. Three quarters only of these columns are seen, the fourth being let into the corner, but in the centre there projects a pilaster, which forms an acute angle; between the pilasters is an entrance forming an arched doorway, five palms broad and thirteen palms five inches high, but above this level it is filled in with solid masonry even to the capitals of the columns and pilasters, being united with two other pilasters similar to those which form the acute angle beside the columns, and these decorate the sides of the sixteen windows constructed around the circle of the tribune, each window having a clear light twelve and a half palms wide, and about twenty-two palms high.

The windows are adorned on the outside by an architrave of varied character two palms and three quarters broad, and on the outside they are in like manner decorated with a similarly varied range of pediments and arches intermingled, being broader without and narrower within, for the purpose of increasing the light; they are lower also inside than out, to the end that they may throw light on the frieze and cornice. Each window is enclosed between pilasters corresponding in height to the columns on the outside, so that there are thirty-six columns without and thirty-six pilasters within;† over the pilasters on the inside is the architrave,

* In other words, they are thirty-six palms broad, and nineteen and a half deep.—*German Edition of Vasari.*

† For the reasons given respecting the piers, this must be thirty-two.—*Masselli.*

which is four palms five inches high, while the frieze is four palms and a half, the cornice being four palms and two thirds, with a projection of five palms; and over this is a range of balusters, to the end that one may walk around in security.* For the more commodious ascent to the platform whence the columns ascend, there is another flight of steps, with two branches, which rise to the summit of the columns, capitals, architrave, frieze, and cornice; so that this staircase, without interrupting the light of the windows, passes at the upper end into a spiral stair of the same breadth until it attains to the platform, whence the Cupola begins to turn.

All these arrangements, divisions, and decorations are so varied, commodious, strong, and rich, the base gives such effectual support to the two vaults of the Cupola which are turned upon it, the whole work is so admirably conceived and so ably executed, that the eyes of one who understands and is capable of judging, can see nothing more graceful, more beautiful, or more ingenious. As to the masonry, and all that respects the stability of the work, every part has received the utmost strength and power of duration, while infinite judgment is displayed in the conduits for carrying off water by concealed channels, and in every other minutia: at a word, the whole work, so far as it has hitherto proceeded, is brought to such perfection that all other edifices shrink into nothing when compared therewith. Very deeply it is to be regretted that those in power have not put everything into Michelagnolo's hands, to the end that before the death of this extraordinary man we might have had this immense and beautiful erection completed. Up to this point Michelagnolo has finished the masonry of the building, it now remains that we commence the vaulting of the Cupola, of which, since we have the model, we will continue to describe the arrangement as he has left it to us. The centres of the arches are directed on three points which form a triangle as below.

A B
C

The lowermost, or point C, determines the form, height, and width of the first half circle of the Tribune,† which

* These balustrades have not been erected.

† Vasari calls the Cupola a "Tribune," almost throughout the whole of this description.—*Ed. Flor.*, 1832-8.

Michelagnolo has ordered to be constructed of well-baked bricks, the thickness given to the wall being four palms and a half above as well as below, leaving a space in the middle which is four palms and a half wide at the foot, and this is to be occupied by the stairs leading from the cornice, whereon are the balustrades, to the lantern; the arch of the interior of the second vaulting, which is broader below and narrower above, proceeds from the point B, which gives four palms and a half as the thickness of the lower part. The last arch which represents the outer side, and is also enlarged below while it is restricted above, departs from the point A.* At the upper part this arch gives the entire space in which are the stairs, whose height is of eight palms, so that men can walk upright therein, the thickness of the vault being gradually diminished to the extent that, while it has four palms and a half at the foot, it has three palms and a half only at the head. The vaultings, exterior and interior, are so well conjoined and connected that one supports the other; of the eight parts into which it is divided at the base, four are left hollow above the arches, to diminish the weight, while the four others are bound and secured to the piers in such sort that their durability may well extend to all time.

The central stairs between the two vaultings are made in the following manner. Those which start from the point whence the vault springs have each two branches, and proceeding through one of the sections they cross each other in the form of the letter X, until they attain the summit of the vaulting over the centre of the arch C. Having thus ascended the half of this arch by a direct line, the remainder is commodiously surrounded by a flight which turns easily, until the summit, whence the lantern commences, is attained; around this there is a smaller range of double pilasters and windows similar to those in the interior, all corresponding with that diminution of the compartments which takes place above the piers, as will be described below.

Over the first great cornice within the tribune commence those concave compartments into which the vaulting is divided and which are formed by sixteen projecting ribs; these have

* The complaints of all commentators, Italian and German alike, as to the obscurity of this description, are here renewed with increased energy, but the elucidations they attempt cannot be reproduced in this place, and we content ourselves with referring our reader to the authorities before cited.

the width of two of those pilasters which separate the windows placed under the vault of the Cupola at their base, but they constantly diminish up to the opening for the lantern: they rest on a pedestal of breadth equal to their own and twelve palms high, based on the platform of the cornice which passes around the tribune; over this and between the ribs are eight large ovals, each twenty-nine palms high, while above them is a range of rectangular compartments twenty-four palms high and somewhat broader at the lower than the upper edge; but where the ribs approach each other more nearly, then come circles, fourteen palms high, over each square, so that there are eight ovals, eight squares, and eight circles; each range being less deeply concave, as well as smaller than that beneath it: a most rich and beautiful design. Michelagnolo proposing to form the ribs, and framework of all these compartments in carved work of travertine.*

There remains that we mention the superficies and ornaments of the exterior vaulting, which rises from a basement twenty-five palms and a half high, reposing on a socle which has a projection of two palms, as have the mouldings at the head. The master proposed to cover the whole roof with lead, as was done for the old Church of San Pietro, he divided it into sixteen spaces, which commence at the point where the double columns end, and are placed between them; in the centre of each space he formed two windows, making, thirty-two in all, and serving to light the staircases between the two vaultings: to these he added projecting corbels supporting the segment of a circle; the whole forming a kind of roof which serves to throw off the rain. In the line of the columns and in the centre of the space between them, the ribs were made to spring from that point where the cornice ends, they were broader at the base and narrower at the summit; sixteen in all, and of five palms in width. In the centre of each there was a channel formed, a palm and a half broad, and in this were stairs of about a palm high, by which an ascent can be made to the opening left for the lantern. These are to be of travertine, constructed in such sort as shall defend them from the effects of the frost and rain.

The design for the Lantern makes that structure diminish

* "In this, as well as in every other part," remarks a German writer, "many changes have been made."

in the same proportion with all the other parts of the work, becoming gradually smaller in exact measure, and ultimately closing with a small temple having round columns, which stand in pairs, as do those below; they have pilasters behind them, and rest on a socle, so that one can pass around from pilaster to pilaster, looking down upon the windows, the the interior of the cupola, and the church. An architrave with frieze and cornice surrounds the whole, and projects over the two columns, immediately above which are spiral shafts and niches, rising together to the summit of the coping, which begins to contract at about one third of their height in the manner of a circular pyramid, until it reaches to where the ball and cross are to form the completion of the structure. I might here add numerous details, such as the precautions taken against earthquakes, the conduits for water, the various lights and other commodious arrangements, but I refrain, since the work is not yet finished, and it shall suffice me to have touched on the principal parts. All the details, moreover, are within reach of the reader's eyes, and can be seen; this slight sketch will therefore be sufficient to inform such as know nothing of the building.*

The completion of this model was a great satisfaction, not only to the friends of Michelagnolo but to all Rome; he continued to direct the works until the death of Pope Paul IV.; and when Pius IV. was chosen in his place, that Pontiff, although employing Piero Ligorio, who was architect of the Vatican, to construct the little Palace in the wood of the Belvedere, yet made many offers of service and showed much kindness to Michelagnolo. The *Motu-proprio* of Paul III., Julius III., and Paul IV., in respect to the fabric of San Pietro, was confirmed by His Holiness, who likewise restored a portion of those allowances which our artist had lost during the Pontificate of Paul IV. He employed him in many of his own buildings, and during his reign the works of San Pietro likewise proceeded busily. Among other things Michelagnolo was required to prepare the design for a monument to the memory of the Pope's brother, the Marquis of Marignano, which the Cavaliere Lione Lioni of Arezzo, an excellent sulptor and the friend of Michelagnolo, was commissioned

* For minute details our readers may consult Ferrabosco, *Libro dell' Architettura di San Pietro del Vaticano finito col disegno di Michael Angelo Buonarroti*, Rome, 1620.

to construct in the Cathedral of Milan, as will be related in its due place.

About the same time the Cavaliere Lioni made the Portrait of Michelagnolo, (a very close resemblance,) in a medal; on the reverse of which, and in compliment to the master, was a blind man led by a dog, with the following legend:—

DOCEBO INIQUOS VIAS TVAS, ET IMPII AD TE CONVERTENTUR.

This pleased Michelagnolo greatly,* and he presented Lioni with a model in wax of Hercules killing Antæus, accompanied by several of his designs. Of Michelagnolo we have no other portrait except two in painting, one of which is by Bugiardino, and the other by Jacopo del Conte, with an alto-rilievo in bronze by Daniello Ricciarelli; but from that of the Cavaliere Lione there have been made so many copies, that I have myself seen a vast number both in Italy and other countries.

In the same year, Giovanni Cardinal de' Medici, son of Duke Cosimo, went to Rome to receive the Hat from Pope Pius IV., when Vasari, who was his friend and servant, determined to go with him, remaining there willingly for a month to enjoy the society of Michelagnolo, whom he held very dear, and visited constantly. Vasari had taken with him, by order of his Excellency, the model in wood of the Ducal Palace of Florence, together with the Designs for the new Apartments, which had been built and painted by himself. These models and designs Michelagnolo desired to see, since, being old, he could not visit the works themselves; they were extensive, varied, and replete with divers inventions and phantasies, exhibiting Stories of Uranus, Saturn, Ops, Ceres, Jupiter, Juno, and Hercules; each apartment being adorned with histories, in numerous compartments, of one of those Gods. The apartments beneath these were decorated with stories from the Lives of Heroes belonging to the House of Medici, beginning with Cosimo the Elder,† and proceeding through the times of Lorenzo, Leo X., Clement VII.; the Signor Giovanni,‡ the Duke Alessandro, and,

* For details respecting the medals struck in honour of Michael Angelo, see the notes of Manni, to the *Vita* by Condivi. See also Litta, *Famiglie Illustri Italiane*.

† Cosmo, *Pater Patriæ*.

‡ Giovanni delle Bande Nere, father of Cosmo I.

finally, of Duke Cosimo. There were portraits of these personages, moreover, with those of their sons, and of many among the renowned of old times, whether distinguished for statesmanship, in arms, or for their learning, and being almost all portraits taken from the life. A Dialogue written by Vasari, in which the whole of these paintings were explained, and the connexion of the fables in the upper rooms, with the histories in the lower apartments set forth, was read by Annibale Caro to Michelagnolo, who was much pleased with the same. This Dialogue, Vasari proposes to publish, when he shall find time to do so.*

These things caused a discussion to arise respecting the Great Hall, which Vasari had desired to alter, because the ceiling thereof was too low, giving it a stunted appearance, and it had besides too little light. For these causes Vasari wished to raise it, but the Duke had not yet given him leave to do so: it was not that his Excellency feared the cost, but he dreaded the danger that there might be in lifting a roof thirteen braccia, yet, judicious as he was, he now agreed to have the opinion of Michelagnolo on the subject. The model of the Hall in its early condition was then laid before the master, as was also that of its improved state, with all the Stories designed as they were to be painted therein. Having examined all this, Michelagnolo was so much pleased that he became rather the partizan than the judge of the work, the rather as all the precautions taken for the security and promptitude of its execution were also apparent to his perceptions; and when Vasari returned to Florence, Michelagnolo wrote by him to the Duke, declaring that his Excellency ought to execute that undertaking, which he affirmed to be worthy of his greatness.

Now Duke Cosimo himself also repaired that same year to Rome with his consort, the Duchess Leonora, when Michelagnolo went to see his Excellency, who received him with much favour, causing him, from respect to his great genius, to be seated near himself, and conversing with him very familiarly of all the works in painting and sculpture which he had commanded to be performed, and still proposed to execute in Florence, more especially of the Hall above-mentioned. Michelagnolo then encouraged Cosimo anew to that

* It was published at Florence in 1588, by Giorgio Vasari, the nephew of our author.

undertaking, expressing his regret that he was himself no longer young enough to do him service, for he did truly love that Prince. Among other things, the Duke told him how he had discovered the method of working porphyry, and as Michelagnolo did not believe that possible, his Excellency sent him the Head of Christ, executed in porphyry by the sculptor Francesco del Tadda (as we have said in the first chapter of our *Theories*), which astonished him greatly. Michelagnolo visited the Duke several times afterwards, during the stay of the latter in Rome, to the great satisfaction of both; and when the most illustrious Don Francesco de' Medici, son of Duke Cosimo, was in Rome a short time afterwards, the master visited him likewise; being much pleased with the respect and affection shown to him by the noble Prince, who always spoke to him with uncovered head; so great was his reverence for that extraordinary man. To Vasari, Michelagnolo wrote, declaring, that it grieved him to be so old and infirm that he could do nothing for his Excellency, and he went about Rome looking for some fine piece of antiquity, that he might send the same to Florence as a present for that Signore.

About this time Pope Pius required from Michelagnolo a design for the Porta Pia, and the master made him three, all singularly beautiful. Of these the Pontiff chose the least costly, and this has been erected, to the great credit of the artist.* Finding, moreover, that His Holiness would gladly have the other gates of Rome restored, he made numerous designs for the same, as he also did one, at the request of Pope Pius, for the new Church of Santa Maria degli Angeli constructed in the Baths of Diocletian, when that building was brought into the service of Christians. The design of Michelagnolo surpassed those of many other excellent architects, by the singular consideration displayed therein for the requirements of the Carthusian monks, who have now nearly completed the edifice. His Holiness, with all the prelates and those of the Court who have seen it, have indeed been amazed at the judgment with which he has availed himself of the whole skeleton of those Baths, whereof he has made a Church with so beautiful an entrance, that the expectation of the architects has been much surpassed, to the infinite honour

* The Porta Pia has never been finished.

of the master.* He designed a Ciborium for the Sacrament also, which the Pope desired to have made for this church; it has been executed, for the most part, by Jacopo Ciciliano, an excellent artist in bronze, whose castings succeed so well and are so delicately fine, that they require but little chiselling, for in this respect Jacopo is a distinguished artist, and greatly pleased Michelagnolo.

Now the Florentines in Rome had often talked of beginning in good earnest to set about the Church of San Giovanni in the Strada Giulia. All the heads of the richest families among them assembled with that view, promising to contribute according to their means for that purpose, and a good sum of money was got together. A discussion then arose as to whether it were better to pursue the old plans or to have something newer and better; when it was at length determined that a new edifice should be raised on the old foundations; the care of the whole being committed to three persons, Francesco Bandini, Uberto Ubaldini, and Tommaso de' Bardi. By these persons an application for a design was made to Michelagnolo, to whom they represented that it was a disgrace for the Florentines to have spent so much money without any profit, adding, that if his genius did not avail to finish the work, they should be wholly without resource. The master assured them, with the utmost kindness, that the design they required should be the first thing he would lay hand on; remarking, moreover, that in this his old age he was glad to be occupied with things sacred, and such as might contribute to the honour of God. He furthermore declared, that it rejoiced him to do something for his own people, to whom his heart was ever true.†

At this time Michelagnolo had with him the Florentine sculptor Tiberio Calcagni, a youth who greatly desired to improve in his art, and who, having gone to Rome, had also given his attention to architecture. Being pleased with his manners, Michelagnolo had given him the Pietà which he had broken, as we have said, with a head of Brutus in marble, larger than life, which he had copied, at the request of his friend Messer Donato Giannotti, for the Cardinal

* The building was altered in 1749 by the architect Vanvitelli, an altar being constructed in the place of the principal entrance and other changes, which are much to be regretted, being also made.

† For details respecting this affair, see Gaye, *Carteggio*, vol. iii.

Ridolfi, from a cornelian of the highest antiquity belonging to Messer Giuliano Cesarino; a beautiful thing it is, and this he now desired that Tiberio should finish.* He could, indeed, no longer execute the more delicate parts of his architectural designs, and therefore employed Tiberio, who was a modest and well-conducted youth, to complete them under his direction. For this church, therefore, he now required him to take the ground-plan of the original foundation which he brought to Michelagnolo; the latter instantly caused him to inform the Commissioners, who did not expect to find anything yet accomplished, that he had fulfilled their wishes, showing them at the same time five plans of beautiful churches, which surprised them greatly. He then bade them choose one; but they refused, preferring to abide by his own decision. Yet, the master insisting that they should make a selection, they all with one accord declared for the richest; whereupon Michelagnolo is reported to have told them, that if they brought that design to completion they would do more than either Romans or Greeks had ever done in their best of times;† words which certainly never proceeded from his mouth, neither at that time nor at any other, seeing that he was always most reserved and modest.

It was finally determined that Michelagnolo should direct the work, while Tiberio should execute it, and the Commissioners, to whom our artist promised his best services for the church, were entirely satisfied with that arrangement. The plan was then given to Tiberio, that he might copy it in all parts, with due order; and the master commanded that a model in clay should be prepared, which he showed Tiberio how to fix up firmly. This, which was of eight palms, Tiberio completed in ten days, and it pleased all the Florentine community; wherefore they caused him afterwards to make one in wood, which is now in their Consolate,‡ and a beautiful church it is as ever man beheld, grand, rich, and varied. The building was commenced accordingly; but when five thousand crowns had been expended thereon, the works ceased for lack of funds to Michelagnolo's infinite

* The bust, which was never finished, is now in the Florentine Gallery of the Uffizj.

† Or this may be read, "more than either Romans or Greeks had done for their temples."

‡ According to Bottari this model perished in a fire.

vexation.* He then procured for Tiberio the commission to finish, under his direction, a Chapel which the Cardinal of Santa Fiore had commenced in the church of Santa Maria Maggiore; but this also remained unfinished at the death of the Cardinal, of Michelagnolo, and of Tiberio himself; the early demise of the latter being an event much to be regretted.

Michelagnolo had been seventeen years in the Fabric of San Pietro, and the Commissioners had more than once attempted to remove him, but not succeeding, they laboured continually to throw obstacles in his way, hoping to weary his patience, seeing that he was now old, and could endure but little. At this time it chanced that Cesare da Castel Durante, overseer of the works, died; when Michelagnolo, to the end that the building should not suffer, and until he could find a successor after his own heart, sent Luigi Gaeta thither in his place, a very young man certainly, but not without experience. Some of the Commissioners had, however, been frequently trying to bring Nanni di Baccio Bigio into that undertaking, he having urged them much to do so,† and promising great things; they now, therefore, thinking of managing everything in their own fashion, sent away Luigi Gaeta, when Michelagnolo, much displeased by this, would no longer go to San Pietro; and they, the Commissioners, then began to give out that a substitute must be provided, he being able to do no more, and having himself declared, as they said, that he would no longer trouble himself with that work. These things coming to Michelagnolo's ears, he sent Daniello Ricciarelli of Volterra, to the Bishop Ferratino, one of the Commissioners, who had told Cardinal Carpi that Michelagnolo had assured a servant of his that he would have no more to do with the building. Daniello now informed the Bishop that it was not Michelagnolo's wish to give it up: but Ferratino replied that he was sorry the master had not made his purpose known, adding nevertheless that a substitute was needful, and that he would have gladly accepted Daniello himself, a reply with which Michelagnolo appeared to be satisfied. The bishop then

* The Church was ultimately finished by Giacomo della Porta.—*Masselli.*

† For details of much interest respecting this affair, see Gaye, *Carteggio*, &c., vol. iii.

gave the rest of the Commissioners to understand, in the name of Michelagnolo, that a substitute was to be appointed; but instead of presenting Daniello, he put forward Nanni Bigio in his place: the latter was accordingly accepted and installed, nor had any long time elapsed before he caused a scaffolding to be raised from the Pope's stables which are on the side of the hill, to the great apsis which looks towards that side, declaring that too many ropes were consumed in drawing up the materials, and that it would be better to raise them by means of his scaffolding.

Being made acquainted with this proceeding, Michelagnolo repaired to the Pope, whom he found on the Piazza of the Capitol; and speaking somewhat loudly, His Holiness made him enter a room, when the master exclaimed, "Holy Father! a man of whom I know nothing has been placed by the Commissioners in San Pietro as my substitute, but if they and your Holiness are persuaded that I can no longer fulfil my office, I will return to take my rest in Florence, where I shall be near that great Prince who has so often desired my presence, and can finish my life in my own house; wherefore I beg the good leave of your Holiness to depart."* The Pope, whom that proposal did not please, sought to pacify the master with kind words, and bade him come to Araceli on the following day, to talk of the matter. Having there assembled the Commissioners, His Holiness inquired the cause of these things; and they, declaring that the building was in danger of being ruined by the errors committed therein, which he knew was not the case, the Pope commanded Signor Gabrio † Scierbellone to examine the structure, and require Nanni, who had made these assertions, to show where the errors might be found.

The master being examined accordingly, and Signor Gabrio

* A singular observation of Michael Angelo in respect to his reasons for not returning to Florence, will be found in the well-known *Autobiography* of Benvenuto Cellini, who relates that when he pressed Michael Angelo to return, on the part of Duke Cosimo, the master looked fixedly into his face, and with a meaning smile replied, "And you, Benvenuto, how do you like abiding with him?" "This smile and question," remarks an Italian writer, "need no comment;" and if the reader will recall the fate of the hapless Sforza Almeni, mentioned in vol. iv. of the present work, p. 321, note ‖, he will perhaps agree with our author's compatriot, that no comment is required.

† Agabrio, as he is subsequently called.

finding all the reports to be false and malignant, Nanni was dismissed with few compliments, and in the presence of many nobles, being reproached at the same time with the destruction of the Bridge of Santa Maria, and with having promised to clean the Harbour of Ancona at small cost, whereas he had injured that Port more in one year than the Sea had ever done in ten. And this was the end of Nanni Bigio's employment in San Pietro,* where Michelagnolo had employed seventeen years merely in the care of so fixing the arrangement of all its parts, that they should not be altered; the envious persecutions to which he was subjected, making him fear that changes in the building might be effected after his death: but he has thus brought things to such a state, that the work has now a fair prospect of being securely completed. By all this we see that God, who protects the good, has defended him while he lived, having extended his hand over the fabric and the master, even to his death. Then Pope Pius IV., who survived him, commanded the superintendents to alter nothing that Michelagnolo had arranged; while Pius V., his successor, continued with even greater authority, to command that the designs of Michelagnolo should be followed with unvarying exactitude, nay, when the architects Piero Ligorio, and Jacopo Vignola, were directing the fabric, he caused the former, who presumptuously proposed certain changes, to be dismissed with little honour, and the whole charge was then made over to Vignola.

That Pontiff was indeed as zealous for the honour of the edifice, as for the glory of the Christian faith; and in the year 1565, when Vasari went to pay his respects to His Holiness—as well as in the next year, when he was again summoned to Rome—the Pontiff spoke of nothing but the regard that was to be paid to the designs left by Michelagnolo; and, to obviate all disorder, he commanded Vasari to repair to the Bishop Ferratino, in company with Messer Guglielmo Sangalletti, the private treasurer of His Holiness, on the part of Pope Pius, and to direct that prelate, who was chief of the builders, on all occasions to guide himself by the important records and memoranda which Vasari would give him; to the end that no malignant or presumptuous person should ever prevail to alter a single point of those arrangements made by the admirable genius of Michelagnolo. On this occasion, Messer

* He was afterwards re-instated. See Gaye, *loc. cit.*

Giovambattista Altoviti, a good friend of Vasari and of these arts, was also present, and when Ferratino had heard the discourse made to him by Vasari, he solemnly promised to observe, and see observed, every order and arrangement left by Michelagnolo, adding that he would himself be the protector, defender, and preserver of the labours performed by that great man.

Returning to Michelagnolo himself, I have to relate, that about a year before his death, Vasari secretly prevailed on Duke Cosimo, to move the Pope, through Messer Averardo his Ambassador, to the end that since Michelagnolo was now much debilitated, His Holiness should keep a careful eye on those by whom he was surrounded, and should cause him to be visited at his house, for the due preservation of his designs, cartoons, models, and other property, taking measures, in the event of any sudden accident, such as may well happen to the very old; and this, in order that whatever might belong to, or be needful for, the fabric of San Pietro, the Sacristy and Library of San Lorenzo, or the Façade of the last-named Church, might not be taken away, as so frequently happens, nor were these precautions, which were all duly attended to, without a satisfactory result.*

In the Lent of this year, Leonardo, the nephew of Michelagnolo, resolved to go to Rome, as though divining that his kinsman was now near the end of his life, and the promise of this visit was all the more welcome to the latter, as he was already suffering from a slow fever. He caused his physician, Messer Federigo Donato, to write to Leonardo, hastening his arrival; but his malady increased, notwithstanding the cares of those around him: still, retaining perfect self-possession, the master at length made his will in three words, saying he left his soul to God, his body to the earth, and his goods to his nearest relations. He recommended his attendants to bethink themselves, in the passage from this life, of the sufferings endured by Our Saviour Christ; and on the 17th of February, in the year 1563, and at 23 o'clock, according to the Florentine computation, (in 1564 after that of Rome,) he departed to a better life.†

* But few drawings were found among the property of Michael Angelo, his people affirming that he had burnt many of them before his death. See Gaye, *loc. cit.*

† Aged eighty-eight years, eleven months, and fourteen days.

Michelagnolo found his chief pleasure in the labours of art; all that he attempted, however difficult, proving successful, because nature had imparted to him the most admirable genius, and his application to those excellent studies of design was unremitting. For the greater exactitude, he made numerous dissections of the human frame, examining the anatomy of each part, the articulations of the joints, the various muscles, the nerves, the veins, and all the different minutiæ of the human form. Nor of this only, but of animals, and more particularly of horses, which he much delighted in, and kept for his pleasure, examining them so minutely in all their relations to art, that he knew more of them than do many whose sole business is the care of those animals. These labours enabled him to complete his works, whether of the pencil or chisel, with inimitable perfection, and to give them a grace, a beauty, and an animation, wherein (be it said without offence to any) he has surpassed even the antique. In his works he has overcome the difficulties of art, with so much facility, that no trace of labour appears in them, however great may be that which those who copy them find in the imitation of the same.

The genius of Michelagnolo was acknowledged in his lifetime, and not as happens in many cases, after his death only; and he was favoured, as we have seen, by Julius II., Leo X., Clement VII., Paul III., Julius III.,* Paul IV., and Pius IV.; these Pontiffs having always desired to keep him near them, as indeed would Soliman, Emperor of the Turks, Francis, King of France, the Emperor Charles V., the Signoria of Venice, and lastly Duke Cosimo de' Medici: all very gladly have done, each of those monarchs and potentates having offered him the most honourable appointments, for the love of his great abilities. These things do not happen to any except men of the highest distinction, but in him all the three arts were found in such perfection, as God hath vouchsafed to no other master, ancient or modern, in all the many years that the sun has been turning round.†

* Julius III. bore him a strong personal affection. It was that Pontiff who induced Condivi to write the Life of Michael Angelo, of which His Holiness accepted the dedication.

† Let our readers be pleased to remember that Galileo was an infant in his cradle when our good Giorgio thus wrote, the philosopher not having been born until two days before Michael Angelo died.

His powers of imagination were such that he was frequently compelled to abandon his purpose, because he could not express by the hand those grand and sublime ideas, which he had conceived in his mind, nay, he has spoiled and destroyed many works for this cause; and I know too that some short time before his death he burnt a large number of his designs, sketches, and cartoons, that none might see the labours he had endured, and the trials to which he had subjected his spirit, in his resolve not to fall short of perfection. I have myself secured some drawings by his hand, which were found in Florence, and are now in my book of designs and these, although they give evidence of his great genius, yet prove also that the hammer of Vulcan was necessary to bring Minerva from the head of Jupiter. He would make his figures of nine, ten, and even twelve heads long, for no other purpose than the research of a certain grace in putting the parts together which is not to be found in the natural form, and would say that the artist must have his measuring tools, not in the hand but in the eye, because the hands do but operate, it is the eye that judges; he pursued the same idea in architecture also.

None will marvel that Michelagnolo should be a lover of solitude, devoted as he was to Art, which demands the whole man, with all his thoughts, for herself. He who resigns his life to her may well disregard society, seeing that he is never alone nor without food for contemplation; and whoever shall attribute this love of solitude to caprice or eccentricity, does wrong; the man who would produce works of merit should be free from cares and anxieties, seeing that Art demands earnest consideration, loneliness, and quietude; she cannot permit wandering of the mind. Our artist did nevertheless greatly prize the friendship of distinguished and learned men, he enjoyed the society of such at all convenient seasons, maintaining close intercourse with them, more especially with the illustrious Cardinal Ippolito de' Medici, who loved him greatly. Having heard that an Arab horse which he possessed was much admired for its beauty by Michelagnolo, the Cardinal sent it to him as a present, with ten mules, all laden with corn, and a servant to take care of those animals, which the master accepted very willingly. The most illustrious Cardinal Pole was also a very intimate friend of Michelagnolo, who delighted in the talents and virtues of that Prelate.

The Cardinals Farnese and Santa Croce, the latter afterwards Pope Marcellus, with the Cardinals Ridolfi and Maffeo, Monsignore Bembo, Carpi, and many other Cardinals and Prelates, were in like manner among his associates, but need not all be named here. Monsignore Claudio Tolomei was one of his intimates, and the Magnificent Messer Ottaviano de' Medici was his gossip, Michelagnolo having been godfather to one of his sons. Another of his friends was Messer Bindo Altoviti, to whom he gave that cartoon of the Chapel, wherein Noah is represented as inebriated and derided by one of his sons, while the other two compassionately seek to veil the degradation of their father.

Messer Lorenzo Ridolfi, Messer Annibale Caro, and Messer Giovan Francesco Lottini, of Volterra, were likewise among the friends of Michelagnolo, but more then all the rest did he love Messer Tommaso de' Cavalieri, a Roman gentleman, still young and much inclined to these arts. For him, and to promote his acquirement of drawing, he made superb cartoons, beautiful heads in red and black chalks, with a Ganymede carried to heaven by the Bird of Jove,* a Tityas with the Vulture devouring his heart, the Chariot of the Sun with Phaeton therein falling into the river Po, and a Bacchanalia of Children, each and all of which are most admirable. Michelagnolo also made the Portrait of Messer Tommaso in a cartoon the size of life; he, who never painted the likeness of any one either before or after, seeing that he hated to take anything from the life, unless it presented the very perfection of beauty. These drawings were afterwards increased by those which Michelagnolo made for Sebastiano del Piombo, to the end that he might put them into colours, and which were obtained by Messer Tommaso, who has a great delight in these works,† which are indeed most admirable, and well merit to be kept as he keeps them in the manner of relics, but he very liberally permits artists to use them at their pleasure. The friendships of Michelagnolo were all for deserving and noble persons, he having much

* This was purchased in Florence by our countryman, Bouverie, when on his way to Egypt. A picture after this drawing is in the Imperial Collection at St. Petersburg, and there are copies of the drawing at Vienna, Berlin, and Milan, as well as in London.

† A large portion of these drawings passed from the Palazzo Farnese to the King of Naples.—*Ed. Flor.*, 1832-8.

judgment in all things, Messer Tommaso induced him to execute numerous drawings for his friends, among others an Annunciation in a new manner for the Cardinal di Cesis; this was afterwards painted by Marcello of Mantua, and placed in the marble Chapel constructed by that Cardinal in the Church of the Pace at Rome. Another Annunciation, also painted by Marcello, is in the Church of San Giovanni Laterano, and the design for this is in the possession of Duke Cosimo; given by Lionardo Buonarroti, after the death of his uncle, to his Excellency, who keeps it like a jewel, with a figure of Christ in the Garden, and other cartoons and sketches from the hand of Michelagnolo.* The Duke also possesses a statue five braccia high, representing the Goddess of Victory, with a captive lying beneath her;† he has besides a group of four Captives, merely rough hewn, but which may well serve to teach all men how statues may be extracted from marble without injury to the stone.

The method of proceeding is to take a figure of wax, or other firm material, and lay it in a vessel of water, which is of its nature level at the surface; the figure being then gradually raised, first displays the more salient parts, while the less elevated still lie hidden, until, as the form rises, the whole comes by degrees into view. In the same manner are figures to be extracted by the chisel from the marble, the highest parts being first brought forth, till by degrees all the lowest parts appear; and this was the method pursued by Michelagnolo, in these figures of the Captives,‡ which his Excellency would fain see adopted as models by his academicians.

Michelagnolo loved the society of artists, and held much intercourse with many among them, as, for example, with Jacopo Sansovino, Il Rosso, Pontormo, Daniello da Volterra, and the Aretine Giorgio Vasari, to whom he showed infinite kindness. It was by him indeed that Vasari was led to the study of architecture, Michelagnolo intending some day to make use of his services, and gladly conferring with him on matters connected with art. Those who affirm that he was

* Many of these works, and of incontestable authenticity, are in the Collection of the Florentine Gallery.

† See ante, p. 248, note †.

‡ Now in the Boboli Gardens.

not willing to instruct others are wrong, he would assist all with whom he was intimate or who asked his counsels. I have been present many times when this has happened, but I say no more, not desiring to proclaim the defects of others.* It is true that he was not fortunate with those whom he took into his house, having chanced upon disciples wholly incapable of imitating their master. The Pistolese, Pietro Urbino, had ability but would never give himself the trouble to work. Antonio Mini was sufficiently willing, but had not quickness of perception, and when the wax is hard it does not take a good impression. Ascanio della Ripa took great pains, but no results have been displayed, whether in designs or finished works; he spent several years over a picture of which Michelagnolo had given him the cartoon, and, at a word, the hopes conceived of him have vanished in smoke. I remember that Michelagnolo, having compassion on Ripa's hard labours, would sometimes help him with his own hand, but it was all to little purpose. Had he found a disciple to his mind, he would have made studies of anatomy, and written a treatise on that subject, even in his old age, as he often said to me, desiring to do this for the benefit of artists, who are frequently misled by want of knowledge in anatomy. But he distrusted his power of doing justice to his conceptions with the pen, having little practice in speaking, although in his letters he expressed his thoughts well and in few words. He delighted in the reading of our Italian poets, more especially of Dante, whom he honoured greatly and imitated in his thoughts as well as copied in his inventions. Like Petrarch also, he was fond of writing madrigals and making sonnets, many of which are very serious, and have since been made subjects of commentary. Messer Benedetto Varchi, for example, has read an admirable lecture† before the Florentine Academy, on that beginning: —

*Non ha l'ottimo artista alcun concetto*
*Ch' un marmo solo in se non circonscriva.*

Michelagnolo sent a large number of these verses to the most illustrious Marchesana di Pescara, receiving replies

* Giovann' Bologna, when very young, showed Michael Angelo, then in his eightieth year, a model which he had finished with infinite care, but the master, passing his fingers over it, altered every part, saying, "Learn to sketch before you attempt to finish."

† Two rather, which were published at Florence in 1594.

both in verse and prose from that lady, of whose genius he was as much enamoured as she of his. She went more than once from Viterbo to Rome to see him, and Michelagnolo designed for her a Pietà, with two Angels of infinite beauty; an admirable work, as is also a figure of Christ on the Cross, raising his head to heaven, and commending his spirit to his Father;* and one of Our Saviour at the Well with the Woman of Samaria, both executed for the Marchesana. He delighted in the reading of scripture, like a good Christian as he was, and greatly honoured the writings of Fra Girolamo Savonarola, whom he had heard in the pulpit. He was an ardent admirer of beauty for the purposes of art; and from the beautiful he knew how to select the most beautiful, a quality without which no master can produce perfection; but he was not liable to the undue influence of beauty, as his whole life has proved. In all things Michelagnolo was exceedingly moderate; ever intent upon his work during the period of youth, he contented himself with a little bread and wine, and at a later period, until he had finished the Chapel namely, it was his habit to take but a frugal refreshment at the close of his day's work; although rich, he lived like a poor man; rarely did any friend or other person eat at his table, and he would accept no presents, considering that he would be bound to any one who offered him such: his temperance kept him in constant activity, and he slept very little, frequently rising in the night because he could not sleep, and resuming his labours with the chisel.

For these occasions he had made himself a cap of paste-board, in the centre of which he placed his candle, which thus gave him light without encumbering his hands. Vasari had often seen this cap; and, remarking that Michelagnolo did not use wax-lights, but candles made of unmixed goat's tallow, which are excellent, he sent the master four packets of the same, weighing forty pounds. His own servant presented them respectfully in the evening, but Michelagnolo refused to accept them; whereupon the man replied: "Messere, I have nearly broken my arms in bringing them from the bridge hither, and have no mind to carry them back; now, there is a heap of mud before your door which is thick enough to hold them upright, so I'll e'en stick them up there, and set

* "Of these works," observe the Italian commentators, "there are copies innumerable, nearly all of which pretend to be the original."

them all a-light." But, hearing that, the master bade him lay down the candles, declaring that no such pranks should be played before his house.

He has told me that, in his youth, he frequently slept in his clothes, being wearied with his labours he had no mind to undress merely that he might have to dress again. Many have accused him of being avaricious, but they are mistaken; he has proved himself the contrary, whether as regards his works in art or other possessions. He presented rich productions of various kind, as we have seen, to Messer Tommaso de' Cavalieri and Messer Bindo, with designs of considerable value to Fra Bastiano: while to his disciple, Antonio Mini, he gave designs, cartoons, the picture of the Leda, and all the models in clay or wax that ever he had made, but which were left in France as we have said. To Gherardo Perini, a Florentine gentleman and his friend, he gave three plates of most beautiful heads, which have fallen since his death into the hands of the most illustrious Don Francesco, Prince of Florence, by whom they are kept as the gems which they truly are. For Bartolommeo Bellini he made the Cartoon of a Cupid kissing his mother Venus; a beautiful thing, now at Florence, in the possession of Bellini's heirs. For the Marquis del Vasto, moreover, he made the Cartoon of a *Noli me tangere;* and these two last-mentioned works were admirably painted by Pontormo, as we have before related. The two Captives he gave to Signor Ruberto Strozzi; and the Pietà, in marble, which he had broken, to Antonio, his servant, and Francesco Bandini.

Who is it then that shall tax this master with avarice, seeing that the gifts he thus made were of things for which he might have obtained thousands of crowns; to say nothing of a fact which I well know, that he has made innumerable designs, and inspected buildings in great numbers, without ever gaining one scudo for the same? But to come to the money which he did gain: this was made, not by offices nor yet by trafficking or exchanges, but by the labour and thought of the master. I ask also, can he be called avaricious who assisted the poor as he did, who secretly paid the dowry of so many poor girls, and enriched those who served him? As witness Urbino, whom he rendered very rich; this man, having been long his disciple, had served him many years when Michelagnolo one day said to him, "When I die what wilt thou do?" "Serve some one else," replied Urbino. "Thou poor creature!" returned Michelagnolo, "I must save thee from that;" whereupon he gave him two thousand crowns at one time, a mode of proceeding befitting the Cæsars and high Princes of the world. To his nephew also, he has more than once given three and four thousand crowns at a time, and has finally left him ten thousand crowns, besides the property in Rome.

Michelagnolo had remarkable strength of memory, insomuch that, after having once seen a work of any other artist he would remember it so perfectly that, if it pleased him to make use of any portion thereof, he could do so in such a manner that none could perceive it. In his youth he was once supping with some painters his friends, when they amused themselves with trying who could best produce one of those figures without design and of intense ugliness, such as those who know nothing are wont to scratch on the walls. Here his memory came to his aid, he remembered precisely the sort of absurdity required, and which he had seen on a wall; this he reproduced as exactly as if he had had it before his eyes, surpassing all the painters around him: a very difficult thing for a man so accomplished in design, and so exclusively accustomed to the most elevated and finished works of mastery as was Michelagnolo.

He proved himself resentful, but with good reason, against those who had done him wrong, yet he never sought to avenge himself by any act of injury or violence; very orderly in all his proceedings, modest in his deportment, prudent and reasonable in discourse, usually earnest and serious, yet sometimes amusing, ingenious, and quick in reply; many of his remarks have been remembered and well merit to be repeated here, but I will add only a few of these recollections. A friend once speaking to him of death, remarked that Michelagnolo's constant labours for art, leaving him no repose, must needs make him think of it with great regret. "By no means," replied Michelagnolo, "for if life be a pleasure, yet, since death also is sent by the hand of the same master, neither should that displease us." To a citizen who observed him standing at Or San Michele, to look at the San Marco of Donato, and who inquired what he thought of that statue, he replied, that he had never seen a face looking more like that of a good man; adding, "If

St. Mark looked thus we may safely believe what he has written." Being once shown the drawing of a boy who was recommended to his favour, and told, by way of excuse for defects, that he had not been long learning, he answered, "It is easy to perceive that." A similar remark escaped him when a painter who had depicted a Pietà was found to have succeeded badly; "It is indeed a pity," observed the master.

When Michelagnolo heard that Sebastiano Veniziano was to paint a Monk in the Chapel of San Pietro a Montorio, he declared that this would spoil the work; and being asked wherefore, replied, that "as the monks had spoiled the world, which was so large, it could not be surprising that they should spoil that Chapel which was so small." A painter had executed a work with great labour, and spent much time over it, but acquired a good sum when it was finished; being asked what he thought of the artist, Michelagnolo replied, "While he is labouring to become a rich man, he will always continue a poor painter." A friend of his who had taken orders, arrived in Rome, wearingt he garb of a pilgrim, and meeting Michelagnolo, saluted him, but the latter pretended not to know him, compelling the monk to tell his name at length, when Michelagnolo, feigning surprise at his dress, remarked, "Oh, you really have a fine aspect; if you were but as good within as you seem without, it would be well for your soul." The same monk had recommended a friend of his own to Michelagnolo, who had given him a statue to execute, and the monk then begged him to give something more; this also our artist good-naturedly did, but it was now found that the pretended friend had made these requests only in the certainty that they would not be granted, and suffered his disappointment to be seen; whereupon Michelagnolo declared that such gutter-minded men were his abhorrence; and, continuing to take his metaphors from architecture, he added, "channels that have two mouths rarely act well."

Being asked his opinion of an artist who, having copied the most renowned antique marble statues and imitated the same, then boasted that he had surpassed the ancients, he made answer to this effect:—"He who walks on the traces of another is but little likely to get before him; and an artist who cannot do good of himself, is but poorly able to make good use of the works of others." A certain painter, I know not who, had produced a picture wherein there was an ox that was better than all besides, when, being asked why the artist had made that animal more life-like than the rest, Michelagnolo replied, "Every painter draws himself well." Passing one day by San Giovanni, in Florence, he was asked his opinion of the doors, and said, "They are so beautiful that they deserve to be used as the gates of Paradise." Seeing a prince who changed his plans daily, and was never in one mind, he remarked to a friend, "The head of this Signore is like a weather-cock; it turns round with every wind that touches it." Going to see a work in sculpture which was about to be fixed in its place, the sculptor took great pains to arrange the lights, that the work might be seen well, when Michelagnolo said:—"Do not trouble yourself; the principal question is, how it will bear the light of the Piazza,"—meaning to imply that when a work is given to public view, the people judge it, whether good or bad. There was a great prince in Rome who desired to pass for a good architect, and had caused certain niches to be made wherein he meant to place figures; each recess was three times the height of its depth, with a ring at the summit, and here the prince had various statues placed, but they did not turn out well. He then asked Michelagnolo what he could put into the niches. "Hang a bunch of eels in that Ring," replied the master.

With the Commissioners of San Pietro there was associated a gentleman who professed to understand Vitruvius, and to criticize the works accomplished. "You have now a man in the building who has great genius," remarked some one to Michelagnolo; "True," replied our artist, "but he has a bad judgment." A painter had executed a story, for which he had taken so many parts from drawings and other pictures, that there was nothing in it which was not copied: this being shown to Michelagnolo, and his opinion requested, he made answer, "It is very well; but at the day of Judgment, when every body shall retake its own limbs, what will this Story do, for then it will have nothing remaining?"—a warning to those who would practise art that they should do something for themselves. Passing once through Modena, he saw many beautiful figures which the Modanese sculptor, Maestro Antonio Bigarino, had made of terra-cotta, coloured to look like marble, which appeared to him to be most excellent productions; and as that sculptor did not know how to work in marble, he said, "If this earth were to become marble, woe to the antiques."

Michelagnolo was told that he ought to resent the perpetual competition of Nanni di Baccio Bigio, to which he replied: "He who strives with those who have nothing gains but little." A priest, who was his friend, said to him, "'Tis a pity that you have not married, that you might have left children to inherit the fruit of these honourable toils;" when Michelagnolo replied, "I have only too much of a wife in my art, and she has given me trouble enough; as to my children, they are the works that I shall leave; and if they are not worth much, they will at least live for some time. Woe to Lorenzo Ghiberti, if he had not made the gates of San Giovanni; for his children and grandchildren have sold or squandered all that he left; but the gates are still in their place." Vasari was sent one night by Pope Julius III. to the house of Michelagnolo for a design, and the master was then working at the Pietà in marble which he afterwards broke, knowing by the knock, who stood at the door, he descended with a lamp in his hand, and having ascertained what Vasari wanted, he sent Urbino for the drawing, and fell into conversation on other matters. Vasari meanwhile turned his eyes on a Leg of the Christ on which Michelagnolo was working and endeavouring to alter it; but to prevent Vasari from seeing this, he suffered the lamp to fall from his hand, and they remained in darkness. He then called to Urbino to bring a light, and stepping beyond the enclosure in which was the work, he remarked: "I am so old that death often pulls me by the cape, and bids me go with him; some day I shall fall myself, like this lamp, and the light of life will be extinguished."

With all this he took pleasure in the society of men like Menighella, a rude person and common-place painter of Valdarno, but a pleasant fellow; he came sometimes to see Michelagnolo, who made him a design of San Rocco and Sant' Antonio, which he had to paint for the country people; and this master, who would not work for kings without entreaty, often laid aside all other occupation to make designs of some simple matter for Menighella, "dressed after his own mind and fashion," as the latter would say. Among other things Menighella received from him the model of a Crucifix, which was most beautiful; he formed a mould from this also, whence Menighella made copies in various substances, and went about the country selling them. This man would sometimes make Michelagnolo laugh till he cried, more especially when he related the adventures he met with; as, for example, how a peasant, who had ordered the figure of San Francesco, made complaints that the painter had given him a grey dress, he desiring to have a finer colour, when Menighella put a pluvial of brocade on the back of the Saint, which gladdened the peasant to his heart.

He favoured, in like manner, the stone-cutter Topolino, who imagined himself an excellent sculptor, although, in fact, a very poor creature. He passed much time at the quarries of Carrara, sending marbles to Michelagnolo, nor did he ever despatch a cargo without adding three or four little figures from his own hand, at the sight of which Michelagnolo would almost die of laughing. At length, and after his return, he had rough-hewn a figure of Mercury in marble, which he was on the point of finishing, when he begged Michelagnolo to go and see it, insisting earnestly that he should give his true opinion of the work. "Thou art a fool to attempt figures, Topolino," said the master; "for dost thou not see that, from the knee to the foot, this Mercury of thine wants a full third of a braccio of its due length? and thou hast made him a dwarf and a cripple?" "Oh, that is nothing," replied Topolino, "if it has no other fault I shall find a remedy for that, never fear me." The master laughed again at his simplicity and departed; when Topolino, sawing his Mercury in two below the knee, fastened a piece of marble nicely between the parts, and having thus added the length required, he gave the figure a pair of buskins, the fastenings of which passed beyond the junctures. He then summoned the master once more; and Michelagnolo could not but wonder as well as laugh, when he saw the resolutions of which those untaught persons are capable, when driven by their needs, and which would certainly never be taken by the best of masters.

While Michelagnolo was concluding the Tomb of Julius II., he permitted a stone-cutter to execute a terminal figure, which he desired to put up in San Pietro in Vincola, directing him meanwhile by telling him daily, "Cut away here,"—

"level there,"—"chisel this,"—"polish that," until the stone-cutter had made a figure before he was aware of it; but when he saw what was done, he stood lost in admiration of his work. "What dost thou think of it?" inquired Michelagnolo. "I think it very beautiful," returned the other, "and am much obliged to you." "And for what?" demanded the artist. "For having been the means of making known to me a talent which I did not think I possessed."

But now, to bring the matter to a conclusion, I will only add, that Michelagnolo had an excellent constitution, a spare form, and strong nerves. He was not robust as a child, and as a man he had two serious attacks of illness, but he was subject to no disease, and could endure much fatigue. It is true that infirmities assailed him in his old age, but for these he was carefully treated by his friend and physician, Messer Realdo Colombo. He was of middle height, the shoulders broad, and the whole form well-proportioned. In his latter years he constantly wore stockings of dog-skin for months together, and when these were removed, the skin of the leg sometimes came with them. Over his stockings he had boots of Cordovan leather, as a protection against the swelling of those limbs, to which he then became liable. His face was round, the brow square and ample, with seven direct lines in it; the temples projected much beyond the ears, which were somewhat large, and stood a little off from the cheeks; the nose was rather flattened, having been broken with a blow of the fist by Torrigiano, as we have related in the Life of that artist; the eyes were rather small than large, of a dark colour, mingled with blue and yellowish points; the eye-brows had but few hairs; the lips were thin, the lower somewhat the larger, and slightly projecting; the chin well-formed, and in fair proportion to the rest of the face; the hair black, mingled with grey, as was the beard, which was divided in the middle, and neither very thick nor very long.

This master, as I said at the beginning, was certainly sent on the earth by God as an example for the men of our arts, to the end that they might profit by his walk in life, as well as learn from his works what a true and excellent artist ought to be. I, who have to thank God for an infinite amount of happiness, such as is rarely granted to those of our vocation, account it among the greatest of my blessings that I was born while Michelagnolo still lived,* was found worthy to have him for my master, and being trusted by him, obtained him for my friend, as every one knows, and as the letters which he has written to me clearly prove. To his kindness for me I owe it that I have been able to write many things concerning him, which others could not have related, but which, being true, shall be recorded. Another privilege, and one of which he often reminded me, is, that I have been in the service of Duke Cosimo. "Thank God for this, Giorgio," has Michelagnolo said to me; "for to enable thee to build and paint, in execution of his thoughts and designs, he spares no expense, and this, as thou seest well, by the Lives thou hast written, is a thing which few artists have experienced."

Michelagnolo was followed to his tomb by a concourse of all the artists, and by his numerous friends, receiving the most honourable sepulture from the Florentine nation, in the Church of Sant' Apostolo, within a sepulchre of which church he was laid, in the presence of all Rome, His Holiness expressing an intention to command that a monument should be erected to his memory in St. Peter's.†

Leonardo, the nephew of Michelagnolo, did not arrive in Rome until all was over, although he travelled post in the hope of doing so. When Duke Cosimo heard what had happened, he resolved that, as he had not been able to do the master honour in his life, he would cause his body to be brought to Florence, where his obsequies were to be solemnized with all possible splendour; but the remains of the artist had to be sent out of Rome in the manner of a bale, such as is made by merchants, that no tumult might arise in the city, and so the departure of the corpse be prevented.

But before the body could arrive, the news of the master's death having been noised abroad, the principal painters, sculptors, and architects assembled in their Academy, on the requisition of their Prorector, who was at that time Don

* Condivi represents Raphael as expressing the same thought.

† "A great honour," observes Bottari, "since none but Pontiffs have been thus distinguished, with the exception of two Queens, who have abandoned thrones for the Catholic faith." See also Moreni, *Illustrazione storica-critica*, &c., &c.

Vincenzio Borghini, they being obliged by their rules to solemnize the obsequies of all their brethren. They had done this most affectionately, and to the satisfaction of every one, in the case of Fra Giovan-Agnolo Montorsoli, who was the first that had died after the creation of the Academy; and it was now fitting and proper that they should resolve on what was to be done for the due honouring of Buonarroto, who had been unanimously elected first Academician and head of them all. To this proposal all replied, that, being obliged, as they were, to the genius of that great man, they desired that nothing should be omitted which could contribute to do him honour, but that everything should be accomplished in the best manner possible. That decided, and to avoid the daily assemblage of so many men, which was very inconvenient to them, as well as for the more effectual arrangement of the preparations, four persons, all of eminent reputation and distinguished in their arts, were chosen to direct the same. These were the painters Agnolo Bronzino and Giorgio Vasari, with the sculptors Benvenuto Cellini and Bartolommeo Ammannato; who were appointed to consult among themselves, and with the Prorector, as to all the arrangements to be made; they being empowered to dispose of everything belonging to the Academy: this charge they undertook the more willingly, as they saw that all the artists, young and old, came forward readily with offers to prepare, each in his several vocation, such pictures and statues as were needed for the ceremony.

It was first resolved that the Prorector and Syndics should lay all before the Duke in the name of the Academy, requesting from his Excellency such countenance and aid as they might require, the first thing to be asked being permission for the solemnization of those obsequies in the Church of San Lorenzo, which belongs to the illustrious house of Medici, and where are the greater part of Michelagnolo's works in Florence. His Excellency was also requested to permit Messer Benedetto Varchi to pronounce the funeral oration, to the end that the greatness and excellence of Michelagnolo might be suitably set forth in the eloquence of so distinguished a man as was Varchi, but who, being in the particular service of his Excellency,* could not undertake that office without his permission, although they were certain that he

* In quality of Historiographer.

vould not of himself refuse to do so, being most kindly of ıature as well as much attached to the memory of Michelgnolo. All this duly settled, and the Academicians having lispersed, the Prorector wrote to the Duke as follows :—

"The Academy and Company of Painters and Sculptors ıaving resolved, if it please your Excellency, to do honour n some sort to the memory of Michelagnolo, not only from ı consideration of what is due to the genius of him who was, perhaps, the greatest master that has ever lived, and one more particularly their own, he belonging to their common country, but also as being moved by a sense of the benefit accruing to the arts from the perfection of his works, and by the obligation laid upon them to prove their gratitude to his memory, do hereby repeat this their desire, expressed to your most illustrious Excellency in their former epistle, and do entreat from you, as their sure resource, a certain amount of assistance. I then, being requested by them and being (as I think) bound thereto, by the fact that, with your Excellency's good pleasure, I am again of their company this year under the title of your Prorector, am moved to compliance, as the undertaking appears to me worthy of upright and grateful men ; but still more as knowing the protection extended by your Excellency to the arts, and that in this age you are the sole resource and shield of distinguished men. Insomuch that you do herein surpass your illustrious ancestors, although they also conferred innumerable favours on the men of these vocations ; witness the Magnificent Lorenzo, who, long before his death, caused a statue to be erected in the Cathedral to Giotto,* with a monument in marble to Fra Filippo,† all at his own cost ; to say nothing of many other great and noble acts that might be named. Considering all these things, I have taken courage to recommend to your illustrious Excellency the petition of this Academy, to the effect that they may duly honour the genius of Michelagnolo, who was the disciple and especial pupil of the School created by the Magnificent Lorenzo. For this that they desire to do shall be not only to their great contentment, but also to the infinite satisfaction of all men ; it will, furthermore, be no slight spur to the professors

* A bust and inscription rather.

† At Spoleto, as related in the Life of Fra Filippo.

of these arts, and a proof to all Italy of the high mind and great goodness of your most illustrious Excellency, whom may God long preserve in happiness, for the advantage of your people and for the good of art."

To this the Duke replied as follows :—

"REVEREND AND WELL-BELOVED,—The promptitude which the Academy has shown, and is showing, in its preparations to honour the memory of Michelagnolo Buonarroti, who has passed from this life to a better, has consoled us much for the loss of so extraordinary a man ; and not only will we do as you request, but will endeavour to have his remains brought to Florence, as, according to what we hear, was his own desire. All this we write to the Academy to encourage the members in their purpose of honouring the talents of that great man in the best manner possible ; and so may God keep you in joy."

Of the letter, or memorial, mentioned above, as addressed by the Academy to the Duke, the following are the words:—

"MOST ILLUSTRIOUS, &c.—The Academy and the Men belonging to the Society of the Arts of Design, established under the grace and favour of your Most Illustrious Excellency, having heard with what care and zeal you have caused the body of Michelagnolo Buonarroti to be claimed by your ambassador in Rome, have assembled and unanimously resolved to celebrate his obsequies in the best manner possible to them. Knowing therefore that your Excellency was honoured by Michelagnolo as much as he was favoured by your Excellency, they pray you of your infinite goodness and liberality to be pleased to permit, first, that the solemnities shall be held in the Church of San Lorenzo, which was built by your ancestors, wherein are so many fine works, both in architecture and sculpture, by his hand, and near which it is your purpose to erect an abode which, for the Academy and Company of Design, shall be as it were an abiding seat of study, whether in architecture, painting, or sculpture.

"Secondly, we beg that you will commit to Messer Benedetto Varchi the charge, not only of composing the funeral oration, but also of pronouncing it with his own lips, as at our entreaty he has freely promised to do, provided your

Illustrious Excellency shall consent. Thirdly, we pray that you will be pleased, out of that same goodness and liberality, to assist the Academy in all which these obsequies may demand, beyond their own power, which is very small, to supply. All and every of these things have been discussed in the presence and with the consent of the very magnificent and reverend Monsignore, Messer* Vincenzio Borghini, Prior of the Innocents, the Prorector of your most Illustrious Excellency, for the said Academy and Company. And your petitioners, &c."

To this the Duke replied :—

"OUR WELL-BELOVED,—We are well content fully to grant your petitions, for the great love that we have ever borne to the rare genius of Michelagnolo Buonarroti, and which we still bear to all of your vocation. Do you therefore execute whatever you propose to do for his obsequies, and we, on our part, will not fail to supply what you may need. We have, meanwhile, written to Messer Benedetto respecting the oration, and to the Director concerning all else that occurs to us as needful in this matter. And herewith we bid you farewell. From Pisa."

The letter to Varchi was as follows :—

"MESSER BENEDETTO, OUR WELL-BELOVED, — The affection we bear to the great genius of Michelagnolo Buonarroti, makes us desire that his memory shall be honoured and celebrated in all ways, wherefore it will be pleasing to us, if, for our love, you will accept the care of the oration which is to be pronounced at his obsequies, according to the arrangements made by the deputies of the Academy: still more will it please us if this oration be spoken by yourself. Fare you well."

Messer Bernardino Grazzini also wrote to the above-named deputies, telling them that the Duke was displaying all the zeal that could be desired in that cause, and adding that they might assure themselves of all help and favour from his Most Illustrious Excellency.

While these arrangements were proceeding in Florence,

* *Sic.* Nor was this mode of expression unusual at the time when Vasari wrote.

Leonardo Buonarroti, the nephew of Michelagnolo (who had departed post for Rome on hearing of his uncle's sickness, but had not found him living), had been told by Daniello da Volterra, the intimate friend of Michelagnolo, as well as by others who had been about his person, that he had requested and even entreated them to have his body taken to Florence, his most noble country, to which he had ever borne the tenderest affection. Leonardo therefore had promptly and with great resolution, but also very cautiously, had the body taken out of Rome, and had sent it towards Florence in the form of a bale, as if it had been some kind of merchandise. And here we are not to conceal the fact that this ultimate determination of Michelagnolo confirmed what many did not believe, but which was nevertheless true, namely, that his having remained away from Florence for so many years had been caused by the effect of the air only, the sharpness of which, as experience had taught him, was injurious to his constitution.* That of Rome, on the contrary, more temperate and mild, had kept him in health to nearly his ninetieth year, preserving all his faculties in perfection, and giving him so much strength, his age considered, that he had not been compelled to cease entirely from his labours, till the very last.

The sudden and almost unexpected arrival of the body, not having permitted such dispositions for its reception as were afterwards made, it was placed, by desire of the deputies, in the vault of the Company of the Assumption, which is beneath the steps at the back of the High Altar in the Church of San Pietro Maggiore. This was on the 11th of March, which was a Saturday, and for that day nothing more was done. The next day, which was the second Sunday in Lent, all the painters, sculptors, and architects assembled quietly around St. Peter's, whither they had taken nothing more than a pall of velvet, richly decorated and embroidered all over with gold, and this they placed over the bier as well as coffin, on which there lay a crucifix. At nightfall they gathered silently around the corpse, when the oldest and most distinguished masters each took one of a large number of torches, which had been brought for that purpose, the

* Vasari was the devoted servant of Duke Cosimo, and had not the slightest suspicion of Michael Angelo's real motive for avoiding Florence; he therefore accepted the master's excuses in good faith.

younger artists at the same moment raising the bier; this they did with so much promptitude that blessed was he who could approach near enough to get a shoulder under it, all desiring the glory of having to say in after years that they had borne to earth the remains of the greatest man ever known to their arts.

The sight of a certain number of persons assembling round San Pietro, had caused others to stop, and the rather as a rumour had got abroad, that the body of Michelagnolo had come, and was to be carried to Santa Croce, although everything had been done to keep the matter secret, as I have said, that a great crowd might not be attracted, which could not fail to cause confusion, and also because it was desired that all then to be done should proceed with more quiet than pomp, all display being reserved to a more convenient time. Yet the contrary happened in both these things; for as to the crowd, the news passing from mouth to mouth, the Church was completely filled in the twinkling of an eye, so that at length it was not without the utmost difficulty that the corpse could be taken from the Church to the Sacristy, there to be freed from its wrappings, and placed in the receptacle destined to receive it. Then for the pomp—although the number of priets, wax-lights, and mourners clothed in black, are without doubt imposing and grand in funeral ceremonies, yet it cannot be denied that the sight of all the distinguished men, some of whom are now highly honoured, and others promising to be still more so in the future, gathered in so much affection around that corpse, was also a very grand and imposing spectacle.

And of a truth the number of such artists, (and they were all present), was at that time very great in Florence; the Arts have indeed ever flourished there in such sort, that without offence to other cities, I believe I may say that their first and principal abode is in Florence, as that of the Sciences was at Athens. But besides the number of artists, there were so many citizens following them, and such masses of people joined the procession in the streets through which it had to pass, that the place would hold no more, and what is greater than all, nothing was heard but the praise of Michelagnolo. True art has indeed so much power, that after all hope of further honour or profit from a distinguished man has ceased, yet for its own merit and qualities it is ever beloved and admired. For all these causes, that demonstration was more precious and more truthful than all the pomp of gold and banners that could have been displayed.

When the remains, with this magnificent attendance, had been carried to Santa Croce, the Monks performed the ceremonies customary for the dead; when the corpse was removed (but not without the greatest difficulty, because of the concourse of people) to the Sacristy, where the abovenamed Prorector, who was there by virtue of his office, thinking to gratify many thereby, and also (as he afterwards confessed) desirous of seeing him dead whom he had not seen living, or at so early an age that he had lost all memory of him; the Prorector, I say, resolved to have the cerements taken off. This was done accordingly, and whereas he, and all of us who were present, expected to find the body decomposed, since the master had been dead twenty-five days, and twenty-two in the coffin, we found it altogether perfect, and so totally free from odour that we were almost tempted to believe he lay in a sweet and quiet sleep. The features were exactly as in life, except that they showed the pallor of death; the limbs were unaltered, and the face and cheeks were firm to the touch, as though but a few days had elapsed since Michelagnolo had passed away.*

When the great press of people had departed, arrangements were made for placing the body in a tomb of the church which is near the altar of the Cavalcanti family, beside the door leading into the cloister of the Chapter House. But meanwhile the news had spread through the city, and so great a concourse hastened to look upon the corpse, that the tomb was not closed without much difficulty, and if it had been day instead of night, we must have left it open many hours to satisfy the general wish. On the following morning, while the painters and sculptors were preparing the solemnities, many of those distinguished persons who have ever abounded in Florence, began to append verses, both in Latin

* The tomb of Michael Angeio was opened in the last century, when the corpse was found still well preserved. Bottari, who had his intelligence from the senator, Filippo Buonarroti, one of the few persons who entered, describes it as "dressed in a long robe of green velvet, and with slippers on the feet;" but in the *Memorie Fiorentine inedite*, the master is said to have been found wrapped in a "mantle of black damask, wearing boots with spurs, and having a hat with a bordering of fur on the head." See the *Carteggiio nedito*, vol. iii. p. 133.

and the vulgar tongue, on the above-named tomb, and this was continued for some time. Many of these compositions were afterwards printed, yet these made only a small part of the number written.

But to come to the obsequies; these were not solemnized on St. John's day, as had been intended, but were deferred to the 14th of July,* when the three deputies (for the fourth, Benvenuto Cellini, who had been indisposed from the first, had taken no part in the matter), having chosen the sculptor, Zanobi Lastricati, as their Proveditor, resolved to exhibit some ingenious invention worthy of their art, rather than a pompous and costly ceremonial. For, having to celebrate such a man as Michelagnolo, and this having to be effected by men of those vocations which he exercised, who are always more amply furnished with the wealth of mind than with other riches; it was most appropriate, as the deputies and their Proveditor agreed, that he should be honoured, not with regal pomp or superfluous vanities, but with ingenious inventions and works full of spirit and beauty, proceeding from the knowledge, ability, and promptitude of hand of our artists, thus honouring Art by Art. It is true that we might have reasonably expected to obtain from his Excellency all the money we should require, seeing that he had already given whatever we had asked, but we were nevertheless convinced that from us was expected a preparation; rich from its ingenuity and art, rather than the grandeur and cost of a pompous display. But although this was the conviction of the deputies, the magnificence of the ceremonial was equal to that of any ever solemnized by those academicians, and was no less remarkable for true splendour than for ingenious and praiseworthy inventions.

The arrangements finally made were as follows. In the central nave of San Lorenzo and between the two lateral doors, one of which opens on the street and the other on the cloister, was erected a Catafalque of a square form, twenty-

* Some of the Italian commentators affirm this date to be inaccurate, and cite in support of their opinion the *libretto* describing the ceremonies, published at the time by the Giunti, and with the title, *Esequie del divin Michael Angelo Buonarroti celebrati, &c., 28th June*, 1564. But Vasari has told us that the ceremony was "deferred;" and doubtless it was so, to the 14th of July, as he says, for was he likely to be mistaken as to the date of a solemnity in which he took so active a part? Let the reader judge.

eight braccia high, eleven long, and nine broad, the whole surmounted by a figure of Fame. On the basement of the Catafalque, and at two braccia from the floor, on that side which looks towards the principal door of the Church, were two River-gods, the Arno and the Tiber. The first bore a cornucopia with its flowers and fruits, to signify that the labours of our vocations in the city of Florence are such and so rich in fruits as to fill the world, but more especially adorning Rome with their beauties; a thought well carried out by the attitude of the other river, for the Tiber, extending one arm, had the hand full of the flowers and fruits poured forth from the horn of the Arno, which lay beside and opposite to the Tiber. The enjoyment by this last of the Arno's fruits also implied that Michelagnolo had spent much of his life in Rome, and there produced those works which astonish the world. The Arno had a Lion beside him as his device, and the Tiber a Wolf, with the infants Romulus and Remus; both the River-gods being colossal figures of extraordinary beauty and excellence, and having the appearance of marble. The artist who executed the Tiber was Giovanni di Benedetto of Castello,* a disciple of Baccio Bandinelli; the Arno was from the hand of Battista di Benedetto, a disciple of Ammannato, both young men of much promise.

From the basement there rose a structure five braccia high, having a cornice at the upper and lower parts as well as at the angles; space for the reception of pictures was left in the centre of each side. The picture on the part where the River gods were, and which, like all the others, was in chiaro-scuro, represented the Magnificent Lorenzo, in his garden, an old man receiving Michelagnolo as a child, having seen certain indications of his genius, which may be said to have intimated, in the manner of flowers, the rich fruits afterwards so largely produced by the grandeur and force of that genius. This story was painted by Mirabello,† and by Girolamo del Crocifissaio,‡ as they were called, and who, being companions and friends, undertook to do it together. The attitude of Lorenzo, whose figure was a portrait from the life, exhibited great animation; his

* Giovanni Bandini. See Baldinucci, vol. x. p. 183.

† Mirabello da Salincorcio, a disciple of Ghirlandajo.

‡ Girolamo Macchietti, a scholar of Michele di Ridolfo Ghirlandajo.

reception of Michelagnolo was most gracious: the boy stood before him with looks of reverence, and having been examined, was in the act of being passed over to the masters by whom he was to be instructed.

In the second story, or that on the side of the lateral door, which opens into the street, was Pope Clement, who, far from resenting the part taken by Michelagnolo in the siege of Florence, as is commonly believed, was careful to assure his safety, gave evidence of much friendly feeling towards him, and employed him in the works of the New Sacristy and Library of San Lorenzo, in which places how admirably he acquitted himself we have already set forth. This picture was painted with much facility and softness by the Fleming Federigo,* called the Paduan. Michelagnolo was showing the Pope the plan of the Sacristy; and behind him, borne partly by angels, and partly by other figures, were carried the models of the Library, the Sacristy, and the statues which have been completed, all well composd and carefully executed. In the third picture, which faced the High Altar, was a long Latin inscription, composed by the very learned Messer Pier Vettori, the meaning of which in the Italian tongue, was as follows:—

"The Academy of Painters, Sculptors, and Architects, by favour of the Duke Cosimo de' Medici, their chief, and the supreme protector of these arts, admiring the extraordinary genius of Michelagnolo Buonarroti, and acknowledging the benefits received from his divine works, have dedicated this monument, erected by their own hands, and consecrated with all the affection of their hearts, to the eminence and genius of the greatest painter, sculptor, and architect that has ever existed."

The Latin words were these:—

*Collegium pictorum, statuariorum, architectorum, auspicio opique sibi prompta Cosmi ducis auctoris suorum commodorum, suspiciens singularem virtutem Michaelis Angeli Bonarrotæ, intelligensque quanto sibi auxilio semper fuerit præclara ipsius opera, studuit se gratum erga illum ostendere, summum omnium, qui unquam fuerint,* P. S. A. *ideoque monumentum hoc suis manibus extructum magno animi ardore ipsius memoriæ dedicavit.*

This inscription was supported by two Angels weeping, and each extinguishing the torch which he held in his hand, as

* Friedrich Lambert, a native of Amsterdam who setted in Florence.

if lamenting the loss of that great and extraordinary genius. In the picture of that side which turned towards the door of the Cloister was Michelagnolo engaged in constructing the fortifications of the Heights at San Miniato, and which were considered impregnable: this was by Lorenzo Sciorini, the disciple of Bronzino, and a youth of much promise. The lowermost part, or what may be called the base of the whole fabric, had a projecting pedestal on each side, and on each pedestal was a colossal figure, having another at its feet in the manner of a captive, and of similar size, but in the most singular and abject attitude. The first, or that on the right as you approach the High Altar, was a youth of slender form, and a countenance full of life and spirit, representing Genius, and with two small wings on his temples, as Mercury is sometimes depicted: beneath his feet, and executed with remarkable ability, was a figure with asinine ears, representing Ignorance, the mortal enemy of Genius.* These were both by Vincenzio Danti, of Perugia; of whom and of his works, which are much distinguished among the young sculptors of the day, we shall speak more at length hereafter.

On the Pedestal opposite to this, and facing the new Sacristy, was a female figure representing Christian Love; for this, being made up of religion, and every other excellence, is no less than an aggregate of all those qualities which we call the cardinal, and the Pagans the moral virtues, and was thus appropriately placed in the monument of Michelagnolo, since it beseems Christians to celebrate the Christian virtues, without which all other ornaments of body or mind are as nothing. This figure, which had Vice, or Impiety, trampled beneath its feet, was by Valerio Cioli, an excellent youth of much ability, and who well merits the name of a judicious and diligent sculptor. Opposite to the above, and on the side of the old Sacristy, was a figure of the goddess Minerva, or Art; and this was placed there with much judgment, since after a pure life and upright walk, which among the good are ever to be held the first, it was Art that gave to Michelagnolo, not honour and riches only, but so much glory, even in his life, that he may with truth be said to have then enjoyed, more than most of our illustrious artists obtain from their works even after death; nay, to him it was given even to overcome envy, seeing that by common consent, and without any contradiction, the reputation of being the first and greatest has been accorded to his name. For this reason the figure of Art had Envy beneath her feet; the latter, an old woman, meagre, worn, and with viperous eyes, which, together with all her countenance and every feature, were breathing poison and bitterness; she wore a girdle of snakes about her waist, and had a serpent in her hand. These figures were executed by a youth of very tender age, called Lazzaro Calamec of Carrara, who, though still but a child, has given evidence of most distinguished talent, both in painting and sculpture.

It was by his uncle, Andrea Calamec, who was a disciple of Ammannato, that the two figures placed on the fourth pedestal were prepared; these were opposite the organ, and looked towards the principal door of the Church. The first of the two represented Diligence; for those who act but feebly, and effect but little, cannot hope to attain the excellence of Michelagnolo, who, from his fifteenth to his ninetieth year, never ceased to labour earnestly, as we have said above. This figure, most appropriate to the monument of such a man, exhibited the appearance of a bold, powerful youth, having small wings a little above the wrist, to intimate the promptitude and facility of his operations. Beneath him, as his captive, was Indolence or Idleness; a heavy, weary-looking woman, bearing an impress of sleepy dulness over all her person.

These four groups, arranged as here described, formed a beautiful and magnificent composition, and had all the appearance of being in marble, the *terra* having been covered with a coat of white, which had succeeded admirably. From the level platform on which they were placed, there rose another basement, also quadrangular, and about four braccia high, but neither so long nor so broad as that below, which surpassed it by all the space occupied by the figures above-described. On each side of the second basement was a Picture six and a half braccia wide and three high; and over these arose a platform, similar to but smaller than that beneath, on each angle of which was a projecting socle occupied by a seated figure, somewhat larger than life. These four statues, all of women, were readily perceived, by the instruments beside them, to be Painting, Sculpture, Architecture, and Poetry, and were judiciously placed here, as the Life of Michelagnolo, above written, may fully prove.

Proceeding from the principal door of the Church towards the High Altar, the first painting in the second range of the Catafalque appeared, and referring to the Statue of Architecture, it presented Michelagnolo standing before Pope Pius IV., with the Model of the wonderful Cupola of San Pietro in his hand. This Story was over that in which Lorenzo receives Michelagnolo in his garden, the invention and manner of which were highly commended; it was painted by the Florentine Piero Francia; and the Statue of Architecture, which was to the left of the Story, was by Giovanni di Benedetto, of Castello, who, so much to his credit, also executed the Tiber, one of the rivers in front of the Catafalque, as we have before said. In the second Picture, continuing towards the right and approaching the lateral door into the street, was a Picture to accompany the Statue of Painting, and representing Michelagnolo engaged in the execution of that so much, yet never sufficiently, lauded work, the Last Judgment; that, I say, which serves as the example to all in our vocation of foreshortening, and every other difficulty of the art. To the left of this Painting, which was executed with much grace and diligence by the disciples of Michele di Ridolfo, was the Statue of Painting by Battista del Cavaliere, a youth no less distinguished as a sculptor, than for the modesty and excellence of his life.

In the third Picture, or that towards the High Altar and above the inscription, was a Story relating to Sculpture, and showing Michelagnolo taking counsel with a female figure known to be Sculpture by her accompaniments; the artist has around him certain of the works executed by his hand in that branch of art, and the Figure holds a Tablet, with the words of Boëthius: *Simili sub imagine formans.* Beside this picture, which was painted in a very good manner by Andrea del Minga, was the Statue of Sculpture, extremely well executed by Antonio di Gino Lorenzi. The fourth of these pictures, or that towards the organ, related to the Statue of Poetry, and exhibited the master intent on the writing of some composition. Around him, in a graceful hand, robed as the poets describe them, were the Nine Muses and before them Apollo, crowned with laurel, and bearing the Lyre in one hand; while in the other he held a second Crown of Laurel, which he appeared about to place on the head of Michelagnolo. Near to this graceful and beautiful

Story, which was painted in an admirable manner, with figures exhibiting attitudes of infinite animation, by Giovanmaria Butteri, was the Statue of Poetry, the work of Domenico Poggini, a man of much experience in the casting of bronze, the making of dies for coin, and the execution of medals; nor was he less remarkable as a writer of poetry.

Thus it was then that the Catafalque was adorned, and as it diminished at every stage there was a walk entirely around each platform; it was indeed not unlike the Mausoleum of Augustus in Rome; or rather, being of square form, it was more like the Septizonium of Severus; not that near the Capitol, which is commonly called so by an error, but the true one, near the Baths of Antoninus, of which there is a plate in the *Nuove Rome*.

Up to this point the Catafalque had three stages; the first on which were the River-gods, the second where were the groups, and the third on which stood the single figures. From the platform of the last stage there rose a base or socle, one braccio high, much smaller than the platform on which it was placed; and above the ressaults of which were seated the Statues, as before-mentioned, while around it were the words, *Sic ars extollitur arte.* On the socle was a Pyramid, nine braccia high, on two sides of which, that towards the principal door namely, and that towards the High Altar, were two oval compartments, each bearing the head of Michelagnolo in relief; a Portrait from the life, and admirably executed by Santi Buglioni.

On the summit of the Pyramid was a Ball in due proportion with the same, and supposed to be placed there as representing one that might contain the ashes of him so highly honoured; while above the Ball was a figure, larger than life, with the appearance of marble, and representing Fame in the act of commencing her flight to cause the glory and praise of that greatest of masters to resound through the whole world; she being about to place to her lips a trumpet which terminated in three mouths for that purpose.

This figure of Fame was by the hand of Zanobi Lastricati, who, in addition to all his labours as Proveditor for the whole, would yet, to his great honour, assist with the force of his genius and the labour of his hand also. The height of the Catafalque, from the floor to the head of the Fame, was twenty-eight braccia, as we have said. Besides the Catafalque, the Church was hung with baize and serge, not around the central columns only, as is customary, but about all the surrounding Chapels also; nor was there any space between the pilasters, which stand on each side of those Chapels and correspond with the Columns, which had not some ornament of painting, or which did not present a beautiful and imposing aspect.

To begin with one end, in the space of the first Chapel, which is beside the High Altar, and proceeding towards the old Sacristy, there was a picture six braccia high and eight long, wherein, with a new and almost poetical invention, Michelagnolo was displayed as having attained the Elysian fields. On his right hand were figures larger than life, representing the most renowned of the great painters and sculptors of antiquity, each made clearly manifest by some particular sign; Praxiteles, by the Satyr which is in the Vigna of Pope Julius III.; Apelles, by the portrait of Alexander the Great; Zeuxis, by that picture with the grapes which deceived the birds; and Parrhasius with the pretended curtain covering the picture. The others, also, were in like manner made known by other signs.

On the left of Michelagnolo were the masters of modern times, all those who have been most illustrious in these arts, from Cimabue downward that is to say. Thus Giotto was known by a small portrait of Dante as a youth, depicted in the same manner as that by his hand which is still to be seen in the Church of Santa Croce. Masaccio was a portrait from the life; as was also Donatello, who had besides his Zuccone of the Campanile beside him. Filippo Brunelleschi was made known by the copy of his Cupola of Santa Maria del Fiore; then followed (portraits from the life and without any other sign) Fra Filippo, Taddeo Gaddi, Paolo Uccello, Fra Giovann' Agnolo, Jacopo Pontormo, Francesco Salviati, and others; all surrounding Michelagnolo with a welcome similar to that offered by the masters of antiquity, and giving evidence in their looks of their love and admiration for him, no other than was done for Virgil when the other poets received him on his return, as feigned by the divine poet Dante, from whom the invention was taken, as was likewise the verse which was added and which was exhibited on a scroll held in the hand of the River-god Arno, which lay at the feet of Michelagnolo in a most graceful attitude, and with features of singular beauty.

*" Tutti l'ammiran, Tutti amor gli fanno."*

This picture, which was by the hand of Alessandro Allori, the disciple of Bronzino, an excellent painter and most worthy scholar of so great a master, was very highly extolled by all who beheld it. In the space of the Chapel of the Holy Sacrament, at the end of the cross aisle, was a picture five braccia long and four broad, wherein was Michelagnolo surrounded by all the School of the Arts; little children, boys and young men of every age up to twenty-four, all offering to him, as to something sacred and divine, the first-fruits of their labours, paintings, sculptures, models, &c., all which he was courteously receiving, instructing them at the same time in questions of Art, while they gave ear to his precepts with reverent attention, and were looking at him with exquisite expressions of countenance, and in attitudes truly beautiful and graceful. In effect the composition of this picture is such that it could not in a certain sense have been done better; nor, as respects some of the figures, could anything more beautiful be desired; for which cause Battista, the disciple of Pontormo, by whom it was painted, received infinite praise. The verses at the foot of this picture were as follows:—

*Tu pater et rerum inventor, tu patria nobis*
*Suppeditas præcepta tuis ex, inclyte, chartis.*

Descending from this picture towards the principal door of the Church, just before you arrived at the organ, was another, six braccia long and four broad, in the space of a Chapel, and on this was depicted the extraordinary favour conferred by Julius III., when, desiring to avail himself of the great master's talents, he invited him to the Vigna Julia, and caused him to be seated beside himself. Here then Michelagnolo was seen in conversation with the Pontiff, while the cardinals, bishops, and other great personages of the Court remained standing around them. This event, I say, was here depicted with such admirable composition and so much relief, the force and animation of the figures was so remarkable, that it could not perhaps have been much better had it proceeded from the hand of an old and experienced master. Wherefore, Jacopo Zucchi, a young disciple of Giorgio Vasari, by whom it was executed in so good a manner, was judged to have hereby proved that the best hopes of his future progress might reasonably be entertained. Not far from this, and on the same side, a little beneath the organ that is to say, the able Flemish painter, Giovanni Strada,* had painted a picture six braccia long and four high, wherein he depicted an event from the period of Michelagnolo's visit to Venice, at the time of the Siege of Florence. The master is in the Guidecca, a quarter of that most noble city so called; and is receiving a deputation of Venetian gentlemen, whom the Doge, Andrea Gritti, had sent to visit him and make him offers of service. In this work the painter above-named showed much knowledge and judgment, the whole composition and every part of it doing him much honour, seeing that the propriety and grace of the attitudes, the animation of the faces, and the life-like movement imparted to each figure, gave proof of rich inventive power, great knowledge of design, and infinite grace.

We now return to the High Altar, and looking towards the new Sacristy: in the first picture exhibited there, which was that in the space of the first Chapel, was represented another signal favour enjoyed by Michelagnolo, and which was here depicted by Santi Titi, a young man of great judgment, and who had practised painting extensively in Florence as well as in Rome. This favour, to which I think I have before alluded, was conferred at the visit paid by the master to the most illustrious Signor Don Francesco Medici, Prince of Florence, when the latter was in Rome about three years before Michelagnolo died. No sooner did Buonarroti enter the room, than the Prince rose from his seat; and, to do honour to the truly venerable age of that great man, he would have him be seated in his own place, although Michelagnolo, who was exceedingly modest, refused to accept that courtesy. Then, standing before him with the utmost respect, the Prince listened to his words with all the reverence and attention that could have been shown by a son to the best of fathers. At the feet of Don Francesco, in the painting of Santi Titi, was a Boy admirably depicted, who held the beretta, or ducal cap, of the Prince in his hand, and around the group stood soldiers dressed in the antique fashion, and executed in a very good manner. But

* He was with Vasari ten years. See Borghini, *Riposo*; also Baldinucci, vol. vii. p. 61.

best of all were the figures of Michelagnolo and the Prince, which were so full of animation that the old man appeared to be truly speaking, and the youth to be attentively listening to his words.

In another picture, nine braccia high and twelve long, which was opposite to the Tabernacle of the Sacrament, Bernardo Timante Buontalenti,* a painter much favoured by the most Illustrious Prince, had painted the Rivers of the three principal parts of the world, representing these River-gods as having all come, downcast and sorrowful, to lament and condole with the Arno for their common loss. These rivers were the Nile, the Ganges, and the Po; the first had the Crocodile for his symbol, with a sheaf of corn to intimate the fertility of his country: the Ganges had the Gryphon and a coronal of gems; and the Po a Swan, with a chaplet of black amber. The River-gods, conducted into Tuscany by Fame, whose figure was seen hovering above them, were standing around the Arno, who was crowned with cypress, and, holding aloft his exhausted urn in the one hand, had a branch of cypress in the other: beneath the feet of the Arno was a Lion. Then, to intimate that the spirit of Michelagnolo had ascended to the regions of bliss, the judicious painter had depicted a Story or Splendour in Heaven, significant of the celestial light; and towards this the soul of Michelagnolo, in the form of a little angel, was seen ascending, with the following verse:—

*Vivens orbe peto laudibus æthera.*

On each side of this picture were pedestals with statues holding back a curtain, within which those River-gods, the soul of Michelagnolo, and the figure of Fame appeared. The statues on the pedestals had figures beneath their feet, that on the right of the Rivers respecting Vulcan. He has a torch in one hand; and beneath him, in an attitude of much constraint, is Hatred, labouring to free himself from the weight imposed on his neck by the foot of his conqueror. The Symbol of this group was a Vulture with the verse which follows:—

*Surgere quid properas Odium crudele? Jaceto.*

Signifying that supernatural, nay, almost divine excellence,

* Also frequently mentioned in the works of Borghini and Baldinucci. He was a painter, sculptor, architect (civil and military), and a most ingenious theatrical machinist.

should by no means be either envied or hated; the second statue, representing Aglaia, one of the Graces, and the wife of Vulcan. She was placed there to signify Proportion, and had a Lily in her hand, partly because flowers are dedicated to the Graces, and also because Lilies are considered to be not inappropriately used in funeral ceremonies. The figure beneath this statue represented Disproportion (or Deformity), her symbol was an Ape, and over her was the following verse:—

*Vivus et extinctus, docuit sic sternere turpe.*

Beneath the River-gods were the two verses following:—

*Venimus Arne, tuo confisa ex vulnere mæsta*
*Flumina, ut ereptum mundo ploremus honorem.*

This picture also was considered very fine for its invention, for the composition of the story, the beauty of the figures and that of the verses, as also because the painter had not executed the work by commission as the others had done, but had spontaneously, and with the help of certain among the obliging and respectable friends which his abilities had gained him, thus done honour to the master by these his labours. For this cause, therefore, Bernardo both deserved and obtained the greater commendation.

In another picture, six braccia long and four high, which was near the side-door opening on the street, Tommaso da San Friano, a young painter of much ability, had depicted Michelagnolo when despatched by his country as Ambassador to Pope Julius II., as we have said that he was sent, and for what causes, by Soderini. Not far distant from this picture, a little lower down than the side door that is to say, was one of similar size by Stefano Pieri, a disciple of Bronzino, and a very studious careful youth. He had paid several visits to Rome no long time previously, and now painted Michelagnolo as seated in an apartment in conversation with Duke Cosimo, which he frequently did at that period, as we have sufficiently related in other places.

Above the black cloth with which, as we have said, the Church was hung all round, in all the spaces where there were no pictures or stories, were placed images of death, escutcheons, devices, and other objects of like sort, all differing from those usually seen, and exhibiting much ingenuity. Some of the figures of death, as if lamenting that they had robbed the world of such a man, held a tablet with these rords, *Cœgit dura necessitas*, with a globe of the world, out f which was growing a Lily bearing three blossoms, but the talk of which was broken, the ingenious invention of the ,bove-named Alessandro Allori. Other figures of Death vere represented with various peculiarities, but one among hese was more especially commended. This was extended n the Earth, and a figure of Eternity holding a palm in the ıand, stood over it with one foot planted on the neck and ooking disdainfully at Death, appeared to say, that whether ıcting by force or his own will, he had effected nothing, ince, despite of him, Michelagnolo must live to all eternity. The motto was *Vicit inclyta virtus*. This was the invention of Vasari.

Nor will I omit to mention, that between these figures of Death was mingled the device of Michelagnolo, which was three coronals or circlets, interwoven in such sort that the circumference of one crossed alternately through the centres of the other two. This Michelagnolo used either because he meant to signify that the three arts of Sculpture, Painting, and Architecture were so bound and united that each received benefit and ornament from the other, and neither can nor ought to be divided; or perhaps (he being a man of so high a genius), because he had some more subtle meaning in view. But the Academicians, considering the perfection to which he had attained in all three, one having aided and embellished the other, changed these three circlets into three crowns interwoven, with the motto, *Tergeminis tollit honoribus*, to signify that the crown of perfection had been merited by him in all these arts.

On the pulpit whence Varchi pronounced the funeral oration, which was afterwards printed, there was no ornament placed, since, being that in bronze and marble, which had been executed in mezzo and basso-rilievo by the excellent Donatello, whatever decoration had been attempted must have proved infinitely less beautiful than itself. But on the pulpit opposite to this, and which had not then been raised on its columns,* there was placed a picture four braccia high, and somewhat more than two wide, on which a figure of admirable design and execution was painted by the Perugian sculptor, Vincenzio Danti, of whom we have

* This also was designed by Donatello, but was completed by his disciple, Bertoldo, as related in the first volume of the present work, p. 485.

already made mention, and shall speak further hereafter. It represented Fame, or Honour, under the semblance of a youth in a fine attitude, and bearing a trumpet in the right hand, while his feet are planted on the figures of Time and Death, to show that Fame and Honour, in despite of Death and Time, maintain those who have powerfully acted in this life, in the perpetual memory of their fellow men.

The Church being prepared in this manner was furthermore adorned by numerous lights, and was filled by an incalculable number of the people; all of whom, abandoning every other care, had thronged to behold that honourable solemnity. When the procession entered the building, there first came the Prorector of the Academy, accompanied by the Captain and Halbardiers of the Duke's Guard, and followed by the Syndics, the Academicians, and all the Painters, Sculptors, and Architects of Florence. These having taken their places between the Catafalque and the High Altar, where they had for some time been awaited by a large number of nobles and gentlemen, all seated according to their rank, a solemn mass for the dead was begun, with music, and all the ceremonies usual on the highest occasions. That finished, Varchi mounted the pulpit above-mentioned, to fulfil an office which he had last undertaken for the most illustrious lady, the Duchess of Ferrara, daughter of Duke Cosimo, and had never accepted since; then, with that elegance of manner, those modes of utterance, and that tone of voice, which are indeed peculiar to that distinguished man, he described the merits, life, and works of the divine Michelagnolo Buonarroti.

And assuredly it is to be reputed as a great happiness for Michelagnolo that he did not die before the creation of our Academy, seeing that his funeral ceremonies were solemnized by that Society with pomp so magnificent and so honourable. Very fortunate was he, likewise, in having departed before Varchi was removed from this life to that of eternal blessedness, since he could not have been eulogized by a more eloquent or more learned man. The funeral oration pronounced by Messer Benedetto was printed no long time afterwards, as was also another equally beautiful oration, made in praise of Michelagnolo and of Painting, by the most noble and most learned Messer Leonardo Salviati, then a youth of but twenty-two years old, although distinguished by his compositions of all kinds, both in Latin and the vulgar tongue, to the extent which we all know, and which will be further made manifest to the world by his future efforts.* But what shall I say, or what can I say, that will not be too little, of the ability, goodness, and foresight displayed by the very reverend Signor Prorector, Don Vincenzio Borghini? if it be not that, with him for their chief guide and counsellor, the highly distinguished men of that Academy and Company succeeded to perfection in the solemnization of those obsequies. For although each of them was capable of effecting much more in his particular branch of art than he was called on to accomplish on that occasion; yet can no undertaking be brought to a successful conclusion unless one sole head, in the manner of an experienced pilot and captain, have the direction and government of the work.

Now the whole city could not sufficiently examine the above-named preparations in one day, it was therefore decided, by command of the Signor Duke, that the ornaments should remain, and the Church continued thus adorned during several weeks, for the satisfaction of his people, as well as for that of the strangers who came from the neighbouring places to see it. The multitude of epitaphs, and verses in Latin and Italian composed in honour of Michelagnolo by many able men, are not repeated here, because they would fill a book of themselves, and have besides been printed by others. But I will not omit to say, that after all the honours above described, the Duke commanded that a place of sepulture should be given to the master in Santa Croce, the Church in which Michelagnolo had desired to be buried, that being the place of burial of his ancestors. To Leonardo, the nephew of Michelagnolo, his Excellency gave all the marbles for the tomb of his uncle, which the able sculptor, Battista Lorenzi, was commissioned to construct, after the designs of Georgio Vasari; the same artist having also to execute the bust of Michelagnolo.

Three statues are to adorn this tomb, to be executed, one by Battista Lorenzi, one by Giovanni dell' Opera, and the third by Valerio Cioli, Florentine sculptors, who are now occupied with the same, and these figures, together with the

* The vast learning of Salviati has been justly eulogized, but his unfair and pedantic criticism of Tasso greatly diminished his reputation.

tomb, will soon be finished and in their places. The work is at the cost of Leonardo Buonarroti, with the exception of the marbles; but his Excellency, that nothing may be wanting to the honour of so great a man, proposes to place his bust* with an inscription, in the Cathedral, wherein there are the busts and names of many other distinguished Florentines.†

---

## DESCRIPTION OF THE WORKS‡ OF FRANCESCO PRIMATICCIO, PAINTER AND ARCHITECT OF BOLOGNA.

[BORN 1490—DIED 1570.]

HAVING hitherto treated of such of our artists as are no longer in life among us, from 1200 that is to say, down to the current year 1567, and having, for many reasons, placed at the last Michelagnolo Buonarroti, although two or three have died since his departure, I have now considered that it cannot be other than useful to make mention of many noble artists still living, but well meriting to be enumerated among those already recorded. And this I do the more willingly, because all are my friends and brethren, while the three principal are so far advanced in years that few more labours can now be hoped for from their hands, although custom induces them still to continue working. After these I will also briefly name those who, under their discipline, have attained the first places among the artists of the present day; with a few others, who are proceeding to the acquirement of perfection in their art.

* This intention was never fulfilled.

† For the numerous details respecting Michael Angelo, which the short space allotted to the notes of the present volume have rendered it impossible to add in the course of this biography, the reader is referred to Condivi, Duppa, and the other authorities as above cited. Fea, *Notizie*, &c., may also be consulted with advantage, as may likewise Manni, *Addizioni Necessarie*, &c., &c., Florence, 1774; Hautcorne, *Vie de Michael Angelo Buonarroti*, Paris, 1783; *Alcune Memorie di Michael Angelo Buonarroti*, &c., Rome, 1823; and the *Onologia scientifico-letteraria, di Perugia*, for 1834. See also D'Agincourt, Lanzi, Cicognara, &c.

‡ Primaticcio and the artists following him being still alive when Vasari wrote, he does not say "their Lives," but "Description of their Works."

I begin with Francesco Primaticcio, proposing to speak afterwards of Tiziano Vecellio, and Jacopo Sansovino. Francesco was born in Bologna, of the noble family of the Primaticci, which is much celebrated by Fra Leonardo Alberti, and by Pontano. In his first youth he was destined to commerce, but this vocation did not please him: being of elevated mind and spirit he began to practise design, to which he was much inclined by nature, nor did any long time elapse before he gave many proofs, sometimes in drawing, and sometimes in painting, of the ability which finally raised him to distinction. Proceeding afterwards to Mantua, where Giulio Romano was then working for Duke Federigo, at the Palace of the T, Francesco found means to gain a place among the many other young men who were labouring with Giulio at that undertaking.

Here, devoting himself with infinite diligence to the studies of his art, during six years; Francesco learned to work admirably in stucco, as well as to handle the colours; wherefore, among all the young men who then laboured in the palace, Francesco was considered one of the best. Nay, his design and colouring were thought the best of all, and the proof that they were so may be seen in a large apartment, for which he executed a double range of ornaments, comprising a vast number of figures in stucco, which represent the ancient Roman soldiery. He executed many of the paintings also, which are still to be seen in that palace, after the designs of Giulio. These things caused Francesco to be much favoured by the Duke, and when King Francis of France, having heard of the decorations with which he was adorning his palace,* wrote, requesting that a young man who understood painting and stucco-work might be sent him, the Duke despatched Francesco, who repaired to France accordingly in the year 1531. Twelve months earlier, the Florentine painter, Rosso, had entered the service of the French king, as we have said, and had executed many labours for that Monarch, more especially the pictures of Bacchus and Venus, and Cupid and Psyche; yet the first stucco work executed in France, and the first frescoes of any

* For details respecting these works, the reader is referred to Cadioli, *Descrizione delle pitture e sculture di questa città di Mantova*, 1763. See also Bottari, *Descrizione Storica*. The *Dissertazione sulle lettere ed arti Mantovane* of Bettinelli, may likewise be consulted with advantage.

account, are said to have been commenced by Primaticcio, who decorated many apartments in that manner, with Halls and Loggie also, for the French Monarch.

King Francis, being much pleased with the conduct and proceedings of our artist, sent him, in the year 1540, to Rome,* there to attempt the purchase of some antiques in marble, and herein Primaticcio served the King so diligently that what with heads, trunks, and entire figures, he bought in no long time one hundred and twenty-five pieces. At the same period Francesco caused Barozzi da Vignola and others to copy the Bronze Horse of the Capitol; the greater part of the *rilievi* on the Column,† the Statue of Commodus, the Venus, the Laocoon, the Tiber, the Nile, and the Statue of Cleopatra, which are in the Belvedere, and all which were afterwards to be cast in bronze.

Meanwhile, Il Rosso having died in France, and a long gallery, which had been commenced after his designs, and adorned with paintings and stucco-work, remaining unfinished, Primaticcio was recalled to Paris; wherefore, having embarked with the marbles above-mentioned and his casts from the antique, he returned accordingly. But before attending to any other occupation, Primaticcio caused the greater part of those antiques to be cast, when all succeeded so well that they might be taken for veritable works of anti quity, as may still be seen in the Queen's garden at Fontainebleau, where they were placed, to the great satisfaction of King Francis, who may be said to have there made another Rome. And here I must not omit to mention that Francesco had masters in casting of such excellence, as to have his works brought to a degree of perfection which rendered polishing almost needless.

These castings completed, Primaticcio undertook the gallery left unfinished by Rossi, which he decorated in a short time with paintings and stuccoes in greater number than had ever before been executed for any one place.‡ The

* Malvasia accuses Rosso of having caused Primaticcio to be sent to Rome, that he might rid himself of a rival. Benvenuto Cellini, on the contrary, declares that Primaticcio had "put the wish to possess antiques into the king's head, in the hope of thereby depreciating his (Benvenuto's) works."

† The Column of Trajan that is.

‡ For details respecting these works, see Caima, *Lettere d'un vago Italiano*, vol. iv. See also the *Tresors des Marveilles de la maison royale de Fontainebleau*, Paris, 1642.

King, therefore, perceiving that he had been well served during the eight years that Primaticcio had been with him, appointed the painter to be one of his chamberlains; and shortly after, in 1544 that is to say, his Majesty made him Abbot of San Martino. Yet Francesco has not ceased to labour in painting and stucco for his sovereign, nor for King Francis only, but for the other monarchs who have since governed France. In this he has had many assistants, Bolognese and others; Giambattista, the son of Bartolommeo Bagnacavallo for example, who, in the many works which he has executed for Primaticcio, has proved himself no less able than was his father.

Ruggieri of Bologna,* has also been for some time with Primaticcio, and is said to be still in his service, as was Prospero Fontana,† whom Francesco invited to leave Bologna for that purpose, but he fell sick shortly after his arrival, and was compelled to return home. These artists are truly able men; and I, who have not unfrequently employed them both, Bagnacavallo at Rome, and Fontana at Rimini and Florence, can safely affirm them to be so. But among all those who have served the Abbot Primaticcio, none have done him more honour than Niccolò da Modena, of whom we have made mention before;‡ he has indeed surpassed all others, having decorated a hall called the Ball-room entirely with his own hand, after the designs of the Abbot. The figures are as large as life, and so numerous that they can hardly be counted; they are painted in a light and graceful manner, the colouring exhibiting so much harmony that they might be taken for oil-paintings. Niccolò has also painted sixty pictures in the Great Gallery, all after the designs of the Abbot, the subjects taken from the Life of Ulysses; but the colouring of these works is much darker than that of the Ball-room, and this comes perhaps from the fact that he has here used no other colouring than earths, which he has taken pure as they are presented by Nature, scarcely mingling any white with them; he has charged the darker parts with shadow to such an extent that the figures have much force and relief, and they are painted with so much

* The reader may consult Masini, *Bologna Perlustrata.*

† See Malvasia, *Viti*, vol. i. p. 215, *et seq.*

‡ In the fourth volume of the present work, p. 515, *et seq.* See also Zanotti, *ut supra.*

harmony that one might suppose them all done in one day: for this the artist merits high praise, as he does for having executed all *a fresco*, without ever touching them *a secco*, as so many now do.

The ceiling of this Gallery is also decorated with stucco-work and paintings by these and other young artists, but all after the designs of the Abbot, as is likewise the old Hall with a lower gallery which is over the Pond. This last is adorned with works of greater merit than any other apartment of the place, but to describe them fully would lead me too far. At Meudon, and in a vast Palace called the Grotto, belonging to the Cardinal of Lorraine, the Abbot Primaticcio has executed many decorations; the building is of such immense extent, it has so large a number of apartments, such extensive Loggie and so many stair-cases, public and private, that it resembles those edifices of the ancients which they called *Thermes;* but without descending to particulars, there is one apartment called the Pavilion, which is indeed most beautiful; among the decorations are rich cornices replete with fine figures, and the foreshortenings exhibited in this work are very fine.* Fountains decorated with figures in stucco, ornaments in shell-work, and other marine productions, contribute to the beauty of the place, the vaulting being likewise beautifully adorned with stuccoes by Domenico del Barbiere, a Florentine painter, who has given much proof of ability, not in these reliefs only, but in design and colouring also. Another of our countrymen, called Ponzio,† a sculptor, has likewise produced figures in relief for this palace, and has acquitted himself very creditably.

But the works here executed are so numerous that I must restrict myself to the mention of the principal ones produced by the Abbot, with the intent that I may show the distinction to which he has attained in design, in painting, and in architecture.‡ Not that I would refuse the labour of describing them all, had I the minute information respecting them which I have of works executed here. The excellence

* This Palace, our author's description of which Bottari calls "somewhat exaggerated," was destroyed for the purpose of making a Fort on the site.

† This is the *Maitre Ponce* of the French writers.

‡ The reader, who shall desire minute details, may consult Waagen, *Kunstwerke und Künstler in Frankreich*. See also the *Kunstblatt* for 1836.

of Primaticcio in design is made manifest by a drawing, now in my book, which he has sent me, and which I greatly value for his sake as well as for the perfection of the work.

King Francis I. being dead, the Abbot remained with King Henry, whom he served while he lived, and on his death was, by Francis II., made Commissioner-general of all the public buildings in France; a most honourable office, formerly exercised by Monsignore de Villeroi. Since the death of Francis II., Primaticcio, retaining the same office, has served the present King; by whose order, and that of the Queen-mother, he has commenced the Tomb of the above-named King Henry. This is to be constructed in the centre of a chapel having six sides, on four of which are to be the tombs of his four sons; the fifth side being occupied by the altar, and the sixth by the door. Many fine bronzes and statues in marble are to enrich this work, which will doubtless prove to be worthy of so great a King, as well as of so excellent an artist as is the Abbot of San Martino. In his best years, Primaticcio displayed the utmost ability and universality in all things appertaining to our arts; and in the service of his royal masters, he has laboured not only for their buildings, paintings, and stucco-works, but also in the preparations for their various festivities and solemnities, wherein he has shown much ingenuity and power of invention.

He has ever been most liberal and affectionate towards his friends and relations, as well as towards the artists who have served him. In Bologna, more particularly, he has conferred many benefits, and has bought houses of much convenience and beauty for his kindred; witness that now inhabited by Messer Antonio Ancelmi, who married the niece of Primaticcio; another niece, sister of the first mentioned, has also been honourably married by him, and with a good dowry. His life has ever been that of a gentleman rather than a painter; but he is always most friendly to those of our vocation, as I have said: when he sent for Prospero Fontana, for example, he took care to forward a good sum of money for his journey to France; but this, Fontana having fallen sick, could not return by his labours or otherwise; wherefore, when I passed through Bologna in 1563, I spoke to the Abbot on that subject for Prospero; and Primaticcio was so kind that, before I left the city, I saw a writing from his hand, whereby he freely presented to Fontana the whole sum in question. These things have caused him to be much beloved among the artists, who speak of and honour him as a father.

But to say something more of Fontana. This artist was employed in Rome, to his great credit, by Pope Julius III.; first at the Palace of the Vigna Julia, and next at that of the Campo Marzio, which was then in the possession of the Signor Balduino Monti,* but is now in that of the Signor Cardinal, Ernando de' Medici, son of the Duke Cosimo. In Bologna he has produced many works in oil and fresco, more particularly in the Church of the Madonna del Baracane, where there is a picture in oil by his hand of St. Catherine disputing with the philosophers and doctors in the presence of the tyrant, which is considered an exceedingly beautiful work.† Fontana has likewise executed several pictures in fresco in the principal chapel of the Palace, inhabited by the Governor.

The excellent painter, Lorenzo Sabatini, has also been much befriended by Primaticcio, who, knowing the excellence of his manner, and the great facility of which his many works in Bologna present full proof, would have taken him to France, had he not been burdened with so large a family, but he has a wife and several children. In the year 1566 Vasari availed himself of Lorenzo's services for the preparations made in Florence at the marriage of the Prince with the Queen Joanna of Austria, employing him to execute six figures in fresco between the Great Hall and the Hall of the Dugento; beautiful figures they are, and truly worthy of praise. But since this able painter is still making progress I will say no more, except that the studies in which he is known to pass his time give promise of much future excellence.‡

And now, speaking of the Abbot and of other Bolognese artists, I will take the opportunity of mentioning Pellegrino,§ a painter of admirable genius, and one who gives the highest hopes. In his first years he studied the works of Vasari in the Refectory of San Michele-in-Bosco at Bologna, with those of other masters in good repute; and in the year 1547

* Pope Julius III. was a Monti.

† This picture is still in the Church.

‡ For the Life of this artist see Malvasia, *Felsina Pittrice*. The six figures of the vestibule still remain, but are much injured by the dust which covers them.

§ Pelligrino Tibaldi, already mentioned in vol. iv. of the present work.

he proceeded to Rome, where he laboured until 1550, in the designing and copying of the most notable works to be found there. At this time and afterwards, he was employed in the works then in course of execution by Perino del Vaga at the Castel Sant' Angelo: he also painted a Battle-piece in fresco on the ceiling of the Chapel of St. Denis in the Church of St. Louis of the French; and herein he acquitted himself so much to his credit, that, although Girolamo Sicciolante of Sermoneta had executed many works in that chapel, yet those by Pellegrino were by no means inferior; nay, many considered him to have surpassed that artist in the design and colouring of his pictures, whether in boldness or grace. These works afterwards caused Pellegrino to be employed by Monsignore Poggio, who, having built a palace on the Esquiline Hill,* where he had a Vigna outside the Porta del Popolo, desired that Pellegrino should paint certain figures on the front, and should also decorate a Loggia on the side of the Tiber; this he painted accordingly with much care; and it is considered a beautiful and graceful production.

In the court of a house belonging to Francesco Formento, which is situate between the Strada del Pellegrino and the Parione, this artist painted a Façade and two figures besides. In the Belvedere he painted a large Escutcheon of Arms with two figures, by order of the stewards of Pope Julius III.; and at the church of Sant' Andrea, outside the Porta del Popolo, which that Pontiff had erected, he painted figures of San Pietro and Sant' Andrea, both which were much commended. The design for the San Pietro we have now in our book, with other drawings carefully executed by the same artist. Being subsequently despatched to Bologna by Monsignore Poggio, Pellegrino painted numerous stories in fresco at a Palace † which that prelate possessed there; among these there is a very beautiful one, wherein the artist surpassed himself, whether as to the composition, the excellence of the figures, or the beauty of the draperies, insomuch that he has not since produced anything superior to this.

At the Church of San Jacopo in the same city, Pellegrino commenced a chapel for the same Cardinal Poggio; but this was afterwards finished by Prospero Fontana. Being subsequently taken by the Cardinal of Augusta to the Madonna

* The Pincian, and not the Esquiline Hill.

† This is now the Palace of the University.

di Loretta,* Pellegrino there adorned a Chapel for that prelate with the most beautiful paintings and stucco-work. In the ceiling, within rich compartments, is the Birth of Christ, and his Presentation in the Temple; the centre of the vaulting has the Transfiguration, with Moses, Elias, and the Disciples. On the altar-piece is the Baptism of Our Saviour by St. John; and here the artist has painted the Portrait of the above-mentioned Cardinal in a kneeling position. The side walls exhibit San Giovanni Preaching to the People on the one, and the Beheading of that Saint on the other. Pellegrino also depicted the Last Judgment in another part of this Church, with certain figures in *chiaro-scuro*, in the place where the Theatines now have their Confessional.

Being subsequently invited to Ancona† by Giorgio Morato, he there painted a large picture in oil, of Our Saviour Baptized by St. John, for the Church of Sant' Agostino: on one side of this picture are St. Paul and other Saints, while on the Predella there are numerous small figures, which are very graceful. For the same Giorgio Morato, Pellegrino executed a beautiful framework of stucco around the picture of the High Altar, in the Church of San Ciriaco on the Hill, with a figure of Christ in full relief, which was greatly extolled. This artist has executed a grand and beautiful frame-work for the High Altar of San Domenico at Ancona, and was also to have painted the picture for the same; but he having fallen into disaccord with the Signore, who was causing the work to be done, it was given to Tiziano Vecellio instead, as will be related in due time. At a later period, Pellegrino undertook the Loggia of the Merchants of Ancona, a building of which one side turns towards the sea and the other towards the principal street. The vaulting, which is entirely new, he has adorned with paintings and large figures in stucco: he has given his best attention to the work, which has accordingly proved to be a very beautiful and graceful performance: to say nothing of the many fine figures, there are foreshortenings among certain of the nude forms which are most admirable, and it is manifest that he has very carefully imitated the works of Michelagnolo in the Chapel at Rome.

* The Cardinal of Augusta (Augsburg) was Otto Truchses of Waldburg.

† See Ricci, *Memorie Storiche delle Arti, &c., della Marca d'Ancona*, Macerata, 1834.

Now there are no architects or engineers of any great :count in those parts, and finding none who know better ıan he does, Pellegrino has taken it upon himself to work in :chitecture, and to direct the fortifications of certain places ı that province: perceiving that painting is more diffiılt and perhaps less profitable than architecture, he has artly abandoned the first to take charge of the defences at ıncona, as well as other towns in the States of the Church, ut more especially at Ravenna. Pellegrino has lately comıenced a Palace at Pavia for the Cardinal Borromeo, and ıis building is to be used for the High School; but not aving totally ceased to paint, he is now occupied with a tory in fresco for the monks of Monte Oliveto. Of this tory, which is in the Refectory of San Giorgio, Pellegrino howed me the design not long since: it is a very fine one, nd the work will, without doubt, be very beautiful. But ince this artist is not more than thirty-five years old, and is till making progress, this that I have said of him shall uffice for the present.*

I will be very brief in speaking of Orázio Fumaccini,† lso a Bolognese painter. Over one of the doors of the Hall ıf Kings in Rome he painted a Story, as we have said,‡ vhich is an extremely good one, and in Bologna he has proluced several paintings of merit. Although still very young ıe conducts himself in such a manner that there is every ıope of his proving equal to those of his compatriots who ıave gone before him, and of whom we have made mention n these our Lives.

The people of Romagna likewise, moved by the example of :heir neighbours, the Bolognese, have produced many noble works in our Arts; for to say nothing of Jacopone da Faenza, who painted the Apsis of San Vitale in Ravenna, as we have related, there have been and are many besides of great excellence. Maestro Luca de' Longhi, of Ravenna, a man of studious habits and quiet reserved character, has painted many beautiful pictures in oil, with numerous

* Pellegrino was subsequently invited to Madrid by Philip II., and designed the Escurial. For details respecting him, our readers may consult Ximenes, *Descripcion de L'Escorial*, and Ponz., *Viage de España.*

† Samacchini, or Sommacchini, as Vasari calls him, in the Life of Taddeo Zucchero. See Malvasia, *ut supra.*

‡ In the Life of Taddeo Zucchero; see *ante*, p. 196.

portraits from the life, in his native city and its neighbourhood. Among other productions by Longhi, are two sufficiently graceful little pictures, which the reverend Don Antonio da Pisa, then Abbot of the Monastery, caused him to paint, no long time since, for the monks of Classi, many other works have also been executed by this painter. It is certain that Luca Longhi, being studious, diligent, and of admirable judgment as he is, would have become an excellent master had he not always confined himself to Ravenna, where he still remains with his family: his works are accomplished with much patience and study; and of this I can bear testimony, since I know the progress which he made during the time of my stay in Ravenna, both in the practice and comprehension of Art. Nor will I omit to mention that a daughter of his, called Barbara, still but a little child, draws very well, and has begun to paint also in a very good manner and with much grace.

Livio Agresti of Forlì, was at one time the rival of Luca, but after he had painted certain Stories in fresco in the Church of the Spirito Santo, and executed some few other works, he left Ravenna and repaired to Rome. Here he studied design with great zeal and acquired considerable facility, as may be seen in certain façades, and other works in fresco, executed by Livio at that time. The first works painted by this artist at Narni are also tolerably good ones; and in the Church of the Spirito he has produced frescoes and Stories in one of the Chapels, which are executed with much care and patience, wherefore they are justly praised by every one. This last work procured Livio, as is said, the commission for painting one of those smaller stories, which are over the doors in the Hall of Kings in the Palace of the Vatican; and here he acquitted himself in such sort that his work may bear comparison with any to be seen there. The same artist painted seven pictures on cloth of silver, to serve as hangings for a chamber for the Cardinal of Augusta, by whom they were sent to Spain as a present for King Philip, and in that country they are considered very beautiful.

Another picture on cloth of silver was painted by Agresti for the Church of the Chietini * in Forlì, where it now is. At length, having acquired good and bold design, become a

* The Theatines.

ractised colourist and obtained much power in composition, s well as a fine and varied manner, he was invited by the bove-named Cardinal to Augsburg, where he continues to xecute works of great merit.

Highly distinguished in many respects among the artists f Romagna is Marco da Faenza (for so, and no otherwise, s he called),* who has indeed extraordinary facility in resco; bold, resolute, and powerful, he excels most of our oung artists, especially in *grottesche*, not having an equal n the present day, or any one who can approach the perection of his works in that kind. The labours of this artist nay be found in all parts of Rome, and the greater portion of he ornaments in at least twenty rooms of the Ducal Palace n Florence are by this artist, with the decorations of the ceilng in the Great Hall, painted by Giorgio Vasari, as will be elated in the proper place. The ornaments prepared in he Great Court for the coming of the Queen Joanna, and executed in a very short time were also for the most part by his hand. And this shall suffice me to have said of Marco, since he is still living, is making admirable progress, and in the best of his activity.

At Parma, and in the service of the Duke Ottaviano Farnese, there is now a painter called Miruolo, also, as I believe, of Romagna,† who, besides works executed in Rome, has painted many stories in fresco, at a small palace which the above-mentioned Signor Duke has erected within the fortifications of Parma, and where there are some Fountains constructed in a graceful manner by Giovanni Boscoli, a sculptor of Montepulciano. This Giovanni, after having worked in stucco for many years with Vasari in the Palace of Duke Cosimo at Florence, has ultimately settled at Parma in the service of the Signor Duke, who has given him a handsome stipend. Here this artist is still producing works of great beauty, and worthy of his admirable genius. In these same cities and districts there are many other good and noble artists, but since they are young, we will defer to a more convenient season the honourable mention which their works shall have merited.

And this shall be the end of the works of the Abbot Primaticcio, but I will add that, he having made a Portrait

* His family name was Marchetti.—*Ed. Flor.*, 1832-8.

† This artist was a Bolognese. See Masini, *Bologna Perlustrata*.

with the pen, of the Bolognese Painter Passerotto, his intimate friend, which Portrait has come into our hands, we have placed it in our Book of Designs from the hands of eminent painters.

---

## WORKS OF THE PAINTER, TITIAN OF CADORE.

[BORN 1477—DIED 1576.]

TITIAN was born in the year 1480,* at Cadore, a small place distant about five miles from the foot of the Alps; he belonged to the family of the Vecelli, which is among the most noble of those parts. Giving early proof of much intelligence, he was sent at the age of ten to an uncle in Venice, an honourable citizen, who seeing the boy to be much inclined to Painting, placed him with the excellent painter Gian Bellino, then very famous, as we have said. Under his care the youth soon proved himself to be endowed by nature with all the gifts of judgment and genius required for the art of painting. Now Gian Bellino, and the other masters of that country, not having the habit of studying the antique, were accustomed to copy only what they saw before them, and that in a dry, hard, laboured manner, which Titian also acquired; but about the year 1507, Giorgione da Castel Franco, not being satisfied with that mode of proceeding, began to give to his works an unwonted softness and relief, painting them in a very beautiful manner; yet he by no means neglected to draw from the life, or to copy nature with his colours as closely as he could, and in doing the latter he shaded with colder or warmer tints as the living object might demand, but without first making a drawing, since he held that, to paint with the colours only, without

* This is one of the rather numerous inaccuracies of this Life, for such details respecting which, as cannot here find place, our readers may consult Northcote, *Life of Titian;* Lodovico Dolce, *Dialogo della Pittura;* Boschini, *Carta del Navegar Pittoresco;* Cean Bermudez, *Diccionario Historico;* Pungileoni, (in the *Giornale Arcadico* for August and September, 1831); or Cadorin, *Dell' Amore ai Veneziani di Tiziano Vecellio,* &c., with many other works, for the name and titles of which we cannot here find space.

ıny drawing on paper, was the best mode of proceeding and nost perfectly in accord with the true principles of design.

But herein he failed to perceive that he who would give ırder to his compositions, and arrange his conceptions intel-igibly, must first group them in different ways on the paper, o ascertain how they may all go together; for the fancy annot fully realize her own intentions unless these be to a ertain extent submitted to the corporal eye, which then aids ıer to form a correct judgment. The nude form also demands nuch study before it can be well understood, nor can this ver be done without drawing the same on paper; to be ompelled always to have nude or draped figures before the yes while painting, is no small restraint, but when the hand ıas been well practised on paper, a certain facility both in lesigning and painting is gradually obtained, practice in ırt supervenes, the manner and the judgment are alike ›erfected, and that laboured mode of execution mentioned bove, is no more perceived. Another advantage resulting rom drawing on paper is the store of valuable ideas which radually fill the mind, enabling the artist to represent ıatural objects from his own thoughts, without being compelled o hold them constantly before him, nor does he who can lraw, need labour to hide his want of design beneath the ttractions of colouring, as many of the Venetian painters, Giorgione, Il Palma, Il Pordenone and others, who never aw the treasures of art in Rome, or works of the highest ›erfection in any other place, have been compelled to do.

Having seen the manner of Giorgione, Titian early re-olved to abandon that of Gian Bellino, although well rounded therein. He now therefore devoted himself to his purpose, and in a short time so closely imitated Gior-ione that his pictures were sometimes taken for those of hat master, as will be related below. Increasing in age, udgment, and facility of hand, our young artist executed ıumerous works in fresco which cannot here be named in-lividually, having been dispersed in various places; let it uffice to say, that they were such as to cause experienced nen to anticipate the excellence to which he afterwards ttained. At the time when Titian began to adopt the nanner of Giorgione, being then not more than eighteen,*.

* Ticozzi remarks that this must be an error of date, since Giorgione ould otherwise not have been himself more than sixteen or seventeen.

he took the portrait of a gentleman of the Barberigo family who was his friend, and this was considered very beautiful, the colouring being true and natural, and the hair so distinctly painted that each one could be counted, as might also the stitches in a satin doublet, painted in the same work; at a word, it was so well and carefully done, that it would have been taken for a picture by Giorgione, if Titian had not written his name on the dark ground.

Giorgione meanwhile had executed the façade of the German Exchange, when, by the intervention of Barberigo, Titian was appointed to paint certain stories in the same building, and over the Merceria.* After which he executed a picture with figures the size of life, which is now in the Hall of Messer Andrea Loredano, who dwells near San Marcuola: this work represents Our Lady in her flight into Egypt, she is in the midst of a great wood, and the landscape of this picture is well done; Titian having practised that branch of art, and keeping certain Germans who were excellent masters therein for several months together in his own house: within the wood he depicted various animals, all painted from the life, and so natural as to seem almost alive. In the house of Messer Giovanni Danna, a Flemish gentleman and merchant, who was his gossip, he painted a portrait which appears to breathe, with an *Ecce Homo*, comprising numerous figures which, by Titian himself, as well others, is considered to be a very good work. The same artist executed a picture of Our Lady, with other figures the size of life, men and children, being all taken from nature, and portraits of persons belonging to the Danna family.

In the year 1567, when the Emperor Maximilian was making war on the Venetians, Titian, as he relates himself, painted the Angel Raphael, with Tobit and a Dog, in the Church of San Marziliano. There is a distant landscape in this picture, wherein San Giovanni Battista is seen at prayer in a wood; he is looking up to Heaven and his face is illumined by a light descending thence: some believe this picture to have been done before that on the Exchange of the Germans, mentioned above, was commenced. Now it chanced that certain gentlemen, not knowing that Giorgione no longer worked at this façade, and that Titian was doing it (nay, had already given that part over the Merceria to

* See Zanetti, *Varie Pitture a fresco dei principali Pittori Veneziani.*

public view) met the former, and began as friends to rejoice with him, declaring that he was acquitting himself better on the side of the Merceria than he had done on that of the Grand Canal, which remark caused Giorgione so much vexation, that he would scarcely permit himself to be seen until the whole work was completed, and Titian had become generally known as the painter; nor did he thenceforward hold any intercourse with the latter and they were no longer friends.

In the year 1508, Titian published a wood engraving of the Triumph of Faith; it comprised a vast number of figures; our first Parents, the Patriarchs, the Prophets, the Sybils, the Innocents, the Martyrs, the Apostles, and Our Saviour Christ borne in triumph by the four Evangelists and the four Doctors, followed by the holy Confessors: here Titian displayed much boldness, a fine manner, and improving facility. I remember that Fra Bastiano del Piombo, speaking on this subject, told me that if Titian had then gone to Rome, and seen the works of Michelagnolo, with those of Raphael and the ancients, he was convinced, the admirable facility of his colouring considered, that he would have produced works of the most astonishing perfection, seeing that, as he well deserved to be called the most perfect imitator of Nature of our times, as regards colouring, he might thus have rendered himself equal to the Urbinese or Buonarroto, as regarded the great foundation of all, design. At a later period Titian repaired to Vicenza, where he painted the Judgment of Solomon, on the Loggetta wherein the Courts of Justice are held; a very beautiful work. Returning to Venice, he then depicted the façade of the Grimani; at Padua he painted certain frescoes in the Church of Sant' Antonio, the subjects taken from the life of that Saint;* and in the Church of Santo Spirito he executed a small picture of San Marco seated in the midst of other saints, whose faces are portraits painted in oil with the utmost care; this picture has been taken for a work of Giorgione.

Now the death of Giovan Bellino had caused a Story in the Hall of the Great Council to remain unfinished, it was that which represents Federigo Barbarossa kneeling before

* Not in the Church, but the *Scuola* of St. Anthony. Ridolfi, *Maraviglie*, &c., declares that these works obscure the glory of Titian.

Pope Alessandro III., who plants his foot on the Emperor's neck.* This was now finished by Titian, who altered many parts of it, introducing portraits of his friends and others. For this he received from the Senate an office in the Exchange of the Germans called the Senseria, which brought him in three hundred crowns yearly, and which those Signori usually give to the most eminent painter of their city, on condition that from time to time he shall take the portrait of their Doge or Prince when such shall be created, at the price of eight crowns, which the Doge himself pays, the portrait being then preserved in the Palace of San Marco, as a memorial of that Doge.

In the year 1514, the Duke Alfonso of Ferrara had a small apartment decorated in certain of its compartments by the Ferrarese painter Dosso; the Stories were of Eneas, Mars, and Venus; and in a Grotto was Vulcan with two Cyclops working at the forge. The Duke then wished to have some pictures by Gian Bellino, who painted on one of the walls a Vat of red wine surrounded by Bacchantes, Satyrs, and other figures male and female, all inebriated, with Silenus entirely nude mounted on his ass, a very beautiful figure; around this group are crowds of figures with grapes and other fruits in their hands, and this work is so carefully coloured that it may be called one of the finest ever executed by Gian Bellino, although there is a certain harshness and stiffness in the draperies, he having imitated a picture by the Fleming, Albert Dürer, which had just then been brought to Venice. It was placed in the Church of San Bartolommeo, an extraordinary work painted in oil, and comprising a crowd of figures. Within the Vat abovementioned Gian Bellino wrote the following words :—

*Joannes Bellinus Venetus, p.* 1514.

This picture the great age of the master had prevented him from completing; and Titian, as being more eminent than any other artist, was sent for to finish it; wherefore, desirous of progress and anxious to make himself known, he depicted two Stories which were still wanting to that apartment: the first is a River of red wine, beside which are singers and players on instruments half inebriated, females as well as men. There is one nude figure of a sleeping Woman which is very beautiful, and appears living, as indeed

* This story was left unfinished, not by Bellino, but Giorgione, and the description of it by Vasari is not strictly accurate. See Ridolfi, *ut supra.*

do the other figures. To this work Titian affixed his name.* In the second picture, which is near the above, and is seen on first entering, there are numerous figures of Loves and beautiful Children in various attitudes: the most beautiful among these is one who is fishing in a river, and whose figure is reflected in the water. This greatly pleased the Duke, as did the first picture. These children surround an Altar, on which is a statue of Venus with a shell in her hand; she is attended by Grace and Beauty, exquisite figures, which are finished with indescribable care.† On the door of a press Titian painted the figure of Christ, from the middle upwards, a most beautiful and admirable work; a wicked Hebrew is showing to Jesus the coin of Cæsar: other pictures, executed in the same place, are declared by our artists to be among the best ever produced by Titian, and are indeed singularly fine. He was consequently rewarded very largely by the Duke, whose portrait he also took, representing him as leaning on a large piece of artillery. He portrayed the Signora Laura likewise, who was afterwards wife of the Duke; and this too is an admirable work: nor is it to be denied that the labours of those who toil for art have great energy when stimulated by the liberality of Princes.

About this time Titian formed a friendship with the divine Messer Ludovico Ariosto, and was by him acknowledged as an admirable painter, being celebrated as such in his Orlando Furioso.

*. . . . . E. Tizian che onora*
*Non men Cador che quei Venezia e Urbino.*

Having then returned to Venice, Titian painted a picture in oil, for the brother-in-law of Giovanni da Castel-Bolognese; a nude figure of a Shepherd, to whom a Peasant Girl offers a Flute: around the group is a beautiful Landscape: that work is now at Faenza, in the house of the above-named Giovanni. For the High Altar in the Church of the Minorite Friars, called the Ca Grande, this artist painted a picture of our Lady ascending into Heaven, with the Twelve Apostles beneath. But of that work, which was painted on cloth, and perhaps not carefully kept, little can now be seen.‡

* This is the Bacchus and Ariadne of our National Gallery.

† Boschini tells us that when this picture was sent to Spain, Domenico wept for the loss sustained by Italy in its departure.

‡ This work is now in the Venetian Academy of the Fine Arts.

In the same Church, and in the Chapel of the Pesari family, Titian painted a Madonna with the Divine Child in her arms; San Piero and San Giorgio are beside her, and the owners of the Chapel are kneeling around the group. These persons are all portraits from the life; among them are the Bishop of Baffo* and his brother, who had just then returned from the victory which that Bishop had obtained over the Turks.† At the little Church of San Niccolò in the same Convent, Titian also painted a picture, comprising figures of San Niccolò, San Francesco, Santa Caterina and San Sebastiano; the latter is nude, and has been exactly copied from the life without the slightest admixture of art, no efforts for the sake of beauty have been sought in any part, trunk or limbs: all is as Nature left it, so that it might seem to be a sort of cast from the life; it is nevertheless considered very fine, and the figure of Our Lady with the Infant in her arms, whom all the other figures are looking at, is also accounted most beautiful.‡ This picture was drawn on wood by Titian himself, and was then engraved and painted by others.

After the completion of these works, our artist painted, for the Church of San Rocco, a figure of Christ bearing his Cross; the Saviour has a rope round his neck, and is dragged forward by a Jew; many have thought this a work of Giorgione: it has become an object of the utmost devotion in Venice, and has received more crowns as offerings than have been earned by Titian and Giorgione both, through the whole course of their lives. Now Titian had taken the Portrait of Bembo, then Secretary to Pope Leo X., and was by him invited to Rome, that he might see the city, with Raffaello da Urbino and other distinguished persons; but the artist having delayed his journey until 1520, when the Pope and Raffaello were both dead, put it off for that time altogether. For the Church of Santa Maria Maggiore he painted a picture of St. John the Baptist in the Wilderness; there is an Angel beside him that appears to be living; and a distant Landscape, with trees on the bank of a river, which are very graceful.§ He took portraits of the Prince Grimani and Loredano, which were considered admirable, and

* The Bishop of Paphos, Monsignore Jacopo da Pesaro.

† This picture is still to be seen in the Church of the Frari, at Venice.

‡ Now in the Vatican. See Grattani, *Quadri dell' Appartamento Borgia.*

§ This work also is in the Venetian Academy.—*Ed. Ven.*

not long afterwards he painted the portrait of King Francis, who was then leaving Italy to return to France.*

When Andrea Gritti was elected Doge, our artist made his Portrait also; a beautiful thing it is, the likeness being in the figure of Sant' Andrea, who makes one of a group, consisting of Our Lady, San Marco, and himself. The picture is now in the Hall of the College. He painted other portraits of the Doges likewise, that being in his office, as we have said; and these were Pietro Lando, Francesco Donato, Marcantonio Trevisano, and Veniero; but in respect to the two Doges and brothers Pauli,† he was excused, because he had become very old at the time of their election.

The renowned poet, Pietro Aretino, having left Rome before the sack of that city, and repaired to Venice, then became the intimate of Titian and Sansovino, which was both honourable and useful to the former, who was by that circumstance made known wherever the pen of the writer had reached, more especially to certain powerful princes, as will be related in due time. To return, meanwhile, to the works of Titian: it was by him that the Altar-piece of San Piero Martire, in the Church of S.S. Giovanni and Paolo, was painted. San Piero, a figure larger than life, is seen extended on the earth, in a wood of very large trees, he is fiercely assailed by a Soldier, who has already wounded him so grievously in the head, that although still living, the shadows of death are seen on his face. The countenance of another Monk, who is flying from the scene, exhibits the utmost terror. In the air are two nude figures of Angels descending from Heaven in a blaze of light, by which the picture is illumined: these are most beautiful, as is indeed the whole work, which is the best and most perfectly finished, as it is the most renowned of any that Titian has yet executed.‡ This painting having been seen by Gritti, who was ever the friend of Titian as well as of Sansovino, he caused the former to receive a commission for the Story of a great Battle-piece, to be painted in the Hall of the Grand Council, and representing the route of Chiaradadda. The soldiers are contending furiously, while heavy rain is falling on them.

* Now in the Louvre.

† Priuli.—*Ed. Ven.*

‡ It was taken to Paris, among other spoils of the French, but was restored to Venice in 1816.

The work is wholly copied from the life, and is considered the best, most animated, and most beautiful picture in the Hall.* In the same Palace, at the foot of one of the staircases, our artist depicted a Madonna in fresco.

No long time after, Titian painted a Picture for a gentleman of the Contarini family, the subject was Our Saviour at Table with Cleophas and Luke; but the gentleman, considering that the beauty of the work rendered it worthy to be seen in public—as it certainly is—presented it, he being a lover of his country, as a gift to the Signoria, when it was kept for some time in the apartments of the Doge, but it is now placed in a more public position, and where it can be seen by all, over the Door of the Hall leading to that of the Council of Ten namely.† About the same time our artist executed a picture of the Virgin ascending the Steps of the Temple, for the Scuola of Santa Maria della Carità: the Heads in this work are all portraits from the life.‡ He also painted a small Picture of St. Jerome doing Penance, for the Scuola of San Faustino; this was much commended by artists, but was destroyed by fire about two years since, together with the whole church.

In 1530, when the Emperor Charles V. was in Bologna, Titian, by the intervention of Pietro Aretino, was invited to that city by the Cardinal Ippolito de' Medici, and there he made a magnificent Portrait of his Majesty in full armour. This gave so much satisfaction that the artist received a present of a thousand crowns for the same.§ Out of these he had subsequently to give the half to Alfonso Lombardi the sculptor, who had made a model of that monarch to be executed in marble, as we have related in his Life.

Having returned to Venice, Titian there found that many gentlemen had begun to favour Pordenone, commending exceedingly the works executed by that artist in the Ceiling of the Hall of the Pregai, and elsewhere. They had also procured him the commission for a small Picture in the

* This work perished, with many others, in the conflagration of the Palace. There is one in the Louvre of similar character, and by the hand of Titian, but this may be that painted for the Marchese Federigo Gonzaga in 1531. See Gaye, *Carteggio inedito d'Artisti*, vol. ii. p. 164.

† Not now in the Palace.

‡ Now in the Gallery of the Venetian Academy.

§ Now in the Royal Gallery of Madrid.—*Förster.*

Church of San Giovanni Elemosynario, which they intended him to paint, in competition with one representing that Saint in his Episcopal habits, which had previously been executed there by Titian. But whatever care and pains Pordenone took, he could not equal nor even approach the work of the former. Titian was then appointed to paint a picture of the Annunciation for the Church of Santa Maria degli Angeli, at Murano; but those who gave the commission for the work, not wishing to pay so much as five hundred crowns, which Titian required as its price, he sent it, by the advice of Pietro Aretino, as a gift to Charles V., who being greatly delighted with the work, made him a present of two thousand crowns.* The place which the Picture was to have occupied at Murano, was then filled by one from the hand of Pordenone.

When the Emperor, some time after this, returned with his army from Hungary, and was again at Bologna, holding a conference with Clement VII., he desired to have another portrait taken of him by Titian,† who, before he departed from the city, also painted that of the Cardinal Ippolito de' Medici in the Hungarian dress, with another of the same Prelate fully armed, which is somewhat smaller than the first; these are both now in the Guardaroba of Duke Cosimo.‡ He painted the portraits of Alfonso, Marquis of Davalos, and of Pietro Aretino, at the same period, and these things having made him known to Federigo Gonzaga, Duke of Mantua, he entered the service of the latter, and accompanied him to his states. At Mantua our artist made a Portrait of the Duke which appears to breathe, and afterwards executed that of his brother, the Cardinal. These being finished, he painted twelve beautiful Heads of the Twelve Cæsars, to decorate one of the Rooms erected by Giulio Romano, and when they were done, Giulio painted a Story from the Lives of the Emperors beneath each head.§

* The present was to the Empress Isabella, as we learn from a letter of Pietro Aretino, and the two thousand crowns came from her, and not from the Emperor.—*Ed. Flor.*, 1832-8.

† This portrait also is believed to be at Madrid.

‡ The first of these portraits is in the Pitti Palace, the second is in the Louvre.

§ Ridolfi speaks of these heads as in one of the Royal Collections in England, but they are not now to be found; and the twelve heads said to be by Titian in the Royal Gallery of Munich, are believed by many to be those here in question.

In Cadore, the native place of Titian, that artist has painted a picture wherein is Our Lady, San Tiziano, the Bishop,* and his own Portrait in a kneeling position. In the year that Pope Paul III. went to Bologna, and thence to Ferrara, Titian having gone to the court, took the Portrait of His Holiness, a very fine work. He also painted that of the Cardinal Santa Fiore; both of these works, for which he was very well paid by the Pope, are now in Rome; one in the Guardaroba of Cardinal Farnese, the other in the hands of those who became heirs of the Cardinal Santa Fiore: many copies have been taken from them, and these are dispersed throughout Italy. About the same time our artist made the Portrait of Francesco Maria, Duke of Urbino; and this is so wonderfully beautiful, that it was celebrated by Messer Pietro Aretino in a sonnet, which begins thus:—

*Se il chiaro Apelle con la man dell' Arte*
*Rassembrò d' Alessandro il volto e il petto.*

In the Guardaroba of the same Duke there are two female heads by Titian, which are very pleasing, with a recumbent figure of Venus, partially covered with flowers, and transparent draperies, the whole exceedingly beautiful and finely finished.† There is a half-length of Santa Maria Maddalena, with dishevelled hair, which is likewise very beautiful,‡ with Portraits of Charles V., King Francis, as a youth, the Duke Guidobaldo II., Pope Sixtus IV., Julius II., Paul III., the old Cardinal of Lorraine, and Soliman, Emperor of the Turks; all from the hand of Titian, and exceedingly fine In that same Guardaroba, among many other things, is an antique Head of the Carthaginian Hannibal, cut in a cornelian, with a beautiful bust in marble by Donatello.

In the year 1541 Titian painted the picture of the High Altar, in the Church of the Santo Spirito in Venice, the subject being the Descent of the Holy Spirit on the Apostles; the Almighty is represented in fire, and the Spirit as a Dove. This picture having shown signs of deterioration in a very short time, Titian had much discussion with the monks of Santo Spirito respecting it, and was ultimately obliged to

* This Bishop is said to have been of Titian's family.

† This is the Venus of the Tribune of the Uffizj, known to most of our readers.

‡ Also at Florence, but in the Pitti Palace

-paint the work, which is that now on the Altar.* At Brescia itian painted the picture of the High Altar in the Church ' San Nazzaro, which he did in five divisions: the centre as the Resurrection of Our Lord, with soldiers around the pulchre; in the sides are San Nazzaro, San Sebastiano, the ngel Gabriel, and the Virgin receiving the Annunciation. n the Cathedral of Verona he painted the Assumption of )ur Lady into Heaven, with the Apostles standing beneath; his is held to be the best modern painting in that city.† In he same year, 1541, this master painted the Portrait of Don )iego di Mendoza, then Ambassador from Charles V. to 'enice; that beautiful portrait is a full-length, standing pright; and from that time Titian began the custom, since ecome frequent, of painting portraits at full-length. In the ame manner he made the likeness of the Cardinal of Trent, hen a youth, and for Francesco Marcolini he took the Portrait of Pietro Aretino; but this is not so fine a one as hat which the same person caused to be taken, and sent himself as a present to the Duke Cosimo de' Médici, to whom he also sent the Head of the Signor Giovanni de Medici, father of the Duke. This last was taken from a cast made from the face of Giovanni after his death, at Mantua, which cast was in possession of Pietro. The portraits are both in the Guardaroba of the Duke with other noble pictures.‡

In the same year Giorgio Vasari was in Venice, where he passed thirteen months, employed, as I have said, in the decoration of a ceiling for Messer Giovanni Cornaro, and certain works for the Company of the Calza, when Sansovino, who was directing the construction of Santo Spirito, caused him to make designs for three large pictures in oil, which were to be executed in the ceiling of Santo Spirito, and which Vasari was to paint; but Giorgio having departed, the three pictures were given to Titian, who executed the same most admirably, having taken especial pains with the foreshortening of the figures. In one of these

* This picture is now in the Church of Santa Maria della Salute.—*Ed. Ven.*

† This also was taken to Paris, but was restored, and is now in its original place.

‡ The portrait of Pietro Aretino is now in the Pitti Palace; that of Giovanni in the Uffizj.

pictures is the Sacrifice of Isaac by his father Abraham; in the second, David taking off the head of Goliath; and in the third, Cain killing Abel.* About the same time Titian painted his own Portrait, that this memorial of himself might be left to his children; and in the year 1546, being invited to Rome by the Cardinal Farnese, he repaired to that city accordingly. There he found Vasari, who had then returned from Naples, and was painting the Hall of the Chancery for the Cardinal Farnese, by whom Titian was recommended to his care, whereupon Giorgio kept him faithful company in his visits to the remarkable objects of Rome.

Having rested himself for a few days, Titian then received rooms in the Belvedere, and was commissioned to make another full-length Portrait of Pope Paul III., with that of Farnese,† and of the Duke Ottavio; all of which he executed to the great satisfaction of those Signori, who then prevailed on him to paint a half-length figure of Christ, in the manner of the *Ecce Homo*, as a present for the Pope. But this work, whether it were that the paintings of Michelagnolo, of Raffaello, of Polidoro, and of others, had made him lose courage, or from some other cause, although a good picture, did not appear to the painters equal in excellence to others of his productions, more particularly his portraits. Now it chanced that Michelagnolo and Vasari, going one day to see Titian in the Belvedere, beheld a picture, which he had just then finished, of a nude figure representing Danæ, with Jupiter transformed into a shower of gold in her lap,‡ many of those present beginning to extol the work (as people do when the artist stands by) praised it not a little: when, all having left the place, and talking of Titian's work, Buonarroto, declared that the manner and colouring of that artist pleased him greatly, but that it was a pity the Venetians did not study drawing more, "for if this artist," said he, "had been aided by Art and knowledge of design, as he is by nature, he would have produced works which none could surpass, more especially in imitating life, seeing that he has a fine genius, and a graceful animated manner."

* These pictures are now in the Sacristy of the Oratory of Santa Maria della Salute.

† The portrait of Pope Paul III. is believed to be now in Naples; that of Farnese is in the Corsini Gallery in Rome.

‡ Now in the Museo Borbonico at Naples.

And it is certainly true that whoever has not practised design extensively, and studied the best works, ancient and modern, can never attain to the perfection of adding what may be wanting to the copy which he makes from the life, giving to it that grace and completion whereby Art goes beyond the hand of Nature, which very frequently produces parts that are not beautiful.

Titian left Rome enriched by many gifts from those Signori, more particularly by a benefice of good income for Pomponio his son; but first his second son, Orazio, had completed the Portrait of Messer Battista Ceciliano, an excellent player of the violin, which is a good work, Titian himself having made certain Portraits besides, for Guidobaldo Duke of Urbino. Arrived at Florence, he was amazed at the sight of the fine works in that city no less than he had been by those of Rome. He then visited Duke Cosimo, and offered to take his portrait; but the Duke did not give himself much trouble in the matter, perhaps because he had no mind to offer a slight to the many noble artists of his own city and dominions.

Having reached Venice, Titian then finished an Allocution (as they call it) for the Marquis del Vasto, and which that Signore had made to his soldiers. He afterwards executed the portrait of Charles V., with that of the Catholic King, and of many other persons. These labours completed, Titian painted a small picture of the Annunciation for the Church of Santa Maria Nuova, and afterwards, using the assistance of his disciples, he painted a Last Supper in the Refectory of S. S. Giovanni and Paolo,* with a picture for the High Altar of the Church of San Salvatore, the subject of which was the Transfiguration; and an Annunciation for another Altar in the same Church. But these last works, though there are good qualities in them, were not much esteemed by the master himself, and have not the perfection seen in many of his other paintings. The productions, but more especially the portraits of Titian, are so numerous that it would be almost impossible to make the record of them all. I will therefore speak of the principal only, and that without order of time, seeing that it does not much signify to tell which was painted earlier and which later. He took the Portrait of Charles V. several times, as we have

* This picture perished in a conflagration.—*Ed. Ven.*

said, and was finally invited by that monarch to his Court; there he painted him as he was in those last years; and so much was that most invincible Emperor pleased with the manner of Titian, that once he had been portrayed by him, he would never permit himself to be taken by any other person. Each time that Titian painted the Emperor he received a present of a thousand crowns of gold, and the artist was made a Cavalier, or Knight, by his Majesty, with a revenue of two hundred crowns yearly, secured on the Treasury of Naples, and attached to his title.

When Titian painted Filippo King of Spain, the son of Charles, he received another annuity of two hundred crowns; so that these four hundred added to the three hundred from the German Exchange, make him a fixed income of seven hundred crowns, which he possesses without the necessity of exerting himself in any manner. Titian presented the Portraits of Charles V. and his son Filippo to the Duke Cosimo, who has them now in his Guardaroba.* He also took the portrait of Ferdinand King of the Romans, who was afterwards Emperor, with those of his children, Maximilian that is to say, now Emperor, and his brother: he likewise painted the Queen Maria; and at the command of the Emperor Charles, he portrayed the Duke of Saxony, when the latter was in prison.† But what a waste of time is this! when there has scarcely been a noble of high rank, scarcely a prince or lady of great name, whose portrait has not been taken by Titian, who in that branch of art is indeed an excellent painter.

He painted King Francis I. of France, as we have said. Francesco Sforza, Duke of Milan; the Marquis of Pescara, Antonio da Leva, Massemiano Stampa, the Signor Giovambattista Castaldo, and other Signori in vast numbers. He has, moreover, produced various works at different times, besides those above mentioned. At Venice, for example, and by command of Charles V., he painted a large Altarpiece, the subject of which is the Triune God Enthroned; Our Lady is present with the Infant Christ, who has the Dove over his head, and the whole ground is of fire, to signify Eternal Love; while the Father is surrounded by glowing Cherubim. On one side of this picture is the Emperor, and

* The portrait of Philip is in the Pitti Palace.

† This portrait is in the Gallery of the Belvedere at Vienna.

n the other the Empress, clothed in linen garments; they re kneeling in prayer with folded hands, and are surrounded y numerous Saints. The composition of this work was in ccordance with the orders of his Majesty, who was then giv- ng evidence of his intention to retire, as he afterwards did, rom mundane affairs, to the end that he might die in the nanner of a true Christian, fearing God and labouring for is own salvation. This picture the Emperor told Titian hat he would have taken to the Monastery, where his Majesty afterwards finished the course of his life; and being work of extraordinary merit, it is expected that engrav- ngs thereof will be published in a short time.*

The same master painted for the Queen Maria a figure of Prometheus bound to the Mount Caucasus and torn by the Eagle of Jupiter; with one of Sisyphus in Hell loaded with his stone,† and Tityus devoured by the Vulture. All these were transmitted to her Majesty, with a figure of Tantalus of the same size, that of life namely, on cloth and in oil. He painted a Venus and Adonis also, which are admirable; the Goddess is fainting as she sees herself abandoned by Adonis, who is accompanied by dogs, which are singularly natural.‡ In a picture of the same size, Titian painted Andromeda bound to the Rock with Perseus delivering her from the Sea-monster; a more beautiful painting than this could not be imagined; and the same may be said of another,§ Diana Bathing with her Nymphs, and turning Actæon into a Stag. He painted a figure of Europa likewise, borne over the Sea by the Bull. These pictures are in the possession of the Catholic King, and are held in high esteem for the animation imparted to them by the master, whose colours have made them almost alive.

It is nevertheless true that his mode of proceeding in these last-mentioned works is very different from that pursued

* It was engraved by Cornelius Cort. The picture accompanied Charles V. to the Monastery of St. Just, and on his death was taken to the Escurial, where it remains.—*Ticozzi*.

† This picture and the Prometheus are at Madrid.

‡ The original work is at Madrid; that in our National Gallery is a replica.

§ Since Vasari speaks of "another Diana," although he has mentioned no other, he was most probably thinking of the Diana and Calisto of Titian, which, with that above-mentioned, is also at Madrid. There are replicas of both pictures in the Bridgewater Gallery, and at Vienna.

by him in those of his youth, the first being executed with a certain care and delicacy, which renders the work equally effective, whether seen at a distance or examined closely; while those of a later period, executed in bold strokes and with dashes, can scarcely be distinguished when the observer is near them, but if viewed from the proper distance they appear perfect. This mode of his, imitated by artists who have thought to show proof of facility, has given occasion to many wretched pictures, which probably comes from the fact that whereas many believe the works of Titian, done in the manner above described, to have been executed without labour, that is not the truth, and these persons have been deceived; it is indeed well known that Titian went over them many times, nay, so frequently, that the labour expended on them is most obvious.* And this method of proceeding is a judicious, beautiful, and admirable one, since it causes the paintings so treated to appear living, they being executed with profound art, while that art is nevertheless concealed.

In a picture three braccia high and four broad, Titian painted the Infant Christ in the arms of the Virgin, and receiving the Adoration of the Magi; the work comprises numerous figures one braccio high, and is a very good one, as is another which he copied himself from this and gave to the Cardinal of Ferrara (the elder).† Another work by this master, representing Christ derided by the Jews, was placed in a chapel of the Church of Santa Maria delle Grazie at Milan.‡ For the Queen of Portugal he painted a picture of Christ scourged at the Column; this, which is somewhat less than life, is very beautiful. For the High Altar in the Church of San Domenico, in Ancona, he painted a picture of Christ on the Cross, with Our Lady, San Giovanni, and San Domenico at the foot of the same; this also is very beautiful, and in the bold manner described above. The picture at the Altar of San Lorenzo, in the Church of the Crocicchieri at Venice, is by Titian; it represents the Martyrdom of San Lorenzo, with a building crowded with figures; in the midst of them lies the foreshortened figure of San Lorenzo on the Gridiron, beneath

* "To those who sufficiently understand the matter," remarks Bottari.

† Now at Madrid; that in our National Gallery is a replica.

‡ This picture was taken to Paris, and has not been restored.

which is a great fire, and the executioners stand around it. The time being night, there are two servants with torches giving light to those parts of the picture, that are beyond the reach of the fire beneath the gridiron, which is a large and fierce one; but the light it throws, as well as that of the torches, is overcome by a flash of lightning which descends from heaven, and cleaving the clouds, shines brightly over the head of the Saint and the other principal figures. In addition to these three lights there is that of lamps and candles, held by those at the windows of the building. All this produces a fine effect, and the whole work is, in short, executed with infinite art, genius, and judgment.*

At the Altar of San Niccolò, in the Church of San Sebastiano, there is a small picture by Titian, representing St. Nicholas, so animated as to seem alive; it is seated in a chair painted to imitate marble, and an angel is holding the mitre; this was executed for the advocate Messer Niccolò Crasso.† At a later period, our artist painted a half-length figure of Mary Magdalene for the Catholic King; her hair falls about her neck and shoulders, her head is raised and the eyes are fixed on Heaven, their redness and the tears still within them, giving evidence of her sorrow for the sins of her past life. This picture, which is most beautiful, moves all who behold it to compassion;‡ when it was finished, a Venetian gentleman, . . . . . . Silvio, was so much pleased therewith, that, being a zealous lover of painting, he gave Titian a hundred crowns for the picture, and the master had to make another for the Catholic King, which was however no less beautiful.

Among the Portraits by Titian is that of a Venetian citizen his friend, called Sinistri; and of Messer Paolo da Ponte, whose daughter, called the Signora Giulia da Ponte, a most beautiful damsel, and a gossip of Titian, the latter also took; as he did the Signora Irene, another lovely maiden accomplished in music, in learning, and in design, who died about eight years since, and was celebrated by the pens of almost all the Italian writers.§ Titian also made the like-

* This picture had nearly perished when Bottari wrote.

† Restored some years since by the Count Bernardino Corniani.—*Ed. Ven.*

‡ See the *Kunstblatt* for 1846. See also Gaye, *Carteggio*, vol. ii.

§ Irene di Spilembergo, the disciple of Titian. See Maniago, *Storia delle Belle Arti del Friuli*.

ness of Messer Francesco Filetto, an orator of happy memory, with that of his son in the same picture, the last appears to be living, and the portrait is now in the possession of Messer Matteo Giustiniani, a lover of these arts, who has had his own likeness taken by the painter Jacomo da Bassano,* a fine work, as are many others dispersed through Venice, and also by Bassano, who is particularly excellent in small pictures, and in the painting of animals.

Titian made a second Portrait of Bembo, when the latter had become a Cardinal that is; he also took Fracastoro,† and the Cardinal Accosti of Ravenna, whose portrait the Duke Cosimo has in his Guardaroba. The sculptor Danese has the portrait of a gentleman of the Delfini family by this master in his possession; and Messer Niccolò Zono tells us that he saw the likeness of Rossa, the wife of the Grand Turk, a lady of sixteen, with that of Cameria her daughter, both by the hand of Titian, and wearing dresses and ornaments of great beauty. In the house of the lawyer, Messer Francesco Sonica, a gossip of Titian, is the portrait of that Messer Francesco by the hand of our artist, with a large picture, representing the Madonna in the Flight to Egypt; she appears to have just descended from the Ass, and has seated herself on a stone by the wayside; St. Joseph stands near, as does St. John, a little child who is offering to the Saviour the flowers gathered by an angel from the branches of a tree which is in a wood, wherein are numerous animals; the ass is browsing near. This picture, a very graceful one, has been placed by the Signor Francesco in a palace which he has built near Santa Justina in Padua.

For the Florentine Monsignore Giovanni della Casa, a man illustrious for learning as well as birth, our artist painted a beautiful Portrait of a gentlewoman whom Della Casa loved when he was in Venice, and by whom the master was honoured for the same, with the exquisite sonnet which begins thus:—

*Ben veggo io, Tiziano, in forme nuove*
*L'idolo mio, che i begli occhi apre e gira.*

As also with that which follows it.

This admirable painter likewise sent a picture of the Last Supper to the Catholic King; this work, which was

* For whose Life, see Ridolfi, *Vite de' Pittori Veneti*.

† An eminent physician and Latin poet of the time.

seven braccia long, was a performance of extraordinary beauty; and besides these, with many others of minor importance which we omit, he has still in his house, among numerous sketches and pictures commenced, the Martyrdom of San Lorenzo, of size similar to the above, which he also proposes to send to the Catholic King. He has likewise a large canvass exhibiting Christ on the Cross, the thieves on each side, and the executioners beneath, which he is painting for Messer Giovanni d'Arna; and a picture which was begun for the Doge Grimani, father of the Patriarch of Aquileia. For the Hall of the Great Palace of Brescia, Titian has commenced three large pictures, which are to form part of the decorations of the ceiling,* as we have said when speaking of the Brescian painters, Cristofano and his brother. He also began a picture many years since for Alfonso, first Duke of Ferrara, the subject is a nude figure of a woman bowing before the Goddess Minerva; there is besides another figure, and in the distance is the Sea, with Neptune in his Chariot; but the death of Alfonso, according to whose fancy the work was composed, caused the picture to remain incomplete, and it is still in Titian's hands.

Another work, brought to a state of considerable advancement, but not finished, is Our Saviour appearing to Mary Magdalen in the Garden; the figures are of the size of life, as are those of another of equal size where Christ is placed in the Sepulchre, while the Madonna and the other Maries stand around: and among other good things to be seen in his house is a picture of the Madonna, with, as it is said, a portrait of himself, finished four years since, and which is very beautiful and natural.† There is, likewise, a figure of San Paolo reading, a half-length figure, which is so fine that it may well be that same which was filled with the Holy Spirit. All these works, with many others which I omit, to avoid prolixity, have been executed up to the present age of our artist, which is above seventy-six years. Titian has been always healthy and happy; he has been favoured beyond the lot of most men, and has received from Heaven only favours and blessings. In his house he has been visited by whatever Princes, Literati, or men of distinction have gone to or dwelt

* They were destroyed by fire.—*Ed. Flor.*, 1832-8.

† Now among the portraits of painters in the Uffizj.

in Venice; for, to say nothing of his excellence in art, he has always distinguished himself by courtesy, goodness, and rectitude.

Titian has had some rivals in Venice, but not of any great ability, wherefore he has easily overcome them by the superiority of his art; while he has also rendered himself acceptable to the gentlemen of the city. He has gained a fair amount of wealth, his labours having always been well paid; and it would have been well if he had worked for his amusement alone during these latter years, that he might not have diminished the reputation gained in his best days by works of inferior merit, performed at a period of life when nature tends inevitably to decline, and consequent imperfection.

In the year 1566, when Vasari, the writer of the present History, was at Venice, he went to visit Titian, as one who was his friend, and found him, although then very old, still with the pencils in his hand and painting busily. Great pleasure had Vasari in beholding his works and in conversing with the master. Titian then made known to Giorgio, Messer Gian Maria Verdezzotti, a young Venetian gentleman of great ability, the friend of Titian, and a man well versed in design as well as a tolerable colourist, which he has proved by some very beautiful Landscapes from his own hand. This youth, by whom Titian is loved and revered as a father, has two figures painted in oil within two niches by that artist, an Apollo and a Diana that is to say.

It may be affirmed then, that Titian, having adorned Venice, or rather all Italy, and other parts of the world, with excellent paintings, well merits to be loved and respected by artists, and in many things to be admired and imitated also, as one who has produced, and is producing, works of infinite merit; nay, such as must endure while the memory of illustrious men shall remain.

Many young men have been with Titian for the purposes of learning; yet the number of those who may truly call themselves his disciples is not great, seeing that he has never given much instruction; yet all may learn more or less from the works of a master, once they have acquired the power of comprehending them. Among those about Titian meanwhile was a certain Giovanni, a Fleming,* who became a

* Johann Calcar, or Calker. See Lanzi, *Storia Pittorica*. See also Bryan, *Dictionary of Painters and Engravers*.

good master, whether for large or small figures, and in portraits was most admirable, as may be seen by his works at Naples, where he lived for some time, and where he ultimately died. By his hand, and they must do him honour to all time, were the designs for anatomical studies which the most admirable Andrea Vessalio caused to be engraved on copper and published with his works.* But the artist who has most successfully imitated Titian, was Paris Bordone; who, born in Treviso, of parents, one a Trevisano, the other a Venetian, was taken, at the age of eight, to certain of his mother's kindred in Venice. Here, having studied grammar and become an excellent musician, he was sent to Titian, but did not spend many years with that master, whom he perceived to have but little disposition to instruct his disciples, even though entreated by them to do so, and encouraged thereto by the patience and good conduct of those young men. Bordone resolved to leave him therefore, but grieving much that Giorgione was no longer alive at that time, the manner of the latter pleasing him greatly; as did still more his reputation of being an excellent and affectionate teacher to all who desired to learn from him. Since he could not do better, therefore, Bordone set himself to imitate the manner of Giorgione to the utmost of his power, and by earnest labour in the copying of his works, he rendered himself so good an artist that he obtained an excellent reputation. He was thus only eighteen when he received the commission for painting a picture in the Church of San Niccolò, which belongs to the Minorite Friars; but Titian, having heard this, contrived by means of friends and favours to get it out of his hands, perhaps to prevent his giving proof of his ability at so early a period; perhaps, also, induced by the love of gain.

Paris was subsequently invited to Vicenza, there to paint

* This great anatomist was born at Brussels. He was condemned to death for having opened the body of a Spaniard whom he affirmed to have been dead, but who is said to have only appeared to be so. The crime was, however, not fully proved, and his sentence was commuted by the intervention of Philip II., for a pilgrimage to the Holy Land. On his return from this journey, Vessalio was shipwrecked, and died of hunger on a desert part of the island of Zante, in the year 1564. His portrait, painted by Titian, is in the Pitti Palace, and his magnificent work, *De humani corporis fabrica*, (some of the plates in which are said to have been designed by Titian) will doubtless be known to many of our readers.

a story in fresco, in the Loggia of the Piazza where the courts are held. This commission he accepted willingly, although Titian had himself painted a picture representing the Judgment of Solomon in that place; and having executed a story of Noah and his Sons, Paris was considered to have acquitted himself extremely well, both as regarded design and execution, insomuch that the work, being no less beautiful than that of Titian, both are considered by those who do not know the truth to be by the same hand.*

Having returned to Venice, Bordone painted certain nude figures at the foot of the Rialto; and, after this proof of his ability, he was employed to decorate the Façades of many houses in Venice. He was then invited to Treviso, where he also executed numerous Façades and other works, more particularly Portraits. Among these was that of the illustrious Messer Alberto Unigo, with those of Messer Marco Serravalle, Messer Francesco da Quer, the Canon Rovere, and Monsignore Alberti. In the Cathedral of that city he painted a picture at the request of the Signor Vicar; it is in the middle of the church, and represents the Birth of Christ. This being completed, he painted a Resurrection of Our Lord in like manner. In the Church of San Francesco he painted a picture for the Cavaliere Rovere, with another in San Girolamo, and one in Ognissanti, exhibiting varied heads of Saints, male and female. These are all beautiful, and display much variety in the attitudes and vestments.† There is also a picture, by the hand of Paris, in the Church of San Lorenzo; and in San Polo he painted three chapels: in the principal of these he represented the Resurrection of Christ; the figures are as large as life, and are accompanied by a vast number of Angels. In the second chapel he painted Saints with Angels around them; and in the third, is Our Saviour Christ in the air with Our Lady, who presents San Domenico to her Divine Son. All these works have made Bordone known as an able painter, and a citizen firmly attached to his native place.

In Venice, where he has almost always lived, he has executed numerous works at various times; but the most

* These works have both perished.—*Bottari.*

† This story is now in the Venetian Academy, as is that of the Fisherman mentioned below. See Zanotto, *La Pinacoteca Veneta.*

beautiful and most praiseworthy performance ever executed by Bordone, was a Story in the Scuola of SS. Giovanni e Polo, in which the Fisherman presents St. Mark's ring to the Signoria of Venice. We have here a building beautifully painted in perspective, around which are seated the Senators, with the Doge; many of the heads being portraits from life, of great animation, and admirably executed. The beauty of this work, so well painted in fresco, caused Bordone to be employed by many gentlemen, and he executed numerous pictures in the great Palace of the Foscari, near St. Barnabas; among others, a figure of Christ descended to the Gates of Hell, whence he is delivering the Holy Fathers; a picture considered to display great merit. In the Church of St. Job, at the Canal Reio, Bordone painted a very beautiful picture; and at San Giovanni he executed another, with one in each of the Churches of Santa Maria della Celeste, and Santa Marina.

But knowing that he who would succeed in Venice must pay great court to one and another, Paris, who was a man of reserved habits, and had no taste for certain modes of proceeding, which he saw to prevail around him, resolved to accept whatever should be offered to him in other places, and to take what Fortune might give, without being obliged to go begging for employment. He therefore seized an occasion which presented itself, and in 1538 went to France, where he entered the service of King Francis, and painted numerous Portraits of Ladies for that Monarch, with other pictures of different kinds. At the same time he executed a singularly beautiful Church picture, for the high ecclesiastic, Monsignore de Guise, with one of Venus and Cupid, for his chamber. For the Cardinal of Lorraine he painted the *Ecce Homo*, with a Jupiter and Io, and many other works. Paris likewise sent the King of Poland a picture of Jupiter and a Nymph, which was considered a very fine one. Two others which he despatched to Flanders, were also reputed to be most beautiful. One of these represented Mary Magdalene in the Hermitage, accompanied by Angels; the other was a Diana bathing with her Nymphs; both of which our artist painted by commission from the Milanese Candiano, physician to the Queen Maria, who intended them as presents for her Highness.

At Augsburg, Paris Bordone undertook works of great

importance, for the Fugger Palace; the payment for these was three thousand crowns; and in the same city he executed a large and beautiful picture, wherein he exemplified all the five rules of architecture, in a building painted in perspective, for the Priners, who are great men in that place, and for whom he also painted a cabinet picture, which is now in the possession of the Cardinal of Augsburg.* At St. Augustine, in Crema, this artist painted two pictures, in one of which is the portrait of the Signor Giulio Manfrone, who is fully armed, and represents St. George. The same painter has executed many works, which are much praised at Civitale di Belluno, more particularly a figure of Santa Maria, and one of St. Joseph, which are greatly admired. He sent the Portrait of Signor Ottaviano Grimaldo, the size of life, to Genoa, with a picture of the same size, representing a female figure.

Proceeding at a later period to Milan, Bordone painted a picture for the Church of San Celso in that city; it represents certain figures in the air, with a most beautiful landscape beneath them. This he is said to have done at the request of the Signor Carlo da Roma, in whose Palace he also painted two large pictures in oil; the first representing Mars and Venus in the net of Vulcan; the second, King David looking at Bathsheba, who with her Maids is bathing at the fountain. He also painted the Portrait of the Signor Carlo, with the likeness of his Consort, the Signora Paula Visconti, and some Landscapes; these last are of no great size, but are exceedingly beautiful. About the same time our artist painted several of Ovid's Fables, for the Marquis Astorga, by whom these pictures were taken into Spain; he also executed many works for the Signor Tommaso Marini, but these require no further mention. This then shall suffice me to say of Paris Bordone, who being now seventy-five years old,† lives quietly in his own house, working only at the request of princes, or others of his friends, avoiding all rivalry, and those vain ambitions which do but disturb the repose of man, and seeking, as he says, to avoid having the serene tranquillity of his life invaded by those who, proceeding by dubious paths, do not seek truth, but rather malignity, and are totally devoid of charitable purpose. He, on the contrary,

* None of these works can now be found in Augsburg.

† It was at this age that Bordone died, according to Ridolfi, *Vite*, &c.

accustomed to a simple and upright life, desires no contention with the subtleties and craft of those who proceed less openly. This master has lately executed a singularly beautiful picture for the Duchess of Savoy; it represents Venus and Cupid, sleeping under the guard of a servitor, and is so admirably executed, that words do not enable me to praise it sufficiently.

I must not here omit to mention that the art of Mosaic, almost abandoned in all other place, is encouraged and kept in life by the most Serene Senate of Venice, and of this Titian has been the principal cause; seeing that so far as in him lies, he has ever laboured to promote the exercise thereof, and to procure respectable remuneration for those who practise the art. Various works have thus been undertaken in the Church of San Marco, the old Mosaics having been almost wholly restored, and this mode of delineation being now brought to all the perfection of which it is susceptible, exhibits consequently a very different aspect from that displayed in Florence and Rome, at the time of Giotto, Alesso Baldovinetti, the Ghirlandai, or the Miniaturist Gherardo. All that has been done in Venice has been executed after the designs of Titian and other excellent painters, who have made coloured Cartoons for the same; thus the works are brought to perfection, as may be seen in the portico of San Marco, where there is a Judgment of Solomon, so beautiful that it could scarcely be executed more delicately with the pencil and colours.* In the same place is the Genealogical Tree of Our Lady, by Ludovico Rosso; the Sibyls and Prophets are admirably represented in this work, which is carefully conjoined, and displays excellent relief. But in the art of Mosaic there are none who have distinguished themselves more highly in our times than have Valerio and Vincenzio Zuccheri, natives of Treviso,† many stories by whom may be seen in San Marco; those from the Apocalypse may more particularly be specified: in this work the four Evangelists, under the form of various animals, are seen to surround the Throne of God: the Seven Candle-

* For details respecting these works, our readers may advantageously consult the learned Zanetti, *Della Pittura Veneziana*. The Judgment of Solomon is by Vincenzio Bianchini.

† According to Federici, these brothers, more correctly called Zuccati, were not of Treviso but Da Ponte, and the name of the one was not Vincenzio, but Francesco. See *Memorie Trevisane*.

sticks, and other things, are also represented so admirably well, that to him who looks at them from below, they appear to be paintings in oil. There are besides numerous small pictures by those artists, and these are filled with figures which look—I do not say like paintings only—but like miniatures, and yet they are made of stones joined together. There are portraits, moreover, of various personages; the Emperor Charles V. that is to say, with Ferdinand his brother, who succeeded him in the Empire, Maximilian, son of Ferdinand and now Emperor, the most Illustrious Cardinal Bembo, the glory of our age,* and the Magnifico . . . all executed so carefully, with so much harmony, so admirable a distribution of light and shadow, and such exquisite tints of the carnatians (to say nothing of other qualities), that no better or more perfect works of the kind could possibly be conceived.

Bartolommeo Bozzato has also worked on the Church of San Marco: he is the rival of the Zuccheri, and has acquitted himself in a sufficiently praiseworthy manner; but that which has most effectually contributed to the success of all these artists, has without doubt been the superintendence of Titian, with the designs prepared for these Mosaics by his hand. In addition to the above-mentioned and others, who have been disciples of Titian, there was besides a certain Girolamo,† of whom I know no other name than Girolamo di Tiziano.‡

---

## THE FLORENTINE SCULPTOR, JACOPO SANSOVINO.

[BORN 1477—DIED 1570.]

THE family of the Tatti has its records in the communal books of Florence, and that from so early a period as the year 1300; but the house took its origin from Lucca, one of

* The portrait of Bembo is in the Uffizj. Vasari calls him the "glory of our age," on account of his literary distinction.

† Girolamo Dante.

‡ For some part of the numerous details which we had proposed to add to various parts of this Life, our readers must be referred to Ridolfi; *Vite* &c.; Zanotti, *Pinacoteca Veneta;* Zanetti, *Della Pittura Veneziana;* and the other authorities, whose names alone we have here space to indicate.

he most noble cities of Tuscany; always remarkable for active and honourable men: this house of Tatti was most especially favoured by that of Medici, and from the Tatti family descended that Jacopo of whom we are now to write. He was the son of an Antonio, a very estimable person, and of Francesca his wife, who gave birth to the child in the month of January, 1477.* In his first years the boy was sent, as is usual, to acquire the rudiments of learning, wherein he displayed much intelligence: he soon began to study drawing of himself, and gave evidence, in a certain sort, that nature had disposed him to the study of design rather than that of letters, since he went very reluctantly to school, and was most unwilling to undertake the difficult acquirement of grammar.

His mother, whom he strongly resembled, perceiving this, and desiring to aid his genius, caused him to be secretly taught drawing, with the intention of making him a sculptor, perhaps in emulation of the rising glory of Michelagnolo Buonarroto, then very young. She may, perhaps, have also thought it a favourable augury that the latter and her son Jacopo were both born in the same street, the Via Santa Maria namely, which is near the Via Ghibellina. But the boy was meanwhile on the point of being devoted to trade, which he liked even less than grammar, and he opposed himself in such sort to this purpose, that his father ultimately permitted him to follow his own inclination.

At that time there had come to Florence the sculptor, Andrea Contucci, of Monte Sansovino, a place near Arezzo, much talked of in our days as the birthplace of Pope Julius III. Having acquired a great name in Spain as well as in Italy, Contucci was the best sculptor and architect, after Michelagnolo, then known to our Art: he was then occupied with the execution of two figures in marble; and with him Jacopo was placed that he might study the art of the sculptor. Andrea soon perceived that the young man promised to become very eminent, and neglected no precaution calculated to render him worthy of being known as his disciple; he became much attached to him moreover, and being as much loved by Jacopo in return, Contucci taught the youth with much

* Temanza, *Vite dei piu celebri Architetti e Scultori Veneziani*, says 1479, but the date given by Vasari is proved, by reference to other authorities, to be the correct one.

affection, and it was thus soon believed that the disciple would ultimately equal his master, nay perhaps surpass him. The attachment of these two was indeed of such a character that being almost like father and son, Jacopo was no longer called De' Tatti, but Sansovino, and as he was then named, so is he now and ever will be called.

When Jacopo began to exercise his art he was so powerfully aided by Nature, that although he was not particularly studious, nor very diligent in his work, yet in whatever he did there was a grace and facility, with a certain ease, which was very pleasing to the eyes of the artists, seeing that every draught, sketch, or outline of his, displayed a boldness and animation which it has been given to but few among the sculptors to possess. The intercourse and friendship subsisting in their childhood between Jacopo and Andrea del Sarto, was also very useful to them both; pursuing the same manner in design, they exhibited a similar grace in execution, the one in painting, the other in sculpture; and as they frequently conferred together on the difficulties of Art, Jacopo meanwhile making models for Andrea, they assisted each other greatly. And that this is true we have proof in the picture of San Francesco, executed for the Nuns of the Via Pentolini, and in a San Giovanni Evangelista, which was taken from an exquisite mould in *terra*, which Sansovino made in those days, in competition with Baccio da Montelupo.

For it chanced that at this time the Guild of Porta Santa Maria was about to have a statue in bronze, cast for a niche of Or San Michele, which is opposite to the Wool-Shearers: but although Jacopo's model was the more beautiful, yet Montelupo, as being an older master, obtained the commission. This model, which is a most exquisite one, is now in possession of the heirs of Nanni Unghero. Sansovino was then the friend of Nanni, for whom he prepared the large models in clay, of Angels in the form of children, with one for a figure of San Niccolò, of Tolentino, which were afterwards carved in wood, with the aid of Sansovino; all these figures being of the size of life. They were placed in the Chapel of San Niccolò, in the Church of Santo Spirito.

Becoming known, by the productions here enumerated, to all the Florentine artists, and being considered a young man of great genius and excellent character, Jacopo, to his nfinite delight, was taken to Rome by Giuliano da San Gallo, architect of Pope Julius II., when the statues of the Belvedere attracting him beyond measure, he set himself to copy the same. Now Bramante, who was also architect to Pope Julius, holding the first place, and having rooms in the Belvedere, chanced to see the designs of Jacopo, with a nude figure of clay, in a recumbent attitude, holding a vase for ink, which he had also made; and these things pleased him so much that he began to favour the youth, and ordered him to make a large copy in wax, of the Laocoon, which he was also having copied by other artists, intending to cast it in bronze. These artists were Zaccheria Zacchi,* of Volterra, the Spaniard, Alonzo Berughetta, and Vecchio, of Bologna. When all had completed their work, Bramante showed the models to Raffaello Sanzio of Urbino, inquiring of him which he thought the best. It was then judged by Raffaello that Sansovino had greatly surpassed the others; wherefore, by the advice of Domenico, Cardinal Grimani, Bramante was commanded to have the model of Jacopo cast in bronze. The mould was prepared accordingly, and the metal, being cast, succeeded to perfection; being then polished, the group was given to the Cardinal, who valued it all his life no less than the antique, and at his death he bequeathed it as a work of great importance to the most Serene Signoria of Venice, by whom, after it had been kept for some years in the Hall of the Council of Ten, it was finally given to the Cardinal of Lorraine, who took it to France, in the year 1534. While Sansovino was thus daily acquiring reputation in Rome, Giuliano da Sangallo, who had kept him in his own house in the Borgo Vecchio, fell ill, and leaving Rome, was taken in a litter to Florence, for change of air. Thereupon Bramante found a dwelling for Jacopo, still in the Borgo Vecchio; but in the Palace of Domenico della Rovere, Cardinal of San Clemente, where Pietro Perugino was at that time lodging, he being engaged with the painting of a ceiling, for Pope Julius, in a room of the Torre Borgia.

There, Pietro having remarked the fine manner of Sansovino, caused him to prepare numerous models in wax for his use; among the rest a Deposition from the Cross, in full relief, with many figures, the ladders used for the depo-

* Temanza calls this artist Zari.

sition, and other things; a very beautiful work it was. All these models were afterwards collected by Messer Giovanni Gaddi, and they are now in his house on the Piazza of the Madonna in Florence.* Sansovino then became known to the Cortonese painter, Maestro Luca Signorelli; to Bramantino da Milano; Bernardino Pinturicchio; Cesare Cesariano, who was at that time in high repute for his Commentaries on Vitruvius; and to many other persons of genius and renown flourishing at that period. Bramante then desired that Sansovino should be presented to Pope Julius, and commissioned him to restore certain works of antiquity, which he did with so much care and grace that His Holiness, and all who beheld them, considered it impossible that they could have been done better.

Stimulated by the praises he received, and eager to surpass his previous performances, Sansovino then devoted himself so zealously to his studies that, being of a somewhat delicate constitution, he became seriously ill, and was compelled to return to Florence for the saving of his life; happily, however, his native air, the aid of youth, and the cares of his physicians, quickly restored him to health. Now, Messer Piero Pitti was then desirous of having a Madonna in marble executed for that front of the Mercato Nuovo, in Florence, where the clock is, and as there were many able young artists as well as old masters then in Florence, he thought the work ought to be given to him who should make the best model. He consequently had one prepared by Baccio da Montelupo, another by Zaccheria Zacchi, of Volterra, who had also returned that same year to Florence, with one by Baccio Bandinelli, and a fourth by Sansovino. They were then compared; when Lorenzo Credi, an excellent painter as well as a man of much judgment and goodness, declared the honour and the commission to belong of right to Sansovino, an opinion wherein the other judges, artists, and all who understood the matter fully concurred.

But although the work was adjudged to him accordingly, the procuring and bringing down the marbles were so much delayed by the envy and malicious contrivances of Averardo da Filicaja, who greatly favoured Bandinello and detested

* In the year 1766, the Deposition came into the possession of our countryman, Ignatius Hugford, but its ultimate fate is not known to the present writer.

ansovino; that the latter, in consideration of these delays, as ordered meanwhile to execute one of the large figures of ne Apostles in marble, which were to be placed in the Church f Santa Maria del Fiore. He therefore made the model of San Jacopo (of which, when it was finished, Messer Bindo ltoviti took possession;) and, working with all diligence, he onducted the Statue very successfully to completion. An dmirable figure it is, showing in every part the patient tudy with which it has been executed; the arms and hands re clearly and finely detached; the draperies are well rranged, and the whole is finished with so much art, and xhibits such perfect grace, that no better work in marble an be seen.* And here Sansovino showed the method in which draperies should be executed, in such a manner as o detach them clearly from the figure, having treated these vith so much delicacy, and rendered them so natural, that in ome parts he has brought the marble to the subtlety of texure usual in the folds, edges, and hems of the real vestment, work of great difficulty, and demanding much time, skill, nd patience, if the attempt be to succeed in such sort as to xhibit the perfection of art. This Statue remained in the House of Works, from the time when it was finished to the nd of the year 1565, when it was placed in the Church of Santa Maria della Fiore, to do honour to the arrival of the Queen Joanna of Austria, wife of Don Francesco de' Medici, Prince of Florence and Siena. It is considered to be a work of extraordinary merit, as are the figures of the other Apostles, executed by different masters for that place, as we have related in their Lives.

At the same time Sansovino executed for Messer Giovanni Gaddi, a Venus on a Shell, in marble; this was a most beautiful figure, as was the model for the same, which was in the house of Messer Francesco Montevarchi, but was destroyed in the flood of 1558. Sansovino executed a Boy also for Giovanni Gaddi, with a Swan, which was as beautiful a work as could be made of marble; he did many other things for the same person, who still has these productions in his house.

* This admirable statue has been accused of a defect in the right leg, "but this," remarks Bottari, "is an accident caused by the fracture of the rich drapery, which originally descended to the foot of the statue, but was accidentally broken. See also the *Riposo* of Borghini, who has successfully defended Sansovino against his critics.

For Messer Bindo Altoviti he directed the construction of a most costly Chimney-piece, in macigno, finely carved by Benedetto da Rovezzano, and which was erected in his house at Florence, where Sansovino executed a Story in small figures with his own hand, as the Frieze of that chimney-piece; representing therein the God Vulcan and other heathen deities, all of great beauty. But most beautiful of all were two Boys placed on the summit of this work, and supporting the Arms of the Altoviti family; but these have been taken away by the Signor Don Luigi di Toledo (who now dwells in the house of Messer Bindo,) and have been placed on a Fountain in the garden, which Don Luigi possesses behind the Servite Monastery.

Two other Children of extraordinary beauty, also in marble and by the hand of this master, are in the house of Giovan Francesco Ridolfi; these being likewise the supporters of an Escutcheon of Arms. The works here described, caused Sansovino to be considered a most excellent and graceful artist by all Florence, and by every one connected with art; wherefore Giovanni Bartolini, having built a house in the Gualfonda, requested him to execute a Bacchus in marble, represented by a youth the size of life; when, the model being made by Sansovino, was found to be entirely satisfactory, and Giovanni having supplied him with the marble, he set to work with a good will, that gave wings both to his thoughts and hands. But the figure was not hastily done; on the contrary, he studied it with the most intense care, and to promote the perfection of the form, he set himself to copy the figure of a certain disciple of his, called Pippo del Fabbro,* whom he kept standing naked the greater part of the day.

Having completed this statue, it was adjudged to be the best ever executed by a modern master, Sansovino having overcome a difficulty no longer attempted; one arm of the

* "The Blacksmith's Joe" that is to say. Of this poor boy, our author, in his first edition, remarks that he would have become an able artist, but he adds the melancholy conclusion that this long remaining unclothed during cold weather or the severity of his studies, destroyed his health, and disturbed his mind, he was perpetually placing himself in the attitude of the Bacchus, or in that appropriate to other statues, in which he would stand for hours together, silent and immoveable, as if he were in fact a statue. In this condition he remained, with few intervals, until his early death.

gure being fully detached and raised in the air, while a 'azza, cut from the same piece of marble, is held aloft in he hand, or rather, so delicate and subtle is the work, by he fingers, whereon it is so lightly poised, that they scarcely ppear to touch it. The attitude of the figure is, besides, so vell calculated for effect, as seen on all sides, it is so nicely alanced, and so admirably arranged; the form is so well pro-ortioned, the limbs are so finely attached to the trunk, and he whole statue is so exquisitely finished, that while looking it, or even touching it, one would be more disposed to believe t the living flesh than a mere piece of stone. At a word, he renown this work has obtained is not in any way more than, or even equal to, its due; it was visited while Giovanni lived, with the utmost admiration, alike by natives and strangers; but Giovanni being dead, his brother Gherardo gave it to the Duke Cosimo, who keeps it in his apartments with other beautiful statues.* For the same Giovanni, Sansovino made a Crucifix in wood, which is now in the house of the Bartolini family, with many works by the ancients and by Michelagnolo.

In the year 1514 rich preparations were to be made in Florence for the arrival of Leo X. in that city, when the Signoria and Giuliano de' Medici gave orders for triumphal arches of wood, which were to be constructed in various parts of the city. For many of these Sansovino made the designs; and, in company with Andrea del Sarto, he undertook to adorn the whole façade of Santa Maria del Fiore; this they decorated with statues, stories, and architectural ornaments in wood, after a manner which it would be well if we could have retained, instead of that in the Teutonic manner which we now have. I say nothing of the canopies in cloth, with which, on the festivals of San Giovanni and other solemnities, it has been customary to cover the Piazza of Santa Maria del Fiore and that of San Giovanni, having spoken of them sufficiently elsewhere, but confine myself to the remark, that beneath this canopy Sansovino decorated the façade with a triumphal arch of the Corinthian Order,

* Now in the western corridor of the Uffizj. In the year 1762, when the building was partially destroyed, this work was broken to pieces by fire, but was put together with indescribable care and patience after a cast which had happily been made from it just before the conflagration, by the painter, G. Traballesi.

double columns, rising on a great basement on every side, with large niches between them, wherein were figures of the Apostles in full relief. Above these were stories in mezzo-rilievo, having the appearance of bronze, the subjects taken from the Old Testament; some of them may still be seen in the house of the Lanfredini on the Lung' Arno. Over all were projecting architraves, friezes, and cornices, with varied and beautiful frontons. In the angles of the arches, and beneath them, in the thickness of the same, were beautiful stories painted in chiaro-scuro by Andrea del Sarto, and the whole work was such that when Pope Leo saw it, he declared it to be a pity that the front of the church, as erected by the German Arnolfo, had not been of similar character.

On the same occasion, Sansovino made a Horse, formed of clay and shearings of wool, which was erected on a pedestal of masonry; the animal was rearing, and beneath him lay a figure of nine braccia; this work also pleased the Pope greatly by its power and boldness, wherefore Sansovino was taken by Jacopo Salviati to kiss the feet of His Holiness, who received him very kindly. The Pontiff then returning to Florence after his conference with King Francis I. at Bologna, Sansovino received orders to construct a Triumphal Arch at the gate of San Gallo; and, not degenerating from his former self, he completed it as he had done the others, enriched with statues and pictures finely executed, that is to say, and beautiful to a marvel.

His Holiness having afterwards resolved that the façade of San Lorenzo should be constructed in marble, Sansovino, while Raffaello and Michelagnolo were expected from Rome, prepared a design for the same by order of the Pope, who, being pleased therewith, caused Baccio d'Agnolo to make from it a model in wood, which was most beautiful; Buonarroto had meanwhile prepared another, and was commanded to repair with Sansovino to Pietrasanta, where the two artists found marble in plenty; but the difficulties of transport caused the loss of so much time that when they returned to Florence, the Pope had gone back to Rome. They both followed him, however, with their models, each for himself; but when Jacopo arrived, Michelagnolo was already showing his model to the Pope at the Torre Borgia; and whereas the former had expected to receive the commission for a part of the statues, at least under Buonarroto, who had given him reason to expect as much, he found on arriving in Rome that Michelagnolo was determined to keep all for himself. Nevertheless, and as he did not wish to have his journey for nothing, Sansovino resolved to remain in Rome for the study of architecture as well as sculpture. He then undertook the execution in marble of a Madonna with the Divine Child in her arms, for the Florentine Francesco Martelli; this group, somewhat larger than life and admirably finished, was placed on an Altar within the principal door of the Church of Sant' Agostino, on the right of the entrance.* The plaster model for the work, Sansovino gave to the prior of the Salviati, who placed it in a chapel of his palace, beside the Piazza of San Pietro at the end of the Borgo Nuovo. No long time afterwards he made a Statue of San Jacopo in marble, four braccia high, for the Altar of a Chapel which Cardinal Alborense had built in the Church of the Spaniards in Rome; this also, which is in a very graceful attitude and exhibits infinite judgment, procured the artist a great increase of fame; and while he was yet engaged therewith, he received the commission to prepare plans and models for the Church of San Marcello, which belongs to the Servite Monks: this Church Sansovino afterwards erected, and a very beautiful structure it is.

Continuing to be employed in architecture, Sansovino next built a beautiful Loggia for Messer Marco Cosci; this is in the Flaminian Way, on the road leading from Rome to the Pontemolle. For the "Brotherhood of the Crucified," which belongs to the Church of San Marcello, he made a Crucifix in wood, to be carried in procession, which is very graceful; and for Antonio Cardinal di Monte he commenced a large building at his Vigna outside Rome, near the Acqua Vergine. It may be also, that a Portrait of the elder Cardinal Monte, which is now over a door in the Palace of Signor Fabiano at Monte Sansovino, is by his hand. He built a commodious house for Messer Luigi Leoni, with a palace in Banchi, which belongs to the Gaddi family; this was afterwards purchased by Filippo Strozzi; it is handsome and richly decorated as well as very commodious.

Now in those days the Germans, Spaniards, and French had each built churches for themselves in Rome, wherein they were now performing the offices, when the Florentines,

* Still in the church.

favoured by Leo X., requested permission also to erect a church. Orders being given by the Pope accordingly to Ludovico Capponi, who was Consul of the Florentines, it was resolved that a large Church, dedicated to St. John the Baptist, should be constructed behind the Banchi, at the commencement of the Strada Julia on the shore of the Tiber; and this, whether for size, magnificence, cost, or beauty of design, was to surpass all the others. For that work Raffaello da Urbino, Antonio da Sangallo, Baldassare da Siena, and Sansovino prepared designs in competition; and the Pope having seen all, declared that of Jacopo the best, he having made a tribune at each angle of the church, with one of larger size in the centre, resembling that in the plan which Sebastiano Serlio gives in the second book of his work on Architecture. In this opinion all the heads of the undertaking agreed with the Pope, Sansovino received many proofs of favour, and the foundations for a portion of the church, about twenty-two yards in length, were begun. But there was not space enough for the building, more especially as it was determined to have the front of the Church opposite to that of the houses in the Strada Julia; the builders were consequently obliged to impinge upon the stream of the Tiber to the extent of full fifteen braccia, which pleased many, all the more, because the display as well as cost was the greater; it was therefore commenced as I have said, and more than forty thousand crowns* was spent thereon, a sum for which they might have erected half the walls of the Church.

The works were proceeding rapidly, when Sansovino had a fall, which injured him so severely, that he determined to be taken to Florence, leaving the care of those foundations to Antonio da Sangallo. But no long time afterwards, the death of Pope Leo depriving the Florentines of so great a support and so splendid a Prince, caused the abandonment of the works, which remained suspended during the Pontificate of Adrian VI. Pope Clement afterwards succeeding, Sansovino was ordered to return, and the Church was recommenced, with the original designs. At the same time our artist undertook the sepulchral monuments of the Cardinals of Aragon and Agen; he began to prepare the marbles, and

* In the Life of Antonio San Gallo, Vasari has said "12,000," but the above is considered more likely to be correct.

made models for the figures; all Rome was indeed then being in his hands, and works of the utmost importance came pouring in upon him from all sides: his merits had been acknowledged by three Pontiffs, Pope Leo in particular having given him a Knighthood of St. Peter, which he, fearing he should die in his sickness, had sold. But it now pleased God to punish that city, and abase the pride of the Romans; wherefore it was permitted, that on the 6th of May, 1527, Bourbon should come with his army, and all Rome should be sacked and given up to fire and sword.

This ruin, amidst which so many men of genius came to an evil end, compelled Sansovino, to his infinite loss, to depart from the city, and he took refuge in Venice, whence he proposed to repair to France, where he had been invited to enter the service of the King. But halting in Venice, to provide himself with necessaries, having been despoiled of all, the Doge Andrea Gritti, a true friend of distinguished men, was told that he was there and desired to see him; the rather as Cardinal Grimani had given him to understand that Sansovino would be just the person they wanted to restore the Cupolas of San Marco, which is the principal Church of the Venetians, seeing that they, having become very old, and being, moreover, weak in the basements, and not well put together, were cleft in many parts, and threatened with absolute ruin. The Doge therefore caused our artist to be called, and receiving him very favourably, after many conversations, he gave him to know that he wished, or rather entreated, him to find a remedy for this misfortune, which Sansovino promised to do. Commencing the work accordingly, he raised scaffoldings within the Cupola, and, after much toil, contrived to secure the whole structure, by means of massive beams, well and firmly chained together by strong iron bands; he then added curtains of wood-work to the whole fabric, within and without, which done, he raised new walls, refounding the piers by which the mass was supported, and so fortifying the entire building that its stability was assured for ever. All Venice stood amazed at his success, and the Doge was perfectly satisfied: nay, what was more to the purpose, that most illustrious Senate, convinced of his ability, appointed Jacopo Protomaster of the Signori Procuratori of San Marco (the highest office conferred by the Signoria on its architects and engineers), assigning to him the house of his predecessor, who had just died, with a suitable stipend.

Having entered on his office, Sansovino began to fulfil the duties thereof with diligence; those connected with the books and accounts of expenditure, as well as with the building, giving his most earnest care to the details of that employment, which are very numerous, and displaying the most courteous consideration for the Senators. And not only did he devote himself zealously to whatever could promote the grandeur, beauty, and ornament of the Church, the Piazza, and the whole city, to an extent never before done by any man who had held his office; but by the ingenuity of his inventions, the promptitude of his actions, and the prudence of his administration, he lessened the outlay and improved the revenue, so that the Signoria was burdened with little if any expense. Among the ameliorations made by Jacopo, was the following:—In the year 1529, there were butchers' stalls between the two columns of the Piazza, with a number of small wooden booths, used for the vilest purposes, and a shame as well as deformity to the place, offending the dignity of the Palace and the Piazza, while they could not but disgust all strangers who made their entry into Venice, by the side of San Giorgio.

Sansovino, therefore, having convinced Andrea Gritti of the excellence of his plan, caused these booths and stalls to be removed; he then erected the butchers' shops where they now are, and, adding to these certain stalls for the dealers in vegetables, he increased the revenues of the Procuranzia by seven hundred ducats yearly, while he beautified the Piazza and the city by the same act. No long time afterwards, he observed that by removing one house in the Merceria (near the clock, and on the way to the Rialto), which paid a rent of twenty-six ducats only, he could open a street into the Spadaria by which the value of the houses and shops all around would be much increased, he took down that house accordingly, thereby adding a hundred and fifty ducats to the income of the Procuranzia. He built the Hostelry of the Pellegrino, moreover, on the same site with another on the Campo Rusolo; and these together brought in four hundred ducats. His buildings in the Pescaria and other parts of the city, houses as well as shops, and erected at various times, were also of the utmost utility; and altogether the Procuranzia gained by means of Sansovino, an addition of no less than two thousand ducats per annum, so that they might well hold him in esteem.

At a subsequent period, our artist received orders from the Procurators, to commence the rich and beautiful Library, opposite to the Public Palace. The orders of architecture, Doric and Corinthian, the fine carvings, columns, capitals, cornices, half-length figures, and other decorations, executed without any consideration for the amount of cost, all contribute to display an aggregate of beauty which renders the building a marvel.* The stucco work, the stories which decorate the Halls, the rich pavements, the staircases adorned with pictures (as has been related in the Life of Battista Franco), every part, at a word, is most admirable; to say nothing of the rich ornaments which give majesty and grandeur to the principal entrance; and all prove the vast ability of Sansovino. These works caused a notable change in the mode of building at Venice; for whereas it was before the custom for houses and palaces to be erected all after one old fashion, without any variation, either on account of the difference in site, or for the sake of convenience; they now began to build with new designs, a better manner, and some attention to the ancient rule of Vitruvius, whether as regarded their public or private constructions.

But returning to the Library: the best judges, and those who have visited many other parts of the world, declare it to be without an equal.

Sansovino then built the Palace of Messer Giovanni Delfino: it stands on the Grand Canal, beyond the Rialto, and opposite the Riva del Ferro: the cost of the fabric was thirty thousand ducats. The Palace of Messer Leonardo Moro, at San Girolamo, also of great cost, and much resembling a fortress, is in like manner by Sansovino, as is that of Messer Luigi de' Garzoni, which is thirty paces larger in every direction than the Exchange of the Germans:

* The vaulting of this fabric fell in while it was in course of construction, when the favoured architect was instantly thrown into prison, condemned to pay a fine of a thousand ducats, and deprived of his title of Protomaster. It is true that the Signoria, finding him to have been falsely accused, released him at once, and shut up his accusers in his place, restoring him to all his honours, and re-paying nine hundred of his thousand ducats; but such, as our readers will remember, by many an instance, was the Venetian justice—first hang your man, then try him.

it lies without the city, at Ponte Casale that is, and has the convenience of water conducted through every part of the building, which is adorned with fine figures, by the hand of Sansovino. But more beautiful than all is the Palace of Messer Giorgio Cornaro, on the Grand Canal: it surpasses all the others in majesty, grandeur, and convenience; nay, is reputed to be, perhaps, the most splendid residence in Italy.

Omitting the private buildings constructed by Sansovino, I restrict myself to recording that he also erected the Scuola and Brotherhood of the Misericordia, at the cost of a hundred and thirty thousand ducats: an immense fabric it is, and, when completed, will be the most superb edifice in Italy. The Church of Francesco della Vigna, which belongs to the Barefooted Friars, is also the work of this artist, and a very great and important one; but the façade was by another master.* The Loggia of the Corinthian order erected around the Campanile of San Marco, was of Sansovino's design: it has a rich decoration of columns, with four niches, wherein are four beautiful figures, in bronze, somewhat less than life: these also, with various figures and stories in basso-rilievo, are by the hand of Jacopo. This Loggia forms a beautiful basement to the Campanile, which is thirty-five feet wide on one of its fronts, and that is about the extent of Sansovino's work: from the ground to the cornice, where are the windows of the belfry, the Campanile measures a hundred and sixty feet, and from the cornice to the corridor twenty-five. The dado above the cornice is twenty-eight and a half feet high, and from the platform of the corridor to the obelisk are sixty feet. On the obelisk is placed the small quadrangular basement, which supports the figure of the Angel, it stands six feet high; and the Angel, which turns with every wind is ten feet high; so that the entire Bell-tower is two hundred and ninety-two feet high.

But one of the richest, most beautiful, and most imposing edifices of this master is the Zecca (Mint) of Venice, constructed wholly of stone and iron, without a particle of wood, to secure it from the danger of fire. This is so commodiously arranged within, for the convenience of the many labourers working there, that in the whole world there is

* "And what a master!" exclaims an Italian commentator; "no less than Palladio himself."

not so strong or so well-ordered a treasury as that of Venice. It is all in the Rustic order, and this, not having been previously adopted in that city, caused much admiration there. The Church of Santo Spirito, on the Lagunes, is also by Sansovino; a graceful and pleasing work.* The façade of San Gimignano, which gives splendour to the Piazza,† with that of San Giuliano in the Merceria, are both by that master, as is the rich Tomb of Prince Francesco Veniero. He built the new Vaults at the Rialto likewise; and the design of these works is excellent, furnishing a commodious market to the peasantry and others who daily flock to Venice with their merchandise.

At the Misericordia, Sansovino undertook a new and remarkable construction for the Trepoli; that family had a large Palace, with apartments of regal splendour, on the Canal, but being badly founded within the waters, it was feared that the edifice would in a few years fall to the ground. Sansovino reconstructed the foundations, however, with immense masses of stone, gave further support to the house itself with a marvellous system of piles, and the owners now inhabit their palace with the most perfect security. Nor have these numerous fabrics prevented our artist from daily producing, for his recreation, great and beautiful works in marble and bronze. Over the Holy Water Vase belonging to the monks of the Ca Grande, for example, he has placed a figure of San Giovanni Battista in marble, which is most beautiful, and justly extolled. At the Chapel of the Santo,‡ in Padua, moreover, there is a beautiful story in marble, representing a miracle of Sant' Antonio,§ by his hand: it is in mezzo-rilievo, and is greatly valued by the Paduans.

For the entrance to the Palazzo of San Marco, Sansovino is now preparing two colossal figures of Neptune and Mars, to signify the power of the Republic, both by land and water. They are seven braccia high, and promise to be very beautiful. He has executed a fine statue of Hercules, for the Duke of Ferrara; and in the Church of San Marco,

* Now demolished.—*Ed Venet.*

† "This church also was cruelly demolished in 1807, thereby depriving the Piazza di San Marco of a rich ornament."—*Ibid.*

‡ St. Anthony, who is so called in Padua, *par excellence.*

§ See Cicognara, *Storia della Scultura Moderna*, tom. ii.

there are six stories of mezzo-rilievo, in bronze, by his hand: They are one braccio high, and one and a half long: the subjects are taken from the Life of the Evangelist; they are to be placed around a pulpit, and are greatly admired for their variety.* Over the door of the same Church is a Madonna in marble, also by Jacopo; it is the size of life, and considered very beautiful. The bronze door of the Sacristy divided into two parts, and adorned with Stories from the Life of Christ, admirably executed,† are in like manner by his hand; and over the Gate of the Arsenal he has erected a fine statue of Our Lady in marble, with the Divine Child in her arms. All these works have not only adorned the city, but have daily increased the renown of Sansovino; they have furthermore caused him to receive frequent proofs of the estimation in which he is held by the Signoria, with gratifying marks of their liberality, while they have procured him the respect and admiration of artists, no work in sculpture or architecture being undertaken in his time at Venice without his advice and concurrence.

And well did Sansovino deserve to be held in esteem by the Venetians, artists, nobles, and people, seeing that by his knowledge and judgment the city has been, so to say, renewed, while he has taught her builders the true science of architecture, as I have said before. Three beautiful statues in stucco, by Jacopo Sansovino, are now to be seen in the hands of his son. These are a Laocoon, a Venus standing upright, and a Madonna surrounded by Angels. They are the most beautiful figures to be found in Venice. This son has also sixty designs for Churches and other buildings, all of Sansovino's invention, and so beautiful that since the time of the ancients nothing better has been seen, or even imagined. I hear that their owner is about to give them to the world, and has already caused some portions of them to be engraved, together with plates of some of those fine buildings which his father erected in various parts of Italy.

Thus constantly occupied, as we have said, in works public and private—out of the city, as well as in it (for

* They are in the Presbytery of the Church.—*Ed. Ven.*

† In the angles of the frame are six heads, three of which are portraits of Titian, Pietro Aretino, and Sansovino himself.—*Ibid.* See also Cicognara, as before cited.

strangers, also, had constant recourse to Sansovino, for models, designs of buildings, statues or advice: as, for example, the Dukes of Ferrara, Mantua, and Urbino); this artist was nevertheless ever ready to oblige, and more especially was he devoted to the Signor Procuratori, by whom no work was ever undertaken, either in Venice or elsewhere, without his counsels and aid. Nay, they not unfrequently employed him for their friends and themselves without offering him any remuneration, he refusing no labour that could give them satisfaction. Sansovino was most especially beloved and valued by the Prince Gritti, a firm friend to men of genius, by Messer Vettorio Grimani, brother of the Cardinal, and by the Cavalier Messer Giovanni da Legge, who were all Procurators. Messer Marcantonio Giustiniano, who had known him in Rome, was also the friend of Jacopo: these great and illustrious men, well practised in the affairs of the world, and having full knowledge of our Arts, were all well aware of his value, and the esteem in which he deserved to be held; doing him justice, therefore, they declared, and all the city agreed with them, that the Procuranzia never had had, and never would have, his equal. Nor were they unacquainted with the estimation in which he was held at Rome and in Florence, nay, throughout all Italy, by all great Princes and men of intellect; hence they were firmly persuaded that not only Sansovino himself, but his descendants also, would be duly honoured by that city for his extraordinary efforts and abilities.

Jacopo Sansovino, as to his person, was of the middle height, but rather slender than otherwise, and his carriage was remarkably upright; he was fair, with a red beard, and in his youth was of a goodly presence, wherefore he did not fail to be loved, and that by dames of no small importance. In his age he had an exceedingly venerable appearance; with his beautiful white beard, he still retained the carriage of his youth: he was strong and healthy even to his ninety-third year, and could see the smallest object, at whatever distance, without glasses, even then. When writing, he sat with his head up, not supporting himself in any manner, as it is usual for men to do. He liked to be handsomely dressed, and was singularly nice in his person. The society of ladies was acceptable to Sansovino, even to the extremity of age, and he always enjoyed conversing with or of them. He had not been particularly healthy in his youth, yet in his old age he suffered from no malady whatever, insomuch that, for a period of fifty years, he would never consult any physician even when he did feel himself indisposed. Nay, when he was once attacked by apoplexy, and that for the fourth time, in his eighty-fourth year too, he would still have nothing to do with physic, but cured himself by keeping in bed for two months, in a dark and well-warmed chamber. His digestion was so good that he could eat all things without distinction: during the summer he lived almost entirely on fruits, and in the very extremity of his age would frequently eat three cucumbers and half a lemon at one time.

With respect to the qualities of his mind, Sansovino was very prudent; he foresaw readily the coming events, and sagaciously compared the present with the past. Attentive to his duties, he shunned no labour in the fulfilment of the same, and never neglected his business for his pleasure. He spoke well and largely on such subjects as he understood, giving appropriate illustrations of his thoughts with infinite grace of manner. This rendered him acceptable to high and low alike, as well as to his own friends. In his greatest age his memory continued excellent; he remembered all the events of his childhood, and could minutely refer to the sack of Rome and all the other occurrences, fortunate or otherwise, of his youth and early manhood. He was very courageous, and delighted from his boyhood in contending with those who were greater than himself, affirming that he who struggles with the great may become greater, but he who disputes with the little must become less. He esteemed honour above all else in the world, and was so upright a man of his word, that no temptation could induce him to break it, of which he gave frequent proof to his lords, who, for that as well as other qualities, considered him rather as a father or brother than as their agent or steward, honouring in him an excellence that was no pretence, but his true nature.

Sansovino was liberal to all, and so effectually devoted to his kin that he deprived himself of many enjoyments the better to aid them; yet he always lived honourably and with good credit, as a man looked up to by all. He sometimes permitted himself to be overcome by anger, which in him vas an exceedingly violent passion, but one that soon passed ›ver, and a few gentle words often sufficed to brings tears nto his eyes. His love for his art was immense ; nay, that he knowledge of sculpture might be the more widely dif'used, Sansovino brought up numerous disciples, establishing vhat might almost be called a Seminary of that art in Italy.

Among those of his disciples who attained the most disinguished name, were the Florentines Niccolò Tribolo and Solosmeo ; Danese Cattaneo of Cattaro, a Tuscan of great 'epute, not in sculpture only, but in poetry also; Girolamo of Ferrara, the Venetian Jacopo Colonna, Luco Lancia of Naples, Tiziano of Padua, Pietro da Salò, the Florentine Bartolommeo Ammannato, now Sculptor and Protomaster of the Grand Duke of Tuscany; and finally Alessandro Vittoria of Trent, who was admirable for his portraits in marble. These, with the Brescian Jacopo de' Medici, were all among his disciples ; and they, renewing the memory of their master, have executed many honourable works in divers places.

Sansovino was much esteemed by princes, among others by Alessandro de' Medici, Duke of Florence, who sought his advice when constructing the fortifications of that city. Duke Cosimo also, when Sansovino, in the year 40, paid a visit to his native place for certain affairs of his own—Duke Cosimo, I say, not only requested his opinion in respect to those defences, but also endeavoured to fix the master in his own service, offering him a very large stipend with that view. On his return from Florence, moreover, the Duke Ercole of Ferrara, detained him for some time at his court, and made every effort to keep him at Ferrara; but Sansovino, accustomed to Venice, and finding himself much at his ease in that city, where he had spent the greater part of his life, would listen to none of these proposals, the rather as he greatly loved the Procuratori, and was much honoured by them.

He was in like manner invited to Rome by Pope Paul III., who wished him to undertake the care of San Pietro, in place of Antonio da San Gallo, and Monsignore della Casa, then Legate at Venice, did his best to prevail on our artist to consent, but it was all in vain ; he declared that he would not exchange his life in a Republic for that under an absolute Prince. King Philip II. of Spain, also, when on his way to Germany, conferred many marks of favour on Sansovino whom he saw in Peschiera. This master was exceedingly desirous of glory, and, to the end that his memory might survive him, he spent much of his property for others, greatly injuring his descendants thereby. The judges of Art affirm that, although yielding on the whole to Michelagnolo, yet Sansovino was the superior of that artist in certain points. In his draperies, his children, and the expression which he gave to his women, for example, Jacopo never had an equal. The draperies by his hand are, indeed, most delicately beautiful; finely folded, they preserve to perfection the distinction between the nude and draped portions of the form. His children are soft flexible figures with none of the muscular development proper only to adults; the little round legs and arms are truly of flesh, and in nowise different to those of Nature herself. The faces of his women are sweet and lovely; so graceful withal, that none can be more so, as may be seen in certain figures of the Madonna, in those of Venus, and in others by his hand.

This master, so renowned in Sculpture, and so great in Architecture, had lived by the grace of God, who had endowed him with that ability which rendered him illustrious to the degree that we have described, up to the age of ninety-three years; when, feeling himself somewhat weary of body, he lay down in his bed to repose himself. He felt no kind of illness, and frequently proposed to rise and dress himself, as being in perfect health, but remaining thus for about six weeks he felt himself becoming weaker, and requested to have the Sacraments of the Church administered to him; this having been done, although he still expected to live some years, Sansovino departed on the 2nd of November, 1570, and, notwithstanding that the years of his life had come to their end in the pure course of Nature, yet all Venice lamented his loss.*

He left a son called Francesco, born in Rome in the year 1521, and who became a very learned man in Law as well as Letters. From this son Sansovino had three grandchildren, a boy called after his grandfather Jacopo, and two girls, one called Florence, who died early, to the infinite

* For more minute details respecting this artist, the reader is referred to the *Vite de' piu celebri Architetti e Scultori Veneziani* of Temanza, vol. i. See also the *Venetian Edition of our Author* by Antonelli.

orrow of Sansovino; and the other named Aurora. The emains of Jacopo Sansovino were borne with great honour o his own Chapel in San Gimignano,* where his son placed marble Statue, which had been executed by the great naster himself, on his tomb. The following epitaph was lso inscribed thereon, as the memorial of so much excellence :—

*Jacobo Sansovino Florentino P. qui Romæ Julio II., Leoni X., Clementi VII., Pont. Max. Maxime gratos, Venetiis Architecturæ Sculpturæque ntermortuum decus. primus excitavit, quique a Senatu ob eximiam virtuem liberaliter honestatus summo civitatis mœrore decessit,* FRANCISCUS F. HOC MON. P. VIXIT ANN. XCIII. OB. V. CAL. DEC. MDLXX.

The Florentines in Venice also celebrated publicly the obsequies of Jacopo at the Church of the Frari, having made honourable preparations for the same, and the funeral oration was performed by Messer Camillo Buonfigli, who is also an excellent person.†

---

## THE ARETINE, LIONE LIONI, AND OTHER SCULPTORS AND ARCHITECTS.

[Flourished for the most part from the end of the 15th, to somewhat beyond the middle of the 16th century.]

WHAT we have previously said of the Aretine Sculptor, the Cavalier Lione Lioni, having been spoken incidentally, it will not be amiss that we should here enumerate in order the works performed by him, and which well merit to be retained in the memory of future ages. Lione first studied the art of the goldsmith, and in his youth produced many good works, more especially dies for medals, cut in steel, and representing portraits from the life; nay, so excellent did he become in a

* When the Church of San Gemignano was demolished, the remains of Sansovino were first removed to that of San Maurizio and afterwards to the private Oratory of the Seminario della Salute.

† To this Life of Sansovino, some of the Florentine and Venetian editors of our author's works (but not the Roman Bottari), have added an account of his disciples and their labours, but this the want of space prevents us from re-producing here. Such of our readers as may desire to see the same will find it in the Edition of Stefano Audin, Florence, 1822, and in that of Antonelli, Venice, 1828, and in the Passigli Edition (1832-8).

few years, that his ability made him known to many princes, more particularly to the Emperor Charles V., who, perceiving his value, employed him in occupations of more importance than that of preparing medals.

No long time after the first presentation of Lione to the Emperor, that monarch commissioned him to execute a Statue of himself in bronze; this figure, which was somewhat larger than life, Lione invested with a splendid suit of armour, by means of two very thin plates of metal, which could easily be put on or taken off: the effect is most graceful, and the artist has managed his work so perfectly, that whoever sees the figure clothed would never suppose it to be sometimes nude; and whoever sees the nude Statue would find it difficult to believe that it could ever be armed. Resting on the left foot, the Emperor's right foot is placed on a chained figure, lying beneath him, and representing Rage or Fury, with a torch, and various arms. On the pedestal of the Statue, which is now in Madrid, are the words:—

CÆSARIS VIRTUTE FUROR DOMITUS.

Having completed that figure, Lione then made a large die for the purpose of striking medals of the Emperor, with Jupiter launching his thunderbolts at the Titans, on the reverse. For these works his Majesty gave the artist a pension of a hundred and fifty ducats per annum, secured on the Mint of Milan, with a commodious house in the Contrada de' Moroni. Charles also made him a Knight, conferring at the same time a patent of nobility on his descendants; and while Lione was in Brussels, he had rooms in the palace of the Emperor, who sometimes amused himself by going to see the artist at his work.

Lione subsequently made a Statue in marble, of the Emperor, with others of the Empress and King Philip; he executed a Bust of Charles also, which was to be placed in a high position, between two rilievi in bronze. He made a bust in bronze, of the Queen Maria, likewise; with one of Ferdinand, then King of the Romans; another of Maximilian, now Emperor, and many more, which were placed in the gallery of the Palace at Brindisi, by Queen Maria, at whose command they were executed. But they did not remain there long, seeing that Henry, King of France, set fire to the building out of vengeance, and left the following ords written on the walls:—"*Vela fole Maria;*"* I say out vengeance, because that Queen had done nearly the same ing to Henry, some years previously However this may , the gallery made no progress, and the Statues are now rtly in the Palace of the Catholic King at Madrid, and rtly in Alicant, a sea-port whence her Majesty intended ship them to Granada, where all the Spanish Kings are ried. On his return from Spain, Lione brought with him vo thousand ducats in money, besides the many gifts and vours which he had received from that Court.

For the Duke of Alva, Lione Lioni has executed a bust f himself, with one of Charles V., and another representing King Philip. For the most reverend D'Arras, now called he Grand Cardinal Granvella, he has executed numerous ieces in bronze, of an oval form, each of two braccia, and livided into compartments, with half-length figures in them. One of these exhibits Charles V.; another, King Philip; and third, the Cardinal himself; all portraits from the life, and each placed on a basement adorned with little figures of nfinite grace. For the Signor Vespasiano Gonzaga, Lione has made the portrait of Alva, in a large bust of bronze, which Vespasiano now has in his house; and for the Signore Cesare Gonzaga, he has executed a Statue four braccia high, also in bronze, and having a figure beneath him, around which is entwined a Hydra. This group is intended to signify the bravery and excellence of Ferrante, the father of Cesare, who had overcome the wickedness and envy which had sought to bring him into disgrace with Charles V., in regard to the affairs of the government of Milan. This Statue wears the Toga, it is armed partly in the ancient and partly in the modern manner, and is to be taken to Guastalla, as a memorial of that Don Ferrante, who was indeed a most valiant Captain.

The same artist, as we have related elsewhere, constructed the Tomb of the Signor Giovan-Jacopo de' Medici, Marquis of Marignano, and brother of Pope Pius IV.; this Tomb is in

* Bottari tells us that Mariette explained to him these obscure words in the following story. "In the year 1533 Queen Mary set fire to the Chateau of Folembrai; and in the year following Henry, to avenge himself for this, attacked and burnt a small fortress in Upper Hainault, which had been built by the Queen; on the ruined walls of the fort he then attached the words, "Voilà pour Folembrai," out of which Vasari, his copyist, or his printer, has made the "*Vela fole Maria*" of the text.

the Cathedral of Milan. The monument is about twenty-eight palms long and forty high. The tomb is of Carrara marble, adorned with four columns, two white and two black, which were sent from Rome by the Pope, as a great rarity; there are also two larger columns of a vari-coloured marble, resembling jasper; these columns are all arranged under the same Cornice, in a manner no longer used, but as the Pope desired that they should stand, His Holiness having caused the whole to be arranged after the designs of Michelagnolo, with the exception of five figures in bronze, which are by the hand of Lione. The first and largest of these figures is the Statue of the Marquis, larger than life, and standing upright; he has the baton of a General in one hand, and rests the other on a helmet, richly decorated, which is placed on a genealogical tree. To the left of this figure is a smaller statue, representing Peace; and on the right a second, which signifies Military Virtue, both seated. Of the other two, which are on the upper part of the tomb, one represents Providence, the other Fame, and between them is a beautiful basso-rilievo in bronze, representing the Nativity of Christ. At the summit of the whole are two figures in marble, and these support an escutcheon of arms bearing the balls of the Medici. For this work Lioni was paid seven thousand eight hundred crowns, according to an agreement made in Rome, between the most Illustrious Cardinal Morone and the Signor Agabrio Serbelloni.

The same artist has executed a Statue, also in bronze, for the Signor Giovambattista Castaldo; this, with certain decorations, is to be placed in some Monastery, of which I do not know the name. For the Catholic King, Lioni has executed a figure of Christ, more than three braccia high, with the Cross and other mysteries of the Passion; this work is much admired. He has now in hand the Statue of the Signor Alfonso Davalo, the renowned Marquis del Vasto, the commission for which he has received from the Marquis of Pescara, son of Davalo. The figure, which is four braccia high, is expected to prove a beautiful casting, seeing that he is giving the utmost care to the execution of the same, and has always been singularly fortunate in the casting of his bronzes.

This Lione, to prove the boldness of his spirit, the fine genius which he has received from Nature, and the favour always granted to him by Fortune, has erected a house, at great cost and with infinite beauty of architecture, in the Contreda of the Moroni at Milan. This is so filled with fanciful inventions, that there is perhaps not such another in all the city. On the façade are six figures in stone, which stand on pilasters; they represent Captives, and are six braccia high. Between them, in niches made to imitate the antique, are windows, terminal figures, and cornices, entirely different from those in general use, but all very graceful. The decorations of the lower part are in admirable harmony with those of the upper part, and the frieze represents various instruments used in the arts of design. From the principal door you pass through a vestibule into the Court, wherein there are erected four columns, which support a copy, in plaster, of that Equestrian Statue of Marcus Aurelius, which is on the Capitol. By thus placing this statue in that place, Lione is supposed to have dedicated his house to Marcus Aurelius, but the signification which he meant to attach to the Captives before-mentioned is matter of conjecture. In addition to this Horse, Lione Lioni has collected into that beautiful and commodious habitation of his, very numerous casts in plaster, of such works of merit as he could obtain, whether ancient or modern, and in bronze as well as marble.

A son of this master, called Pompeo, is now in the service of the King of Spain, and is by no means inferior to his father in the preparation of steel dies for casting medals. Pompeo also produces figures in plaster, of extraordinary beauty, and is the competitor in that Court of the Florentine Giovampaolo Poggini, who is also in the service of King Philip, and has executed many beautiful medals. But as to Pompeo, having served the King many years, it is now his purpose to return to Milan, and there enjoy his Aurelian house, with all the other acquisitions made by that true friend of distinguished men, his excellent father.

I will now say a few words respecting medals and dies of steel, in which I believe I may truly affirm, that the moderns have approached the ancient Romans as respects the beauty of the figures, while in the excellence of the letters and some other particulars, they have surpassed them. And of this we have proof in twelve reverses to the medals of Duke Cosimo (among other things), lately executed by Pietro Paolo

Galeotti. These represent Pisa restored by the Duke almost to her pristine condition, he having drained the marshes around the city and effected other improvements; the Aqueducts whereby Florence has been supplied with water brought from divers places; the magnificent and beautiful edifice erected for the magistrates; the Union of the States of Florence and Siena; the erection of a City and two Fortresses in the Island of Elba; the Column brought to Florence from Rome, and set up in the Piazza della Trinità; that work of public utility, the preservation, enlargement, and completion of the Library of San Lorenzo; the institution of the Knights of San Stefano; the resignation of the government to the Prince; the fortification of the State; the Militia, or armed bands of the country; and finally, the Palace of the Pitti, with its magnificent and royal gardens, fountains, and other decorations. Of these works I do not now propose to give the legends, or their explication, intending to speak of these elsewhere; but they are all very beautiful, and are executed with much care, in a very graceful manner; as is the head of Duke Cosimo, which is a work of perfect beauty. Medals and other works in stucco are also made in the present day, with the utmost perfection, as I have said before. The Anconitan, Mario Capocaccia, for example, has just completed busts and portraits in coloured stuccoes, enclosed within small cases, which are of the most perfect beauty. Among them is one of Pope Pius V., which I saw no long time since, and another of the Cardinal Alessandrino. I have likewise seen very fine portraits of similar character by the sons of the Perugian painter, Polidoro.

But to return to Milan. About a year since I was again looking over the works of the sculptor Gobbo,* of whom we have spoken before, but I saw nothing beyond the common, with the exception of an Eve, a Judith, and a Sant' Elena, in marble, which are placed around the Cathedral, with two other statues representing the dead bodies of Lodovico il Moro, and of Beatrice his wife, which are to be placed on the tomb by Giovan-Jacomo dalla Porta, sculptor and architect to the Duomo of Milan.† This Giovan Jacomo pro-

* Cristofano Solari, called Il Gobbo (the Hunchback), and mentioned in the Life of Ridolfo Ghirlandajo, see vol. iv. p. 543.

† For the Life of this artist, see Baglioni, *Vite de' Pittori*.

duced many good works in his youth, under the discipline of the said Gobbo, and the works just alluded to are finished with much propriety. This artist has also executed many sculptures for the Certosa of Pavia, more especially at the Tomb of the Counts of Virtù, on the front of the church. From Gio-Jacomo, his nephew Guglielmo* acquired the art of the sculptor, and, about the year 1530, he gave the most earnest attention to the copying of Leonardo da Vinci's works, from which he derived great advantage. Having accompanied his uncle to Genoa, when the latter was invited thither in 1531, to erect the Sepulchre of San Giovanni Battista, he furthermore devoted himself with much zeal to the study of design, under Perino del Vaga, but did not neglect his labours in sculpture, and executed one of the six pedestals to be seen at that Sepulchre in so effective a manner that he was then commissioned to prepare all the rest.

Guglielmo afterwards produced two Angels in marble, which are now in the Compagnia of San Giovanni, and for the Bishop of Servega he made two portraits in marble, with a figure of Moses, larger than life, which was placed in the Church of San Lorenzo. Having subsequently executed a Ceres in marble, which stands over a door of the house of Ansaldo Grimaldi, Guglielmo made a figure of Santa Caterina, the size of life, to go over the Gate of the Cazzuola in that city, with the Three Graces, also in marble, and four Children, which were sent to Flanders, to the Grand Esquire of the Emperor Charles V., accompanied by another statue of Ceres, of the size of life. All these works were produced by these artist in six years, and in 1537 he repaired to Rome, where he was warmly recommended to the good offices of the Venetian painter, Fra Bastiano del Piombo, by his uncle Giovan-Jacomo, who was the friend of that Frate. Sebastiano then presented Guglielmo to Michelagnolo, as Giovan-Jacomo had begged him to do; and Buonarroti, perceiving that Guglielmo was a spirited and industrious artist, began to conceive an affection for him. He therefore set him first of all to restore certain antiquities in the Casa Farnese, and in these he acquitted himself so well that Michelagnolo put him into the service of the Pope, having previously seen a further specimen of

* The Life of Guglielmo della Porta will also be found in Baglioni, *ut supra.*

his ability in a tomb, principally of metal, erected by Guglielmo for the Bishop of Sulisse, at the Botteghe Scure. This work, adorned with many graceful figures and stories in bassi-rilievi, that of the Bishop himself namely, with those of the Cardinal Virtues, and others, was ultimately sent to Salamanca in Spain.

While Guglielmo was restoring the antiquities of the Casa Farnese, which are now in the Loggia before the Upper Hall, it chanced that Fra Bastiano, who held the office of the Leaden Seal, departed this life, when Guglielmo contrived in such sort, by means of Michelagnolo and others, that he obtained the office in question, with the commission for erecting the Sepulchre of Pope Paul III., which was to be placed in San Pietro. For this tomb he used the models of the Cardinal and Theological Virtues, which he had prepared for that of the Bishop of Sulisse,* but with improved design, placing four Children, with inscriptions, at the four angles, and adding the seated statue of the Pontiff, in the act of giving the benediction: this last figure, which is seventeen palms high, is in bronze. Fearing that the mass of the metal might get cold, and so endanger the success of his casting, Guglielmo kept it in the lower furnace constantly heated, and caused it to be brought gradually into the mould above; this unusual mode of proceeding turned out so well, that the work came forth clean and equal, as wax, so that the very surface was suffered to remain as it came from the fire, having no need of polishing. This figure may be now seen under the first arches of the Tribune in the New San Pietro.

To this Sepulchre, which according to the design of Guglielmo was to be entirely isolated, there were to be added four figures in marble, which he had himself prepared with admirable inventions, as he had been directed to do by Annibale Caro, who had received the care of the same from the Pope and Cardinal Farnese. One of these represents Justice, a nude figure, recumbent amidst beautiful draperies, and with the cincture of the sword across the breast, the sword itself being concealed: in one hand are the fasces of Con-

* Or, according to a letter from Annibale Caro, to Elio da Capo d'Istria, Bishop of Pola, relating to this tomb, the Bishop *Del Solis*. See the *Sienese Edition* of our author, where this letter was published for the first time, in a note, by the Padre Della Valle.

sular Justice, and in the other is a flame of fire: the countenance is youthful, the hair waving, the nose aquiline, the whole aspect full of fine expression. The second figure is Prudence; her form is that of a matron, but one still young, she has a mirror in her hand, with a closed book, and is partly nude, but also partially draped. The third is Abundance, a maiden crowned with ears of corn, and bearing the horn of plenty in one hand, with the ancient corn-measure in the other; her dress is such as to render the nude form visible beneath its folds. The fourth and last of these figures represents Peace; it is that of a matron with a child, which has its eyes taken out, and bears the Caduceus of Mercury. For the same tomb, and likewise under the direction of Annibale Caro, this artist also prepared a Story in bronze,* with two figures of River-gods; the one representing a lake, and the other a river in the domains of the Farnese family. There was also to have been an eminence, covered with lilies and the Bow of Iris; but many of these things were omitted, for reasons which have been mentioned in the Life of Michelagnolo.† It is true, that to judge from the beauty of these works, they would have had a good effect if erected in the position destined to them; meanwhile, it is also true, that the light of the place itself is that which finally decides the effect that a work will have, whether as to its whole or in the details.

This Fra Guglielmo has been for some years preparing fourteen Stories from the Life of Christ, which are to be cast in bronze; each of them is four palms broad and six high, with the exception of one, which is twelve palms high and six wide. This last exhibits the Birth of Christ, with figures of very fanciful invention. The other thirteen represent:—the first, Our Lady, with the Infant, proceeding to Jerusalem on an Ass; it comprises two figures in high relief, with many others in half and low relief. This is followed by the Last Supper, with thirteen well-composed figures, and an exceedingly rich building; then follow the Washing of the Disciples' Feet; Christ in the Garden, with five figures, and a crowd of infinitely varied character; Our Saviour led before Annas, with six large figures, many others beneath

* This rilievo was never placed on the tomb.—*Bottari.*

† See also the *Lettere Pittoriche*, vol. iii. The reader may likewise consult the letter of Annibale Caro as before cited.

them, and one in the distance; the Scourging; the Crowning with Thorns; the *Ecce Homo;* Pilate Washing his Hands; Christ Bearing his Cross, with fifteen figures; Christ Crucified, with eighteen figures; and the Deposition from the Cross. All these compositions, if cast, would certainly prove a work of extraordinary merit, seeing that it has been prepared with infinite care and labour.

Pope Pius IV. had intended to employ Guglielmo to execute one of the Gates of San Pietro, but His Holiness being overtaken by death, had not time to set the artist to work. Fra Guglielmo has been lately making models in wax, for the decoration of three altars in San Pietro. The Deposition of Christ from the Cross namely; St. Peter receiving the Keys of the Church; and the Descent of the Holy Spirit; which will doubtless be very beautiful stories. At a word, this artist has had and has many favourable occasions for distinguishing himself by fine works; and the rather as the office of the Piombo, producing a sufficient income, gives the recipient leisure for study, and permits him to labour for glory alone, which cannot be done by those who have not such an advantage. Yet, from 1547 to the present year of 1567, Fra Guglielmo has produced no finished work. For it is the peculiarity of this office that it renders him who holds it fat and lazy; the truth of which may be proved by the fact, that before he obtained it, Guglielmo had executed many busts and other works in marble besides those we have named. It is true that he has made four large figures of Prophets in stucco, which are in the niches between the piers of the first large arch of San Pietro, and did also employ himself to some extent for the Chariots used in the Festival of the Testaccio and other maskings which were held some years since in Rome.

A disciple of this artist was a certain German called Guglielmo, who, among other works, has executed a rich and beautiful frame, decorated with several figures in bronze which are imitations of the best antiques, for a Study (as they call it) in wood work, which the Count of Pitigliano presented to Duke Cosimo. These little figures are copies of the Equestrian Group on the Capital, of that on the Monte Cavallo of the Farnese Hercules, the Antinous and the Apollo of the Belvedere; to these were added the Heads of the twelve Cæsars, with others, all executed with infinite care.

Milan also had another sculptor called Tommaso Porta,* but he died during the present year. This artist worked admirably well in marble, he imitated antique heads so perfectly that his productions in that kind have been sold for those of antiquity, and his masks have never been equalled. I have one of these last myself; it is in marble, and I have placed it in a chimney-piece of my house at Arezzo, where all men take it to be an antique. Tommaso likewise executed the heads of the twelve Cæsars, of the size of life, and these, too, are singularly fine. Pope Julius III. took them, and kept them in his own apartments for many months as a work of great rarity, His Holiness then presented the artist with an office of a hundred crowns per annum, but the envy of Fra Guglielmo, as it is thought, co-operating with that of others, caused the heads eventually to be sent back to the sculptor; they were, however, finally purchased at a good price by the merchants, who sent them into Spain. None of the copyists of the ancient works have surpassed Tommaso, and I have therefore thought him worthy of a memorial, the rather as he has departed to a better life, leaving behind him a very fair reputation for his ability and excellence.

The Florentine sculptor Nanni di Baccio Bigio, of whom we have spoken in other places, gave some hope of future distinction in his youth, and when the disciple of Raffaello da Montelupo, by the manner in which he executed certain small works in marble. Repairing to Rome with the sculptor Lorenzetto, he gave his attention to architecture as his father had done, but at the same time received the commission for a Statue of Pope Clement VII., which is now in the Choir of the Minerva, and for a Pietà in marble, copied from that of Michelagnolo. This last was placed in Santa Maria *de' Anima*, the Church of the Germans, as a work of great merit, which it certainly is. No long time after having finished it, Nanni Bigio made another of similar kind for the Florentine merchant Luigi del Riccio, and this is now in a chapel belonging to that Luigi in the Church of San Spirito;† nor was the merchant less extolled for his

* Of the same family with Giovan-Jacomo and Guglielmo.

† Where it still remains.

liberality towards his native city than was the sculptor for the love and care with which he had finished the Group.

Ultimately Nanni Bigio devoted himself more especially to architecture, under Antonio da Sangallo, and while the disciple of the latter, Nanni Baccio worked with him at the Church of San Pietro, where he fell from a scaffold sixty braccia high, and hurt himself so grievously that it was a marvel he escaped with life. This artist has erected many buildings both in Rome and without the city; many others and of more important character he has laboured to obtain the care of, as we have said in the Life of Michelagnolo. The Palace of Cardinal Montepulciano in the Strada Gulia is Nanni's work, as is one of the Gates of Monte Sansavino, erected by order of Pope Julius III., with a reservoir of water not yet finished; a Loggia and entire apartments added to the Palace formerly built by the elder Cardinal di Monte. The house of the Mattei family, with many other edifices, either completed or in course of construction at Rome, are in like manner the work of Nanni Bigio.

The Perugino Galeazzo Alessi is also among the most renowned architects of our day. In his youth he was chamberlain to the Cardinal of Rimini, and among his first works were certain apartments in the Fortress of Perugia, which he rebuilt at the desire of that prelate, completing them in so beautiful a manner and rendering them so commodious, that, the small space he had to work in considered, they caused amazement in all who saw them; the Pope and all his court having been more than once accommodated therein. After the execution of many other works for the same prelate, Galeazzo, to his great honour, was invited to enter the service of the Genoese republic. His first work was to restore and fortify the Port and Pier, which he greatly improved, extending the former into the sea for a considerable distance, and adding a semi-circular haven richly adorned with rustic columns and niches, while at the extremities of the half-circle are two Bastions which defend the same.

On the piazza above the pier and behind the haven, on the side towards the city, Galeazzo furthermore erected a very large *Portico* of the Doric order, for the accommodation of the Guard; and above this building is a platform for the Artillery, of the same size with itself, and extending besides over the two bastions and the gate. This is continued over the pier also, in the manner of a cavalier, and defends the port from all attack, whether from within or without. The work is now completed, and the city is furthermore about to be enlarged and beautified after the designs of the same master, who is acquiring great honour by these and other works. The model he has exhibited has already been approved by the Signoria, and the new Street which he has laid out in Genoa has so many palaces in the modern manner, erected along the range thereof after his designs, that many affirm it to be as magnificent a street as can be found in any city of Italy; nay, for the many rich palaces which the Genoese nobles have built by the persuasions and under the direction of Galeazzo, to say nothing of its noble width and extent, some declare that it has no equal. All the Genoese confess themselves greatly indebted to the architect meanwhile, he having been the inventor as well as executor of works by which their city is so much embellished. Galeazzo has laid out other streets leading from Genoa, and among them that which, departing from the Ponte Decimo, commences the road into Lombardy. He has restored the city wall towards the sea, moreover, and has added the Tribune with a Cupola to the Cathedral. Many private residences have been constructed by this master, the Country House of Messer Luca Justiniano for example, with that of the Signor Attaviano Grimaldi. The Palaces of two Doges are in like manner among his works, as is one for the Signor Battista Grimaldi and many others, which need no further mention.

But I will not omit to say that the Lake and Island so beautifully adorned with rich and fancifully decorated Fountains, which belongs to the Signor Adano Centurioni, are also of Galeazzo's design, as is the Fountain of the Captain Learco, near the city, a truly noble work. He has, indeed, constructed numerous fine fountains for many persons, but more beautiful than all else is the Bath which has been formed after his design, in the house of the Signor Battista Grimaldi at Bisagno. This, which is of a round form, has a basin in the centre within which eight or ten persons can bathe commodiously. Warm water is poured into the basin from four heads of marine monsters, which appear to proceed from the basin itself; while the cold water is supplied by as many frogs which are placed above the heads of those monsters. Around the basin, into which there is a commodious descent by circular steps, there is a space in which two persons can walk together conveniently.

The wall of the building is divided into eight compartments, in four of which are large niches, each of them having a circular basin, but slightly raised from the ground, and half within the niche, while the other half projects beyond it; this basin, which is large enough for a man to bathe therein, receives cold and hot water from the horns of a great mask which takes the same in again at its mouth. In one of the other four compartments is the door, the remaining three divisions having windows and seats in them. These eight compartments are separated by terminal figures which support the cornice whereon the circular vaulting of the whole fabric reposes: from the centre of the ceiling hangs a large ball of crystal, on which is depicted the celestial sphere, and within this is the Globe of the Earth, from various parts of which proceed lights to illumine the Bath, when any one desires to use it at night: these lights render the whole building as clear as it is at mid-day. I omit all description of the ante-room, dressing chambers, and small bathing room, which are finely adorned with stuccoes, and do not enumerate the pictures which embellish the place, that I may not be more prolix than is needful; suffice it to say, that they are by no means unworthy of the structure.

The Milanese Palace of the Signor Tommaso Marini, Duke of Terra-Nuova, has been also erected after the design of Galeazzo; and by the same artist, very probably, are the façade of the building, now in course of erection at San Celso, with the circular Hall of the Exchange, the lately-commenced Church of San Vittore, and many other edifices. When Galeazzo has not been able himself to be present, he has sent designs for Palaces, Churches, and other buildings, into every part of Italy; but of these I will not now speak further, what I have said being sufficient to make him known as an excellent and able architect.*

There is one artist more, whom, as he is one of our Italians, I will not omit to mention, although I do not know the par-

* For details respecting Galeazzo Alessi, the reader may consult Milizia, *Memorie degli Architetti*, tomo ii. p. 1.

culars of his works; this is Rocco Guerrini, of Marradi, ow in France, where, as I am told, he is proving himself a ery good architect, more especially as regards fortifications, aving effected many creditable and useful works during aese last wars.

Here, then, and at this last moment, that I may not efraud any one of the credit due to his abilities, I have aentioned certain sculptors and architects now living, of rhom I have not had a convenient opportunity for speaking lsewhere.

---

## THE MINIATURIST, DON GIULIO CLOVIO.

[BORN 1498—DIED 1578.]

THERE never has been, and for many ages there probably never will be, a more admirable and more extraordinary miniaturist, I mean a painter of minute objects, than Don Giulio Clovio, who has far surpassed all that have hitherto distinguished themselves in that manner.

He was born in Sclavonia, or Croatia, at a town called Grisone, in the Diocese of Madrucci; his family was of Macedonian origin, and he was baptized Giorgio Giulio. From his childhood he was kept to the study of letters; but he took to design by instinct, and, desirous of improvement, he came to Italy when he had attained his eighteenth year, attaching himself to the service of Marino Cardinal Grimani; labouring for three years in the studies of design, with so much zeal, that his progress went much beyond what had previously been expected from him. Proof of this may be seen in certain designs for medals, and their reverses, which he executed for the above-named Prelate at that time; they are drawn with the pen with infinitely minute detail, and are finished with an extraordinary, nay, almost inconceivable, care and patience.

Perceiving, therefore, that he was more powerfully aided by Nature for minute works than for larger ones, Giulio determined, and very wisely, to become a miniaturist, a decision to which he was advised by many friends, who remarked that his works in that manner were graceful and beautiful to a marvel. Among these counsellors was Giulio Romano, a painter of illustrious name, from whom Clovio first learned to use tints and colours prepared with gum and in tempera.

Among the first works painted by Giorgio Giulio was a Madonna, which he copied, as being a spirited and beautiful thing, from a book of the Life of our Lady, and which was one of the first of Albert Dürer's wood-engravings. Acquitting himself well in this, Giulio was introduced, by means of the Signor Alberto Carpi, who was then serving in Hungary, to the notice of Lodovico, King of that country, and of Maria his Queen, the sister of Charles V. To that Monarch he took a Judgment of Paris in chiaro-scuro, which gave infinite satisfaction; and to the Queen he presented the Roman Lucrezia killing herself, with other things, which were all considered to be very beautiful. But Ludovico dying, and the affairs of Hungary falling into confusion, Giorgio Giulio was compelled to return to Italy, where he had scarcely arrived before Cardinal Campeggio (the elder) took him into his service. He was thus accommodated to his liking, and painted a Madonna for that prelate, with some other small works. He also disposed himself to study Art with more zeal than ever, and set himself with all his power to copy the works of Michelagnolo.

These his good intentions were nevertheless interrupted by the unhappy sack of Rome in 1527, when the poor man, taken prisoner by the Spaniards, and finding himself in evil case, had recourse, in the extremity of his wretchedness, to the help of God, making a vow, that if ever he got safe out of that miserable ruin, and escaped from those modern Pharisees, he would immediately make himself a monk. Being delivered by the favour of Heaven accordingly, and having reached Mantua, he attached himself to the Order of the Scopetine Canons Regular, and took the habit in the Monastery of San Ruffino. He then received a promise to the effect, that, besides the quiet repose and leisure to serve God there afforded him, he should also be allowed time to work occasionally, as it were for recreation, at his miniatures.

In taking the religious habit, Giorgio Giulio retained his second name, and at the end of a year made his profession, remaining quietly among those Monks, with an occasional hange from one monastery to another, for the space of three 'ears; but always doing something in his art. It was at his time that he completed a large Choral-book, with most lelicate miniatures and beautiful borderings, among which vas a Story of Our Saviour Christ appearing to Mary Magdalen in the Garden, and this was considered most ingularly beautiful. Encouraged by success, Don Giulio next painted the Woman taken in Adultery; the group comprising many figures, of much larger size than his works usually exhibit, and being copied from a picture executed in those days by Tiziano Vecellio,* a most excellent painter.

Not long after the completion of these works, it chanced that Don Giulio, removing from one monastery to another, as is the manner of those Monks, or Friars, had the misfortune to break his leg; whereupon, being taken by the brotherhood, for his better attendance, to the Monastery of Candiano, he remained there for some time. But he did not recover, perhaps because, as is frequently the case among those Monks, he was treated badly by the Brotherhood as well as by the doctors.† The accident coming to the ears of Cardinal Grimani, by whom Don Giulio was much valued for his ability, that Prelate obtained permission from the Pope to take him into his own service, when our artist, throwing off the habit, and having had his leg cured, went to Perugia with the Cardinal, who was Legate in that city, where Don Giulio executed for him the works which follow: an Office of Our Lady, with four most beautiful Stories; an Epistolary, with three large Stories from the Life of St. Paul, one of which was soon afterwards sent into Spain; with a most exquisite Pietà, and a Crucifix, which came, after the death of Grimani, into the hands of Messer Giovanni Gaddi, Clerk of the Chamber.

These works made Don Giulio known at Rome as an able artist, and Cardinal Alessandro Farnese, who has always assisted, favoured, and desired to have about him, distin-

* Vasari has not mentioned this picture in the Life of Titian, but there is one on the subject in question, in the Brera at Milan, which has been engraved by Anderloni as a work of Titian's, but has usually been considered one of Palma Vecchio's.

† The accomplished churchman Bottari will not have us believe this, and maintains that Don Clovio continued the friend of these Canons all his life, which may well be, even though our author were not far wrong, placable and good as the miniaturist is known to have been.

guished and able men, having heard the fame and seen the works of this artist, took him into his service, and there he has remained ever since, even to his present advanced age. For this Signore, Don Giulio has executed a vast number of most beautiful illuminations and miniatures, but of these I propose to name a part only, since to mention them all would be impossible. In one of his small pictures he has painted the Madonna with the Divine Child in her arms, and Pope Paul III. kneeling before her; the last is a portrait from the life, and so good a resemblance that this minute form appears to be living, nor do the other figures want anything but the actual breath of life. This picture was sent, as the extraordinary work that it really is, to the Emperor Charles V., then in Spain, and that Monarch was quite astonished at the beauty and excellence thereof.

The Cardinal then caused our artist to commence the miniature stories and illuminations for an Office of the Madonna, written in fine letters by Monterchi, who is very clever at that work. For this production Don Giulio resolved to put forth his utmost efforts, and gave so much care to every part of it that no work of the kind could ever receive more; he has, in fact, here effected such amazing things with his pencil, that one fails to comprehend how the eye and hand can have gone so far. The series is divided into twenty-six small stories arranged in pairs, and representing the symbol with that which is symbolized: each picture is surrounded by a delicate bordering of figures and fancies, in harmony with the subject represented, nor will I refuse to take the trouble of briefly describing them, seeing that it is not every one who can obtain a sight of this work.

The first plate, where the office for Matins commences, represents the Angel of the Annunciation, and the border is formed of children whose beauty is miraculous; on the opposite plate is Isaiah speaking to the Hebrew King. In the second, which is for the Lauds, we have the Visitation, the frame-work of which imitates metal; and on the opposite plate are Justice and Peace embracing each other. For the Primes there is the Birth of Christ, with Adam and Eve eating the apple in the terrestrial Paradise on the opposite plate, the frames of both are filled with figures nude and draped, some human, others of animals. At the Horary office called the Terza, are the Shepherds with the Angels

ppearing to them; and opposite to this is the Tibertine
ybil, showing to the Emperor Octavian the Virgin in
Ieaven with the Son born to her; both are adorned with
gures and coloured ornaments of various kinds, among
vhich is the head of Alexander the Great, with the Portrait
f Alexander Cardinal Farnese. At the *Sesta* is the cir-
umcision of Christ; and in the figure of Simeon we have
likeness of Pope Paul III.; portraits of Mancina and
Septimia, gentlewomen of Rome, of great beauty, are also
o be found in the story itself. A beautifully formed deco-
ation surrounds this and the next picture, which represents
St. John baptizing Christ, and wherein are exhibited many
nude figures.

For the Nones we have the Adoration of the Magi, with the visit of the Queen of Sheba to Solomon opposite thereto, and both together have a framework, at the foot of which is the whole Festival of the Testaccio, represented in figures not so big as ants; a thing which cannot be seen without amazement, that the point of a pencil can have been made to produce such perfection in objects so minute: this is indeed one of the most extraordinary works ever effected by mortal hand, or seen by eye of man. All the colours or liveries given by the Cardinal Farnese to his people on that occasion are clearly to be distinguished in this singular production.* At Vespers we have the Flight into Egypt, with the Submersion of Pharaoh in the Red Sea on the opposite side, the framework exhibiting much and varied beauty of ornament. For Complins there is the Coronation of Our Lady in the Heavens, with a multitude of Angels, opposite to which is the Story of Esther crowned by Ahasuerus, the framework of both being appropriately decorated.

At the Mass of the Madonna, Don Clovio has given us a framework painted to imitate Cameos, and representing Gabriel announcing the Word to the Virgin; the pictures within are, Our Lady with the Infant Christ in her arms, and God the Father creating the Heavens and the Earth. Opposite to the Penitential Psalms is the Battle in which Uriah the Hittite was exposed to death by command of King David; and here there are horses and riders with the warriors wounded and dead, depicted in a manner that is

* Which the reader may examine at his leisure, since it is still in the Museo Borbonico at Naples, and in a state of excellent preservation.

miraculous; the picture opposite to this shows King David in his repentance, the framework being composed of grotteschine and other ornaments.

But let him who has a mind to be utterly amazed, cast an eye on the Litanies, where the artist has minutely interwoven the letters which form the names of the Saints; and in the margin above is the Most Holy Trinity in Heaven, surrounded by innumerable Angels, together with whom are the Apostles and other Saints. Opposite to this is the Madonna, also in Heaven with the Holy Virgins; and in the margin beneath is the Procession in which Rome performs the Solemnity of the Corpus Christi. Here we have the various officials bearing torches, with the bishops, the Cardinals, and the Holy Sacrament, carried by the Pope, who is followed by the remainder of the Court, and the Guard of Lancers; finally there is the Castel Sant' Angelo, whence they are firing salutes; the whole being a thing well calculated to astound and awaken the admiration of the most acute intellect.

In the commencement of the Office for the Dead, we have Death himself, who is represented as triumphing over Kingdoms and the mighty of the Earth, as over those of the lowest degree. Opposite to this is the Resurrection of Lazarus, and herein is Death again perceived in combat with certain figures on horseback. For the Office of the Crucifixion, the artist has depicted Christ on his Cross, opposite to which is Moses lifting aloft the brazen Serpent; and for that of the Holy Ghost he has chosen the Descent of the Spirit on the Apostles, with the building of the Tower of Babel by Nimrod placed opposite thereto.

Nine years did Don Giulio labour over this work, which could never be paid for, so to speak, whatever the price that might be given for it; the variety of fanciful ornaments, the divers attitudes and movements of the figures, nude and draped, male and female, placed in the most appropriate manner for the embellishment of the whole, with the beauty of every detail, and the studious care given to all points, are not to be described; the diversity and excellence of this production are indeed such as to make it seem not of human so much as of divine origin. The figures, the buildings, and the landscapes are all made duly to recede by the art of the master, and the nice arrangement of his colours; the laws of perspective are observed in every particular, and whether near or far, each portion of the work maintains its due place and is viewed with surprise and admiration; the trees, to say nothing of other parts, are so well done that they seem to have been made in Paradise.

In the stories and inventions of these pictures there is the most admirable design; in the compositions the most perfect order; the vestments are singularly rich and varied; while the whole work is conducted in such a manner that one thinks it could not possibly have been executed by the hands of men; wherefore it is perfectly true, as we said at the first, that in this performance Don Giulio has surpassed both the ancients and moderns, having been the Michelagnolo in little of our day.

The same artist executed a small picture, with minute figures, for the Cardinal of Trent; and this was so beautiful that the Prelate sent it as a present to Charles V. He subsequently executed a Madonna for the same Cardinal, with a Portrait of King Philip II., which were in like manner presented for their beauty to the Catholic King above mentioned. For Cardinal Farnese, Giulio painted Our Lady with the Divine Child in her arms; Sant' Elizabetta, the little San Giovanni, and other figures being in the same picture, which was sent to Rigornes in Spain. In another picture, which the Cardinal Farnese still retains, this artist painted San Giovanni Battista in the Desert: the work exhibits a beautiful Landscape with Animals; and Don Clovio made a second, exactly like it, for the same Prelate, who sent the work into Spain for King Philip. A Pietà by his hand was also presented by Farnese to Pope Paul IV., who kept it in his own apartments till he died. A story exhibiting David cutting off the head of Goliath, was given by the same Cardinal to Madama Margherita of Austria, who sent it to King Philip her brother, with another, which that most illustrious Lady caused Don Clovio to paint, as the companion of the above; this last is a Judith taking off the head of Holofernes.*

Many years since, Don Giulio stayed for some months with Duke Cosimo, and during that time he executed several works for his Excellency; some of these were sent to the

* Della Valle, in the Sienese Edition of Vasari, has given the letter written to the Princess Margaret by Don Clovio, and sent with this work.

Emperor and other great personages; the rest were kept by the Duke for himself. Among other works he copied a small Head of Christ, from one of great antiquity in the Duke's possession, which formerly belonged to Godfrey King of Jerusalem, and which is said to be a more exact resemblance of the Saviour than any other in existence. Don Giulio also executed for His Excellency a Crucifix with the Mary Magdalen at the foot thereof, which is a work of infinite beauty.* The same artist likewise painted a small picture, the subject a Pietà, of which we have the design in our book,† with another, also by the hand of Don Clovio, representing Our Lady dressed in the Hebrew manner, and holding the Infant Christ in her arms; she has a choir of Angels around her, with several nude figures, representing Souls in the act of recommending themselves to her mercy. But to return to the Signor Duke: that Prince has ever greatly admired the abilities of Don Clovio, and taken pains to procure his works; nay, had it not been for the respect due to Cardinal Farnese, he would not have permitted our artist to leave him at the time when he remained, as we have said, during some months in his service at Florence.

Besides the works above-mentioned, Duke Cosimo has a small picture by Don Clovio, representing Ganymede borne to Heaven by Jupiter turned into an Eagle: this was copied from that designed by Michelagnolo, and which is now in the possession of Tommaso de' Cavalieri, as we have said elsewhere. The Duke has also in his writing-room a figure of San Giovanni Battista, seated on a stone, with some Portraits by the same artist, which are truly admirable. Don Clovio formerly painted a Pietà, with the Maries and other figures, for the Marchioness of Pescara, with one exactly similar for Cardinal Farnese, who sent it to the Empress, sister of King Philip, and wife to the Emperor Maximilian. Another work, executed with infinite care, and representing St. George killing the Dragon, with an exquisite Landscape, was sent by Farnese to his Imperial Majesty; but this was surpassed in design by a larger picture, which Don Giulio painted for a Spanish gentleman; the subject is the Emperor

* Now in the Directory of the Uffizj: the colour is somewhat faded, but considering the lapse of time, three hundred years, the work may be called well-preserved. It bears the inscription, *Julius Macedo, fa.* 1553.

† In the Pitti, in the "Hall of the Education of Jupiter."

Trajan, as he is represented on those medals which have the Province of Judea on the reverse. This picture also was sent to Maximilian, now Emperor.

For Cardinal Farnese Don Giulio has executed two other pictures; in one of these is a nude figure of Christ with the Cross in his hand: the second also represents Our Saviour, but here he bears the Cross on his shoulder, and is led by the Jews, who are accompanied by an immense crowd of people, to Mount Calvary. Behind him is Our Lady with the other Maries, in attitudes and with expressions that might move a heart of stone to pity. In two large plates, for a Missal, the artist has furthermore depicted for the same Cardinal, Our Saviour Christ instructing the Apostles in the Doctrines of the Gospel in the one, and the Last Judgment in the other. They are both so beautiful, or rather so admirable and amazing, that I stand confounded when I think of these works, and feel persuaded that there can be nothing in miniature, I do not say done, but even imagined, which could surpass them in beauty.

In many of these works, more particularly in the Office of the Madonna, there are figures not larger than a very small ant, which yet have all the parts so distinctly drawn and so perfectly formed, that they could not be more correctly exhibited in figures the size of life; and there are besides innumerable portraits of men and women dispersed over these pictures, which are no less faithful likenesses than they might have been, had they been of the size of life, and proceeded from the hands of Titian or Bronzino. Some of the little figures in the frames also, whether draped or undraped, being painted in imitation of cameos, have all the effect of colossal figures, although so excessively minute: such was the extraordinary ability and enduring patience which Don Giulio exhibited in his works.*

Of these I have desired to give the world this notice, that such as cannot see those productions, for they are almost all in the hands of Princes or other great personages, may at least know something of them and of him. I say *almost* all, because I know some private persons who have small cases, containing beautiful portraits, by his hand, of Sovereigns, of their friends, or of ladies whom they have loved.

* A small round portrait of Don Giulio in oil, at a very advanced age, is in the Uffizj, but is not certainly known to be by his own hand.

But be this as it may, we are certain that the works of this master are not in public places where they may be seen by all, as are for the most part the paintings, sculptures, and buildings of others who practise these our arts.

Now Don Giulio, although being old he does not study or do anything, but seek the salvation of his soul by good works, and a life spent wholly apart from mundane affairs, being in all respects an old man, and living as such,* does yet continue to work occasionally, amidst the repose and comfort by which he is surrounded in the Farnese Palace, where he most willingly and courteously shows his productions to those who visit him for the purpose of seeing the same, as they would any other of the wonders of Rome.†

## OF DIVERS' ITALIAN ARTISTS.

THERE is now living in Rome, and certainly a very able artist in his vocation, the painter Girolamo Sicciolante of Sermoneta, of whom, although we have already named him in the Life of Perino del Vaga, whose disciple he was,‡ and whom he assisted greatly in his works at the Castel Sant' Angelo and elsewhere, it will yet be well to say here also what his merits so amply deserve. Among the first works of Girolamo was a picture twelve palms high, which he painted in oil at the age of twenty, and which is now in the Abbey of San Stefano near Sermoneta, his native place. In this work are figures of SS. Pietro, Stefano, and John the Baptist, with several Children. After this performance, which was much extolled, he painted a picture, also in oil, for the Church of Sant' Apostolo in Rome, a Dead Christ namely, with the Madonna, San Giovanni, the Magdalen, and other figures, all executed with exceeding care.§

* He died in 1578, at the age of eighty, and is buried at San Pietro in Vincola, where the reader will find his portrait, a basso-rilievo in marble. It is in the Tribune, and is accompanied by an inscription.

† Baglioni also, *Vite*, &c., has written the Life of Don Giulio Clovio, but has made few additions to that here given by Vasari.

‡ He was first the disciple of Leonardo, called Il Pistoja. See Lanzi, *History of Painting*, vol. i. pp. 406 and 430.

§ Now at Berlin, in the Collection of Count Raczynslay.

The entire ceiling of the marble chapel constructed by Cardinal Cesis in the Pace, was then decorated by Girolamo with stucco-work, forming compartments within which were four pictures, exhibiting the Birth of Christ, the Adoration of the Magi, the Flight into Egypt, and the Slaughter of the Innocents; a very commendable work, and one giving proof of good invention, fair judgment, and great diligence. In the same Church, and no long time after the completion of the above, Girolamo painted a beautiful picture of the Birth of Christ; this work, which is fifteen palms high, is placed near the High Altar. For the Sacristy of the Church of Santo Spirito in Rome he painted a picture in oil, representing the Descent of the Holy Spirit on the Apostles; this also is a very graceful production. The Chapel of the Fuccheri family in the Church of Santa Maria *de' Anima*, which is that of the German nation, was painted in fresco by this artist: who depicted events from the Life of Our Lady therein, the Altar-piece had previously been executed by Giulio Romano. For the High Altar of San Jacopo of the Spaniards, Girolamo painted a large picture, exhibiting a most beautiful composition of Christ on the Cross surrounded by Angels, while on each side is another picture nine palms high, with a single figure; St. James the Apostle on the one side namely, and the Bishop Sant' Alfonso on the other; from all these pictures it is manifest that the artist studied with much diligence, and they are executed with great care.

At the Church of San Tommaso, which is in the Piazza Giudea, Girolamo painted a chapel in fresco depicting therein the Birth of Our Lady, the Annunciation, and the Nativity of Our Lord: the chapel is that opposite to the Court of the Cenci Palace. He painted stories from the History of Rome in a Hall of the Palace of Cardinal Capodiferro;* and for the Church of San Martino in Bologna he painted the picture of the High Altar, which was greatly extolled.† For the Signor Pier Luigi Farnese, Duke of Parma and Piacenza, in whose service Girolamo Sermoneta passed some time, he executed numerous works, more especially a picture eight palms high, now in Piacenza and intended for a chapel; it represents Our Lady, St. Joseph, St. Michael, and St. John the Baptist, with an Angel.

* Which afterwards became the property of the Spada family.

† Now in the seventh Chapel of the Church of San Martino, in Bologna.

On his return from Lombardy our artist painted a Crucifix in the Church of the Minerva, this is in the passage leading to the Sacristy: for the Church itself he painted another, and he afterwards executed a Santa Caterina and Sant' Agata in oil. In San Luigi, Girolamo painted a fresco in competition with the Bolognese Pellegrino Pellegrini and the Florentine Jacopo del Conte. In a picture sixteen palms high, painted no long time since for the Church of Sant' Alò, which is opposite to the Misericordia and belongs to the Company of the Florentines, this artist depicted a Madonna, and St. James the Apostle, with the Bishops St. Alò and San Martino. For San Lorenzo in Lucina, he painted St. Francis receiving the Stigmata, a picture destined for the chapel of the Countess of Carpi. In the Hall of the Kings moreover, and during the Pontificate of Pius IV., Girolamo painted a Story in fresco over the door of the Sistine chapel, as we have said: this represents Pepin, King of the Franks, presenting Ravenna to the Roman Church, while he leads Astolfo king of the Lombards into captivity; of this we have the design in our book, with many others by the same hand. Finally, he has now in process of execution the chapel of Cardinal Cesis in Santa Maria Maggiore, where he has already completed a large picture of the Martyrdom of St. Catherine, who is seen amidst the wheels; a beautiful picture, as are many others which he is now painting with great care in this chapel as well as at other places. I do not name the portraits and other smaller works of Girolamo, because they are very numerous, and what I have here said will suffice to make him known as an able and excellent painter.*

Having mentioned in the life of Perino del Vaga, that the Mantuan painter, Marcello, had worked under him for many years, executing pictures from which he had acquired a great name, I will here add a few more particulars respecting him. In the Church of Santo Spirito, Marcello painted the chapel of San Giovanni Evangelista with its Altar-piece, adding the Portrait of a certain Commendator of Santo Spirito, by whom the Church was built, and who constructed the chapel: this Portrait is a very fine one, and the Altar-piece is beautiful. A Frate del Piombo, seeing

* According to Lanzi, his best work is in the Church of St. Bartholomew, at Ancona.

the good manner of this work, then caused the artist to paint a Disputation of Christ with the Doctors, over that door of the Pace which leads into the convent: that also is a very beautiful production; but this master, taking more pleasure in making portraits and executing other small works than in those of more important character, abandoned the latter and has painted a vast number of likenesses, among which are some of Pope Paul III., which are admirable as to resemblance and very beautiful pictures.

From the designs and after the works of Michelagnolo, this Marcello has also made numerous little pictures, among which is the whole of the Last Judgment, which he has executed extremely well. Nay, of a truth, for small things it could not be easy to find better pictures; wherefore, that most kindly gentleman, Messer Tommaso de' Cavalieri, who has always favoured Marcello, employed him to paint for the Church of San Giovanni Laterano an Annunciation, after the design of Michelagnolo, which is a very beautiful thing. The design, by Michelagnolo's own hand, was presented to the Duke Cosimo by Leonardo Buonarroti, nephew of Michelagnolo, together with other designs of fortifications, architectural works, and similar productions of great excellence. And this shall suffice for Marcello, who is still working at these small pictures, which he finishes with a care and patience that are truly remarkable.*

Of the Florentine Jacopo del Conte,† who, like the abovementioned artist, lives in Rome, I shall have said enough, if to the remarks before made concerning him I here add some few particulars. This artist, then, taking much pleasure from his earliest youth in drawing from the life, desired to make that his principal vocation, although he has occasionally executed a good number of frescoes and other pictures, both in Rome and elsewhere. Of his portraits (not proposing to name them in detail, which would make too long a story) I will only say that, from Pope Paul III. downwards, he has taken likenesses of all the Pontiffs who have since occupied the Papal seat, with those of the Ambassadors

* Marcello Venusti left a son, called Michelagnolo, who neglected painting for art-magic, but after suffering "*a good penance inflicted on him by the Holy Inquisition*," writes a commentator *of our own day* (let the date be remarked), "was restored to the paths of truth."

† A disciple of Andrea del Sarto, for whose Life see Baglioni, *loc. cit.*

and other important personages of their Courts. He has likewise portrayed the military leaders and great men of the House of Colonna, with those of the Orsini family, as he did the Signor Piero Strozzi, with a large number of bishops, cardinals, and other great prelates and nobles, to say nothing of many literary persons and other men of distinction, all which caused him to acquire a considerable reputation in Rome, as well as great gain; insomuch that he dwells at his ease in that city with all his family.

This artist drew so well even from his childhood, that he gave great hope of future excellence, and would doubtless have fulfilled the same, but he devoted himself, as I have said, to that for which he felt most inclined; yet the works he performs are not unworthy of commendation. There is a Dead Christ by his hand, in the Church of the Popolo for example, with a figure of San Luigi, and certain stories in the chapel of St. Denis, which is in the Church dedicated to the first-mentioned Saint, both of great merit. But the best work that he ever produced were the two stories in fresco, formerly executed, as we have said, for the Company of the Florentines at the Misericordia,* with a Deposition from the Cross, wherein are the Thieves, with Our Lady in a swoon, all painted with infinite care and to the great credit of the artist. There are besides, numerous pictures and figures from his hand, dispersed through Rome; with full-length portraits nude and draped, male and female, many of them very beautiful, because the originals were so. Jacopo has also portrayed many Princesses, Ladies, and Gentlewomen, who have been in Rome at different times; among others I know that he took the Signora Livia Colonna, a lady most noble for illustrious birth, for great ability, and for incomparable beauty.

And this shall suffice for Jacopo del Conte, who is still living and working.

I might here mention the names and works of many among our Tuscan artists, and those from other parts of Italy, but I pass over them lightly; some have ceased to work, from their advanced age; others, still young, are but beginning to make attempts, and will more effectually render themselves known by their works than can be done by writings. But of

* The Church of San Giovanni Decollato, where the pictures still are. *Ed. Flor.*, 1831-8.

Adone Doni of Assisi, who is still living, and working, I will add some few particulars, although he has been mentioned in the life of Christofano Gherardi. There are many pictures by his hand in Perugia, and through all Umbria, more particularly in Fuligno; but his best works are at Santa Maria degli Angeli in Assisi, and in the little Chapel where St. Francis died. Here he has depicted Stories from the Life of the Saint; they are painted in oil on the wall, and have been much praised. In the Convent at that place he has likewise painted the Passion of Christ, in fresco; this is at the upper end of the Refectory, and does him much honour; he is besides greatly beloved for the courtesy and liberality of his disposition and conduct.

There are two young men of our calling at Orvieto; the one a painter called Cesare del Nebbia; the other a Sculptor, . . . . . . . * both promising to place their native city, which has hitherto always had to employ foreign masters for her embellishment, in a condition to dispense with such aid, seeing that, if they continue as they have begun, she will not need to employ strangers. There is also now working at Orvieto, in Santa Maria that is to say, which is the Cathedral of that city, a certain Niccolò dalle Pomerance, who, having painted the Resurrection of Lazarus by Our Saviour, has proved by this, and other works in fresco, that he merits a name among the artists above-mentioned.†

We are now come to the end of our Italian masters still living, and I will therefore only say further, that I have heard some mention of a certain Ludovico, a Florentine sculptor, who, as I am told, has produced good works in England, and at Bari, but as I know nothing of his kindred or family name, and have not seen any of his productions, I cannot (as I fain would) do more than allude to him by these few words.

* Della Valle, in the Sienese Edition of our Author, fills up this lacuna by the words, " Lo Scalzo, a rival of Michelagnolo," and of this Scalzo he speaks further in his *Storia del Duomo d'Orvieto.*

† Niccolò Circiniano dalle Pomerance, who was the master of Cristofano Roncalli, called Il Pomarancio.

## OF DIVERS FLEMISH ARTISTS.

Now in many places I have already spoken of the works performed by certain Flemish artists, of much excellence, and more especially of their engravings, but this I have done somewhat vaguely, and will therefore here add the names of some others, who have been in Italy for the purpose of acquiring knowledge in art, and who have for the most part been known to myself, although I have not been able to obtain notices of their works, they meriting, as I think, to be here recorded for their industry, and the labours they have endured for our arts.

I say nothing further of Martin d'Olanda* Giovan Eyck of Bruges, and Hubert his brother, who in 1510 brought to light the invention of painting in oil, because I have spoken of them elsewhere: the latter, having left many works by his hand, as we have before related, in Ghent, Ypres, and Bruges, where he lived and died honourably. But I proceed to say, that after them came Roger Van der Weide, of Brussels, who executed numerous works in various places, but more especially in his native city. In the Town Hall, for example, are four beautiful pictures in oil, the subjects relating to matters that appertain to the administration of justice. This master had a disciple named Hansse,† from whose hand we have a small picture in Florence, representing the Passion of Christ, which is now in possession of the Duke. Next followed the Flemings, Ludvig der Loviano Luven,‡ Peter Christo,§ Justus of Ghent,‖ Hugo of Antwerp,¶ and many others, who never left their native country,

* Martin Schöngauer. Our readers know that Vasari frequently confounds Holland, Flanders, and Germany.

† Hans Memling, called in the Life of Antonello, *Anse*.

‡ This is the Dutch painter, Dierk Von Stuerbout.—*German Edition of Vasari.*

§ Peter Christophson; many small works by whom are at Frankfort. See the *Kunstblatt* for 1841, p. 15, and for 1843, p. 230.

‖ See the *Kunstblatt* for 1841, p. 16. See also Bryan, *Dictionary of Painters*, and the *Handbook* of Kugler, where (vol. ii. of English Edition) there is an elaborate description of his celebrated picture, the Last Judgment, in the Church of St. Mary, at Dantzic.

¶ Hugo Von der Goes. Works by this artist may be seen at Berlin, Munich, &c., and there is one in the Church of Santa Maria Nuova, at Florence.

and constantly abode by the Flemish manner; nay, even Albert Dürer, though he did come into Italy, as we have before said, yet always held to the same manner, exhibiting extraordinary animation and power in his heads, as is well known to all Europe.

But leaving these, with Luca d'Olanda,* and others, in the year 1532, I became acquainted, in Rome, with a certain Michelo Cockuysen,† who gave considerable attention to the Italian manner, and painted many frescos in that city, more particularly two Chapels in Santa Maria *de' Anima.* He subsequently returned to his country, where he proved himself an able artist. I hear that among other works, he copied, for the King of Spain, a picture by Giovanni Eyck, which is in Ghent. The subject of this painting, which was sent into Spain, is the triumph of the *Agnus Dei.* A short time after, Martin Hernskerck,‡ was studying at Rome, an excellent master of figures and landscape he is, and in Flanders he has produced numerous pictures, with designs for engravings, these last have been executed by Jeronimo Cocca (as we have said elsewhere), and whom I also knew while I was at Rome, in the service of the Cardinal Ippolito de' Medici. All these artists have been excellent inventors of Stories, and careful observers of the Italian manner.

In the year 1545, I became known to, and contracted much friendship with Giovanni Calcar, a Flemish painter of great merit, who so successfully practised the Italian manner, that his works were not always perceived to be those of a Fleming; but he died at Naples, while still young, and when the fairest hopes had been conceived respecting his future progress. The anatomical drawings for the work of Vesalio were made by Calcar. But before these, Divile da Lovarico§ had been in high repute as a good master, in that manner, with Quintin,‖ who came from the same country, and who faithfully adhered to the truth of Nature in all his figures, as did a son of his called Giovanni. Gios di Cleves¶ was a

* Lucas of Leyden.

† Michael Coxcie.

‡ The principal work of this master is the Theban Legion in the High Church of Zante.

§ Dierk Von Stuerbout.

‖ Quintin Metsys.

¶ Johann Van Cleef; much valued by Henry VIII., and whose vanity is said to have driven him mad.

great colourist, and an admirable portrait painter, in which branch of art he was much employed by King Francis of France, for whom he painted many of his nobles and ladies.

Renowned painters of those lands have been, and in part still are, Giovanni d'Hemsen;* Mathias Cook, of Antwerp;† Bernhard, of Brussels;‡ Giovanni Cornelis, of Amsterdam;§ Lambert of the same place;‖ Heinrich, of Dinant; Joachim von Partenier, of Bovines, and Johann Schoreel, Canon of Utrecht, who took from Italy into Flanders many new modes of painting. In addition to these, I may name Giovanni Bellagamba, of Douai; Dierich d'Haarlem,¶ of the same place; and Francesco Mostaert,** who displayed much ability in landscapes painted in oil, and in the painting of phantasies, dreams, and other imaginations. He was imitated by Girolamo Hertoghen Bos, and Peter Breughel of Breda. A certain Lancelotto was excellent at painting fires, nights, meteors, devils, and such like; while Piero Coek displayed much invention in his stories, and made excellent Cartoons for tapestry and cloth of arras; he had also a good manner, and considerable practice in architecture; wherefore he has translated into the German tongue, the architectural work of the Bolognese, Sebastiano Serlio.

Giovanni di Mabuse was almost the first who took the true method of representing nude figures and poetical inventions, from Italy into Flanders. The great Tribune of the Abbey of Middleburg in Seeland, is by his hand. Of all these I have received notice from the painter, Maestro Giovanni della Strada,†† of Bruges, and from Giovanni Bologna of Douai, the sculptor,‡‡ both Flemings and excellent artists, as we shall furthermore observe in the treatise on the Academicians.

As to such of the masters belonging to those parts as are

* The principal works of this artist are in the Imperial Collections at Vienna.

† Brother of Hieronimus.

‡ Bernhard Von Horley. His works are also at Vienna.

§ This is the painter Vermeyen.—*German Edition of Vasari.*

‖ Lambert Susterman.

¶ This is again Dierk Von Stuerbout.

** Who worked principally in Spain.

†† Called Stradano. He was ten years with Vasari. See Borghini, *Riposo*, vol. ii. See also Baldinucci, *Notizie de' Professori*, tomo vii. p. 136.

‡‡ For details respecting whom, see Baldinucci, *Notizie*, &c., *ut supra.*

still living and in repute, the more remarkable among them, both for paintings and copper-plates, is Franz Floris,* of Antwerp, disciple of Lambert Lombardo. This artist is considered an excellent one in every branch of his vocation, and it is said that none can exhibit more effectually the expression of grief, gladness, or other passions: he is also much admired for the originality of his fancies, so that, comparing him to the Urbinate, his people call him the Flemish Raphael. It is true that the plates from his works do not very satisfactorily prove to us the justice of that appellation; but however excellent the engraver, he rarely gives full effect to the design and manner of him who first conceived the work. A fellow disciple of Floris was Guglielmo Cay† of Breda, who also studied at Antwerp; a sober-minded, grave, and judicious man, who studied nature with infinite care, and was endowed with good powers of invention. His pictures are remarkable for their harmony, and have much grace and softness, if not equal force and boldness, with those of his fellow student Floris. Cay is, in short, considered to be an admirable artist.

Michele Cockuysen, of whom I have spoken above, remarking that he had taken the Italian manner into Flanders, is also much celebrated among the Flemish painters, being one who imparts an imposing gravity and force to his figures, for which cause the Fleming, Messer Domenico Lampsonio, of whom we shall have more to say in due time, speaking of the artists before mentioned and of Michele, declared that they resembled a fine trio in music, wherein each performer plays his part to perfection. Among the Dutch artists, Antonio Moro,‡ of Utrecht, painter to the Catholic King, is also greatly admired, and of his colours it is said, that in whatever he pleases to design, these colours rival nature herself, and effectually deceive the spectator. Lampsonio writes to me that Moro, who is a man of the most pleasing manners and greatly beloved, has lately painted a resurrection of Christ, with two Angels, and SS. Piero

* Born at Antwerp in 1520, and died there in 1570.

† Wilhelm Kay, or Key, is said to have died of grief for the death of Count Egmont, whose fate he heard Alva determine while painting the portrait of that scourge of his kind and disgrace to humanity.

‡ Anton Moor, a disciple of Johann Schoreel, and good portrait painter.

and Paolo, which, as he tells us, is a production of singular beauty.

A good colourist and esteemed original in his inventions, is Martin Vos,* who paints admirably from the life; but for the execution of fine landscapes, Jacob Grimmer,† Hans Bolz,‡ and some few other artists of Antwerp, are said to be unequalled: yet, I have not been able to obtain minute particulars of these able men. Peter Arsen,§ called Lungo, has painted a picture with folding wings, in his native city of Amsterdam; the subject, Our Lady with Saints. This work cost two thousand crowns. Lambert of Amsterdam‖ is also much spoken of as a good painter. He passed many years in Venice, and obtained considerable practice in the Italian manner. He had a son named Federigo, of whom, as he was one of our Academicians, I propose to speak elsewhere. Peter Breughel of Antwerp, and Lambert Van Hort, of Amersfort in Holland, are also excellent; while Gilis Mostaert,¶ brother of the above-named Franz, is considered a good architect. Peter Pourbus** likewise, although still but a youth, has already given proof that he will eventually become a distinguished painter.

And now, that we may not be wholly unacquainted with the miniaturists of those lands, I add that the masters named below are excellent in that branch of art. Marino of Siressa,†† Lucas Hurembout‡‡ of Ghent, Simon Benich of Bruges,§§

* A scholar of Floris, born 1520, died 1604. For details respecting the numerous masters named thus rapidly, the reader is referred to the authorities before cited, or may consult Bryan, *Dictionary of Painters and Engravers.*

† A disciple of Michael Coxcie and Christian Queeborn.

‡ An engraver as well as painter.

§ Called Long Peter, for his great height; painted principally still-life and glass windows for chambers.—*Förster.*

‖ Lambert Sustris, flourished and lived principally at Munich. He is not to be confounded with Lambert Lombard, or Susterman.—*German Edition of Vasari.*

¶ The twin brother of Franz, and so like him that their own father could not always distinguish the one from the other.

** This must be Franz, the son of Peter, who was born in 1513, and was not a youth when Vasari wrote this (in 1567). Franz Pourbus was an excellent portrait painter, as was his son, also called Franz.

†† Of this artist the present writer can find no authentic account.

‡‡ Gerard Lucas Horebout was in the service of Henry VIII., and died at London in 1558.

§§ Who likewise passed some time in England.

and Gherardo, also of Ghent.* There are besides certain women who have herein distinguished themselves; as, for example, Susanna, the sister of Lucas above-named, who was invited to England by Henry VIII., and lived there in great honour her whole life long; Clara Skeysers of Ghent, who died unmarried at the age of eighty; Anna, daughter of the physician, Maestro Segher; Levina, daughter of the above-named Maestro Simon of Bruges, who was nobly married in England by Henry VIII., was held in great esteem by Queen Mary, and is now in much favour with Queen Elizabeth, have all obtained a name in this art; as hath also Caterina, the daughter of Maestro Giovanni d'Hemsen, who went into Spain, and entered the service of the Queen of Hungary with a very good stipend. There are besides many other excellent miniaturists among the women of those parts.†

In the art of glass and window painting there have also been many masters of great ability in those countries. Among them are Art Van Hort of Nymvegen;‡ Borghese,§ of Antwerp; Jacob Felart;‖ Dittick Stas of Campen; and Johann Ack of Antwerp; by the last of whom are the windows in the Chapel of the Sacrament, in the Church of St. Gudule, at Brussels. We have also two able Flemish painters in Tuscany, Walter and George namely, who have painted several windows for the Duke, at Florence, after the designs of Vasari.

In architecture and sculpture, the most renowned artists among the Flemings are Sebastian d'Oia of Utrecht,¶ who served Charles V. in his Fortifications, as he afterwards did Philip II. Wilhelm of Antwerp, Wilhelm Cucur of Hol-

* This Gerard of Ghent is believed by Morelli, *Notizia di disegno*, &c., to be Gerard Van der Meer; other authorities consider him to be Gerard Horebout. He painted twenty-five miniatures in a MS. for the Library of San Marco in Venice.

† Of these ladies the present writer can find no well-authenticated details of interest.

‡ Arnold Von der Hout; sometimes, but incorrectly, called the inventor of burning the colours into glass. "He is probably," says the German Förster, "the same person with the above-named Lambert Van Hort."

§ Mentioned by Guicciardini, in his description of the Netherlands, but believed to be the same with Simon Benich.

‖ Named by Guicciardini, but unknown to the German writers, as are the two artists whose names follow that of Felart in the text.

¶ He died in 1557, at the age of thirty, but his works are not known.

land,* a good architect and sculptor; Johann Van Dale, a sculptor, poet, and architect; with Jacob Brucer,† a sculptor and architect, who has executed numerous works for the Queen Regent of Hungary; these and some others have all distinguished themselves. The latter mentioned was master of Giovanni Bologna of Douai, our academician, respecting whom we shall have more to say hereafter.

Johan Van Minescheren, of Ghent, is likewise held to be a good architect, and Matteo Manemacken, of Antwerp, is reported to be an excellent sculptor; the latter is now with the King of the Romans. Cornelius Floris, a brother of the above-named Franz, is distinguished in sculpture and architecture; it was by him that the art of executing grottesche was first taken into Flanders. Wilhelm Palidamo, the brother of Heinrich, with Johann Van Sart, of Nymwegen, a most diligent and able sculptor; Simon of Delft, and Gios Jason, of Amsterdam, all give earnest attention to sculpture, as does likewise Lambert Suave, of Liege; all have indeed attained considerable reputation: the last-named of these masters is an excellent architect and engraver of prints with the burin. He has been followed by George Robin, of Ypres, Divick Volcaerts, and Philip Galle;‡ the two last, both of Amsterdam; with Lucas, of Leyden, and many others, have all been in Italy, to design the antiquities, and improve themselves in their art, when they have for the most part returned to their country, and become excellent artists.

But all these have been much surpassed by the before-mentioned Lambert Lombard of Liege, a distinguished man of letters, a most judicious painter, and an admirable architect, the master of Franz Floris, and of Wilhelm Cay. Of the ability displayed by this Lambert and others, I have received notices in the various epistles sent me by Messer Domenico Lampsonio of Liege, a person admirably skilled in letters, and possessing infinite judgment in all things; he was attached to the service of Cardinal Pole, while that

* Believed to be the before-mentioned Peter Koek.—*Förster*.

† Jacob von Breuck, who performed important works at St. Omer and Mons, about 1520-24.

‡ He was born at Haarlem in 1537, and died in 1612, and was the first of a family of artists; for details respecting whom the English reader may consult Bryan, *Dictionary of Painters*, &c.

Prelate lived, having accompanied him to England, and is now Secretary to Monsignore, the Prince Bishop of Liege. Messer Domenico Lampsonio, I say, formerly sent me the Life of Lambert, written in Latin, and I have often received greetings from him in the name of many of our artists, belonging to those lands. One of his letters, dated Oct. 30th, 1564, is of the tenor here following:—

"During four years I have had it in my mind to thank your honourable worship for two important benefits received at your most courteous hands, I know that this exordium may appear strange to you as coming from one whom you have never seen or known; and so it might be, if you, in like manner, were unknown to me; but the matter stands on this wise, my happy fortune, or more properly the goodness of God, had put into my hands your most excellent writings concerning the architects, painters, and sculptors, but at that time I did not understand a word of Italian, whereas now, although I have never seen Italy, yet I thank Heaven that by reading your works I have acquired such little knowledge as emboldens me to write to you as I am now doing. Your writings have inspired me with a wish to learn your language, what perhaps no other book could have done, and to the study of this I was furthermore impelled by the profound and natural love which from my childhood I have borne to those three arts whereof you treat, but most especially to that which gratifies every age, sex, and condition, doing good to all and hurting none, your own art of painting. It is true that when I commenced the reading of your works I was in perfect ignorance respecting those arts, and had no judgment in the matter, but by the frequent and reiterated perusal of your writings, I have acquired so much that, even though it be but little, or almost nothing, does yet suffice to add a cheerfulness and joy to my life, procuring me a pleasure which I value above all the honours, enjoyments, or riches of this world.

And the little whereof I speak is this, that I design or occasionally paint in oil the natural objects before me, more particularly figures nude or draped, but I have not courage to go further and attempt such things as require a firmer and more practised hand, landscapes, trees, waters, clouds, fires, meteors, &c., although it is true that in a case of necessity, and up to a certain point I could perhaps show that the above-named reading of your works has enabled me to do some little even in these matters.* For the present I have nevertheless contented myself with the limning of portraits, and the rather as the numerous duties, necessarily enforced upon me by mine office, do not leave me leisure for more.

"It was my wish, that I might show you my gratitude for having by your means acquired a most beautiful language, and learned to paint, to have sent you herewith a small portrait of my face, taken by myself with the aid of a mirror, but I am doubtful whether this my letter will find you in Rome or not, seeing that you may perhaps now be at Florence or in your native city of Arezzo."

In addition to the above, this letter contains many other particulars which need not be repeated here, and in other epistles that have followed, the writer has begged me, in the name of many able men of those countries, who have heard that these Lives are about to be reprinted, to add three Treatises on sculpture, painting, and architecture to the same, with designs, by way of elucidation, where such might be needful, and so to enforce the rules of art, as Albert Dürer, Sebastian Serlio, and Leon Battista Alberti have done, and whose writings have been translated by the Florentine gentleman and academician, Messer Cosimo Bartoli.

And this I would have done more than willingly, but my intention has been solely to write the Lives and record the works of our Artists, and not to teach the arts, or the method by which the lines are to be drawn in painting, architecture, and sculpture. The work has besides for many causes already grown much upon my hands, and has perhaps become too long, even without the addition of all those three Treatises thus proposed to me. Yet I could not have abridged more closely, or done otherwise than I have done, since it was not fitting that I should defraud any man of his due praise and honour, nor yet that the world should be deprived of the

* The writer of this courteous and gratifying letter, which it rejoices us to imagine our good Giorgio as reading, here alludes to the practical Treatise of our Author, which does not appear in the present edition, which comprises the "Lives" only; his letters and other works not entering into our present plans.

pleasure and profit which I hope that it may derive from the knowledge of the distinguished persons here named, and from these my labours.

---

## OF THE ACADEMICIANS OF DESIGN, PAINTERS, SCULPTORS AND ARCHITECTS; AND OF THEIR WORKS, MORE PARTICULARLY THOSE OF BRONZINO.

HAVING so far written the Lives of the most eminent painters, sculptors, and architects, who have passed to a better life, from the time of Cimabue down to the present day; and having mentioned those still living as occasions were presented to me, there now remains that I say something of the Artists belonging to our Academy of Florence, respecting whom I have not hitherto found opportunity for speaking to sufficient purpose. Beginning with the first and oldest, therefore, I proceed to the Florentine painter, Agnolo, called Il Bronzino, a truly excellent artist, and one most worthy of all praise.

Having been many years with Pontormo, as we have before said,* he acquired the manner of that master to such perfection that their works have frequently been taken one for the other, so exactly did the two artists, for a certain time, resemble each other. And it is of a truth not a little wonderful, that Angelo should have acquired Pontormo's manner so completely, seeing that the latter was always somewhat rude and repulsive, even with his most beloved disciples, not liking indeed that any one should see his works until they were entirely finished. The patience and affection displayed by Agnolo to Pontormo were nevertheless such, that Jacopo could not choose but treat him well, and love him like a son.

The first works of any importance executed by Bronzino were performed while he was still but a youth, at the Certosa of Florence, in two Arches; one on the inside and one on the outside of the door which leads from the great Cloister

* In the Life of Pontormo, vol. iv. See also Borghini, *Riposo*, where we find that Bronzino was born in one of the suburbs of Florence of very poor parents.

into the Chapter House. That on the outside has a Pietà, with two Angels in fresco; that within is a nude figure of San Lorenzo extended on the gridiron: the last is painted in oil on the wall. These paintings gave the first proofs of that excellence which was seen in the works of Bronzino, when arrived at mature age. For the chapel of Ludovico Capponi, in the Church of Santa Felicità, at Florence, this artist painted two Evangelists within two circular compartments, as we have said before;* and in the Ceiling of that chapel he also painted certain figures. In the Abbey of Florence, which belongs to the Black Friars, Bronzino painted a fresco in the upper Cloister; this represents St. Benedict cast naked among thorns, and is an admirable work.† In the garden of the Nuns, called the *Poverine*, he painted a beautiful Tabernacle in fresco, depicting therein Our Saviour Christ appearing to Mary Magdalen in the form of the Gardener; and in the Church of the Trinità, which is also at Florence, there is a picture in oil by the same hand, on the first pilaster to the right, representing the Dead Christ, Our Lady, San Giovanni, and Santa Maria Maddalena, all figures which are executed in an admirable manner and with great care. He painted numerous portraits and other pictures at the same time, from which he obtained a very great reputation.

The siege of Florence being at an end, and the agreement having been made, as we have related, Bronzino repaired to Pesaro, where, in addition to the beautiful Case of the Harpsichord before alluded to, as executed for the Duke Guidobaldo, of Urbino, he painted the portrait of that sovereign; and took, besides, the likeness of a Daughter of Matteo Sofferoni, which last was a truly exquisite and deservedly extolled painting. Bronzino also worked at the Imperiale, a villa of the above-named Duke, where he painted certain figures in oil on the corbels of a Ceiling, and would have done more had he not been recalled to Florence by his master Pontormo, for the purpose of assisting the latter in completing the Hall of Poggio-a-Cajano.

Arrived in Florence our artist painted, as it were for pastime, and in his leisure hours, a small picture of our Lady; this work, which he did for Messer Giovanni de Statis, Auditor of the Duke Alessandro, was very highly commended. Shortly

* See vol. iv. p. 358, *et seq.*

† Still in existence, but showing marks of injury.

afterwards Bronzino painted the portrait of Andrea Doria, for Monsignore Giovio, who was his friend; and for Bartolommeo Bettini he painted the portraits of Dante, Petrarch, and Boccaccio, half-length figures of great beauty, with which Bettini has filled a lunette in his chamber. Having finished these pictures, Bronzino took the likeness of Bonaccorso Pinadori, as he did that of Ugolino Martelli, with those of Messer Lorenzo Lenzi, now Bishop of Fermo; of Pier Antonio Bandini, and of his wife. Nay, at this time, Agnolo took the portraits of so many persons that, to name them all, would lead me too far; let it suffice to say that they were all most natural, executed with extraordinary care, and finished with a delicacy which left nothing to desire.

For Bartolommeo Panciatichi, Bronzino painted two large pictures of the Madonna, with other figures, and these are beautiful to a marvel; he also took the portraits of Bartolommeo and his wife, both so natural that they appear to be living, and want nothing but the breath of life. For the same person Agnolo painted a picture of Christ on the Cross; and this is executed in a manner which proves that the artist really drew from a dead body fixed to a cross, so complete is the perfection of every part. For Matteo Strozzi he painted, in fresco, a Pietà, with Angels in a Tabernacle, at Matteo's villa of San Casciano.* This was a beautiful work, as was also a Birth of Christ, which he painted for Filippo d'Averardo Salviati, in a small picture, the minute figures of which are unequalled, as every one knows, seeing that the work is now engraved. For Maestro Francesco Montevarchi, a distinguished naturalist, Bronzino painted a Madonna, with some small pictures, which are very graceful. He also assisted his master, Pontormo, to paint the Villa of Carreggi, where he executed five figures on the corbels of the vaulting; Fortune, Fame, Peace, Justice, and Prudence namely, with some Children, which are admirably done.

The Duke Alessandro being then dead, and Duke Cosimo elected, Bronzino assisted Pontorno at the Loggia of Castello; and for the nuptials of the most illustrious Lady Leonora de Toledo, wife of Duke Cosimo, he painted two Stories of chiaro-scuro in the Court of the Medici Palace. On the Pedestal which supported the Horse made by Tribolo, he

* This Tabernacle, observes Bottari, is at some distance from the Villa. The painting he described as then (1750) in a grievous condition.

executed Stories in imitation of bronze, as we have before said, representing therein the deeds of the Signor Giovanni de' Medici. These pictures of Agnolo's were the best painted for that solemnity; wherefore the Duke, perceiving Bronzino's ability, commanded him to begin a Chapel for the Signora Duchess, a lady excellent above all that have ever lived, and whose infinite merits render her worthy of eternal praise. In the vaulting of this Chapel, which was not of large size, Bronzino painted beautiful Children, with four figures of Saints, S.S. Francesco, Jeronimo, Michelagnolo, and Giovanni namely, all executed with extreme love and care. On the three walls of the Chapel, the space in two of which is interrupted by the door and window, our artist painted three Stories from the Life of Moses, one on each wall that is to say; on the side of the door is the Story of the Serpents falling on the People; and here are figures, some dying, some dead, and others recovering after having looked on the brazen serpent. On the side wherein is the window we have the Fall of Manna; and in the unbroken wall of the remaining side is the Passage of the Red Sea, with the Submersion of Pharaoh.

The last-mentioned Story has been engraved at Antwerp, and the whole work, completed with all the care possible to a production in fresco, is such that it has not its equal.* The Altar-piece of the Chapel, painted in oil, exhibited Our Saviour Christ deposed from the Cross, and lying in the lap of the Virgin; but this was taken away by Duke Cosimo, who sent it as a work of extraordinary merit to Granvella, the most influential personage then about the Emperor Charles V. The same artist has therefore painted a similar picture, and placed it over the Altar, between two others which are no less beautiful, and which represent the Virgin, with the Angel of the Annunciation.† Before the first altar-piece was removed, however, there were in the place of these a San Giovanni Battista and a San Cosimo; but the Signora Duchess, having changed her mind, these were put into the Guardaroba, and the Virgin with the Angel were painted for the Chapel in their stead.

The Signor Duke, convinced by these and other works of Bronzino's abilities; perceiving, too, that he was particularly

* These frescoes are still in the Palazzo Vecchio.

† Now in the Gallery of the Uffizj.

successful in paintings from the life, which he executed with the utmost care and fidelity, caused his own portrait to be taken, with that of the Signora Duchess, his consort, in another picture; and the likeness of Don Francesco, their son, and Prince of Florence, in a third. The Duke, then young, was represented in white armour, and with one hand on his helmet. No long time after the completion of the above, Bronzino, having pleased the Signora Duchess, was commissioned to take her portrait once again, but in a different manner from the first, and with her son, the Signor Don Giovanni, beside her.* Our artist also portrayed La Bia, the natural daughter of Duke Cosimo, as he subsequently did all the other children of the Duke; some for the first and others for the second time; the Signora Donna Maria, that is to say, the Prince Don Francesco, Don Garzia, and Don Ernando, in various pictures, which are all in the Guardaroba of his Excellency, with the portrait of Don Francesco di Toledo; that of the Signora, mother of his Excellency; and of Ercole, second Duke of Ferrara, as well as many others.

For two years following, Bronzino likewise made the scenic decorations for dramatic representations given in the Palace at the Carnival, and which were considered very beautiful; he also painted a picture which was sent into France to the King Francesco. This represented a nude figure of Venus embraced by her son Cupid: the Pleasures, Loves, and Sports are on one side; and on the other, Fraud, Jealousy, and Passions of similar character.

The Signor Duke having caused Pontormo to commence the Cartoons for cloth of arras in silk and gold, to be woven for the Hall of the Council of the Dugento, and having had two Stories of the Hebrew Joseph executed by Pontormo, with one by Salviati, he ordered that Bronzino should prepare the remainder. Thereupon our artist designed fourteen pieces, all of that excellence and perfection which those who have seen them will remember. But these works giving him too much labour, and requiring too great an expenditure of time, he caused the greater part of the Cartoons to be executed after his own designs, by Raffaello dal Colle, of Borgo a San Sepolcro, who acquitted himself to admiration therein.

Now Giovanni Zanchini had caused a rich chapel to be constructed in the Church at Santa Croce at Florence, and

* This portrait of the Duchess and her son is also in the Uffizj.

opposite to the chapel of the Dini family; for this, which is situate to the left of the entrance and encloses the marble tombs of his forefathers, Giovanni commissioned Bronzino to paint the Altar-piece, requiring him to represent Our Saviour Christ descending to the Gates of Hell to recall the spirits of the Holy Fathers thence. Having set hand to the work accordingly, Agnolo conducted it to completion with the utmost diligence, exhibiting therein many nude figures of men and women, old and young, with children, all displaying various attitudes and singular beauty. There are many Portraits from the life in this work, among them those of Jacopo Pontormo and Giovambatista Gello, a Florentine academician of considerable reputation, with the Painter Bacchiacca, of whom we have before made mention. Among the female figures also are the Portraits of two noble and truly beautiful Florentine maidens, Madonna Costanza da Sommaia, who became the wife of Giovambatista Doni, and Camilla Tedaldi of Corno, who has now passed to a better life.* Not long afterwards, our artist executed another large and beautiful picture, representing the Resurrection of Christ; this was placed in the chapel of Jacopo and Filippo Guadagni, which is near the choir of the church of the Servites, the Nunziata namely;† and at the same time Bronzino executed the picture which replaced, in the chapel of the Palace, the one that had been sent to Granvella; a most beautiful thing it is, and well worthy of the position which it occupies. For the Signor Alamanno, Salviati Bronzino then painted a Venus with a Satyr beside her; the first named figure is so truly exquisite, that it is indeed the Goddess of Beauty in very presence.

Having been invited to Pisa by the Duke, our artist there took certain Portraits for his Excellency, and for Luca Martini his friend, nay, rather the friend and well-beloved of all distinguished men; he painted a beautiful Madonna likewise, with the portrait of Luca himself bearing a basket of fruit: this alludes to the fact that Martini had been the Duke's administrator in the drainage of the marshes and other waters, which had made Pisa insalubrious, but by the removal whereof the district had been rendered healthsome and fruitful. Nor did Bronzino depart from Pisa before he had

* Now in the Uffizj, in the larger Hall of the Tuscan School.
† Still in its place, as indicated in the text.

received, by the intervention of Martini, a commission from Raffaello del Setaiuolo the Superintendent of the Cathedral, to paint the Altar-piece for one of the chapels of that church. In this picture he represented a nude figure, Christ bearing his Cross namely; around him are many Saints, and among them San Bartolommeo, flayed alive, is depicted to such perfection, that he does indeed appear to be a true study of anatomy, and really flayed, as was the case with that saint, so carefully has the painter studied the dissected form, and so successful is the imitation which he has made of the reality before him. This picture was placed in a chapel, whence another, by the hand of Benedetto da Pescia, a disciple of Giulio Romano, had been removed.*

Bronzino subsequently portrayed the Dwarf Morgante for the Duke, depicting him in two manners, the front and back view namely, and displaying all the hideous deformity of those strangely contorted limbs, entirely nude ; nor do these Portraits fail to be fine and admirable in their way. For Ser Carlo Gherardi of Pistoja, who from his youth had been a friend of Bronzino, that artist executed various pictures at different times; the portrait of Ser Carlo namely, a beautiful figure of Judith placing the Head of Holofernes in a basket, and a figure of Prudence looking at herself in a glass; this last he painted on the cover by which the picture of the Judith is closed. He executed a Madonna for the same person, and this is one of the most beautiful ever painted by Bronzino. The Portrait of the Duke, when he had attained his fortieth year, was also taken by this master, with that of the Signora Duchess, and both are as faithful likenesses as they possibly can be.

Now Giovambattista Cavalcanti had caused a Chapel in the Church of Santa Spirito at Florence to be decorated with fine vari-coloured marbles, which he had brought over the sea at great cost; and having here placed the bones of Tommaso his father, he caused the bust of the same to be sculptured by Giovann' Agnolo Montorsoli, and gave Bronzino the Altar-piece, which the latter painted to admiration. The subject chosen was Our Saviour Christ appearing to Mary Magdalen in the form of the Gardener; while in the distance are the two other Maries ; all these figures being executed with indescribable care.

* Benedetto Pagni of Pescia.

Jacopo Pontormo had left the Chapel of San Lorenzo unfinished at his death, and the Signor Duke commanded that Bronzino should complete the same, when he added many nude figures wanting to the lower part of the Deluge, giving infinite perfection to that portion of the work. In the Resurrection of the Dead also, many figures were wanting, and in the space of about a braccio high, but along the whole width of the wall, Bronzino executed these in the beautiful manner we see. Between the windows, in a part left wholly unadorned, he likewise depicted a San Lorenzo stretched naked on the Gridiron, and with Angels in the form of children around him; and here Bronzino displayed judgment superior to that shown by Pontormo his master in the same place; he also depicted the Portrait of his said master in a corner of the chapel, and to the right of San Lorenzo.

The Duke subsequently ordered Bronzino to paint two large pictures, one, a Deposition from the Cross, with numerous figures, to be sent to Porta Ferrajo in the Island of Elba, where it was destined to adorn the Convent of the Barefooted Friars, which his Excellency had built in his city of Cosmopoli;* the other, a Birth of Christ, being intended for the new Church of the Knights of San Stefano, which has since, together with their Palace and Hospital, been erected in Pisa after the designs of Giorgio Vasari. Both these pictures were painted with all the art, diligence, design, invention, and beauty of colouring that can be conceived, nor was less than that due to a Church erected by so great a Prince, and one who founded and endowed the above-mentioned order of Knights.†

Bronzino has furthermore depicted the great men of the House of Medici, on plates of metal, all of the same size, beginning with Giovanni di Bicci, and Cosimo the Elder, and coming down to the Queen of France in that line. In the other line he has gone from Lorenzo, brother of the Elder Cosimo, down to the Signor Duke Cosimo, and his children; all these portraits are ranged in due order, behind

* This picture was washed by certain ignorant persons with a strong lye and much injured, but it is now in the Academy of the Fine Arts at Florence, where it will soon be, so far as possible, restored to its former state.—*Masselli.*

† When Cosimo obtained the relics of St. Stephen from the Pope, he caused the Altar to be entirely reconstructed of porphyry, and the picture of Bronzino was removed.—*Ibid.*

the door of a writing chamber,* which Vasari has caused to be added to the new rooms of the Ducal Palace, and wherein are many antique statues of bronze and marble, with small pictures by modern artists, exquisite miniatures, and a large number of medals, in gold and silver, all arranged in the most perfect order. These portraits of the Illustrious persons of the House of Medici are all exceedingly animated pictures, as well as most faithful likenesses; and it is a great thing in Bronzino, that whereas many artists fall off in their age, he, on the contrary, does even better now than in the best years of manhood, as his works are daily proving.

No long time since, he painted a picture about a braccio and a half high, in the Monastery of the Angeli at Florence, for Don Silvano Razzi, a Monk of Camaldoli, who is very much his friend; the subject is St. Catherine, and the figure is so beautiful that it may bear comparison with any one that has been executed by this noble artist; nay, it seems to want only that spirit and voice with which the Saint confounded the tyrant, and confessed her beloved Lord, even to her latest breath. The father has accordingly no possession which he values more highly than that truly graceful picture. Agnolo likewise painted a portrait of Don Giovanni, Cardinal de' Medici, son of Duke Cosimo, and this was sent to the Court of the Emperor, for the Queen Joanna; the same master afterwards portrayed Don Francesco, Prince of Florence, a most faithful likeness, and so carefully finished, that it has the effect of a miniature.

At the marriage of the Queen Joanna, of Austria, wife of the above-mentioned Prince, Bronzino painted three great pictures, which were placed on the Bridge of the Carraja, as will be related hereafter. He represented therein certain stories, from the Nuptials of Hymen, which were so beautiful that they did not seem like paintings executed for a festival, but were rather like works intended to be permanently fixed in some most honourable position, where they might endure for ever. A few months since, he furthermore painted a small picture, full of minute figures, that have not their equal, and may rather be called fine specimens of miniature. Nor is Bronzino less enamoured of his art now, in his sixty-fifth year, than he was as a youth; he has lately undertaken two

* They are now in the Gallery of the Uffizj, in a room appropriated to the Directory of the building.—*Ed. Flor.*, 1832-8.

stories in fresco, which the Signor Duke desires to have painted on the wall beside the Organ, in the Church of San Lorenzo, and we cannot doubt but that he will here prove himself that excellent Bronzino, whom we have always known him to be.*

This master has besides taken great pleasure in poetry, and has written many stanzas and sonnets, some of which have been printed; but he is above all remarkable (as regards poetry) for his success in rhymes written after the playful manner of Berni;† nor have we any one in our day who is more ingenious, varied, fanciful, and spirited, in this jesting kind of verse, than Bronzino, as all will see, if the whole of his works should some day be printed, as it is believed and hoped that they will be. Our artist is, and ever has been, most liberal of all that he possesses, and most kindly in all things, as it is possible for any one, even an artist, noble as he is, to be; gentle of disposition, he has never offered injury to any one, and has ever loved the distinguished men of his own vocation, as well we know who have lived on terms of close friendship with him for three and forty years, from 1524 that is, to the present year of 1567; since it was at the first mentioned period, when he was labouring at the Certosa, with Pontormo, that I first began to know and love this man; I then going, as a youth, to draw from the works of Jacopo, at that place.‡

Bronzino has had may followers and disciples, but the first (to speak now of our own Academicians) is Alessandro Allori, who has been ever beloved by his master, not as a disciple only, but as if he were his own son; they have

* One only, a Martyrdom of San Lorenzo, was painted, and that still retains its place.

† The burlesque poems of Bronzino are declared by the Academy Della Crusca to be models of their manner. Seven of them will be found (as the present writer is informed) among the early printed works of Berni, others in an edition published at Naples in 1723, but dated, "Florence and London." The whole were printed, but, as it is said, from an incorrect copy, at Venice, in 1822, and a part of Bronzino's Canzoni and Sonnets was published for the first time at Florence in 1822-3.

‡ Borghini, in his *Riposo*, says that Bronzino died in his sixty-ninth year, but does not give the date. "In a Book of the Guild of Painters, however, I (Bottari) have found him mentioned as down for the tax, on the 1st of November, 1572, but the tax is not marked as *paid*;" whence we may infer that Bronzino died towards the end of that year, or the commencement of the following; about four years after Vasari wrote the above, that is to say.

lived, nay, still do live together, in all the love which is usually found to exist between a good parent and his child. Alessandro then, in the pictures and portraits executed up to his present age of thirty years, has proved himself to be the worthy disciple of so great a master, and is constantly seeking to attain by diligence and perpetual study, to that highest perfection to which all noble and elevated minds aspire. He has painted the Chapel of the Montaguti, in the Church of the Nunziata, entirely with his own hand; the Altar-piece in oil that is to say, and the walls and ceiling in fresco. On the Altar-piece we have Christ and the Madonna in the heavens; they are seated in judgment and beneath them are numerous figures, well executed, and in various attitudes, which are copied from the Last Judgment of Michelagnolo Buonarroti. On the same side of the Chapel are four large figures, representing Prophets, or perhaps Evangelists; and on the ceiling are Sibyls and Prophets, executed with infinite thought and care, Allori having endeavoured to imitate Michelagnolo in the figures.*

On the wall to the right, as you face the Altar, is Christ disputing with the Doctors in the Temple. The Child, whose attitude is good, appears to be replying to the arguments of the Doctors, all of whom, with other figures standing near, exhibit a rich variety in the countenances, attitudes, and vestments: there are among them numerous portraits ot the friends of Allori, which are very faithful as to resemblance. On the wall, opposite to this picture, is Christ driving the Traders from the Temple, a work wherein there are many parts which merit praise. Over these two pictures are Stories from the Life of the Virgin; and in the ceiling are figures of no great size, but graceful and well arranged; there are besides landscapes and buildings, which prove the love which Allori bears to art, and the care with which he seeks perfection in design and invention.†

In the upper part of the wall opposite the Altar is the Story of Ezekiel with the dry bones, which become re-

* All the painters here mentioned by Vasari belonged to the School of Michael Angelo; Alessandro Allori, who was the nephew of Bronzino, being one of those who most deserve mention. He had a son called Cristofano, who would never follow the paternal manner, but, adhering to that of Correggio, declared that in painting his father was a heretic.

† Those pictures have been retouched.

clothed with flesh; here this young artist has shown the zeal with which he laboured to acquire the anatomy of the human form,* and in this, his first important work, as well as in the rilievi and paintings executed for the nuptials of his Highness, he has given an excellent specimen of his powers and awakened many hopes. Allori is thus continually labouring to render himself a good painter, and in the above-named as well as in certain smaller works (more especially in a little picture after the manner of a miniature executed for Don Francesco Prince of Florence, which is highly praiseworthy) he is studying to obtain facility and to form a fine manner.†

Another youth called Giovanni Butteri, also the disciple of our academician Bronzino, has likewise displayed much readiness and facility; in that which he did, for example, when the obsequies of Michelagnolo were solemnized, and at the arrival in Florence of her most Serene Majesty Joanna, as well as in other works of minor importance.‡

The painter Cristofano dell' Altissimo was also the disciple, first of Pontormo and afterwards of Bronzino; after having in his youth depicted numerous works in oil and some portraits, Cristofano was sent by Duke Cosimo to copy the many portraits of illustrious personages which are in the Gallery of Monsignore Giovio, and which that distinguished person, one of the most learned men of our own day, has collected. The Duke has besides many other works executed for him by the cares of Giorgio Vasari. The list of all these portraits shall be added to the index of this work,§ but here we will not speak more of them than to say that Cristofano has acquitted himself very zealously of his commission, having already copied more than two hundred and eighty of those pictures for the Guardaroba of the

* "The Ezekiel never has been, nor could have been painted here," remarks an Italian commentator, "the space not sufficing to contain it; but there is a work on that subject by Allori, in the garden of a house in the Via Ghibellina, and Vasari may have mistaken the site of the work."

† For the vast number of works executed by Allori after the publication of these Lives, and for other details concerning him, which cannot here find place, the reader is referred to Baldinucci, *Decennali*, tom. x. p. 171, *et seq.* In the Uffizj is a work executed by Allori, when in advanced years, and which bears his name, *Allessandro Bronzino Allori*.

‡ This artist never passed beyond mediocrity.

§ The list appeared in the *Giunti Edition* of our author, accordingly.

Duke, where they are arranged in three lines, as will be related when we speak further of the ornaments of that apartment: the copies consist of popes, emperors, kings, and other princes, with military leaders, men of learning, and persons of eminence; at a word, from whatever cause they have become illustrious.

We also shall of a truth be all deeply indebted to the care of Giovio and the Duke,* seeing that from this beginning, not only the apartments of princes but the chambers of private persons are now being adorned with portraits of one or another among these illustrious men, as the partialities of country, family, or friendship shall decide. Cristofano, then, has fixed himself to this kind of work for which his genius, or perhaps I should say inclination, disposed him; and he has done little besides, as finding that he derives honour and profit in abundance from this.

Stefano Pieri and Lorenzo dello Sciorina† are likewise disciples of Bronzino; they both distinguished themselves in the obsequies of Michelagnolo, as well as for the marriage of his Highness, and that in a manner which has caused them to be placed among the number of our academicians.

From the same school of Pontormo and Bronzino, came also Battista Naldini, of whom we have spoken elsewhere;‡ and who, having passed some time in Rome, after the death of Pontormo, has made considerable improvement, insomuch that he has become a bold and able painter, as is seen by various works executed by his hand for Don Vincenzio Borghini, who has employed him frequently and assists him very much, as he does Francesco da Poppi, a young artist, and also one of our academicians. This Francesco has acquitted himself exceedingly well in the preparations for the marriage of his Highness, as have other young men whom Don Vincenzio is constantly employing and assisting. Vasari likewise has availed himself of Battista's services for more than two years, and still continues to do so for the works of the Ducal Palace in Florence, where, in emulation with the many other young artists who also work at that

* These portraits hang along the Corridor of the Uffizj, and their number has been much increased since Vasari wrote.—*Masselli.*

† The first worked principally for other painters, the second was distinguished only for a certain correctness of design.

‡ For whose Life, see Baldinucci, *Notizie de' Professori.*

place, he has made great improvement, and may now consider himself equal to any of the younger men of our Academy. Among other qualities in this youth which please men of knowledge, is that he is prompt, and performs his work without effort. In a picture which Battista has painted in oil for the Black Friars of the Abbey of Florence, he has represented a Story of Christ bearing his Cross, wherein there are many good figures, and he has now works on hand which will suffice to make him known as an able artist.

Not inferior to any of these in genius, talent, and worth, is Maso Mazzuoli,* called Maso of San Friano, a young man, now about thirty or thirty-two years old, who acquired the first principles of his art under our academician Pier-Francesco di Jacopo di Sandro, of whom we have spoken elsewhere. This Maso, besides having shown us of what he is capable, and what may be hoped from him in many small pictures, has lately displayed two large paintings, which do him great honour and give universal satisfaction, since he has exhibited therein much invention, correct design, a good manner, infinite grace, and admirable harmony of colouring. One of these pictures, which is in the Church of Sant' Apostolo in Florence, is the Nativity of our Saviour Christ; and in the other, which is in the Church of San Pietro Maggiore, and is as beautiful as it could have been if executed by an old and experienced master, we have the Visitation of Our Lady to St. Elizabeth; a work which does indeed display much forethought and judgment: the heads, the attitudes, the draperies, the buildings, every part of it, at a word, is full of beauty and grace. This artist, as one of our Academy, and a man of most obliging disposition, acquitted himself well in the obsequies of Buonarroti; and in the preparations made for the nuptials of the Queen Joanna, he distinguished himself very highly.

And now, as in the Life of Ridolfo Ghirlandajo, and other places, I have spoken of Michele, Ridolfo's disciple, and, of Carlo da Loro, I will say nothing more of them here although they are of our Academy, having already mentioned them sufficiently.

But I will not omit to relate that Andrea del Minga, another of our academicians, who has performed and is per-

* Tommaso d'Antonio Manzuoli, not Mazzuoli.—*Ed. Flor.*, 1832-8.

forming numerous works of merit, was also a disciple and follower of Ghirlandajo; as were likewise Girolamo di Francesco Crocifissaio,* a youth of twenty-six years old, and Mirabello di Salincorno, both painters, who have executed, and are executing, numerous works in oil and fresco, with portraits also. These artists, too, give hope of a very successful future, and some years have now elapsed since they painted in company certain frescoes, which are very fair works, and may be seen in the Church of the Capuchins, outside of Florence. In the obsequies of Michelagnolo, and the nuptials above-mentioned, they likewise did themselves great honour. Mirabello has furthermore painted numerous portraits, that of the most Illustrious Prince among others, and this he has taken many times with those of various persons, now in the possession of divers Florentine gentlemen.

The Fleming, Federigo di Lamberto, of Amsterdam, son-in-law of the Paduan Cartaro, also greatly honoured our Academy as well as himself, in the obsequies and nuptials aforesaid, and has besides given proof of much judgment, very correct design, and a good manner, in many pictures in oil, large and small, with other works. But if he has merited commendation up to the present time, much more will he do so in the future, since he is still labouring with manifest progress in Florence, which he appears to have adopted as his country, and where the emulation and competition existing among so many young men is of infinite advantage to those artists.

A very fine genius and extraordinary wealth of felicitous fancies, are likewise displayed by Bernardo Timante Buontalenti,† who acquired the first principles of design, when in his childhood, from the works of Vasari, and has since made so much progress, that he is now in the service of the most illustrious Signor, Don Francesco Medici, Prince of Florence, with whom he has been for some years, and who favours him greatly, having long kept, and still keeping him constantly employed. Buontalenti has thus executed for his Excellency many works painted in miniature, after the manner of Don Giulio Clovio, as, for example, numerous portraits and stories in small figures, which are finished with

* Girolamo Macchietti.

† For details respecting this gifted and versatile artist, let our readers consult Baldinucci, *Decennali*, vol. vii. p. 3.

great care. The same artist has made a splendid library table, by command of Don Francesco, constructing the work of ebony, divided into compartments by columns of eliotrope, oriental jasper, and lapis lazuli, which have bases and capitals of chased silver. The work is furthermore enriched with jewels, beautiful ornaments of silver and exquisite little figures interspersed with miniatures and termini of silver and gold in full relief, united in pairs. There are besides other compartments formed of jaspers, agates, eliotropes, sardonyxes, carnelians, and other precious stones, to describe all which here would make too long a story: let it suffice to say that in this work, which now draws near its completion, Bernardo has given proof of a most admirable genius, and one ready for every purpose.

Don Francesco accordingly avails himself of his services for various labours; in the construction of machines for lifting weights for example, and many other ingenious inventions. Bernardo has also discovered a method by which Rock-crystal may be readily melted and purified; of this substance he has made Vases and Stories of various colours. This artist meddles with every kind of art; and in a short time we shall see such Vases of porcelain as will equal in beauty the most perfect of those executed in the highest antiquity, of which they will have all the qualities. Another excellent master in these works is Giulio da Urbino, who is now in the service of the most illustrious Duke Alfonso II. of Ferrara; this Giulio makes Vases of amazing beauty from earths of different kinds; and in porcelain he forms them of the most exquisite shapes. From the same clays he likewise makes octagons, circles, and squares for pavements, all of extraordinary hardness, and so neatly arranged in imitation of vari-coloured marbles, that they appear to be made of the stones themselves, rather than of mere imitations formed out of clay. Of all these things our Prince is in possession of the processes and modes of manipulation.

His Excellency has also lately commenced the construction of a small table richly adorned with jewels, and which he proposes to make the companion of one which belongs to his father Duke Cosimo. Not long since, moreover, he completed a small table after the design of Vasari, which is a very splendid production, being wholly formed of oriental alabaster intermingled with great pieces of carnelian, jasper, eliotrope, lapis, and agate, with other stones and jewels worth twenty thousand crowns. The execution of this table was confided to Bernardino di Porfirio of Leccio, a place in the neighbourhood of Florence. Bernardino is admirable in works of this kind, and has executed an octangle of ebony and ivory, inlaid with jaspers, for Messer Bindo Altoviti, after the designs of Vasari. This Bernardino is still in the service of their Excellencies.

But returning to Buontalenti I add, that, contrary to the expectation of many, he proved himself capable of painting large figures equally well with small ones, by that great Story which he prepared for the obsequies of Michelagnolo, as we have before related. He was employed, to his great credit, at the nuptials of our Prince also; for certain maskings that is to say, for the Triumph of Dreams, of which I propose to speak elsewhere, and for the Interludes of the Dramatic Spectacle given at the Palace, as other writers have related at full length. Nay, had Bernardo attended to the studies of art in his first youth (he is now but thirty years old), as he did to the construction of fortresses, in which he spent much time, he would now perchance have attained to an unusually high degree of eminence; it is indeed even yet expected that he will do so, although somewhat later, seeing that he is all genius and talent, and has besides the further advantage of being constantly employed by his sovereign in the most honourable occupations.

The Fleming, Giovanni della Strada, is also one of our Academicians; and to good design, a rich fancy, and admirable power of invention, this artist adds an excellent method of colouring; he has worked much in fresco, in oil, and in tempera, during the last ten years, under the direction and from the designs of Giorgio Vasari, in the Ducal Palace: Giovanni may indeed declare himself the equal of any painter in the Duke's service. But his principal occupation just at present is to prepare Cartoons for arras, also after the designs of Vasari, which the Duke and Prince are causing to be made in divers manners to correspond with the paintings executed by Vasari in the upper parts of the various chambers of the Palace, to the end that the tapestries below may be in harmony with the pictures above. For the Halls of Saturn, Ops, Ceres, Jupiter, and Hercules, Giovanni has made very beautiful Cartoons for about thirty pieces of arras, with others, also very fine, for the upper rooms occupied by the Princess; and of these, four are devoted to the virtues of women, and display histories of Roman, Hebrew, Greek, and Tuscan ladies, taken from the lives of Sabina, Esther, Penelope, and Gualdrada. For ten panels of a Hall wherein is delineated the Life of Man, Giovanni has also made Cartoons, as he has for the five lower rooms, which are occupied by the Prince, and which are decorated with stories from the Lives of David, Solomon, Cyrus, and others.

For the Palace of Poggio-a-Cajano, wherein twenty rooms are to be supplied with arras, now daily making progress, Giovanni has made Cartoons of Hunting-pieces after the invention of the Duke; they exhibit all kinds of animals of the chase, and portray the various modes of fowling and fishing, with the most singular and beautiful fancies. In this work, the variety of animals, birds, fish, landscapes, and vestments, with the hunters, on foot and on horseback, the fowlers in various attitudes, and the nude figures of the fishermen, have proved this Strada to be a truly able man, well skilled in the Italian manner. It is his purpose to live and die at Florence, in the service of his illustrious lords, and in the company of Vasari and the other Academicians.

Another disciple of Vasari, and also an Academician, is the Florentine Jacopo di Maestro Piero Zucca,* now about twenty-five or twenty-six years old; having assisted Vasari in the greater part of his works at the palace, but more especially in the ceiling of the Great Hall, by his industry, care, and diligence, he has acquired so much knowledge of design and facility in the handling of colours, that he may be considered among the first of the young painters in our Academy. The works which he executed alone in the obsequies of Michelagnolo, and at the marriage of the Prince, with others for certain of his friends, in all which he has displayed intelligence, boldness, care, grace, and judgment, have made him known as a clever youth and able painter, but still more may yet be hoped from him in the future, when he will doubtless do as much honour to his country as any other of her painters.

Among the younger artists of the Academy, Santi Tidi†

* For the many works executed by Jacopo Zucchi, in Rome and elsewhere, see Baglioni, *Vite*, p. 45.

† Santo Tito, not Tidi. See Borghini and Baldinucci, *ut supra*.

may likewise be accounted an ingenious and able master. Having laboured for many years in Rome, as we have said elsewhere, he has now returned to enjoy himself in Florence, which he considers his home, although his family belongs to Borgo-a-San Sepolcro, where it holds a very honourable place. This artist certainly acquitted himself perfectly well in all that he did for the funeral of Michelagnolo, and the wedding of the most Serene Princess, but he distinguished himself principally in the stories, which, with incredible labour, he depicted for the theatre which he constructed on the Piazza San Lorenzo, for the most illustrious Paolo Giordano Orsino, Duke of Bracciano, on the occasion of the same marriage. Here, on great pieces of canvas, he delineated stories from the Lives of the most distinguished men of the Casa Orsina. The ability of Santo Tidi may however be more accurately judged from two pictures by his hand, one of which is in Ognissanti, or rather San Salvadore di Fiorenza (for so is that Church now called), which formerly belonged to the Padre Umiliati, but is now the Church of the Barefooted Friars. In the upper part of this work is the Madonna, and beneath are S.S. Giovanni, Girolamo, and others; the second picture is in the Chapel of the Guardi in the Church of San Giuseppe, which is behind that of Santa Croce; it is a Nativity of Christ painted with great care, and presenting numerous portraits from the life. This artist has besides executed many pictures of the Madonna, and various portraits both in Rome and Florence; he has also worked in the Vatican, as we have said before.

Other young painters, some Florentine and some belonging to other parts of the Tuscan States, who were employed for the before-mentioned solemnities, are also members of our Academy. Among them may be named Alessandro del Barbiere, now about twenty-five years old, who, among other works, depicted the front of the Great Hall for those Nuptials, under the direction and with the designs of Vasari. Here the Piazzas of all the cities in the Duke's dominions were delineated, and in the execution of this painting Alessandro certainly acquitted himself well, giving evidence of much judgment and offering fair hopes of future success. Many others among Vasari's disciples and friends, have likewise assisted him in these and other works, Domenico Benci for example, with Alessandro Fortori of Arezzo, Stefano

Veltroni, the cousin of Giorgio, and Orazio Porta, both of the Monte San Savino; Tommaso del Verrocchio also has been one among these assistants.

There are besides many excellent foreign artists in the same Academy, but of these we have spoken at length in various places; it shall therefore here suffice to mention their names, to the end that they may not fail to be enumerated with the other Academicians. These then are: Federigo Zucchero, Prospero Fontana, and Lorenzo Sabatini, of Bologna; Marco da Faenza, Tiziano Vecellio, Paolo Veronese, Giuseppe Salviati, Il Tintoretto, Alessandro Vettoria; the sculptor Danese; the Veronese painter, Battista Farinato; and the architect, Andrea Palladio.*

But now, to say some few words of the sculptors who are Academicians, and of their works, in which I do not intend to be very diffuse, nevertheless, because they still live, and are for the most part of high fame, I add that the Florentine citizen, Benvenuto Cellini (to begin with the oldest and most honoured), now a sculptor, was without an equal, when, in his youth, he gave his attention to the art of the goldsmith; nor, perhaps, for many years was there any to compare with him in that calling, and in the execution of figures whether in full or low relief, nay, in all the other works proper to the vocation of the goldsmith. He set jewels and adorned the settings themselves with minute figures, so well formed and often so fancifully imagined that better would not well be conceived. The medals of gold and silver which Benvenuto also executed in his youth, can scarcely be sufficiently extolled. For Pope Clement VII. he made the brooch of a Cope or Pluvial, wherein he set a diamond, beautifully surrounded by minute figures of children in gold plate, and finished above with a figure of God the Father, most admirably executed. Wherefore, besides the payment, Benvenuto received from His Holiness the office of a mace-bearer.

The same Pontiff afterwards gave him a golden goblet to make; the cup was to be adorned with figures of the Theological Virtues, and this Benvenuto executed with marvellous art. At that time there was none among the many by whom

* A name so well known to our readers as to need no further mention in the closely restricted space for notes which alone now remains at our command.

medals were made for Pope Clement, who succeeded better than did Cellini, as is well known to those who have seen or possess any of the same. He therefore received the care of the dies for the Roman Mint; nor have more beautiful coins ever been seen than are those then stamped in Rome. After the death of Clement, Benvenuto returned to Florence, where he also struck the dies with the head of Duke Alessandro for the Mint of Florence, executing the same so admirably and with such care that they are now kept as might be the most beautiful ancient medals, and with good reason, seeing that in these Cellini surpassed himself.

Having ultimately turned his attention to Sculpture and casting in metal, Benvenuto performed numerous works in France, some of which were in bronze, gold, and silver, he being for a certain time in the service of Francesco King of that realm. Having subsequently returned to his native country, he entered the service of Duke Cosimo, by whom he was at first employed in goldsmiths' work, but who finally gave him commissions for works in sculpture. The Perseus, in metal, cutting off the Head of Medusa, which is near the gate of the Palace in the Piazza del Duca; is by the hand of Cellini; it stands on a pedestal of marble, decorated with most beautiful figures in bronze, each about one braccio and a third in height. This whole work was executed with so much care, and has in truth been completed to such perfection, that it worthily occupies the above-named position, where it stands together with the Judith of that most renowned and admirable sculptor Donato. Nor is it a little extraordinary that Benvenuto, so long occupied with works of such minute character, should so successfully have executed a statue of such size and importance.

He has also made a Crucifix in marble, which is in full relief and the size of life, the most beautiful work of its kind that could well be seen; wherefore the Signor Duke has had it brought to the Pitti Palace, as a thing greatly valued by himself; and it is to be placed in the Chapel, or rather small Church, which is now constructing there; nor can this church be provided in our times with any ornament more worthy of itself, or of so great a Prince, than this Crucifix, which it would be difficult to commend sufficiently.

I might easily find much more to say respecting the works of Benvenuto Cellini, who has given proof in all his productions of a bold, proud, animated, prompt, and forceful character; he is, indeed, a man but only too well disposed and able to hold his own by word in the presence of Princes, as well as ready with hand and spirit in matters of art; yet I will not here say more, because he has himself written a Treatise concerning his Life and Works, with one on the Art of the Goldsmith, on founding and casting in Metal, as well as on other matters appertaining to those arts: he has spoken of Sculpture likewise with much more eloquence and to more purpose than might, perhaps, be possible to myself; wherefore, as regards Benvenuto, it shall suffice me to have thus indicated some few among the best of his principal works.*

Francesco, the son of Giuliano da Sangallo, a sculptor and architect, also one of our Academicians, and now seventy years old, has likewise produced numerous works in sculpture, as we have said in the Life of his father. The three figures in marble, somewhat larger than life, which are on the Altar in the Church of Or San Michele, are by his hand. They are much extolled, and represent Sant' Anna, the Virgin, and Our Saviour Christ as a Child. Some other Statues, also in marble, on the Tomb of Piero de' Medici at Monte Cavallo, are likewise by his hand, as is the Sepulchre of the Bishop of Marzi in the Nunziata; and that of the historian Monsignore Giovio.† The same master has also executed many fine works in architecture at Florence and elsewhere; and his many valuable qualities, with the services performed by his father Giuliano, have secured to him the good-will of the House of Medici, for which cause the Duke Cosimo gave him the place of Architect to the Cathedral of Florence, when the death of Baccio d'Agnolo left that office vacant.

Of Ammannato, who is among the chief of our Academicians, I need not speak further, since we have said enough of him in describing the works of Jacopo Sansovino, and I will but add, that the very able Sculptor, Andrea Calamec of Carrara, also an Academician, was his disciple: the latter

* Benvenuto Cellini frequently speaks of Vasari in a manner which proves his ill-will to that master, whom he doubtless—rude and eccentric as he was—very frequently offended, yet no one could discover any trace of resentment in what is here said by our upright and impartial author.

† The tomb of Giovio is in a recess, near the side door of the Cloister of San Giovanni Laterano.

executed numerous works under the direction of Ammannato; but having been invited to Messina after the death of Martino, to occupy the place formerly held in that island by Fra Giovann' Agnolo, he there died. Battista di Benedetto, a youth who has already given evidence of future success, was also the disciple of Ammannato; his many works produced thus early show him to be in nowise inferior to the above-mentioned Andrea, or to any other of the young sculptors who are Academicians, whether in genius or judgment.

The Sculptor and Architect, Vincenzio de Rossi, of Fiesole, also a member of the Florentine Academy, is in like manner worthy of a memorial in this place, in addition to what has been said of him in the Life of Baccio Bandinelli, whose disciple he was.* Having left his master, Vincenzio, though still young, gave a favourable specimen of his ability in a group, representing San Giuseppe with Our Saviour Christ, a child of about ten years old, which he executed for the Ritonda; both of these figures being in a very good manner, and giving evidence of great facility. He afterwards constructed two Tombs in the Church of Santa Maria della Pace, the figures of those within them are in a recumbent position on the sarcophagi; and on the external front are figures of Prophets in half-relief, which are of the size of life, and have acquired for Vincenzio the name of an excellent Sculptor. This caused him to be commissioned by the Roman people to execute the Statue of Pope Paul IV., which was placed on the Capitol, and wherein he acquitted himself exceedingly well; but this work had not a long life, seeing that when the Pontiff died, his Statue was destroyed by the populace, ever prone to persecute fiercely to-day those whom they were yesterday exalting to the skies.

At a later period, Vincenzio executed two Statues, somewhat larger than life, carved in one piece of marble; the subject is Theseus, King of Athens,† who has carried off Helen, and holds her in his arms; beneath his feet there lies

* Many details of interest respecting this sculptor will be found in Borghini, *ut supra*.

† A commentator thinks it well to assure us that this must needs be Paris, and not Theseus. Our friend is right without doubt, but the dear Giorgio has already told us that his eyes were more familiar with the painter's palette than with the page of the mythologian, *et hoc genus omne*.

the figure of a Trojan; Statues more graceful, or more carefully executed than these are, could not well be imagined: it chanced therefore, that when Duke Cosimo visited Rome, he went to see such modern works as he thought worthy of remark, no less than the ancient productions; when, being shown these Statues, and justly commending them, they were courteously presented to his Excellency, by Vincenzio, who at the same time offered his services to the Duke. It is true that when Duke Cosimo had transported the Statues to his Palace of the Pitti, he paid a very good price for the work, and having brought Vincenzio with him likewise, he commissioned him no long time afterwards to execute the Labours of Hercules, in marble; commanding him to represent the same in figures, larger than life, and in full relief. With these Vincenzio is now occupied, he has already completed the Slaying of Cacus, and the Combat with the Centaur, and as the work is of an exalted and difficult character, so, as it is hoped, will it prove an excellent production of art; Vincenzio possessing a fine genius, with much judgment, and being very thoughtful in the conduct of all matters of importance.

Nor will I omit to mention, that under the discipline of this artist, the young Florentine citizen, Ilarione Ruspoli is devoting himself to Sculpture in a manner which does him great honour; and when the obsequies of Michelagnolo, with the marriage so frequently alluded to, presented him with an opportunity, he showed equal excellence of design and facility in the production of statues, with the other Academicians of his age.

Francesco Camilliani, a Florentine Sculptor and Academician, who was the disciple of Baccio Bandinelli, after having proved himself an excellent Sculptor, by many good works, has consumed fifteen years in executing ornaments for Fountains. One of these, which he has made for Don Luigi di Toledo, at his Garden in Florence, is certainly most surprising; the decorations which surround it, are various figures of men and animals, represented in divers attitudes, but all graceful and effective; the entire work is indeed rich and magnificent, nay, truly regal, and has been completed without sparing any amount of cost thereon.* Among the

* This Fountain, comprising 644 pieces of marble, was sold to the city of Palermo, in the year 1573, for the sum of 20,000 crowns, and the

rest, are two larger than life, which represent the rivers Arno and Mugnone; they are exceedingly beautiful, more especially the Mugnone, which may bear comparison with the best statues of the most eminent masters. At a word, all the architecture and decorations of this garden are by Francesco, who, by the magnificence of the various Fountains, which he has constructed therein, has rendered it such, that it has not its equal in Florence, nor perhaps in Italy; nay, the principal Fountain, which is now on the point of completion, will be the most rich and sumptuous that can be seen in any place, whether for the splendid ornaments, or for the vast abundance of waters, which will never fail at any time.

The Flemish Sculptor, Giovanni Bologna, of Douai,* is also of our Academy, and his remarkable ability has caused him to be much in the favour of our Princes. He is indeed a young man of singular talent, and it is by him that the new Fountain on the Piazza of San Petronio,† opposite to the Palace of the Signori, at Bologna, has been constructed: among other ornaments, there are four Syrens at the angles, which are exceedingly beautiful, as are also the Children and fanciful Masks by which it is surrounded. But the most remarkable part of this work is a figure of Neptune, six braccia high, placed over the centre of the Fountain, and which is a most beautiful casting, the figure being studied and executed to perfection. And, not to speak now of what this artist has produced in clay, terra-cotta, wax, and other materials, he has executed a beautiful Venus, in marble, and almost completed a Sampson, the size of life, in combat with two Philistines, for the Signor Prince. He has likewise made the figure of Bacchus, in bronze, larger than life and in full relief, with a Mercury in the act of flight, which is very ingenious, the whole figure resting on the point of the foot: this has been sent to the Emperor, Maximilian, as the extraordinary work that it certainly is.‡ But if Giovanni

architect Camillo Camilliani went to that city for the purpose of superintending its erection.—*Ed. Flor.*, 1832-8.

* For the Life of this admirable sculptor and architect, see Baldinucci, *Decennali*, tom. vii. p. 87.

† Not on the Piazza of San Petronio, but before the Palace of the Podestà.—*Ed. Flor.*, 1832-8.

‡ This work was most probably not sent to Maximilian, for although some affect to believe that the one so long adorning the Fountain of the

Bologna has hitherto produced fine works, still finer may we expect from him in the future, seeing that the Signor Prince, after giving him rooms in the Palace, has lately commissioned him to execute a Statue, of five braccia high, representing the Goddess of Victory, with a Captive;* and this work, which is to be placed in the Hall, opposite to one by Michelagnolo, being accomplished, Giovanni will be employed in many other great and important undertakings for the same Prince, thus obtaining a wide field for the display of his powers.

Beautiful models by the hand of Giovanni Bologna are now in the possession of the Florentine gentlemen, Messer Bernardo Vecchietti, and of Maestro Bernardo the son of Mona Mattea, the Duke's master builder, who has erected, with great ability, all the edifices designed by Vasari. Nor less remarkable, for his fine genius, than Giovanni and his friends, is Vincenzio Danti of Perugia,† a youth who, under the protection of Duke Cosimo, has adopted Florence as his country. Vincenzio first gave his attention to the art of the goldsmith, in which calling he produced works of incredible excellence; and having afterwards taken to casting figures in metal, he had the courage, in his twentieth year, to undertake the Statue of Pope Julius III., four braccia high: the Pontiff is seated in the act of giving the Benediction, and the Statue, which is very fairly executed, is now on the Piazza in Perugia. Having subsequently come to Florence and entered the service of Duke Cosimo, Vincenzio made a beautiful model in wax, somewhat larger than life, which

Villa Medici, and which all now admire in the Florentine Gallery, to be a replica, yet this is by no means probable (for reasons into which our narrow space does not here permit us to enter), and the less so, as no trace whatever can be found of that which, supposing this to be a replica, was sent to the Emperor. The Mercury of the Florentine Gallery is without doubt the original work.

* This group, which is erroneously ascribed to Vincenzio Danti, by Cinelli, who has been followed by Cicognara and others, is in the Hall of the Palazzo Vecchio. Baldinucci, speaking of Bologna, tells us that "he made a model of Victory with a Captive, to the excellence of which the completed work is not, of a truth, fully equal." This model may be seen in the Court of the Florentine Academy.

† For details respecting this distinguished sculptor and military architect, who was besides no mean poet, let the reader consult Baglioni, as before cited, p. 56. See also Pascoli, *Vite de piu celebri Pittori del Secolo*, XVII., vol. iii. p. 137.

represented Hercules strangling Antæus : this was intended for the principal Fountain in the Garden of Castello, which is a Villa of the Duke's, but having made the mould, either because of his ill fortune, or that the metal had been burnt, or for some other cause, he could not succeed in the bronze casting, although he twice attempted it.

Vincenzio then resolved no longer to subject his labours to the caprices of that malicious Fortune ; he therefore began to work in marble, and in a short time completed two figures in the same block of stone : these represent Honour and Deceit, the latter fallen beneath the feet of the former.* This he completed with so much care, that while looking at it you think the artist can never have done anything but handle the mallet and chisels through his life long ; the head of Honour, which is exceedingly beautiful, has waving hair which is so finely worked that it looks exactly as does that of Nature ; and Vincenzio has also displayed profound knowledge of the nude form in this group, which is now in the Court of the house belonging to the Signor Sforza Almeni in the Via de' Servi.

At Fiesole, Vincenzio executed various decorations for the same Signore Sforza, in his gardens that is to say, and around certain fountains. He subsequently produced numerous bassi-rilievi ; these, which are in marble and bronze, and were considered very beautiful, are, for the most part, in possession of the Signor Duke : in that branch of sculpture Vincenzio is perhaps not inferior to any other master. This artist furthermore cast the grated doors of the chapel lately made in the Palace for the new apartments painted by Giorgio Vasari, and with them a work in basso-rilievo, which serves to close a cabinet in which the Duke keeps writings of importance ; he also executed another, which represents Moses raising the Serpent in the Wilderness ; this last is about a braccio and a half high, by two and a half broad. By order of Duke Cosimo, Danti then executed the Door of the Sacristy in the Deanery of Prato, with a marble

* This group, which is now in the Boboli Gardens, represents a youth with "an old man, tied hands and feet, whom he seems about to carry by means of a girth across his shoulder, as a peasant carries a lamb to market," observes an Italian commentator. He adds that, "To discover that the group represents Honour and Deceit, we must first be *told* that they do so."

Sarcophagus above it, whereon there is a figure of Our Lady, three braccia and a half high; the Infant Christ, entirely nude, is near her, and two children are added, these last holding between them the head, in basso-rilievo, of Messer Carlo de' Medici, natural son of Cosimo the Elder and formerly Dean of Prato, whose remains, after having long remained in a tomb of bricks, have been placed in the above-mentioned sarcophagus or sepulchre, with which they have been honoured by Duke Cosimo. It is, however, true that the work, which is a singularly beautiful one, is in a very bad light, and does therefore not appear to be what it really is.

Vincenzio then decorated the building used by the superintendents of the Mint; executing the arms of the Duke, supported by two nude figures larger than life, in the Loggia which looks on the Arno; one of these supporters represents Equity, the other Severity, or Firmness: our artist is now also in daily expectation of the marble for a statue larger than life to represent the Signor Duke, and of which he has already made the model: this is to be placed in a seated position over the Arms above-mentioned, as the completion of that work,* which is very soon to be effected, with the whole façade, all designed by Vasari, who is the architect of that fabric. Danti has besides now in hand a Madonna, somewhat larger than life; she is standing upright, and holds the Infant Christ, a child of about three months old, in her arms; when it is completed this group will be a very beautiful thing. These works, with many others, Vincenzio is bringing to completion at the Monastery of the Angeli in Florence, where he lives quietly in the society of the monks, who are very much his friends, occupying the rooms formerly inhabited by Messer Benedetto Varchi, of whom he is now executing a Portrait in basso-rilievo, which will be exceedingly beautiful.

Vincenzio has a brother in the Order of Friars Preachers, he is called Fra Ignazio Danti,† is very learned in Cosmography, and a man of distinguished ability in letters, insomuch that the Duke Cosimo has committed to his care a

* In the place destined for the work of Danti was erected the statue of the same Duke, but standing.—*Ed. Flor.*, 1832-8.

† The Dominican, Ignazio Danti, a well-known mathematician and cosmographer.—*Masselli.*

work of which none more perfect in design, or more important in the results to be expected from it, has ever been executed in that kind. His Excellency, that is to say, has caused a room of considerable extent to be prepared on the second floor of his palace, as a continuation of and addition to the Guardaroba; around this room he has had cabinets arranged seven braccia high, and richly carved in walnut wood, intending to place within them the most valuable and beautiful works of art in his possession; and on the doors of the same he is causing fifty-seven pictures, about two braccia high and of proportionate width, to be painted in oil on the wood in the manner of miniatures. The subjects delineated are the Ptolomaic Tables, measured by Don Ignazio with the most exact perfection, and corrected according to the latest authorities; sea-charts of the utmost accuracy are added, the scale and degrees being adjusted with all possible care, and all having the ancient as well as modern names; the division made of these works being as follows:—

At the principal entrance into the room are seen four pictures executed on the sides of the cabinets, and representing in perspective the halves of four spheres, those below showing the Earth and those above the Heavens, with all their signs and celestial figures. Proceeding towards the right we have all Europe depicted in fourteen compartments, the pictures succeeding each other to the centre of the wall which is at the head of the room, and opposite to the principal door, that namely whereon is placed the Horologe with its wheels, and the daily motions made by the planets in their spheres; I mean, that so much renowned clock made by the Florentine Lorenzo della Volpaia.* Above the compartments representing Europe, are those of Africa in eleven divisions; these extend to the Horologe itself, beyond which and on the lower part is Asia, which occupies a consecutive range of fourteen compartments, extending to the principal door. There are besides the West Indies, which commence from the clock, and continue to the principal door; the whole series forming the fifty-seven divisions before-mentioned.

On the lower part of the walls and immediately beneath the geographical delineations, in an equal number of compart-

* Of whom our readers will remember that mention has been made in the Life of Alessio Baldovinetti, and other parts of this work.

ments, will be the various plants and animals produced by the respective countries, all depicted from Nature. Over the cornice of the said cabinets, which completes the decoration, there are to be ressaults dividing the pictures, and on these will be placed certain antique busts in marble, representing the Emperors and Princes by whom those lands have been possessed, so far as those portraits are known to exist or can be procured. The ceiling is entirely in carved wood-work, and within the compartments of the same are twelve large pictures, in each of which are to be four of the Celestial Signs, making in the whole forty-eight; the figures are to be but little less than the size of life, each accompanied by its Stars. On the walls beneath are three hundred portraits of distinguished persons belonging to the last five centuries, or somewhat more; they are painted in oil; but, that I may not make too long a story, I refer the mention of their names to the Tables of my work. All have frames of similar size, very richly carved in oak, and produçing an exceedingly fine effect.

In the two pictures occupying the centre of the ceiling, each of which is four braccia wide, are the celestial signs; these can be thrown back by means which cannot be perceived; and in a space representing the concave are to be two large spheres, one representing the Earth: this will be made to descend by a concealed windlass, and will then be balanced on a support adequate to that purpose, so that when fixed, all the pictures and maps on the cabinets will be reflected therein, each part being thus readily found in the sphere. On the other globe the forty-eight Celestial Signs will be arranged, in such sort that all the operations of the Astrolabe may be performed most perfectly by the aid thereof. The plan of this work has proceeded from the Duke Cosimo, who desired to have all these parts of Earth and Heaven brought for once fairly together in their just positions, exactly and without errors, to the end that they might be observed and measured, either apart or all together, as might be desired by those who study and delight in this most beautiful science. I have, therefore, thought myself bound to make a memorial of the same in this place, for the sake of Fra Ignazio; and that his ability, with the magnificence of that great Prince, who has judged us worthy to enjoy the benefits of so honourable a labour, may be made known to all the world.

But to return to the men of our Academy. I add somewhat concerning the sculptor, Antonio di Gini Lorenzi, of Settignano, although he has already been mentioned in the Life of Tribolo. Here then, as in its due place, I proceed to say that this artist, under the direction of his master Tribolo, completed the Statue of Esculapius, which is at Castello, with four boys on the principal fountain of that place. He has also lately executed certain ornaments round the new fish-pond of Castello, which is at the upper part of the grounds, and in the midst of various trees, all evergreens; and in the beautiful gardens at the stables near San Marco, he has just completed most exquisite decorations, formed of marine animals, in white and vari-coloured marble, for a Fountain standing entirely apart. At Pisa this Antonio constructed the Tomb of the renowned philosopher and eminent physician, Corte, executing the statue of the same, with two beautiful boys in marble for that monument. He is now, by command of the Duke, preparing birds and animals in vari-coloured marbles for the ornaments of fountains, all works of much difficulty, and which render Antonio Lorenzi well worthy to be accounted among the other Academicians.

A brother of this Antonio, called Stoldo di Gino Lorenzi, and now thirty years old, has also executed works in sculpture, which give him the right to be considered among the first young artists of his profession. At Pisa he has executed a Madonna with the Angel of the Annunciation, which has made him advantageously known as a young man of good genius and fair judgment. From Luca Martini he received the commission for a statue which was presented by the Duchess Leonora to the Signor Don Garcia her brother, who has placed it in his Garden on the Chiaja at Naples. The same artist has made an Escutcheon of the Signor Duke's Arms at Pisa, under the direction of Giorgio Vasari; this is placed over the principal gate in the centre of the façade of the palace belonging to the Knights of San Stefano in Pisa, of which Order the Duke is Grand Master. The shield, which is very large, is in marble, and the supporters are figures of Religion and Justice, both exceedingly beautiful, and justly extolled by all who understand the subject. Stoldo Lorenzi has also constructed a fountain by command of the Duke, for his garden of the Pitti, the design being that of the Triumph of Neptune, exhibited in the superb maskings given by his Excellency on the Marriage of the Prince.

And this shall suffice to say of Stoldo Lorenzi, who, being young, is constantly making improvement and acquiring honour among his brother Academicians.

Of the same family of the Lorenzi, of Settignano, is Battista, called Del Cavaliere, from having been the disciple of Baccio Bandinelli,* and who has executed in marble three Statues larger than life, receiving his commission for the same from the Florentine citizen, Bastiano della Pace, who has had them made for the Guadagni family, now resident in France, where they have placed them in their gardens; they are, a nude figure of Spring, with others of Summer and Winter, one of Autumn being also to be prepared for the same persons. Those who have seen these Statues declare them to be singularly beautiful, and they have obtained for Battista the distinction of having been chosen by the Duke to execute the Sarcophagus, with its ornaments; and one out of three Statues, which are to be executed for the Tomb of Michelagnolo Buonarroti, now about to be constructed by his Excellency and Lionardo Buonarroti, after the design of Giorgio Vasari. In this work Battista is acquitting himself with much credit, more especially as regards certain Boys, and the half-length figure of Buonarroti himself.

The second of the three Statues, intended for this tomb, and which are to represent Painting, Sculpture, and Architecture, has been given to Giovanni di Benedetto, of Castello, also a disciple of Bandinelli and an Academician, who is employed in the works of Santa Maria del Fiore; the bassirilievi around the Choir are by his hand, and are now approaching their completion. In this work Giovanni is closely imitating his master, and his mode of conducting the same is such as to give hope of great success in the future; nor can this hope fail to be realized, since he is both earnest in study and diligent in labour.

The third figure is adjudged to the sculptor and Academician, Valerio Cioli, of Settignano, his previous works having given fair ground for expectation that he will render the Statue worthy of being placed on the sepulchre of so great a

* Who received the honour of the Cavalierato, or knighthood.

man. Valerio, now twenty-six years old, has been in Rome where he restored certain antiquities in marble for the Cardinal of Ferrara; to these Statues, which are in the garden of that Prelate at Montecavallo,* Valerio has added, in some cases arms, in others legs; to one a foot, to another some other part wanting thereto; and he has done the same for many others which the Duke has placed in the Palace of the Pitti, as the ornaments of a large hall which is therein. His Excellency has also caused Valerio to execute the Statue of the Dwarf Morgante, in marble; this figure, entirely nude, is so accurately true to the life that there has perhaps never before been a monster (*sic*) so well portrayed, so carefully executed, and so faithfully rendered as is this Morgante. The same artist has been commissioned to execute, in like manner, the Statue of Piero, called Il Barbino, also a dwarf, and great favourite of our Duke, for his learning, ingenuity, and pleasing dispositions. At a word, the performances hitherto accomplished by this Valerio have caused him to be considered worthy of the commission for a Statue destined to adorn the tomb of him who is the chief master of all these Academicians and artists of ability.†

With respect to the Florentine sculptor, Francesco Moschino, having spoken of him to some extent in other places,‡ it shall suffice to say here that he also is an Academician; and that, under the protection of the Duke, he is constantly working at the Cathedral of Pisa. At the marriage of the Prince he prepared the decorations for the principal Gate of the Ducal palace, and acquitted himself to admiration.

Of Domenico Poggini, in like manner, having before mentioned him § as a good sculptor and able man, who has produced numerous medals of great beauty, with other works in marble and castings in metal, I will say no more of him here than that he is justly enumerated among our Academicians; that he acquitted himself well in certain statues among the preparations for the marriage of the Prince; and that he has lately executed a Medal of Duke Cosimo, admirably

* Now the Pontifical Palace, or the Quirinal, well known to all who have visited Rome.

† The statue by Valerio is that representing Sculpture.

‡ See the Life of Mosca, vol. iv. p. 385.

§ In the Life of Valerio Vicentino.

beautiful, and perfectly true to the life. Poggini still continues his labours.

The Academician, Giovanni Fancegli, or, as some call him, Giovanni di Stocco, has produced many works in marble and stone, which have proved to be good sculptures. Among others an Escutcheon of Arms, bearing the Balls of the Medici, with two Boys, and other ornaments. This has been placed over the two grated windows in the front of the house belonging to Ser Giovanni Conti, in Florence, and is much extolled. Much the same may be said of Zanobi Lastricati, a good and able sculptor, who has produced and is producing numerous works in marble and bronze, which have rendered him worthy of being received into the Academy and as the companion of those above-mentioned. Among other works by this artist, one much commended is a Mercury, executed with all the care which such a performance demands, and which is now in the Court of the Palace of Messer Lorenzo Ridolfi.

Lastly: there are certain young sculptors who acquitted themselves very creditably in the preparations made for our Prince's nuptials, and have been accepted by the Academy; these are, Fra Vincenzio, of the Servites, a disciple of Fra Giovanni Montorsoli; Ottaviano del Collettaijo, a disciple of Zanobi Lastricati; and the architect, Pompilio Lancia, son of Baldassare da Urbino, and disciple of Girolamo Genga. This Pompilio distinguished himself very particularly at the marriage, in the Mask called that of the Genealogy of the Gods, which was arranged, for the most part, and more especially as to the machinery, by his father, Baldassare.*

* Our author has here added a paragraph, introductory to his *Descrizione dell' Apparato*, &c., &c.; but as that part of his works does not appear in our Translation, we omit the paragraph.

# DESCRIPTION OF THE WORKS OF GIORGIO VASARI, PAINTER AND ARCHITECT OF AREZZO.

[BORN 1512*—DIED 1574.]

HAVING hitherto treated of the works of others with as much care, sincerity, and uprightness as I have been able to command, I will now, at the end of these my labours, gather together, and make known to the world, such works as by the Divine Goodness I have myself been permitted to accomplish. For although these have not attained to the perfection that I could desire, yet whosoever shall examine them with unprejudiced eyes, will perceive that they have been executed by me with study, care, and loving labour; wherefore, if they be not worthy of praise, they will at least be allowed to merit excuse. They are laid open, moreover, to the eyes of all, and cannot be concealed. Wherefore, as their defects may perchance be described by some other, it were better that I should myself confess the truth, and accuse them with my own lips of those imperfections, whereof none can be more firmly convinced than myself. But of this I am sure, that if no excellence be discovered in my works, there will at least be found an ardent wish to do well, as I have before said, with great and enduring industry, and a true love for these our Arts.

And now shall it happen, according to the laws usually prevailing, that having thus openly confessed my shortcomings, a great part thereof shall be forgiven to me.

To begin then with my first beginnings, I observe that these have been sufficiently insisted on, in remarks previously made concerning the origin of my family,† my birth, my childhood, and the affection with which I was led into the paths of Art, more especially that of Design, by my father Antonio, who perceived me to be much disposed thereto. Of all these things I have spoken in the Life of Luca Signorelli of Cortona, my kinsman, in that of Fran-

* That our author was born in 1512 is ascertained from a letter written by him to Francesco de' Medici, on the 10th April, 1573, where he says, "This time I feel weary, nay, exhausted; I am now sixty years old, and the fatigues to be endured in these works are such that my life can support them no longer. See Gaye, *Carteggio inedito de Artisti*, vol. iii. p. 371.

† In the Life of Lazzaro Vasari. See vol. ii. of the present work, p. 49, *et seq.*

cesco Salviati, and in certain other parts of this work, wherein fair occasions for the same have presented themselves; I will therefore not reiterate the same things. It is, however, well that I should repeat one fact, which is, that having copied whatever good pictures there are in the Churches of Arezzo, the first principles of Art were imparted to me with some order by the Frenchman, Guglielmo da Marsiglia, of whom we have described the Life and works in a previous page. In the year 1524 I was taken to Florence by desire of Silvio Passerini, Cardinal of Cortona, and there studied design for a short time under Michelagnolo, Andrea del Sarto, and others. But in the year 1527, the Medici, more particularly Ippolito and Alessandro, to whose service, thus in my childhood, I had been closely attached by means of the above-named Cardinal, being then exiled from Florence, my paternal uncle, Don Antonio, caused me to return to Arezzo, my father having died of the Plague but a short time previously.

Now the said Don Antonio, mine uncle, kept me at a distance from the city, in the hope of saving me from the infection of that pestilence; wherefore, that I might not be idle, I began to paint certain frescoes for the peasantry of the neighbourhood, although I had at that time scarcely ever touched colours: but in doing this I perceived that to exercise one's powers in that manner, wholly alone and without aid, is of great use, teaching much and imparting considerable facility.*

In the year 1528, the Plague having ceased, I executed my first work in Arezzo, which comprises three half-length figures of SS. Agata, Rocco, and Sebastiano; this was seen by the much-renowned Painter Rosso, who came in those days to Arezzo, and he, perceiving something good in such parts as were taken from Nature, was pleased to say that he would willingly make my acquaintance; when he rendered me effectual aid, both with designs and counsels.

Nor did any long time elapse before I obtained by his means, a commission from Messer Lorenzo Gamurrini to

* At the end of the Life of Tommaso di Stefano, called Giottino, Vasari declares himself to have profited greatly in his first youth by the repainting of certain figures; those of San Jacopo and San Filippo more particularly, which Giovanni Tossicani, a disciple of Giottino, had depicted in a Chapel of the Episcopal Church of Arezzo.

paint a picture for which Rosso made me the design, and which I afterwards executed with all the study, labour, and care that I could possibly command, being anxious to improve, as well as to acquire some little reputation and name. And now, had but my power equalled my desire, I should soon have became a tolerably good painter, so earnestly did I labour, and so anxiously did I study my art; but I found the difficulties of success much greater than I had believed them to be.

Not losing courage, nevertheless, I returned to Florence; but seeing that it must still be long before I could attain to such a position as would enable me to assist the three sisters and two brothers, all younger than myself, whom I had left to me by my father, I set myself to practise the art of the goldsmith. This did not last long,* seeing that in the year 1529, the army having encamped before Florence, I went with my good friend, the goldsmith Manno, to Pisa, where, abandoning the practice of goldsmiths' work, I painted a fresco on the arch over the door of the building wherein the Old Company of the Florentines are wont to assemble, with some pictures in oil, the commissions for which I obtained by means of Don Miniato Pitti, then Abbot of Agnano, outside Pisa, and of Luigi Guicciardini who was at that time in Pisa.

The war meanwhile became daily more violent, and I resolved to return to Arezzo; but not being able to do so by the direct and ordinary route, I crossed by the mountains of Modena to Bologna, where, finding that certain triumphal arches, decorated with paintings, were about to be erected for the Coronation of Charles V., I had an opportunity of employing myself, even though but a youth, to my honour as well as profit. Nay, being tolerably well skilled in design, I might have found the means of establishing myself, and occupying my time in that city; but the wish that I felt to rejoin my family and friends impelled me to seize an opportunity which presented itself for travelling in good company, and I returned to Arezzo. Here I found that my affairs, by the diligent care which my uncle Don Antonio had taken of them, were in a very satisfactory state; and thus tranquillized in mind, I devoted myself to design, and even ventured

* Bottari says not more than four months.

to execute certain little pictures in oil, but they were not of any importance.

Meanwhile Don Miniato Pitti had been made either Abbot or Prior, I know not which, of Santa Anna, a Monastery of Monte Oliveto in the district of Siena, when he sent for me, and I painted for him as well as for Albenga, the General of his Order, several pictures and paintings of various kinds. Subsequently, the same ecclesiastic being appointed to the Abbacy of San Bernardo in Arezzo, commissioned me to paint two pictures in oil, figures of Job and Moses namely, on the balustrade of the organ; and the work having pleased those Monks, they furthermore employed me to paint certain frescoes in the ceiling and on the walls of the Portico before their Church.* These were the four Evangelists, with a figure of the Almighty Father in the ceiling, and some other figures, the size of life, on the walls. And in these, although, as an inexperienced youth, I did not effect what might have been done by a more practised artist, yet I did what I could; and those Monks, having consideration for mine early years and small experience, were not displeased with my labours.

The work was but just completed, when the Cardinal Ippolito de' Medici, travelling to Rome, passed through Arezzo, and taking me to Rome in his service, I was there enabled, by the courtesy and favour of that Noble, to devote myself for many months to the studies of design, as I have related in the Life of Salviati. And here I may with truth affirm, that this advantage and the studies of that period were indeed my true and principal master in this art, although I had without doubt profited, and not a little, by the instructions received from those whom I have before mentioned, nor had an ardent desire to learn ever departed or been absent from my heart, insomuch that my perpetual care was to draw with unwearying diligence night and day. A great advantage of that time was the competition with young men, then my equals and companions, who afterwards became for the most part most excellent in our arts: the desire of glory was indeed ever a sufficiently powerful stimulus to mine exertions, as was the sight of the extraordinary success, and the advancement to rank and honour, by which so many artists had been rewarded.

* These frescoes, which were executed by our author at the age of eighteen, are still in the Portico of the church.

Wherefore I sometimes said to myself, Why should it not be in my power to attain, by assiduous labour and study, to that eminence and greatness which so many others have acquired? They, too, were but of flesh and bones as I am. Impelled by these strong impulses therefore, and by the need which I perceived my family to have of me, I disposed myself to endure every extremity of fatigue, and to shrink from no labour, no hardship, no watchfulness, and no effort, that might contribute to the desired end. With this aim constantly in view, I set myself to design all the best works that I could find, nor was there anything remarkable at that time, whether in Rome, Florence, or any other place wherein I sojourned, that I did not copy in my youth, works ancient and modern, in sculpture and architecture as well as paintings. To say nothing of the advantages obtained from designing the ceiling and chapel of Michelagnolo, there was no work by Raphael, Polidoro, or Baldassare of Siena, which I did not likewise copy, in company with Francesco Salviati, as has been related in his Life.

And to the end that each of us might have designs of every work, we did not both copy the same thing on the same day, but different ones, and when night came we copied each other's drawings for the purpose of sparing time, and also to advance our studies; nor did we ever breakfast in the morning, except on what we ate while standing, and that very frugally.

After these excessive labours, the first work that proceeded from my hand, or, as it were, out of my own forge, was a large picture with figures the size of life, representing Venus surrounded by the Graces, who are adoring and doing her homage. The commission for this painting I received from the Cardinal de' Medici; but I need not say much of its qualities, since it was but the work of a youth. Indeed, I would not mention it here, were it not that I find pleasure in the recollection, even of these first beginnings, and of the aids then afforded to me for the acquirement of my art; let it suffice to say then, that the above-mentioned Prelate and other persons gave me to understand that there was a certain something intimating a good foundation, vivacity, facility, and boldness therein.* Among other particulars I had taken it into my

* A more extended description of this painting will be found in a letter written by Vasari to Niccolò Vespucci, and dated Rome, Feb. 8th, 1540. See the Passigli edition of our author's work, Florence, 1838.

head to add the figure of a Satyr half hidden amidst the foliage, while he observes the Goddess and her attendant Graces with manifest enjoyment. This part so greatly pleased the Cardinal, that he caused me to be clothed anew from head to foot, and gave me a commission for painting a larger picture, also in oil, the subject a Battle of Satyrs, with Fawns, Sylvan Deities, and Cupids, which made a kind of Baccanalia. Setting hand to this work, therefore, I made the Cartoon, and then sketched the subject in colours on the canvas, which was ten braccia long.*

But the Cardinal was then obliged to depart for Hungary; wherefore, having made me known to Pope Clement, and left me under the protection of His Holiness, he commended me to the keeping of his first Gentleman of the Bed-chamber, the Signor Jeronimo Montaguto, with letters to the effect that, if I should desire to avoid the air of Rome for that summer, I was to be received at Florence by the Duke Alessandro. And well would it have been for me had I done so; for the heat and fatigue of my prolonged stay in Rome, with the air of that place, caused so serious an illness, that before I could recover it became needful to transport me in a litter to Arezzo. I was however ultimately cured, and about the 10th of December following, I went to Florence, where I was received with a friendly aspect by the above-named Duke, and was shortly afterwards consigned to the care of the Magnificent Ottaviano de' Medici, who took me into his protection in such sort, that ever after, during his life, I was held by him in the place of a son. Nor have I ever ceased to cherish the beloved memory of that my true friend, but rather have revered, and do revere it, as that of one who was to me a most affectionate father.†

* Of this picture, Giorgio sent the description to Ottaviano de' Medici. See *Lettera* ii., in the Edition of Vasari above named.

† "Who would not become the friend of Vasari," exclaims the Padre Della Valle, "if it were only for the sentiments of gratitude which he so manifestly entertained for all who had offered him kindness? How candidly does he relate whatever passes, how freely confess every obligation of whatsoever kind." Very right you are, Della Valle, and truly may we affirm that those who have ventured to accuse our admirable Giorgio of ingratitude, injustice, presumption, or prejudice, have either never read more than garbled extracts of his works, or are themselves most justly chargeable with the defects they attribute to the kindly, upright, and most impartial Biographer.

Having returned to my wonted studies, I obtained the advantage, by the intervention of Messer Ottaviano, of a free admission, at whatever hour I pleased, into the New Sacristy of San Lorenzo, where are the works of Michelagnolo, who had then gone to Rome; these I studied, therefore, for some time, with much diligence, just as they were lying on the ground, that is to say. Then, setting to work, I painted, in a picture of three braccia, the figure of our Saviour Christ when dead, and in the act of being borne by Nicodemus, Joseph, and others, to the Sepulchre. Behind them come the Maries weeping. The Duke Alessandro took this painting,—a good and fortunate commencement for my labours, seeing that the work was not only held in estimation by that Prince while he lived, but was placed after his death in the apartments of Duke Cosimo, whence it has passed into those of the Prince his son, where it still remains. I have often wished to retouch and improve it in certain parts, but have never been permitted to do so ?*

After having seen this, my first work, the Duke Alessandro ordered me to finish that apartment on the ground floor of the Palazzo de' Medici, which had been left incomplete by Giovanni da Udine, as we have related elsewhere. Here then I depicted four Stories from the Life of Cæsar; the first showing him as he swims the river with the Commentaries in his mouth and his sword in his hand; in the second he is causing the writings of Pompey to be burnt, that he may not see the works of his enemies; in the third he is making himself known to the pilot when assailed by a storm at sea; and in the fourth is the Triumph of Cæsar, but this last was never entirely finished.†

At this time, although I was but little more than eighteen years old, the Duke assigned to me a provision of six crowns per month, with a place at table for myself, board for a servant, rooms for my habitation, and other advantages. I felt persuaded that I was far from deserving so much, but I did all that I knew how to do with love and diligent zeal; nor did I shrink from inquiring of those who knew better

* For details respecting this picture, see the letter of Vasari to the Cardinal Ippolito de' Medici, *Lettera* iv. of the Edition *ut supra.*

† These paintings are believed to have perished when the palace was altered and enlarged on its acquisition by the Riccardi family, to whom it still belongs.

than myself concerning such things as I did not know, wherefore I was afterwards assisted, both in works and counsels, by Tribolo, Bandinello, and others.

In a picture some three braccia high then, I portrayed about this time the Duke Alessandro, armed and taken from the life; the arrangement adopted for this work was in some respects peculiar; the Duke's seat, for example, was formed of captives chained together, and there were other phantasies. I remember also that, to say nothing of the resemblance of the countenance, which is a faithful one, I desired to reproduce the burnished gloss and peculiar gleaming of the clear, bright, shining arms, and was fairly in danger of losing my wits in that matter, so desperate were my struggles to produce the desired effects, and so painfully did I copy every the smallest minutia from the objects themselves. But, despairing of a satisfactory approach to the truth, I took Jacopo da Pontormo, whose abilities I greatly respected, to see the work, when, having examined the same, and perceiving my discouragement as well as the earnest zeal of my labours, he said to me kindly, "My son, so long as these lustrous arms shall stand in all their glitter beside this picture, the work will appear to thee a mere thing painted, seeing that although the *biacco* is the most potent light and lustre that can be used by Art, yet is the steel itself inevitably more bright and lustrous than the *biacco*. Take away these weapons then, and thou shalt see that thy feigned arms are not so bad a work as thou art supposing them to be." When the picture was ultimately completed I gave it to the Duke, who presented the same to Messer Ottaviano de' Medici, and in his palace it remains to the present day, in company with the Portrait of Catherine, the sister of Duke Alessandro, then a girl, but afterwards Queen of France, and that of the Magnificent Lorenzo de' Medici the Elder.* In the same Palace are three other pictures, executed in youth by my hand: Abraham about to Sacrifice Isaac, Our Saviour Christ in the Garden,† and the Last Supper of Our Lord with his Apostles.

Meanwhile the Cardinal Ippolito, in whom all my best hopes were placed, being dead, I began to understand that

* See Letters v. and vii. of the Passigli Edition. The portrait of Alexander, of which there is an outline in the *Firenze Illustrata*, will be found in the Uffizj.

† For the picture of Abraham, see *Lettera* vi., and for that of Christ in the Garden, *Lettera* ix., *loc. cit.*

the promises of this world are for the most part but vain phantoms; and that to confide in one's self, and become something of worth and value, is the best and safest course. After the works above-named, perceiving the Duke to be principally interested in fortifications and buildings of various kinds, I set myself to study Architecture, that I might the more effectually render him service, and in this labour I expended much time. The preparations for receiving Charles V. on the visit of that Emperor to Florence in 1536 were then to be made; and in giving orders for the same, Duke Alessandro commanded those deputed to the care thereof to join me with them, as has been related in the Life of Tribolo, for the designing of all the arches and other decorations to be erected in honour of the Monarch's entry.*

This being done, I also received for my benefit the appointment, not only for preparing the great Banners of the Castello and Fortress, as we have before said, but also the commission for constructing that Façade in the manner of a triumphal arch, which was erected at San Feliçe in Piazza, with the decorations of the Gate of San Piero Gattolini; the Arch was forty braccia high and twenty wide. These works were indeed too great for my strength; but what was worse, the favour by which I obtained them, attracted a host of envious rivals around me, and at their suggestion, about twenty men who were assisting me in the execution of those banners and the other operations, left me on the spur of the moment, in the midst of my labours, hoping thereby to render my completion of those important undertakings impossible.

But I had in some sort foreseen the malignity of those persons, whom I had nevertheless always endeavoured to assist; wherefore, partly by working day and night with my own hand, partly by the help of painters who came to me from other places, I contrived, in despite of their efforts, to keep the works in progress; and, attending closely to my business, I sought to overcome the difficulties thus presented, while I replied to the malevolence of these enemies by the works themselves. Meanwhile, Bertoldo Corsini, who was then Proveditore-general to the Duke, had reported to

* For details concerning these preparations, see letters xi. and xii., as above cited.

his Excellency that I had undertaken an amount of work beyond what it was possible for me to have ready in time, more especially as my want of men had much delayed the preparations, when Alessandro sent for me and repeated what he had heard. To this I replied, that the works were making fair progress, as his Excellency might assure himself by inspection at his pleasure; adding that the result of my labours would be their best encomium.

Having left the Duke thereupon, no long time elapsed before he secretly came to the place where I was working; and when he had seen all, he became to some extent aware of the malignity with which those who had received no cause for doing so were persecuting me. When the time came, moreover, all was found to be completed and in its due place, at the moment required, to the perfect satisfaction of Duke Alessandro, as well as of the whole city; while the works of those who had been more earnestly busied with my affairs than with their own, had in several instances to be put up in an unfinished state. The festivals being concluded, I received from the Duke, in addition to the four hundred crowns due to me for my works, three hundred more, which were taken from those who had failed to deliver their performances completed at the time agreed for. With the help of my savings and these sums, I then married one of my sisters; and a short time afterwards I was enabled to make another of them a nun in the Convent of the Murate at Arezzo, giving to that convent, in addition to the dowry or alms, a picture of the Annunciation by my hand, with a Tabernacle of the Sacrament therein; this was placed in the Choir where the services are performed.*

The Company of the Corpus Domini having then given me a commission for the picture of the High Altar in San Domenico, I painted a Deposition from the Cross therein; and shortly afterwards I commenced for the Company of San Rocco, the Altar-piece of their Church in Florence.†

* The Monastery of Santa Chiara, called *delle Murate*, has long been suppressed, and the fate of this work is not known.

† Vasari does not mean that the Church of the Company was in Florence; it was at Arezzo, but that he executed the Altar-piece in the first-mentioned city. For details relating to the works here in question, see the admirable letter of our Giorgio to Baccio Rontini (*Lettera* xvi., *loc. cit.*) See also *Lettere* xiii. and xv. The first addressed to Francesco Rucellai, the second to Niccolò Serguidi.

And now, while I was seeking to obtain renown, riches, and honour, beneath the protection of Duke Alessandro, the poor Prince was cruelly assassinated, and every hope of fortune which I had promised to myself by means of his favour was thus taken from me. Wherefore, having thus in a few years lost Pope Clement, Ippolito, and Alessandro, I resolved, by the advice of Messer Ottaviano, to follow no longer the fortune of Courts, but to think of Art alone, although it would have been easy for me to have fixed myself with the new Duke, Signor Cosimo de' Medici. Proceeding, therefore, with the before-mentioned Altar-piece and Façade for San Rocco at Arezzo, with the frame thereof, I began to take order for repairing to Rome, when, by means of Messer Giovanni Pollastra,* I was invited (as it pleased God, to whom I have ever commended myself, and whose goodness I acknowledge, and ever have acknowledged) to Camaldoli, of which Congregation Messer Giovanni was the chief; the fathers of that Hermitage desiring me to examine the works which they were about to have executed in their Church.

Here the Alpine solitude and profound stillness of the place delighted me greatly; and although I perceived that at the first those venerable fathers, seeing me to be so young, began to doubt of the matter; yet, taking courage, I discoursed to them in such a manner that they resolved to accept my services, and permitted me to execute the pictures in oil and fresco, which they had determined to have painted in their Church. Now the fathers desired that the picture of the High Altar should be painted before any other part of the work, but I proved to them by good reasons that it was better first to complete one of those for the minor altars in the middle aisle, when, if this pleased them, I could proceed with the rest. I refused, moreover, to make any fixed agreement as to the price at that time, considering that if my work pleased the monks they might pay me what they found right, but if it did not satisfy their expectations I was ready to keep the picture for myself; and they, finding these conditions upright and favourable to themselves, were content to have the work commenced at once.

The subject they chose was Our Lady holding the Infant Christ in her arms, with San Giovanni Battista and San

* To whom our author addressed a most pleasing letter on the subject of his abode at the Camaldoli. See *Lettera* xvii., *loc. cit.*

Jeronimo, both of whom had been hermits, living in the woods and deserts. I then descended to their Abbey of Camaldoli, where I quickly prepared a design, which being found to please the fathers, I then began the picture. This was completed, and fixed in its place at the end of two months, to the great satisfaction of those hermits (as they gave me to understand) as well as my own: and during those two months I furthermore discovered how much more favourable to study is a calm repose and agreeable solitude, than the tumult of cities and courts; I perceived, likewise, that my error had been great when I had before placed my hopes in men, and made my pleasure of the levities and follies of the world. That picture being finished, as has been said above, I at once received the commission for the remainder of the chapels in the aisle, the Stories and other paintings in fresco that is to say, which were to be executed in the upper and lower parts of the same, all which I was to execute in the succeeding summer, since it would be scarcely possible to work in fresco amidst those mountains during the winter season.*

Having then returned to Arezzo, I finished the picture of San Rocco, depicting Our Lady with six Saints, and a figure of the Almighty Father therein: the latter having certain arrows in his hand, to signify the pestilence which he is in the act of launching on the city; while San Rocco and other Saints are interceding for the people. On the wall are numerous figures in fresco, and these, as well as the Altar-piece itself, are—as they are.

I was then sent for by Fra Bastiano Graziani, a Monk of St. Agostino, at Monte Sansovino, who invited me into the Val di Caprese, and gave me a large picture in oil to paint for the High Altar of the Church of Sant' Agostino in the above-named Monte.† Having made our agreement for the same, I then repaired to Florence for the purpose of visiting Messer Ottaviano de' Medici; and remaining there some few days, I had no small difficulty to avoid the temptation of

* Many of our author's works still remain there; one at the High Altar namely, two beside the same, one in the Infirmary, three in the Chapter House, and two in the choir above the church.

† One of the best of Vasari's works; it is an Assumption, and was painted after the many months of study in Rome to which he alludes immediately below.

once more attaching myself to the service of Courts, which I had determined not to do. By many good reasons, however, I did finally come off conqueror, and resolved that, before doing anything else, I would repair by all means to Rome, yet I did not succeed entirely in my purpose, seeing that my departure was delayed until I had made a copy for Messer Ottaviano, of the picture representing Pope Leo, Giulio Cardinal de' Medici, and the Cardinal de' Rossi, which Raffaello da Urbino had formerly painted, the Duke desiring to reclaim the original, which had remained until that time in the possession of Messer Ottaviano: the copy here in question is now in the house of that Noble's heirs. For himself, when I left him for Rome, he gave me a letter of exchange for five hundred crowns on Giovambattista Puccini (who was to pay me that sum at sight), saying as he gave it me: "Use this for the better promotion of thy studies, and if ever thy leisure shall serve thee, thou shalt return it to me either in works or money, at thy own pleasure."

Arriving in Rome in the month of February, 1538, I remained there till the end of June, devoting myself to designing, in company with my young scholar, Giovambattista Cungi of the Borgo,* all such antiquities or other works as I had not secured during the previous visits made to Rome, more particularly such things as were in the grottoes beneath the earth. Nor did I now omit any production of sculpture or architecture, but drew and measured them all; insomuch that I may truly affirm the designs made by me at that time to have been no less than three hundred, all which afforded me both advantage and pleasure, when looking over them in after years, and refreshing my memory as to the works of art in Rome. Nor did the profit which I had obtained from all these labours and studies fail to be perceived on my return to Tuscany, by the picture which I then painted at Monte Sansovino, and in which I delineated an Assumption of Our Lady, with a somewhat better manner: beneath are the Apostles, standing around the tomb, with SS. Agostino and Romualdo.

I subsequently went to the Camaldoli, as I had promised those Eremite Fathers to do; when I painted the Birth of Christ on the vaulting of the middle aisle, representing the splendour of Our Saviour incarnate as supplying the sole

* Mentioned in the Life of Cristofano Gherardi. See vol. iv.

light to the picture, of which the time was the night. Around the Divine Child are the Shepherds in adoration. I furthermore endeavoured to imitate the rays of the rising sun, by means of the colours, and portrayed every object in those works from the life, and with the light that made them approach as nearly as possible to the reality. Then, as the light within the cabin could not illumine the roof and exterior, I caused the upper and surrounding portions of the picture to receive light from the splendour of the angels who are hovering in the air, and singing the *Gloria in excelsis Deo*. The Shepherds also produced light in certain parts by the sheaves of lighted straw which they carried about in their hands; in other parts, the moon, the stars, and the Angels appearing to the Shepherds, supply the light.

As to the building, I formed it of certain antiquities after my own fancy, with broken Statues and other things of similar character. At a word, I conducted the whole to the best of my knowledge and ability, and although I could not by hand and pencil attain to such a performance as I fain would have produced, the picture has nevertheless pleased many; wherefore, Messer Fausto Sabeo, a very learned man, who was then keeper of the Pope's Library, made several Latin verses in honour of the same, as after him did many others; but moved, perhaps, more by great kindness than by the merit of the work. However this may be, if there be any thing good in the picture, that good was the gift of God. On the completion thereof, the Fathers determined that the paintings which were to be executed on the façade should be entrusted to my care, when I depicted a view of the Hermitage itself over the door, with a figure of San Romualdo and that of a Doge of Venice, who was a holy man, on one side;* and a Vision seen by the above-named Saint in the place where he afterwards made his Hermitage, on the other. There were besides certain phantasies, grottesche, and other things, as may be seen there. This being done, the Fathers commanded me to repair thither in the following summer, with commission to paint the picture for the High Altar.

Meanwhile, the above-mentioned Don Miniato Pitti, who was then visitor to the Congregation of Monte Oliveto,

* "Perhaps," remarks Bottari, "our author here alludes to San Pietro Orseolo."

having seen the picture at Monte Sansovino, and the works at Camaldoli, declared to the Florentine Don Filippo Serragli, Abbot of San Michele-in-Bosco, whom he met at Bologna, that as the Refectory of that distinguished Monastery was to be painted, it was his opinion that the work should be given to myself and no other. Wherefore, being summoned to Bologna, I undertook the execution of the same, although it was a matter of no small importance; but first I determined to examine all the most renowned paintings in that city, whether by the Bolognese or other artists.

The pictures at the upper end of this Refectory were divided into three compartments; in the first was to be represented Abraham preparing food for the Angels in the valley of Mamre; in the second, Christ in the house of Mary and Martha, declaring to the latter that Mary hath chosen the better part; and in the third, San Gregory at table with twelve poor men, among whom he perceives the Saviour Christ himself.* Thereupon, setting hand to the work, I represented in the last St. Gregory at table in a Monastery, served by the White Monks of his order, that being the wish of those Fathers. The Holy Pontiff, San Gregorio, presents the portrait of Pope Clement VII.; and among those of many ambassadors, princes, and other high personages who are standing around and beholding him, is the portrait of the Duke Alessandro de' Medici, which I placed there in memory of the benefits and favours received by me at his hand, and in consideration of the family to which he belonged; there are also the portraits of many others of my friends. Among those who serve the poor at table, moreover, I depicted certain Monks of that Monastery who were mine intimates, with certain foreigners, of whose services I availed myself there. The Almoner and the Cellarer were of the number; and I likewise portrayed the Abbot Serraglio, the General Don Cipriano of Verona, and Bentivoglio. The vestments of the Pontiff were copied from the real textures, velvets, damasks, and cloths of gold and silver, with silks, and such like; the service of plate for the table, the vases, with the decorations of animals and other objects of similar kind, I caused to be executed by Cristofano dal Borgo, as I have said in his Life.

* The first of these pictures is in Milan, the other two are in Bologna; they are accounted among Vasari's best works.—*Ed. Flor.*, 1832-8.

In the second picture I endeavoured to produce variety; whether as regarded the heads, the draperies, the buildings, or other parts; but more especially did I seek to express the affection with which our Saviour Christ instructed Mary, and the prompt devotion of Martha in arranging her feast and attending her guest, while she complains of being left by her sister to all the weight of those ministrations: to say nothing of the feelings evinced by the Apostles, or of many other things, which I laboured to set forth in that picture as was befitting. As to the third Story, I depicted the three Angels (I do not myself know how it occurred to me), in the midst of a celestial light which seems to emanate from themselves, while the rays of the Sun fall brightly on a cloud which surrounds them. The old Abraham is paying his adorations to one, although he sees three; while Sarah stands laughing and marvelling how that which has been promised to her shall come to pass; Hagar, meanwhile, is departing from the house bearing Ishmael in her arms. The light from the Angels illumines the servants who are preparing the meal; and some of these, unable to endure the splendour of the rays, place their hands before their eyes, seeking to cover them from the too great brightness; this variety, seeing that the deep shadow and the strong light give force to a picture, caused the one now in question to show more relief than did the other two; the effect of each was indeed quite unlike that of the other two. But very different would all have been, could I but have found power fully to express my thoughts, seeing that both then and afterwards, I was constantly seeking, with new inventions and phantasies, to accomplish the difficult and laborious in Art.

This work, then, whatever it may be, was completed in the space of eight months, with a Frieze ornamented in fresco,* architectural embellishments, carved seats, tables, and every other ornament or requisite for the whole work and for the use of the Refectory; and for the price of the whole I contented myself with two hundred crowns, as being one who aspired to glory rather than to gain; for which

* The Frieze is still in the Refectory; the two pictures of Christ in the house of Mary and Martha, and St. Gregory at Table, are in the Gallery of Bologna; the latter bears the following inscription:—*Giorgio Aretino faceva,* CDXL.

cause my friend, Messer Andrea Alciati, caused the following words to be written beneath the picture :—

*Octonis mensibus opus ab Arretino Georgio Pictum, non tam precio, quam amicorum obsequio, et honoris voto, anno 1539, Philippus Serralius pon. curavit.*

At the same time I painted two small pictures, one of a Dead Christ, and the other of the Resurrection, which were placed by the Abbot, Don Miniato Pitti, in the Church of Santa Maria di Barbiano, which is outside of San Gimignano in the Val d'Elsa. These works completed, I returned instantly to Florence, seeing that the Trevisan, Maestro Biagio,* and other Bolognese masters, believing that I proposed to settle in Bologna, and might, in that case, take their works out of their hands, had begun to disquiet me from the first, and did not cease to do so ; but they injured themselves thereby more than they did me, who could not but laugh at certain of their furies, and at the modes of their proceeding in my regard.

Having arrived in Florence, I copied the Portrait of Cardinal Ippolito, a large half-length figure, with some other pictures for Messer Ottaviano de' Medici, and with these I occupied my time during the insupportable heats of that summer; but having finished the same I returned to the quiet and freshness of Camaldoli, there to paint that picture of the High Altar before alluded to. The subject of the work is Christ deposed from the Cross, and all the study and labour at my command did I bestow thereon. But as it appeared to me, that by time and effort I was making a certain progress, and the first sketch which I had prepared for it no longer satisfied me, I gave it a new ground and recommenced it, making it as we now see.

Detained in the place by the charms of that solitude, I lingered there for some time after the completion of the above, and then painted for Messer Ottaviano, a youthful San Giovanni, the figure nude, and represented amidst rocks and mountains, which I copied from the district around me. Nor had I well put an end to this picture before Messer Bindo Altoviti, arriving at Camaldoli, and by my good fortune being pleased with the works executed there, resolved

* Biagio Pupini, called also Maestro Biagio della Lame. He is mentioned in the Lives of Bartolomeo Bagnacavallo and of Benvenuto Garofolo.

that I should paint a picture for his Church in Florence, Sant' Apostolo namely. Messer Bindo had repaired to Camaldoli for the purpose of procuring a large quantity of fir-trees, required in the fabric of San Pietro, and which were supplied by the Cella di Sant' Alberigo, a place belonging to those fathers, whence they were conveyed to Rome by the Tiber; but before his departure I received from him the commission for that picture.

Having then completed the façade of the Chapel at Camaldoli, which I painted in fresco, and where I made experiments on the union of oils with that manner—succeeding very nearly to my satisfaction—I departed from the Hermitage and went to Florence, where I executed the picture in question. But I had not before painted a work of the kind in that city, and desired to give a specimen of what I could do, the rather as I had many rivals, and was infinitely desirous of reputation. I therefore disposed myself to put forward my best efforts; and, to obtain freedom of mind for my work, I first married my third sister; I also bought a house, which was in course of construction at Arezzo, with the site for laying out beautiful gardens in the suburb of San Vito, one of the best positions for purity of the air to be found in that city.

In October of the year 1540, then, I began Messer Bindo's picture; the subject selected being a Conception of the Virgin, because such was the designation of the Chapel for which it was intended. But the due treatment of that subject appeared to me to present certain difficulties; wherefore Messer Bindo and I, taking counsel of such among our common friends as were men of letters, determined finally to arrange it as follows.

The Tree of the Original Sin was represented in the centre of the painting, and at the roots thereof were placed nude figures of Adam and Eve bound, as being the first transgressors of God's commands. To the principal branches were then also bound Abraham, Isaac, Jacob, Moses, Aaron, Joshua, David, and the rest of the kings, lawgivers, &c., according to their seniority, all fastened by both arms, excepting only Samuel and San Giovanni Battista, who are bound by one arm only, to intimate that they were sanctified before their birth. At the trunk of the Tree, and with the lower part twining about it, is the Old Serpent, but the upper part of the form has the shape of Man, and the hands are confined behind the back; on his head is one foot of the glorious Virgin, which is trampling down the horns of the demon, while the other foot is fixed on a Moon. Our Lady is clothed with the Sun and crowned with twelve stars, being sustained in the air, within a splendour of numerous angels, nude, and illuminated by the rays which proceed from the Madonna herself. These same rays, moreover, passing amidst the foliage of the Tree, give light to the figures bound to the branches; nay, they seem to be gradually loosening their bonds, by the power and grace which they derive from her out of whom they proceed. In Heaven meanwhile, that is at the highest point of the picture, are two Children bearing a scroll, on which are the following words:—

*Quos Evæ culpa damnavit, Mariæ gratia solvit.*

To no work, so far as I can remember, had I then given more study, or devoted myself with more love and care thereto, than I had done to this; but nevertheless, if perchance I may have contented others, I did not satisfy myself, although I alone know what time, what consideration, and what labour I spent thereon, the care expended on the nude figures for example, and that given to the heads, or rather, at a word, to every part of the work.* Messer Bindo presented me for the same, with a sum of three hundred crowns; and in the year following he showed me infinite kindness, at his own house at Rome, treating me with so much courtesy, that I shall be ever grateful to his memory. I then also made for Messer Bindo a small picture or copy, almost in the manner of a miniature, from the work here in question.†

Now about the period when, having completed the picture of Sant' Apostolo, I had seen it put up in the Church, I painted a Venus for Messer Ottaviano de' Medici, with a Leda, which I took from the Cartoons of Michelagnolo. In a large picture, moreover, I executed a San Girolamo in penitence, making the figure of the Saint the size of life; he is in contemplation on the death of Christ, whom he has

* Still in the church, and tolerably well preserved, but the picture has been somewhat injured by a common-place painter, who has added drapery to the figure of Adam.

† This copy is now in the smaller room of the Tuscan School, in the Gallery of the Uffizj.

before him on a Cross, and is striking his breast, while he drives far from him those mundane thoughts which did not cease to assail him, even in the most remote deserts, as he most fully tells us in his own writings. To express this condition of things intelligibly, I depicted Venus, with Cupid in her arms, and leading a laughing Love by the hand; she is flying from the place made sacred by that devotion, and has suffered the quiver and arrows of her son to fall to the earth. The arrows which Cupid has shot at the Saint turn broken towards himself, while others, caught as they are falling, are brought back to Venus by her Doves.*

These pictures were, without doubt, accomplished to the best of mine ability, and at the time they may perchance have pleased me, yet I do not know that they would do so at my present age. But as art is difficult in itself, we must be content to accept from each that whereof he is capable. This, however, I may say, and can affirm it with truth, that all my pictures, inventions, and designs, of whatever sort, have always been executed, I do not say with very great promptitude only, but with more than ordinary facility, and without laboured effort.† A proof of this will be found, as I have related elsewhere, in the large picture, painted by me in six days only, at San Giovanni in Florence, in the year 1542, for the baptism of the Signore Don Francesco Medici, now Prince of Florence and Siena.

After the completion of these works, I would fain have gone to Rome, in compliance with the wishes of Messer Bindo Altoviti, but I could not bring my purpose to bear, having been instantly pressed by the Aretine Poet, Messer Pietro, then in much renown and my intimate friend, to

* Now in the Royal Gallery of the Pitti.

† For this rapidity of execution, which doubtless did wrong to his talents, Vasari has been reproached rather than extolled by later times, and with justice, up to a certain point, since it is certain that we do not now ask how long a time the master gave to his work, but how that work was accomplished. We are nevertheless to remember that if our admirable author prided himself in the promptitude of his execution, that came from the uprightness of character, which, causing him most justly to revolt from the unprincipled conduct of certain among his contemporaries who unreasonably deferred, or, on too many occasions, even neglected altogether, to fulfil engagements for which they had received payment, may have caused him, in the pride of rectitude, and the recollection of his own fidelity to his engagements, somewhat to over-estimate the quality n question.

visit Venice, where he greatly desired to see me. I was, therefore, compelled to repair thither, but did so all the more willingly, as I wished to see the works of Titian and other masters, which that journey enabled me to do. I also then saw the works of Correggio in Modena and at Parma, with those of Giulio Romano at Mantua, and the Antiquities of Verona, which I visited on my way to Venice. Finally, having arrived there, I presented two pictures, which I had painted from the Cartoons of Michelagnolo, to Don Diego di Mendoza, who sent me two hundred crowns of gold.

I had not been any long time in Venice before I prepared, at the request of Messer Pietro, the decorations for a festival, which the Signori of the Calza* were then about to give, and for the execution of which I had in my company Battista Cungi and Cristofano Gherardi of Borgo San Sepolcro,† with the Aretine Bastiano Flori; all able and practised artists, of whom I have spoken sufficiently in other places. I also painted nine pictures in the Palace of Messer Giovanni Cornaro, near San Benedetto; those namely which are in the wainscot work of a certain apartment in that building. These and other works of no small importance being completed, I took my leave of Venice on the 16th of August, 1542, although overwhelmed with commissions, which had come unsought to my hands, and returned to Tuscany.

Here the first thing I did was to paint a picture representing all the Arts connected with, or which depend on, that of Design, in the ceiling of a room which had been constructed by my order in the above-named house of mine. In the centre is a figure of Fame; she is seated on the Globe of the world, and is sounding a golden trumpet, while she casts from her one of fire, which signifies Calumny. Around her figure it is that all the Arts, each holding his appropriate instruments in the hand, are arranged; but as I had not time to complete the entire work, I left eight oval compartments vacant, proposing to execute therein the portraits

* A Society instituted at Venice, in the commencement of the fifteenth century, by men of rank, who kept the people in good humour by their various festivals, while they also assisted and encouraged many young and able artists. For their ensign, the *Calza*, whence they took their name, see Martinelli, *Del Costume Veneziana*, p. 127.

† In whose Life, which may be considered as the complement to that of Vasari, other works of our author are enumerated. See vol. iv. of the present work.

from the life, of men most eminent for distinction in our arts. At the same time I painted a Birth of Christ in fresco, the figures life-size, for the Nuns of Santa Margherita, in a Chapel of their garden situate in Arezzo; and when I had thus expended the remainder of the summer and a part of the autumn in my native place, I departed for Rome. Most kindly received in that city by Messer Bindo Altoviti, and greatly favoured by him, I painted a picture in oil, representing the Deposition from the Cross, in figures the size of life, the Saviour being laid on the ground at the feet of the Virgin mother; while in the air is Phœbus veiling the face of the Sun, and Diana that of the Moon. In the Landscape thus obscured are seen Mountains rent by the earthquake which took place at the Crucifixion of our Lord; the dead bodies of Saints in different attitudes being seen to proceed from their tombs,* some in one manner and some in another.

When this picture was finished, it had the good fortune not to displease the greatest sculptor, painter, and architect that ever lived in our times, or perhaps in those preceding them; and by his intervention, I was made known to the most illustrious Cardinal Farnese, to whom the work was shown by Giovio and Messer Bindo. For that Prelate, then, I was consequently commissioned to execute a picture, eight braccia high and four wide, which represented, according to his own fancy, the figure of Justice with the twelve Tables and a Sceptre, on the point of which is a Stork.† The head of Justice bears a helmet of iron and gold, with three plumes of three different colours, the symbol of upright judgment. The upper part of the figure is undraped; at her waist she has the seven Vices, which are her enemies, bound to her girdle by chains of gold; these are Corruption, Ignorance, Cruelty, Fear, Treachery, Falsehood, and Calumny; on whose shoulders is raised the figure of Truth, wholly nude, and presented to Justice by Time, with a gift of two Doves, as emblematic of Innocence. Justice, meanwhile, is placing a crown of Oak-leaves on the head of Truth, as the symbol of strength of mind. All these things I expressed with the utmost care and to the best of my ability.

* Now in the Pamphili Gallery.—*Ed. Flor.*, 1846-51.

† This work remained in the Farnese Palace until the year 1760, when it was taken to Naples.

At this time I paid much attention to the counsels of Michelagnolo, whose advice I took in respect of all my works, he, in his goodness, giving me numerous proofs of affection; and among other marks of kindness he advised me, after having seen some of my designs, to set myself anew, and with a better manner, to the study of Architecture, which I should very probably never have done, had not that most excellent man said what he did to me, but this modesty commands me to refrain from repeating.

At the Feast of San Piero in that year, the heat at Rome was insupportable; and having spent in the city the whole winter of 1543, I then returned to Florence, where, in the house of Messer Ottaviano de' Medici, which I might even call my own, I painted for his gossip, the Lucchese Messer Biagio Mei, a picture of which the thought was that represented in the one executed for Messer Bindo, and placed in the church of Sant' Apostolo; but the work, excepting only the composition, was varied in every particular: being finished, it was placed in the chapel of Messer Bigio, which is in the church of San Piero Cigoli in Lucca. In a second picture of similar size, seven braccia high and four wide that is to say, I depicted Our Lady with SS. Jeronimo, Luca, Cecilia, Marta, Agostino, and Guido the Hermit; this was put up in the Cathedral of Pisa, where there are many others by the hands of eminent artists.

I had no sooner completed the above than the Superintendent of works to that Cathedral commissioned me to paint another, in which, as there was also to be the Madonna, I sought variety by placing the Dead Christ in the lap of the Virgin at the foot of the cross, while the Thieves remain on their crosses above them; the Maries, Nicodemus, and the Saints to whom the chapel for which the picture was destined is dedicated, stand around the group; all which varied the composition and added grace to the story.

Returning to Rome in 1544, I made numerous pictures for different friends, of which it is not needful to make any record; but I may name one which I painted for Messer Bindo Altoviti, who had again received me into his own house; this was a Venus, which I executed from the design of Michelagnolo. For the Florentine merchant, Galeotto da Girone, I painted a Deposition from the Cross in oil, and this was placed in the chapel of Girone, which is in the church of Sant' Agostino in Rome.* But to the end that I might execute this picture, with others which Tiberius Crispus, the Castellan of Sant' Angelo, had commissioned me to paint, with the greater convenience, I had gone into the Trastevere, to the Palace beneath Sant' Onofrio, formerly commenced by the Bishop Adimari, and finished by Salviati the Second,† when, finding myself exhausted, and becoming ill, in consequence of the many fatigues to which I had subjected myself, I was compelled to return to Florence. There I painted some other pictures, and among them one which afterwards became the property of Luca Martini, wherein there were the Portraits of Dante, Petrarch, Guido Cavalcanti, Boccaccio, Cino da Pistoja, and Guittone d'Arezzo; the likenesses being accurately copied from older portraits. There were subsequently many copies of these heads made from this work.

In that same year of 1544, I was invited to Naples by Don Giammatteo of Antwerp, General of the Monks of Monte Oliveto, to the end that I might paint the Refectory of a Monastery of theirs, built by the King Alfonso I. But when I arrived in Naples and saw the Refectory, I was on the point of declining to undertake the work: the architecture of that Monastery being ancient, and the low ceilings, with their pointed arches, being almost wholly deprived of light, I feared there would be but little honour to be gained thereby. Persuaded, nevertheless, by Don Miniato Pitti and Don Ippolito da Milano, my intimate friends, I did finally agree to accept the commission; but seeing that no good could be effected in that place without a vast amount of ornaments which might dazzle the eyes of those who should examine the work, by the multiplicity and variety of the figures, I resolved to have all the ceiling of the Refectory worked in stucco; thus doing away, by rich compartments in the modern manner, with all that old-fashioned appearance and that heaviness of the arches. And here I was much aided by the tufa with which those walls and that ceiling were constructed, for this can be cut as one would cut wood, or rather bricks not perfectly baked, so that I found it possible to hollow out concavities of various forms at my pleasure, squares, ovals, or octangles; whereunto I could

* The picture is no longer in the church.

† Cardinal Salviati the younger.

also add such projections as I desired, simply by affixing pieces of the same tufa, attached and well secured with the aid of nails and clamps. I thus brought the ceiling to somewhat fairer proportions by means of those stuccoes, which were the first modern works of the kind executed in Naples.*

On the walls and at the ends of the Refectory I painted six pictures in oil, each seven braccia high, three at each end that is to say. In three of these pictures, those over the entrance namely, are Stories representing the Fall of Manna, with Moses and Aaron, who are gathering it up; and here I took much pains to give variety to the attitudes and vestments of men, women, and children, expressing also the feelings with which they collected that manna, and their gratitude to God for the same. At the upper end of the Refectory is Our Saviour Christ at table in the house of Simon, Mary Magdalen is bathing his feet with her tears, and wiping them with her hair; her attitude, and the expression of her countenance, showing her repentance of the sins she has committed.†

This Story is divided into three compartments; in the centre is the supper, and to the right a buttery, with its credenza or beaufet, covered with vases in varied and fanciful forms; to the left is the Seneschal superintending the bringing forward and placing of the dishes. The ceiling was also divided into three parts, in one of which the subject treated of is Faith, in the second it is Religion, and in the third, Eternity: each of these figures, representing those ideas, is in the centre of its compartment; and around them are eight Virtues, intimating to the Monks, who eat in that Refectory, the qualities required for the perfection of their lives. The remaining spaces of the ceiling I enriched with grottesche divided into forty-eight compartments, and serving as a sort of framework or bordering to the forty-eight Celestial Signs. In six divisions, beneath the windows of the place, moreover, which last I enlarged and decorated, I painted six Parables of Christ, the subjects whereof are appropriate to that place. And to all these pictures the richly executed carving of the seats is made to correspond.

* Della Valle tells us that this passage is said to have greatly displeased the Neapolitans, who, as the Padre affirms, have taken considerable pains to prove the assertion inaccurate.

† These pictures are now at Naples (in the Museo Borbonico).

This being finished I painted a picture, eight braccia high, for the High Altar of the Church; the subject, Our Lady presenting the Infant Christ to Simeon in the temple;* a work of which the invention and arrangement were new. And here it may be allowable to remark the somewhat extraordinary fact, that there had been no masters since Giotto, who in that great and noble city had accomplished works in painting of any importance; although it is also true that productions from the hand of Perugino and Raffaello da Urbino had been transported thither. Wherefore I now laboured to the very utmost of my power, in the hope of producing something that might arouse the genius of men in that country, and incite them to attempt works of high and honourable character. Subsequently then, whether from this cause or from others, from that time to this there have been many beautiful productions completed in those lands, whether in stucco-work or painting.

In addition to the pictures above-mentioned, I painted frescoes on the ceiling of the Strangers' Lodgings in the same Monastery; Christ bearing his Cross namely, with numerous Saints, who, in imitation of their Lord, are also bearing their crosses on their shoulders; the figures are of the size of life: and in this work I desired to intimate that he who would truly follow Christ must learn to bear the adversities of the world, and that with enduring patience. For the General of the Order I painted a large picture of Christ walking on the waves and extending his hand to Peter, who, having gone to meet him, is in fear of drowning; and in another picture, painted for the Abbot Capeccio, I delineated the Resurrection.

These works completed, the Signor Don Pietro di Toledo, Viceroy of Naples, commissioned me to paint in fresco a Chapel, which he had in his Garden at Pozzuolo, adding other ornaments in very delicate stucco-work. Directions had been given by the same noble for the construction of two great Loggie, but that design did not take effect for the following cause: between the Viceroy and the Monks there had arisen a dispute, and the civil magistrate, with his followers, had come to the Monastery to apprehend the Abbot and some of his Monks, who had quarrelled for precedence with the Black Friars, when the two bodies had met in a

* The Presentation is also in the Borbonico.

procession. But the Monks, aided by some fifteen or sixteen young men, who were helping me in my stucco-works, having made resistance, certain of the Sbirri were wounded, this compelled my assistants to take refuge in the night-time, some here, others there, and I was left almost alone. Thus I was not only prevented from making the Loggie, but was impeded also in the execution of twenty-four stories from the Old Testament, and from the Life of San Giovanni Battista, which, as I did not choose to leave them in Naples, I took with me to finish them in Rome, whence I afterwards sent them to their destined place.

I then spent several months on the stalls and presses of walnut-wood, made after my own designs and architecture, in the Sacristy of San Giovanni Carbonaro,* a monastery of the Eremite Monks, who are Observantines of Saint Augustine, and for whom a short time previously I had painted a picture of Christ crucified, in a chapel outside of their church.† This, to which I had added a rich frame of stucco-work, was executed by me at the desire of Seripando, the General of their Order, who was afterwards made a Cardinal. In the centre of the staircase at the same Monastery, I likewise depicted San Giovanni in fresco; he is looking at Our Lady, who, standing on the Moon, is clothed with the Sun and crowned with twelve stars.

At Naples, I furthermore painted the Hall of a house belonging to the Florentine merchant, Messer Tommaso Cambi, who was my friend, adorning the four walls of the same with pictures of the Seasons. On a terrace, moreover, where I constructed a fountain for Messer Tommaso, I likewise executed paintings of Sleep and Dreams. For the Duke of Gravina I painted an Adoration of the Magi, which he took with him into his states; and for Orsanca, the Viceroy's secretary, I delineated five figures around a crucifix, with many other pictures.

But although well received by the Neapolitan nobles, very liberally remunerated, and finding commissions daily multiplying on my hands, I nevertheless decided that, as my young men had departed, and I had executed a very fair sufficiency of works, during the year that I had passed in

* There are still fifteen small pictures by Vasari in the Sacristy of San Giovanni a Carbonari, at Naples.

† This also retains its place.

Naples, it would be better for me to return to Rome; and having done so, the first thing I did after my arrival was to paint four immense pictures, in oil and on cloth, for the doors of the Organ of the Epispocal Church in Naples, for the Signor Rannuccio Farnese, who was then Archbishop of that city. On the outer side of these doors were placed five Saints, Patrons of Naples; and on the inside was the Birth of Christ with the Shepherds, and King David singing from his Psalter the words, *Dominus dixit ad me.* I also finished the above-named twenty-four pictures, with some for Messer Tommaso Cambi, which were all sent to Naples.

These works completed, I painted five pictures for Raffaello Acciaiuoli, by whom they were taken into Spain; these represented the Passion of Christ.* The same year, Cardinal Farnese, desiring to have the Hall of the Chancery, in the Palace of San Giorgio, adorned with Paintings, Monsignore Giovio, anxious to see the work in my hands, advised me to prepare various designs and inventions, which were nevertheless not put into execution. Ultimately, however, the Cardinal determined on having the Hall painted in fresco, and with all the expedition possible, desiring to have it ready for his use at a certain fixed time. The Hall is rather more than a hundred palms long, fifty wide, and about fifty high. At each end it was determined to have one large picture, and on one of the side walls two, but on the other, which was broken by windows, there could not be stories, and there was consequently only a repetition of the ornaments forming the divisions of the opposite side.† And here, to avoid reproducing the basement or socle, which had always been painted beneath pictures of this kind, and with the view to attain variety of effect, I caused a range of steps, rising at least nine palms above the floor, to be constructed in various forms, each picture having its separate flight. On these steps I placed figures in harmony with the subject represented above them, these ascending until they came to the platform or level, whence the pictures commenced.

It would, however, be a long and, perchance, fatiguing story, were I to describe all the particulars of these pictures; I will therefore only touch on the principal features. The whole

* Of these works the present writer can find no trace.

† The pictures, which have been mentioned in the Life of Cristofano Gherardi, are still in existence.

of the stories are from the Life of Pope Paul III.; and in each of them is the Portrait of that Pontiff, taken from the life. In the first, wherein are represented the Expeditions, so to speak, of the Roman Court, on the Tiber, are seen Embassies from various nations, some sent to beg favours, others to offer tribute to the Popes; and here there are numerous Portraits from nature. In large niches placed over the doors, which are on each side of the Story, are two figures of great size, the one representing Eloquence, the other Justice; over the first are two figures of Victory, sustaining a bust of Julius Cæsar; and over the second, two similar figures bearing that of Alexander the Great. Over all are the Arms of the Pope, the supporters of the Escutcheon being Liberality and open-handed Generosity.

On the principal façade is the same Pontiff rewarding merit, by the bestowal of marriage portions, knighthoods, bishoprics, and cardinals' hats. Among those who receive the same are Sadoleto, Polo, Bembo, Contarino, Giovio, Buonarroto, and other men of distinction, all portraits from the life: there is also a figure which represents Sovereign Favour, and is placed within a large niche; she holds a Cornucopia filled with various dignities, all which she pours out upon the earth: the figures of Victory above her head support the bust of the Emperor Trajan. There is also Envy, eating Vipers, and appearing to burst with their venom.

In the other story is Pope Paul, intent on various works of architecture, more especially on that of San Pietro at the Vatican; and therefore we have kneeling before His Holiness the figures of Painting, Sculpture, and Architecture, who are laying before him the plan of that church, and receiving his commands for the completion of the work. Here there is, moreover, the figure of Resolution, which, opening its breast, displays the heart within. Promptitude is likewise seen, accompanied by Riches; and in the niche is Abundance with Victories, holding a bust of the Emperor Vespasian. In a niche above this, and which divides one story from the other, is a figure representing the Christian Religion, having also two Victories over her head, who bear the bust of Numa Pompilius. The Escutcheon of Arms surmounting this story is that of the Cardinal San Giorgio, by whom the Palace was built.

In the Story opposite to that of the Expeditions of the

Court, is the Universal Peace made among all Christians by means of the same Pontiff, Paul III., more particularly between the Emperor Charles V. and Francis King of France, both portraits. Here Peace is seen to burn the Arms of War; the Temple of Janus is in the act of being closed; and Fury is lying in chains. The large niches which stand on each side of the Story are occupied, one by Concord, with Victories supporting the bust of the Emperor Titus; the other by Charity with Children, the Victories over her bearing the head of Augustus: at the summit of all are the Arms of Charles V., the supporters of which are Victory and Joy.

The whole work is enriched with inscriptions and beautiful mottoes by Giovio, one more particularly, which records the fact of these paintings having been executed in a hundred days, as I, being then young, took pains that they should be, because I thought only of complying with the wishes of the Cardinal who had an especial reason for desiring to have them finished at a certain day. But of a truth, if I laboured hard in making the cartoons and in studying my work, I confess to having committed an error in confiding the execution of the same to my young assistants, for the sake of having them completed the more rapidly and within the time when the Hall was required, since it would have been better that I had toiled a hundred months, so only I had done all with my own hand. For although I might not, even in that case, have accomplished all that I could have desired, for the service of the Cardinal and mine own honour, yet I should, at least, have had the satisfaction of having effected all with my own hand and done my best. But this error caused me to resolve that I would never undertake works again of which I could not paint the whole myself, permitting nothing more than the mere sketch to be effected by others after my own designs.*

The Spaniards, Bizzera and Roviale, who assisted me to

* After the candour of this admission there seems little justice, and less generosity, in reproaching our good Giorgio with his too disinterested wish to oblige the Cardinal, as is so frequently done; his own evident sense of the injury suffered by his reputation was assuredly a sufficient punishment, and his resolve to sin no more should be accepted as an ample *amende*. It may be true that he did not always maintain this resolve, but let him who has never broken a resolution throw the first stone.

a considerable extent in this Hall, attained great practice and facility thereby, as did also the Bolognese Battista Bagnacavallo, the Aretine Bastian Flori, Giovan Paolo of the Borgo, Fra Salvador Foschi of Arezzo, and many other of my disciples.

Now at this time, and when my day's work was done, I went frequently to see the most illustrious Cardinal Farnese at his supper, where there were always present, entertaining him with admirable and honourable discourses, Il Molza, Annibale Caro, Messer Gandolfo, Messer Claudio Tolomei, Messer Romolo Amasei, Monsignore Giovio, and many other literati and men of distinction, of whom the Court of that Prelate is ever full.

One evening among others, the conversation fell on the Museum of Giovio, and of the portraits of illustrious men placed there in admirable order and with appropriate inscriptions, when, passing from one thing to another, as is done in conversation, Monsignore Giovio said that he always had felt, and still did feel, a great wish to add to his Museum and to his book of "Eulogies," a Treatise concerning men who had distinguished themselves in the Arts of Design; from Cimabue down to our own times. He spoke at some length on the subject, giving proof of much knowledge and judgment in matters respecting our arts. It is nevertheless true, that as he was treating only on generals and did not enter into the matter very closely, he often made some confusion among the artists cited, changing their names, families, birth-places, &c., or attributing the works of one to the hand of another, not describing things as they were precisely, but rather treating of them in the mass.

When Giovio had finished his discourse, the Cardinal, turning to me, said, "What think you, Giorgio; would not this be a fine work, a noble labour?" "Admirable, indeed; most illustrious my lord," replied I, "provided Giovio be assisted by some one belonging to our calling, who can put things into their right places, and relate them as they have really occurred; and this I say because, although the discourse he has just concluded is admirable, yet he has often made assertions that are not correct, and said one thing for another." "Could not you, then," replied the Cardinal, being incited thereunto by Giovio, Caro, Tolomei, and the rest,—"could not you supply him with a summary of these matters, and with notices of all these artists; their works being arranged in the order of time, whereby you would confer that benefit also on your arts?" This, although I knew the undertaking to be beyond my strength, I was yet willing to attempt, with such power as I possessed, and promised to do it according to the best of my ability.

Thus having sat down to collect my notes and memoranda, which I had prepared even from my boyhood, for my own recreation, and because of a certain affection which I preserved towards the memory of our artists, every notice respecting whom had always been most interesting to me, I put together all that seemed to be suited for the purpose, and took them to Giovio. Having commended my pains, the latter then said, "My dear Giorgio, I would have you undertake this work yourself, for I see that you know perfectly well how to proceed therein; whereas I have not myself the courage to attempt it, not knowing the various particulars with which you are acquainted, nor possessing that judgment respecting the different manners of the artists which you have attained. Thus, even had I the heart to undertake this labour, the best I should make of it would be a little Treatise after the manner of Pliny. Do you, therefore, what I say, Vasari; for, by the specimen you give me in this narration, I perceive that you will succeed admirably well."

Finding that I was, nevertheless, but slightly disposed to do as he recommended, Giovio caused Caro, Molza, Tolomei, and others of my intimate friends, to join their persuasions to his own; wherefore, having finally taken my resolution, I set hand to the work, intending to give it to one or other of them, when it was finished, to the end that he might look it over, and having brought the work into good order, might get it published under some other name than mine own.*

* In the following year our author sent a portion of the Lives to Caro accordingly, when the latter replying, in a letter which the reader will find in vol. i. of his *Lettere Famigliari*, encourages him to continue, exhorts him not to depart in any instance (as he had sometimes done) from the general simplicity of his own natural style, and ends by assuring him that he was performing "a beautiful and useful work." From this letter, as well as from internal evidence, to which we cannot here refer more minutely, it is manifest that the Lives of Vasari were written by himself, and not by Don Silvano Razzi or others, as some have affirmed.

In October of the year 1546 I left Rome, and repaired to Florence, where I painted a Last Supper, for the Nuns of the renowned Convent of the Murate, and in the Refectory of their house. The commission for this work I received from Pope Paul III., who had a sister-in-law there, she who had been Countess of Pitigliano namely.* I subsequently executed a Marriage of the Virgin Martyr, St. Catherine, who is accompanied by two other Saints, being commissioned to do so by Messer Tommaso Cambi, who designed the picture for a sister of his, then Abbess in the Convent of Bigallo, outside of Florence.† That completed, I painted two large pictures in oil, for Monsignore de' Rozzi of the family of the Counts of San Secondo and Bishop of Pavia, one a San Jeronimo, the other a Pietà; both of which were sent into France.

In the year 1547, I undertook, at the request of Messer Bastiano della Seta, Superintendent to the Cathedral of Pisa, to finish a picture which had been commenced in that church; and for my friend, Simon Corsi, I executed a Madonna, in oil, of very large size. While occupied with these works, I had also brought almost to its conclusion my book of the Lives of our Artists, nothing more remaining than to have it arranged in a good form; when, just at this time, I made the acquaintance of Don Gian Matteo Faetani of Rimini, a monk of Monte Oliveto, and a very learned as well as intelligent person, who desired that I should execute certain works in the Church and Monastery of Santa Maria di Scolca at Rimini, of which he was Abbot. He then, having promised to get the work transcribed by one of his Monks, who was an excellent penman, and to correct it himself,‡ I repaired to Rimini, there to execute the picture for the High Altar of the above-named church, which is about three miles from the city.

* On the suppression of the Convent, this picture was removed to the Altar of the Most Holy Sacrament, in the Church of Santa Croce.

† "After various changes, this picture was sold in the year 1757 to the painter, Ignatius Hugford," observes an Italian commentator; but the present writer has not been able to ascertain its subsequent destiny.

‡ "Let the proof here given of Vasari's freedom from presumption not fail to be remarked," exclaims a compatriot of our author. Observe, too, the candour of his confession, that these writings were subjected to the correction of others; but this confession itself is a clear proof that the work was his own, and not that of another, with which it is obvious that he would not have taken any such liberty.

The subject of this work was an Adoration of the Magi; it comprised a vast number of figures, which in that solitary place I was enabled to execute with great pains and study, imitating, as well as I could, the varieties existing between the followers of each King's Court, those of all the three being mingled together; but their complexions, vestments, and decorations, render it easy to decide to which King every courtier and follower belongs. The central portion of the picture is accompanined by two others, one on each side; these contain such parts of the Courts as could not find place in the first, with horses, elephants, and giraffes. For the different Chapels also I painted separate figures of Prophets, Sybils, and Evangelists in the act of writing. In the Cupola or Tribune I painted four large figures, all singing the praises of Christ and the Virgin, Orpheus and Homer namely, who have mottoes in Greek; with Virgil, having the motto, *Jam redit et virgo*, &c.; and Dante, who has the following lines:—

*Tu se' colei, che l'umana natura*
*Nobilitasti sì, che il suo fattore*
*Non si sdegnò di farsi tua fattura.**

There are, besides, many other circumstances and accessories which need not be mentioned here.†

Continuing meanwhile to proceed with my book, I painted at this same time a large picture in oil for the Church of San Francesco in Rimini; it was intended for the High Altar, and represents the Saint receiving the Stigmata from Christ at the Mountain of La Vernia, which is given as it is in Nature, but as those rocks are entirely grey and San Francesco with his companion are also clothed in grey vestments, I caused Our Saviour Christ to appear in a splendour of Glory, within which are numerous Seraphim also; the work is thus varied; and the Saint, with other figures, being wholly illumined with the light of that glory, while the landscape, lying in shadow, exhibits a variety of changing colours; many persons declared themselves not displeased with the

* Thou, thou art she who hast ennobled high
The human nature, so that He who formed
Hath not disdained through Thee to live as man.

† One of the finest of our author's paintings, and still (1846) in good preservation; but the pictures of the Cupola have disappeared; the intonaco had peeled off, according to Piacenza, and the walls were therefore whitewashed.

picture, and it was much praised by the Cardinal Capo di Ferro, then Legate of the Romagna.*

Being then invited from Rimini to Ravenna, as I have said elsewhere, I painted a Deposition from the Cross, in the new Church of the Abbey of Classi, which belongs to the Order of the Camaldolines, and at the same time I executed numerous designs, small pictures, and other works of minor importance for many of my friends. These were indeed so numerous and so varied, that it would be difficult for me to remember even a part of them, while it might perchance be fatiguing to the reader to hear so many minutiæ.

The building of my house in Arezzo had meanwhile been completed; and, returning to my home, I now made the designs for painting the Hall, three chambers, and the façade, principally by way of amusing myself through that summer In these designs I depicted among other things, all the places wherein I had myself laboured, as if they had in a manner brought tribute (by the gains which I had made through their means) towards the building of my house. But at that time I did not complete more than the ceiling of the Hall (the wood work whereof is tolerably rich), adorning the same with thirteen large pictures, wherein are represented the Celestial Deities, while the nude forms of the four Seasons of the year are placed in the angles; they appear to be examining a large picture which occupies the centre, and presents a figure of Art trampling Envy beneath her fect, while she takes Fortune captive by the hair of her head, and strikes both with a staff. These figures are all the size of life; and a thing which then pleased many in this work, was the circumstance that, Fortune being in the midst, the spectator, in passing around the Hall, sometimes sees Envy surmounting Fortune and Art at one part, while at another part he sees Art surmounting both Envy and Fortune, as is known frequently to happen in real life.

On the walls around are Abundance, Liberality, Wisdom, Prudence, Labour, Honour, and other figures of similar character; and beneath them are stories of the ancient masters, Apelles, Zeuxis, Parrhasius, Protogenes, and others, with varied compartments and other minutiæ, of which, for the sake of brevity, I omit further mention. On the ceiling,

* This work also is well preserved, and bears the master's name, inscribed with his own hand.—*Piacenza.*

in the carved wood-work of one of the chambers, I painted a large circular painting of God blessing the seed of Abraham, and promising the infinite multiplication of the same; on four pictures, moreover, which surround that just mentioned, I painted figures of Peace, Concord, Virtue, and Temperance.

Always delighting in and respecting the memory and works of the ancients, and perceiving that the method of painting in tempera has fallen into neglect, I felt a great desire to resuscitate that mode of delineation, and executed the whole work in tempera accordingly; a manner which certainly does not merit to be either despised or neglected. At the entrance to this chamber, I depicted, almost by way of jest, a Bride, who, with a rake in her hand, appears to have gathered up, and carried with her, whatever she could obtain from the house of her father; while, in the other hand, which is stretched before her, as she is about to enter the habitation of her husband, she has a lighted torch, by way of intimation that she bears with her, wherever she goes, a fire which consumes and destroys all things.

While I was thus passing my time, the year 1548 arrived, when Don Giovan Benedetto of Mantua, Abbot of Santa Fiore e Lucilla, a Monastery of the Black Friars, taking much pleasure in painting, and being a friend of mine, requested me to paint the Last Supper, or some work of similar kind, at the upper end of their Refectory. Desiring to do him pleasure, therefore, I thought over the matter, considering how I might best contrive something out of the common in that place; and taking counsel with the good father, it was determined that I should paint there the Marriage of the Queen Esther with King Ahasuerus: the picture, fifteen braccia long, to be in oil, but first to be fixed in its place, and afterwards executed. And this method (I, who have tried, can safely affirm it) is that which ought always to be adopted, if it be desired that the picture shall have its true and appropriate lights in all parts; seeing that to paint the picture in any other place, whether higher or lower than that where it is to be fixed, is to endanger the effect; since the lights, shadows, and other properties of the work are frequently much affected by the change.

In this picture then, I did my utmost to produce an aspect of dignity and majesty; but am not myself the competent judge as to whether I have succeeded or not.* Servants of different degrees, pages, esquires, soldiers of the guard, the credenza, the beaufet musicians, a dwarf, and whatever may be supposed requisite to a royal banquet, are all to be clearly distinguished. Among the rest is the Seneschal, superintending the service; he is accompanied by numerous pages, servants in livery, esquires, and other attendants. At the two ends of the table, which is of an oval form, are nobles, and other great personages, standing, as is the custom, to look upon the feast. The King Ahasuerus, haughty of aspect, yet with a truly regal dignity, and face expressing his love for the Queen, presents to her a cup of wine with his right hand, while he supports himself by leaning on the left arm. In fine, if I were to believe what I then heard from the people, and what I still hear from all who see this work, I might be tempted to imagine that I had effected something; but I know too well how the matter stands, and what I would have accomplished had the hand been only capable of performing what the spirit had conceived. This, however, I may freely admit, namely, that I gave my best care and attention to the execution of the picture.† On a corbel of the ceiling, above this painting, is a figure of Our Saviour Christ, presenting to Queen Esther a Crown of flowers. The figure is in fresco, and was placed there to signify the spiritual import of the story, denoting that, repulsed by the old Synagogue, Christ espoused the New Church of his faithful Christians.

About this time, I painted the Portrait of Messer Luigi Guicciardini, brother of Messer Francesco, who wrote the History. Messer Luigi was that year Commissary of Arezzo, and, being my intimate friend, he had made me buy a considerable property in land, called Frassineto, situate in the Valdichiana. This has been the very salvation of my

* Whoever shall compare the unrestrained liberality with which our beloved Giorgio bestows his praise on the works of others, will be certain that this is true and not feigned modesty. He will remember how remarkable is the contrast which those warm eulogies present to the reserved and really diffident manner in which, not here only, but always, the admirable Vasari speaks of his own performances.

† This great work still exists; the Refectory now serves as the Hall of Assembly for the Academicians. See Gaye, *Carteggio inedito*, vol. ii. p. 378. See also Gualandi, *Memorie originali Italiane di Belle Arti*, serie i. p. 85.

family, and will be the best possession of my successors, if, as I hope, they should know how to prove true to themselves. The portrait, which is now in possession of Messer Luigi's heirs, is said to be the most faithful in resemblance of all the infinite number that I have taken. But I will make no further mention of the portraits made by my hand, since it would be tedious to enumerate these likenesses; and, to tell the truth, I have avoided painting them whenever I could do so.*

These works completed, I was commissioned by the Aretine, Fra Mariotto da Castiglioni, to paint a picture of Our Lady with SS. Anna, Francesco, and Salvestro, for the Church of San Francesco, in the territory of Arezzo, and at the same time, I undertook to prepare, for the Cardinal di Monte, afterwards Pope Julius III., and my great patron, who was then Legate of Bologna, the design and ground-plan of an important edifice, which was afterwards erected at the foot of Monte Sansovino, the native place of the Cardinal, and whither I did myself repair many times by order of that Prelate, who took great pleasure in building.

When I had finished all here in question, I went to Florence; and that summer I painted, on a banner to be borne in procession by the Company or Brotherhood of San Giovanni di Peducci of Arezzo, the figure of that Saint preaching to the people on one side, and the same San Giovanni in the act of baptizing Our Saviour Christ on the other. This picture I sent to my house at Arezzo so soon as it was finished, with directions for its being remitted to the men of the Company. Now it happened that the Frenchman, Monsignore Giorgio, Cardinal d'Armagnac, passing through Arezzo, and going, for other causes, to see my house in Arezzo, did likewise see this banner or standard; wherefore, being pleased with the same he made great efforts to obtain it, and offered a very large sum as the price thereof, proposing to send it to the King of France: but I would not break my promise to those who had commissioned me

* "It is true that Vasari painted many portraits," remarks Masselli, "and it is also true that in these he appears greater than himself. This difference proceeds, as I believe," he further adds, "from the fact that while taking a portrait he was compelled to keep the reality before him, and could not avail himself of that facility of hand which he turned to account in his larger compositions. See the *Passigli Edition of our Author*, Florence, 1832-8.

to paint it; many said I might have made another for the Brotherhood, but I could not be sure of succeeding equally well.

No long time afterwards I painted a picture for Messer Annibale Caro, and which he had long before requested me to execute, in one of those letters of his which are now printed;* the subject, taken from Theocritus, is Adonis dying in the arms of Venus; this work, at a later period and almost against my will, was taken into France and given to Messer Albizzo del Bene, together with a Psyche, looking with a lamp at Love, who was sleeping, but, being touched by a spark from the lamp, is awakening. These figures, which were of life-size and entirely nude, caused Alfonso di Tommaso Cambi, then a most beautiful youth, and very learned and accomplished, as well as good, kindly, and courteous, to desire that I would make a Portrait of himself, also nude and of life-size, in the character of Endymion, that hunter beloved of the Moon; the fair form of the youth and a landscape, of fanciful composition, amidst which it is seen, receive their light from the splendour of the moon; which, penetrating or rather dissipating the darkness of the night, gives the view a tolerably natural and pleasing appearance, for I laboured with all diligence to imitate the peculiar tints communicated by the pale yellow light of the moon to such objects as are struck by the same.

At a later period I painted two pictures to send to Raugia, in one of these is a Madonna, in the other a Pietà; and shortly afterwards I painted Our Lady with the Divine Child in her arms, and Joseph beside her, in a large picture for Francesco Botti. This work, which I certainly executed with all the care of which I was capable, Francesco took with him into Spain. Having finished these labours, I went that same year to see the Cardinal Monti at Bologna, where he was Legate, and remained with him some days. There was one subject of conversation, among many others,

* This letter is the second in the second volume of the *Lettere Pittoriche*, and is in the first volume of those of Annibale Caro. At the end of it are a few words relating to the Lives of the Artists, and these afford a further proof that the work was wholly by Vasari, and by no other hand; they are as follows:—"Of your other work" (the Lives namely), "there needs not that I speak here, since you are determined that we shall read them over together; but meanwhile, do you finish them entirely, for I am convinced that I shall have little to do unless it be to praise them."

on which he said so much, and sought to persuade me with so many good reasons, that, thus pressed by him, I resolved at length to do what I had never before chosen to do, that is to take a wife; and I married accordingly, as was his desire, a daughter of the noble Aretine citizen, Francesco Bacci.

Having returned to Florence, I painted a large picture of Our Lady, with numerous figures, according to a new invention. This was taken by Messer Bindo Altoviti, who gave me a hundred crowns of gold for the same; and it is now in his house at Rome, to which city Messer Bindo took it.* I painted many other pictures at the same time, as for example, for Messer Bernardetto de' Medici, for the eminent physician, Messer Bartolommeo Strada, who was my friend, with other things for many others, also my friends; but of these works I need make no further mention.

Now in those days, Gismondo Martelli had died in Florence, and having left orders in his will that a picture, with Our Lady, and certain Saints, should be painted for the Chapel of that noble family, which is in the Church of San Lorenzo, I was applied to, for the execution of the same, by Luigi and Pandolfo Martelli, with Messer Cosimo Bartoli, all my friends. Wherefore, having received permission from Duke Cosimo, patron, and chief superintendent of that Church, I accepted the work, but on condition that, in allusion to the name of the Testator, I should be permitted to execute a Story from the Life of San Sigismondo, choosing the subject thereof at my pleasure. This agreement concluded, I remembered having heard that Filippo di Ser Brunellesco, the architect of the Church, had erected all the Chapels, with a view to the execution therein, not of small paintings, but of one large picture, occupying the whole space in each one; for which cause, regarding the honour to be derived from the work, rather than the moderate sum which I was to obtain from the owners of the chapel, who intended to have a small picture, of few figures only, I depicted the death, or more properly the martyrdom, of the King, San Sigismondo, in a great picture, ten braccia wide and thirteen high, showing himself, his Queen, and their two

* Bottari tells us that in his time there were no longer any of the pictures which Vasari speaks of himself as having painted for Bindo Altoviti, to be found in the possession of that family.

sons, on the point of being thrown into a well by another King, or rather tyrant.

The Story was arranged in such sort that the frame-work of the Chapel, which is a half circle, was made to represent the Gate of a large Palace of rustic architecture, and through this gate a view was obtained into a square court surrounded by columns and pilasters of the Doric order, between which was seen a wall of eight sides; the ascent to the same being by a flight of steps: up these steps the myrmidons of the tyrant were bearing the two sons of San Sigismondo, whom they were about to cast naked into the well. Within the Loggia on one side, I depicted the people regarding that frightful spectacle; and, on the other, the left namely, are executioners, who, having seized the wife of King Sigismond, are dragging her towards her death: near the principal door is a group of soldiers binding San Sigismondo, whose resigned and patient attitude proves him to suffer that martyrdom willingly; he is looking upwards at angels who are hovering in the air, and showing him the palms and crowns of martyrdom prepared for his queen and children as well as for himself, a sight which appears to be mightily sustaining and consoling to him.

I also took great pains to express the cruelty and fierceness of the wicked tyrant who stands at the upper end of the Court, observing the progress of his vengeance and the death of San Sigismondo. At a word, so far as in me lay, I strove to give every figure its appropriate expression and proper attitude, with promptitude of action and whatever else was required: the degree of my success I leave others to decide, but I may say that I gave all the labour, care, and study to the work that my utmost efforts could command.*

Meanwhile Duke Cosimo desired that the Book of the Lives, already brought to conclusion by the aid of my friends, and with all the diligence that I could use—the Duke desired, I say, that this book should now be printed, whereupon I gave it to the ducal printer Lorenzo Torrentino, and the work was commenced. But the "Theories"† had not

* The colours of this picture scaled off, until the canvas remained bare, when it was removed, and an altar being erected in the place, a picture of the Annunciation was fixed over it. This happened in the year 1711.

† The Treatise on the Practice of Architecture, Sculpture, and Painting, that is to say.

yet been completed when the death of Pope Paul III. took place, and I thought I should be compelled to leave Florence before the printing could be finished. For it had chanced that going out of the city gate to meet Cardinal Monte, who was passing through on his way to the Conclave, I had no sooner made my bow to that prelate and spoken a few words with him, than he said to me, "I am going to Rome, and shall infallibly be elected Pope; wherefore, if thou hast anything to desire, hasten to follow me, so soon as the news shall arrive, without waiting any other invitation than that I now give thee, or seeking any further intelligence."

Nor was this prognostic a vain word; being at Arezzo during the Carnival of that year, I was making arrangements for certain festivals and maskings, when there came a messenger with the news that the aforesaid Cardinal had become Pope Julius III. Mounting my horse, therefore, without delay, I proceeded to Florence, whence, hastened by the Duke, I departed at once for Rome, to be present at the Coronation of the new Pontiff, and to make arrangements for the festivities consequent thereon.

Arrived at Rome, and dismounting at the house of Messer Bindo, I went immediately afterwards to kiss the feet of His Holiness, which, when I had done, his first words were to remind me that the prediction he had uttered had not proved to be untrue. Having been crowned, and the confusion which always accompanies a change having passed, Pope Julius was anxious, first of all, to acquit himself of a duty to the elder and first Cardinal di Monte, by erecting a Tomb for that prelate at San Piero in Montorio. The designs and models were made accordingly; and it was constructed in marble, as I have related at length in another place.* The Altar-piece for the Chapel was meanwhile painted by myself, and I depicted thereon the Conversion of St. Paul; but to vary it somewhat from that of Michelagnolo, in the Paolina, I represented the saint still young, according to his own relation, and at the moment when, having fallen from his horse, he is conducted by the Soldiers to Ananias, from whom, by the imposition of hands, he receives his lost sight, and is baptized.†

But in this work, either on account of the restricted space,

* In the Lives of Simone Mosca, Michelagnolo, and Jacopo Sansovino.

† This picture is still in the Chapel.—*Ed. Flor.*, 1846-51.

or from some other cause, I did not entirely satisfy myself, although others did not appear to be displeased; Michelagnolo more particularly, was not dissatisfied. I also painted another picture for the same Pontiff, in a Chapel of the Palace namely; but this, for the causes before related,* I afterwards took to Arezzo, and placed at the High Altar of the Decanal Church.†

If, however, I had satisfied neither myself nor others in this picture any more than in that of San Piero a Montorio, there would have been no cause for surprise, seeing that I was in perpetual attendance on the Pontiff, who kept me constantly in action, either for architectural designs or other works. It was myself, for example, with whom originated the first arrangement and plans of the Vigna Julia, which the Pope then caused to be constructed at an incredible cost; and although the works were executed by others, it was I who made drawings of all the fancies which Pope Julius invented for that place, and which were afterwards examined and corrected by Michelagnolo; when Jacopo Barozzi da Vignola completed various apartments, halls, and chambers of the Vigna, with their appropriate ornaments from his designs. The lower Fountain, however, is after my own design, and was executed by Ammannato, who subsequently remained to construct the Loggia, which is above the Fountain. That artist could, nevertheless, not show what he was capable of, nor do anything in its due order in that place, because the Pope was daily taking into his head some new fancy, which had then to be instantly put into execution,‡ under the orders, given daily, of Messer Pier Giovanni Aliotti, Bishop of Forlì.§

In the year 1550, I had to go twice to Florence for certain affairs, and on the first of these occasions I completed the picture of San Sigismondo. The Duke, who came to see it in the house of Messer Ottaviano de' Medici, where it was that I executed the same, was so much pleased therewith,

* In the Life of Francesco Salviati.

† This picture forms the front of the Altar in the above-mentioned church.—*Ed. Flor.*, 1846-51.

‡ The exterior of this edifice is not wanting in a certain inelegance of proportion, but the deformities of the interior amply justify the remark of Vasari.—*Masselli.*

§ This is the prelate whom Michael Angelo called *Tantecose*, or Busy-body.

that he said to me, "When your engagements in Rome are completed, return to Florence, and enter my service, when I will show you what I desire that you should do."

Having returned to Rome, I took measures for the completion of all my works commenced there, and among other things I painted a picture for the Company or Brotherhood of the Misericordia; this, which was destined for the High Altar of that Brotherhood, was the Beheading of St. John the Baptist, and having fixed it in its place in the year 1553, I desired to return to Florence. But I was compelled to remain, for the purpose of constructing two very extensive Loggie for Messer Bindo Altoviti, in whose service I could not fail to be ever ready. These Loggie I decorated with stucco work and fresco paintings. One of them was erected at his Vigna, and that with a new species of architecture, for the arches being of so great a width, it was difficult to turn them without danger; I had them formed, therefore, of wood-work, canes, and matting, on which I caused stucco and fresco to be executed, as if the niches had been of masonry, as indeed they appear, and are supposed to be, by all who see them, supported as they are by very fine antique columns of vari-coloured marble, and enriched with various ornaments of similar kind.*

The second of the two Loggie mentioned above was erected on the ground-floor of Messer Bindo's house at Ponte, and is covered with Stories in fresco. I subsequently painted four large pictures in oil, representing the Four Seasons of the year, for the ceiling of an ante-chamber; and these finished, I was compelled to further delay by the request of my intimate friend, Andrea del Fonte, that I would paint the Portrait of his wife; this I did, giving him at the same time a large picture of Christ bearing his Cross, with figures copied from nature, which I had executed for a kinsman of the Pope, to whom I did not ultimately think proper to give it. For the Bishop of Vasona I painted a Dead Christ, supported by Nicodemus and two Angels; with a picture, representing the Birth of Our Lord, for Pier Antonio Bandini; the latter a Night-piece, with certain varieties in the composition thereof.

* Bottari observes that Baglioni has mistaken the sense of this passage, making Vasari describe a range of painted columns, whereas the paintings are stories, and the columns are really marble.

Now while I was occupied with these works, I took care to observe what the Pope was from time to time proposing to accomplish, and finally I became convinced that but little was to be expected from that Pontiff, for whose service one did but labour in vain; wherefore, although I had already prepared the Cartoons for painting in fresco the Loggia which is above the Fountain of the beforementioned Vigna, I resolved that nothing should thenceforth prevent me from entering the service of Duke Cosimo; more particularly as I was much pressed to do so by Messer Averardo Serrestori and the Bishop of Ricasoli, his Excellency's Ambassadors in Rome, as well as by the letters of Messer Sforza Almeni, cupbearer and first chamberlain of the Duke.

Having therefore repaired to Arezzo, intending thence to pass on to Florence, I was compelled to paint a figure of Patience, the size of life, in a large picture for Monsignore Minerbetti, the Bishop of that city, who was my friend and very good lord. This figure was in the same manner with that afterwards used as the impress for the reverse of his medals by the Signor Ercole, Duke of Ferrara.* These things being completed, I hastened to kiss the hand of Duke Cosimo; by whom, in his kindness, I was received with much favour; and while the subject of what I was first to undertake was in consideration, I caused the Façade of Messer Sforza Almeni's house to be painted in *chiaro-scuro* by Cristofano Gherardi dal Borgo, after my designs and with the compositions described at length in another place.†

Now at that time I was one of the Signori Priors of Arezzo, whose office it is to govern the city, but being called to his service by the letters of the Signor Duke, I was released from the duties of that office; and on my arrival in Florence I found that his Excellency had commenced the construction of those apartments in his Palace which look towards the Piazza del Grano, and which were then in progress under the direction of the wood-carver Tasso, then

* This figure, which Vasari designed with the advice of Michael Angelo and Annibale Caro, is described by the biographer in *Lettera* xix. of his Epistles, as given in the Passigli edition. See vol. ii. p. 1439.

† In the Life of Gherardi, vol. iv. of the present work. Four letters respecting these frescoes, and addressed by Vasari to Sforza Almeni, will be found as above-cited; they are those numbered from 27 to 30.

architect to the Palace: but the roof was so low that all the rooms wanted elevation, and had altogether a poor and stunted appearance. To raise the rafters would, nevertheless, have been a long operation; and I therefore advised the Duke to introduce a decoration formed in wood-work above the cross beams of the ceilings, with compartments two braccia and a half in extent, supported on corbels, which gave an elevation in the whole of nearly two braccia above the beams, as these last were first laid: that proposal pleased the Duke much, and he gave orders for its being instantly put into execution, commanding Tasso to prepare the wood carvings and frame-work, within which, in the square compartments that is to say, there was to be painted the Genealogy of the Gods, a subject afterwards to be continued in the succeeding apartments.

While these things were thus in preparation, I therefore, having had permission from the Duke, went to pass two months between Cortona and Arezzo, partly to complete the arrangement of certain of my affairs, and partly to finish a work in fresco commenced at Cortona on the Façade and ceiling of the house belonging to the Company of Jesus; where I painted stories from the Life of Christ, with others representing the Sacrifices described in the Old Testament, as offered to God from Cain and Abel, down to the time of the Prophet Nehemiah. At the same time I also arranged the designs and models for the edifice of the Madonna Nuova, constructed outside of that city. The works for the Brotherhood being completed, I then repaired to Florence with all my family; and in the year 1555, commenced my labours in the service of Duke Cosimo.

I then began and finished the paintings on the walls and ceiling of the before-mentioned Hall, called the Hall of the Elements, depicting therein eleven pictures, which represent the wrongs done to Uranus by the Titans. And in the ceiling of a room adjacent, I painted the Histories of Saturn and Ops, with that of Ceres and Proserpine on the ceiling of a large chamber. In a still more extensive apartment near this, I then painted Stories of the Goddess Berecenthia, and of Cibele, in triumph, with the four Seasons, on a ceiling, which is exceedingly rich. On the walls beneath, I furthermore delineated the twelve Months. In the ceiling of a room, which is not so richly decorated, I then painted the Birth of

Jupiter, with his nourishment by the Goat Amalthea, and the other more important circumstances related concerning him. In another room on the ground-floor, and beside that just mentioned, but richly adorned with marbles and stucco-work, are Stories of Jupiter and Juno; and finally, in the room succeeding the above, is the Birth of Hercules and all his Labours; those which could not be contained in the ceiling having been added to the frieze of each room, or executed in cloth of arras, corresponding to the various stories which the Signor Duke has caused to be woven after Cartoons prepared by myself.

Of the *grottesche*, ornaments, and pictures of the staircases, with other minute details prepared by my hand for those apartments, I will say nothing, not only because I propose to speak of them at greater length in another place,* but also because every one can see and judge of them for himself.

While these rooms were receiving their paintings, others, which are on a level with the Great Hall, and in a direct line with the same, were in process of construction; they are furnished with exceedingly convenient staircases, public and private, and by these access may be gained most commodiously from the lowest even to the highest chambers of the Palace.

Tasso, meanwhile, had died; and the Duke, who had a great wish to have this palace (which had been constructed at various times almost as it were by chance, and more for the convenience of the officials than with a view to good effect) brought into something like good order, determined to improve the same so far as should be found possible, resolving that in course of time the Great Hall should be painted, and that the Audience-chamber, commenced by Bandinello, should be completed. To bring the building into harmony therefore, making that which was to be done in accordance with the part already finished, he commanded me to prepare

* In the "Ragionamento" namely, first published after the death of our author, by his nephew Giorgio Vasari, in the year 1588. They have since gone through many editions, and will be found in that fine one of our author's collected works, first edited by Montani, then continued by Masselli, and published by Passigli in Florence, to which we have so frequently referred in the course of this Life.

various plans and designs, deciding at length, that a model in wood should be made, after that one of these plans which had best pleased him, to the end that he might the better arrange all the apartments according to his mind, as also that he might then direct the changes required in the old staircases, which appeared to him inconveniently steep, ill-contrived, and very defective, as in truth they were.

To this work, although a difficult undertaking and beyond my powers, I set hand, and to the best of my ability prepared the large model required, which is now in his Excellency's possession, but rather in obedience to his commands than as having any great hope that I should succeed. Yet, when this model was finished, whether it were his good fortune or mine, or the result of the great desire which I felt to satisfy him, it pleased his Excellency greatly; wherefore, commencing the work accordingly, that fabric has, by little and little, been brought, now doing one thing and now another, to the state in which we at present see it.*

While the remainder of the apartments were in course of construction, the first eight rooms completed in the new buildings were decorated with very rich works in stucco of varied compartments; these, comprising saloons, chambers, and a small chapel, all on the level of the Great Hall, were adorned with various pictures, and a large number of portraits, all belonging to history, and commencing with that of Cosimo the Elder; each room, moreover, received its name from some great and renowned person descended from that Signore. In one of these chambers are depicted the principal actions of the above-named Cosimo himself, with the virtues, which were more peculiarly his own; the Portraits of his children, taken from the life, are also there; and he is accompanied by his most distinguished friends and principal servants. In other rooms are the stories of Lorenzo the Elder, Leo X., Pope Clement, the Signor Don Giovanni, father of our Illustrious Duke, and that of Duke Cosimo himself.† In the chapel is a large and very beautiful picture

* Piacenza, speaking of Vasari's architectural works, extols more particularly the staircases of this palace, remarking that they are exceedingly commodious, "insomuch, that he who ascends them, attains the highest floor of the building almost without perceiving that he has ascended."

† The paintings in question still exist.

by the hand of Raffaello da Urbino,* placed between two others painted by myself, and representing SS. Cosimo and Damiano, to whom that chapel is dedicated.

In like manner the four upper rooms, appropriated to the Signora Duchess Leonora, are adorned with the actions of illustrious women, Greek, Hebrew, Latin, and Tuscan, each chamber exhibiting the life of a personage belonging to one of those nations; but I have spoken of these elsewhere, and shall mention them further in the Dialogue, which, as before said, will be soon published to the world, and to speak of all here would make the relation too long.

For these my labours, persistent, severe, and difficult as they were, I was richly rewarded by the liberality of the Duke, from whom I received handsome gifts in addition to my allotted stipend, seeing that he presented me with an excellent and commodious house in Florence as well as one in the country, to the end that I might devote myself the more easily to his service. In my native city of Arezzo, moreover, his Excellency has honoured me with the supreme magistracy of the Gonfaloniere and other offices, adding the privilege of permission to substitute a citizen to perform the active duties thereof in my place. To my brother Ser Pietro, also, the Duke has given profitable employments in Florence, and has bestowed important favours on my kinsmen in Arezzo, for which cause I shall never be satisfied with declaring the obligations I owe to that Signore for his many favours conferred on me.

Returning to my works, I proceed to say, that the illustrious Duke had resolved to put in execution a thought which he had long conceived, that namely of having the Great Hall adorned with paintings, an idea entirely worthy of his greatness and the extent of his genius.† Of this work he spoke to me in a light and jesting manner. I know not whether because he thought that I should certainly make good despatch therewith, and that he would thus see it finished in his own days, or whether for some concealed and,

* This is the Holy Family, called the *Madonna dell' Impannata*. Now in the Royal Palace of the Pitti.

† This is the Hall which was to have been painted by Leonardo da Vinci and Michael Angelo, and wherein there was also to be a fine picture by Fra Bartolommeo. The paintings of Vasari are in good preservation, those in oil on the ceiling, meanwhile, are more esteemed than are the frescoes on the walls.

as all his reasons ever were, prudent cause; but the end of the matter was, that I received a commission to raise the roof thirteen braccia above its then height, being commanded to make the ceiling in wood-work with rich gilding, and to paint stories in oil on each compartment of the same.

This great and important undertaking, if not above my courage, might yet, perhaps, have proved above my strength; but whether it were that the confidence reposed in me increased my ability, or that the good fortune which the Duke has in all things prevailed here also, or that the hope of distinction, with the occasion offered me by so fine a subject, added to my powers, or that (and this I ought to place before all besides) the grace of God supplied me with force, certain it is that I took it upon me to begin the work, and, as is seen, have brought it to conclusion, in contradiction to the opinions expressed by many, not only in less time than I had promised or than the work merited, but also in less than I had expected, or than his illustrious Excellency had ever hoped to see it completed in; and, as it chanced, he had good reason to be pleased as well as surprised, since the completion could not have taken place at a moment of greater need or on a more fortunate occasion.

This (that the cause of so much haste and solicitude may be understood) was no less than the Marriage of our illustrious Prince with the daughter of the late Emperor and sister of the present, which, having been in treaty for some time, was then concluded on; and it seemed to me to be my duty to make all possible effort, that this Hall, one of the principal apartments of the Palace, and that wherein the most important acts were to be solemnized, should be in such a condition as to permit of the owners availing themselves thereof. And here I submit to the consideration, not only of those connected with our arts, but of all other persons who may have seen these works, whether, the extent and variety of the same being taken into the account, this important and pressing occasion should not be accepted as my excuse, even though I may not, in that eager haste, have fully satisfied all the just demands of those numerous subjects presented there: subjects taken both from earth and sea;—storming of cities in one place for example, and building of the same in another; batteries, assaults, and skirmishes, intermingled with other subjects, such as councils, ceremonies, ancient and modern, triumphal processions, and many more, the mere sketches, designs, and cartoons for which, to say nothing of all else, is a matter demanding a very long time.

The nude figures, moreover, in the perfection whereof consists the beauty and excellence of our arts, with the landscapes, wherein those figures are exhibited, all of which I had to depict from Nature herself in the place to be displayed, were of themselves a laborious work ; as were the many portraits, which I also took from the life, of generals, captains, and other military chiefs, whose figures, with those of their soldiers, appeared in the stories to be described. At a word, I may with truth affirm, that in this work I was called on to depict almost every thing that could present itself to the mind and thought of man, an almost infinite variety of persons, faces, vestments, and ornaments, with arms of all kinds, morions, helmets, and cuirasses, horses with their caparisons and defences, artillery of all sorts, and every other implement demanded for battles on land; to which must be added ships, and whatever belongs to those on the sea, or to the navigation of the ocean, with tempests and storms, rains, snows, and other matters, of which I cannot record even the names.

But whoever examines the work will easily comprehend the vast amount of labour, and the many weary vigils and nights of wakefulness that I have supported in the execution thereof, and in combining, with all the knowledge I could command, some forty large stories, each ten braccia square, and comprising very large figures of every kind. And if some of my disciples and dependants were there assisting me, it is also true that they sometimes gave me effectual aid, and sometimes the contrary, seeing that, as they well know, I have not unfrequently had to repaint all they had done with my own hand, and to go over the whole picture, that every part of it might be in the same manner.

These stories treat of the History of Florence, from its first foundation to the present day ; dividing the town into its Quarters ; they also describe the cities which have submitted to, or been subjugated by, Florence and the enemies she has overcome, with the war of Pisa (to speak more particularly) on one side, and that with Siena on the other. There is also a war carried on by the popular government, for the period of fourteen years ; with another, which was brought to an end by the Duke in fourteen months. These events collectively will be found partly on the ceiling and partly on the walls, which are eighty braccia long and twenty high; the frescoes I am still proceeding with, and of these I shall speak in the Dialogue before-mentioned. All this I say, for no other cause than the wish I have to show the earnest persistence with which I have laboured and do labour in these our arts; and with what just reasons I may excuse myself when I have in some places (and I am conscious these are many) fallen short in my works of what might and ought to have been effected.*

I may here add that, about this time I was charged with the care of designing and laying before his Excellency the various Arches of Triumph to be erected for the Nuptials, a great part of which I had likewise to construct. I was also commissioned to complete the remainder of the preparations so largely made in Florence for the Marriage of the illustrious Signor Prince; and had, moreover, to delineate in ten pictures, each fourteen braccia high and eleven wide, all the Piazzas of the principal cities in the Florentine dominions, with the most important edifices and distinctive characteristics of the same. Furthermore, I had to see that part of the Hall which had been commenced by Bandinelli brought to completion, and to make a scene for the opposite

* What can be more candid, upright, and creditable to the writer, whether as an artist or a man, than this dignified and most satisfactory exposition of his motives and proceedings? Consider also the character of the man, grateful and affectionate; his first impulse on receiving kindness was to do kindness, but in double measure, in return. Highly favoured and liberally treated by the Duke, the first wish of our admirable master's heart was to gratify Cosimo in his turn; to this wish he sacrificed his reputation, as well as his repose, consciously sacrificed it, dear as fame was to him, as is fully manifest. Compare this mode of proceeding with that of other artists of the period; paid for works which no entreaty could prevail on them to complete; no sense of shame or higher motive could force them to fulfil their engagements: take the unprincipled and selfish Bandinelli, for example. Had Vasari been equally devoted to the interest, or supposed interest—for whose true interest can really consist in wrong doing?—of his own sole self, many proofs concur to convince us that his powers would have been proved equal on all points, as they are acknowledged to have been in many, to those of the greatest masters, Raphael and Michael Angelo alone perhaps excepted. All honour to the dear and upright Giorgio, therefore; and let us hope that his life of affectionate devotion had its rewards in a better kind of satisfaction than could have been derived by those more careful of their own interests and reputation, from the questionable proceedings whereby they but too frequently permitted themselves to seek their object.

end of the same, larger and richer than any that had ever been made before: finally, I had to construct the principal staircases of the Palace, with their vestibules, the court, and the columns, in that manner which every one may see, and which has been described above. To all which must be added fifteen pictures, representing that number of cities belonging to the Empire and the Tyrol;* all being copies from the places described.

Nor has the time that I have given to the putting forward of the Loggia, and to the great Fabric for the magistrates, been of unimportant duration, since I commenced the same; for this building, which looks on the Arno, is one of the most difficult and dangerous that I have ever erected, seeing that its foundations have had to be laid in the river; and it may be almost called an edifice constructed in the air.† But it was not possible to avoid doing as we have done, since, to say nothing of other causes, the great corridor, which, crossing the Arno, proceeds from the ducal Palace to the Palace and Gardens of the Pitti, had to be appended to the fabric above-named. That corridor, too, was completed under my directions, and with my designs, within the space of five months, although it is a work which one might imagine unlikely to be finished in less than five years.

There was, besides, committed to my care the charge of causing to be reconstructed and enlarged, for those nuptials, that machinery which had been used for the festivities solemnized in the great Tribune of the church of Santo Spirito, and which had formerly been held at San Felice in Piazza; all which was brought to such perfection as could be attained, insomuch that the dangers formerly incurred at those festivals are no longer to be feared. The Palace and Church erected for the Knights of San Stefano in Pisa,‡ is also a work of mine; as is likewise the completion of the

* These are Hertzig, Hall, Neustadt, Constance, Ebersdorf, Inspruck, Vienna, Presburg, Lintz, Fribourg (in Breisgau), Grätz, Kloster-Neubourg, Stein, Passau, and Prague.

† Considered one of the finest of our author's architectural works. Many important letters respecting it, written partly by Vasari himself, partly by others, will be found in the work of Gaye so frequently cited, the *Carteggio inedito di Artisti* namely. See vol. iii. p. 55, *et seq.*

‡ On this edifice the Duke is said to have proposed expending 15,000 crowns, but Vasari found means to erect a building sufficient to the purpose for a sum of 3,000. See Gaye, *loc. cit.*

Tribune, or rather Cupola of the Madonna dell' Umiltà in Pisa, which is one of great importance.* In all which, if I have produced anything that can be called good, I render thanks to God, without seeking to excuse my imperfections, which I know better than any one can tell them to me,—I give thanks to God, I say, from whom I hope to have furthermore so much assistance as shall enable me to complete that great undertaking of the walls of the great Hall, to the satisfaction of my Signor and Prince, who for thirteen years has afforded me so many good opportunities for the performance of honourable works to my credit as well as profit. If I can accomplish this, I shall then consider myself old, weary, and worn enough to retire to my repose.

And if from various causes my previous works have been executed with somewhat too much of haste, I hope to accomplish this one at my leisure, since the illustrious Duke does not wish me to proceed rapidly, but would have me do it at my ease, affording me all that rest and those recreations which I could myself desire to have. Last year, for example, being weary and exhausted with all the undertakings mentioned above, his Excellency gave me permission to amuse myself for some months; wherefore, I set off on my travels, and passed through little less than all Italy, revisiting a vast number of my old friends and signori, with the works of numerous masters, as I have related in another place. Lastly, I finished my visits with Rome, and being about to return to Florence, I went to kiss the feet of the most holy and blessed Pope Pius V., when His Holiness commanded me to paint him a picture so soon as I should have returned to Florence, and send it to his Convent and Church of the Bosco, which he was having built in his native place, near Alessandria della Paglia.

Having returned to Florence accordingly, and having received this command from His Holiness, whose many acts of favour I could not forget, I painted an Adoration of the Magi; and when he knew that it was finished, the Pontiff gave me to understand, that for his satisfaction, and because he desired to confer with me respecting certain of his plans, he would have me proceed myself to Rome with that picture, desiring most particularly to speak to me concerning the Fabric of San Pietro, which His Holiness proved himself to

* Alluded to at the end of Bramante's Life, when speaking of the Pistojese, Ventura Vitoni. See vol. ii. of the present work.

have much at heart. Having made my arrangements, with a hundred crowns which Pope Pius sent me for that purpose, and sending the picture before me, I repaired to Rome accordingly,* where, after I had remained a month, and had held much discourse with His Holiness, advising him not to permit that any changes should be made in the plans of Michelagnolo for the construction of San Pietro, and preparing certain designs which he required, I received his commands to paint, for the High Altar of the above-named Church at the Bosco, not a picture such as is usual, but an immense construction, in the manner of a Triumphal Arch,† with two large paintings, one before, the other behind, and about thirty stories in smaller pictures,‡ all of which were brought to completion with tolerable success.

At this time I obtained from His Holiness the gracious favour of his permission to erect a chapel and decanate in the Deanery of Arezzo, and he sent me the Bull free of cost in the kindest manner. It is the principal chapel of that Church, and is placed under the invocation of my patron Saint, and that of my house: it was endowed by myself, and painted with my own hand, being offered as an acknowledgment (although it be but a small one) of the Divine Goodness, and an evidence of my thankfulness for the infinite favours and benefits which the Supreme Ruler of all things§ hath vouchsafed to confer upon me.

* Where he arrived in February, 1567; Vasari found the Pope much pleased with the picture, and was commanded to examine, not only the works of San Pietro, but the Sistine Bridge, which was showing symptoms of weakness and decay. See *Carteggio inedito*, vol. iii. p. 233.

† Which no longer exists.

‡ In one of these pictures is a Last Judgment; this may still be seen in the Choir of Santa Croce del Bosco, the church in question. Vasari makes mention of the same in a letter to the Prince Francesco, as also in two others, one to Concino, the second likewise to Don Francesco. See *Carteggio*, &c., vol. iii. pp. 237, 239, 241.

§ The expression here used by Vasari is, "His Majesty," a phrase which, like that of Messer Domeniddio (see *ante*, p. 133), I should have been unwilling to disturb in its simplicity, had it not been for the fact that this phrase, then of such high and solemn import, has now become a comparatively common-place one, a mere title. Its use, as synonymous with "The Host," will be familiar to such of our readers as are acquainted with Spain and the Spaniards, "Su Majestad" being the words by which they intimate that portion of the Sacrament permitted to the use of the laity. Vasari was a true "Conservative" of his day, a profound lover of order, and he could find no term more vividly expressive of his deep adoration than that which he here adopted.

The picture of this my Chapel is very similar in its form to that of the Bosco mentioned above, which has partly caused me now to recollect it, for this also is isolated, and has in like manner two pictures, one of which, already alluded to elsewhere,* is in the front; and the other, representing San Giorgio, is behind. On each side of them are, furthermore, figures of certain saints, and beneath are the lives of the same, depicted in small compartments: while in a rich tomb, under the altar, are their remains, with some of the principal relics belonging to the city of Arezzo. In the centre, moreover, there is a Tabernacle for the Sacrament, which is well and handsomely arranged, seeing that it corresponds with both the Altars, but is adorned with such stories from the Old Testament as have relation to that Mystery,† and of which we have made some mention elsewhere.‡

Now I had forgotten to say that in the year preceding, when I had first gone to Rome to kiss the feet of the Pontiff, I had taken my way by Perugia, for the purpose of fixing in their appointed places three large pictures, which I had painted for the Black Friars of San Piero in that city, and which were then appended in their Refectory. The central picture of these three represents the Marriage of Cana in Galilee, when Christ performed the miracle of changing water into wine: in that on the right hand is the prophet Elisha, who, throwing meal into the bitter compound which his disciples could not eat, caused every hurtful quality of that which had been spoiled by the coloquinth to disappear.§ The third picture exhibits San Benedetto, who, in a time of grievous famine, and when all means of nourishment for his monks had failed him, receives from a lay-brother the announcement that camels loaded with corn are at the door, and who sees that the Angels of God are miraculously bringing a large quantity of flour to his relief.

For the Signora Gentilina, mother of the Signor Chiappono and of the Signor Paolo Vitelli, I painted a large picture in Florence, which I afterwards sent to her at Città

* This is the picture restored to Vasari by Pope Pius IV., as mentioned in the Life of Salviati.

† Of the Host namely.

‡ In the Life of Lazzaro Vasari. See vol. ii. of the present work, p. 55.

§ In this picture is the portrait of Vasari himself. It is now in the Church, and has been placed in the Chapel of the Sacrament.

di Castello; the subject is the Coronation of Our Lady: in the upper part is a choir of Angels, and beneath are numerous figures larger than life. This picture was placed in the Church of San Francesco in that city.* For the Church of Poggio a Cajano, a villa belonging to the Signor Duke, I painted Our Saviour Christ lying dead in the lap of his Mother; San Cosimo and San Damiano are in contemplation of the Virgin, and a weeping Angel, seen in the air above, is bearing the Mysteries† of our Saviour's Passion. In the Church of the Carmine at Florence there was placed, about the same time, a picture also by my hand, which I had painted for the Chapel of Matteo and Simon Botti, my intimate friends; in this there is Christ Crucified, with Our Lady, San Giovanni, and the Magdalene weeping.‡ I afterwards painted two large pictures, for Jacopo Capponi; the subjects of these, which were to be sent into France, are, of the one, Spring; of the other, Autumn; the figures in both are large, and each exhibits a certain novelty in the composition. In another and still larger picture, I delineated a Dead Christ sustained by two Angels, above whom is seen the figure of the Almighty Father. For the Nuns of Santa Maria Novella in Arezzo, I painted an Annunciation of the Virgin, with two Saints beside her, which I sent to their convent about this time or shortly before;§ and for the Nuns of Luco di Mugello, who are of the Order of Camaldoli, I painted a picture which is now in their inner Choir; it represents Christ Crucified, with Our Lady, St. John the Baptist, and Mary Magdalen.

For Luca Torrigiani, who is my intimate and very good friend, I painted a large picture, which he, desiring to have a work from my hand among the many productions of our arts in his possession, now keeps in his house; the subject is Venus, a nude figure surrounded by the Graces, of whom one adorns her head, while the second holds a mirror, and the third pours water into a vase. This picture I laboured to execute to the very best of my ability, as well to content

* Where it still remains.

† Our readers will not require to be reminded that the material emblems are here alluded to.

‡ Bocchi, *Bellezze di Firenza*, has described and greatly eulogizes this picture, which is still in the church.

§ This is now in the Louvre, having been taken to Paris in 1813.

my own mind as to satisfy the expectation of so dear and kind a friend. I also (compelled against my will to do so) took the Portrait of Antonio de' Nobili, Commissioner-general of his Excellency, and well inclined to myself. For the same person I depicted the Head of Our Saviour Christ, painting it after the words in which Lentulus writes of the Redeemer's countenance; both these pictures were executed with great care, as was also another, similar to that just mentioned, but somewhat larger, which I first intended for the Signor Mondragone, but which is now in the possession of Don Francesco de' Medici, Prince of Florence and Siena; I having presented it to his Highness on account of his love to our arts, and also that, when looking thereon, he may remember that I love him and am his friend.

I have now in hand, and hope soon to finish, a large and very fanciful picture which I intend for the Signor Antonio Montalvo, lord of the Sassetta, first gentleman of the bed-chamber to the Duke, and much valued by his Excellency. This Signor Antonio is likewise so dear and intimate a friend of my own (not to say a superior), that I am anxious to produce a something which shall serve as a pledge of the affection I bear him; and if my hand do but correspond to my desires, the result shall be such as to prove how much I honour him, and how dear to me is the remembrance of one so worthy to be respected and so well beloved; while I would fain contribute to make his memory descend to a future time, seeing that his labours are ever willingly given to promote the interests and the progress of all who belong to our vocation, or take pleasure in the arts of design.*

For the Prince, Don Francesco, I have lately painted two Pictures, which he has sent to Toledo, in Spain, for a sister of the Signora Duchess Leonora, his mother, with a small one, in the manner of a miniature, which he keeps for himself, and wherein there are forty figures, great and small; the composition, which is a very beautiful one, being his own. For Filippo Salviati I completed a picture, no long time since, which is to be sent to Prato, for the Nuns of San Vincenzio; in the upper part of this work is a Coronation of the Virgin, as having just then arrived in Heaven, and

* This picture is still in the Palace of the Marquis Ramirez di Montalvo, descendant of Vasari's friend and protector, Antonio.

beneath are the Apostles, all of whom are larger than life:* there are, besides, other figures and stories, the whole being surrounded by ornaments which are in a manner that is quite new.

The Signor Duke, who is of a truth most excellent in all things, takes much pleasure, not only in the building of palaces, cities, fortresses, gates, loggie, and piazzas, with the laying out of gardens, construction of fountains, and works of similar kind, all beautiful, magnificent, and most useful to his people, but he has also infinite delight, as a Catholic prince, in the restoration and improvement of the holy churches of God, therein imitating the great King Solomon. Wherefore he has lately caused me to remove the screen and rood-loft of Santa Maria Novella, which had long deprived that Church of its beauty,† when I made a new and rich Choir behind the High Altar; this has given the Church quite a new aspect; and as nothing can be entirely beautiful which has not harmony and correctness of proportion, the Duke has ordered that rich ornaments in stone, of a new kind, shall be constructed between the columns in the side-aisles; they are placed immediately beneath the arches, and with their altars in the centre; they serve as Chapels, and are all in one out of two manners. The pictures, which are to be seven braccia high and five wide, are to be placed within the ornaments, and will be painted at the pleasure of those who may own these Chapels.

Within one of them, for example, I have already executed a picture, after my own design, for the most reverend Monsignore Alessandro Strozzi, Bishop of Volterra, my old and most beloved patron, depicting therein a figure of Christ Crucified, according to the Vision of Sant' Anselmo that is to say; with the Seven Virtues, without which we cannot ascend the seven degrees to Jesus Christ: there are also other allusions to the Life of Sant' Anselmo in that picture.‡ In the same Church, nay, within another of the above-men-

* The work here in question serves as a kind of Canopy to the imitation of an organ.—*Masselli.*

† This removal caused great regret to many, and not without reason, since it involved the destruction of numerous frescoes, among which were some by Mataccio, but unhappily not even these were spared.—*Ed. Flor.*, 1846-51. See also Gaye, *Carteggio*, &c., vol. ii. Appendix, p. 480.

‡ This picture is no longer in the Church of Santa Maria Novella, nor can its present place be ascertained.

tioned ornaments, I also painted, by commission from the excellent Maestro Andrea Pasquali, physician to the Signor Duke, a Resurrection of our Lord Christ, which I have brought to completion in such sort as it has pleased God to inspire me with the ability to effect, for the satisfaction of the same Maestro Andrea, who is my very good friend.

The same great Duke has commanded that similar changes shall be made in the vast Church of Santa Croce, in Florence; that the screen shall be removed namely; the Choir placed behind the High Altar, bringing the latter somewhat forward, and placing upon it a rich Tabernacle for the holy Sacrament, to be newly constructed in carved stone-work, richly adorned with gilding, stories, and figures.* There are, furthermore, to be fourteen Chapels made beside the walls, as in Santa Maria Novella, but at greater cost and with richer ornaments than those, because Santa Croce is much larger than Santa Maria Novella. In the pictures which are to be in these Chapels, and which are to correspond with the two by Salviati and Bronzino,† all the principal events in the Passion of Our Lord are to be depicted, down to the moment when he sends his Holy Spirit on the Apostles. With this last named picture, the Descent of the Holy Spirit namely, I am even now employed, painting it for Messer Agnolo Biffoli, Treasurer-general of the Princes, and my singular good friend;‡ the design for the Chapels, and the ornaments in stone, I have already made. No long time since I finished two large pictures which are in those buildings, beside San Pietro Scheraggio, that belonging to the Court of Conservators; in one of these is the Head of Christ, and in the other a Madonna.

But since it would take me too far were I to describe minutely the many other Pictures, or to enumerate the

* Moisè, in his *Illustrazione Storico-artistica di Santa Croce*, has published a letter, wherein Vasari describes to Duke Cosimo with his own hand the mode in which he proceeded with this work. The Altar and Tabernacle are in wood, and were carved by Dionisio Nigetti.

† The picture of Bronzino is in the Uffizj; that of Salviati retains its place in the church.

‡ The pictures painted by Vasari for Santa Croce were three; they all remain in the church, and represent Christ bearing his Cross, the Descent of the Holy Spirit, and St. Thomas touching the wounded side of Our Lord. There is besides a fourth, the Last Supper namely, as mentioned in a previous note.

designs and models that I have made, I omit all mention thereof, as well as of the maskings which I have prepared; wherefore, having said enough and more than enough of myself, I will add nothing further, unless it be the remark that, however great and important have been the works which I have executed for Duke Cosimo, I have never been able to attain, much less surpass, the greatness and boldness of his genius: of this there is proof in the purpose he has conceived of erecting a third Sacristy beside San Lorenzo, very large, and similar in manner to that formerly constructed there by Michelagnolo,* but all of different marbles, and mosaic. Here he proposes to have deposited the remains of his departed children, of his father and mother, of the illustrious Duchess Leonora his consort, and of himself; all in tombs worthy of his power and greatness. Of this I have already prepared him a model after his own taste, and as he has himself ordered me to make it; when completed, then, this will be a new Mausoleum of truly regal magnificence.†

And now it shall suffice me to have spoken thus much of myself, who have thus arrived, amidst many labours, to the age of fifty-five; but I am prepared to live so long as it shall please God, to his honour and for the service of my friends; and, so far as in me lies, will be ever ready to promote and work for the progress of these most noble arts.‡

[*End of the Life of Vasari, as written by himself.*]

* That subsequently erected is larger than the one by Michael Angelo. It was built after a design by the Prince Don Giovanni, brother of the Grand Duke Ferdinand I. The first stone was laid in 1604.—*Masselli.*

† In the year 1836, the Commendator Pietro Benvenuti, of Arezzo, completed the painting of the Cupola, on which he had spent thirty years. —*Masselli.*

‡ Vasari finished the printing of his Lives in 1568, in which year he also made his will, writing it with his own hand. This document, which will be found in the second volume of the *Carteggio*, pp. 502—518, affords further proof of our author's admirable uprightness of mind and kindliness of heart. It bears date, the 25th of May, 1568.

## ADDENDA.

PIACENZA, in the Turinese edition of the *Decennali* of Baldinucci, has made various additions to the notices previously given of our Author by the accomplished churchman, Bottari; and of these we here reproduce such portions as seem best calculated to complete the biography left unfinished by the subject of it, supplying what was still wanting by reference to other authorities. From Bottari we find that in 1570 Vasari was once more in Rome, invited thither by Pope Pius V., who had requested the permission of Duke Cosimo to that effect, where he painted three Lunettes in the ascent, called the Cordonate, which connects the Court of San Damaso with the Loggia, &c., painted by Raphael. In the Sala Regia, also, there are numerous pictures by his hand; that over the entrance from the Scala Regia, for example, and which represents the Excommunication of the Emperor Frederick by Pope Gregory IX. The large picture, between the door of the Sistine Chapel and that of the Scala Regia, the Victory of Lepanto namely, is also by Vasari. "All these," says Bottari, "are the work of Giorgio; but certain large figures, representing the Holy Church, Spain, and the Republic of Venice, are by Lorenzino, of Bologna."

The picture next to this, a very beautiful one, is also by Giorgio, although it has been attributed to Taddeo Zucchero, but that painter died five years before the naval combat represented therein had taken place. It is true that the large figures are by Lorenzetto. The picture of Gregory IX., conducted by Santa Caterina, of Siena, and removing the Apostolic Seat into France, is another of Vasari's works; the name and native place of the artist are written in the Greek character thereon, and this painting has more of Vasari's usual manner than has that mentioned immediately before it. The Death of Coligny is in like manner by his hand, as were the Cartoons for other pictures here painted, but which were coloured by his disciples.

The Altar-piece in the private Chapel of San Pio, which represents the Death of St. Peter Martyr, is likewise by our artist; and the Cartoons for other pictures in the same Chapel are by his hand, but were executed by his disciples. The Vaulting of the first Chapel, belonging to the private apartments of His Holiness, and wherein is the Descent of the Fallen Angels, was commenced in December, 1570; and in January, 1571, Vasari had already completed the designs for all the three Chapels, as well as nearly painted three pictures. On the 10th of February he wrote to the Prince, Francesco de' Medici, informing him that he had brought to conclusion fifty-six pieces of the Cartoons for the three Chapels, and had sketched twelve large Cartoons for that of San Michele, with no other assistance than that of Sandro di Baldassare;* having been impelled to this excess of haste by his wish to return to the Hall of the Palace in Florence, where he hoped to recommence his labours in the month of July then following.

One of the three Chapels above-named, that dedicated to San Pietro Martire namely, was thrown open to public view on the 30th of April in that year (1571); and with all these works on his hands, the Pope was still daily committing some new one to the care of the master; now it was to superintend the buildings in San Pietro; now to conduct the waters of the Acqua Vergine, from Salona to Rome; anon, to repair the Church of San Giovanni Laterano, or to execute other undertakings of similar character.

From May to December of 1571, we have no records, but Vasari may be presumed to have returned to Florence before the month of July, as his letters prove that he much wished to do; since we find that the paintings of the Great Hall, so frequently alluded to, were given to public view on the 5th of January, 1572.†

But the master did not long remain in Florence, Pope Pius V. having again requested Duke Cosimo to permit him to return to Rome; and among other works he then executed a picture of San Girolamo in the Desert. But not all the labours here pressed on his attention by the Pope could divert his thoughts from a great undertaking, entrusted to

* Among the Cartoons made for the Pope were twelve large Stories, four from the History of Tobit, four from the Life of St. Stephen, and four from that of St. Peter Martyr. The remainder of the Cartoons are for the ceilings, among these the Fall of the Angels and the stories of Tobit still exist. These pictures have been usually attributed to Federigo Zucchero, but Gaye (see the *Carteggio*, vol. iii. p. 292) has proved them to be the works of Vasari.

† For numerous details of much interest relating to this period, see Gaye, *Carteggio inedito*, vol. iii. p. 293. See also p. 305, note.

his care by Duke Cosimo, the painting of the Cupola of Santa Maria del Fiore, in Florence, namely, for the continuance of which Rome was at that moment a most commodious residence, since Vasari had there the Ceiling and other works of Michelagnolo, and in effect his letters soon began to make mention of a commencement of the Cartoons for the Cupola. His Holiness, meanwhile, resolved to have three Pictures painted in the Sala Regia, which should immortalize the memory of an event in which he had taken an essential part, the Battle of Lepanto namely; but the Cartoon for the third of these was not more than half completed* when Vasari was called on to begin the sketches of two other pictures for the same Pontiff; one of these represents the Magdalen borne to Heaven by Angels; the other, St. Jerome extracting the Thorn from the Foot of the Lion. The death of Pope Pius interrupted these labours, and Vasari returned to Florence, reposing for some days at Arezzo on his way, and writing thence to the Prince Francesco, to the effect that he was returning to his service in the expectation that he (the Prince) would close his eyes; the master sent at the same time the Cartoons which he had prepared for the Cupola.

In October of the same year, 1572, we find Vasari occupied in various labours for the Duke. He designed a Palace for him at the Capraia, in the Pisan territory, a small Church at Colle Mingoli, and some Fountains at the Castello. His preparations for painting the Cupola still continued, but he was at this time much disquieted by the fear of a summons to Rome; and in effect a letter from the Cardinal Buoncompagno soon announced to him that the new Pontiff, Gregory XIII., required his assistance for continuing those works of the Sala Regia, which he had already commenced; wherefore he was enjoined to transport himself to Rome with his best speed. Always anxious to gratify the Pontiff, the Duke opposed no resistance, but despatched his Giorgio to Rome with orders to obey Pope Gregory in all things, and expressing his satisfaction that the Holy Father "should have service from his men"—the phrase invariably used by Duke Cosimo on similar occasions.

Vasari deferred his departure nevertheless, being very

* A minute description of these paintings, written by Vasari himself, in a letter to the Prince Francesco, and dated February 2nd, 1572, will be found in Gaye, *ut supra*, see vol. iii. p. 307—309.

unwilling to leave Florence, but the Duke, conversing with him one day, suddenly said: "Giorgio, I do not see how we are to escape from this going to Rome of thine; for as that is the first thing His Holiness has requested from me, I do not think I can refuse it; there are, besides, none of our people at the Papal Court, and the intercourse that thou wilt assuredly have with His Holiness cannot but be useful to us; wherefore, get thyself ready, and before the weather breaks up I will despatch thee to the Pope, writing to him that I think his using what belongs to me a great kindness, but that he must speedily send thee back, because we want to finish our Cupola. This winter, meanwhile, thou canst be preparing thy Cartoons for the same, and as to that Sala (Regia), since thy designs and cartoons are so far advanced, I cannot but think that it will soon be finished. Take a good number of assistants with thee, and get on rapidly, for the Pope is old, and interruptions may again ensue."

Having arranged his domestic affairs, and finished a picture of Humanity and Divinity, the appropriate symbols for which were suggested to him by his friend and counsellor, Don Vincenzio Borghini, Giorgio departed for Rome, where he arrived on the 11th of November, and there found that Pope Gregory desired him to paint the Massacre of St. Bartholomew, which had taken place that same year, and under his own Pontificate. Vasari had but little inclination to recommence his labours, and would fain have given place to the other painters then in Rome; but, unable to refuse, he commenced this work also, which he divided into three Stories.* Duke Cosimo, meanwhile, was constantly urging the master to hasten his movements and return to him; when Giorgio, but too well accustomed to profit by his facility of hand, hurried through with all speed, and on the Corpus Domini of 1573, the Sala Regia was thrown open to public view. This work, which had been commenced by Paul III., had successively occupied twelve painters,† who had employed twenty-eight years in its completion, which was ultimately effected by Vasari (the thirteenth master engaged therein), under the Pontificate of Gregory XIII.‡

* For a minute description of these paintings, see Gaye, as before cited vol. iii. p. 350.

† Their names will be found in the *Carteggio*, vol. iii. p. 361.

‡ Very curious and interesting details respecting these works will be found in Gaye, *ut supra*, vol. iii. p. 343.

This brought infinite credit to Vasari, insomuch that, an inscription being demanded for the Hall from Vincenzio Borghini, the latter composed the following, of which the conceit was suggested to him, it is said, by our Giorgio himself:-

"*In thirty-nine years, which is three times thirteen, under six popes and by twelve excellent painters, this work had been continued, but not completed; wherefore Gregory XIII., Pontifex Maximus, commencing in the first year of his Pontificate, has brought it to conclusion in thirteen months, by the hand of Giorgio Vasari, the thirteenth painter.*"

Very greatly did Vasari rejoice in the completion of this work, and the rather as his friends and benefactors, the principal personages of the papal Court, were never weary of congratulating themselves on the results obtained by his means; and had he possessed his earlier vigour and powers of labour, these nobles would have been only too glad to supply him with opportunities for the exercise of the same.

In the midst of all this triumph our beloved Giorgio was furthermore to be gratified by an invitation from Philip of Spain, who, by the mouth of Marcantonio Colonna, had despatched his request that Vasari would repair to the Spanish Court; but the latter refused, "desiring no higher glory than that already obtained; seeking no increase of riches, and resolving to attempt no new toils: being desirous, in short, of nothing more than the opportunity of reposing himself beneath the shadow of his own magnificent Sovereign." He returned to Florence accordingly, and resumed his labours at the Cupola, the Pontiff expressing infinite grief at his departure, and consoling himself principally with the hope that Duke Cosimo would send the artist to him once more in the winter of 1574. But in the month of June of that year,* worn out by the pains and fatigues of a life unusually active and laborious, the excellent master closed his mortal career, crowned with fame and honours, and very sincerely lamented.

Such was the life, and such the works, of Giorgio Vasari. Richly endowed by nature, he was furthermore aided by earnest zeal for the study of his art, and a persistent industry; but there were defects in his artistic education which

* The death of Giorgio was announced to Prince Francesco on the 27th of June, the day on which it happened, in a letter written by Pietro Vasari, brother of the master. See *Carteggio*, vol. iii. p. 389.

neutralized these advantages to a certain extent; of those defects it is, however, not here our purpose to speak further. As an Architect, Vasari stands deservedly higher than as a Painter; as the Historian of the Arts, he occupies a position, the eminence of which has never been approached; he is the source from which all other writers draw their best and most important materials, and no work on the subject he treated can be opened, but his name shall be found, and that to useful purpose, on every page. We conclude with a few words from Bottari, to whose magnificent edition of our author's works, published at Rome in 1759, we are indebted for many of the most valuable among the notes given in the present volumes.

"Having returned to Florence, the master betook himself to the painting of the great Cupola of the Duomo, but did not finish more than the Prophets which are around the Lantern, because he was interrupted by death; wherefore the completion of the same was confided to Federigo Zucchero.*

"Vasari was in the sixty-third year of his age when he died; his remains were conveyed to his native city of Arezzo, where they were laid in the tomb of his family within the principal Chapel of the Decanal Church, which Chapel belongs to his house, and where very honourable obsequies were solemnized to his memory. His friends were almost all the learned men, and every distinguished artist of his time; while of the less distinguished he was himself the friend and protector. Our Giorgio left behind him a very great reputation; more perhaps for the vast number than for the excellence of his pictures,† but the beauty and perfection of his architectural works are not to be denied, seeing that

* By whom, with the assistance of Passignano and others, it was finished after continual labour, in the year 1577. The compositions, wholly due to Vasari, will be found described by himself in the *Ragionamento del Signor Cavaliere Giorgio Vasari, pittore ed architetto Aretino sopra le invenzioni da lui depinte in Firenza, nel Palazzo di Loro Altezze Serenissime*, &c. It was published in Florence by the nephew of the master, also a "Giorgio Vasari," in 1588, and was afterwards re-published under the title of *Trattato della Pittura*, &c.

† Had Vasari thought less of obliging those to whom he believed himself indebted for kindness, or felt bound by his duties, and more of his own reputation, the result might, or rather would, have been different.

he was, in truth, a most accomplished architect. His highest renown and name in the world will nevertheless be always that derived from this present work—the Lives of Painters, Sculptors, and Architects."

GRATITUDE AND HONOUR TO HIS MEMORY.

# INDEX.

Q.



R.

S.

J. HADDON, PRINTER, CASTLE STREET, FINSBURY.

CPSIA information can be obtained
at www.ICGtesting.com
Printed in the USA
LVHW021946301122
734228LV00004B/224

9 780342 319190